Joe Namath,
Game by Game

Joe Namath, Game by Game

The Complete Professional Football Career

Bryan L. Yeatter

McFarland & Company, Inc., Publishers

Jefferson, North Carolina, and London

Bryan L. Yeatter is also the author of
*Cinema of the Philippines: A History and
Filmography, 1897–2005* (McFarland, 2007)

LIBRARY OF CONGRESS CATALOGUING-IN-PUBLICATION DATA

Yeatter, Bryan L., 1964–
Joe Namath, game by game : the complete
professional football career / Bryan L. Yeatter.
       p.   cm.
Includes bibliographical references and index.

ISBN 978-0-7864-7036-5
softcover : acid free paper ♾

1. Namath, Joe Willie, 1943–
2. Football players — United States — Biography.
I. Title.
GV939.N28Y43 2012   796.332092—dc23   [B]   2012019536

BRITISH LIBRARY CATALOGUING DATA ARE AVAILABLE

On the cover: Joe Namath (12) of the New York Jets in a 17–14 win
over the Miami Dolphins at Shea Stadium on November 24, 1974
(AP Photo/NFL Photos)

Manufactured in the United States of America

*McFarland & Company, Inc., Publishers
Box 611, Jefferson, North Carolina 28640
www.mcfarlandpub.com*

For my mother and father,
who bought me a Joe Namath jersey when I was a boy

Acknowledgments

There are a number of individuals I need to thank for their help and support as I worked on this book. I should start with my research assistants, Ellen Letostak and Cindie Moore. Ellen was always gracious in offering to look things up, despite the fact she loathes football (hates football — loves research). Hating football didn't stop her from enjoying the book as she read through it, however, and I need to also thank her for the editorial suggestions she offered along the way (it never hurts to have an English teacher proofread your work).

Cindie was also always eager to help; if I mentioned being vexed by some elusive bit of information, she would quickly reappear with a computer printout in hand. That would have been enough in itself, but Cindie's most notable quality is her irrepressible buoyancy; it seems impossible to hold a negative thought in her presence, or to fail to be swept up in her sunny disposition. She has a wonderful gift for cheerleading, and we all need cheerleaders.

My brother, Alan Yeatter, was always willing to lend a hand whenever necessary, as was Michael Marshall, who gave me the run of his Premier Copy facility after hours, which was primetime for getting things done.

Football fans are often very useful when one is delving into seasons long past. Their memories and personal collections of memorabilia offer a wealth of information, and a true fan can sometimes be the best historian of all. For that reason I would like to thank Miami Dolphins fan and historian Chris Kellum and Baltimore Colts fan and historian Al Val, who were both helpful despite the fact I was writing about a man they once regarded with all the affection of an archenemy. In fact, Al, a lifelong Colts fan, still views Super Bowl III with a degree of suspicion, I believe.

While naming fans, I can't leave out the Poosers. When Peggy Pooser speaks, there is no mistaking her drawl for anything other than full-on Alabaman, and being from Alabama, she is well versed in regional football lore. But the Poosers are diehard Auburn people, and to them Namath and Bear Bryant were the enemy. Even so, in any great rivalry there is due respect for a worthy adversary, and it was Peggy who first told me of the old adage that, in Alabama, atheists are people who don't believe in Bear Bryant. The Poosers are more of the church of Shug Jordan, however, and if you were to look through the video library of Peggy's late husband, Carlyle Pooser, you would come away with the distinct impression that Auburn never lost a game.

Together, Peggy and Carlyle Pooser raised sons who inherited both their congenial nature and their love of football. John Pooser is always very generous with the libations, and can be counted on to tell (and retell) the story of having attended Auburn's upset victory over Alabama in 1972's famous "Punt, Bama, Punt" game.

I also want to acknowledge Scott Pooser because, well, he kinda *looks* like Joe Namath, and my hope is that in mentioning Alan Pooser as well, I will secure a unanimous vote in making me an honorary Pooser brother. I would make them all honorary Yeatter brothers, but having just one-third of the vote I can only accomplish so much toward that end.

Finally, I want to thank my parents, David Lewis Yeatter and Theresa Joy Marshall, who provided a childhood of wonderful memories for their sons. One that comes to mind in light of this book is their purchase of an 8mm Super Bowl III highlight reel from K-Mart, because their 10-year-old son could not be without it. How many times I watched that film in those pre-VCR days I could not even guess, but every play was burned into my memory, where they remain to this day. There was also the Joe Namath jersey that I would wear to every sandlot game I played in. It is with all my love and gratitude that I dedicate this book to Mom and Dad.

Contents

Introduction

In the history of professional football there are certain names that stand out — Unitas, Sayers, Butkus. To a fan, the mere mention of these names conjures vivid images: frosty breath billowing from Unitas' helmet during a frigid December championship, Sayers in his mud-caked uniform cutting back against the grain and finding daylight, a very intense look on Butkus' face as blood runs down the bridge of his nose. But there is perhaps no name in sport that can bring to mind as many and as varied an array of images as the name Namath, for while the others are inextricably linked to the game of football, Namath encompasses much more. Although he is still largely identified with the game, Joe Namath transcended it like no player before, or even since.

Namath wasn't just a player; he was a celebrity, a personality, and of course a player of another sort. His entire career seemed marked by controversy of one kind or another. An interesting thing is that, although it has been some 30 years since he retired from professional football, Namath is still a figure of controversy. One can find debate raging on the internet concerning the question of whether Namath belongs in the Pro Football Hall of Fame. The points raised against his induction (he was inducted in 1985) are worth exploring, some more valid than others.

What stands out most about the objections to his induction, however, is the lack of adequate rebuttal offered when there is good reason to counter these points. While he was playing Namath had his detractors, then as now, but the difference is that those making the case against him now seem woefully ignorant of certain pertinent facts (rule changes, for instance, which presently benefit passers in a way that Namath and his contemporaries couldn't enjoy). Some have even suggested that *no* quarterback with more interceptions than touchdown passes should be in the Hall of Fame. The point has been raised in relation to Namath's status as a Hall of Famer, yet one would be hard-pressed to find similar objections to other Hall of Fame quarterbacks with more interceptions than touchdowns. Eliminating them all would strike many of the greatest names in the history of the game from the Hall — Y.A. Tittle, Sammy Baugh, Norm Van Brocklin, Bobby Layne, George Blanda; and even Terry Bradshaw, he of the four Super Bowl rings — threw only two more touchdown passes in his career than interceptions. It was a different game then. These rule changes will be discussed in the concluding chapter.

There are those who say that Namath was inducted more for what he brought to the game in terms of popularizing it, and this is a valid point. It is Namath, after all, who is most responsible for turning the Super Bowl into the gargantuan national carnival that it has become. Prior to Namath's appearance in the 1969 Super Bowl, the game had been something of a non-event; there were thousands of empty seats at the 1967 Super Bowl, and the 1968 game only fared better because of ticket markdowns and giveaways. Namath turned it into the much-anticipated event that it remains to this day, and that is a fact.

But what about Namath's actual playing career? Does it merit the attention? Writing about Namath's retirement in the February 18, 1978, edition of *The Sporting News,* in "Future Will

Decide Namath's Ranking as QB," columnist Melvin Durslag remarked that "researchers years hence will be exploring his story, trying to piece together a logical explanation for his fame." Okay, chalk one up for Durslag; we're still writing, exploring, wondering, and trying to figure it all out.

It has been said that baseball is the most humbling of games. A hitter with a .400 average is thought to be doing quite well, but that average only shows that he has failed more often than not. Even so, a hitter who only succeeds four out of every ten tries is well above average. Failure is simply accepted as a part of the game. Apparently football is a more unforgiving sport. Namath's critics will point out, for instance, that he only led his team to three winning seasons (a misleading assessment that will be discussed later).

Nowadays people tend to look at statistics — career totals — thinking the answer lies therein: it doesn't. It may be true that numbers don't lie, but they don't tell the whole story, either. As so many have tried to solve the puzzle of Namath's legend, one thing that hasn't been done is to look at the games, and not just the big ones, but all of them, big and small, important and not-so-important, good, great, awful, and everywhere in between. What does the record say week-to-week? Why did he win? Why did he lose? Maybe in looking over the whole record we can figure out the Namath mystique. Maybe. Whichever side of the fence you're on when it comes to Namath, you'll likely find fuel for your argument. But whether any definitive conclusions can be drawn from such an exploration, one thing is certain: it's going to be interesting, and a whole lot of fun.

1

The Yankee from
Bear Bryant's Court

There is an interesting story related in the book *When Pride Still Mattered,* the excellent biography of Vince Lombardi written by David Maraniss. The time is late summer of 1970, and the great coach is on his deathbed, just days from breathing his last. Dying of cancer, Lombardi is even then thinking of his life's passion — football. As he sleeps, his wife, sitting nearby in the room, is startled when the coach cries out urgently from his bed. "Joe Namath!" he bellowed. "You're not bigger than football! Remember that!"[1]

What was Lombardi dreaming? Why as he lay dying was Joe Namath on his mind? Was he rebuking Namath? Warning him? Football was at the center of Lombardi's universe. Even his wife and children had to accept that they all took a backseat to football in the coach's life, Lombardi's devotion to the game was so complete. The game rewarded Lombardi in return: he is the most revered coach in history — they named the Super Bowl trophy after him!

So why during his dying days was the coach dreaming about Namath? Given his passion for the sport, it seems likely that it shocked Lombardi's sensibilities to see the game he so loved being overshadowed by this one player. Lombardi knew that no single player could be bigger than the game, yet it must have seemed to him like the game had been all but swallowed up by this mammoth personality. It was ridiculous, offensive, impossible — even troubling.

With all due respect to the coach of coaches, he was wrong. For however brief the moment may have been, Joe Namath was indeed bigger than football, and not just bigger — he was *much* bigger. There were the movies (a wonderfully bad spaghetti western, and even more wonderfully awful biker film), the television shows (including guest hosting Johnny Carson's *Tonight Show,* the primo celebrity venue of its day), a Broadway Joe's fast food franchise (albeit short lived), and, of course, the advertising. Namath was hawking everything: Schick razors, Noxzema shaving cream, Brut cologne, Arrow shirts, Dingo boots, Puma shoes, Cutty Sark whiskey, Fieldcrest sheets, Braniff Airlines, La-Z-Boy recliners, Ovaltine chocolate milk mix, Hamilton Beach popcorn makers, Olivetti typewriters, and ... Beauty Mist pantyhose (of course). He had his own television talk show in the New York market (*The Joe Namath Show*), and he ran with the Rat Pack. There was even a song about him, sung by a female choir with wonderfully ebullient girlie voices, declaring Namath's ability to pass a football through a needle's eye.

Yeah, Joe Namath was bigger than football. "I've been away in Europe for several years," Jane Fonda said during an appearance on *The Dick Cavett Show* in the late 1960s. "I knew the name Joe Namath. Everybody in Europe knows him. I heard a lot of things about him. I never heard that he played football."[2]

People who couldn't tell a football from a Frisbee knew who Joe Namath was; people who didn't know the Dodgers had left Brooklyn knew who Joe Namath was; people who couldn't tell a shortstop from a defensive end knew who Joe Namath was. In 1969, *Life* magazine noted that

Namath was "too delicious to spit out, too indigestible to swallow, too noisy to shut up, and too firmly embedded in the minds of millions to vanish without caterwauling for a long, long time."[3]

Football may have made Namath a star, but the game in turn reaped a substantial reward from his celebrity. The very idea of Namath retiring was enough to give the businessmen behind the sport shudders. "Can Football Live Without Joe Namath?" asked a *Sport* magazine article in July of 1972. It doesn't matter that the piece came to the conclusion that, yes, football would ultimately survive even if the man they called Broadway Joe did not return, but the mere fact that the question was raised is very telling, as is the fact that Vince Lombardi would feel compelled from the deepest recesses of his soul to weigh-in on the matter from his deathbed. Joe Namath not bigger than football? The hell you say.

But how did it happen? How *could* it? How did a cocksure kid from Beaver Falls, Pennsylvania manage to eclipse an entire sport? Of course he had talent — that's a given — but so much so that legendary Alabama coach Paul "Bear" Bryant was moved to say that Namath was not merely the greatest athlete he had ever coached, but the best he had ever seen.[4] With Bryant's considerable history as a coach — as a *winning* coach — that's really saying something. Such regard for Namath's abilities extended back to his senior year of high school in 1960, when he led the Beaver Falls Tigers to an undefeated season and the school's first Western Pennsylvania Interscholastic Athletic League title in 35 years. "We always felt that if someone gave Joe two fish and a loaf of bread he could feed the whole world," said Larry Bruno, who coached the team that year.[5] Namath threw for more than 1,500 yards and 12 TDs that season, very impressive for a high school quarterback with a 10-game schedule.

Aside from his impressive ability as a passer, Namath had other qualities to recommend him. The team relied on his leadership, and his skill at reading defenses was already in evidence. In fact, Bruno would later say that his confidence in his quarterback was such that he allowed Namath to call most of the plays himself (99 percent, by Bruno's recollection).[6] And then there was his running.

Given the fact that his bad knees got as much press through the years as his good right arm, it is interesting to contemplate Namath the scrambler, but he was once as dangerous running with the ball as he was throwing it. His sleight of hand was also impressive — sometimes too much so, as it occasionally counted against him. Four times in 1960 Namath ran for touchdowns that were called back due to officials having blown the play dead when the runner Namath had faked the handoff to was tackled. On one occasion Namath ran more than 60 yards for a score only to have it brought back because the play had been blown dead. Yes, even then referees were blind as bats and dumb as rocks.

And all the while, don't you know the scouts were taking notice? Bruno remembered when they started coming around, haunting his office like horny drovers at a brothel, watching game films, checking grades, sitting outside waiting their turn. One college that showed a good deal of interest was the University of Maryland, whose head coach, Tom Nugent, personally made the trip to Beaver Falls to make a play for Namath. His pitch must have been good, because he convinced the young quarterback to choose Maryland. Namath would likely have ended up there, too, if he hadn't been just shy of passing his entrance exam. It was a disappointment Namath would get over easily enough; after all, there were plenty of other schools that would be interested. It was a more crushing outcome for Nugent, who knew that Namath's next choice could well be Penn State, meaning Nugent would then have to face this kid as an opponent for the next few years. Determined to derail that prospect, Nugent had an assistant — an alumnus of the University of Georgia — put in a call to recommend Namath to Georgia. The hope was to place Namath in another conference safely away from Maryland, but Georgia balked at the idea of taking Maryland's castoffs. Their loss, as Namath wound up going to Alabama, where he made an annual tradition of opening the season by taking Georgia to the woodshed.

Namath's arrival at Alabama was very memorable for all present. He was brought to the practice field by assistant coach Clem Gryska, and was greeted by the sight and sound of the legendary Coach Bryant atop his tower barking orders through a megaphone to the players on the field below. In Alabama they had a saying that an atheist was somebody who didn't believe in Bear Bryant. It was only half in jest, for when people heard that deep, gravelly, commanding voice, sure enough they could almost believe they were hearing the voice of God.

Gryska shouted up to Bryant, informing him that he had brought Joe Namath. Then, to the amazement of everyone, Bryant summoned Namath to come up the tower. It was not altogether unheard of for someone to be invited by Bryant to climb the tower, but it was extremely rare, and no one had ever seen a mere player go up there, let alone a simple freshman. Everyone had to be wondering who this kid was, but they could all be certain of one thing: he *had* to be someone special.

Special or not, as a freshman Namath did not make the varsity squad and wound up doing what freshmen mostly do, biding his time, waiting, watching the Crimson Tide roll through an unbeaten season and to a national title in 1961. But come his sophomore year in 1962 there was no holding back, and wouldn't you know that Namath's first game as Alabama's quarterback was against Georgia. How sweet is that?

As beginnings go, it was more than promising. Namath made short work of the Georgia defense, throwing a 52-yard touchdown to Richard Williamson on his first pass only minutes into the game. From there the rout was on, and Namath threw a couple more touchdowns (both to halfback Cotton Clark) as Alabama rolled to an easy 35–0 victory. The Tide looked just as sharp the following Friday night in New Orleans, whipping Tulane 44–6. The Associated Press said that Namath "demonstrated an uncanny eye for spotting receivers, and his fakes were carried off with the aplomb of a magician."[7]

And so it went throughout the season, as Alabama racked up eight straight wins before making the one mistake that would cost them a consecutive national title. Against Georgia Tech, the Tide found themselves down 7–0 before finally scoring a touchdown in the game's final six minutes. They could easily have tied the score with an extra point, but Bryant knew that lose or tie, either one would cost Alabama their number one ranking. He therefore opted to try and win it with a two-point conversion. The play failed, and Alabama ultimately lost 7–6. Even so, Bryant knew he had made the right decision.

Alabama finished the season with two more shutouts, beating Auburn 38–0 to close out their schedule, then blanking Oklahoma 17–0 in the Orange Bowl. The bowl victory marked the fifth shutout registered by the Alabama defense that season, but it was still Namath that reporters were asking about after the game. The Orange Bowl had been the first chance many in the national press had gotten to see him. "Keep your eye on Namath," Bryant told them. "In the next two years you'll be hearing a lot about him."[8]

It was in 1963 that Paul W. Bryant Hall opened. Bryant knew that winning was as much about attitude as it was ability. He wanted his boys to have the best because he wanted them to believe they were the best. For that reason, Paul W. Bryant Hall was a luxury palace among the university's dorms. It had wall-to-wall carpeting, phones in the dorm rooms, color televisions, guest rooms for the players' parents when they came to visit — even maid service! It was the Waldorf-Astoria of the University of Alabama. It was nothing so obtuse as mere elitism: Bryant wanted his players to have the inner pride that came with feeling a cut above. A good example would be the coach's comically disparaging assessment of Auburn before Alabama trounced them in 1962. He pointed out to his players that they were all wearing alligator shoes while the Auburn boys were wearing Thom McAn's. "How the hell you going to lose to a bunch of guys wearing Thom McAn's?" he goaded.[9] Jingoistic? To some, perhaps, but there is no arguing with results: Bryant's boys were winners.

Alabama opened the 1963 season by once more stomping Georgia, coming away with a lop-sided 32–7 victory, and although their 28–0 win over Tulane the following week gave the impression of another strong team, it soon became apparent they weren't firing on all cylinders. Nearing the end of the season the Tide had already dropped two games, and while a 7–2 record would hang nicely on many teams, it seemed altogether uncharacteristic of the team Alabama had become under Bryant. Going into their week 10 meeting with Miami, the Tide would have to dig deep to overcome the season's most crushing blow. It was dealt by — of all people — Bryant himself.

The Monday before the game it was announced that Namath had been suspended for the remainder of the season (the Miami game and the Sugar Bowl against Mississippi) for breaking training rules. The announcement wasn't specific, but Namath's infraction was drinking alcohol, or more precisely, *being seen* drinking alcohol. He wasn't the only one, merely the most recognizable team member said to have been spotted with a beer in hand on a Saturday night. When word got back to the coach, it put him in a quandary. Bryant had no desire to lose his star quarterback, of course, but on the other hand he ran a tight ship and was religious about the rules. Could he in good conscience bend them for one player? Could he allow himself to be accused of favoritism, of being lax, of playing fast-and-loose with the rules? His integrity was at stake, to say nothing of the blow to his authority if he were to be seen as allowing his quarterback to flout the rules. But he also loved Namath. Could he wound him so deeply as to do what the rules prescribed, to suspend him? He must have longed for a way out of the predicament. Bryant, prepared to take Namath's word on the matter, asked him if it were true that he had broken training rules by consuming alcohol during the season. Maybe Namath didn't think it was a big deal, or maybe he thought that his relationship with Bryant was such that the old man would look the other way. Or maybe Namath just respected Bryant too much to lie to him. Whatever the reason, he confirmed that he had indulged on the Saturday night in question. The reality of it was much drabber than some of the stories that were floating around campus (one of which had Namath drunkenly directing traffic in the heart of the city late at night), but Bryant still saw no alternative but to enforce the rules. "Joe has indicated to me he will remain in school and concentrate on his studies,"[10] Bryant said in a statement. He informed the press that, while Namath would be allowed to remain on scholarship, whether or not he rejoined the team the following season would be Namath's decision.

The truth is that Namath was bitter. He had enormous respect for Bryant, but found the punishment extreme. He was forced to move out of Paul W. Bryant Hall: it was like being drummed out of town. He weighed his options — revisiting offers from Major League Baseball teams, playing professional football in Canada, leaving Alabama and going to another University — but cooler heads prevailed. It was Namath's roommate, Butch Henry, who helped him realize that his decision would have repercussions beyond his own bruised feelings. There were many people who would be affected, from family and friends to teammates, and even Coach Bryant. But the experience was hurtful, humiliating: it was like he had been fired by his own father. In the end, Namath chose to stay and win back Bryant's respect. The team, sound as Bear Bryant squads tended to be, managed without Namath in their two remaining games, beating Miami 17–12 and defeating Mississippi 12–7 in the Sugar Bowl (Namath attended the game).

Against Georgia on opening day of the 1964 season, Namath had no trouble picking up where he left off; in fact, he made it look absurdly easy. "Namath disappointed no one," wrote George Smith in the *Anniston Star*, "least of all Bryant, as he piled up 222 yards of total offense — a figure no one in the press box could remember being topped by an Alabama back."[11] Maybe nobody in the press box went back that far, but Namath was 11 yards shy of the school's record set by Bobby Marlow in 1951. That's all right: all Namath did was complete 16 of 21 passes for 167 yards while also running for three touchdowns in his annual drubbing of Georgia. Alabama won, 31–3.

It was much the same story the following week when Alabama hosted Tulane. Namath ran for two touchdowns and passed for a third, as the Tide rolled to a decisive 36–6 win. While their week three romp over Vanderbilt started slowly (Vanderbilt played Alabama to a scoreless standstill in the first half), Namath and the Tide exploded in the second half for a 24–0 win. Namath ran 15 yards for a score, but more significantly threw for two touchdowns, putting him ahead of both Harry Gilmore and Eddie Salem as the school's all-time TD pass leader. Only three games into the season, there was no reason to think Namath would not add handily to his totals to shore up his position in that respect. Ah, but for the slings and arrows of outrageous fortune.

October 10, 1964. It's a day that Joe Namath will surely remember for the rest of his life — it's a day that forever changed his life. People who followed sports knew about Namath's rocket right arm, but from then on everyone would probably hear as much or more about Namath's knees. They would become as fabled as Achilles' heel.

Alabama was hosting North Carolina State, and Namath had hit on seven of eight passes for 52 yards. Still, the game remained scoreless into the second quarter when Namath started the Tide on what would be their first scoring drive of the game. Beginning from the Alabama 31-yard line, Namath drove his team to the North Carolina 34 when he opted to run the ball himself. While cutting back sharply, Namath's right knee gave out: he went down like a sack of potatoes. Nobody had hit him, the knee just gave out. "Namath twisted his knee and we don't know how bad it is," Bryant said after the Tide went on to win, 21–0. "It had swollen up and we got him off of it quick. I had no intention of using him in the second half even if we had lost."[12] And so it all began.

Originally thought to be no more than a twisted knee, Namath played sparingly the remainder of the season. The following week at Tennessee, his knee wrapped tightly, Namath entered the game, as Steve Traylor wrote in the *Anniston Star*, "to shock Tennesseans with his bullet-like passes."[13] Bryant tried playing Namath earlier in the following week's 17–14 victory over Florida, but after taking a hit while scrambling (old habits die hard), Namath limped off the field.

Bryant made the wise choice of playing Namath with caution, if at all, the rest of the year, but then, with Alabama winning week-to-week, the coach could afford such prudence. The only time Bryant felt he didn't have that luxury was in the Tide's game with Georgia Tech in the ninth week of the season. The game was still scoreless approaching halftime when the Tide recovered a fumble at the Tech 49. With less than two minutes remaining in the half, Bryant sent Namath into the game. Namath promptly hit David Ray with a pass inside the 20-yard line, which Ray carried to the one. On the following play, fullback Steve Bowman dove across for the score. Feeling inspired, Alabama gambled successfully with an onside kick, which the Tide recovered at the Tech 48. Namath went right back to work, firing 45 yards to Ray Ogden at the three-yard line, and then tossing a three-yard TD to David Ray to make it 14–0 with 27 seconds left in the half. Namath had led his team to two touchdowns in 1:20. The *Sporting News* called it "the most explosive 80 seconds in all the history of Alabama football," adding that "everything that happened after Namath was anti-climax. He packed the excitement of a season, the thrill of a lifetime, into 80 astonishing seconds and no one who saw him could forget, ever."[14] Alabama would go on to win the game, 24–7.

The Tide finished out their schedule with a hard fought 21–14 victory over Auburn to remain undefeated. Playing more than expected when he was pressed into duty as a result of an injury to his back-up, Steve Sloan, Namath contributed to the victory with a 23-yard TD pass to Ray Perkins. He was six of nine for 76 yards. After the game it was announced that the 10–0 Tide would be playing the 9–1 Texas Longhorns in the thirty-first Orange Bowl.

January 1, 1965 would be the first Orange Bowl played at night before a primetime national television audience. Attendance was counted at 72,647. Alabama (ranked number one) was favored by three points over fifth-ranked Texas. In the weeks leading up to the game, it was decided that Namath would be able to quarterback the Tide come New Year's Day, but his chances of playing at all seemed to disappear a few days before the game when his knee gave out during practice. Steve Sloan would be quarterbacking Alabama in the Orange Bowl.

It wasn't until the final minute of the first period that Texas broke a scoreless tie when running back Ernie Koy ran around right end, and after a key block or two, found himself with clear sailing 79 yards for a score: 7–0, Texas. About five minutes into the second quarter, Texas quarterback Jim Hudson heaved a bomb downfield that hit his receiver, George Sauer, Jr., in stride. Sauer raced the distance for a 69-yard scored: 14–0, Texas.

Alabama had managed to come from behind several times during the 1964 season, but at 14–0 the situation was acquiring a certain urgency. After the game Bryant said he hadn't intended to play Namath at all, but then, the boy *wanted* to play, and this was his final collegiate game. Alabama only brought the ball out to their own 13-yard line on the ensuing kickoff. Beginning from deep in their own end, and trailing by 14, Bryant made the decision to send Namath into the game.

After a short gain by one of the backs, Namath went to work — a 25-yard pass to Ray Perkins, another nine to Perkins, 11 yards to Wayne Trimble, 15 yards to Tommy Tolleson, 14 to Wayne Cook, and finally, seven yards and a touchdown to Trimble. Namath had taken the team 87 yards in 14 plays, 81 of those yards through the air, hitting six of 10 passes. With less than five minutes until halftime, it seemed to be the lift Alabama needed, but the Longhorns managed to score another touchdown with 27 seconds left in the second quarter, making it 21–7 at the intermission.

On their initial possession of the second half, Namath promptly guided Alabama downfield to score on a drive in which he threw for 57 yards in seven completions, the final being a 20-yard touchdown pass to Perkins. The lead now cut to 21–14, the teams exchanged punts until Namath again got the Tide moving. But the drive stalled as the fourth quarter got under way, and rather than go in for a tying touchdown, the Tide could only whittle away at the Texas lead with a 26-yard field goal to make it 21–17.

After intercepting a pass, Alabama took possession at the Texas 34, and it seemed to be the break that would help them finally gain the lead; two passes by Namath gave the Tide a first-and-goal at the six-yard line. But after three runs by Steve Bowman only advanced them to the one-yard line, the Tide found themselves facing a fourth-and-goal. A field goal would only draw them to within a point of Texas, so there was no question that, for Bryant, this was definitely a four-down situation, notwithstanding the fact that there were some nine minutes left to play. What happened next was not without controversy. Namath tried to lunge across on a quarterback keeper, and a massive pileup ensued at the goal line. Namath thought he had made it. "One official called it good but another said wait a minute," Namath said, "then when they talked it over, they put the ball back short of the goal."[15] The final verdict resulting from the conference of officials was that Namath had been stopped just short of the goal: Texas took over on downs.

Through the years there have occasionally been accounts that had the game ending there, some even claiming that it was the last play as time ran out. The truth, however, is that Alabama had two more chances to win it. After taking over in the shadow of their own goalpost, the Longhorns failed to move the ball and had to punt. Alabama wound up with excellent field position, beginning in Texas territory, but Namath was intercepted at the 32 by a linebacker named Pete Lammons — it was Lammons' second pick of Namath in the game. Alabama's final opportunity came when they got the ball back with less than two minutes remaining. After hitting Tolleson with a 26-yard pass to the Texas 41, Namath failed to connect on four straight throws. Texas again took over on downs, this time running out the clock.

Namath had come into a game in which his team was trailing 14–0; with him as their quarterback from the second quarter onward, Alabama outscored Texas 17–7. There was no shame in losing, but it hurt just the same. The following day, many newspapers across the country ran a photo of a distraught Namath being consoled by his coach after the game, the old man's arm resting on the young man's shoulder. "I thought he was the most courageous player I've ever seen," Bryant said, pointing out that Namath was aching to play despite the pain of his injured knee.[16]

Bryant wasn't the only one praising Namath after the game. Texas coach Darrell Royal said that his team had stopped everything but Namath, who Royal said simply could not be stopped. Obviously Namath had won the respect of Royal, who in his enthusiasm seemed to have forgotten that his team *had* stopped Namath — about a half-foot from the goal, by the reckoning of the officials. Still, the impression Namath made on the Texas coach was considerable. "A lot of Texans will be mighty happy that we will never again have to play against Joe Namath," he said.[17] The player who stopped Namath on that critical fourth down, linebacker Tommy Nobis, also felt moved to comment. "You know, that Namath is the best," Nobis said, "really number one."[18]

Others agreed: Namath was voted MVP of the game, even in a losing effort. Well, why not? After all, he had set Orange Bowl records, completing 18 of 37 passes for 255 yards and two touchdowns. More than anyone, Namath had made the 1965 Orange Bowl a game to remember. Two people in attendance that night who were very pleased with what they saw were New York Jets president and co-owner Sonny Werblin and Jets coach Weeb Ewbank. "You should have seen the way everybody came forward on the edge of their seats when Namath came into the game," Ewbank said. "I never saw anything more exciting than that boy."[19]

Ewbank had reason to be excited: as of the end of the Orange Bowl, Namath was no longer Bear Bryant's quarterback. The next day, Namath would become Ewbank's quarterback. Even so, Bryant would forever be Namath's coach, the one man whose authority he would always respect. That would be something Ewbank would have to get used to.

January 2, 1965, the day after the Orange Bowl, in a public ceremony held at a Miami Beach luxury hotel, Namath signed with the New York Jets. Signing that contract and becoming the highest paid player in professional football was likely a balm for having lost the Orange Bowl. Legend has it the signing ceremony was only for show, for no sooner had the final gun sounded to end the Orange Bowl than Sonny Werblin raced onto the field to find the dejected Namath and have him sign the contract right then. Or so it has been said.

Werblin wasn't taking any chances. He had abided by Bryant's request that he not talk to Namath during the season, but in the period between the season-ending Auburn game and the Orange Bowl, Werblin had been very busy, as were his competitors for Namath's services. The NFL's St. Louis Cardinals had been the first to come around. In the week leading up to the Orange Bowl, Werblin had met with Namath several times; Namath had already told Werblin that he wanted to play for the Jets, but Werblin had nothing in writing. Feeling anxious, Werblin called Bryant. He wanted Namath to sign right away, and felt that with Bryant's approval he would. But when Werblin told Bryant that Namath had given his word on the matter, Bryant said nothing more was needed. If Namath gave his word, then come January 2 he would be signing with the Jets. For Werblin, it had been a long time coming: he had been looking for his marquee player since purchasing the franchise in 1963.

During his senior year, Namath had been advised by Bryant to start thinking about his asking price because soon enough the pro scouts would be coming around. It was Bryant who told Namath to set his price at $200,000. That was small potatoes to a man like Werblin. He was used to thinking big; he was used to pageantry, he was used to show business, and he was used to stars. Namath was perfect for him — *he* was perfect for *Namath*.

David "Sonny" Werblin had spent 30 years with MCA (Music Corporation of America), wheeling and dealing, working out television contracts with some of the biggest names in show business. He started at the bottom in 1932 and worked his way up, eventually becoming vice-

president of the company and president of the subsidiary MCA-TV. It was Werblin who orchestrated Jack Benny's move from NBC to CBS, and it was Werblin who swung the deal that brought
Benny back to NBC again. Nobody could put a deal together like Showbiz Sonny. That's how
Werblin had become involved in the AFL in the first place. In the league's early days, Werblin
was asked to work out the AFL's network television contract.

At the time, the AFL's New York franchise — the Titans — was owned by Harry Wismer, a
former sportscaster who got in on the ground floor when the league launched in 1959. Wismer's
love of the game, and of his team, was greater than his business skills. It wasn't that the Titans
were a bad team: they went 7–7 in each of their first two seasons, so despite the fact that they
weren't champions, they did maintain a level of mediocrity against the odds. Working against
the team was an urgent lack of funds: Wismer just couldn't get people to come out and see them.
In New York, if it was football you wanted, it had to be the Giants — now *there* was a team. As
for the Titans, well, few people wanted to sit in a decrepit, ramshackle place like the Polo Grounds
to watch what most regarded as a minor league club.

Of course, the Titans weren't the only team struggling financially during the AFL's first
season, merely the team suffering most demonstrably. In 1960, none of the AFL's eight teams had
shown a profit, but the Titans were certainly bringing up the rear. The situation remained
unchanged after the 1961 season. Wismer was often the butt of jokes among the press, who found
his inflated attendance numbers risible, knowing very well that actual attendance was well below
the numbers Wismer claimed. Werblin once indiscreetly told Wismer that he would like to own
Wismer's team and show him how to run it. The comment infuriated Wismer, and despite
Werblin's claims to have meant nothing by it, he could not allay Wismer's suspicions that he was
out to grab his team. There was no doubt as to the remark's underlying truth: the idea definitely
interested Werblin — interested him *a lot*.

Werblin would get his chance when the Titans' financial situation bottomed out in 1962.
The team was so far in the hole that Wismer could no longer pay his players. The AFL could
not allow its New York franchise to die off, so the league took over paying the team's salaries with
money siphoned off from other teams. After the Titans were taken away from Wismer, he went
to court and fought to keep the team, but to no avail: the Titans were sold in bankruptcy court
for $1 million to the Gotham Football Club, Inc.

The Gotham Football Club was a partnership put together by Werblin who, aside from
being president of MCA-TV, was also director of the Monmouth Race Track in New Jersey.
Werblin brought in Monmouth associates Leon Hess, Townsend Martin, and Phil Iselin, along
with Donald Lillis, president of Bowie Race Track in Maryland and a partner in a Wall Street
brokerage firm.

Werblin immediately set about completely remolding the team. It may have been a partnership, but there was little doubt as to whose team it really was — it was Werblin's all the way.
Because of his keen interest, Werblin was voted president of the club by his partners. On April
15, 1963, within weeks of purchasing the team, Werblin announced that they would thereafter
be known as the New York Jets. Even the team's color would be changed from blue to Werblin's
favorite color of green (he was born on St. Patrick's day). He also announced the hiring of Weeb
Ewbank as the club's head coach. Ewbank had coached the NFL's Baltimore Colts during their
1958 and '59 championship seasons, but after three years without another title, Baltimore owner
Carroll Rosenbloom grew impatient and fired Ewbank. It was a decision he perhaps regretted
down the road. Two months after being fired by Rosenbloom, Ewbank was offered the head
coaching job with the Jets, and even managed to get Werblin to also make him general manager.
Ewbank signed with the Jets on April 12, 1963.

Very little of the Titans club would remain under the new ownership. Only a handful of
players were retained (receiver Don Maynard, linebacker Larry Grantham, running back Bill

Mathis, defensive back Dainard Paulson, and punter Curley Johnson), as was personnel director George Sauer, Sr. Ewbank brought in a whole new coaching staff, young men in their thirties, all but one of which had no professional coaching experience. Among them was 31-year-old offensive line coach Chuck Knox, who would be pivotal in the Namath saga. Knox hailed from the same region of western Pennsylvania as Namath, and was even head coach at Ellwood City High School in the late 1950s when Namath would have played against them with the Beaver Falls Tigers. With that firsthand experience to draw from, Knox certainly knew whereof he spoke in recommending Namath to Werblin and Ewbank.

One thing Werblin knew was lacking for this new production was a suitable theater. Shea Stadium, which was slated to be the team's new home venue, would not be completed in time for the 1963 season, so the Jets would have to endure another year at the Polo Grounds. Werblin was determined to get a bigger turnout nonetheless, which he accomplished with a publicity blitz. The Titans had sold a mere 500 season tickets in 1962: the Jets sold 4,000 during their maiden season in 1963. With the team moving into Shea Stadium the following season, things would surely be better still. Werblin was business savvy in a way Wismer hadn't been. It wasn't just a matter of advertising, but of *smart* advertising. Werblin figured that if the Giants could only accommodate 60,000 people per game, that still left millions of potential patrons to draw from in the nation's most populace city. And that wasn't all: New Jersey was close enough to factor in as well. Once the Jets moved into Shea, Werblin would walk the parking lot during games, checking the license plates on cars. He noticed that many of the cars came from New Jersey, giving him an indication of which fan base to market to. If the football snobs in New York were going to stick with the Giants and look down their noses at the Jets, the folks from Jersey were just fine with Werblin. Their money was just as good, and besides, being from Monmouth, Werblin already had a fondness for Jersey.

Werblin and company also had capital to throw into the venture. When the AFL had begun, league commissioner Joe Foss announced that the league had no intention of getting into a money war with the NFL, but then, why would they? The AFL certainly wasn't pulling in the money the NFL was. Could the AFL even hope to keep up if a bidding war over players ensued? Probably not, and the mere thought of invoking the wrath of the NFL may have made some in the AFL cautious. Not Werblin: they didn't scare him. "The NFL couldn't buy shoe polish from most of the owners in the AFL," Werblin proclaimed.[20] The NFL was put on unofficial notice that the bidding wars were on when the Jets beat their cross-town rivals, the Giants, in landing Ohio State running back Matt Snell, who signed a three-year contract with the Jets in 1964 for $100,000. Snell had been the Jets' first-round draft choice, while the Giants made him their third-round pick. He maintained that it wasn't just the money that made up his mind: after all, the Giants were a wealthy franchise. What swayed him was the fact that Werblin took the time to come and meet with him personally, something the Giants' owners couldn't be bothered to do. In signing with the Jets, Snell became the franchise's first name college player: he was worth the money. Werblin proclaimed his belief in the star system, likening the playing field to a stage. If you expect people to come to your show, you've got to put a star on the stage.[21]

Werblin's plan was coming together. Prior to the start of the 1964 season, Jets season ticket sales were growing, and when they were able to play their home games at Shea attendance increased dramatically, as Werblin knew it would (from 91,000 in 1963 to 298,000 in 1964). Even so, those were still lean times. During their first two seasons—losing seasons—the Jets lost $700,000 in '63 and $648,000 in '64. But Werblin was building toward something, and he knew it wouldn't come overnight. There was one key ingredient still missing. If the show was going to be a hit, Werblin reckoned it all hinged on landing a star—a *real* star, someone with charisma. "I needed to build a franchise with somebody who could do more than just play," Werblin said.[22]

Werblin considered Tulsa's Jerry Rhome, who was setting NCAA passing records, but upon meeting him, Werblin found Rhome decidedly lacking in charisma.[23] This was not what Werblin wanted; it was not what the team needed, nor what the league needed. Meeting Namath was an altogether different experience. Werblin sparked to Namath right away; he took note of how Namath instantly gathered a room's attention by merely walking through the door. *This* was what was needed.

When representatives from the St. Louis Cardinals came to see Namath they reacted to his $200,000 asking price—and request for a brand new Lincoln Continental—with high drama, but they took his demands back with them. Back where? And to who? That was a bit nebulous. They had told Namath that the price was agreeable, their theatrics notwithstanding, but for whom they were really dealing wasn't altogether certain. When Werblin heard the news he immediately upped the ante by informing Namath that he was thinking something more along the lines of $300,000. He might have thought that would get rid of the Cardinals: after all, St. Louis already had a fine quarterback in Charley Johnson, who had led the NFL in passing yardage in 1964. Why would a small-market club like St. Louis chance bankrupting itself over a pricey, untried college player with a bad knee, especially when it didn't appear to be essential to their team in its present situation? Werblin was suspicious. The Cardinals sent vice-president Billy Bidwell to meet with Namath and his attorney, Mike Bite, and Bite called Werblin to give him a heads up about the meeting. Bite wanted to hear the Cardinals out, and Werblin had been dealing long enough to know that was only natural. But he wanted to make it clear to Bite that the Jets would match any offer the Cardinals made.

The meeting was just weird, with Bidwell frequently leaving the room to call his brother, Cardinals president Stormy Bidwell, when certain important points came up. Bite took those opportunities to phone Werblin to ask for advice. After Bidwell continued to leave the room to call his brother, Werblin felt sure the Cardinals were acting on behalf of another party. It had to be the New York Giants: it was the only thing that made sense. The Jets had already burned the Giants with the signing of Snell. Could the Giants endure the humiliation of losing to the Jets again? Besides, if it became known that the Giants were making a play for Namath, might Werblin not throw caution to the wind and escalate things purely out of a sense of rivalry? The Jets did, after all, have a need to prove themselves to the city. If the Giants were bidding for Namath, they figured it was best to remain in the shadows.

Werblin wasn't entirely certain what was going on, but the Bidwell negotiating strategy struck him as odd. Werblin told Bite that the next time Bidwell wanted to go call his brother Stormy, Bite might request to speak to him also. Once he had Stormy on the phone, Werblin told Bite to lay it all out for him: here are the terms, and if Stormy agreed then Namath would sign with St. Louis. If Stormy dodged, then he was dealing for someone else. Bite followed Werblin's instructions, and when he got on the phone with Stormy he told him what Namath wanted. But Stormy couldn't answer—he had to call someone else first. There was no doubt about it now: the Cardinals were fronting. Bite rescinded the offer and said that Namath would be signing with the Jets.

Before negotiations broke down, St. Louis had gone as high as $389,000 (or *somebody* had). But Namath had really already decided to sign with the Jets. Whoever he was dealing with here—the Cardinals, Giants, or whoever—he didn't trust them. Why would he trust anyone who wouldn't come out from behind the curtain and meet with him face to face? *Werblin he trusted.* Werblin struck Namath as an honest man, a man whose sense of fairness was indicative of character and made him the kind of man Namath would feel comfortable working for. Just as importantly, Werblin was a very likeable man.[24]

Reaction to Namath's contract ranged from amazement to disbelief, resentment, and even outrage. Reported sums were generally in the neighborhood of $400,000. It was more than any professional football player had ever gotten. Hell, it was comparable to the entire payroll of most teams in either the NFL or the AFL. "[I]f Namath is worth $400,000 then I'm worth a million," said Frank Ryan.[25] Uh, yeah, who the hell is Frank Ryan? Well, he *was* the quarterback of the Cleveland Browns. How many people remember that?

Cleveland Browns owner Art Modell, exemplifying the frustration of the NFL, said that Namath's contract would be the ruination of professional football.[26] The dreaded bidding war between leagues was on, and it was on full throttle.

Dick Wood did not shy away from expressing the opinion that no player fresh out of college was worth such a price, but then, he had reason to be upset. Wood had quarterbacked the Jets the prior season; with Namath coming to the team, surely Wood's future with the club was more than a little doubtful.[27]

Namath, Werblin, Ewbank — all three were coy when asked how much money was involved. Werblin allowed that it was more than anyone had paid for any single player before, but was quick to add that the team felt Namath was worth the investment. Namath demurred, saying that as the numbers got higher, he left it all to Mike Bite and went out to play golf.[28] Only Bite knew for sure, he said.[29] All told, the final tally was $427,000, broken down as follows: a $25,000 annual salary for Namath for three years, which included no-cut and no-trade clauses, a $225,000 signing bonus in deferred payments, a $7,000 Lincoln Continental, $30,000 lawyer fee for Bite, and $10,000 annual scouting fees for three years for Namath's brothers, Frank and Bob, and his brother-in-law, Tommy Sims.

The sum — so astronomical in its day — was really the catalyst for the merger of the two leagues. The bidding war had to end. A year later, the two leagues agreed to a merger, which was scheduled to take place in 1970. A byproduct of the agreement was the decision for the two leagues to play each other in a championship game: it would come to be known as the Super Bowl. How about that? One could even make a case that Joe Namath brought about the Super Bowl.

Werblin defended the contract, saying that he didn't expect to lose money. If there was one thing Werblin knew, it was box office — Namath *was* box office. Werblin might not have been able to pin star quality down, but he knew it couldn't be faked or manufactured. It was either there or it wasn't, he said, and Namath definitely had it.[30] And now whatever Namath had, the New York Jets would have too.

But Werblin did have a moment of weakness. It may have been brief, but it was expensive. He had suspected that his nemesis, New York Giants owner Wellington Mara, was lurking in the shadows, and maybe he got a little nervous. Namath wanted to play in New York, not some second-rate market like St. Louis. What if the Cardinals came out with it and told him that they couldn't actually afford him, but the Giants could, and were interested. Like most college prospects, Namath was an NFL fan, and like virtually all sports fans, he considered the NFL the superior league. Hell, the AFL had only gotten started when Namath was getting packed for Tuscaloosa. If the money was there, maybe Namath would sign with the Giants. It worried Werblin because, as close as he felt he was to signing Namath, he knew that things could come undone in an instant. Then Werblin would be left with nothing: no brilliant rookie, no charismatic superstar, no franchise-saving — nay, *AFL-saving* — wunderkind: no quarterback that he felt confident he could build a future on. Werblin couldn't help it: he had to hedge his bets. He couldn't be left without a name draft pick at quarterback.

When Werblin was at his most uncertain about how the Namath deal would play out, he entered into talks with Notre Dame quarterback John Huarte. He lacked Namath's ability to captivate a crowd just by showing up, but Huarte had won the Heisman Trophy, so aside from ability he also had a degree of name recognition. Huarte got $200,000 when he signed with the Jets a week after Namath's well-publicized signing. Even though only roughly half of Namath's contract, Huarte's signing was viewed as further evidence of a franchise in the throes of excess. Werblin found himself on the defensive, having to justify it all by explaining what should have been obvious. He did it, he said, because he had to; he had to because he was determined to put together the best football team in the country. If he really wanted to achieve that, how could he not be willing to pay for it? Werblin reasoned that the bonuses would take care of themselves, noting that the team took in thousands of dollars in ticket sales the week after signing Namath.

But $600,000 for two players? And both of them quarterbacks at that. It isn't like he could play them both: it had to be one or the other. The Jets, who had been in need of a good quarterback, now found themselves with a surplus. Aside from Namath and Huarte, there was also Dick Wood, second-year man Mike Taliaferro, Pete Liske, and kicker Jim Turner, who doubled as third-string quarterback. Obviously, some of them would have to go. But what if the ones who didn't pan out in camp and preseason turned out to be the $600,000 worth of bonus babies? Then Werblin's embarrassment of riches would simply be embarrassing. Ewbank publicly conceded that if Namath flopped there would be no saving face for the franchise.[31] Hey, no pressure here, Joe.

Everyone had to wonder, was he worth the money — was he worth twice what Werblin was paying the Heisman winner? Could he take all the relentless publicity that came with playing in New York City? Could he withstand the scrutiny? Would he wither in the spotlight? And what about that knee, by the way? It had been announced that Namath needed surgery. How bad was the knee? Did anyone even know? How much would it limit him? How much would it take away from his game? If too much, then maybe he'd be a washout. What if you don't make it, Joe? "Take everything into account," Namath said, "my injury, all the publicity, all those things you've mentioned, and just throw them away, because *I am going to make it.*"[32]

The first order of business, then, was getting that knee taken care of. Paging Dr. James Nicholas.

Within sports circles, Namath made Dr. James Nicholas something of a celebrity. Nicholas was the orthopedic surgeon who through the years would periodically be called on to piece Namath's knees back together. "When they write my obituary," Nicholas once said, "the first thing they'll mention will be Namath's knees."[33] This despite the fact that Nicholas once counted John Kennedy among his patients: he was part of the surgical team that had performed the spinal surgery on Kennedy in 1954. But Nicholas was right: when he passed away in 2006, the *New York Times'* writeup by Richard Goldstein on July 17 began by crediting Nicholas with performing the surgeries that saved Namath's career.

In mid–January of 1965, more than a hundred print, television, and radio reporters packed Toots Shor's midtown Manhattan restaurant to listen to Werblin's announcement regarding Namath's impending knee surgery. They didn't learn much, just the when and where — January 25 at Lenox Hill Hospital. Werblin could add little else since nobody would really know much until Dr. Nicholas cut the knee open and got a good look inside.

After making the incision, Dr. Nicholas found that the medial meniscus had torn, become detached and bunched up, which was the reason Namath had been unable to get full extension of the leg. The cruciate ligament had also been stretched to the point of becoming very slack. Nicholas removed the shredded meniscus cartilage, then tightened the cruciate by doubling it back on itself. It was determined that the void left by the missing cartilage would have to be filled by body fluids. The work was accomplished in 73 minutes and Nicholas was pleased, feeling that the knee was workable enough for Namath to last four years in professional football. He would, however, have to wear a brace on the knee to stabilize it during play, which Nicholson didn't feel would be so cumbersome as to inhibit Namath.

Press coverage was pretty intense. Everybody wondered how that $400,000 knee would turn out. Namath remained in the hospital for twelve days, so the personnel at Lenox Hill had to grow accustomed to the constant presence of reporters. They weren't used to it, but they had to learn to accept it for the better part of two weeks. Really, the New York Jets hadn't been accustomed to much media attention either, but they too would have to get used to it. Only for them it wouldn't be a matter of twelve days—it would be twelve years.

Throughout the 1960s, Pete Perreault was an offensive lineman for the New York Jets. In 1971 he was traded to the Minnesota Vikings, and for Perreault the contrast was striking. When he was with the Jets, Perreault had grown accustomed to the hullabaloo: the press that met them at the airport, the throng of fans crowding the team bus, screaming girls and autograph seekers waiting outside the hotel, hordes of reporters and television cameras following the team around. When Perreault went to Minnesota, all of this was suddenly absent. It occurred to him that this was what it had always been like for those teams that didn't have Joe Namath. Without Namath, Perreault concluded, you're nothing but a football team.[34]

That kind of media scrutiny began immediately upon Namath's signing with the Jets. It was encouraged by Werblin, of course, who adhered to the show business philosophy that any publicity was good publicity. It would probably be an ego boost to any rookie, but it couldn't have made Namath's situation easier. The New York Jets had not experienced such a media presence at previous training camps. Resentment toward Namath among his new teammates was already palpable, no matter how much they tried to deny or downplay it. It's only natural for a seasoned veteran to resent a young kid getting so much more money and attention.

Rookies tend to be easy to spot in training camp: they are the ones with the wide eyes. There is a vaguely lost countenance they can't help but wear. Sure they want to impress the coaches on the field, but otherwise they are quiet, cautious, a bit nervous; in general, they try not to call too much attention to themselves. In that sense, Namath was not dissimilar from any other rookie. Teammates at that time remembered him as not saying much, and coming across as rather shy. But however discreet he might have preferred to be, keeping a low profile was one luxury Namath didn't get. He didn't need to call attention to himself: it was coming, like it or not.

Of course, Namath was not unaware of the hard feelings some of his teammates were harboring towards him, but Werblin, for one, was unconcerned. He maintained that Namath could take care of himself, and more than that, Namath knew how to handle men.[35] Never having been one to complain, Namath voiced some displeasure over the situation nonetheless. "They should give me a chance to prove myself before they come down on my head like this," he said.[36]

Before the season started, he took occasion to address the team during a players-only meeting. All he was interested in, he told them, was winning. He assumed that they were too, and he assumed as well that each of them had gotten as much in their respective contracts as they could, just as he had. If any of them had a gripe with him, he would be glad to settle accounts with them outside. No takers. Now all he had to worry about was the wellspring of resentment from players on all the other teams. He could win his teammates over; they would like him well enough once they got to know him, and they were, after all, working toward a common goal. For that reason, he could win them over with his passing skills, if nothing else. He couldn't win his opponents over with his passing: if anything, they'd despise him all the more for it. *Those guys wanted to kill him.*

Protecting Namath became the team's top priority. Ewbank insisted his quarterback stay in the pocket. When he did venture out, Ewbank didn't always wait to express his displeasure. "I don't want him to run with the ball," Ewbank said. "I never want him to run with the ball. When he made that long run, he went right past me, and I kept yelling to him to get out of bounds."[37] Ewbank was recalling Namath's 39-yard run in Oakland in 1966, an absurdly leisurely jaunt down the sideline, which had fortunately presented clear sailing for a good distance. Because he didn't want him risking injury by running, Ewbank instructed Namath to drop back deeper in the pocket, not six or seven yards, but ten or even twelve. This would put more distance between Namath and the front line. It would also mean that by the time he got back and set up his receivers would have time to run deeper patterns, which Namath was, of course, inclined to throw.

Targets that they are, quarterbacks require added consideration. With all of the money invested in him, and having already had knee surgery before he even began his pro career, protecting Namath seemed even more important than it might otherwise have been. This was impressed upon the offensive linemen in no uncertain terms. If they missed their block and the team lost Namath for it, they were told, they needn't walk back to the huddle — they could keep right on walking. Tackle Winston Hill spoke of how vital it was for a lineman to keep his man off Namath — vital to Namath's health, and consequently to a lineman's job security.[38]

"We can't let anything happen to Joe," said right guard Dave Herman. "I'm getting paid to keep him healthy."[39] Sure they felt pressure, but there was also a great deal of pride that came with being Namath's first line of defense. They were protecting the most expensive player the game had ever seen, and were therefore trusted with one of the most vital jobs in all of sport. Under the circumstances, how could they not feel special themselves? They also admired Namath, and the fact is they just plain liked the guy and developed a fierce loyalty to him. "If you had to bite a guy in the gonads to take him down," said center John Schmitt, "you'd take him down before you'd let him get to Joseph."[40] These guys knew Namath was their bread and butter.

Running backs were a slightly different story. Sure, they liked Namath too, but running backs are stars in their own right, and as such can resent not getting their share of the spotlight. Let the linemen protect the quarterback; after all, that's their job. They're used to doing the grunt work and getting none of the glory. But any running back with the New York Jets had to understand that this was a passing team, and there was no question as to who the star of the show was. A running back with the Jets had to pass block as well as run: it was mandatory. It was something that weighed on John Riggins when he came to the Jets in 1971. Riggins admitted to worrying about his blocking, saying that the coaches might say you did a bad job if you missed your block and any other quarterback got hurt, but if it was Namath who got hurt when you missed your block, well, Riggins said, the coaches would accept no excuses.[41]

For the most part, Namath's offensive line did an admirable job of protecting him. Through the 1960s, Namath was consistently dropped for a loss less than any quarterback in the league despite his curtailed mobility. The knee injuries he would suffer as a pro were not the result of poor protection, but rather were more freak incidents. Even more exasperating, they tended to come in preseason.

When Namath signed with the Jets in 1965, thirteen-year veteran defensive lineman Dave Hanner of the Green Bay Packers reacted to the reported price tag by saying, "A man who gets that much money doesn't usually want to pay the price."[42] But when it came to paying the price, Hanner was as wrong as wrong could possibly be, for no one could say that Namath did not pay a heavy price during his years as a professional football player: he paid, with interest. Anyone who knew Namath, whether teammate or opponent, came to admire his toughness.

After the 1965 season had ended, Namath was not satisfied with how his right knee felt and requested to have another surgery. The Jets were unwilling to chance it, and the team physicians reasoned that as long as he was able to play a full schedule (which he did) and win Rookie of the Year (which he did as well), then there was no point in gambling by cutting into the knee unnecessarily. Whether they were right or wrong, perhaps it was best for Namath that he didn't get his way, for as it turned out he would be needing another operation soon enough.

Showbiz Sonny was always looking for an angle, always working a deal. Since attendance at exhibition games tended to be significantly lower than for the regular season, Werblin tried to find a way to beef up the count. The Jets' first preseason game of 1966 would be against Houston; Werblin arranged for the game to be played at Legion Field in Birmingham, making it something of a homecoming for Namath. Surely people would turn out to watch their adopted hometown hero. It worked: a record preseason crowd of 57,205 showed up. The game was still in the first quarter when Matt Snell slammed the ball into the ground in frustration after gaining just two yards. Snell thought he heard the whistle signaling the end of the play before he took his frustration out on the ball, but Houston defensive tackle Ernie Ladd grabbed the ball and started to run with it. Namath was in the process of pointing out to the referee that it was a dead ball when defensive end Don Floyd took him down with a block. It might have looked purposeful, but Floyd would say afterward that it wasn't. Floyd — six-three and 245 pounds — took Namath down at the knees. There was a collective gasp throughout the stadium when Namath didn't get back up, and a certain solemnity about the crowd as they watched him limp from the field. Some homecoming.

Upon examining the knee in New York the following day, Dr. Nicholas diagnosed it as merely a minor strain. Nicholas was encouraged by the X-rays, which showed "no damage to the bony structure of the knee."[43] Upon aspirating the knee, Nicholas took the lack of blood in the fluid as a further good sign. Namath was told to stay off his feet for a couple days and he could return to playing in a few weeks. It was certainly an optimistic diagnosis. It was also fantasy: the truth was much worse. How Namath could play an entire season with such an injury would amaze and baffle everyone. Ewbank's hope was that by keeping Namath out of the preseason games the knee would mend by the time the regular season opened, but teammates would recall watching Namath at practice during the course of the season, seeing him often barely able to walk in the days following a game, wincing with every step. Toward the end of the season, his problems were very evident in his play.

It was late in the season when Howard Cosell turned up at a Jets' practice session, and after seeing Namath very visibly suffering through the task of simply walking, Cosell went on television and predicted Namath would be unable to play in the Jets' next game.[44] Namath made a liar out of Cosell: of course he played. What Cosell didn't know was that the pain he observed in Namath at that practice session was the same pain Namath had been enduring all season long. It must have been a great mental strain as well, for not only was he suffering physically, but also had the added psychological burden of knowing that Dr. Nicholas was wrong: it was no simple strain — there was something very wrong.

The day after the 1966 season ended, Namath went to see Nicholas to have him re-examine the knee. Immediately after the examination, Nicholas called Ewbank. Namath had torn cartilage in the knee again: it would have to come out. Ewbank was stunned. He surely thought back to that August night in Birmingham. He couldn't believe Namath had played the entire season on a shredded knee: *nobody* could. While he could have insisted on a more thorough examination of the knee following the injury, Namath was unwilling to sit out the entire season, which is what surgery would have meant. How's that for paying the price, Dave Hanner? And there would be plenty more to come.

That kind of grit was something Namath would exhibit throughout his career, all the more so when the situation — and the opponent — called for it. One opponent that always challenged Namath's fortitude was the Oakland Raiders. The Raiders were cheap shot artists; in fact, they seemed to take a measure of pride in that reputation. When Namath came into the league with his $400,000 contract, the Oakland defense made him a priority. "He's always been fun to play against," said six-foot-eight, 275-pound defensive lineman Ben Davidson. "He's the poor little rich kid."[45]

"I think I like Oakland less than any other team," Namath said. "When I was a rookie they went for my knee and no one else has ever done that."[46] They went for his knee and worse. Going for his knee might end his season, maybe even his career, but it was even said they tried to kill him.

The Jets had beaten the Raiders on a Saturday night at Shea in the fourth game of the 1967 season, which would turn out to be Oakland's only defeat of the season until losing Super Bowl II to the Green Bay Packers in January of '68. Come the thirteenth week of the season, with that loss still the only blemish on their record, the Raiders were happy to be hosting the Jets.

New York led 14–10 at halftime, with Namath throwing for one touchdown and scoring another by diving into the end zone after recovering a fumble, but the second half would be disastrous for the Jets. Early into the third quarter it was six-foot-five, 270-pound Ike Lassiter who crowned Namath, delivering a shot to the head as he released a pass. The blow cracked Namath's face. But it didn't end there. As the Jets fell further behind Namath was forced into passing on almost every down, and the Raiders used each play for target practice.

Although Lassiter's shot to the face had done the most obvious damage, it was Davidson's cheap shot that got all the notice. Chasing Namath out of the pocket, Davidson was frustrated at having been unable to catch him throughout the day, and by then he didn't care if Namath had the ball or not: Davidson was not going to be denied. After Namath threw the ball, Davidson wound up and struck a blow to the head with such force it sent Namath's helmet flying. The officials had been outrageously oblivious to Oakland infractions — hey, they were in Oakland — but this time they flagged it. Namath was slow in rising, and didn't seem altogether sure where he was going when he did get up. At first he wobbled toward the Oakland bench, looking not unlike Foster Brooks making his way to the podium at a celebrity roast, but after center John Schmitt redirected him, Namath gathered himself and made his way back to the huddle. Then he started throwing again. He might not win the game, but he wasn't going to quit. A touchdown pass to George Sauer, another to Don Maynard: the Raiders could only shake their heads in wonder. They had certainly seen men crumble under lesser assaults. "You can't intimidate Namath," said John Madden, then an assistant coach with the Raiders. "He just doesn't scare."[47] Payment enough yet, Hanner?

One of the outcomes of the 1966 merger agreement was that NFL commissioner Pete Rozelle would act as High Sheriff of both leagues pending their co-joining in 1970. Rozelle had zero tolerance for public criticism of game officials by players and coaches, but in this instance Ewbank seemed not to care. "This will probably cost me money, but I've got to say it," Ewbank told the press as he launched into a chastisement of officials "for letting the game get out of hand. I thought the officiating was poor."[48] That was putting it mildly. The game had practically devolved into a donnybrook.

In the locker room after the game, his cheekbone broken, his face grotesquely swollen and discolored, Namath took on the press. They all wanted to know who busted him up. Was it Davidson? Lassiter? Hell, no! Namath told them it didn't even happen in the game. He informed the press that he had hurt himself biting down too hard on a steak bone earlier in the day. You think you put a hurtin' on me Ike Lassiter? How you liking me now Ben Davidson? Punks. Nothin' but six-foot-eight-inch punks. Oakland always took pride in pummeling Namath, and this then should have been their proudest moment. After all, they had beaten him senseless and left him a mess. But Namath was too defiant to allow them the opportunity to revel in it. In the end, they could only admire him for it.

Even then Namath wasn't through. In the following week's season-ender in San Diego he lit the place up, throwing four touchdowns while racking up 343 yards passing. That brought his season total to 4,007 yards, making him the first quarterback in professional football history to throw for 4,000 yards in a season. The record would not be broken until years later when the league extended the season from 14 to 16 games, and otherwise introduced new rules designed to benefit the passing game. Namath did it when the yardage came hard.

Although Namath had led the Jets to their first winning record in 1967, at 8–5–1 they failed to make the playoffs. The 4,007 passing yards seemed wasted in light of that. Being tough enough to withstand thugs like the Raiders was all fine and good, but in the end the only thing that would really chap their asses would be for the Jets to win it all. If the Jets were ever going to be champions, 1968 would be the year to get it done.

The feeling among the players when camp opened that year was that this would be the season when all the pieces fell into place. So much of Namath's legend, of course, rests on that season. It was the year Namath won it all: he was voted the AFL's Most Valuable Player, but probably more significantly to Namath, his teammates voted him the team's MVP for the first time. There was the sweet victory over Oakland in the AFL championship game at Shea Stadium in late December, and ultimately the Super Bowl against Baltimore. The images are unforgettable, and so essential to the Namath legend. There was Namath holding court by the pool of a Fort Lauderdale hotel in the days before the game, smiling, relaxing: what, me worry? Only the Cleveland Browns had beaten Baltimore all year, and Baltimore corrected that one flaw in their record by mopping up the field with the Browns in the NFL championship game, beating them 34–0. What chance did the Jets have? None, said the experts. Namath smiled all the wider. It's as though he knew this was his destiny. What benevolent God would deny him this?

Namath was happy to win the Super Bowl MVP honor as well, but he would have just as gladly seen it go to Matt Snell. What did Namath need with another award? He already had the whole world; in light of that, one more award couldn't mean much. And with the Super Bowl triumph, Namath's celebrity catapulted through the ionosphere. He was paid $60,000 for a mere ten days of work on the film *Norwood*. Yeah, the movie offers were coming in, as were those from advertising agencies. If you want to sell something, get Namath to pitch it. Who could resist buying something that Joe Namath was using? Who didn't want to be like Joe Namath? Everybody wanted a piece of Namath now; there was no bigger celebrity anywhere in the world. It was enough to give a man like Vince Lombardi troubled dreams.

Of course, football, the NFL, Pete Rozelle, they could none of them fail to ride the crest of the wave. In 1970 pro football was going primetime with the launching of *Monday Night Football* on ABC, and ABC Sports president Roone Arledge specifically requested that Namath and the Jets be featured on the first broadcast. Arledge knew that when you launch something, you do it with as much fanfare and mass appeal as possible to maximize the project's initial success. He reasoned that, more than anything else, Namath would lure viewers to that first Monday night broadcast. Rozelle didn't take much convincing: Namath meant ratings — everybody knew it.

ABC-TV publicist Beano Cook likened having Namath on a Monday night broadcast to "having the Pope say your mass."[49] It would remain that way throughout Namath's career, despite the fact that he never once managed a victory on *Monday Night Football*. "Win or lose," said *Time* magazine, "Namath generates more high-voltage excitement than any other player in the game."[50]

Had Lombardi lived just a few more weeks, he would surely have watched that first *Monday Night Football* broadcast on September 21, 1970. He would then have seen the brash Namath brought low. With the Jets trailing by 10 points late in the game, Namath took them 80 yards to score with just four passes, the final being a beautiful 33-yard throw arched perfectly over the shoulder of George Sauer as he glided down the sideline and in for the score, so perfect it almost qualified as a work of art. With the lead cut to three points, Namath had one last shot with two minutes left, one last chance to thrill a national audience with that Namath hoodoo. But it didn't turn out that way. Looking increasingly desperate, Namath tried to hit Emerson Boozer across the middle, but the pass fell very short and was intercepted by linebacker Billy Andrews, who scrambled to his feet and proceeded to race like a mad bull into the end zone. It was pandemonium: 85,000 Cleveland fans went wild as their team celebrated in the end zone. And amid all of the chaos there was Namath, utterly dejected, head hanging low, looking not unlike a little boy who had been shamed in front of everyone. Howard Cosell started to say something but stopped abruptly when the monitor switched to a shot of Namath. For once, Cosell knew better than to talk. He let the image speak for itself. A somewhat melodramatic personality himself, Cosell knew drama when he saw it. His broadcast partner, Keith Jackson, was not as intuitive. Being a broadcaster, Jackson felt inclined to break the silence in the booth, but in light of the images on the screen, his comment was comically inadequate. He could only think to note Namath's seeming depression.

And what would Lombardi have been thinking at that moment? It is just possible that there would have been a tinge of "I told you so" in the old coach, but it isn't likely that Lombardi would have taken any satisfaction from it. How could he? No one knew better than Lombardi how hard it could be. He had seen great players come and go and he had seen what the game could do to a man, how it used men up and discarded them. It's what sport does. No, it doesn't seem likely that Lombardi would have enjoyed the moment. More than likely he would have felt empathy for Namath. Nobody knows like an old coach.

What he couldn't have known — what no one could have known — was that it was really the beginning of the end for Broadway Joe. It was the start of a long, painful decline, years of disappointing, mediocre seasons, injury-shortened seasons, *awful* seasons. The triumphs were fewer from then on, and were seldom of the sort worthy of someone of such renown. In a very real sense, that game was the marking post that divided Namath's career, separating the glory days from those, well, not so glorious.

Even so, there were still those moments — and one has to wonder if they haven't been aggrandized because they involved Namath — when there was still magic in the air. After missing almost two full seasons due to injuries Namath returned in November of 1971, coming off the bench to wow a partisan crowd at Shea Stadium with a three-touchdown performance against San Francisco, a comeback that fell just short when Namath, trailing by three points, threw an interception in the end zone on the game's final play. It quashed an exciting comeback bid, and one might have expected it to have soured what came close to being a glorious reaffirmation, a triumph for the ages. But unlike Mudville, there was still joy in Shea Stadium that day. After the game, fans mobbed the field and people stood applauding long after the gun had sounded. Their team had lost, yet the people not only seemed oblivious to that fact, they even acted as though they had just won a championship. Win, lose, what did it matter? All that really seemed important to the fans was that they had their man back, and more than that, he gave them a game — he gave them a *day* — that they would remember for the rest of their lives. But what if it hadn't been Namath? What if some other quarterback had come into the game and *almost* won it? Would the people have been so forgiving? Would they have been so joyous, so ... awed? Would they have bragged, "I was *there!* I *saw* it! I saw *him!*" Joe Namath not bigger than football? The *hell* you say!

It's interesting now to look back at all the pieces that had to fall into place to make a Joe Namath possible. It all starts with family, of course: it's that way for all of us. Namath's older brothers, Bob and Frank, were tough kids, and they cultivated the same in their younger brother, never treating him gingerly and impressing by example. From them Namath learned never to show weakness to an opponent. What if Namath hadn't had two older brothers instilling that toughness from an early age? What if he hadn't had an early coach and father figure like Larry Bruno? What if Georgia had played it smart and not passed on Namath as simply a Maryland reject, and what if Maryland coach Tom Nugent hadn't gotten in touch with Bear Bryant? What if there had been no Bear Bryant in Namath's life, teaching him the true discipline that went into winning? Perhaps most of all, what if Sonny Werblin hadn't bought a lowly, bankrupt franchise like the New York Titans? Chances are that Namath would have wound up with the New York Giants, and he would have been the same swinging playboy. But like all the other womanizing athletes of that time, few people would have heard of his exploits off the field. Werblin saw to it that his boy was not only in the sports pages, but in the gossip columns as well. It took the showbiz chutzpa of a Werblin to orchestrate it.

But all of Werblin's efforts and publicity acumen would have been in vain had Namath not had either the talent or the charisma to make a paying public give a damn. People came to watch him play because he had the ability to fascinate them. There were better football players, and there were better quarterbacks, but they weren't superstars. Perhaps more than anybody who ever played the game, Namath was the full package. Howard Cosell once described Namath as someone who possessed that rare attribute of having a personality capable of mass communicating.[51] Who can say what that intangible quality was? It was a quality Werblin spotted right away; maybe it took a showbiz savvy person like Werblin to see it for what it was. Most owners look only at athletic talent, but there were plenty of college prospects who had that — there always are. In Namath, Werblin found that rare combination of talent and that something extra as well. "I don't know how to define star quality but Joe has it," said Werblin. "When he walks into a room it changes."[52]

Perhaps you will find yourself feeling a bit wistful as you read along and reach those last few disappointing seasons in Namath's career, but if you should perchance find yourself feeling a touch of melancholy, take heart and imagine that wonderful choir of girlie voices buoyantly shouting that nobody else can throw a football like Broadway Joe.

2

The 1965 Season

Sonny Werblin had addressed his team prior to drafting Namath and Huarte. He wanted the players to know that, for the New York Jets, 1965 was the year of the quarterback, which is why the franchise would be spending so liberally to get one. Dick Wood, the Jets' starting quarterback for the two prior seasons had not been pleased with the news of Namath's signing, probably taking it as a vote of no confidence in his own abilities. He was right: early that summer, the Jets traded Wood to Oakland. Ewbank allowed that the team might win a few games earlier in the season with Wood as their starter, but in the long run they would be no better for it, and they were, after all, looking further into the future.

But Wood wasn't alone. Mike Taliaferro, the Jets' second-year quarterback out of the University of Illinois (where he had been a teammate of Dick Butkus), was also not shy when asked by reporters about the team signing Namath, though his comments were a bit more measured than Wood's. "I could hardly take it as a compliment," Taliaferro said.[1] And then there was reserve quarterback Pete Liske. "I'd lie if I didn't say I was disappointed," Liske remarked.[2] Like Wood, Liske would be departing early.

In June, Namath arrived at the Jets' training camp in Peekskill with five minutes to spare: players had to be in by 6 P.M. Namath arrived at 5:55: his teammates were snickering already. Namath wound up with a three-week head start on Huarte, who had been chosen to play on the college All-Star team that would face the NFL-champion Cleveland Browns in Chicago. The players in Peekskill may have been expecting a prima donna in Namath, but reports out of Chicago regarding Huarte were even less encouraging. Late for practice time and again, Huarte was bumped from second to third quarterback (behind Roger Staubach and Craig Morton) by coach Otto Graham after he turned up almost an hour late for practice the day before the game.

As for Namath, he obviously needed some brush up. "I've been watching Joe throw," said Ewbank. "From favoring that bad knee he has lost his footwork and started throwing with just his arm."[3] But aside from seeing that he had to regain his form, Ewbank was encouraged by how Namath comported himself. The old coach had a habit of spying on his quarterbacks, silently sauntering up behind them when they were in the huddle and listening in. What he heard from Namath was very positive. He didn't hear a rookie: he heard a leader.

Namath's first game action came in a late–July Wednesday night scrimmage between the rookies of both the Jets and Boston Patriots. Namath led his team to a 23–6 victory, completing nine of 19 passes for 106 yards and two touchdowns. The downside was that he also threw two interceptions, but Ewbank was still pleased enough with what he saw, declaring that Namath "didn't make a single glaring error out there."[4] Then again, there were none but rookies out there that night. The real exhibition season would begin a week later.

The night before the Jets' first exhibition game, Huarte impressed the hell out of everybody in Chicago. Entering the game midway through the third quarter with the All-Stars trailing the Browns 24–3, Huarte led his team on two 80-yard touchdown drives in the rain to make the final score a more respectable 24–16. He completed nine of nine throws for 132 yards and two touchdowns, and won MVP honors on the All-Star team by a wide margin over teammate Dick Butkus (66 votes went for Huarte, 27 for Butkus). People couldn't help but wonder if maybe Huarte hadn't been the one deserving of the bigger bonus from the Jets.

The following night in Alexandria, Virginia, Namath didn't exactly dissuade that opinion when the Jets lost to the Houston Oilers 21–16. Taliaferro had started the game, but Ewbank put Namath in to open the second quarter, evoking cheers from the 10,000 spectators who had come to the high school stadium. After several running plays, Namath's first pass was unspectacular — a six-yard throw to Don Maynard. His stats were likewise unspectacular, completing six of 14 passes for 110 yards, but what did impress was his poise in the face of the heavy Houston rush. It was also Namath who had quarterbacked the Jets to 13 of their 16 points in the game. The fans, however, wanted an aerial show, and were therefore disappointed that Namath's passes tended to be mostly underneath the coverage. His longest pass was a 49-yard completion to Bake Turner, but the bulk of those yards were due to Turner's finesse, as he caught a short pass and left his defender grabbing at thin air after putting a move on him. Turner ran it all the way to the five-yard line, which would set up the Jets only touchdown of the game. Otherwise, Namath's other long-gainer was a 30-yard throw, also to Turner. Huarte had suited up for the game but didn't play, having only just joined the Jets' camp earlier in the day after arriving from Chicago.

Namath had gotten a three-week jump on Huarte, which meant not only having been able to learn his playbook, but also having time to begin forming a bond with his teammates. That part was easy for Namath, in spite of the obstacles caused by the attendant publicity and underlying resentment over his bonus money. Really, once the players got to know him, they couldn't help but like Namath, and in that respect Huarte may have been at another disadvantage. Some of the players had misread Huarte's shyness to be an indication of attitude; he seemed to have an unwillingness to mix with the other players, whereas Namath warmed up to them fairly quickly. Misconceptions about Huarte were also not helped by word that he had been complaining about the type of banter among players in the locker room. Welcome to the pros, kid. Even the reporters did their share to make Huarte the butt of jokes in camp when they spread word of how he had asked one of them where the nearest library was: he said he wanted to go somewhere quiet to study his playbook. It may seem innocuous that players were viewing Huarte as unsociable, but the truth is that, in a team sport, feeling at ease with your teammates goes a long way, especially regarding a position requiring the amount of confidence that coaches and players alike must place in their quarterback. Many of the players just didn't seem to be accepting of Huarte.

The Jets' next preseason game was a Friday night meeting with the Boston Patriots in Allentown, Pennsylvania. The crowd of 18,000 was witness to Namath's first touchdown pass (if you discount the rookie scrimmage with Boston in July), but it was a while in coming. Although Namath had started the game, it would not be until 13 minutes into the first quarter that he would even throw a pass, but when he did he made it a good one — a 60-yard touchdown strike to Don Maynard. Namath finished out the first half, completing four of six for 80 yards. After Taliaferro increased the Jets' lead in the third quarter with his own touchdown pass to Maynard — good for 55 yards — Huarte entered the game late in the third quarter. Far from the nine-for-nine he threw in the All-Star game, Huarte only managed to complete two of seven passes against Boston for 31 yards. The Jets won 26–16.

It was Huarte that got the start the following Saturday at Rutgers' Stadium in New Brunswick, New Jersey, and the AFL-champion Buffalo Bills made short work of him. Playing the entire first half, Huarte was only able to complete two of 11 passes for 20 yards while also throwing two interceptions, one of which was picked off by Buffalo lineman Jim Dunaway, who proceeded to run it back 35 yards for a score. More than anything else, that play may have sealed Huarte's fate, for it seemed to be a glaring affirmation of his deficiencies as noted in some scouting reports.

Huarte threw with a side-armed delivery, which, when coupled with his height of six-foot even, was believed by many to be problematic in as much as he would have a hard time getting the ball past a professional defensive line. At six-foot-four, Dunaway was not inordinately tall for a lineman; how would Huarte manage against men ranging from six-five to six-nine? With Huarte leading them in the first half, the Jets could only manage one first down and trailed 27–0 at half-time.

But Namath's numbers in the second half were also pretty dismal, hitting just six of 24 passes for 72 yards. Namath also threw two interceptions. Ultimately the Jets would lose 30–14, their two touchdowns in the second half coming largely by way of the defense. In the third quarter, Gerry Philbin blocked a punt, which Paul Rochester returned 10 yards for a score, and then Dainard Paulson's fourth-quarter interception set up a three-yard TD run by Bill Mathis.

General consensus after the respective performances of Namath and Huarte was that the Jets' starting quarterback position was Taliaferro's to lose. Of course, that is what Ewbank had maintained all along anyway. In Norfolk, Virginia, for their next preseason game, there didn't seem any reason to contradict that belief. Again facing the Patriots, Namath got the start and played the entire first half, but while he led the Jets to a 3–0 advantage, his numbers were poor, completing only two of 13 passes for 35 yards. He did, however, have a number of passes dropped by receivers, fueling talk of his throwing too hard. By contrast, Taliaferro seemed to bring life to the offense in the third period, leading them on two touchdown drives, both of which culminated with four-yard scoring runs by Mathis. Huarte played the final nine minutes of the game, and managed to drive the Jets to the Boston one-yard line when time ran out. The Jets won 17–0.

Ewbank was planning on having three quarterbacks on the roster, but one of the three would be kicker Jim Turner, who would double as the third-string quarterback. That meant that very soon somebody would have to go. For their final exhibition, the Jets again played Buffalo; game time was split fairly evenly between Taliaferro and Namath, with Huarte only playing in the closing minutes. Buffalo manhandled the Jets again, beating them 31–10. Taliaferro's numbers were fair (eight of 17 for 162 yards), but they looked pretty good in comparison to Namath's. While Namath only managed to complete four of his 17 passes, he did account for the Jets' only touchdown, which came on a 35-yard pass to Maynard. Still, his very first pass had been intercepted, and he followed it with ten consecutive incompletions. After the game, two things seemed certain: Huarte was on the outs, and Taliaferro would be the Jets' starting quarterback come opening day.

Associated Press reporter Dick Couch wrote, "The New York Jets' great experiment has ended the laboratory phase with no conclusive results and one frightening possibility … the Jets may have a $400,000 telephone operator on their hands."[5] Nobody wanted to think about it, least of all Werblin, but Namath's preseason numbers were pretty skinny. In the Jets' five preseason games, he had only completed 22 of 74 passes. Taliaferro's experience may have been negligible in 1964, but once more by comparison he looked like a grizzled veteran.

With mounting public interest in who would be piloting the New York Jets come opening day, NBC hoped to scoop everyone a week before the season started by having Weeb Ewbank appear on the show Sports In Action to announce who had won the Jets' starting job in a program titled "Will the Real Jet Quarterback Please Stand Up?" Would it be the $400,000 Namath or the $200,000 Huarte? NBC must have felt like Ewbank flipped them the bird when he proclaimed Mike Taliaferro to be the Jets' starting quarterback for the season opener.

Beyond that, the announcement that many were anticipating came on Tuesday, September 7, when the Jets placed Huarte on waivers. Any team that wanted him had 24 hours to claim him, provided they were willing to pick up his heavy price tag. Given Huarte's preseason numbers, not many expected there to be any takers. When the 24 hours passed without anyone laying claim, the Jets were permitted to place Huarte on their taxi squad, thereby keeping him as a reserve that could be called up if an emergency need arose.

After practice, as the reporters participated in their new favorite ritual of crowding around Namath in the locker room, they asked him who he would have picked to start at quarterback if he were the coach? "That's not very hard," said Namath. "Mike."[6] And so it was.

The Jets opened the 1965 season on September 12 against the Oilers in Houston. The Oilers were supposed to begin playing their home games in the newly built Houston Astrodome, but the outrageous rental fees being sought by the Astrodome sent the team in search of another venue. Although it had never been made available to a professional team before, the Oilers were able to make arrangements to rent Rice Stadium to play their home games. With temperatures in the mid-nineties on opening day, they may have been wishing that they were in the air-conditioned Astrodome, but the truth is that Rice Stadium was the far superior facility. The Astrodome was to be the beginning of artificial football, games played on carpeting in giant, cavernous, temperature-controlled rooms, but for all its boasts it still seated some 20,000 less than Rice Stadium. It may have struck the cynical as a pipedream that a lowly AFL franchise would need the extra seating, but the geniuses behind air-conditioned football, who likely thought that the humidity of Houston in September would keep people away, were proven wrong by a record AFL opening day crowd of 52,680, some 2,000 more than could have been accommodated at the Astrodome. Arena football would have to wait for another day.

The opening day attendance was rather extraordinary, however, and Houston's home games for the remainder of the season would average about 34,000. *Something* had to account for the bigger turnout that day. Many came to the conclusion that it was the presence of two high-priced New York rookie quarterbacks coming to town, but if the people did turn out to see Namath and Huarte, they would be disappointed, for both wound up manning the sideline telephone and relaying information from the coaches in the upstairs booth. Being on the taxi squad, Huarte didn't even suit up for the game.

What the people did see was a hard fought — albeit sloppy — game wherein the two teams combined for a total of 13 fumbles. Matt Snell, who did not fumble once during the entire 1964 season, fumbled twice that afternoon in Houston. He cited the humidity, which had made the ball slicker, without necessarily using it as an excuse.

The score was tied at 14 at halftime, Houston having scored on two touchdown passes from Don Trull to Willie Frazier of 57 and eight yards, and the Jets scoring on runs of 45 yards by Bill Mathis and 12 yards by Snell. The Oilers would gain the upper hand in the second half, however, by way of a series of fumbles by the Jets that would lead to 10 Houston points in 73 seconds. It all began in the third period when Jets punter Curley Johnson was unable to field a bad snap, and fumbled it at the New York 29-yard line. After recovering the ball Houston managed to work their way to a first-and-goal, but rather than settle for a field goal on fourth down they opted to go for it and were stopped an inch from the New York goal line. The Jets took possession there, but three plays later Houston got another gift when Mathis fumbled the ball away at the New York 10. After three plays, the Oilers again found themselves an inch from the New York goal, this time choosing the field goal and a 17–14 lead. Bill Baird then fumbled the ensuing kickoff at the New York 25-yard line, leading to a quick score for Houston when Trull threw his third touchdown pass to Frazier, giving the Oilers a 24–14 lead.

It looked for a moment like Namath would see action when he began warming up in the second half, but Taliaferro put that on ice when he promptly hit Don Maynard with a 23-yard touchdown pass after the Jets recovered a Houston fumble. The score brought the Jets to within three points of the Oilers at 24–21, but kicker George Blanda would extend Houston's lead to six points after hitting a field goal with under five minutes to play.

The Jets maintained that it was not the humidity, but rather bad officiating that cost them the game. Trailing 27–21 with just over two minutes to play, Mathis got behind defender Fred Glick on a pass play, but Glick was able to prevent Mathis from catching up with Taliaferro's throw by grabbing a fistful of Mathis' jersey — and not letting go. On the New York sideline, players and coaches alike were livid. Mathis said afterward that Glick had a hold of his jersey for 10 yards. Saying that the ball had been well thrown, Mathis maintained that, but for Glick holding onto his jersey, the play would in all likelihood have gone for a touchdown. "We all saw it," said Namath after the game. "It was obvious to everyone on the bench."[7]

The Jets had managed to stay in the game right up to the end, but Taliaferro's numbers were not good, completing just four of 21 passes for 58 yards. After the game, Ewbank was asked who would be starting at quarterback the following week. It would be a question that would recur week-to-week, and so Ewbank developed a refrain that could be used as often, telling reporters that he would start whichever quarterback looked best in practice during the week.

Week 2 — Saturday, September 18, 1965
Shea Stadium, New York (attendance: 53,658)

When the Jets returned to New York to host the Kansas City Chiefs at Shea the following Saturday night, they were greeted by another record-setting home opener crowd. Attendance was counted at 53,658, and it became apparent early on who they were there to see: New York's love affair with Joe Namath had begun.

Once more it was Taliaferro who got the start, and once more he could complete but four passes. The Jets had managed a 3–0 first-quarter lead, but that was largely by way of a pass interference penalty that placed them at the Kansas City 15-yard line. When the Jets were forced to settle for a field goal after Taliaferro missed Maynard on a couple of passes, the crowd made its displeasure known. "I was never booed in college," Taliaferro said. "I'm sure I must have been booed before, but I was never so aware of it as I was on Saturday night."[8]

As Taliaferro struggled through the first half, completing four of 12 passes for only 24 yards, the crowd grew increasingly — and more demonstrably — impatient; Ewbank saw less and less reason not to oblige the people by giving them what they wanted. It was Namath they came to see, so why not now? And then it happened. In the second quarter of the game, to the delight of the fans, Joe Namath trotted out onto the field to begin his professional football career in earnest.

The first play Namath called as a pro (yes, he called his own plays, unlike the quarterbacks of today) was a draw play to Bill Mathis that gained four yards. The second was a sweep by Mathis that gained another four. Namath sent Snell into the line on third-and-two, but he only gained a yard, and with fourth-and-one the Jets punted. Three plays, three runs — not exactly what the people wanted to see. To further add to the crowd's disappointment, Willie Mitchell took the punt for Kansas City and returned it 52 yards to the New York 30-yard line. Several plays later, Kansas City quarterback Len Dawson hit Chris Burford for a touchdown from 19 yards out to give the Chiefs a 7–3 lead.

Taking over on the 30-yard line after the kick, Namath this time started off throwing on first down. He hit Maynard for 18 yards, but a holding penalty brought the play back. A screen to Snell lost four yards, and after incompletions to Maynard and Snell, the Jets again had to punt. The half ended with the Chiefs still leading, 7–3.

Receiving the kick in the second half, the Jets took over on their own 33, and with a combination of passing and Snell's running, Namath drove them to the Kansas City 38-yard line. Tight end Dee Mackey dropped a second-down pass, and when Maynard dropped a pass at the 15-yard line on third down, Jim Turner came out to try a field goal. It was partially blocked, and for all their effort the Jets came away with nothing.

After the teams exchanged punts in the third, the Jets squandered an opportunity when lineman Paul Rochester partially blocked a Kansas City punt, causing it to go a mere 11 yards: the Jets took over on the Kansas City 28-yard line. On first down Snell ran for nine yards, on second down he lost two, and on third down he gained the two yards back. With fourth-and-one, the Jets decided to pass on another field goal try and go for the first down. For the fourth straight play, Namath ran Snell: he didn't make it, and Kansas City took over on downs. The third quarter would end with the Chiefs still up 7–3.

Namath had looked good, despite being unable to put any points on the board. The Jets' problems were mainly down to the running game failing to pick up first downs, and the receivers failing to catch passes (Mackey had dropped three already), but in the fourth quarter Namath would make that rookie mistake that would cost the Jets dearly. Four minutes into the final period, with the Jets on their own 36, Namath went back to pass and was carelessly holding the ball away from his body when he was hit and fumbled. Bobby Bell, a former defensive lineman who had been converted to linebacker, made the hit, and it was Bell who also recovered the ball at the New York 24. Kansas City did the smart thing and went for the kill on first down: Dawson again hit Burford for a touchdown. The Chiefs now led 14–3.

After the teams exchanged punts again, the Jets took over on their own 17. Trailing by 11 with time running out, it was a safe bet that Namath would be throwing now, but although everybody — certainly the defense — was expecting him to pass, Namath showed poise under pressure. He hit Bake Turner for 10 yards, and then came back to Turner again for nine more. On second down he went long for Turner, and a pass interference call on the Chiefs gave the Jets a first down on Kansas City's 37-yard line. This time it was Namath who went for the throat, throwing 37 yards to Maynard in the end zone. Maynard had beaten cornerback Fred Williamson, and as he made the catch Williamson attempted to give Maynard one of his famous cheap shots — a forearm to the head — charmingly named "the hammer." Maynard caught the ball, ducked under the blow, and Williamson fell on his face — touchdown Jets. The lead had been cut to 14–10.

There was now much anticipation among the patrons at Shea. As quickly as Namath demonstrated he could strike, the fans were anxious for the Jets to get the ball back to give him one more chance. Sure enough, the Chiefs were unable to mount a time-consuming drive and had to punt. The Jets took over on their own 27 with just over two minutes to play. Namath started by hitting Bake Turner for 11 yards on the final play before the two-minute warning. After throwing incompletions to Turner and Snell, Namath came back with a seven-yard completion to Jim Evans, and with fourth-and-three the Jets had no choice but to go for it. Namath went back to pass and threw deep down the right sideline — there was nobody there. The Jets turned the ball over on downs, and the Chiefs ran out the clock.

Reporters who covered the Jets surmised what had happened: Maynard had broken his pass pattern, as he often did, and Namath threw the ball where he expected Maynard to be. As the reporters crowded around him in the locker room, Namath was having none of the excuses. He said it was nobody's fault, just a mix-up, and when reporters mentioned the passes dropped by Mackey, Namath remarked that he had thrown Mackey some tough ones. "I was glad to get in the game, but I should have done better," said Namath. "I didn't hit the receivers enough."[9] Through the years Maynard has given interviews in which he has claimed that the communication between Namath and his receivers was so good that they only ever had one busted pass play, which Maynard said occurred in Namath's first game. He could only be referring to that final throw against Kansas City.

Ewbank was perturbed by the suggestion that he had caved in to pressure from the crowd when he sent Namath into the game. The truth, Ewbank said, was that Taliaferro had been nursing some sore ribs, and when he failed to hit a wide open Maynard in the second period, the coaches knew that the ribs were still bothering him, and *that* prompted the quarterback change. Ewbank seemed fairly pleased with Namath's performance, and the press also gave him generally favorable notice, considering it to have been a fairly good showing for the first pro action of a rookie quarterback. Namath, on the other hand, was far from pleased. He had completed 11 of 23 passes for 121 yards and a touchdown, but the bottom line for Namath was that the Jets had lost.

Who's going to play quarterback next week, Coach? Whoever looks best in practice.

Week 3 — Sunday, September 26, 1965
War Memorial Stadium, Buffalo (attendance: 45,056)

Namath must have looked better in practice that week, because he got the start in the Jets' third game of the season as they traveled to Buffalo to play the Bills. It was a hell of a task for a rookie getting his first start: the Bills were the reigning AFL champions, and they had the most impressive defense in the league. In their first two games, the Buffalo defensive line had batted down fourteen passes. Buffalo was strong everywhere you looked: this was going to be some test.

The Jets received the opening kickoff and returned it to their own 19-yard line, but after a short run by Snell and two incomplete passes, they quickly had to turn it over. Buffalo then started at midfield, and it took them seven plays to score as quarterback Jack Kemp ran it in himself from four yards out. In the second quarter, Buffalo added a couple of field goals by Pete Gogolak to go up 13–0 before the Jets finally began to move the ball. Namath was able to take the Jets downfield for a 24-yard field goal by Jim Turner, and with the half winding down the Jets got a break when linebacker Wahoo McDaniel recovered a Kemp fumble on the Buffalo 25. Having very little time to work with, Namath went to the pass right away but was dropped for an 11-yard loss by defensive end Tom Day. After quickly using a timeout, Namath came back with a pass to Snell to the three-yard line, followed by a three-yard touchdown toss to Mathis. As the half ended, the Jets had to feel pleased at having closed the gap to 13–10.

But Buffalo came out strong again in the second half, as Kemp guided his team downfield for another touchdown on an 11-yard pass to Elbert Dubenion. Unfortunately for Buffalo, they lost Dubenion for the year on the play as he fell backward awkwardly when he went down, twisting his leg and injuring himself. It was Dubenion's fifth catch of that drive alone.

When the Jets had to punt again, Kemp drove Buffalo down for another Gogolak field goal and a 23–10 lead. Now the game seemed to be slipping away from the Jets. There had been 29 offensive plays run in the third quarter leading up to Gogolak's field goal: Buffalo had run 22 of them. The Jets seemed helpless to do much about it. Because Tom Day had been beating offensive tackle Winston Hill and getting into the New York backfield regularly, Ewbank had instructed Namath to run a screen pass to Day's side. Hopefully they would make some yardage on the play, and more than that, it might make Day think twice about charging so recklessly through the line. Unfortunately, the area left open when Day rushed in was very well manned by other Buffalo defenders. Namath might have thrown the ball away, or he might have taken the loss on a sack, but being a rookie he chose to stick with the play and threw the ball into a crowd. The ball was deflected into the air, and when it came down, wouldn't you know it fell right into the hands of Tom Day?

Taking over on the New York 29, Kemp was able to work the Bills to the two-yard line when, on third-and-goal, he tried to run it in himself. Well, why not? It had worked in the first quarter. But this time the Jets read the play and stopped Kemp cold: in fact, they *knocked* him cold. Gogolak came in to kick another field goal to increase Buffalo's lead to 26–10.

It was now into the fourth quarter, and the Jets had a lot of catching up to do. Naturally, that meant a lot of passing, and Namath quickly moved the Jets downfield, hitting Maynard with passes of 30 and 25 yards before capping the drive with a nine-yard touchdown pass to Dee Mackey. The Jets then opted to go for a two-point conversion, and Namath again hit Mackey for the points. They had now cut the Buffalo lead to 26–18, which put them within one touchdown and two-point conversion of tying the game. It was up to the defense now.

The New York defense was aided in their efforts by Kemp's having been knocked out of the game. Kemp's backup, Daryle Lamonica, was certainly more than capable, but he was coming off the bench cold and facing a New York team that had been given the impetus to fight. Lamonica called three running plays, which only managed to gain two yards, and the Bills were forced to punt. It was their first punt all afternoon, and it couldn't have come at a better time for the Jets. Namath mixed short passes and runs by Snell to work the Jets down to the Buffalo 16-yard line, but the drive died there and New York had to settle for a 23-yard field goal to whittle Buffalo's lead down to 26–21. Still, with 4:46 remaining, there was a chance as long as the defense could again force Buffalo to turn the ball back over quickly. It looked for a moment like it might happen when the Bills were facing a third-and-13 situation, but Lamonica delighted the home crowd with a pass to Ernie Warlick that just managed to get the yardage. From there, Buffalo ran the clock down and scored on a one-yard run by Wray Carlton with only 11 seconds left in the game. The final was a 33–21 win for the Bills, who advanced to 3–0 while the Jets fell to 0–3.

After the game, Buffalo defensive linemen Day and Jim Dunaway both praised Namath's quick release, saying that there was little they could do to get to him as fast as he got the ball off. Ewbank was impressed too, saying that Namath was progressing quicker than he had expected. He had completed 19 of 40 throws for 287 yards with two touchdowns and a pair of interceptions. The only one who didn't seem impressed by his performance was, of course, Namath himself. "I'm disgusted," Namath said. "I learned to win in high school and college and that's what I want to do as a pro."[10]

Others were more forgiving. UPI sportswriter George C. Langford said that Namath "turned in one of the best passing shows any rookie has put on in his first start as a professional Sunday against the roughest defense in the American Football League."[11] Yeah, but they lost the game. Namath still didn't know what it was like to win a professional football game. He would get another chance in week four: he would be starting again.

Week 4 — Sunday, October 3, 1965
Bears Stadium, Denver (attendance: 34,988)

The crowd of 34,988 at Bears Stadium was the largest home attendance the Broncos had ever managed: record attendance seemed to follow Namath around the country. Although they had only won two games in 1964, the Denver Broncos figured on being an improved team in 1965 with the addition of running back Cookie Gilchrist, who had been acquired from Buffalo during the off-season. Gilchrist had been the AFL's leading rusher in 1964 with 981 yards (putting him just ahead of Matt Snell's 948 yards), but Buffalo had been willing to trade him nonetheless because he was not considered a team player. At one point he undermined coach Lou Saban's authority by refusing to go onto the field when Saban wanted to send him into a game. Good runner or not, who needs a player like that? The Bills were a championship team, and they figured they would be good enough without Gilchrist: turns out they were right.

The Jets had plenty reason to be concerned about Gilchrist, though. Giving up an average of 139.7 yards rushing per game, the Jets had the league's worst defense against the run. The week before Denver hosted the Jets, Gilchrist had run for 142 yards as the Broncos got their initial win of the season by beating Boston 27–10. The oddsmakers had made Denver two-point favorites over the Jets, but at 1–2 the Broncos were certainly beatable.

The Jets got off to a slow start, however, failing to gain a first down on either of their first two possessions. By contrast, the Broncos drove downfield well enough on their first series, which ended on the New York one-yard line. The Jet defense tightened there, and when Denver opted to forego a field goal on fourth down and try instead for the touchdown, the Jets stopped them. That was much closer than anyone would come to scoring for the remainder of the first quarter, and it was as close as either team would get to the end zone in the entire first half.

In the second quarter, the Jets got at least close enough for Jim Turner to kick two long field goals (47 and 49 yards), which gave them a 6–0 lead, but toward the end of the second quarter Denver kicked a field goal of their own to close the gap to 6–3 with just 14 seconds left in the half. Denver then tried an onside kick, and when it failed it wound up giving the Jets good enough field position that Namath felt compelled to take a shot downfield: John McGeever intercepted the pass at the Denver 21-yard line, and managed to run it back to the New York 47 before being brought down to end the half.

Jim Turner had accounted for all of the Jets' points in the first half. As the second half began, Turner would also account for one of their better defensive plays as well. When Turner kicked off to start the second half, Odell Barry took the kick for Denver, and after finding a seam in the coverage, broke through and was well on his way to going the distance. As he crossed midfield, the only player left to beat was Turner, who stopped Barry at the New York 40. Still, the good field position enabled Denver to knot the game at 6–6 with another field goal.

The Jets started the second half as they had the first — three-and-out — and when Denver got the ball back they again got within field goal range, and took the lead with a 37-yard kick by Gary Kroner. For the first time in the game, the Jets were trailing. It seemed to ignite the New York offense, and mixing short passes and runs, Namath began to move the team downfield. A nine-yard pass to George Sauer, an eight-yard draw play to Matt Snell, a six-yard pass to Don Maynard, a 12-yard throw to Maynard, another eight-yard run by Snell, then a 14-yard run by Bill Mathis. Namath hit five of five passes in the drive, which culminated with Mathis running it in from three yards out to give the Jets a 13–9 lead. They would hold that lead through most of the fourth quarter, despite a close call early in the period.

Denver's punter, Bob Scarpitto, was also a flanker, and therefore knew how to run with the ball. The Denver coaches left it to Scarpitto's discretion as to when to kick and when to take off and run for a first down. Scarpitto picked the right moment to run with it, for although linebacker Larry Grantham almost managed to catch him at the line of scrimmage, Scarpitto eluded Grantham and took off on a 44-yard dash that went all the way to the New York eight-yard line.

After gaining and then losing yards on their first two plays, Denver found themselves still on the eight with third-and-goal. Quarterback Mickey Slaughter tried hitting receiver Lionel Taylor in the end zone, but the pass was intercepted by Cornell Gordon: the Jets had dodged a bullet, and still held the lead. It would have helped their cause had they been able to beef up their lead a bit, but once more it was three-and-out for the Jets.

The New York defense then came through again, dropping Slaughter for a loss twice in three plays and forcing Denver to punt. But it was three-and-out for the Jets yet again on their next series, as they seemed determined to give the Broncos every possible chance. After receiving the punt, the Broncos took over on their own 16-yard line with 3:35 remaining in the game. They began by moving the ball in good-sized chunks (an 11-yard reverse to Barry, an 11-yard pass to Al Denson), but it was a pass interference call that would yield the most yardage in the drive. Slaughter threw long to Taylor, and although the ball seemed to be well overthrown, when Taylor collided with defender Bill Baird an official on the opposite side of the field threw the flag. Now, who says referees have poor eyesight? The penalty took Denver from their own 38 to the New York 36.

With less than two minutes to play, Slaughter again threw to Taylor, who caught it and was brought down on the 21. Three running plays picked up a first down at the 11, and a pass to Barry gained nine yards to the two. Then, with just 56 seconds remaining, rookie Wendell Hayes ran in for the score and Denver led 16–13.

But the Jets weren't dead yet. With almost a minute left there was time to at least get close enough for a tying field goal, and when Jerry Robinson returned the kick to the New York 30, it made a winning touchdown plausible. Namath started by throwing short: eight yards to Maynard, nine to Snell, then five more to Maynard. Another eight or 10 yards would put the Jets within Turner's range, but Namath didn't go for eight or 10. Sensing that the Broncos would now be playing for the short pass, Namath went for it all. He threw long for Maynard, but the ball was thrown poorly; it hung in the air too long and failed to catch up to Maynard, instead coming down into the hands of Denver's Willie Brown at the 13-yard line. Brown returned it to the 18 before being tackled by Maynard. The play ended the game. The second half ended as did the first, with Namath being intercepted.

After the game Ewbank was fuming over the pass interference call, saying that the official who threw the flag had also made the longest run of the day, coming from some 60 yards away to make the call. The Jets were 0–4. Namath had completed 18 of 34 passes for 152 yards. He threw a pair of interceptions, and no touchdowns.

Week 5 — Saturday, October 16, 1965
Shea Stadium, New York (attendance: 53,122)

The Jets had the week off between their fourth and fifth games and would be returning to New York to host the Oakland Raiders on a Saturday night game at Shea. At 3–2, it was expected that Oakland would be favored over the Jets; it may have seemed a bit surprising that the Raiders were only favored by two points, but despite their 0–4 record the Jets had played their opponents close, and had really lost on some bad breaks (some said bad calls, as well).

After the teams swapped punts and missed field goals through the first period, the scoreless tie was broken in the second quarter when Namath went back to pass from the Oakland 34 and tried to hit George Sauer along the sideline. It was a rocket of a throw that ricocheted off Sauer's shoulder pads and high into the air, coming down into the hands of cornerback Dave Grayson, who took off running down the sideline. The only one back there to stop him was Namath, and with a linebacker leading the way to block for Grayson, Namath didn't stand much chance. Grayson ran it back 79 yards for the score, and the Raiders were up 7–0.

The Jets began their next possession with good field position when Bake Turner returned Oakland's kick to the New York 35. They tried to get the ground game going: Mark Smolinski gained seven, Mathis gained six, Smolinski got another six, then Mathis ran for four more — four plays, two first downs. Following a holding penalty Namath threw for 25 yards to tight end Dee Mackey, advancing New York to the Oakland 27. After another four-yard run by Mathis, Namath tried to hit Maynard in the end zone, but the pass was intercepted by Oakland's Kent McCloughan. There was a matter of a penalty flag, however, as McCloughan was called for pass interference, giving the Jets a first-and-goal on the one-yard line. Mathis took it across from the left side, and the game was tied at 7–7.

After a good defensive series by the Jets, the Raiders were forced to punt from deep in their own territory: Bill Baird fielded the punt for the Jets at the Oakland 41, and ran it back to the 29. Unfortunately, the Jets failed to gain a first down after that and had to settle for a 31-yard field goal by Jim Turner. Still, it put them out in front, 10–7.

Following another Oakland punt, the Jets again found themselves with good field position, starting from at their own 44. Namath quickly went long to Maynard on first down. Racing down the center of the field, Maynard had gotten behind the coverage and caught the ball at the

15. He outraced the defenders the rest of the way for the score, and the Jets found themselves with a 17–7 lead.

With less than two minutes to play in the half, the Jets would have been more than happy to go into the dressing room with a 10-point lead, but that was too much to hope for. Beginning from their own 25, Oakland quickly worked their way downfield with short passes. Quarterback Tom Flores saved the long throw for the capper, hitting Art Powell for the score from 31 yards out, trimming New York's lead to 17–14. The drive had accounted for almost half of Oakland's total yardage in the first half (75 of 152 total yards).

In the second half the teams resumed with exchanging punts until the pattern was broken by a Maynard fumble. After catching a pass from Namath, Maynard lost the ball on the Oakland 33, and the Raiders returned it to the Jets' 48. Six plays later Flores threw 11 yards to Clem Daniels for the score, and Oakland was up 21–17. Oakland added a field goal in the fourth quarter to increase their lead to 24–17.

Aside from the superb and exciting touchdown bomb to Maynard, Namath had not looked good. It showed in the numbers: he had completed just five of 21 passes. Namath's last two series saw the Jets failing to gain a single first down, as he went 0–6 passing. After the Raiders went up 24–17, Ewbank sat Namath down and sent Taliaferro into the game.

On his first series, Taliaferro managed to move the Jets to the Oakland 12, but two incomplete passes into the end zone brought a fourth down. Trailing by seven points, Ewbank kept the offense on the field, and on fourth down Taliaferro again threw an incompletion: the Raiders took over on downs. Still, in the battle for field position, it was not an altogether untenable decision by Ewbank. As it turned out, it would actually be just what the Jets needed.

Taking over on their own 12, Oakland gained just six yards on three running plays. The Jets seemed assured of decent field position on the ensuing punt, but the resulting Oakland error would surpass anyone's expectations. Punter Mike Mercer did his best to field a high snap from center Jim Otto, but he was just barely able to bat the ball back down to the ground. Mercer then tried to pick it up but dropped it again as he saw a wall of green jerseys rushing toward him. The best he could do was to fall on the ball at the three-yard line. How's that for great field position? On the very next play, throwing from the clutches of a blitzing linebacker, Taliaferro lobbed a pass to Maynard at the back of the end zone. It was an outstanding effort by Taliaferro, throwing as he was being spun around and was falling backward to the turf. With the extra point by Turner, the Jets had tied the game.

The Jets' good fortunes would continue in spite of themselves. With some eight minutes remaining, Flores began moving the Raiders downfield, helped a bit by a face-masking penalty on the Jets that contributed 15 yards to Oakland's cause. From the New York 27, Flores threw to Powell, but safety Jim Hudson tipped the ball, and from there the Jets played hot potato with it. After it was tipped by Hudson, Dainard Paulson got a hand on it before it finally ended up in the hands of rookie linebacker Al Atkinson.

But three consecutive runs — Mathis for five, Smolinski for three, and Mathis again for one — saw the Jets facing a fourth-and-one at their own 22-yard line with 2:42 left to play. The logical decision would be to punt, but incredibly Ewbank decided to go for it. The decision to go for it from the Oakland 12 on Taliaferro's first series had made some sense. After all, the Jets were then trailing by seven, and if they didn't make it, the Raiders would still be in the neighborhood of 90 yards from scoring. But *this*? This just seemed crazy. With fourth-and-one from their own 22 and 2:42 remaining, the Jets sent Taliaferro into the line on a quarterback sneak: he didn't make it. The Raiders took over on the New York 22. They were in field goal range without even running a play.

After Clem Daniels gained a yard up the middle, the two-minute warning was given. On the next play — somewhat surprisingly — Flores passed. The throw was almost intercepted by two

Jet linebackers, going in and out of the hands of, first Ralph Baker, and then Atkinson. After Daniels lost two yards on a run, Gene Mingo came out with 1:17 remaining to kick what everyone assumed would be the winning field goal. It was only a 28-yard shot, well within the range of any kicker in the league, but he missed it wide to the left.

After the Jets took over, Taliaferro missed two passes, first to Mathis, then Maynard, before completing one to Bake Turner. But with the play only gaining six yards, the Jets had to punt with 46 seconds remaining. Curley Johnson's 34-yard punt gave Oakland the ball at their own 40, and after Flores hit Roger Hagberg with passes of 11 and 14 yards, the Raiders found themselves on the New York 35. Mingo came back onto the field with 10 seconds left to try to redeem himself with a 42-yard field goal. He missed again, this time both short and wide right. He had missed kicking the winning field goal twice in 67 seconds. The game ended in a tie. Five games into the season, the Jets were still winless; at least this time they managed to avoid another loss. Namath's final numbers were weak: five of 21 for 126 yards with a touchdown, and a matching interception.

Week 6 — Saturday, October 23, 1965
Shea Stadium, New York (attendance: 59,001)

The following week New York had another Saturday night game at Shea Stadium, this time hosting the San Diego Chargers. At 0–4–1, the Jets were thought to pose little threat to the 4–0–2 Chargers. Adding to the Jets' poor prospectus was the fact that San Diego was boasting the league's top rushing offense *and* top passing offense. Oh, and they were tops in defense in those categories as well. They had the league's top passer in John Hadl, the league's leading rusher in Paul Lowe, and the league's top receiver yardage-wise in Lance Alworth. Under the circumstances, it might have been considered a little surprising that the Chargers were only favored by seven points. The Chargers had beaten the AFL champion Buffalo Bills by the score of 36–3 — *in Buffalo!* Then again, one of San Diego's two ties came in Boston, where the winless Patriots played the Chargers to a 13–13 standstill. Perhaps there was reason for hope after all.

Given Namath's poor showing against Oakland, Ewbank decided to give the starting job back to Taliaferro. It would soon enough be apparent that quarterback was hardly the Jets' only problem. Namath or Taliaferro, it didn't seem to really matter, as the Jets proceeded to put on a performance so inept that it could practically fill a 1965 blooper reel by itself.

Interestingly, it was the Chargers who began the game mistake-prone, as Hadl threw an interception to Dainard Paulson in San Diego's first series. The Jets couldn't cash in, however, and had to turn the ball back over. San Diego then punted as well, and the Jets got another break when a Taliaferro pass to Maynard drew an interference penalty that put New York on the San Diego six-yard line. Two runs by Snell and an incomplete pass to Mackey in the end zone forced the Jets to settle for a field goal.

The Jets caught yet another break when Les Duncan fumbled the ensuing kickoff at the San Diego 31, and Mark Smolinski recovered for New York. Taliaferro then went to the air: an incompletion to Maynard, a six-yard completion to Sauer, followed by an incompletion to Sauer. The Jets would have to settle for a field goal again. They should have been so lucky: six-foot-nine Ernie Ladd blocked it. Then the tide began to turn.

As the second quarter got under way the Chargers were well on their way to a score, being positioned at the New York 13. Two plays into the period, Lowe went around right end from eight yards out to score, giving the Chargers a 7–3 lead.

Although the Jets began to move on their next series, they crossed midfield only to have Snell fumble the ball away at the San Diego 36. But after taking over at midfield on their next series, the Jets did manage to draw to within a point of San Diego when Jim Turner kicked a 24-yard field goal.

The Jets' defense continued to play them tough as second-year end Gerry Philbin dropped Hadl for a 15-yard loss to kill another San Diego drive, but San Diego managed to increase their lead in their next series. Starting at their own 33, the Chargers were facing a second-and-nine when Hadl threw across the middle to Alworth, who caught the ball and carried it all the way to the New York 27. Ultimately, the Chargers would be held to a field goal, which put them up 10–6. The Jets had played them surprisingly close in the first half, but the worst was still to come. A Chargers' explosion seemed to be brewing just beneath the surface, waiting for the right moment to erupt. And then it happened...

After receiving the kick to start the second half, the Jets started at their own 27, but penalties kept moving them in the wrong direction. When they weren't being penalized, they were fumbling. Taliaferro threw to Mackey, who fumbled the ball away at the New York 10-yard line. A pass interference call against the Jets in the end zone gave San Diego a first-and-goal on the one, and three plays later Hadl threw to Dave Kocourek for the touchdown. At least the New York defense made them work for it.

Not so on the Chargers' next score, a 59-yard run by Lowe that was about as free and easy as they come. Lowe took a pitchout running around right end, and saw nothing but clear sailing for the distance. He could have stopped to catch his breath along the way. It was now 24–6.

In the fourth quarter the Jets managed another field goal, but it was precious little compared to their constant bungling. While fielding a punt, Kern Carson decided to let the ball drop: it hit his leg and the Chargers recovered on the New York 15. The Jets' defense then rose to the occasion, holding San Diego to another field goal.

With only five minutes left in the game, both teams were inclined to send in their back-up quarterbacks. The crowd at Shea mustered a cheer when Namath entered the game, and he started well enough, firing off a 14-yard completion to Mackey. But his next three passes were incomplete, and the Jets then punted. By contrast, San Diego back-up quarterback Don Breaux came in and threw a 57-yard touchdown to Alworth.

Namath came back out for one last try, but when he completed a throw to Mackey, the tight end fumbled and San Diego recovered the ball. It was that kind of night for the Jets. Maynard had beaten the coverage twice on long routes only to drop the ball in the end zone when Taliaferro delivered on target. He certainly hadn't served Taliaferro well: two long touchdown passes would have been a nice feather in Taliaferro's cap as he continued to fight for his job week-to-week. Ewbank, infuriated, pulled Maynard from the game; the humiliated receiver was booed from the field by the home crowd. Maynard would claim that the lights at Shea had blinded him when he had to look up for the long passes, but Ewbank was having none of it. Ewbank had cost the team 15 yards himself, having been flagged for unsportsmanlike conduct (word was he had called the officials a bad word or two).

By game's end New York had fumbled six times, losing four of them, and been penalized 10 times for 133 yards. Although they had yet to win a game, the Jets had at least managed to remain competitive in their prior losses. Not this time. This time they took a bitch-slapping. In his brief appearance, Namath completed two of five for 21 yards.

Week 7 — Sunday, October 31, 1965
Shea Stadium, New York (attendance: 53,717)

Huarte was making the news again when a story broke that somebody had made the Jets an offer for him; Werblin confirmed that the Jets had turned down an offer for Huarte that was in excess of his $200,000 contract. If the Jets had declined to turn a profit on Huarte, then obviously they had plans for him beyond keeping him to man the sideline phones. With the Jets still winless, and the displeasure now evident in the demeanor of everyone, from players to coaches to Werblin, it was widely speculated that if neither Taliaferro or Namath came through in the upcoming game with Denver, then Huarte would likely be taken off the taxi squad and activated. The pressure was mostly on Taliaferro, as it was announced on the Thursday before the game that he would again be getting the start.

As the Broncos were 3–4 to the Jets' 0–5–1, it must have galled Denver that they were still considered three-point underdogs in the game. However, leaving aside their humiliating loss to San Diego, it was generally acknowledged that the Jets were somehow a better team than their record indicated.

Denver had been having their own quarterback controversy, alternating between Mickey Slaughter and John McCormick. For their Shea Stadium game with the Jets, Slaughter would be getting the start.

The Broncos took the opening kickoff and began working their way downfield until stalling out at the New York 31. Gary Kroner came in to try a 38-yard field goal, but the kick was wide and Denver came away with nothing. They would soon enough get another chance when Taliaferro was intercepted by safety John Griffin on the Jets' second play from scrimmage, and after a 20-yard return, the Broncos took over on the New York 23. They were able to at least get close enough for Kroner to kick a 26-yard field goal, giving Denver a 3–0 lead.

By the time Taliaferro threw three incomplete passes on the Jets' third offensive series, the fans began to boo. The Jets had run eight plays in three possessions, and had yet to gain a first down. But the first quarter ended on a good note for the Jets when linebacker Ralph Baker intercepted a Slaughter pass intended for Cookie Gilchrist and returned it to the Denver 16. Two plays into the second quarter, Taliaferro hit Maynard in the end zone for a 14-yard touchdown, and the Jets took a 7–3 lead.

The good fortune continued: linebacker Larry Grantham intercepted a Slaughter pass to Lionel Taylor, and ran it back to the Denver 32. A nine-yard sack of Taliaferro on third down forced the Jets to settle for a field goal, but Jim Turner's 46-yarder increased New York's lead to 10–3. The Jets would explode for 24 points in the quarter. Taliaferro led them on a 72-yard drive that culminated with a 10-yard TD run by Matt Snell with 1:53 to play in the half. Two key plays in the drive were a 20-yard pass to George Sauer and a 27-yard run by Snell.

The Jets then got the ball back when Slaughter threw long to Taylor and the pass was tipped by Grantham and intercepted by safety Ray Abruzzese, who returned it to the Denver 39. When Taliaferro went long for Maynard in the end zone on the next play, Griffin was called for pass interference, giving the Jets a first-and-goal on the one. Bill Mathis took it in from there, and the Jets' lead was 24–3.

McCormick was in at quarterback for Denver when the second half began, but he seemed as luckless as Slaughter. His second pass was tipped—Grantham again—and intercepted by defensive lineman Verlon Biggs at the New York 49. Biggs ran it to the Denver seven-yard line. Two plays later Mathis scored again, this time from two yards out, and New York led 31–3.

Even when the Jets were generous, Denver could not take advantage. For the second consecutive game Kern Carson let a punt drop and bounce off his leg, and again the opponents recovered. But after taking over on the New York 32, Denver could move no closer than the 30, and after four plays, turned the ball over on downs.

The teams would trade punts to play out the third quarter (the Jets missed a 43-yard field goal as well), but two plays into the fourth period linebacker Wahoo McDaniel intercepted a McCormick pass intended for tight end Al Denson, giving the Jets the ball on the Denver 39. The excited fans cheered all the louder when they saw Namath coming onto the field with the offense.

Although Namath would throw to Snell for seven yards and would scramble for 14 himself, a holding penalty sabotaged the Jets' efforts and forced them to try a 48-yard field goal. It was no good, but missed opportunities by the Jets proved little blessing to the Broncos. Bob Scarpitto fumbled a double reverse on the next play, and Biggs recovered for the Jets on the Denver four-yard line. Two plays later, Carson ran it in for the score: 38–3.

The Broncos then traded two punts for the Jets' one, but the second only traveled 12 yards when Scarpitto shanked it. Namath immediately took advantage with a 30-yard touchdown throw to Sauer. It was now 45–3. There were only 45 seconds left when Denver finally scored a touchdown on a McCormick-to-Taylor pass from 19 yards out, but not even surrendering a TD at the end of the game could take the shine off this one. The Jets had finally won a game. Even better, they won big, 45–10.

Namath's numbers were better than Taliaferro's, hitting five of six for 49 yards and a touchdown to Taliaferro's four of 12 for 40 yards with one touchdown and two interceptions. But it was Taliaferro who had been behind center as the Jets took a commanding 31–3 lead. Maybe who played quarterback a week later would once more be determined by whoever looked better in practice during the week, but one thing seemed certain: Huarte would not be getting his chance.

Week 8 — Sunday, November 7, 1965
Municipal Stadium, Kansas City (attendance: 25,523)

The Jets had to be pleased with getting their initial victory of the 1965 season, to say nothing of the demonstrative way they went about it, but they now faced another hurdle: they would be traveling to Kansas City to play the Chiefs. The road had not been kind to the New York Jets. In fact, they had not won a road game since winning in Denver on November 17, 1963, a string consisting of 12 straight road losses extending back two years. Given their respective records (the Chiefs were 4–3–1), and the Jets' poor performance on the road, it was no wonder that the Chiefs were six-point favorites.

They were only expecting in the neighborhood of 20,000 in attendance for the game at Kansas City's Municipal Stadium, so the Chiefs' organization was very happy when Ewbank announced publicly that, although Taliaferro would be starting at quarterback, there was every chance that Namath would see some playing time. The Chiefs figured the prospect of Namath's playing could possibly bring another 5,000 in attendance. They were uncannily accurate, as attendance come Sunday was counted at 25,523.

The Jets' first possession was a bit of a misfire. After receiving a punt from Kansas City, the Jets started on their own 32; on just their third play from scrimmage, Taliaferro was intercepted by linebacker E.J. Holub, but Holub proceeded to fumble the ball during his runback and Bill Mathis recovered for the Jets at the 33. The Jets got the ball back, and a yard better field position as well. They took advantage of the second chance, working downfield with runs and shorter passes, and when the drive stalled, Jim Turner put the Jets out in front 3–0 with a 19-yard field goal. The Chiefs shot right back to tie the game, however, with a field goal of their own on their very next series.

After the Jets were forced to punt, the Chiefs did more damage on their next possession. On just the third play of the series, Len Dawson spotted Chris Burford racing downfield well behind the coverage. Dawson's aim was true, and Burford caught the ball at the New York 35 and went the distance, 57 yards for a score. It put Kansas City up 10–3.

Taliaferro hit Dee Mackey with a 19-yard pass on the Jets' next possession, but then went for a long pass to Maynard that was intercepted by safety Bobby Hunt on the Kansas City 19-yard line. Hunt ran it back to the Chiefs' 47, but Kansas City could do nothing with the good field position and had to punt the ball back. Starting on the New York 20-yard line, Taliaferro was able to move the Jets downfield — largely on runs by Mathis — but the drive ran out of steam at the Kansas City 17-yard line. Turner salvaged the series with a 24-yard field goal that cut Kansas City's lead to 10–6, which is how it stood at halftime.

Taliaferro was not happy when Ewbank told him at halftime that Namath would be piloting the team in the second half. Ewbank had told Taliaferro to throw short passes. Taliaferro thought he had been: Ewbank disagreed. After receiving the second half kickoff, the Jets began from their 25. Namath threw 10 yards to Sauer and 16 yards to Maynard, mixed with runs by Mathis. From the Kansas City 31 Namath went back to pass, and when a linebacker blitz left an opening in the coverage underneath, Mackey quickly slid into the gap and Namath just as quickly tossed him the ball. Mackey caught it at the 23 and got as far as the 16. He was in the process of being tackled when he spotted Maynard running alongside the play and quickly flipped him the ball. Maynard faked out defensive back Fred Williamson, who grabbed an armful of nothing before falling facedown onto the turf as Maynard ran 15 yards for the score, giving the Jets a 13–10 lead.

The Chiefs came right back, starting on their own 19 and mounting an impressive drive that included two successful fourth-down conversions. But on first-and-goal from the eight-yard line, Dawson rolled out to the left and tried to lob a pass to running back Curtis McClinton in the end zone: Dainard Paulson stepped in front and pulled the pass down at the one-yard line, then made a nifty runback to the 23.

Into the fourth quarter, the teams were swapping punts until Paulson again intercepted Dawson and the Jets took over at the Kansas City 28. They might have at least gotten a field goal out of it, but for a holding penalty that pushed them out of range. The teams then resumed with their fourth-quarter punting exhibition. The Jets had punted four times in the quarter, while the Chiefs had punted twice (the Chiefs had otherwise been intercepted).

With 3:14 left in the game, the Chiefs took possession at their own 20 after a New York punt carried into the end zone. Following a loss of five yards on a draw play, Dawson hit tight end Fred Arbanas over the middle for 35 yards to midfield; Dawson then ran for 11 yards himself to the New York 39. Another pass to Arbanas gained 10 yards and a first down at the 29, and with 1:17 remaining Dawson hit Burford for nine yards to the 20. After again running it himself for two yards and a first down, Dawson then threw out of bounds to stop the clock. With under a minute remaining, the Chiefs missed two passes in the end zone and would have to settle for a tying field goal from 25 yards out: the kick was blocked by defensive back Willie West, who ran unimpeded around the right end of the Kansas City line. The Jets' long road drought had ended. Even better, they could now boast of a winning streak. Namath completed seven of 16 for 81 yards and a TD.

Week 9 — Sunday, November 14, 1965
Fenway Park, Boston (attendance: 18,589)

Riding a two-game winning streak, and having at last gotten the road-loss monkey off their backs, the Jets had to like their chances going to Boston to face the Patriots at Fenway Park. The Patriots were 1–7–1, but there was something somehow unnatural about their inhabiting the Eastern Division's cellar. Many seemed to feel that they were a better team than that, an opinion which may have been attributable to the fact that ever since the AFL's inception the Boston Patriots had been one of the league's most consistent teams, posting a winning record every season but the first. In 1964 they were 10–3–1, and there seemed to be no obvious reason to explain a complete meltdown. But to those closer to the team — i.e., Boston sportswriters — it was thought to be a long time in coming. When Boston was hit by a wave of injuries in preseason, their lack of depth became all too obvious. The local sportswriters put it down to the stinginess of the owners, but in a way that was unfair. When you don't have much of a profit margin, stinginess is more necessity than choice. The Patriots did not draw large crowds. Only 18,589 would attend their game with the Jets, but then it was a cold, wet November day in Boston; surely it would have helped if the Patriots had been in contention. Still, if they got 25,000 out to Fenway that was about as good as they could expect.

But the Patriots hadn't had the fight knocked out of them yet. They had demonstrated an unlikely dominance of Western Division–leading San Diego, for instance. As the Patriots' record stood at 1–7–1, it is interesting that the only games they *didn't* lose were their two meetings with San Diego, who they first played to a 13–13 tie in Boston in week six, and then beat in San Diego 22–6 in week eight. It was one of only two losses San Diego would suffer during the entire season.

Against the Jets the Patriots received the opening kickoff, but Jim Nance only brought it back to the 10-yard line. Three plays into the series, with a third-and-one on the 19, J.D. Garrett ran off tackle, and although he appeared to have gotten the first down, he fumbled after being hit by linebacker Ralph Baker; the ball was picked up by linebacker Wahoo McDaniel, who ran it to the one-yard line. Two plays later, and little more than two minutes into the game, Matt Snell ran it in for a 7–0 Jets lead.

On the Patriots' next series, quarterback Babe Parilli dropped back to pass on a third-and-16 play and had the ball stripped by Gerry Philbin. Verlon Biggs recovered for the Jets on the nine-yard line. It was starting to look too easy — both of the Jets' offensive series had started with first-and-goal. But this time the Jets would fail to make the most of it as Namath — who must have looked better in practice that week — threw three incomplete passes, and New York had to settle for a 16-yard field goal and a 10–0 lead.

Starting their next series on their 23, the Patriots ran Ron Burton around left end. Rocky Rochester hit Burton, Burton fumbled, and Biggs again recovered for the Jets, this time on the 22. Namath went right for the throat on the next play, and hit Maynard with a 22-yard touchdown pass. Less than halfway into the first period, it was now 17–0.

On the Patriots' next series, Boston coach Mike Holovak sent Eddie Wilson in at quarterback. It might have seemed an odd choice since Parilli could not be held accountable for the fumbles of Garrett and Burton, or maybe even his own for that matter (better pass blocking would have prevented that). Perhaps Holovak was hoping that a change at quarterback might give the team some kind of mental lift and somehow stop the hemorrhaging. Wilson lasted only a few plays, however, as he was knocked cold after scrambling with the ball and getting pasted by McDaniel and tackle Jim Harris.

After Wilson was carried off the field, Parilli came back in and succeeded in moving the team close enough for a 35-yard field goal attempt, but that sailed wide. It was still 17–0, but the Patriots could at least take heart in as much as they held the ball for an entire series without fumbling. The two teams then played out the quarter by exchanging punts.

The Patriots finally got on the scoreboard early in the second quarter with a 30-yard field goal. The breaks now seemed to be coming Boston's way as the field goal was made possible by, first a short punt into the wind by Curley Johnson that set Boston up on the New York 41-yard line, and second by a pass interference call that moved them to the New York 23.

But the Jets shot back quickly: on second-and-nine from the 21 Namath threw over the middle to Maynard at the New York 30, and the lanky flanker ran it 41 yards to the Boston 38. Two plays later Namath found Maynard again, hitting him with a beautiful 36-yard touchdown throw. It was now 24–3.

Following another exchange of punts, Parilli was intercepted by Dainard Paulson, but as Paulson was running it back he lost the handle on the ball, and when it hit the ground Parilli fell on it at the New York 47, giving Boston a new set of downs. This time Parilli made good on the opportunity, hitting Jim Colclough with passes of 27 and 11 yards before throwing seven yards to Gino Cappelletti for the touchdown.

Boston was now coming to life. After forcing the Jets to punt, the Patriots took over on their own 45 and Parilli immediately went long to fullback Larry Garron, who took it all the way to the New York five-yard line. On second-and-goal, Parilli threw to Garrett for the score, and that quickly the Jets' lead had been slashed to 24–17. As the half ended, the Jets found themselves in a dogfight. Namath had completed six of his 14 first-half passes for 122 yards, all accountable by Maynard.

In the third period the teams first exchanged punts, and then field goals, Jim Turner hitting from 19-yards out and Cappelletti making good from 30, as the Patriots continued to hold the New York lead to seven points. The Patriots were known as a blitzing team, and Namath began to feel some pressure; on second-and-10 from the New York 20, he was dropped for a seven-yard loss by linebacker Nick Buoniconti, and on the following play he was dropped for a loss of eight by tackles Jim Hunt and Houston Antwine. The Patriots thereby got the ball back in good field position at their own 42, and Parilli got them moving again. Unfortunately for Boston the drive began to lose steam as the third quarter ended, and when they resumed in the fourth they were traveling into the wind. As the fourth quarter got under way, the Patriots ran two unsuccessful pass plays and then, from 34 yards out, a likewise unsuccessful field goal attempt. The score remained 27–20.

The Jets did a lot to secure the victory on their next series. Although it would only get them three points, the drive would eat up so much of the clock that it made it too daunting a task for the Patriots to score twice with what time remained. Mathis ran the ball eight times in the drive, and Snell four times. The runs were crucial to killing time, but the main play in the drive was a third-and-eight pass from Namath to George Sauer that gained 33 yards to the Boston 34. The Jets would ultimately bog down at the seven-yard line, but Jim Turner booted a 14-yard field goal that gave New York a 10-point lead. The drive, which had begun with almost nine minutes to play, went 73 yards in 15 plays and had left less than five minutes on the clock.

Parilli made a valiant effort, passing the Patriots downfield to the Jets' 26 before once again being intercepted by Paulson, who picked it off at the 10-yard line and ran it back to the 15. The Patriots got one last shot after that, but Willie West intercepted Parilli on the New York 20 on the game's final play. The Jets had just won their third straight game; incredibly, it was the longest winning streak in franchise history. It was also the first time Namath had played an entire game in the pros. He got a phone call from Bear Bryant afterward. The coach had watched the game on television, and he thought Namath had shown a lot of poise during that time-consuming fourth-quarter drive. Bryant let Namath know that, as far as he was concerned, Namath had become a professional quarterback that day.

"I think I proved I can handle the blitz," Namath said, and Ewbank agreed. "Joe did a great job," said Ewbank. "He adjusted well to some new Boston defenses. And the Patriots' blitz helped the two touchdown passes as it left one-man coverage on Maynard."[12]

In the Boston locker room Holovak was handing out free sodas to visitors as they entered, sarcastically remarking that his team gives everything away. "We just give these games away," Holovak said without attempting to hide his disgust. "That was like a nightmare, those first few minutes."[13] He stopped castigating his team long enough to praise Namath, saying the Jets' quarterback could really rifle the ball.[14] Namath completed 10 of 25 for 180 yards and two touchdowns.

Week 10 — Sunday, November 21, 1965
Shea Stadium, New York (attendance: 52,888)

The Jets returned to New York to host the Houston Oilers at Shea Stadium, and with a record of 3–5–1 to Houston's 4–5, could move ahead of the Oilers into second place in the

Eastern Division with a win. That could be little more than a moral victory, however, as there was almost zero chance of either team catching Buffalo to win the division. With their three-game winning streak and strong defensive play, the Jets were favored over Houston, despite trailing them in the standings. During their previous three games the New York defense had only given up an average of 55 yards rushing per game, and with the Houston running game being nothing too spectacular, the ground attack was not a major concern. As for Houston's passing game, George Blanda had been doing most of the quarterbacking for the Oilers and had already thrown 20 interceptions (six the week before the Jets game). That was another area in which the Jets had been looking good: in their previous three games, the Jets had intercepted Denver five times, Kansas City twice, and Boston three times. And then there was Namath's week-to-week improvement. For the Jets, it all looked good.

Although they would hardly begin with the same field position they had in Boston the week before, the Jets would score as quickly nonetheless. Bake Turner took the opening kickoff for the Jets and only brought it out to the 15-yard line, but on first down Namath gave Houston something to think about when he went long for Maynard. The pass was broken up by Tony Banfield, but it seemed to have the desired effect of loosening the defense up, and on second down Namath ran a draw play to Mathis. Guard Sam DeLuca and tackle Winston Hill opened a huge gap in the left side of the line for Mathis to bolt through, and once he did, Mathis was helped further by the fact that tight end Dee Mackey had come across from the right side and taken out defensive back Jim Norton. After breaking through the line, Mathis was off to the races. The result was a franchise-record 79-yard run that ended when defensive back W.K. Hicks caught Mathis from behind and pulled him down at the six-yard line. In Boston, the Jets had started their first possession with a first-and-goal: against the Oilers they had to wait until their third play of the game for first-and-goal. Three plays later Namath hit Maynard with a bullet to the right side of the end zone, and the Jets were up 7–0 less than two minutes into the game.

After a Houston punt resulted in a touchback, the Jets started their next series on the 20. Following a three-yard run by Snell, Namath hit Mackey with a 47-yard pass to the Houston 30. The drive would result in an 18-yard field goal, and a 10–0 New York lead.

Three plays later, Willie West intercepted Houston quarterback Don Trull to set the Jets up on the Oilers' 38-yard line. Shortly after the second period got underway, Namath went to Sauer across the middle and underneath the coverage. Sauer — running left-to-right — caught the ball, eluded several tacklers and took it into the end zone for a 20-yard touchdown. The Jets later added another field goal and led 20–0 at halftime. They hadn't even had to punt in the first half (one possession ended when Namath was intercepted by Banfield in the Houston end zone). Not so in the third period, as the two teams would exchange punts throughout. The period would see no scoring, but the Jets would be in the midst of a sustained drive when the third quarter ended.

Mackey had broken his collarbone in the second quarter, and punter Curley Johnson had come in to play tight end. That might sound strange nowadays, but Johnson was a strong, husky player who looked like he could fill any number of positions: in fact, even before Mackey went down hurt Johnson was in at halfback for the winded Mathis after his 79-yard run. Johnson had carried for two yards on second-and-goal from the six. Now in at tight end, again from the Houston six, Johnson caught a touchdown pass from Namath that extended the Jets' lead to 27–0.

The Jets again got the ball back quickly when linebacker Ralph Baker intercepted Blanda (the Oilers had been alternating Trull and Blanda at quarterback all day), giving New York the ball on the Houston 35. Two plays later, Namath threw a perfect 34-yard strike to a wide open Maynard in the end zone. It was now 34–0.

Taliaferro was in at quarterback for the Jets' next series, and he proceeded to lead the team on an impressive drive that started at the New York 28. The drive would fail to put up any more points, however, as Taliaferro was intercepted by Hicks in the Houston end zone.

After Hicks' interception, the Oilers were finally able to get on the board with a three-yard keeper by Trull. But at 34–7 in the fourth, the Jets were in no danger. Even when the Oilers recovered an onside kick and were able to score another touchdown to cut the lead to 34–14, there just wasn't enough time to overcome a 20-point deficit.

The Oilers tried another onside kick, but Jim Hudson recovered for the Jets at midfield. The Jets would then put the finishing touch on their finest performance of the season; on second-and-nine from the Houston 49, Snell ran to the left, and after experiencing too much congestion, reversed field and ran back around right end with Taliaferro and Sherman Plunkett helping to clear the way. Snell took it 44 yards to the five-yard line. Two plays later, Kern Carson scored from four yards out with 22 seconds remaining to make the final 41–14.

Aside from Mathis' team-record 79-yard run, the Jets had set a number of other club records that day. It was now their fourth straight victory, which broke their consecutive victory record of three set the week before; they also had a team record of 284 yards rushing (Snell had 132, Mathis 129), and another club record of 522 total yards. Namath's four touchdown passes had tied a club record, and Jim Turner tied a league record when his two field goals gave him seven straight. Once more the defense had kept the opponent's ground game in check, holding them to only 62 yards rushing, and had snatched another four interceptions, the final theft coming on the last play of the game when Bill Baird picked off a Blanda pass.

As for Namath, he had his best day as a professional, completing 17 of 26 passes for 221 yards, four touchdowns and one interception. Sonny Werblin was certainly pleased with the performance. After the game, Werblin found Namath in the locker room. "Joe," he said, "I'm ready to renegotiate."[15] They both smiled. This was how it was supposed to be.

Week 11— Sunday, November 28, 1965
Shea Stadium, New York (attendance: 56,511)

The Jets were the hottest team in the league; their four-game winning streak was the longest that any AFL team had put together all season. Technically, they still had a mathematical chance of catching division-leading Buffalo, but that would require the Jets to win all four of their remaining games. The way they were playing, the Jets may have felt like they could accomplish it, but what would also be needed would be for the Bills to lose all three of their remaining games (because of their bye week earlier, the Jets were a game behind Buffalo; Buffalo was 8–2–1, the Jets were 4–5–1).

In their eleventh game the Jets would be hosting the Patriots at Shea, and even though they had already beaten them in Boston, the Patriots were not to be underestimated. The frustrated Patriots knew they were better than their 1–8–2 record made them appear, and they were eager to prove it. In their earlier loss to the Jets in Boston, the Patriots had begun the game by fumbling the ball away deep in their own territory on their first three possessions. Even then, they still managed to make a game of it, so if they could just refrain from such nonsense this time, they were confident of their chances.

The Patriots were likely encouraged by the fact that, after receiving the opening kickoff they managed to make it through their first series without fumbling. What wasn't so good was that they still gave the ball up when they had to punt. Even worse, the punt was partially blocked by Jim Harris, and the Jets would begin their first series at midfield. But Namath began by fumbling the snap, and Mike Dukes recovered for the Patriots. Perhaps the Jets were going to be the same generous hosts the Patriots had been in Boston.

Beginning their second series at midfield, the Patriots moved quickly to the 26 when Babe Parilli hit Jim Whalen with a 24-yard pass. But after three incompletions, the Patriots had to settle for a field goal, which Gino Cappelletti hit from 33 yards out for a 3–0 Boston lead.

New York missed a chance to tie the game later in the period when Jim Turner was wide right on a field goal try of 25 yards, but in the second quarter the Jets seemed to be getting into their rhythm. Turner hit a 14-yard field goal, and then on New York's next offensive series Namath hit Bake Turner with a 50-yard touchdown. Neither team could move the ball effectively after that, however, and the second quarter became a punting contest. The half ended with the Jets up 10–3, but not looking terribly sharp. For the Patriots, things seemed dismal: Parilli had only completed one of 11 passes in the half.

The Jets came out with a thoroughly uninspired three-and-out series to start the second half. The Patriots, on the other hand, were able to get close enough for Cappelletti to try a 53-yard field goal: he hit it, and the Jets' lead had been cut to 10–6.

After dropping Namath for losses of 13 and 14 yards on the Jets' next series, the Patriots took over at midfield following the punt and Parilli promptly hit Jim Colclough for 28 yards to the 22. The Jets gave up another five yards with an offside penalty, and Parilli then scrambled to the 10. Back-up quarterback Eddie Wilson was pressed into duty as Parilli had been shaken up on the play, and two plays later Wilson hit Colclough for the score from eight yards out, putting the Patriots back in front, 13–10.

On the Jets' next series Namath was intercepted by Ross O'Hanley at the New York 47, and the Patriots took advantage. Parilli returned to action and hit Tony Romeo for 17 yards. Three plays later, he went to Colclough in the end zone for a 27-yard score to up Boston's lead to 20–10.

After receiving the kick, the Jets closed out the third period with Namath completing a pass to Maynard for 40 yards to the Boston 36. As the final period got underway, Namath threw to Matt Snell for 10 yards and then hit Bake Turner for 21 more and a first-and-goal at the five. On the next play, Snell took it around left end for the score. It was now 20–17, Boston.

After forcing a Boston punt, the Jets went back to work on offense. Namath threw 35 yards to Maynard for a first down at the Boston 45. Namath then went back to Maynard for 32 yards on a third-and-11 play. Another third-down pass, this time to Bake Turner, was just short of the first down, and the Jets were compelled to settle for a tying field goal, which Jim Turner hit from 13 yards out.

The Jets could sense their fifth straight victory now, and when Willie West intercepted Parilli to give the New York offense possession at the Boston 32, the crowd at Shea could sense it as well. Three runs by Snell and Mathis gained 11 yards and a first down, but after two more runs gained only a yard, Namath ran a draw to Mathis on third-and-nine. It only gained two yards; Jim Turner would have to get the lead back for the Jets, which he did by making good on a 26-yard field goal. The Jets were now up 23–20 with just 2:15 left to play.

The Patriots got a good runback by Larry Garron, and began their series from the 34-yard line. Parilli threw 18 yards to Colclough at the New York 48, and a New York penalty moved Boston up to the 43. A 33-yard pass from Parilli to Cappelletti then gave Boston a first-and-goal at the nine-yard line. Parilli threw incomplete to Romeo in the end zone on first down. On second down, Ron Burton ran for seven yards to the two. A third-down pass was thrown right into the hands of Willie West, but the New York defensive back dropped the ball. It was now fourth-and-goal. The Patriots could easily tie the game with a nine-yard field goal, but with just one victory all season, they weren't interested in a tie. Boston coach Mike Holovak had sent word into the huddle when it was first-and-goal that it was going to be a touchdown or nothing. There would certainly be no field goal and no tie. "We had nothing to lose except another game," Holovak said afterward.[16]

There were now 54 seconds remaining. Parilli ran the same play he had missed on first-and-goal, a rollout pass to Romeo. The pass was low, but Romeo went to the ground and made a nice catch for the touchdown. With the extra point, the Patriots led 27–23. But with almost a minute remaining, the Jets still had a shot. That chance disappeared when Dainard Paulson fumbled the kickoff, and Boston recovered the ball on the New York 25. The Patriots ran four running plays and turned the ball over on downs, leaving just enough time for Namath to throw a meaningless pass to Sauer for 13 yards. New York's winning streak had ended.

"I was surprised that he went for the win instead of the tie," Ewbank said of Holovak.[17] He shouldn't have been. A team with a 1–8–2 record has nothing to risk losing. Besides, Ewbank might have gotten a sense of Boston's desperation earlier in the fourth quarter when Holovak went for broke on fourth down with just a half-yard to go at the Boston 45. They made that one, too.

The loss did more than end the Jets' winning streak: it ended their playoff hopes. The Buffalo Bills had the day off, but even without playing they clinched the division; the Patriots had accomplished it for them. Holovak knew it was a crushing loss for the Jets. After the game he apologized to Ewbank. Namath's stats read 16 of 30 for 284 yards, one TD, one interception.

Week 12 — Saturday, December 4, 1965
Balboa Stadium, San Diego (attendance: 32,169)

It was a deflated New York Jets team that headed out west to play Western Division–leading San Diego the following Saturday. They would be in California for 11 days, first to play the Chargers, and then the Raiders in Oakland eight days later. The Jets' worst defeat of the season had been the 34–9 spanking the Chargers had given them at Shea back in October, but there were hopeful signs. Notwithstanding the loss to Boston the week before, the Jets had been playing better in the intervening weeks, while the Chargers, although still leading in the West, had not been. Since beating the Jets in October, the Chargers had gone 1–2–1. Their two losses had been embarrassments, falling 22–6 to the Patriots in San Diego, and 31–7 to the Chiefs in Kansas City.

The New York defense looked eager, intercepting San Diego quarterback John Hadl on each of the Chargers' first two offensive series. In the game's opening series it was Willie West who picked Hadl off at the New York 45, but the Jets missed their opportunity when Jim Turner was short on a 52-yard field goal try. On San Diego's next series, Dainard Paulson intercepted Hadl on the New York 38 and returned it to the San Diego 41. The Jets would end up trying another field goal, but this time it was blocked.

San Diego took possession on their own 39, and they began to do something that no team had done against the Jets for some weeks — they began to run the ball effectively. Keith Lincoln went off right tackle for nine yards, Paul Lowe went behind right guard for five, Lincoln got eight more off left tackle, then got another eight running to the right. Hadl had supplemented the runs with passes of 18 and 12 yards to Lance Alworth. The first quarter ended with San Diego on the New York one-yard line. The second quarter opened with a touchdown run by Lincoln for a 7–0 San Diego lead.

Although the Jets did start to move the ball on their next possession, the series ended abruptly when Namath was intercepted by Kenny Graham at the San Diego 42. The Chargers then resumed with running for big chunks of yardage — Lowe for 13, then again for four more, Lincoln for seven on a pitchout. Hadl was also still throwing to Alworth, hitting him for 12 yards on a crucial third-down play. Hadl finished the drive by hitting Lincoln over the middle, and the fullback escaped a tackle attempt by linebacker Wahoo McDaniel and ran it in for a 25-yard scoring play, making it 14–0.

On the first play of the Jets' next series, Namath went back to pass and fumbled upon being hit: the Chargers recovered the ball on the New York 15-yard line. The New York defense then rose to the occasion: Gerry Philbin chased Hadl out of bounds for an eight-yard loss, and after a four-yard run and an incomplete pass, San Diego had to make do with a 26-yard field goal and a 17–0 lead.

Namath began to move the Jets with shorter passes — Maynard for five, Sauer for 10 and then 15, Snell for eight — but once more the drive was halted when Namath was intercepted, this time by Dick Degen at the San Diego 48. On this occasion, San Diego wound up punting the ball away as the half ended.

Any hope the Jets may have had of a fresh start in the second half took a kick in the teeth on the very first play from scrimmage. After Bake Turner returned the kickoff to the New York 24, Namath was again intercepted by Graham. This time Graham went the distance, running it back 51 yards for a score. That made it 24–0.

Now fairly well behind, Namath again went to the pass on first down — this time he was sacked for a seven-yard loss. After an incompletion, Namath hit Maynard for 22 yards and a first down, and then threw to Mathis for 17. The New York offense finally began to find its rhythm; Namath went to Bake Turner for 12 yards, then Snell for five, and Turner again for 14 more. The drive went 82 yards in 11 plays, and climaxed with Namath throwing 21 yards to Maynard for the score. Namath had completed six of eight passes for 88 yards in the series.

But notions of staging a comeback were quashed pretty quickly when Hadl went long for Alworth and hit him with a 46-yard bomb that upped the score to 31–7. Early in the fourth quarter Hadl again found Alworth, this time for a 36-yard touchdown to make it 38–7. After that, the Chargers were content to run as much time off the clock as they could, and the Jets seemed in no panic to preserve time either. Although the San Diego ground game seemed to be getting the job done, Hadl went for a little trickery on a second-and-eight play, calling for a double reverse to Alworth. Jim Harris hit Alworth and forced a fumble, which was grabbed by Ray Abruzzese, who took off running. Incredibly, it was Alworth who got to his feet and caught up with Abruzzese, tackling him at the nine-yard line.

Taliaferro then came in at quarterback for the Jets. With first-and-goal at the nine, the Jets failed to score in four plays, and turned the ball over on downs. The game mercifully ended, the final being 38–7. For the second time that season, the Jets had their asses handed to them by the San Diego Chargers. Namath was 18 of 34 for 179 yards, with one TD, and three interceptions.

Week 13 — Sunday, December 12, 1965
Frank Youell Field, Oakland (attendance: 19,013)

The Jets and Raiders would be playing the last game to ever be played in Frank Youell Field, a not-so-charmingly antiquated facility that one would not normally suspect of housing a professional franchise but for Oakland's presence there for four years. The Raiders would be moving into the brand new Alameda County Stadium the following year, but on this day it was a chance for the people to drink in Frank Youell Field in all its ramshackle glory one last time. It had rained heavily on Saturday and nobody had thought to cover the field, making it a wonderfully swampy mess come game time Sunday.

Oakland had a lot more to lose that day than did the Jets, who were already out of the race and were really only trying to cling to the prestige of being in second place in their division; Oakland still had a shot at winning theirs. But that would require more than the Raiders could accomplish on their own: they also needed the Oilers to beat the San Diego Chargers in Houston. Even then, Oakland would have to beat San Diego the following week in their season finale. If San Diego beat Houston, then even consecutive Oakland victories over the Jets and Chargers would fail to turn the trick for the Raiders. That would put them in the curious position of having more wins than the Chargers but still finishing behind them, for it would leave San Diego with an 8–3–3 record and a .727 win percentage while Oakland at 9–4–1 would have a .692 win percentage — just one of those quirks.

The Raiders began the game at their own 30 and very quickly shot down to the New York 13-yard line, the main play in the series being a 34-yard catch and run by Alan Miller. But it was all for naught, as Oakland quarterback Tom Flores was then intercepted by Cornell Gordon in the end zone. Gordon had a moment of indecision before unwisely opting to run it out of the end zone: he only brought it back to the New York seven-yard line. The Jets got out of the hole quickly, however, when Namath threw to Maynard for 25 yards, and then again for 20 more. Ultimately, all it got them was a better spot for Curley Johnson to punt from.

The biggest play in the first quarter came as time expired in the period. Flores hit Art Powell streaking down the sideline, and Powell took it 66 yards to the New York 15 before Gordon made a saving tackle. Two plays later Bill Baird was flagged for pass interference in the end zone, giving the Raiders a first-and-goal on the one-yard line. The call did not agree with Ewbank, of course. "I couldn't teach a back a better way to play his man than Baird played Fred Biletnikoff," Ewbank said after the game.[18] From there, it was Clem Daniels for the score and a 7–0 Oakland lead at 1:26 of the second period. The drive had covered 99 yards in just seven plays (it began after Namath had been intercepted at the Oakland goal line).

Oakland later doubled their lead on a 26-yard pass from Flores to Powell, who made a nice diving catch for the score with only 39 seconds left in the second quarter. The Jets hadn't looked terribly bad in the first half, but other than Namath's passes to Maynard, their biggest gainers were a pair of personal foul penalties on Oakland defensive linemen Ben Davidson and Ike Lassiter, both of whom were flagged for hitting Namath late (go figure). Otherwise, it was a half of missed opportunities for the Jets: Namath had been intercepted by Claude Gibson at the Oakland goal line, ending a drive that had seen the Jets move from their 46 to the Oakland 12. Another drive by the Jets stalled when Winston Hill was flagged for holding, and the Jets wound up trying a field goal from 35 yards out — Jim Turner missed, wide left.

After a halftime farewell ceremony for Frank Youell Field, the Raiders caught the Jets off guard with an onside kick to open the second half: Oakland recovered it at the New York 45. Nothing the Raiders did on the ensuing three plays managed to catch the Jets off guard, however, and Oakland punted to the New York 11. From there Namath hit Bake Turner for 14 yards, and Matt Snell ran for 13 yards up the middle. Then Namath again threw to Turner, who had gotten a good five yards on his defender down the sideline. Claude Gibson came over from his safety position, but rather than going after Turner, Gibson went for the ball: he whiffed, and Turner caught it and ran the remaining 38 yards, untouched, for the score. The play covered 62 yards in all: Oakland's lead had been halved.

When the Jets got the ball back after another Oakland punt, they seemed to be aiming at working their way downfield with a ball-control game plan. Beginning at their own 33, the Jets started by running Snell twice, for eight and then four yards and a first down. A quick drop-off pass to Mark Smolinski gained 12 more, and the following pass to Maynard looked designed for another short gain. It was a simple slant-in pattern, which Maynard caught at the 33, but after catching it he eluded defenders Howie Williams and Warren Powers and went the distance 43 yards for a score. The touchdown tied the game with 2:34 remaining in the third period.

In the fourth quarter, with just four minutes left to play, the Jets seemed to be gaining momentum for a go-ahead score. Namath threw over the middle to Mathis for 16 yards, and then Mathis ran a sweep around right end for six yards to the Oakland 40. Namath then tried to hit Bake Turner, but Turner slipped in the damned Youell mud. The ball was intercepted by Dave Grayson at the Oakland 23, and he returned it 18 yards to the 41. "Turner slipped and I looked up and the ball was there," Grayson said after the game. "Namath was really putting it right there all afternoon for his receivers and it was a good break."[19]

Flores threw 17 yards to Ken Herock, then Larry Todd ran for 11, and the referees tacked on another 15 yards when they called Ray Abruzzese for a personal foul. After the drive stalled, the Raiders settled for a 22-yard field goal by Mike Mercer, giving them a 17–14 lead with only 2:28 left to play.

When the Jets got the ball back they started on their own 23, but soon found themselves with a fourth-and-10 situation after three failed passes. With time running out, Ewbank felt they had no choice but to go for it. Namath got the necessary yardage on a pass to Maynard, but the officials wiped the play out with an illegal procedure penalty against the Jets. It was now fourth-and-15, and the Jets had no other option but to go for it again. Namath threw to Turner, but the pass gained only 13 yards and Oakland took over at the New York 31. Three plays later, Clem Daniels ran off right tackle and went 30 yards for a score with only 38 seconds to play. That made it 24–14.

Ewbank sent Mike Taliaferro in for the last desperate try by the Jets. After hitting Maynard for nine yards, Taliaferro threw long for Maynard: the pass was intercepted, and the game ended there. The Raiders had scored their 10 decisive points in the last two-and-a-half minutes of the game.

There were kind words for Namath from Oakland coach Al Davis after the game; in fact, he came across as quite the fan. Words from the Jets' locker room were not so flattering toward Oakland, however. Ewbank, fuming over the late hits Namath took, was especially hostile toward Davidson, saying that he should have been ejected rather than merely penalized. "I've never seen a team hit Joe late like that this year," Ewbank said.[20]

"I want you to put this in the paper," Namath said. "Ben Davidson shows me no class."[21] But Davidson played it off, even complimenting Namath's skills as a quarterback. Davidson otherwise blamed the muddy field for his inability to stop from delivering late hits — excuses 101. And so began one of the most hostile rivalries in football. Incidentally, San Diego staged a fourth-quarter comeback to beat Houston that day. They beat Oakland the following week as well. Against Oakland, Namath had completed 19 of 36 for 280 yards with a pair of TDs and three interceptions.

Week 14 — Sunday, December 19, 1965
Shea Stadium, New York (attendance: 57,396)

The Jets returned home to close out the season against the Buffalo Bills at Shea. The Bills had clinched the division weeks earlier, and at 10–2–1 were far and away superior in their division. The rest of the division — the Jets, Oilers and Patriots — were all in a heated battle for a fairly meaningless second place, the Jets hanging on to it at 4–8–1, while the Oilers were 4–9 and the Patriots 3–8–2. The Patriots were playing the Oilers, so if the Jets were to lose to Buffalo and fall to 4–9–1, and the Patriots were to beat Houston and finish 4–8–2, that would put Boston ahead of the Jets for second place. If Houston won and the Jets lost, Houston would take second with a 5–9 record. The only way the Jets could hope to hold second place in the division would be for them to beat Buffalo. That would be no easy task, of course, particularly since Buffalo coach Lou Saban would be playing his starting lineup in order to keep them sharp for the impending championship game with San Diego on December 26. Adding to the Jets' woes was the fact that Matt Snell would miss the game with a sprained ankle.

On the Tuesday before the game, it was announced that the Jets and the Patriots had come to terms over John Huarte. After the season was over, Huarte would be going to Boston. On the Wednesday before the game, Buffalo quarterback Jack Kemp was announced as the winner of the AFL's Most Valuable Player award, beating out San Diego receiver Lance Alworth by two votes. The following day, Namath was announced as the winner of the AFL Rookie of the Year award, taking 18 of 24 votes (the voting on both was done by a panel of Associated Press sportswriters).

The Jets received the opening kickoff, but after they could do nothing with it in three plays and punted, Buffalo wound up with very good field position, starting from their own 46. They seemed to move almost at will, for the most part, with Wray Carlton gaining 16 yards on three consecutive runs, and Kemp throwing to Paul Costa for eight. But when Kemp went for the touchdown, the New York secondary came through as Bill Baird intercepted the pass in the end zone.

The Jets showed signs of life when Namath hit Maynard with passes of 10 and 16 yards, but that was followed by a Bill Mathis fumble that Buffalo recovered at the New York 49. Fortunately, the Jets' defense had come to play, and twice in three plays Kemp was dropped for a loss. On first down Verlon Biggs took him down for an 11-yard loss, and on third down it was Bert Wilder who threw Kemp for a 17-yard loss. Wilder was in at tackle for Paul Rochester, who was out with a broken knuckle.

Starting their third series from their own 13, Namath took the Jets into Buffalo territory with just one play, a 40-yard pass to Maynard. But when the Jets could only gain three yards on the ensuing three plays, they had to punt again.

Wilder was making good use of his playing time: on first down from the Buffalo 20, Bobby Smith fumbled and Wilder recovered for the Jets on the Buffalo 19. The Jets then did what a team should do when a defense is unexpectedly thrust back into action — they went for it all. Namath threw for Maynard in the back of the end zone and Maynard made a great tight wire catch, toeing the line and just managing to stay in bounds for a score. The Jets led 7–0, but the celebration would be brief as Charley Warner took the kickoff and ran it back 87 yards for a score. Buffalo's own celebration was dampened when a high snap on the extra point was mishandled by Daryle Lamonica, allowing the Jets to keep a 7–6 edge.

The punters were getting quite a workout in the first half, although Curley Johnson had a more interesting half than Buffalo punter Paul Maguire. Late in the first period, Johnson took a high snap from center, and after hauling it down he saw that he would not get the kick off. He pitched a lateral to Wahoo McDaniel, who ran 13 yards for a first down. It was a hollow victory as three plays later, on the second play of the second period, Johnson had to punt again. Later in the period, the Jets got to keep the ball when the Bills were flagged 15 yards for roughing the punter. That second chance for the Jets resulted in an interception, as Namath threw for Maynard only to have it wind up in the hands of Mike Stratton after a deflection by Harry Jacobs. But the New York defense would again turn them away empty handed when Biggs blocked a 40-yard field goal attempt by Pete Gogolak. Just before the half ended Gogolak got another chance, this one from 42 yards out: that one was blocked by Bill Baird.

The Jets missed an excellent opportunity to increase their lead early in the second half. After Namath hit Maynard with a 26-yard pass, the Jets were moved up to the Buffalo 12-yard line courtesy of a personal foul penalty; two plays later, Namath was intercepted in the end zone by George Saimes.

Buffalo punter Paul Maguire seemed determined to have a more interesting second half than Curley Johnson, and when he pulled down a high snap from center, he entertained the idea of running for the first down (it was fourth-and-inches at the Buffalo 30). It was a new acquisition to the Jets — back-up defensive back Arnie Simkus — who changed Maguire's mind. With Simkus fast approaching, Maguire thought better of running and decided to hurry a kick. He shanked it off the side of his foot, and the kick only traveled 13 yards: the Jets took over on the Buffalo 43. Three plays later Namath hurled the ball 36 yards downfield to Maynard, who went up for it at the goal line, right beneath the goal posts. Maynard caught it and landed in the end zone, giving the Jets a 14–6 lead.

Buffalo was in the midst of a sustained drive as the fourth quarter got underway. Lamonica was in at quarterback for the Bills now, and three plays into the final period he hit Charley Warner with an 11-yard touchdown pass. Having botched the extra point on their first touchdown, the Bills were now forced to go for a two-point conversion to tie the game. Lamonica rolled out and tried to run it in himself, but Wilder and Gerry Philbin stopped him inches from the goal line. The Jets' lead remained 14–12.

When Buffalo got the ball back again with some five minutes remaining, they seemed in good shape. Starting at their own 46, they had plenty of time to score, and even a field goal would win it. Despite having time to play with, Lamonica went deep on the first play. It paid off, as he hit Pete Mills for 43 yards to the New York 11. They were already in position for a go-ahead field goal, but with four-and-a-half minutes left Buffalo could now look for the touchdown.

A four-yard carry by Bob Smith got them to the seven, but an offside penalty then pushed them back to the 12. Two runs to the right by Smith got eight yards to the four-yard line, bringing a fourth-and-three. It was only a matter of a 12-yard field goal by Gogolak, but once again Lamonica was forced to field a high snap, and he again bobbled it. He quickly picked it up and threw a desperate pass to John Tracey, but the pass gained only two yards — one shy of what they needed for a first down and two shy of the end zone.

Even then the Jets were unable to run out the clock, and Buffalo got one more shot. Starting at their own 19, time did not favor the Bills at that point, and the game ended with Lamonica passing to halfback Bobby Smith, who ran it to the 38, where he fumbled. Ray Abruzzese picked it up and returned it to the Buffalo 25 as time expired.

The Bills couldn't take the loss too badly. After all, they were already divisional champs, and a week later they would be in sunny San Diego to play the Chargers for the league championship. They would run away with it, beating San Diego 23–0 for their second consecutive AFL title.

The one Buffalo player who had cause to be genuinely disappointed after the loss to the Jets was kicker Pete Gogolak. With three missed field goal opportunities and not even an extra point to his credit, it was the first time in his professional football career that he had failed to score a single point in a game.

As for the Jets, the victory secured their third consecutive 5–8–1 season, and they held on to second place. Even though they had again finished with a losing record, they had still moved up a notch. When they were 5–8–1 in 1963 they had finished in fourth place in their division; their 5–8–1 finish in 1964 got them a third place finish. Now, with a 5–8–1 record yet again, they finished second in the East. As Frank Litsky wrote in the *New York Times*, the Jets had been "improving while standing still."[22]

Despite a handful of good passes to Maynard, Namath had one of the worst days of his rookie season, completing just 17 of 44 passes, but a win was still a win, and it was sweet beating the division champs, no doubt. He also had an impressive 239 passing yards, with two TDs and a pair of interceptions.

As rookie seasons go, Namath's first year was the expected mixed bag. He had completed 164 of 349 passes, only a 48.2 completion percentage. Still, it was higher than Taliaferro's rather anemic 37.8. Namath had also thrown for 2,220 yards and had 18 touchdowns against 15 interceptions. The yardage was impressive, especially in light of the fact that he had only started nine games, and he often played little in those games in which he did not start. His season was impressive enough to win him the AFL Rookie of the Year award, and he was the only rookie named to the AFL All-Star team.

The league had decided on a new approach to the All-Star game in 1965; rather than the usual East versus West game, it was decided that the league champions would play a team of All-Stars from both divisions. Buffalo had defeated San Diego handily in the championship game on

December 26, 1965, so they would be playing the AFL All-Stars at Rice Stadium on Saturday, January 15, 1966. It was a splendid capper to Namath's rookie season.

Buffalo would have a new coach in Joe Collier, who had been named head coach when Lou Saban abruptly left the team after winning the championship to go and coach college ball. San Diego's Sid Gillman would coach the All-Stars. The game was played before a record AFL All-Star game crowd of 35,572. Nobody wondered what had brought them there in such numbers: could it have been a $400,000 rookie superstar?

Gillman started his own quarterback, John Hadl, in the first half, and the All-Stars struggled and fell behind. The Bills went up 10–0 in the first quarter on a 20-yard field goal by Gogolak and a 61-yard fumble runback by George Saimes, which came on a botched field goal by the All-Stars. The teams traded field goals in the second quarter, and the Bills led 13–6 at the half. The second half was something altogether different: the second half belonged to Namath.

Gillman put Namath into the game in the third quarter, and the All-Stars never looked back. Namath came in after Oakland's Dave Grayson intercepted Jack Kemp, and the All-Stars kicked a 32-yard field goal to cut the Buffalo lead to 13–9. On their next possession, Namath led the All-Stars 57 yards in seven plays in a drive that ended with a one-yard touchdown run by San Diego's Paul Lowe. It put the All-Stars in front to stay at 16–13. Namath had also passed 14 yards to San Diego fullback Keith Lincoln in the drive.

Gillman seemed partial to using his own players; perhaps it helped satisfy his need to have his team avenge itself on Buffalo for the humiliation of the championship game, but it didn't sit well with Denver running back Cookie Gilchrist, who felt he did not get adequate playing time. But the Chargers were loving their revenge against Buffalo. San Diego linebacker Frank Buncom intercepted a Kemp pass, and Namath then threw a 43-yard touchdown to San Diego's Lance Alworth. Kemp was then intercepted in the fourth quarter by Boston linebacker Nick Buoniconti, and Namath drove the All-Stars downfield for another score, once more hitting Alworth for a touchdown, this time from 10 yards out. Namath had piloted the All-Stars to a 30–13 lead.

Daryle Lamonica relieved Kemp, who had thrown three interceptions, and managed to lead the Bills to a late score with a 34-yard touchdown pass to Wray Carlton, but by then the game was out of reach and the All-Stars went on to win 30–19. Namath completed six of 10 passes for 89 yards and was voted the game's MVP with 20 votes (second-place Alworth got four votes). There was no shortage of praise for him after the game: Coach Gillman seemed almost speechless, only being able to keep repeating the word "outstanding" when asked his opinion. "He throws a beautiful ball," said Houston receiver Charley Hennigan.[23] Yeah, the praise was sweet, but Namath had something sweeter lined up: Mamie Van Doren was waiting for him outside.

3

The 1966 Season

As training camp got underway there was plenty of optimism about the Jets' prospects for the 1966 season. The main reason was Namath's improvement over the course of his rookie year. Although the Jets had started the 1965 season winless at 0–5–1, they went on to win five of their remaining eight games. The dour demeanor Werblin wore early on lightened considerably once the team started winning. Those in the press box on that November afternoon at Shea Stadium when the Jets beat Houston 41–14 remembered Werblin beaming like a proud father as Namath threw four touchdowns. Things would be better in 1966: everybody knew it.

For one thing, Namath would have some new weapons to work; the Jets had drafted Texas tight end Pete Lammons and Maryland State running back Emerson Boozer. Lammons had also played linebacker at Texas, and he had intercepted Namath twice in the 1965 Orange Bowl. Now Namath would be throwing to Lammons purposefully.

But the Jets had also lost some players due to the expansion draft. The AFL was growing in 1966 with the addition of the Miami Dolphins, who were permitted to pick four players from among each of the other teams in order to help fill their roster. Each franchise could only name 23 players on their respective rosters as off-limits to the expansion draft, so that left a good many players up for grabs. From the Jets the Dolphins took linebacker Wahoo McDaniel, defensive back Willie West, center Mike Hudok and defensive end LaVerne Torczon. There were reasons why most of them were left unprotected: McDaniel was considered expendable because the Jets had a fine, young complement of linebackers with long and bright futures: Al Atkinson would be entering his second year and Ralph Baker his third. The Jets had also drafted rookie linebacker Paul Crane from Alabama, and with veteran Larry Grantham to anchor them, the linebacking corps looked strong. Hudok would be replaced by second-year center John Schmitt, who had spent much of 1965 on the Jets' taxi squad after having suffered a knee injury in his rookie season in 1964.

The loss of West was more problematic, as the Jets had not drafted any defensive backs. They still had Ray Abruzzese, Bill Baird, Cornell Gordon, Jim Hudson, and Dainard Paulson, but they also signed a number of rookies to the squad to act as reserve defensive backs. The most significant addition to the position, however, was seven-year veteran Johnny Sample, who had played for Ewbank in Baltimore and was a member of the Colts' two championship teams in 1958 and '59. He seemed to have problems in the NFL, and consequently moved from team to team before suddenly finding himself blackballed (by his account, anyway). Ewbank was willing to take a chance on Sample: he had experience and proven ability, so Ewbank seems to have felt it wasn't a big roll of the dice.

The quarterback position seemed to be a foregone conclusion. The quarterback controversies of 1965 already seemed a distant memory, as everybody now knew that Namath would certainly be leading the offense. In 1965 Ewbank had said that the job was Mike Taliaferro's to lose: now it was Namath's to lose. Namath was appropriately optimistic. "We have a shot at the whole deal," he said in August, as preseason was about to get underway. "The defense looks a lot better and the offense is smarter. The flankers and the quarterbacks are working together better."[1] He was surely referring to the fact that he had gotten better accustomed to reading his receivers' tendencies, perhaps Maynard in particular.

Werblin, looking to make the preseason lucrative, arranged for the Jets to open the exhibition season in Birmingham, Alabama, at Namath's old college venue, Legion Field. It was a smart move, as a preseason-record 57,205 spectators turned out to see the Jets and the Houston Oilers. Really, they were there to see Namath — they didn't get to see him long. Trailing 3–0 in the first quarter, Namath drove the Jets to the Houston 23-yard line. Then, on a run by Matt Snell that gained only two yards, the trouble began: after the play, actually. Snell said he had heard the whistle and when he got up he left the ball on the ground: Why not? He didn't need it anymore. But Houston defensive lineman Ernie Ladd grabbed the ball, jumped to his feet and took off running. The Jets all began to yell to the official that the play was already blown dead, but just then 245-pound Don Floyd threw a block on Namath. He threw it low.

The players on the sideline were furious and began screaming at both Floyd and the officials. Meanwhile, Namath stayed on the ground. When Dr. Nicholas came onto the field to examine Namath he tried to calm the quarterback down, telling him that the injury didn't appear to have anything to do with the prior knee surgery and that it was likely a simple sprain. Namath, however, told Nicholas that his knee felt as if it was merely hanging by a thread, saying, "It's gone I tell you."[2]

Ewbank declined to offer an opinion as to whether or not it was a cheap shot, saying that he had his eye on the ball and missed the block, but he did say that his players on the sidelines seemed to have no doubts as they were angrily accusing Floyd.[3] Larry Grantham was quoted in the *New York Daily News* as saying that the Jets had put Floyd on notice that he was a marked man come September 18 when the Jets and Oilers were scheduled to play at Shea Stadium.

Houston coach Wally Lemm was indignant over talk of a cheap shot. He refused to allow Floyd to tell his side of events, saying that there was no reason for Floyd to answer any questions about the play and that the game films told the whole story. "The Jets can say anything they want to but it's all very clear in the movies," Lemm said.[4] He went on to explain that Floyd wasn't even aware that it was Namath, but in the heat of the moment had simply blocked the first green jersey he saw. It was, he said, a very ordinary play. Lemm expressed his belief that if the play had involved any other player — even another quarterback — it would have been a non-issue, but being that it was Namath, well, there was the cause of the hullabaloo.

Ewbank said it never should have happened and laid the blame on poor officiating, the referees having allowed a dead play to continue. Namath was just disappointed. "Of all the times for this to happen," he said, "just when we are getting moving."[5] Namath had requested another knee operation after the 1965 season had ended, but the Jets had declined. They felt that he was playing well enough and that another surgery would be simply risky and unnecessary. It would be a different story after finishing the 1966 season. The truth is, Namath needed the surgery after being injured in Birmingham, but when Dr. Nicholas made an examination the following day in New York, he found no damage to the bony structure of the knee, and there was no blood in the fluid upon aspiration. To Nicholas, it all pointed to a non-serious injury. Namath was told to stay off his feet for a few days and he could return to playing in two-to-three weeks.

After Namath limped to the locker room that Saturday night in Birmingham, Mike Taliaferro had come into the game and led the Jets to a 16–10 triumph over the Oilers. He would continue to lead the team through an undefeated preseason, as Ewbank felt that it was best to let Namath rest the right knee in order to be in the best possible shape for the season. But playing as well as he was, was it fair to Taliaferro not to let him play in the opener in Miami? It would seem the quarterback controversy was beginning anew.

Week 1—Friday, September 9, 1966
Orange Bowl, Miami (attendance: 34,403)

The Jets actually had the first week of the 1966 season off, so the following week, the opening game of their season was actually in the second week of the league's season. The Jets traveled to Miami to meet the expansion Dolphins in the Orange Bowl on a Friday night. Ewbank said that both Namath and Taliaferro were ready and able to play, and both looked good. He claimed to be undecided as to who would start the game. The Dolphins prepared for both. "We know both are good passers," said Miami coach George Wilson, "and that Taliaferro has led them to four straight victories."[6]

It was Taliaferro who got the start against Miami; in fact, favored by 16 points, Ewbank was thinking that he might be able to keep Namath out of the game entirely and give him another week's rest for the home opener against Houston the following week. But Taliaferro's performance made Ewbank a bit restless.

The Jets opened the scoring in the first period when Verlon Biggs dropped Miami quarterback Rick Norton in the end zone for a safety and a 2–0 New York lead. Norton, a rookie from Kentucky, was Miami's big investment, costing them $300,000.

Later in the first period Taliaferro hit George Sauer with a 20-yard touchdown strike to put the Jets up 9–0, but throughout the half Taliaferro looked erratic, completing just four of his 17 passes for 61 yards. When the second quarter went scoreless, the Jets went into the locker room still leading 9–0, and Ewbank felt a change was in order. He initially thought the team might be able to get by with Taliaferro at quarterback, but with just a nine-point lead at halftime, Ewbank decided that the Jets would be pushing their luck in going any further without Namath.[7]

Namath entered the game in the third period and immediately got the offense moving. But after driving to the Miami 21-yard line, the drive stalled and Jim Turner came in to kick a 28-yard field goal. He made it, but a holding penalty forced him to kick again. Holding penalties were 15 yards at that time, and so Turner's retry would be from 43 yards out — he missed, and the Jets came away with nothing.

The Dolphins had also made a quarterback change. Still trailing 9–0, Wilson decided to send veteran Dick Wood in at quarterback: it doesn't seem to have been a smart move on Wilson's part. The former Jet had been acquired by Miami from Oakland in the expansion draft, and if Wood had any notions of showing up his former team, they quickly evaporated when he was intercepted by Johnny Sample at the New York 41. Namath then drove the Jets 59 yards for a touchdown, which Bill Mathis accomplished on a four-yard run. The big play of the drive was a 24-yard pass from Namath to Pete Lammons. That upped the Jets' lead to 16–0. Sample then intercepted Wood again, which led to a 45-yard field goal by Turner and the third period ended with the Jets ahead 19–0.

But Miami kept fighting, and perhaps the Jets let down a bit with such a sizeable lead. Actually luck had much to do with Miami's resurgence. Wilson put Norton back into the game, and early in the fourth quarter he threw an 18-yard pass to Bo Roberson. The ball bounced off of Roberson and Miami's Dave Kocourek snatched it out of the air without slowing down. Kocourek raced 25 yards for a touchdown on a play that covered 43 yards in all. The New York lead had been cut to 19–7, still a comfortable fourth-quarter advantage.

The Jets had reason to be more concerned midway through the fourth quarter, however, and the Dolphins had better cause to entertain ideas of staging an upset. Namath was intercepted by Pete Jaquess, who ran 27 yards with the theft for a Miami touchdown. Suddenly it was 19–14, and the Jets seemed in a struggle to win a game they were picked to easily run away with. Ultimately, they would hang on to win, but really, the game was hardly as close as the final 19–14 score would suggest. But for a freak bounce on Miami's only offensive score, and an additional defensive score, the game could well have been a shutout. In fact, the Jets' defense had only given up 111 yards all told. The Miami quarterbacks had a dismal night, Norton completing only eight of 20 passes while Wood hit on just two of 15.

Namath's numbers weren't exactly stellar either. In fact, they were almost identical to Norton's (ever-so-slightly better, with Namath going eight of 19 for 100 yards with an interception, Norton hitting eight of 20 for 97 yards with one TD and one interception), but then, having missed basically the entire preseason, he was bound to be a little rusty. Namath said afterward that the knee only bothered him when he tried to run with the ball. In the third period he had been forced to run from the pocket and was brought down by rookie linebacker Frank Emanuel after gaining three yards. "If I had had the wheels I would have shown those cats something," Namath said. "I wanted to make a move on that Emanuel so bad, but I couldn't. One move and I'd have been in to score."[8]

Week 2 — Sunday, September 18, 1966
Shea Stadium, New York (attendance: 54,681)

It was yet another AFL-record home opener crowd that welcomed the Jets at Shea Stadium the following week when they hosted the Houston Oilers. An audience of 54,681 came out to witness what was being described as something of a grudge match. But Floyd wasn't the most pressing concern for the Jets as far as Houston's defensive line was concerned; the Oilers had a front four that would make most of the league envious. Tackle Ernie Ladd was six-nine and weighed 315 pounds, while Houston's other tackle, Pat Holmes, was six-five and 265. "It sure is nice to have those big fellows on your side," said Houston quarterback/kicker George Blanda.[9]

The Jets had been given the first week of the season off, so with their opening win over Miami they were 1–0 to Houston's 2–0. The Oilers had bullied the Denver Broncos on opening day, beating them 45–7, and in their second game they had shut the Oakland Raiders out, 31–0. Obviously they were a team to be taken very seriously. Conversely, the Jets' 19–14 win in Miami was nowhere near the thrashing that they were expected to deal out that night.

The Oilers got out to a 3–0 first-quarter lead when Blanda booted a 49-yard field goal, but before the quarter ended the Jets shot back as Namath let fly a picture-perfect 67-yard bomb to George Sauer that put New York up 7–3. Namath had thrown the pass from his own 22-yard line — it reached Sauer perfectly in stride at the Houston 27, and Sauer bolted to the end zone. The Jets would not look back.

Even though Blanda kicked a 30-yard field goal in the second quarter to draw Houston to within a point at 7–6, the Jets were about to embark on a 31-point run to put the game out of reach. Namath threw a perfectly executed reverse-field screen to Matt Snell: after faking a handoff to Bill Mathis, Namath rolled out right, and with the entire flow of the play headed in that direction he then turned left and flipped a pass to Snell. The few Houston defenders who were in any position to try and change direction to catch Snell were superbly shielded out of the play by center John Schmitt, tackle Sherman Plunkett, and tight end Pete Lammons. The result was a 25-yard touchdown that gave the Jets a 14–6 lead.

On Houston's next series, Blanda was intercepted by linebacker Al Atkinson with less than two minutes to play in the half, and Namath took advantage by tossing a 13-yard TD to Lammons. Only 78 seconds had elapsed between scores, and the Jets led 21–6 at halftime. In the first half the Oilers had already given up three times the points they had allowed in their first two games combined, and there was plenty more to come.

The Jets ran off another 17 points in the third quarter as Namath hit Don Maynard with touchdown passes of 55 and 37 yards and Jim Turner kicked a 32-yard field goal to make the score 38–6. For Houston, Blanda managed an 11-yard touchdown pass to Sid Blanks before the quarter ended, but by then the game was a laugher.

With 12 minutes left to play, Ewbank decided to be merciful and he took Namath out of the game, but even that did not stanch the flow of New York points. Mike Taliaferro was in at quarterback, and rookie halfback Emerson Boozer got his first taste of action in the pros: Boozer promptly scored on a 39-yard run to up the Jets' lead to 45–13. It was quite an effort: Boozer started right, but quickly stopped in his tracks and changed direction up the middle. He was met there by three would-be tacklers — he ducked underneath them and left all three grabbing at each other. He was immediately met by a second wave of tacklers, again a trio. He ran right between the first two, did a nifty spin to avoid the third, and he was off and running. Boozer was eventually grabbed at the five-yard line, but dragged two tacklers to the end zone to score.

Even punter Curley Johnson got in on the fun, subbing at tight end and catching an 18-yard touchdown from Taliaferro. When all was said and done, the Jets had scored a franchise-record 52 points. In 1965 Namath had the best game of his rookie season when he threw four touchdowns against Houston at Shea Stadium in a 41–14 triumph. This time he bested that — his five touchdown passes on this day tied a team record set by Johnny Green in 1962, when the Jets were still the Titans.

The only one who didn't seem impressed was Namath himself. He was dissatisfied with his completion percentage as he had hit just 12 of 31 passes, but he had thrown for 283 yards along with his five touchdowns. He also had no interceptions. "I'm not too pleased about my accuracy," he said. "I'm not satisfied with those statistics, but we won and that's important."[10]

One thing Namath *was* very pleased about was his pass protection. He should have been: those Houston goliaths that everyone was concerned about were almost non-entities in the game, as neither Namath nor Taliaferro were sacked all day. Ewbank was certainly pleased, saying that Sam DeLuca and Dave Herman were especially deserving of praise for their performances.[11] Namath also gave kudos to his lineman, saying that on the 67-yard touchdown he had enough time to look at four potential receivers before going long to Sauer.

Defensive back Bobby Jancik was burned on the two Maynard scores. Jancik found Namath's delivery vexing. "On long bombs he doesn't wind up like most quarterbacks do," Jancik said. "His motion is about the same for a 10-yard pass as it is for 60 and it's deceptive as hell."[12]

The New York defense had done its share as well, intercepting Blanda four times and holding Houston to 71 yards rushing. For the second time in as many games, Johnny Sample grabbed two interceptions.

With the victory the Jets went to 2–0, and as the Eastern Division's only unbeaten team, they moved ahead of Houston, who fell to 2–1.

Week 3 — Sunday, September 25, 1966
Bears Stadium, Denver (attendance: 29,878)

The 2–0 Jets traveled to Denver to face the 0–2 Broncos. Given the way in which the Jets had beat up on the Oilers the week before, it might have been expected that they would make short work of the Broncos, who had lost to Houston 45–7 on opening day and been beaten by Boston 24–10 the week after. But it was a fairly listless New York team that showed up in Denver.

Although the Jets were heavily favored, it would seem as though they had used up a month's worth of points at Shea Stadium the previous week and were now running on empty. If they had played a better team they would have had real trouble. As it was, the Broncos were trouble enough.

Perhaps because he had so much success throwing long against Houston, Namath may have been anticipating similar results against the Broncos, but he only hit six of his first 19 passes and the Jets failed to score in the first half. Denver's quarterback, John McCormick, was having problems of his own, completing only one of eight throws before leaving the game after being flattened by Verlon Biggs. Denver's new head coach, Ray Malavasi, who was making his debut that day, sent backup quarterback Mickey Slaughter into the game, and Slaughter got Denver on the board with a 67-yard touchdown throw to running back Charlie Mitchell. Denver would take that 7–0 lead into halftime, but really, other than the long touchdown play, nobody had done much impressing offensively in the half.

Because the long passes had been missing, Ewbank told Namath to work at ball control in the second half. It was a good move, and in the third quarter the Jets were able to get in range for Jim Turner to kick a 40-yard field goal to cut Denver's lead to 7–3. Later in the period the Jets worked their way to the Denver 12-yard line, but on third down and less than a yard to go Matt Snell was thrown for a loss back to the 17. The Jets were forced to settle for another field goal, which Turner made good on from 24 yards out to cut Denver's lead to one point.

Early in the fourth quarter the Jets took possession on their own 44, and Bill Mathis got them started on a drive with a 19-yard run to the Denver 37. A draw play to Snell picked up another 15 yards, and after a couple of running plays failed, Namath converted on third down by throwing to Maynard for 16 yards and a first-and-goal. Again, two runs went nowhere, and on third down Namath threw to Snell for a score from five yards out. It was the fourth quarter and the Jets had only then taken the lead for the first time in the game.

Later in the fourth, Turner would add a 35-yard field goal to make the final 16–7. It had hardly been a sharp performance, particularly coming against a lesser opponent as it did, but it kept the Jets atop the Eastern Division at 3–0, as Houston and Buffalo were both 2–2 and sharing second place. Once more the offensive line had given Namath good protection: he was not dropped for a loss all day. He completed 16 of 35 for 206 yards, one touchdown and two interceptions.

Week 4 — Sunday, October 2, 1966
Fenway Park, Boston (attendance: 27,255)

The Jets were 10-point favorites against the Patriots the following week, but the rather wan performance they had given in Denver seemed to carry over in Boston — well, for three quarters, anyway. They fell behind 7–0 in the first quarter when Boston quarterback Babe Parilli correctly guessed that the Jets would be keying on fullback Jim Nance; Parilli faked a handoff to Nance before giving it to halfback Larry Garron, who took it six yards for a touchdown.

It wasn't until the final five minutes of the half that the Jets got on the board with a five-yard touchdown run by Matt Snell that tied the game, but even then it took a botched play to make it possible. The Jets were initially going to settle for a field goal, but when punter Curley Johnson — kicker Jim Turner's holder on field goals — fumbled the snap, he picked it up and took off running: he gained four yards and got the first down, enabling the drive to continue. Boston managed to regain the lead with a 17-yard field goal by Gino Cappelletti before the half ended.

Namath had a very poor first half, completing just nine of 22 passes for 78 yards, and neither he nor the team in general seemed to show improvement in the third period. Part of the problem for Namath was Boston defensive tackle Houston Antwine, who had been a constant presence in the Jets' backfield. He hadn't been able to drop Namath for a loss, but Antwine had been in his face often enough to be very disruptive. For some reason, it took the Jets the better part of three quarters to devise a plan to double-team Antwine.

Meanwhile, the Boston offense beefed-up its lead in the third period, with Parilli throwing a 19-yard touchdown to Gino Cappelletti and Garron scoring again just 2:13 later, this time from two yards out. After Garron's second touchdown, the Patriots were up 24–7 and looking merely to run as much time off the clock as possible. Bad move. Namath had been a help to Boston's 14-point burst when he threw two interceptions in the third quarter, but the Patriots couldn't count on him continuing to facilitate their lead. Perhaps they simply assumed their lead was substantial enough.

After Garron's third-quarter score, the Patriots became exceptionally conservative — Parilli would throw only two passes in the last 17 minutes of the game, one incompletion and one interception — and Boston would fail to gain a single first down after the touchdown that had put them up 24–7 in the third.

By contrast, Namath was forced into throwing constantly in a desperate bid to catch up. George Sauer became his favorite target, as Sauer was frequently able to get open against Boston's Don Webb. Namath had only completed nine passes in the first half: in the fourth quarter he would complete nine to Sauer alone. Part of the difference was the double-teaming of Antwine.

As the fourth quarter got underway, the Jets started on their own 38 and Namath took his team down to score, hitting four of five passes accounting for 53 of the drive's 62 yards. It climaxed with Namath passing to Snell for a 10-yard touchdown on the same reverse-field screen that had gone for a score against Houston two weeks earlier. That cut the lead to 24–14.

With Boston playing so conservative, the Jets were keying on the run and were able to force a punt after just three plays on the Patriots' next series. When the Jets got the ball back, Namath hit Bake Turner with a 42-yard pass that took New York from their own 44 to the Boston 14. Three plays later Namath hit tight end Pete Lammons at the two-yard line and Lammons fell into the left corner of the end zone as he was being tackled. It was now just a three-point game with 8:03 still left to play.

Boston again failed to gain a first down, and after they punted the Jets took possession on their own 30. Namath drove New York to the Patriots' 23-yard line, but there the drive stalled and Jim Turner came in to try to tie the game with a 30-yard field goal. He missed it wide left. The score remained 24–21, Boston.

Still vainly trying to use up the clock, Boston again ran three plays and punted, but when the Jets got the ball back this time there was little time left to play with. With just over a minute remaining in the game, Namath passed to Bill Mathis for a 16-yard gain to the Boston 18. By the time the Jets had stalled at the 10-yard line only 32 seconds remained, and Jim Turner kicked a 17-yard field goal to tie the game. Boston, of course, did nothing after that, and time expired with the game ending in a tie.

During the first three quarters of play Namath had completed 14 of 33 passes for 133 yards; in the fourth quarter he was 14 of 23 for 205 yards, making his game totals 28 of 56 for 338 yards, two TDs, two interceptions. It had been a demoralizing fourth quarter for the Patriots. Boston coach Mike Holovak was fuming after the game. "We had 'em 24–7 with 12 minutes to go in the last period and then we let them score 17 big points," Holovak said. "We certainly were not satisfied with a tie. Heck, here we were supposed to be 10-point underdog and we're all upset because it was a tie."[13] Actually, maybe Boston should have been satisfied with a tie, for had Jim Turner hit both his fourth-quarter field goal attempts…

The Jets went to 3–0–1 and kept their place atop the Eastern Division.

Week 5 — Saturday, October 8, 1966
Shea Stadium, New York (attendance: 63,497)

The following Saturday night it was an AFL-record crowd once more at Shea Stadium, as 63,497 turned out to see a showdown between the league's only two remaining undefeated teams: the 3–0–1 Jets would be taking on the 4–0 San Diego Chargers. The AFL could be pleased at having the league's two top teams fill a primetime slot. It was to be San Diego quarterback

Steve Tensi's first start as a pro since being drafted out of Florida State in 1965 — he wouldn't last long.

Although San Diego got on the scoreboard first, topping off a 73-yard drive with a 14-yard field goal in the first quarter, the Jets would move out front before the quarter ended. Tensi would only complete two of his 10 passes in the game, and it was his last throw that would be his undoing. From the San Diego 30, Tensi faded back to pass and threw across the middle to Lance Alworth just beyond midfield. Linebacker Al Atkinson stepped in front and picked it off at the Jets' 48, then ran it back to the San Diego 42. Soon after, Namath threw to Matt Snell in the flat: Snell caught the ball at the 10-yard line, weaved between two tacklers and dove into the end zone for a 17-yard score.

John Hadl replaced Tensi at quarterback, and San Diego drew to within 7–6 in the second quarter when the Chargers' Kenny Graham intercepted Namath at the New York 33 to enable the Chargers to kick a 17-yard field goal. From there the teams traded field goals in the closing minutes of the half, the Jets' Jim Turner hitting from 33 yards out with 1:10 left in the half, and San Diego's Dick Van Raaphorst booting a 42-yarder on the last play of the half. The Jets were clinging to a 10–9 lead at the break.

The third quarter went scoreless, with Namath being intercepted twice in the period, but things livened up considerably in the fourth when Hadl dumped a screen pass off to fullback Keith Lincoln, who got a couple superb blocks from tackle Ron Mix and halfback Jim Allison along the right sideline to spring him: Lincoln took it 67 yards for a touchdown. The Chargers now led 16–10 with 10 minutes to play in the game.

Starting from their own 34 after the kickoff, the Jets moved very quickly when Namath threw to Bill Mathis over the middle and Mathis ran it all the way to the San Diego 22, a gain of 44 yards. After a swing pass to Snell lost seven yards, Namath hit Maynard for 17 yards to the 12. The rest of the drive belonged to rookie Emerson Boozer, who carried for four yards to the eight, and then ran it in from there on the next play. With the extra point, the Jets regained the lead at 17–16 with 6:23 left in the game.

That would be plenty of time for the Chargers to get in range for at least a winning field goal. As it turned out, they would get two cracks at it. On their first shot, Hadl took the Chargers down close enough for Van Raaphorst to try a 30-yarder. Van Raaphorst had made nine of 10 to that point in the season, but on this occasion it was blocked by Paul Rochester.

The Jets could do little to run out the clock, and were forced to punt it back to San Diego. After hitting two long passes to Alworth and Gary Garrison, Hadl had the Chargers on the New York 14-yard line with under half-a-minute to play. Van Raaphorst came out to kick a game-winning 21-yard field goal: he missed it wide right. He had missed his chance to kick the winning field goal twice in the final three minutes of the game. The Jets were now the only unbeaten team in the AFL. Namath completed 11 of 22 for 129 yards, one touchdown and three interceptions.

Week 6 — Sunday, October 16, 1966
Rice Stadium, Houston (attendance: 39,823)

At 4–0–1, the Jets were flying high when they traveled to Texas to play the Oilers, who had gone on a skid since the Jets humiliated them at Shea Stadium back in September. Houston had gone into that game 2–0 with two very impressive blowouts under their belts, but since losing to the Jets 52–13, the Oilers had lost their next two games as well and were now 2–3. They were fortunate, however, to have the week off before their rematch with the Jets, which gave them two weeks to prepare. "They may be a little mad about what we did to them last time," said Ewbank.[14] That was a safe assumption. The Oilers had another advantage — the Jets had never won in Houston.

One thing that might have made the Jets more relaxed was the announcement that six-foot-nine defensive tackle Ernie Ladd had been benched in favor of Scott Appleton. At six-three and 260 pounds Appleton was no featherweight, but he certainly wasn't the giant Ladd was. Still, Houston coach Wally Lemm had been unhappy with Ladd's performance. Ladd had been pretty well nullified by Sam DeLuca in the Oilers' previous meeting with the Jets, and perhaps Lemm was looking to shake things up a bit.

The Jets started off poorly from the beginning. On just the third play from scrimmage Bill Mathis fumbled and Appleton recovered the ball for Houston on the New York 35. Three plays later, John Henry Johnson ran 33 yards for the initial score four minutes into the game.

On the Jets' next series Namath was intercepted by Jim Norton, who returned the ball 47 yards to set up a Houston field goal. The first quarter ended with Houston up 10–0, courtesy of the Jets' overly generous comportment. But Houston didn't need New York turnovers to hand them all of their points. The Oilers would score two more touchdowns, a 42-yard touchdown pass from George Blanda to Sid Blanks in the second quarter, and a four-yard pass from Blanda to Charley Hennigan in the fourth, that came on drives of 65 and 95 yards.

As for the Jets' scoring, well, there wasn't any. For the first time in 33 games, the Jets had been shut out, the final score being 24–0. The last time the Jets had been held scoreless was in 1963 when they had been blanked by Kansas City. When the Jets and Oilers had played in September, George Blanda had thrown four interceptions. This time Namath returned the favor; aside from Norton's interception, W.K. Hicks had grabbed two and Johnny Baker got one. Namath had again escaped without being sacked, but that was a misleading statistic, for the Houston defense was pressing hard toward him all day. After sitting out the first quarter, Ladd came into the game and for the next three quarters led a charge that had Namath on his heels. Finishing just 16 of 37 for 143 yards and four interceptions, it was not a good day for Namath. "I don't think we ever nailed him with the ball, but he was rushing his throws," said Lemm, who also said that Ladd's performance had earned him his starting job again.[15]

Maybe it wasn't quite as gaudy as the Jets 52–13 win in September, but being a shutout it probably tasted just as sweet. Houston lineman Pat Holmes said that it had been easy for his team to get up for their rematch with the Jets, the debacle in New York still being fresh in mind.[16] Hennigan saw it as a reawakening, recalling that in 1962 the Oilers had been 1–3–1 and then went undefeated the rest of the season. The comparison wouldn't hold up, but even if the victory failed to ignite the Oilers for a championship run, it did accomplish one thing — it burst the Jets' bubble. Both Ewbank and Namath would dismiss the loss as a mere bump in the road, but if that were the case, it was an awfully big bump. Truth is, it sent the Jets reeling.

Week 7 — Sunday, October 23, 1966
Shea Stadium, New York (attendance: 58,135)

Ewbank had brushed the loss to Houston off as merely a bad day, which will happen to a team throughout the course of a season. Namath likewise downplayed it, reminding reporters that while they had lost one game in six, the previous year they were still winless after six games. But of course it has a lot to do with attitude, and even a single loss can alter a team's outlook.

The Jets were going back to New York, and they had the Oakland Raiders coming to town. Oakland was trailing San Diego in the Western Division, but at 3–3 they were still in the chase. A victory against the Jets would go a long way toward improving Oakland's chances. As for the East, whereas the Jets might have expected Buffalo to be their main concern, they suddenly found that it was Boston that had crept up and was nipping at their heels.

In the first quarter against Oakland the Jets missed two scoring opportunities when Jim Turner failed to make good on field goal attempts of 46 and 28 yards. Later in the period Jim

Hudson presented the New York offense with another opportunity when he intercepted Oakland quarterback Tom Flores and set the Jets up at midfield. After Namath threw 38 yards to Maynard, the Jets found themselves with a first-and-goal at the Oakland four-yard line, but when two running plays failed to score, they were facing a third-and-goal at the two. Namath took the snap from center, faked a handoff and rolled left. Pete Lammons was in the end zone running left and waving his hand. Perhaps Lammons was merely acting as a decoy, because the truth is it didn't look like Namath ever entertained the idea of throwing. The entire left side was free and clear and Namath strolled in for the first touchdown of his professional career.

The Jets' 7–0 lead lasted until midway through the second quarter when Curley Johnson shanked a punt that traveled only 21 yards, giving Oakland the ball at the New York 35. Two plays later Flores threw a 31-yard touchdown to Art Powell, and the game was tied.

The Jets drove 67 yards to break the tie with 2:12 remaining in the second period. Namath had hit Bill Mathis with a 26-yard pass that took the Jets to Oakland's one-yard line, but again, two runs (by Snell and Mathis) failed to cross the goal line. That first score must have given Namath touchdown fever, for once again on third down he scored on a keeper, this time an old-fashioned quarterback sneak right up the middle. The drive had been aided by four Oakland penalties, and the Raiders had amassed an incredible 90 yards in penalties in the first half. The Jets led 14–7 at the half, and held that lead through the third period, which went scoreless.

Oakland did get another generous break just before the period ended, however, when the Jets' Sammy Weir called for a fair catch on Mike Eischeid's punt and then dropped it: Oakland recovered on the New York 27. The quarter ended with Flores throwing an 18-yard pass to Clem Daniels to give Oakland a first-and-goal at the Jets' nine-yard line.

After a gain of a yard opened the fourth quarter, Flores ran a quarterback draw on second-and-goal from the eight: he took it right up the middle to score and tie the game at 14. The Raiders then got a major assist by the officials: in the Jets' next series Namath threw to George Sauer, who was immediately hit by Dave Grayson at the Oakland 48 and dropped the ball; Gus Otto grabbed the ball for Oakland and took off running. Incredibly, the officials, perhaps being caught up in the excitement of the moment, ruled it a fumble and allowed the play to continued. Otto ran 23 yards to the New York 29. It isn't just that such a call would never stand in the modern age of instant replay reviews, but it was a call so egregiously foolish that it is almost unimaginable that it would have stood in any era. Officiating in professional football is notoriously the worst of any professional sport, but this call was beyond any excuse. In short, it was an obvious incomplete pass.

The Raiders failed to make the most of the opportunity and could gain only four yards in three plays, but the field position so generously granted them by the referees had at least guaranteed Oakland a field goal try: Eischeid made it from 32 yards out, and the Raiders took a 17–14 lead.

The Jets regained the lead when Namath directed them on an 80-yard drive in which he hit five of six passes. He threw a flare to Snell for 21 yards, hit Maynard for 12, Lammons for seven, and Mathis for 18. A 14-yard run by Snell set the Jets up on the one-yard line, and on the next play Snell finished the job by scoring, putting the Jets back up 21–17 with 5:01 remaining in the game. The Raiders still had plenty of time.

Beginning on their own 17-yard line, Flores took the Raiders on a masterful drive. It started very badly for them when two rushes by Clem Daniels left Oakland facing a third-and-11. Flores then threw a flair pass to Hewritt Dixon that gained 12 yards and the first down. After gaining six yards in two plays, the Raiders again found themselves facing a crucial third-down. The Jets blitzed, and Flores was able to avoid it and throw deep downfield for Art Powell, who hauled it in at the New York 35 and ran it to the 24 before being brought down. The play covered 42 yards. Then, with 1:47 left to play, Flores passed across the middle to Dixon at the 10-yard line. Dixon made it to the two-yard line before he was brought down.

On first-and-goal, Daniels couldn't gain any ground off right tackle. He likewise failed to gain on second down. On third down Flores tried to run it in but was marked less than a yard from the goal line. Trailing by four points, there was no doubt that it was a four-down situation, and on fourth down Dixon went through the left side of the line. When Dixon went into the end zone standing, the clock showed two seconds remaining in the game. It was Oakland's only score of the day that hadn't been accountable by either New York turnovers or official incompetence, but it was good for a very dramatic win.

Namath was in a foul mood after the game. Some reporters tried to console him by pointing out that, statistically speaking, he had a good game. The Raiders had gone into the game with the league's number one defense, but the Jets had still amassed almost 400 yards. "We lost the damn game didn't we," Namath remarked. "My whole performance doesn't count. We lost, so that's that."[17]

The game had set the Jets back to 4–2–1. There was more bad news for the Jets, and good news for the Raiders: Boston had beaten San Diego, 35–17. That put the Patriots only a half-game behind the Jets in the East, while the Raiders moved to within a half-game of the Chargers in the West.

Namath had completed 19 of 32 passes for 272 yards, and otherwise had a first for the season: Dan Birdwell had dropped him for a 12-yard loss, Namath's first sack of the year. "He made a ceremony of it," Namath quipped after the game. "This is number one, Mr. Namath," Birdwell said after getting up. "Yeah," said Namath, "it sure was."[18]

Week 8 — Sunday, October 30, 1966
Shea Stadium, New York (attendance: 61,552)

The Jets looked to right themselves and end their two-game losing streak when the reigning AFL-champion Buffalo Bills came to Shea Stadium in week eight. Although New York got out to an early 3–0 first-quarter lead on a 28-yard field goal by Jim Turner, the tide shifted in the second quarter, as Buffalo scored 13 unanswered points. A one-yard touchdown run by quarterback Jack Kemp and field goals by Booth Lusteg of 36 and 10 yards gave the Bills a 13–3 halftime lead. Aside from Buffalo's scoring, something else started in the second quarter: Namath heard his first boos. He had never been booed at Alabama, certainly not in Beaver Falls — only in New York.

If the second quarter was bad, the third was a disaster. The second half opened with Buffalo's Charley Warner returning the kickoff 95 yards for a score, giving the Bills a 20–3 lead. When the Jets got the ball, Namath immediately threw to Maynard for a nice 50-yard catch and run that took the Jets to the Buffalo 15-yard line, but on the very next play Namath was intercepted by defensive end Roland McDole. Buffalo then drove downfield and scored on another one-yard run by Kemp. It was now 27–3, and after Lusteg added a 38-yard field goal later in the third, the score stood at 30–3.

By the fourth quarter the boos had faded, though that was partially because many of the fans had already started to leave. Those who remained may have been imagining another amazing comeback like the one Namath had engineered against Boston a month earlier, and Namath and the Jets began to give them reason to entertain such thoughts. Namath hit Pete Lammons with a 34-yard touchdown pass to cut Buffalo's lead to 30–10, but 20 more points was a tall order in one quarter.

It helps when the defense chips in, however, and Bill Baird managed to intercept a Jack Kemp pass and run it back 39 yards for another score. The lead was now 30–17. The fans were no longer booing: now they were watching, waiting, and probably hoping. The Bills dampened that enthusiasm with their lone score of the quarter, a 17-yard field goal, but Namath managed a 19-yard touchdown throw to Maynard that cut the Buffalo lead to 10 points. That's as close as it got. The final was 33–23.

The Jets had made a valiant fourth-quarter effort, but Namath had played perhaps the worst game of his young career, throwing five interceptions. In the fourth quarter, when the Jets appeared to be toying with staging a comeback, Namath was intercepted twice in a three-minute stretch with about eight minutes left to play. That effectively sank the comeback hopes. After the game, Namath appeared to be more upset by the loss than by the booing of the fans. A reporter asked him if he'd ever been booed before. "Are you trying to start something," Namath angrily responded.[19]

Speaking to reporters in the Buffalo locker room after the game, Kemp defended Namath, saying that although the loss might keep anyone from surmising that Namath had a good day, it couldn't be said that Namath had lost the game for the Jets.[20] Actually, Kemp's numbers were nothing to boast of either, hitting only 16 of 40 passes, with three interceptions and no touchdowns. Namath's numbers were a mixed bag; the five interceptions were atrocious, of course, and his completion percentage was below 50 percent, hitting 24 of 53 throws. On the plus side, he set a personal best with 343 passing yards, and also threw two touchdowns. But Kemp and the Bills won and Namath and the Jets lost, which turned out to be very important indeed in the standings.

The loss knocked the Jets out of first place. At 4–3–1 they were now tied with Buffalo for second place in the Eastern Division. Boston's 24–21 victory over Oakland gave the Patriots the lead in the East with a 4–2–1 record. The Jets had a week off now, and for their next game they would be playing … the Buffalo Bills. No kidding.

Week 9 — Sunday, November 13, 1966
War Memorial Stadium, Buffalo (attendance: 45,738)

Teams don't ordinarily get the chance to avenge a defeat by meeting the same opponent in their very next game. It was a scheduling quirk that had the Jets playing two consecutive games against Buffalo. The Jets had a week off in-between: Buffalo did not, and in the interim the Bills had defeated the Miami Dolphins 29–0 to gain an advantage over the Jets in the standings. Meanwhile, Boston had lost, knocking them into a second-place tie with the Jets.

The first quarter saw both teams struggling to mount any offensive threat, and only Buffalo would cross midfield. The Bills had started on their own 14 and managed to drive to the New York 27 before a 15-yard penalty for offensive pass interference had set them back, pushing them out of field goal range and forcing them to punt.

In the second quarter it was the Jets who came closest to scoring, but even then it was not until the half had almost ended. Starting at their own 11, New York had reached the Buffalo three-yard line where they stalled and sent Jim Turner in for a sure three-pointer. But the Jets were not satisfied with the idea of a 3–0 lead, and when holder Jim Hudson took the snap he tried to throw to tight end Pete Lammons: the pass was broken up, and the Jets wound up with nothing. The first half ended scoreless, and Namath and Buffalo quarterback Jack Kemp were having a hard time of it, both being harassed into throwing early and inaccurately.

The third quarter played out much the same until the Jets got in range for a 43-yard field goal late in the period. The Jets had started the series on their own three-yard line, and when they found themselves with a third-and-five at the eight Namath threw from his own end zone and hit George Sauer with a 51-yard strike that took New York to the Buffalo 41. After they failed to make another first down (it was essentially a one-play drive), Turner kicked the field goal for a 3–0 lead.

The New York score seemed to awaken Buffalo from a trance, and after returning the ensuing kick to their own 36, the Bills went to work. Kemp hit Wray Carlton for 32 yards on the last play of the third quarter, and then began the fourth quarter by hitting Carlton again for 14 more. The drive ended with Kemp throwing 14 yards to receiver Elbert Dubenion for the score and a 7–3 lead.

The Jets seemed determined to bounce right back, and they drove to the Buffalo 28 before again bogging down. Turner once more came in for a field goal try, this one from the 35, but it was blocked by tackle Jim Dunaway, who not only blew through the line to block it, but picked the ball up and took off running. Dunaway — all 289 pounds of him — rambled 72 yards for a score.

It was toward the end of the game that the Jets drove from their own 11 to the Buffalo one-yard line only to turn the ball over on downs: they went down in defeat, 14–3. Namath had once again waited until the fourth quarter to come to life against Buffalo. In the game's first three quarters combined, he had only completed eight of 20 passes for 150 yards, while he went 11 of 16 for 136 yards in the fourth, making his totals 19 of 36 for 286 yards (one interception). One person who was impressed was Buffalo defensive end Tom Day. "That Joe Namath called a great game," Day said. "He caught us off guard down there on the goal line but (the plays) just didn't work for him."[21]

With the victory, Buffalo remained atop the Eastern Division at 6–3–1, while Boston's 27–21 victory over Houston kept them in second place with a 5–3–1 record. The Jets had fallen to third at 4–4–1. Having begun the season 4–0–1 they were now four games deep in a losing streak. Fortunately, they only had to play the Miami Dolphins next.

Week 10 — Sunday, November 20, 1966
Shea Stadium, New York (attendance: 58,664)

At 2–7 the Miami Dolphins weren't likely to pose much threat; in fact, they seemed the perfect remedy for a losing streak. The Jets could've used an easy mark about then, not merely because of their four-game tailspin but also due to the fact that their starting backfield was out, for the most part. Matt Snell was sidelined with a separated shoulder, and nagging injuries would force Bill Mathis to be played sparingly. It presented rookie Emerson Boozer with a good opportunity to get some significant playing time.

Wisdom may have dictated that the lowly Dolphins would be little contest, even for a team in disarray and dealing with significant injuries, but Miami began the game by surprising the Jets. With two field goals in the opening period, the Dolphins held a 6–0 lead as the first quarter ended. The crowd at Shea was getting restless again, and the booing had already begun. It wasn't until late in the second quarter that the Jets seemed to get into a rhythm. Namath hit George Sauer with a 33-yard pass that took the Jets deep into Miami territory, and Boozer went in from a yard out three plays later to put the Jets up 7–6. The Jets padded that lead just before the half ended when Namath passed 24 yards to Mark Smolinski to set up a Jim Turner field goal of 10 yards; Boozer had accounted for 22 yards in the drive. New York led 10–6 at halftime.

It was Boozer who received the second half kickoff from Miami, and he gave the Jets a significant cushion to begin the half by running the kick back 96 yards for a score. He took the ball on a bounce at the four-yard line on the left side of the field, and after getting a good initial block from Smolinski, he did a tight wire run up the sideline, going the distance, untouched, to give the Jets a 17–6 lead. Jim Turner would add field goals of 26 and 18 yards during the third period, and the Jets would enter the fourth quarter leading 23–6.

The booing had long since died off, of course, the fans by then being contented with the performance. A fourth-quarter touchdown pass from Dick Wood to Joe Auer of 11 yards drew Miami to within 10 points at 23–13. But it mattered little, as the Jets shot back with a 49-yard drive that was capped by a one-yard touchdown run by Smolinski with 1:49 left to play. In the end, the Jets won 30–13.

Namath had a pretty good day, completing 17 of 30 for 236 yards. He had thrown no touchdowns, but had also avoided being intercepted. Boozer had certainly done his share, but the one getting most of the praise on offense was George Sauer, who had caught seven passes and accounted for 142 of Namath's passing yards. That gave Sauer 48 pass receptions for the season, tying him with Kansas City's Otis Taylor and San Diego's Lance Alworth at the top of the AFL receiving list.

But the victory failed to move the Jets up from third place in the East. The Patriots had tied Kansas City to stay a half-game ahead of the Jets, while Buffalo's 42–20 win over Houston kept the Bills well ahead of the pack, their 7–3–1 record giving them some breathing room above Boston's 5–3–2 and the Jets' 5–4–1. The good news for the Jets was that their home stand would continue the following week. The bad news was they would be hosting Western Division–leading Kansas City, whereas Boston would get to play Miami. The chances of moving into second place were looking remote.

Week 11— Sunday, November 27, 1966
Shea Stadium, New York (attendance: 60,318)

The Kansas City Chiefs came into Shea Stadium with an 8–2–1 record and were looking to end San Diego's three-year dominance in the Western Division. Should the Chiefs beat the Jets and the Chargers lose to Denver (admittedly an unlikely occurrence), then the Chiefs would be the new champions of the West. The Jets, on the other hand, were striving to keep hope alive for one more week. A loss would go a long way toward closing the book on their 1966 playoff hopes. If they lost, they would have to see both Buffalo and Boston go down in flames for the remaining few games of the season in order to hope to capture the East.

The Jets took a first-quarter lead after Gerry Philbin forced a fumble by Kansas City quarterback Len Dawson, and lineman Jim Harris recovered for New York on the Kansas City 48. Namath then threw 43 yards to George Sauer to set up a one-yard touchdown run by Mark Smolinski that made it 7–0. But before the quarter ended, the Chiefs tied the game when Dawson hit Chris Burford with a 19-yard scoring pass.

Throughout the second quarter the teams exchanged field goals, Mike Mercer hitting from 32 yards out to put Kansas City up 10–7, Jim Turner hitting from 18 to tie it again, and then Mercer putting the Chiefs back up again with a 15-yarder. It looked like the Jets would again tie the game when Turner came in for an attempt from 29 yards, but the momentum swung back Kansas City's way when linebacker Bobby Bell pushed through the line and blocked the kick. Bell then picked the ball up and ran it to the New York 45. It helped the Chiefs go up 16–10 at halftime by setting up Mercer's third field goal of the quarter.

In the third quarter the Chiefs built an impressive lead on long touchdown drives that resulted in scoring runs by Mike Garrett and Curtis McClinton, and the Jets found themselves trailing 29–10 going into the fourth quarter. It may have looked like a positive for the Jets when somebody stepped on Dawson's left hand and sidelined him for the rest of the game with a ruptured blood vessel, but backup Pete Beathard did a more than adequate job, hitting seven of 10 passes in piloting the Chiefs on long scoring marches.

Down by 19 points in the fourth, it was looking fairly hopeless for New York, but the Jets caught that fourth-quarter magic once more when Namath hit George Sauer with an 18-yard touchdown, and then took the Jets downfield to score again with an eight-yard touchdown pass to Smolinski. Suddenly it was only a 29–24 Kansas City lead.

But Beathard then drove the Chiefs within range for Mercer to kick a 33-yard field goal with 2:36 left to play. Still, the Jets had a chance: they could tie the game with a touchdown and a two-point conversion. In the end, their comeback hopes died when Namath was intercepted by Willie Mitchell in the last minute of play. Namath's final numbers were 18 of 36 for 263 yards, with two TDs and one interception.

The Jets fell to 5–5–1, and with both Buffalo and Boston winning their respective games, New York's postseason aspirations grew that much dimmer. Kansas City, on the other hand, emerged as divisional champs that day, as Denver surprised everyone by beating San Diego.

Week 12 — Saturday, December 3, 1966
Alameda County Coliseum, Oakland (attendance: 31,144)

When the Jets had played the Raiders in Oakland in 1965 it was in a mud bowl at Frank Youell Field. They would play under similar conditions when the Jets came to Oakland's Alameda County Coliseum for the first time on a Saturday afternoon in week 12. At 7–5, Oakland was already out of the Western Division race, but even at 5–5–1 the Jets still had a very slim shot in the East.

The first meeting between the two teams in October at Shea Stadium had been a nail-biter that saw Oakland score the winning touchdown in the final two seconds of play. Although the contest in Oakland would not come down to the final few seconds, it was close enough, and was in many ways a more interesting and exciting contest.

The game was still scoreless late in the first quarter when Namath, of all people, took off on a 39-yard run from his own 38 that carried the Jets to the Oakland 23. Namath had fled the pocket, rolling to his left with Ben Davidson on his heels. Davidson wanted it bad, but as he extended his arm to try and grab Namath, Davidson slipped in the mud and fell. Namath kept running down the left sideline, which was clear most of the way. It wasn't until reaching the Oakland 36-yard line that he ran across a potential tackler in defensive back Joe Krakoski, but Namath was sprung for an additional 13 yards by an excellent block by George Sauer. From the sideline, Ewbank had been screaming at Namath to get out of bounds, but Namath kept running; he continued to skirt the sideline until diving headfirst onto the turf at the 23 when confronted by an unmolested tackler.

The drive continued when Namath hit Don Maynard with a 13-yard pass that gave the Jets a first-and-goal on the Oakland two-yard line. But after two runs by Matt Snell failed to score, Namath threw incomplete on third-and-goal and the Jets were forced to settle for a 3–0 lead on a nine-yard field goal by Jim Turner.

On the first play of the second quarter Namath was intercepted by Rodger Bird. The Raiders then went 59 yards in seven plays to take the lead on a five-yard pass from Tom Flores to fullback Hewritt Dixon, who had beaten linebacker Larry Grantham on the play. But the Raiders' 7–3 lead didn't last long, as Namath shortly read a safety blitz on a third-down play and quickly rifled the ball to Bill Mathis at the 48-yard line: Mathis ran the distance, untouched, for a 70-yard scoring play that put the Jets back up 10–7.

The Raiders would regain the lead on a 77-yard drive that resulted in a 32-yard touchdown pass from Flores to Art Powell, who was all alone near the end zone: his defender, Bill Baird, had slipped in the mud. The Raiders then had an opportunity to extend their lead just before halftime when they drove to the New York 36, but on that occasion Flores was intercepted by safety Jim Hudson at the three-yard line. The Raiders led 14–10 at the half.

Early in the third quarter the Jets worked their way downfield, with Namath converting a third-and-eight play by hitting Emerson Boozer with a 26-yard pass, followed by a 30-yard pass to Sauer. But when the drive stalled the Jets sent in Jim Turner, who brought them to within a point of the Raiders with a 37-yard field goal.

The Raiders then fired a blank, driving to the New York 33, but producing no points when Mike Eischeid missed a 37-yard field goal try. He got another shot when Namath was intercepted by linebacker Dan Conners at the Oakland 40, and Conners ran it back to the New York 23, but this time Eischeid's kick was blocked by Verlon Biggs.

Still trailing 14–13, the Jets went down to score on a drive that saw Namath hitting key passes to successfully convert on three third-down plays. First, he hit Sauer with a 14-yard pass to the New York 38 to keep the drive going, and then amazingly converted on a third-and-29 play when he threw 44 yards to Mathis. After a 28-yard run by Boozer, the Jets found themselves on the Oakland four-yard line, but when they failed to score on their first two downs Namath again had to convert on third down, which he did by hitting Sauer in the end zone with a five-yard touchdown pass. That gave the Jets a 20–14 lead at the close of the third quarter.

The Raiders came storming right back as the fourth quarter began; Flores threw 43 yards to tight end Billy Cannon to the New York 31, and then threw 31 yards to Powell for the score. It was a two-play 74-yard drive, and as quick as that the Raiders were back on top, 21–20. They would increase that lead even quicker.

On the Jets' first play of their next series, Namath went back to pass and was hit by Davidson as he released the ball. The ball went up into the air and was grabbed by Conners again, who ran it 28 yards for a touchdown. The Raiders had scored two touchdowns in 43 seconds, and now led 28–20 just 1:37 into the period.

Namath's bad fortunes continued; he threw a 55-yard touchdown pass to tight end Pete Lammons, but the play was nullified by a holding penalty, after which he was then intercepted again, this time by defensive back Warren Powers at the New York 25. Powers got to his feet and took off running, making it into the end zone only to be told that the referees had blown the play dead. Still, it gave the Raiders excellent field position, which they squandered by only gaining three yards in the ensuing three plays. But at this point, with under five minutes left to play, a field goal was almost as good as a touchdown as it would increase Oakland's lead to 11 points and force the Jets to score twice to hope to overcome. Eischeid came in for a 29-yard field goal try: he missed it. The Jets had dodged a bullet.

With time running out, Namath drove the Jets into Oakland territory only to be intercepted by Bird again at the Raiders' 34-yard line. With only two minutes left to play, it was up to the defense now: they came through, forcing the Raiders to punt after three quick plays. The Jets still had a shot to tie the game with a touchdown and a two-point conversion, but with only one minute left, a lot would depend on field position.

Eischeid was not having a good day at all. Doing both the kicking and punting, he had already missed three field goals. Now, at a critical moment, he shanked the punt. It only went 12 yards and gave the Jets possession of the ball at the Oakland 47-yard line. On the very next play, with 53 seconds left in the game, the Jets caught the defense off guard. Everybody was expecting a pass, but Namath ran a draw play to Boozer. Well, why not? With almost a minute left and being only 47 yards away, there was a little time to play with, and if a draw could pick up a good chunk of yardage — 10 or maybe 15 yards — it would be a big help. The play worked better than they probably dared dream. Davidson admitted to having been completely fooled. "I read pass on the play and put on an inside rush," Davidson said. "They blocked me away from Boozer, who was running through there."[22] Matt Snell took out linebacker Gus Otto, and Boozer then darted straight through four potential tacklers at the 40-yard line. He outran a diving attempt at a tackle by linebacker Bill Laskey at the 25, and then twisted free of the clutches of Bird at the 15. Bird might have gotten a crack at Boozer sooner, but as Boozer was avoiding Laskey, Bird was being shielded-out nicely by Sauer. The last tackler to take a shot was lineman Ike Lassiter, who had been trailing the play all along. But Lassiter had also been shielded-out by Sauer, albeit unknowingly on Sauer's part. Sauer had his back to Lassiter and was looking to his left at Otto, who had managed to shake Snell and catch up. Sauer didn't even see that Lassiter was approaching from the right, but when Sauer slowed down to let Boozer run by, it forced Lassiter to cut around behind him, which left Lassiter only able to make a desperate dive for Boozer at the four-yard line. Boozer slid free and went into the end zone. It was an outstanding run, executed extremely well.

Namath said afterward that the Jets had figured the Raiders would be laying back deep, expecting a pass play.[23] They figured right. But the Jets still needed the two-point conversion to tie the game: they got it when Namath threw to Sauer on a bootleg. Oakland had been fooled again. They remembered Namath's touchdown run on the bootleg back in October, and when the Raiders saw him roll out they probably figured he was going to try it again. He didn't. The game ended in a 28–28 tie. Namath had completed 20 of 42 for in impressive 327 yards. He had two TDs, but five interceptions.

Oakland Tribune writer Bob Valli wrote that after the game the Oakland players seemed more upset with a tie than they usually were after a loss. The Jets could take satisfaction in having avoided a loss, but the tie really had the same effect on their playoff chances — it killed them. They had needed a win.

Week 13 — Sunday, December 11, 1966
Balboa Stadium, San Diego (attendance: 25,712)

The Jets continued their western trip by playing San Diego the following Sunday. They had beaten the Chargers in October, but that really seemed like more than two months ago: it was like a whole different season. The Jets had gone 1–5–1 since beating San Diego in New York on that Saturday night at Shea. Of course, the Chargers had problems of their own, going 2–4–1 since then. Somebody was due; perhaps it was just a matter of who was hungriest.

In the first quarter the Jets went up 3–0 on a 36-yard field goal by Jim Turner, and before the period was over they had increased their lead to 9–0 after Matt Snell scored on a one-yard TD run (Turner missed the extra point).

San Diego turned things around in the second quarter when they scored two touchdowns, the first an eight-yard pass from John Hadl to Gary Garrison, and the second a nine-yard scoring run by Jim Allison. The Jets did manage a 30-yard field goal before halftime to cut San Diego's lead to 14–12 at the break, but in the second half New York errors helped open the floodgates, and as the gap widened the Jets simply found it too daunting to keep up.

In the third quarter Paul Lowe broke a 57-yard run that carried San Diego to the New York one-yard line. Lowe scored on the next play, but that one-yard touchdown run was hell on his rushing average, dropping him below 10 yards per carry.

Trailing 21–12, the Jets shot back when Namath correctly read a safety blitz and called an audible: he threw quickly over the middle to tight end Pete Lammons, who took it 53 yards for a score. Such are the perils of blitzing. The Jets had again cut the lead to two points, but they would be their own worst enemy thereafter.

The New York defense succeeded in stopping San Diego, but Bake Turner fumbled the ensuing punt and San Diego recovered at the Jets' 41. John Hadl would account for 31 yards on the Chargers' series, first running for 20 yards on a rollout, and then running 11 yards for a touchdown.

In the fourth quarter, a New York drive was halted when Namath was intercepted by linebacker Rich Redman, and the Chargers turned around and went 80 yards to score on a three-yard pass from Hadl to Jacque MacKinnon. Mike Taliaferro then came in to relieve Namath, but he too was intercepted. It led to another touchdown run by Lowe, this one from nine yards out, giving San Diego a 42–19 lead. The Jets could only manage a late touchdown when Bill Mathis scored on a three-yard run, which made the final 42–27.

With the loss, the Jets fell to 5–6–2, the first time during the season that their record had dropped below .500. Namath had completed 10 of 21 throws for 166 yards, with one TD and a pair of interceptions. He was leading the AFL in most passing categories, including passing attempts, completions, and yardage — at 3,092 — but his 27 interceptions were also the most in either league.

Week 14 — Saturday, December 17, 1966
Shea Stadium, New York (attendance: 58,921)

The Jets returned to New York to finish out their season by playing Boston at Shea on a Saturday afternoon. Since the worst that they could finish would be 5–7–2, they at least knew that there was no danger of winding up with a fourth consecutive 5–8–1 record. Other than that, the game was of no real consequence to the Jets — they were going to finish third in the East no matter what. For Boston, it was a far different story.

At 8–3–2, the Patriots were looking to win the Eastern Division: either a win or a tie with the Jets would accomplish it. Boston was really not wanting a tie — they had played the Jets to a 24–24 stalemate at Fenway back in October, and if they hadn't let the Jets come back and tie the game with 17 fourth-quarter points, they would have already wrapped up the division.

Buffalo, at 8–4–1, was hoping for a third straight Eastern Division title, so their hopes rested on the Jets beating Boston on Saturday and themselves defeating Denver on Sunday. If the Jets lost to Boston, Buffalo would finish second in the division whether they beat Denver or not. Buffalo had beaten the Jets twice during the season, so the Jets certainly owed them no more favors, but the Bills appealed to them anyway, sending a flood of telegrams to Shea Stadium during the week to encourage them.

The Patriots had lost only once in their previous 10 games, while the Jets had only won once in their last eight. Under the circumstances, it was understandable that the Patriots would be favored. On their first offensive series, the Patriots certainly played like a team on a mission, working their way downfield to a first-and-goal situation only to see quarterback Babe Parilli fumble the ball away at the 10-yard line. After forcing the Jets to punt the Patriots again marched downfield, this time scoring when Parilli capped the 59-yard drive with an 18-yard TD pass to Gino Cappelletti.

But the Jets bolted right back, going 80 yards in just four plays. On the first play of the series, Emerson Boozer ran 54 yards to the Boston 26. Three plays later Namath hit Don Maynard in the end zone from 18 yards out, and the game was tied at 7–7.

The Patriots did manage to cross midfield on their next series, but Cappelletti was both short and wide on a 54-yard field goal try: Boston's troubles began shortly thereafter. Early in the second period, with the Jets facing a second-and-10 from their own 20, Boston was called for pass interference on a Namath pass to Maynard. After a holding penalty set the Jets back, Namath threw to Pete Lammons for 22 yards and a first down at the Boston 42. Boston then continued to help the drive along, first with a personal foul penalty, and then another pass interference call that set the Jets up on the one-yard line. Two plays later Boozer went in to score, and the Jets were up 14–7 with 12 minutes to play in the half. It had been another 80-yard drive, although more than half of this one had been accountable by Boston penalties.

The Patriots were moving the ball well on their next possession, but when the drive stalled and they were forced to settle for a 38-yard field goal try, Cappelletti missed again. With the half winding down, Namath then took the Jets downfield quickly. He threw 25 yards to Maynard, 16 to Snell, then 21 more to Maynard. The Jets got as far as the Boston five-yard line, but on fourth down, and with less than a foot to go for the first down, they chose a 12-yard field goal by Jim Turner and a 17–7 lead.

Early in the second half it was obvious that Boston was in trouble. After forcing the Patriots to punt on their first series, the Jets took over on their own 31 and drove downfield in 11 plays to score again. Namath had thrown 24 yards to Maynard, then to Snell for gains of 16 and nine yards, and wound up by hitting Maynard in the end zone from eight yards out to give the Jets a commanding 24–7 lead.

Now playing with a sense of urgency, the Patriots went 80 yards in just four plays, Parilli throwing 18 yards to Cappelletti, 44 to Larry Garron, and then hitting Jim Whalen for 18 yards and a score. Parilli bobbled the snap on the extra point, and Cappelletti's rushed kick hit the crossbar, so the Patriots only wound up with six points. But with the lead now cut to 24–13 the Boston defense was playing with renewed purpose, and they quickly forced the Jets to punt. Really, the Jets had done a lot to sabotage the series themselves with two holding penalties.

Boston took over on their own 36, and Parilli quickly got them up and running again when he threw 35 yards to Art Graham on the first play of the series to put the Patriots on the New York 29. But three plays later the drive was abruptly halted when Parilli was intercepted by Bill Baird at the nine-yard line.

It was a disastrous reversal of fortune for the Patriots: rather than taking a bite out of the Jets' lead, they instead saw that lead balloon to 31–13 when the Jets went 87 yards in just three plays. The final 77 yards came when Namath read a safety blitz coming and fired quickly to George Sauer, whose defender, Don Webb, had fallen down as Sauer cut toward the middle. With no safeties to contend with, Sauer had a lonely 56-yard run the rest of the way to the end zone.

Struggling to get back in it, the Patriots drove to the New York 40, but once more it was Baird who proved Parilli's foil, this time intercepting him at the New York 22 to end the third period. When Boston did get the ball back for their initial possession of the fourth period they went 74 yards in nine plays to score on a one-yard run by Jim Nance. Parilli then hit running back Bob Cappadona with a pass on the two-point conversion, and the lead was cut to 10 points at 31–21.

But Boston's hopes once more dimmed when the Jets went 82 yards in seven plays to score again, this time on a 25-yard run by Snell. The other big gainer on the drive was a 25-yard pass from Namath to Maynard that took the Jets from their own 45 to the Boston 30. Now down 38–21, the Patriots continued to fight.

When they got a good return from Joe Bellino on the ensuing kick, the Patriots found themselves starting from close to midfield. Four plays later Parilli hit Art Graham with a 15-yard score, again cutting the lead to 10 points. But when Mark Smolinski recovered Boston's onside kick for New York, the Jets were then able to run out the clock.

In the Boston locker room after the game, Patriots coach Mike Holovak was beside himself. "I wish I knew, I wish I knew," he kept repeating.[24] "They did things to us on offense no other team has done all year."[25]

Buffalo Bills owner Ralph Wilson was in attendance at Shea. After the game he sought out Sonny Werblin in the New York locker room. His jubilation was obvious; when he found Werblin he dropped to one knee and bowed down to him. In his giddiness, Wilson was offering to have champagne brought in for Werblin, Ewbank, the players — everybody. His enthusiasm was understandable, but did he really think that the Jets could share in his celebration? The Jets had just finished a mediocre season. At 6–6–2 they weren't losers, but they weren't winners either. In sport, a tie is often described as having all the appeal of kissing your sister. If a tie game is like kissing your sister, what does that make a 6–6–2 season? Think about that one.

Namath wasn't particularly celebratory. Billy Sullivan, owner of the Boston Patriots, made his way to the Jets' locker room as well. Namath was almost apologetic when Sullivan congratulated him: he told Sullivan that he would have preferred Boston to Buffalo as representatives of the division in the championship. "But I got to play my game," he said.[26] After Sullivan had left, Namath told reporters that he felt that Boston was more deserving of the division title — they had, after all, beaten Buffalo twice during the season — but not at the Jets' expense. In Namath's estimation, the Jets, at 6–6–2, were still losers.

But it had been a great game for the team. The Jets set a new club record with 528 total yards on offense (Snell and Boozer had each run for over 100). Ewbank said that his team should have been playing like that all season: he knew they could, and he knew that they were better than third place.

Praise for Namath's performance after the game was unanimous. He had played a superb game, completing 14 of 21 passes for 287 yards; he had thrown three touchdowns, and had not added to his league-leading interception tally. What made his performance impressive beyond its normal worth was that he was really in no condition to play. Namath didn't show up when the team was supposed to report to the stadium, and as the day wore on and game time approached, he was still missing. When he eventually did turn up, it was uncomfortably close to game time and it was obvious to everyone that he had been out all night. He looked more like a man ready to call it a night rather than go out and call a game. It may have been his best performance of the season, and chances are he wouldn't remember much of it. Go figure.

Nineteen sixty-six had begun very promisingly with the team's 4–0–1 start, and there was no immediate reason to foresee a meltdown. Early in the season, Larry Felser wrote in *The Sporting News* that the Jets seemed well on their way to their first Eastern Division title, and more than that, he predicted an AFL MVP award for Namath and Coach of the Year for Ewbank. "They might as well give Joe Namath this year's MVP award right now," Felser wrote, adding that Namath "has it all wrapped up."[27] Boston fullback Jim Nance won the AFL MVP award that year after rushing for an AFL-record 1,458 yards. Nor did Ewbank win Coach of the Year — that went to Mike Holovak, also of Boston.

One reason that the team began to stumble as the season wore on was a common lament, that being one of injuries. Whether or not a team is capable of making a title run is often down to how healthy their players stay, particularly key players, of course. One blow to the Jets was the inability to keep a healthy offensive backfield (Snell had dealt with both a sprained ankle and rib injuries), but there is no doubt that Namath's knee was the major obstacle. Although he hadn't missed any games, the effect his August injury had on his performance was obvious as the season wore on. When Namath was asked by reporters about his knee during the season and the possibility of further surgery, he made no secret of his feelings: he was not merely agreeable to the idea, he was eager. But then, he knew better than anyone else that things weren't right with the knee.

The day after the season-ending Boston game, Namath went to see Dr. Nicholas to have the knee reexamined, and upon closer inspection Nicholas realized that the injury was far more serious than he had originally thought. Namath knew that even before the Jets' season fell apart. While they were still winning he was telling reporters that he would like to have surgery on the knee again. As the pain increased week-to-week, Namath seemed to adopt a weary pessimism about his condition, saying that he was worse off than he had been before the surgery in 1965. "I don't know how long it will hold up," he said. "I don't think it has properly healed."[28] On a bad day his perspective could be far gloomier, saying at one point during the season that he felt his knees were ruined for life.[29] Cortisone shots helped throughout the season, as did an increasing reliance on Johnny Walker Red. It was both a way of medicating the pain, and helping to forget what lay ahead down the road. "The hurting doesn't bother me. It will always hurt," he said. "What bothers me is that maybe my legs will just give out some day."[30]

"I could tell the way he was setting himself up when he dropped back that something was wrong," Ewbank said. "I'd ask him and he'd say, 'Don't worry, it'll be all right.'"[31] The truth is, even though he wanted another operation, Namath didn't want to miss the season, so he decided to just tough it out.

In late December it was announced that Namath would again be undergoing surgery on his right knee. It was a more complicated operation than his first knee surgery. Assisting Dr. Nicholas this time would be Dr. Philip D. Wilson, Jr. and Dr. Frank E. Stenchfield, who had examined Namath's knee for the Army when he had been classified 4F. Namath went back into Lenox Hill Hospital on December 28, 1966; the surgery took one hour and 45 minutes, the doctors removing torn lateral cartilage and repairing a torn cruciate ligament. They also transferred a tendon to help stabilize the knee where it was weakened. There were bone fragments to remove as well, which had probably been the byproduct of playing with a shredded meniscus. With the meniscus in tatters it was a matter of bone grinding on bone.

Namath held a press conference from his hospital bed afterward, saying that he felt better than he expected to. He was very optimistic about the new mobility that the surgery would give him and was looking forward to the 1967 season. The 1966 season had seen him completing under 50 percent of his throws, hitting 232 of 471 (49.3 percent), but he had thrown for an impressive 3,379 yards. He had also thrown only 19 touchdowns against 27 interceptions, but with the knee now more functional everybody was hoping that his completion percentage would rise and his interception count drop — a little mobility might accomplish it. Then again, while the interception count was high, so was the pass count. The truth is that Namath's 27 interceptions still only gave him a 5.7 interception percentage. As Namath liked to point out at the time, Johnny Unitas — largely regarded as the best quarterback in professional football — had an interception percentage of 6.9 that same year (Namath had thrown 27 interceptions in 471 attempts, Unitas 24 in 348 attempts). Namath held on to a magazine article that quoted Unitas as saying that, if a quarterback knows what he is doing he won't get intercepted. Pretty dumb comment, Namath thought.

4

The 1967 Season

Namath's knee surgery in December of 1966 promised to give the offense a new dimension. Saying that Namath had more mobility than he had at any time since joining the Jets, Ewbank revised the team's playbook to include more play-action passes and rollouts. The coach was also pleased by the way Namath was able to set himself before throwing, which he hadn't been able to do nearly so well on the bad knee a year before. Ewbank felt that the team could now open up more on offense; Matt Snell concurred, saying that the Jets' offensive schemes were no longer as stoic as they had been. "Last year we were like the Green Bay offense," Snell said. "Now we have action, fakes. Things are happening."[1]

But the week before the Jets' first exhibition game Namath began to experience pain in the left knee, supposedly his good one. It was diagnosed as a case of tendonitis, which the doctors reasoned had been the byproduct of favoring his right knee. Until it subsided the doctors suggested more cortisone shots.

The night before the Jets' exhibition season got under way, a situation arose. After receiving word that his brother was in the hospital, Namath felt the need to escape the confine of Peekskill Military Academy, where the Jets held camp, and so he asked Ewbank for permission to leave for the night. Ewbank asked him to wait until Saturday — the night after the game — but Namath was not in the mood to negotiate, and so he left against Ewbank's wishes. Namath's night in New York was initially seen by his teammates as a matter of flouting the rules, but Namath agreed to address the team to explain to them that he was not out for a night on the town, but had a personal matter to contend with and needed some time to get away and think. Although he hadn't mentioned any specifics of what was weighing on his mind, the other players were satisfied that he was sincere, and were willing to forget it. Not so Ewbank, who levied a fine against Namath over the objections of Werblin. Whether or not the fine stuck has never been known.

Despite all the publicity the incident brought, the team didn't seem the least distracted when they traveled to Bridgeport to play the Boston Patriots in front of 16,000 spectators at Kennedy Memorial Stadium. The results were ridiculous, even for an exhibition game. Namath played only the first quarter, but by the time he left the game the Jets had already built up a 28–0 lead. The first score came after Boston punter Jim Swanson fumbled the snap from center, leading to a two-yard touchdown run by Emerson Boozer five plays later.

There were just over five minutes left in the opening period when the Jets began to pour it on. Namath took his team downfield with a few sharp passes, and then Boozer ran it in again, this time from 21 yards out. Linebacker Al Atkinson then intercepted a Babe Parilli pass and ran it back for another score to give the Jets a 21–0 lead. Boozer would add another touchdown on an eight-yard run before the first quarter ended, and then both he and Namath sat out the rest of the game. By halftime the Jets were up 42–0; the Patriots had only managed one first down in the half. It wouldn't be until the final 7:30 of the game that Boston would score, and by then they were playing against the Jets' third-stringers. Namath had completed four of six throws for

48 yards in his one quarter of play. The final score of 55–13 had to be humiliating for Boston coach Mike Holovak, who had won the AFL Coach of the Year award the prior season.

A week later the Jets were in Birmingham to play the defending AFL-champion Kansas City Chiefs on a Saturday night. Namath completed 11 of 30 throws for 136 yards during the first half, but the Jets trailed 6–0 at halftime. The game livened up a bit when the backups took over in the second half, as the Chiefs built up a 20–0 lead before Mike Taliaferro drove the Jets downfield to score. The final was a 30–17 victory for Kansas City.

The Jets' third exhibition would be their first meeting with an NFL team. In 1966 the two leagues had reached a merger agreement, and while the merger itself would not truly occur until 1970, the first Super Bowl in January of 1967 was a byproduct of the agreement (Green Bay had beaten Kansas City handily, as everybody knows). Pending the official joining of the leagues, preseason games would provide the only meeting of AFL and NFL clubs outside of the Super Bowl. The Jets' first NFL opponent would be the Philadelphia Eagles, who would play the Jets in Cincinnati.

Although the Jets got out to a 13–3 lead, both Namath and Matt Snell left the game in the second quarter with injuries — Snell with a foot injury, and Namath, well, his knee (what else?) — and the Eagles took advantage. After scoring on a 42-yard halfback pass to cut the Jets' lead to 13–10 with under three minutes to play in the first half, the Eagles then took the lead when Fred Brown blocked a Curley Johnson punt and ran it in for a score. The Eagles led 17–13 at halftime, but blew the game open in the second half; in the end Philadelphia triumphed 34–19. Although he played less than a half, and the Jets were leading when he left, Namath did not have a particularly good night, completing just three of 10 passes for 20 yards. The injuries to Namath and Snell were minor (Namath left the game with what was described as a strained left knee), but it was still not worth chancing them in an exhibition. At least it was the left one, which meant the surgery performed on the right knee was still holding up. The game was also marked by brawling, with the referees ejecting New York defensive backs Cornell Gordon and Johnny Sample, and Philadelphia halfback Tim Brown and tight end Mike Ditka.

The Jets' next exhibition game took them to Charlotte, North Carolina to play the Houston Oilers in front of a crowd of 15,000 at Memorial Stadium. Namath was sharper this time, hitting 11 of 14 for 110 yards as he again played just the first half, which turned out to be the half that the Jets scored all of their points. After a couple of field goals that put New York up 6–0 in the first quarter, Boozer scored on a five-yard run, set up largely by a 29-yard pass from Namath to Mark Smolinski. The Jets led 13–0 at the half, and wound up winning 13–7, Houston's only score coming with just 57 seconds left in the game. The victory did come at a price for the Jets, however, as they lost guard Sam DeLuca and backup quarterback Mike Taliaferro to injuries. Both would require surgery. Taliaferro would come back; DeLuca's career was over.

The Jets' exhibition season wrapped up with a game against the Buffalo Bills in Mobile, Alabama. The Jets came into the game with a 2–2 preseason record, while Buffalo had until then gone winless in the preseason. Again Namath played the first half only, and although the Jets trailed 21–20 at the intermission, he had a good half passing, completing 15 of 19 for 210 yards.

Buffalo got out of the gate fast when Allen Smith took the opening kickoff back 94 yards for a score, but Namath tied the game quickly when he threw a 67-yard touchdown pass to Bake Turner on the Jets' first play from scrimmage. The Jets then went up 10–7 on an eight-yard field goal by Jim Turner, but Buffalo regained the lead when quarterback Tom Flores — acquired in a trade with Oakland for second-string quarterback Daryle Lamonica — threw 19 yards to Paul Costa for a score. Buffalo immediately added to their lead on the ensuing kickoff when the Jets fumbled the kick and Paul Maguire scooped up the ball and ran it in from the 12 to put the Bills up 21–10. Namath threw an eight-yard TD pass to Boozer and the Jets then closed to within a point of Buffalo when Jim Turner kicked a 47-yard field goal before the end of the half.

With Taliaferro out, Jim Turner—the team's third-string quarterback—took over for Namath in the second half, but he could only pilot the Jets to a fourth-quarter field goal as he completed four of 10 passes for 40 yards. Buffalo scored 10 points in the second half—their only touchdown of the half coming when Hagood Clarke intercepted Turner and ran it back 40 yards for a score—and went on to notch their only preseason triumph, 31–23.

Preseason is always a mixed bag, so finishing 2–3 (or 1–4 for that matter) is no great cause for alarm. Ewbank certainly didn't seem out of sorts; in fact, he seemed quite pleased. "What took all the sting out of it," the coach said of the loss to Buffalo, "is that Joe Namath had such a fabulous first half."[2] Ewbank pointed out that, aside from the points gained by Buffalo against the Jets' kicking teams, the Jets completely dominated in every statistic, and by his reckoning they had delivered a message to the defending division champs. If the Jets were chagrined at winding up their preseason by losing to their division rivals, they could make up for it soon enough—they would open their season against the Bills ten days later in Buffalo.

Week 1—Sunday, September 10, 1967
War Memorial Stadium, Buffalo (attendance: 45,748)

After a scoreless first quarter, the Jets finally got on the board halfway through the second period when Namath hit Don Maynard with a bullet pass to the sideline at the Buffalo seven-yard line: Maynard eluded a tackle and took it in for a 7–0 lead. The Jets added to the lead with just 21 seconds left in the half when Namath threw a beautiful 56-yard bomb to Maynard that put New York up 14–0.

The Bills had started Tom Flores at quarterback, but with their offense going nowhere, Buffalo coach Joe Collier decided to give Jack Kemp a shot in the second half. After leading the Bills to two AFL championships and three consecutive Eastern Division titles, Kemp had somehow fallen out of favor with Collier, and when Buffalo traded second-stringer Daryle Lamonica to Oakland for Flores, it seemed that Collier was eyeing Flores for the spot all the way. As for Kemp, he was not able to get much started in the third quarter against the Jets, and the Bills were lucky that all the Jets could muster in the period was a field goal to increase their lead to 17–0.

A 17-point lead is ordinarily a fairly nice cushion to go into the final quarter with, but for the Jets the fourth quarter was a nightmare. Just over two minutes into the fourth, Kemp threw a 24-yard touchdown to Art Powell that cut the New York lead to 17–7. Two-and-a-half minutes later Kemp threw to Powell for another score, this time from 27 yards out. Now the Jets' lead was down to 17–14.

There was only 2:27 left when Buffalo kicker Mike Mercer tied the game with a 51-yard field goal; there were only four seconds left when he won it with a 43-yard field goal. Buffalo, trailing 17–0 as the fourth quarter began, scored 20 points in the final period to win it. For the Jets, it was an exasperating meltdown.

The most obvious reason for the Jets' disgusting collapse was the unfortunate departure of cornerback Cornell Gordon midway through the third period. Gordon had blocked a Mercer field goal attempt earlier in the game, and on his final play of the game—and, as it turned out, of the season—he had intercepted Kemp, and while in full stride during the runback, he took a shot from Buffalo receiver Elbert Dubenion. He hadn't even seen Dubenion coming. Looking downfield, Gordon was suddenly chopped down at the knees: he had to be helped off the field. It was Gordon's replacement, Solomon Brannan, who would get burned by Art Powell for the two touchdowns.

Losing Gordon for the season was certainly costly enough, but it got worse: in the game's final minutes the Jets also lost Matt Snell to a knee injury. Snell would go in for surgery soon after, and would miss much of the season. Ewbank had said that the Jets had a good chance of making a championship run if Namath could stay healthy. The problem was turning out to be keeping everybody else's knees healthy. Namath finished the game 11 of 23 for 153 yards, two TDs and no interceptions.

Week 2 — Sunday, September 24, 1967
Bears Stadium, Denver (attendance: 35,565)

The 0–1 Jets traveled to Denver to face the 1–2 Broncos. In a peculiar bit of scheduling, the Jets' second game was Denver's fourth game of the year. The Jets had been given the opening week of the season off, and had also been given a week off in-between their first and second games; such a leisurely schedule.

Denver got off to a quick start against the Jets, scoring on their fourth play from scrimmage just 2:26 into the game when quarterback Steve Tensi hit Eric Crabtree with a 49-yard touchdown pass to cap a fast 80-yard drive. Otherwise, Tensi had flipped a swing pass to fullback Wendell Hayes that accounted for another 27 yards in the series.

On Denver's second series they wound up getting close enough for kicker Roger LeClere to kick a field goal to put the Broncos up 10–0. But the Jets battled back by traveling 80 yards in five plays just before the end of the first quarter. Namath started the series with a 46-yard pass to Don Maynard, and the drive concluded with a three-yard sweep by Emerson Boozer that cut Denver's lead to 10–7.

Denver was still moving the ball almost at will, however, and would score two quick touchdowns in the second quarter, first on an 18-yard pass from Tensi to Al Denson, and then a four-yard run by Bo Hickey that set the Broncos up nicely with a 24–7 lead. Denver had scored on each of their first four offensive series. But as the Jets knew all too well, such a lead could be overcome. The Jets had blown a 17-point lead in the final quarter against Buffalo; now trailing by 17 against Denver, they had more than half the game remaining to get it back. They would get most of it back before the end of the first half. Boozer finished another 80-yard drive by running it in, this time from a yard out, and shortly afterward Namath hit George Sauer with a 31-yard touchdown pass that brought the Jets to within three points at halftime.

It was early in the third quarter when the Jets tied the game on a 17-yard field goal by Jim Turner. The Jets then appeared to be driving toward the go-ahead score late in the third, but Namath was intercepted by Goldie Sellers. The New York defense managed to get the ball back quickly, however, when linebacker Al Atkinson recovered a fumble at the Houston 39-yard line, and four plays into the fourth quarter Namath hit fullback Mark Smolinski with a three-yard touchdown pass to put the Jets up for good at 31–24.

Later in the fourth quarter, Boozer went in for his third touchdown of the game, again from three yards out, to make the final 38–24. Without Snell, the Jets' running game was considerably lacking: Boozer had only gained 44 yards and had averaged just 2.4 yards per carry, while Snell's replacement, Mark Smolinski, only gained 16 yards. But Namath had made the difference, having the best game of his professional career, completing 22 of 37 passes for 399 yards, and two TDs. The longer Snell was out, however, the easier it would become for opposing defenses, as the Jets' often lackluster running game would allow opponents to key on Namath and the passing game.

Week 3 — Sunday, October 1, 1967
Shea Stadium, New York (attendance: 61,240)

Returning to New York for their home opener at Shea, the Jets faced the 1–1 Miami Dolphins. The Jets were still without Snell, who had gone in for surgery on his left knee the Friday before the game: he would be out at least six weeks. Having thrown for a personal best of 399 yards the week before, Namath was enough for Miami to worry about. Well, Miami coach George Wilson was worried anyway. "If Namath gets a hot hand like he did against us last year," Wilson said, "New York will be rough."[3]

As for some of the Miami defenders, they seemed more cavalier about the threat posed by the Jets' passing game. One Miami player — speaking under cover of anonymity — pointed out that Namath had not thrown a touchdown pass against the Dolphins in either of the two meetings between the teams in 1966. He then corrected himself by sarcastically adding that the Dolphins had intercepted a Namath pass and ran it back for a score in Miami. One has to wonder why a second-year franchise like the Miami Dolphins would be tempting fate with such careless and inane crowing, but the truth is that, while it was still early in the season, the Dolphins had the league's leading pass defense at that point. They had only allowed an average of 63 net yards passing in their first two games, and so *perhaps* they were feeling overcome by a strutting pride; *perhaps* it was time to take them down a peg ... or two. In reality, the impressive stats posted by the Miami defensive secondary were misleading: Kansas City, who had shut Miami out 24–0 the previous week, hadn't really needed to bother passing that much.

Miami got off to a bad start against the Jets, with quarterback Bob Griese being intercepted by Johnny Sample on his very first pass. The Dolphins were able to prevent the Jets from capitalizing, however, and the first period went scoreless. Only two plays before the end of the quarter Griese was put down hard by defensive end Verlon Biggs and suffered an injury to his shoulder. Rick Norton would quarterback the Dolphins the rest of the game, and he drove the Dolphins 70 yards in seven plays to open the scoring. He threw 31 yards to Doug Moreau, and Joe Auer then gained another 31 yards on two running plays that carried Miami to the New York six-yard line. Sammy Price ran it in from there to put Miami up 7–0, but that only seemed to light a fire under the Jets' asses.

After the kickoff, Namath immediately went to work, throwing 62 yards to Don Maynard, and hitting Maynard again for 25 more to the Miami one-yard line. Emerson Boozer then scored to tie the game 3:24 into the second period. It had taken the Jets just four plays to even the score.

Namath then drove the Jets downfield for the go-ahead score, throwing 21 yards to Pete Lammons, 20 yards to Maynard, and another 20 to George Sauer. The drive resulted in a Jim Turner field goal at 8:10 of the second period that put New York up 10–7. The Jets would increase their lead just before halftime; from the Miami 49, Namath passed over the middle to Boozer, who caught the ball in stride, shook off an attempted tackle by Miami's Pete Jacquess and then raced some 30 yards up the middle of the field to score with just 46 seconds left in the half. "I saw Jacquess there," Boozer said. "I figure most guys think I'm going to swerve right or left. I rammed him and kept my balance."[4] The Jets held a 16–7 lead at halftime (a two-point conversion failed).

By halftime Namath had already thrown for 274 yards, 216 of that in the second quarter. The Jets had only run seven rushing plays in the first half: who needs a running game? They got right back to work in the second half, scoring on their first two offensive series of the third quarter and increasing their lead to 29–7. After receiving the second half kickoff, the Jets embarked on a 10-play, 80-yard drive that climaxed with Namath throwing a perfectly executed 13-yard screen pass to Mark Smolinski. Namath back-peddled to the 25-yard line before tossing the ball to Smolinski at the 17. Smolinski then followed center John Schmitt and tackle Winston Hill into the end zone.

Namath threw his third touchdown of the game when he hit Boozer with a five-yard TD on a third-and-goal play. For the second consecutive week Boozer had scored three TDs, and also for the second consecutive week Namath set a personal best in passing yardage. He left the game in the fourth quarter, having completed 23 of 39 for 415 yards, with three TDs and one interception. He had also set an AFL record by passing for 398 yards without an interception, breaking the record of 375 yards set by Al Dorow in 1960. Namath's lone interception came in the fourth quarter on a busted play involving — who else — Don Maynard.

Namath had been made aware of the comment by the Miami player earlier in the week regarding his never having thrown a touchdown against the Dolphins. "Go get that guy from Miami and see what he's got to say now," Namath said to reporters after the game.[5] Miami coach George Wilson was more than a little agitated, remarking that he wished his players would learn when to shut up.

The Miami defensive backs were awed. Cornerback Jim Warren had watched Namath pump the ball — once, twice, three times — as he waited and anticipated the pass. When it finally came Warren said he was still helpless to stop it. "It was just pop, pop, pop, right down the field," said the Dolphins' other cornerback, Dick Westmoreland, "And there's that man standing back there putting the ball in everyone's arms."[6] Miami may have swaggered into New York, but now they couldn't wait to slink out of town.

Week 4 — Saturday, October 7, 1967
Shea Stadium, New York (attendance: 63,106)

For the second game of a three-game home stand, the 2–1 Jets would be playing the 3–0 Oakland Raiders on a Saturday night. During the week Namath made no secret of his feelings about the Raiders, telling reporters that he wanted to beat Oakland more than any other team. Namath had never beaten the Raiders: the best the Jets had managed against them since Namath's rookie season was to tie them twice (once in 1965, and then again in '66). But Namath went further than that in his comments, going on to accuse the Raiders of playing dirty. "You have to expect to get hit when you're a quarterback," he said, "but not with the cheap shots that you get from Oakland."[7]

The comment didn't sit well with Oakland general manager Scotty Stirling, who said that no one but Namath had ever accused guys like Ben Davidson and Dan Birdwell of taking cheap shots. What, those pussycats? Of course not. As for the Oakland coaches, they had more pressing concerns than a little loose talk. They had seen the films of Namath riddling the Denver and Miami defenses for 399 and 415 yards respectively, and their game plan became simple — get to Namath. They might not drop him for a loss, but they at least wanted to keep him off his game with constant pressure, and for that reason they planned a strategy of frequent blitzing.

To look at Namath's first-half numbers, one might have thought that Oakland's strategy worked just fine: Namath only completed two of 12 passes in the first half. When he did hit, however, it cost the Raiders. With the game still scoreless in the first quarter, Namath threw 30 yards to Don Maynard, who was tackled by safety Howie Williams at the Oakland 14. Emerson Boozer and Mark Smolinski took over from there; Boozer ran for four yards, Smolinski for three, and then Boozer went in for the score from seven yards out. What was becoming apparent was that, in their eagerness to eradicate the pass, Oakland was allowing the New York ground game to run off some big gainers.

In the second quarter, with the Jets still leading 7–0, the Raiders managed to get to Namath, dropping him for a loss at the New York nine-yard line. The Jets were forced to punt from deep in their own territory, and the Raiders found themselves looking at a short field when they took possession at their own 44. But three plays later linebacker Larry Grantham intercepted Oakland quarterback Daryle Lamonica at the New York 48 and proceeded to run it back 36 yards to the Raiders' 16.

Again, the Jets stayed on the ground and Boozer went around right end for nine yards. Three plays later Bill Mathis went in for a score from a yard out to put New York up 14–0 with

11:35 to play in the half. It was a determined effort by Mathis, who tried to go over top, but after being repelled, then bulled his way around left tackle.

Later in the second quarter, Namath was intercepted by Willie Brown, and when Lamonica converted a third-and-10 play by hitting Billy Cannon at the New York 26, it seemed as though the Raiders would be back in the game. But three incomplete passes forced Oakland to attempt a 33-yard field goal, which kicker George Blanda missed.

After that, Namath was again intercepted by Brown, but as hard as Brown seemed to be working to get Oakland back in the game, Grantham was working just as hard to keep them out of it. Just two plays after Brown's interception Grantham again intercepted Lamonica, giving the Jets the ball back at their own 38 with under five minutes left in the half. The New York ground game was still ripping off good yardage, as the Raiders continued to key on the pass. A draw play to Boozer picked up 14 yards, and the Jets embarked on a time-consuming drive in which Namath ran Boozer and Smolinski most of the way. After converting a key third down with a 14-yard pass from Namath to Maynard, the Jets got a 27-yard field goal from Jim Turner to increase their lead to 17–0 with 45 seconds left in the half.

The Jets received the kick to open the second half, and put together a drive that wound its way to the Oakland 24-yard line before stalling out; still, it enabled them to increase their lead to 20–0 once Jim Turner hit a 31-yard field goal. Late in the third quarter the Raiders finally put together a drive of their own in which Lamonica threw 37 yards to Hewritt Dixon before completing the drive with a 15-yard touchdown pass to Bill Miller.* Subsequent Oakland offensive series went nowhere, however, and the Jets fairly well put the game out of reach with just under eight minutes left to play. In a drive that covered 62 yards in six plays, Namath threw 38 yards to Mathis to take the Jets down to the Oakland 10. Boozer scored from seven yards out soon afterward, and the Jets took a commanding 27–7 lead.

Lamonica hit Warren Wells with a 25-yard scoring pass late in the game after Oakland recovered a fumbled punt at the New York 48, but the Jets were never in imminent danger. The game ended as a 27–14 New York victory; it would be Oakland's only loss of the season until getting beaten by Green Bay in the Super Bowl.

Namath's numbers were not impressive—nine of 28 for 166 yards, with two interceptions and no touchdowns—but he had played a smart game, victimizing Oakland's blitz with draw plays. What had primarily sunk the Raiders was their inability to adjust their defensive game plan. Well, that and the Jets' defense, which had harassed Lamonica the entire night while holding Oakland to just 55 yards rushing. Aside from Grantham's two interceptions, Bill Baird and Johnny Sample had each stolen a Lamonica pass.

After the game, Oakland coach John Rauch faced the inevitable question from reporters— what did he think of Namath? "He ranks with the best in football in all the things a quarterback has to do," Rauch replied. "He has a very quick release, he is very accurate, he throws equally well long or short, and he reads defenses well."[8]

Week 5 — Sunday, October 15, 1967
Shea Stadium, New York (attendance: 62,729)

The first-place Jets closed out their three-game home stand against the Houston Oilers, their closest rivals in the Eastern Division. At 2–2, the Oilers were only one game behind the 3–1

The score is uniformly—and erroneously—listed as a five-yard TD pass by all sources. A look at the play, however, clearly shows that the Raiders had possession at the New York 15-yard line when Lamonica went back to pass. Miller makes the catch at the nine-yard line, fakes out Jim Hudson, and takes it into the right side of the end zone for the score. The persistent listing of the play as a five-yard pass rather than 15 would seem to be a simple matter of a typo that was never caught and has led to the play's mislabeling ever since.

Jets, so the game would have obvious and immediate ramifications. At the time, the Jets had the only winning record in the division, and New York and Houston had only each other to worry about as both Buffalo and Boston were floundering and the second-year Miami Dolphins were still trying to find themselves.

The Jets went downfield to score on their first offensive series against the Oilers, as Namath hit Don Maynard with passes of 18 and 20 yards and Emerson Boozer capped the drive with a five-yard touchdown run 4:42 into the opening quarter. The 7–0 lead would hold through the first period, and when safety Jim Hudson intercepted Houston quarterback Pete Beathard in the second quarter, Namath immediately added to the lead with a 30-yard touchdown throw to Maynard.

Everything seemed to be going as scripted by the Jets, and a 10-yard field goal by Jim Turner increased the New York lead to 17–0. As the half was nearing its end, Turner had an opportunity to up the New York lead to 20–0 with a 26-yard field goal, and that is where the Jets' fortunes took an outrageous turn. Turner's kick was blocked by defensive end Pat Holmes, and defensive back Ken Houston gathered up the ball and took flight: he ran 71 yards with it, and with just eight seconds remaining in the half Houston was on the board. The Jets had hoped to go into halftime with a 20–0 lead, but instead found themselves up just 17–7. The change in momentum would carry over into the second half, giving the Oilers renewed purpose, and the Jets festering doubts. Perhaps they were reminded of the 17-point lead they squandered in the fourth quarter in their opening game against Buffalo.

The Jets received the opening kickoff of the second half, but on just their second play from scrimmage, a Namath pass to George Sauer wound up in the hands of Houston defensive back Miller Farr, who ran the ball back 51 yards for a score. Suddenly, without their offense having done a thing — and a mere 46 seconds into the second half — the Oilers were very much in the game, trailing just 17–14.

On the Jets' next offensive series they drove to the Houston 21-yard line before Farr again intercepted Namath, this time running the ball back 67 yards to the New York 20. A few plays later, just so nobody could claim that the Houston offense hadn't contributed anything, Beathard threw a four-yard touchdown pass to Monte Ledbetter, giving the Oilers a 21–17 lead. The natives at Shea were not merely restless, but downright agitated, and they began booing lustily. The Jets would manage a 26-yard field goal to shave Houston's lead to 21–20 with under four minutes to go in the third, but their following series undid that. Before the third quarter could end, Namath tried to hit Pete Lammons, and Ken Houston stepped in front, snatching the ball on the run. He kept running — 43 yards for a touchdown — putting Houston up 28–20.

The interceptions persisted in the fourth quarter: Namath's fourth errant throw was taken by Jim Norton, and then, with less than seven minutes left to play, Farr grabbed his third interception of the game as the Jets were poised to score. Farr only returned this one to the Houston nine-yard line, and the Jets were therefore almost assured of good field position for one more try if they could force the Oilers to punt. The defense did even better: when the Oilers tried a pass play, defensive end Verlon Biggs tipped the ball and it wound up in the hands of linebacker Al Atkinson at the 15: Atkinson returned the ball to the Houston three-yard line.

After that, it was Boozer who once again ran it in for the score, and with a two-point conversion the Jets could tie the game. The Jets got the two points when Namath zipped a pass to Maynard in the corner of the end zone. Maynard managed to make the catch, despite a pass interference call on Houston. It was now 28–28 with five minutes remaining.

Don Trull came in at quarterback for the Oilers, and suddenly their ground game began yielding results. Houston drove downfield with Hoyle Granger running the ball seven straight times until the drive ran out of steam and Houston attempted a 52-yard field goal. The kick failed, and with just 49 seconds to play the score remained tied.

The New York offense — Namath, really — had put on a schizophrenic performance, the first and second halves being like two separate games, but as outrageous as the second half had been, the final five seconds topped everything. With just enough time for one final play, Namath went back to throw and merely heaved the ball deep. He might have expected George Sauer to be in the area, but the only one in the vicinity of the throw was Houston defensive back W.K. Hicks, who looked like he was fielding a punt at his own 25-yard line. Hicks caught the ball and started up field, finally running into traffic at the New York 45, where Pete Lammons got a hold of him. With time on the clock having expired, Hicks struggled forward to the 40 before pitching a lateral to Ken Houston, but Houston quickly got tangled up at the 30 and then pitched the ball to Larry Carwell. With linebacker Garland Boyette out in front to block for him, Carwell broke toward the right sideline. Maynard tried to catch him from behind but Carwell was just beyond his reach. The last man for Carwell to beat was Namath.

Boyette was in good position to take Namath out, and he did block him, but the play was so close to the sideline that it left Carwell with very little room. When Boyette and Namath went down, there wasn't much for Carwell to do but stumble over top of them: the play — and the game — ended with Carwell going down at the New York four-yard line. The Jets had salvaged a tie.

"I don't know who I tackled," Namath said after the game. "All I know is that he tried to run over me. The whole play was ridiculous. It never should have happened."[9] A reporter pointed out to Namath that he saved the Jets a loss with the tackle, but Namath took little satisfaction in it. In fact, he flatly refused any credit. "That didn't save it," he said. "I'm just lucky we didn't lose it. We wouldn't have been in that position if it wasn't for me. Six interceptions ... I was ridiculous."[10]

He only had one TD to go with the six picks, while completing 27 of 49 for 295 yards. The six interceptions were a single-game club record. Actually, it tied the AFL record as well. All six of Namath's interceptions came in the second half, and the Jets had once more squandered a 17–0 lead. But at least the tie allowed them to hang on to first place in the East. There was more good news on the horizon — they would be traveling to Miami to play the Dolphins next. Ah, a vacation in the sun.

Week 6 — Sunday, October 22, 1967
Orange Bowl, Miami (attendance: 30,049)

The near-gale winds in Miami, gusting at 30 mph, might have made the Jets feel that they were at home in Shea. Namath missed on two of his first three passes, but they were his only throws to hit the ground the rest of the first half, as the Jets went on to score on their first four offensive series. After taking a 3–0 lead when Jim Turner kicked a 20-yard field goal to cap their first drive, the Jets then drove 61 yards in eight plays and took a 10–0 lead when Emerson Boozer went in from a yard out. Namath had hit George Sauer with a 31-yard pass in the drive, but he would almost double that in the next series when Sauer beat the coverage and Namath connected with him on a 61-yard touchdown: Sauer raced, untouched, into the end zone with safety Keith Jacquess trailing helplessly behind. The Jets led 17–0 as the first quarter ended.

The second period was less eventful, but the Jets did score another touchdown just 4:49 into the quarter when Namath flipped a two-yard touchdown pass to Boozer. The Dolphins were struggling with Rick Norton at quarterback, not even crossing midfield until halfway through the second period. Even then, they could penetrate no further than the New York 44. The Jets, who would not even punt until the final two minutes of the half, led 24–0 at halftime. But the second half, while not exactly a nail-biter, would tell a somewhat different story. There were a couple reasons in particular.

After throwing two incompletions early, Namath went on to complete his next 12 straight to finish the first half 13 of 15 for 199 yards and two touchdowns. Leading 24–0, there seemed little reason to leave him in, and with backup Mike Taliaferro having just been reactivated from the injured reserve list for the first time since preseason, Ewbank opted to play Taliaferro in the second half.

That accounted for New York's less productive second half, but what accounted for Miami's better performance after the intermission was Bob Griese's relief of Norton. Griese hadn't played since injuring his shoulder against the Jets at Shea three weeks earlier. In the second half Griese was able to move the Miami offense, and the two teams traded scores in both the third and fourth quarters, with Miami getting the better of New York 14–9 in the half.

Miami scored first in the third period when Griese hit Frank Jackson with a nine-yard touchdown pass, but Taliaferro countered with a 20-yard touchdown throw to Maynard. In the fourth, the Jets got a 26-yard field goal from Jim Turner before Miami closed out the scoring when Griese threw six yards to Karl Noonan for a score. The final saw the Jets come away with a 33–14 win that kept them a game ahead of Houston, who had beaten the Kansas City Chiefs 24–19. Other than that, the Eastern Division was a wasteland, Boston at 2–4–1, Buffalo 2–4, and Miami in the cellar at 1–5.

Week 7 — Sunday, October 29, 1967
Shea Stadium, New York (attendance: 62,784)

The Jets returned home to face the 2–4–1 Boston Patriots at Shea. With a 4–1–1 record, the Jets were impressing people, not merely in the AFL, but even in that *other* league. The AFL and NFL had already agreed to a merger, which was to become final in 1970; until then, the Super Bowl had been the big byproduct of the agreement. The First Super Bowl had been played the previous January, with Green Bay winning handily over Kansas City. It seemed to confirm the widely-held opinion that the NFL was still much superior to the AFL, but not everyone — not even everyone in the NFL — held such a view.

Among the 62,784 spectators at Shea as the Jets and Patriots clashed was Ed Franco, a scout for the Green Bay Packers. Why would Green Bay be scouting the Jets (surely he wasn't there to scout the Patriots)? Saying that the AFL was certainly no "Mickey Mouse league," which was the term commonly used by the AFL's detractors, Franco was primarily interested in having a look at Namath, saying that Namath could play quarterback for any team in the NFL.

The Packers were obviously intending to repeat as Super Bowl champs, and they were keeping an eye on the Jets as their next potential opponents. "I think they'd give us one helluva battle," Franco said. "We'd have to contend with Namath and he's good. Real good."[11] Franco was struck by how Namath threw off or on balance with the same results.

Despite their impressing Franco, the Jets got off to a rough start against Boston that day. Gino Cappelletti kicked a 14-yard field goal to put the Patriots up 3–0 in the first quarter, and by the end of the quarter they had increased their lead to 10–0 when John Charles intercepted Namath and ran the ball back 35 yards for a score. Namath had, on the other hand, tied an AFL record when he completed his first three passes, giving him 15 straight completions going back to the previous game, which tied Len Dawson's record set earlier in the season.

The Jets shaved Boston's lead to 10–7 in the second period when Namath flipped a two-yard touchdown pass to Bill Mathis, but Boston bounded back as Cappelletti caught a 16-yard touchdown pass from Babe Parilli to put the Patriots back up by 10. Cappelletti then added a 41-yard field goal, and late in the half the Jets were down 20–7. There were only 30 seconds left in the first half when Emerson Boozer scored on a two-yard run to cut the lead to a more manageable 20–14 at halftime.

The third quarter belonged to the kickers: Jim Turner tied the game with field goals of 14 and 21 yards before Cappelletti put Boston back up 23–20 with a 33-yard kick. But with 1:52 left in the third period, Turner again tied the game, this time hitting from 26 yards.

In the fourth quarter Boston certainly had opportunity. After penalties had pushed the Jets back and forced them to punt from their own two-yard line, the Patriots found themselves starting from midfield, but they could only go backward from there. On first down defensive end Gerry Philbin and linebacker Ralph Baker caught Parilli for a 12-yard loss. On second down, linebacker Larry Grantham dropped fullback Jim Nance for a one-yard loss, and on third down Verlon Biggs took Parilli down for a loss of three yards. A series that had begun at midfield found the Patriots punting from their own 34.

After receiving the punt, the Jets took over on their own 35 with eleven minutes left to play and Namath engineered what would turn out to be the winning drive. The Jets went the 65 yards in seven plays, five of them passes. From the Boston seven-yard line Namath threw across the middle to Pete Lammons, who took a shot from both Chuck Shonta and Leroy Mitchell at the goal line before falling into the end zone. The score put the Jets up 30–23; it was their first lead of the game and it would stick. Following the New York score, there were still some eight minutes left to play, but the Patriots could not cross midfield for the remainder.

The victory pushed the Jets to 5–1–1 and kept them a game ahead of Houston, still nipping at New York's heels with a record of 4–2–1 after beating Buffalo. It was looking like a wise decision on Green Bay's part to send Franco to scout the Jets. Namath was 22 of 43 for 362 yards, two TDs and two interceptions.

Week 8 — Sunday, November 5, 1967
Municipal Stadium, Kansas City (attendance: 46,642)

The defending AFL-champion Kansas City Chiefs had fallen on hard times, dropping back to third place in the Western Division behind Oakland and San Diego. Unfortunately for the Jets, by the time they traveled to Municipal Stadium in Kansas City the Chiefs seemed to have regathered themselves.

Throughout the first half, the teams kept pace with each other, exchanging scores; the Jets received the opening kickoff and drove 72 yards to a 12-yard field goal, but Kansas City answered back minutes later with a 25-yarder by Jan Stenerud to tie the game. The Chiefs then went up 10–3 when they drove 55 yards in four plays and Len Dawson hit Fred Arbanas with a 20-yard touchdown throw just before the end of the quarter. But early in the second period the Jets drove 70 yards in seven plays and tied the game when Namath tossed a four-yard touchdown to Bill Mathis.

There was just a minute left in the half when cornerback Willie Mitchell intercepted Namath to give the Chiefs the ball at their own 36. Dawson quickly moved his team downfield with sideline throws, getting close enough for Stenerud to kick a 32-yard field goal with three seconds left in the second quarter; Kansas City led 13–10 at the half.

The first half may have been close, but the second half would quickly get out of hand. The Chiefs took the second-half kick and went 69 yards to score on a three-yard run by Mike Garrett, who was having a career day rushing. Only 42 seconds later Willie Mitchell intercepted Namath again, this time running it back 27 yards for a score; as fast as that, the Chiefs were up 28–10. Kansas City would add another touchdown before the end of the third period when safety Johnny Robinson recovered a fumble by Pete Lammons at the New York 14-yard line, leading to a scoring pass from Dawson to Otis Taylor. Kansas City had exploded for 22 points in the third quarter, and led 35–10 going into the fourth.

Early in the fourth quarter Namath took the Jets on a 69-yard drive that culminated in a one-yard score by fullback Billy Joe, but dreams of staging a dramatic comeback quickly evaporated when the Chiefs came right back with another touchdown drive of their own to make the final 42–18.

New York mistakes had been costly: Lammons' fumble and two of Namath's three interceptions had all added up to 18 points for Kansas City, but what really did the Jets in that day was their inability to stop Garrett, who racked up 192 yards rushing on 23 carries. "We haven't had anyone run on us like the Chiefs did," said Ewbank. "Garrett's an excellent football player. We couldn't stop him, that's all."[12]

Mitchell also had a fine day. It was Mitchell who had been burned by Max McGee for seven catches and two touchdowns the previous January in the Super Bowl, and since then he hadn't been able to live it down. "It's amusing how the opposition tries to pick on Willie when he is as fine a cornerback as there is in the league," said Kansas City coach Hank Stram.[13]

For the Jets it was more than a loss: it was a loss with losses. The New York running game was already severely hamstrung by the absence of Matt Snell: late in the game the Jets lost Emerson Boozer as well when he took a low tackle that tore ligaments in his knee. He would go in for surgery the following day and would miss the rest of the season. Boozer was leading the league in TDs with 13 and was well on his way to setting a new AFL record for touchdowns in a season. His absence would certainly be felt. Basically, it left the Jets with no real ground attack. Snell was due back soon, but whether or not he would be in top form so soon was doubtful. The Jets' opponents could thereafter key almost exclusively on the pass.

The only good news for the Jets was that Boston had managed to beat Houston. That meant that, even with the loss to Kansas City, the Jets stayed a game ahead of the Oilers nonetheless and retained first place in the East. Namath was 20 of 40 for 245 yards against Kansas City, with one TD and three interceptions.

Week 9 — Sunday, November 12, 1967
Shea Stadium, New York (attendance: 62,671)

The Jets' week nine opponents, the Buffalo Bills, may have come into Shea with only a 3–5 record, but having blown a 17-point fourth-quarter lead against them on opening day, the Jets knew better than to take them lightly. The Jets took a 3–0 lead 3:40 into the game on a 48-yard field goal by Jim Turner and then increased their lead to 10–0 four minutes later when Namath threw a 47-yard touchdown to George Sauer. It was an excellent play by Sauer, who had to cut inside his defender to jump and make the catch, and then cut back outside again to get into the end zone after his defender had adjusted.

The Jets carried that lead into the second period, but a very sloppy performance then allowed Buffalo to pull even with them. The Bills went 74 yards in 12 plays to score a touchdown in a drive kept alive by not one, but two roughing the punter penalties. Keith Lincoln would eventually run it in from two-yards out to cut the Jets' lead to 10–7. A 17-yard Buffalo field goal later in the period evened the score at 10.

Jim Turner put the Jets back up 13–10 at 6:13 of the third quarter with a 14-yard field goal, but otherwise had a 29-yard attempt blocked in the third, and would also miss a 26-yarder in the fourth as the New York offense struggled.

Trailing by just three points in the fourth quarter, Buffalo had plenty opportunity to win the game. After driving to the New York 30-yard line, the Bills failed to convert a third-and-10 play when Jack Kemp threw to receiver Elbert Dubenion at the 15 only to have cornerback Johnny Sample jar the ball loose with a good shot. On fourth down, Mike Mercer then missed a 36-yard field goal attempt.

On Buffalo's next offensive series Kemp tried to hit Bobby Burnett across the middle, but the ball went off Burnett's shoulder and was tipped up into the air by linebacker Ralph Baker. It came back down into the waiting hands of Sample, who made a very determined 41-yard runback for a touchdown that gave the Jets a more comfortable 10-point lead with 9:52 remaining in the game.

Even then opportunity presented itself to Buffalo: Tom Janik intercepted Namath at the Buffalo 31 and returned the ball 30 yards to the New York 39. The Bills would soon find themselves with a first-and-goal at the New York four-yard line, but when a run by Lincoln yielded no gain, Kemp threw three straight incompletions and Buffalo turned the ball over on downs. Ultimately, the Jets would win 20–10.

With Houston barely managing to beat the 1–9 Denver Broncos, 20–18, the Jets again clung to their one-game lead in the Eastern Division. Matt Snell had returned to play for the Jets, but saw limited action. As for Namath's performance, he hit only 13 of 37 passes, but threw for an impressive 338 yards. He had two interceptions to go with his one touchdown.

Week 10 — Sunday, November 19, 1967
Fenway Park, Boston (attendance: 26,790)

The Jets entered the tenth week of their season ranked number two in both offense (behind San Diego) and defense (behind Oakland), but still held only a tenuous one-game lead over Houston, who rated no better than eighth in offense and fifth in defense. Even the Jets' week 10 opponents, the Boston Patriots, with a 3–6–1 record and out of contention, could stand up to that (fifth in offense; sixth in defense).

Matt Snell had returned from his opening day injury and subsequent surgery, and while he had seen only limited action the prior week against Buffalo, the plan was to get him in early against the Patriots at Fenway. Another positive for the Jets was the fact that two of Boston's defensive front four — right side defensive end Larry Eisenhauer and right side tackle Houston Antwine — were out with injuries.

While the Jets would score early, taking the opening kickoff and driving to a 40-yard field goal, those three points would be all the scoring the opening period would see. The second period, on the other hand, got off to a very quick start. As the first quarter came to an end, Johnny Sample intercepted Boston quarterback Don Trull — a midseason acquisition from Houston — and returned the ball to the Boston 45. Namath then began the second quarter by throwing a 45-yard touchdown strike to George Sauer to put the Jets up 10–0. Boston did answer with a drive that produced a 14-yard field goal, but the Jets then shot back with a 75-yard drive that ended with a three-yard touchdown run by Bill Mathis.

Leading 16–3 just before halftime, the Jets missed an opportunity to build on that lead when Namath lost track of the situation. New York was on the Boston three-yard line with just 30 seconds left in the half, and Namath inquired as to the down: he was informed by an official that it was fourth down. Namath then let the clock run down to seven seconds before calling a timeout, only to find out it was third down. Angry over the misinformation from the officials, Namath went ahead and ran one last play — he was intercepted.

With their 16–3 lead, the Jets played conservatively in the third quarter, keeping the ball on the ground despite having once more lost Snell, who had suffered a concussion in the first quarter. They managed to increase their lead to 23–3 when Billy Joe scored on a four-yard run, and that's how it stood after three quarters. Then came the weird and wonderful fourth quarter.

The Jets' lead reached a more than comfortable 29–3 when Namath lofted a beautiful 75-yard bomb to Don Maynard, but curiously, that score seemed to stir Boston, Trull in particular. After receiving the kick, Boston took over on their own 30-yard line and proceeded to drive 70 yards for a touchdown, which Trull ran in himself. Still, at 29–10, the Jets' lead seemed safe. But when New York failed to move the ball on their next series and punted, Trull, scrambling frantically, again drove the Patriots downfield, once more running the ball into the end zone himself. The Patriots had now scored twice in five minutes to cut the Jets' lead to 29–17 with under two minutes to play.

With time an obvious and major factor, Boston tried an onside kick, which Billy Johnson recovered for the Patriots at the New York 40. Trull then threw down the center of the field to Jim Whalen, who caught the ball at the five-yard line and took it into the end zone. The score was now 29–24 with just 1:06 remaining.

The fans at Fenway were roaring with glee as the Patriots gave it one last shot with another onside kick. It was close, but they just missed recovering it: the Jets took possession and were able to run out the clock.

After the game, Boston coach Mike Holovak was giddy over Trull's fourth-quarter heroics. The Jets, on the other hand, were understandably subdued and dismissive of championship talk. The victory lifted the Jets to 7–2–1, and they were therefore guaranteed of the first winning season in franchise history. Namath again had an impressive yardage total, throwing for 297 yards while hitting 15 of 23, with two TDs and one interception. But when reporters turned the subject to the division title and AFL championship, neither Ewbank nor Namath would take the bait. "We're not even thinking about the championship," Ewbank said. "We still have some rough games left."[14]

"Man, we got a lot of playing to do yet before we make it," Namath said. "We gotta face K.C. and San Diego before we can even think of winning the Eastern Division."[15] And Denver. Oh, hell, don't look past the lowly Broncos that easily.

Week 11 — Sunday, December 3, 1967
Shea Stadium, New York (attendance: 61,615)

New York had a week off after the Boston game. The Patriots had come on strong in the fourth quarter against the Jets, and the Jets may therefore have expected them to make a better showing against Houston the following week; the Patriots did the Jets no favor, however, when they were routed by the Oilers 27–6. When the Jets did get back to work the following Sunday, it was a wet, dreary December day at Shea. More than 61,000 tickets had been sold, but only 32,903 bothered to show up in the rain.

The Jets' opponents, the Denver Broncos, appeared to be an easy mark at 2–10, but weather can sometimes be the great equalizer, and they were about to play a mud bowl at Shea. The first quarter was sloppy and fairly uneventful, but the second quarter would likely have filled most of Denver's highlight reel for the season. For the Jets the trouble began early in the quarter when Namath was intercepted by rookie safety Jack Lentz, who returned the ball 25 yards to set up a 43-yard field goal that gave the Broncos a 3–0 lead 3:26 into the second period.

The Jets got the ball back and just two plays later Lentz intercepted Namath again, this time running it back 47 yards to the New York two-yard line. That was good enough to set up a touchdown run by Bo Hickey that gave Denver a 9–0 lead 4:38 into the quarter (the extra point failed).

The Jets managed to avoid being intercepted on their next offensive series, but the ensuing punt was every bit as costly as Floyd Little ran it back 72 yards for a touchdown and a 16–0 Denver lead with 8:51 left in the half.

On the Jets' next series Namath was intercepted at the Denver 23 by cornerback Goldie Sellers, who returned the ball 47 yards to the New York 30. The Broncos went up 23–0 five plays later when Steve Tensi threw a 10-yard touchdown pass to Al Denson with 4:28 left in the half.

When linebacker John Huard intercepted Namath on the Jets' next series, it led to a 47-

yard field goal and a 26–0 Denver lead with 1:06 left in the half. Hoping to stanch the blood flow, Ewbank benched Namath and sent Mike Taliaferro in at quarterback — Taliaferro was intercepted by linebacker Frank Richter at the Denver four-yard line on the last play of the first half.

The Jets had given a thoroughly obnoxious performance in the second quarter. Of their six offensive possessions, five had resulted in interceptions, while the sixth resulted in a punt that had been run back for a touchdown. Ewbank had pulled Namath after he had played a thoroughly awful second quarter, but if the Jets were going to have a prayer of coming back in the second half, Ewbank knew that there was no question but that Namath would have to be back in the game. With Namath, the Jets always had the capacity to strike quickly.

But Namath's reentry in the third quarter notwithstanding, the Jets seemed in no apparent rush to get back in the game, although they did manage to get on the board with a 39-yard field goal. Mistakes continued to sabotage their efforts, however: Bill Baird fumbled a punt, which was recovered by Denver's Larry Kaminski at the New York 12-yard line. Two plays later Wendell Hayes scored from five yards out to put Denver up 33–3 with 3:23 left in the third period. Mercifully, the Denver scoring ended there.

In the fourth quarter the Jets began to do the things they had been expected to do all along. Namath hit Pete Lammons and Mark Smolinski each with 18-yard scoring passes and threw a five-yard touchdown toss to Bill Mathis, cutting the Denver lead to nine points, but by then it was just too late.

Closing out their season with games against Kansas City, Oakland, and San Diego — the three best teams in the AFL — the Jets could scarcely afford losing to a team like Denver, who they should have beaten easily. To make matters worse, Houston had beaten Miami, and the Jets now found themselves in a first-place tie with the Oilers.

The New York locker room was funereal after the game. "No one had anything to do with this [loss] but me," Namath said. "I fouled up."[16] Namath finished the day 24 of 60 for 292 yards, three touchdowns, and four interceptions.

Week 12 — Sunday, December 10, 1967
Shea Stadium, New York (attendance: 62,891)

The New York running game was in bad shape. Matt Snell may have been back, but it was obvious that he was off his game. Billy Joe had been acquired to take up some of the slack, but he was now nursing sore ribs. It was a definite sign of desperation when the Jets picked up Abner Haynes, who had been waived by Miami. When you start bringing in castoffs from 2–9 teams, you know you've got problems.

Kansas City came to Shea Stadium during the twelfth week of the Jets' season, and both teams kept the ball on the ground for almost the entire first half. Namath threw only six passes in the half while Len Dawson threw 13; between them, there were only 10 first-half pass completions. The decision made sense from Kansas City's perspective; when the two teams had met in Kansas City a month earlier Mike Garrett had a career day, running for 192 yards. Although Garrett would not have appreciable success at Shea, there is at least a rationale for the tendency by the Chiefs to build their game plan around the run.

The decision by the Jets to do the same was bewildering because the Jets had no real ground game, and hadn't since Snell went down in week one. Even when Emerson Boozer was healthy and in the lineup he was not consistently reliable. Part of the reason for the Jets sticking with the run against Kansas City probably had much to do with the tenacious pass rush that Namath was facing. "Our front four put as much pressure on Namath today as we have on anybody all year," Kansas City coach Hank Stram said afterward.[17] They were blitzing as well, so Namath tried to cross the Kansas City defense up with more running plays, but that strategy wasn't going anywhere. The game was still scoreless at halftime.

Kansas City bounded out of the locker room for the second half with more spring in their step, receiving the kick and marching downfield in 11 plays for the game's first points. Dawson was passing more liberally then, throwing to Garrett for 10 and then 26 yards, and hitting Otis Taylor for 20 more; the Chiefs soon found themselves with a fourth-and-goal at the Jets' one-yard line. Initially thinking that the ball was on the four-yard line, Stram sent the field goal team onto the field, but when the offensive unit refused to yield, the Chiefs called a timeout and someone clued Stram in. Stram later confessed to not having been aware of exactly where the ball was, saying that he had been misled by the scoreboard, which he said was still listing the line of scrimmage as being at the four-yard line. After their timeout, Curtis McClinton ran the ball in for the score and a 7–0 lead 6:33 into the half.

It was now time for the Jets' philanthropic bent to take over, and just three plays later they handed the ball back to Kansas City when Bobby Bell forced Snell to cough it up and Bud Abell recovered for the Chiefs at the New York 35. Five plays later Dawson threw 11 yards to Chris Burford for a score, and Kansas City led 14–0 with 4:27 to play in the third quarter.

In the fourth quarter another giveaway seemed to nail it down for Kansas City as Namath was intercepted by Fred Williamson, who ran it back 77 yards for a score with just over nine minutes left in the game. Namath then drove the Jets 80 yards in 10 plays (completing seven straight passes) for their only score, a one-yard run by Mark Smolinski, but all that did was prevent the humiliation of a shutout. Namath finished 14 of 25 for 133 yards, with two interceptions.

Fortunately for the Jets, Houston had been beaten by Oakland that day, so at 7–4–1 the Jets remained tied with the Oilers for the lead in the East. As for the Haynes acquisition, well, that didn't pan out very well. Late in the game Namath handed off to Haynes, who ran into immediate trouble when six-foot-seven Buck Buchanan met him in the backfield. Haynes panicked, turned and pitched the ball back to Namath, who did a creditable job of dodging a couple of tackles and holding the play to a three-yard loss. Ewbank was incredulous at Haynes' poor judgment (to put it kindly) in putting Namath right in harm's way by flipping him the ball with a wall of giant tacklers bearing down. Needless to say, Haynes' days in New York were numbered.

Week 13 — Sunday, December 17, 1967
Alameda County Coliseum, Oakland (attendance: 53,011)

Since losing to the Jets at Shea back in October, the Oakland Raiders had gone on an eight-game winning streak. With that loss to the Jets being the only blemish on their record, the Raiders were anxious to make amends and were therefore most pleased to have the Jets coming to town. The Oakland defense always looked forward to a game with the Jets, but the Raider offense was also wanting another shot at New York. In particular, quarterback Daryle Lamonica had experienced a rough night against the Jets in New York, and he very much wanted to redeem himself.

Namath had made no secret of his feelings about the Oakland defense when he publicly accused them of dirty play in the week before the Jets put Oakland down at Shea, and for some reason the Raiders, who always seemed proud of their cheap-shot reputation, took offense. Likely they were more soured by having been beaten. "I don't know what he means by that," said Ben Davidson in reference to Namath's remarks about Oakland's proclivity for late hits.[18] The hits would be cheaper and later this time around; so much so that even the officials would notice a couple of them.

There was no real doubt that Oakland was the top team in the AFL. At 11–1, they had the league's top-rated offense *and* defense. The Jets, meanwhile, were on a skid, wasting the good fortunes of the first half of the season with a plethora of mistakes: they were really giving games away. The Jets needed the game badly; Houston had beaten San Diego the day before, so the Jets needed to beat Oakland to keep their first-place tie with the Oilers. There was also the fact that, while the Jets would be closing out their schedule against the Chargers in San Diego, the Oilers drew Miami as their week 14 opponent. The deck was definitely stacked in Houston's favor.

In the first quarter the Jets got out in front of the Raiders 7–0 with a 28-yard strike from Namath to Maynard, but Oakland came right back downfield on their next offensive series and cut the lead to 7–3 with a 36-yard field goal. Oakland then managed to get out in front in the second quarter on a drive that saw two passes cover 90 yards. From the eight-yard line Lamonica threw 22 yards to Fred Biletnikoff, who proceeded to run another 50 yards to the New York 20 to complete a 72-yard catch and run. Shortly thereafter, Lamonica threw 18 yards to Warren Wells for a score, and Oakland led 10–7.

But the Jets would come back to recapture the lead before the half was up. It was almost a classic New York Jets blunder, as Matt Snell, trying to dive over to score from the one-yard line, lost the ball. Snell looked to be going over for the score when linebacker Dan Conners punched the ball loose. Defensive back Warren Powers made an attempt to grab it but only managed to slap the ball into the New York backfield. Namath, who had been somewhat casually watching the play after handing off to Snell, suddenly saw the ball fall at his feet: he sprang into action, scooping up the ball, darting to his right, and diving headfirst into the end zone to score. The Jets led 14–10 at the half.

The second half would be a farce. In the third quarter the Raiders dropped Namath for the only time in the game when tackle Tom Keating took him down for a 14-yard loss. But although they hadn't been able to get him down, they had put constant pressure on Namath, hurrying his throws and getting in their shots — some later than others — after he threw the ball. Early in the third quarter, Ike Lassiter came barreling in on Namath like a runaway freight train. Namath got the throw away, but it was costly. The pass was intercepted by linebacker J.R. Williamson deep in New York territory, but more than that, the force of Lassiter's shot to Namath's head had fractured his cheekbone. After that, Oakland went on a 21-point spree. In the third quarter, Lamonica threw a four-yard touchdown to Pete Banaszak and a 47-yarder to Billy Cannon to put the Raiders up 24–14.

The fourth quarter was equal parts football game and gang war. The Jets had an opportunity to cut the Oakland lead to three-points when they drove down to within a half-yard of the Raiders' goal line, but on fourth-and-goal, rather than kick a field goal to cut the lead to seven, the Jets went for it. It was a gutsy call, a call that would have made Bear Bryant proud — it was the right call. Matt Snell didn't make it: the Raiders took over a foot from their own goal. To add insult to injury, Oakland then drove the length of the field to score again. The big play in the Oakland drive was a 72-yard throw to Banaszak. Roger Hagberg would run it in from six yards out to give the Raiders a commanding 31–14 lead.

Despite their lead, the Oakland defensive front four seemed utterly exasperated at having only dropped Namath once. They would complain afterward that the New York line was holding on almost every play, but the officials were not calling it. The frustration eventually erupted for Davidson when he chased Namath out of the pocket and gave him a blow to the head — a very late blow to the head — that sent Namath's helmet flying and left him wobbly and struggling to find his bearings when he got back up. *That one got flagged.* It was one of two roughing the passer calls on the Raiders in the game.

Despite having had his cheekbone broken and been knocked silly, Namath played on, fighting to bring his team back. He hit George Sauer with a 24-yard touchdown pass to shave the lead back to 10 points at 31–21, but a 34-yard run by Banaszak set up a three-yard touchdown run by Hewritt Dixon that again put Oakland up by 17. Namath would throw a five-yard touchdown to Maynard and a two-point conversion to Bill Mathis to make the final 38–29, Oakland.

The loss was a major setback to the Jets' hopes of winning the Eastern Division: not only would the Jets have to beat San Diego, who held second place in the West, but they would also have to hope for last-place Miami to beat Houston. After the game, Ewbank was not bashful in his criticism of the officiating. "I feel we were at a disadvantage after the kickoff," he said. "I hope we never have these officials again."[19]

Namath had completed 27 of 46 for 370 yards (three TDs and three picks), giving him 3,664 yards for the season — a new AFL record — but it was Namath's face that drew most of the attention in the locker room. It was announced that he would have X-rays the following day, but the reporters wanted to know when it happened and who delivered the blow. Many of them assumed that Davidson's late hit was the shot that did it, but Namath wouldn't confirm anything, not even having been injured in the game. He coyly told reporters he had hurt himself earlier in the day gnawing on a tough steak. But surely, everyone wanted to know, the Raiders had given him some horrendous shots. Namath put an ice bag to his face and smiled. "I've been hurt worse," he said.[20]

Week 14 — Sunday, December 24, 1967
San Diego Stadium, San Diego (attendance: 34,580)

The Jets' fate for 1967 had already been determined before they took the field for their final game of the season. They had needed Miami to pull an upset of Houston, but the day before New York faced the Chargers in San Diego, the Oilers had throttled the Dolphins, 41–10. The Oilers felt compelled to rub salt in the wound by sending the Jets a snotty telegram informing the Jets that they had saved second place for them.

With the division title no longer on the line, Ewbank thought he'd have Namath sit out the last game, what with his fractured cheekbone and all, but Namath wouldn't hear of it. Having broken Babe Parilli's 1964 single-season passing record of 3,465 yards the week before, Namath took the field in San Diego wearing a special facemask for added protection and proceeded to make still more history.

Like the Jets, the Chargers had been in a late-season freefall, having lost three straight. But unlike the Jets, who had been in first place all year before finally tumbling from the top, San Diego had spent the season chasing Oakland. On this final Sunday of the regular season, the Chargers' collapse would be complete.

The Chargers did come out looking inspired, taking a 7–0 lead only 1:24 into the game when John Hadl threw a 72-yard touchdown pass to Willie Frazier. The Jets shot back soon enough with a 13-yard scoring pass from Namath to Maynard to even the score, and when Bill Baird intercepted Hadl to give the Jets the ball at the San Diego 39, Bill Mathis scored soon afterward on a one-yard run to give the Jets a 14–7 lead at the end of the first quarter.

But running back Brad Hubbert got San Diego right back in it in the second quarter when he ran a sweep around right end and took it 46 yards for a score. After the Jets failed to move the ball, the Chargers took possession on their own 20, and Hubbert ran a sweep off the right end again — this time for an 80-yard scoring run that put San Diego up 21–14. Hubbert was on his way to a career day.

The teams were exchanging scores on almost every possession, and Namath tied the game again with a 36-yard touchdown pass to George Sauer only to see San Diego go back on top with a 13-yard field goal. The half ended with the Jets managing to get back out in front when Namath threw a 26-yard touchdown to Maynard to make it 28–24 at the break.

The pace would fall off in the second half, but the Jets took a commanding 42–24 lead in the third quarter with another one-yard touchdown run by Mathis and yet another Namath-to-Maynard touchdown throw, this one of 36 yards. The only score after that was a very late San Diego touchdown when backup quarterback Kay Stephenson hit Jacque MacKinnon with an eight-yard touchdown throw with just over two minutes left in the game: that made the final 42–31.

Both teams finished the season 8–5–1, but whereas the Jets could at least take some satisfaction in having just completed their first-ever winning season, the Chargers would have the bitter taste of having lost their last four games after having been 8–1–1. In their final four games, San Diego had been outscored by a combined total of 148–83: it made the Jets' fall look somewhat less absurd. And as for the Houston Oilers, well, they proved a less-than-formidable opponent for the Oakland Raiders in the AFL championship game — certainly far less worthy an opponent than the Jets had been. The Raiders beat the Oilers 40–7 in the championship to earn the right to go to the Super Bowl. Of course, we all know how that came out. Before having their asses handed to them by Green Bay in the Super Bowl, the Raiders had lost only once all season — to the Jets.

As for Namath's performance against San Diego, he set another record, passing Sonny Jurgenson's NFL record of 3,746 yards in a season, a record that Jurgenson had set just a week before. Namath had completed 18 of 26 passes for 343 yards and four touchdowns against San Diego (no interceptions). That put his yardage for the season at 4,007. Nobody had ever thrown for 4,000 in a season. It would be years before anyone would again.

Although the Jets had just accomplished the first winning season in franchise history, it seemed nobody in the organization was pleased. The late-season collapse, the failure to win the division — it all made the accomplishment ring hollow. The players voted Maynard the team's MVP of the season, which gave some of the owners further pause for thought. They were paying Namath pretty well to get the team to a championship, and not only had they failed to win their division once in Namath's three years, but his teammates had never even considered Namath worthy of MVP in that time.

But Namath had a good season, over all. He finished tops in most passing categories in the AFL, including passing attempts, completions, yardage, yards-per-attempt and … interceptions. Namath had thrown 28 interceptions in 1967, fairly well ahead of any other quarterback in the league, but he had also thrown a good many more passes than the others. As far as his interception percentage, well, at 5.7 it was still lower than some and more-or-less comparable to others. It's just a simple matter of arithmetic — more passes means more interceptions. As for touchdowns, only Daryle Lamonica threw more in the AFL in 1967 (30 to Namath's 26), and Namath's yards-per-passing-attempt, at 8.2, was far ahead of everyone else (John Hadl was closest to him with 7.9). On the other hand, when Namath was off, it cost his team badly. The loss to Denver at Shea, the tie with Houston — both were largely attributable to Namath's interceptions.

In January Namath made the trip to Jacksonville, Florida, for the AFL All-Star game. The league had gone back to the traditional East-West format rather than continue with the format adopted in 1965 wherein the All-Stars would play the AFL champions. It was a record AFL All-Star crowd of 38,500 who turned out at the Gator Bowl, and they were all there to see the man who threw for over 4,000 yards that season. Namath gave them a show. The fans were anticipating another Namath-Lamonica duel, and while it may have been slow to materialize, they eventually got what they expected.

Lamonica got the West out to a 21–13 halftime lead before giving way to Len Dawson in the second half. Lamonica had thrown a nine-yard touchdown pass to Lance Alworth and a three-yard score to Willie Frazier (obviously liking the San Diego receivers that afternoon), and after San Diego's Les Duncan had fumbled a punt that led to a 10-yard field goal by the East that opened the game's scoring, Duncan made amends by returning the ensuing kickoff 90 yards for a touchdown.

Namath was rather enjoying his own receivers, hitting Pete Lammons with a 35-yard touchdown in the first half, and then hitting Don Maynard with a 24-yard scoring pass in the fourth quarter that cut the West's lead to 24–19. With time winding down, Namath took the Eastern team downfield to the one-yard line, and then, with 58 seconds left in the game, it was Namath himself who took it in for the score and a 25–24 victory. The winners got $1,000 each, the losers, $400.

Namath had completed 16 of 38 for 249 yards with two touchdowns and … three interceptions. Miami's Bob Griese had come into the game for the East team long enough to complete two of eight passes for 32 yards with one interception. Maynard, who shared offensive MVP honors with Namath, caught nine passes for 128 yards and a TD, while Lammons caught three passes for 48 yards and a touchdown.

With 1967 behind them, the New York Jets now finally knew what it felt like to have a winning season. The problem was, it didn't feel good enough. The Jets felt that they were more than just a good team: they felt they were champions. They felt that they could win it all. They *should have* won it all.

5

The 1968 Season

It would prove to be a very eventful off-season for the Jets. For starters, in March Namath was going in for knee surgery again. There was a twist: this time it was for his left knee — the *good* one! Fortunately, it was only to repair a minor tendon tear, and it was easily the least serious of Namath's surgeries.

Otherwise, there was a fair amount of upheaval within the organization following the 1967 season. Despite the team's winning season, Werblin's partners were not a happy group. They were wondering why, with all the money they had spent, the team had been unable to win the division, particularly with the East being so weak (of the division's five teams, only the Jets and Oilers had posted winning records; Buffalo and Miami had both finished 4–10, while Boston was 3–10–1), and the Jets having led all season before folding in the stretch.

But there was more to it than that. The other owners had made Werblin president of the club, and initially they were content to sit in the owner's box enjoying a free lunch and a football game while Werblin tended to the details. These were, after all, men with businesses of their own to look after (Werblin had given up his position at MCA). For them, the New York Jets had been a hobby: for Werblin it had been a passion.

Somewhere along the way it became more than a matter of impatience among the owners, and resentments of a more personal nature began to surface. The others began to take offense at how the Jets were frequently referred to as Werblin's team, even by Werblin himself. They had been made to feel like mere stockholders rather than partners. "Sonny did a great job," one of the owners was anonymously quoted as saying, "but there had been a lack of communication with the rest of us."[1] Werblin, on the other hand, took issue with the fact that his partners suddenly wanted a more active role in running the team, whereas they had all been more than willing to let him look after things when the team was losing games and losing money.

Donald Lillis was reported to be looking to sell his share of the team, and he wondered publicly how it was that a team's star quarterback could throw for an unprecedented 4,007 yards in a season and still have no more esteem among his teammates than to rate sixth or seventh in the club's MVP balloting. And there was more to suggest that things were amiss: when Werblin hired Ewbank he had told him that he wanted it to be Ewbank's last coaching job, obviously suggesting that the position was Ewbank's until he decided to retire. Now Werblin was fielding questions about the possibility of a coaching change, which he was noticeably not ruling out, telling reporters that he had not come to a decision and would not do so until after the college draft when he had more time to see who might be available.

At a meeting of the owners in January of 1968, Lillis told Werblin that he wanted out. Phil Iselin, Leon Hess, and Townsend Martin followed Lillis' lead, each also offering to sell out to Werblin, but their price was too high. They then offered to buy Werblin out, but their price was too low.

As for Namath, his contract was up, and after recovering from his surgery he met with

Werblin in Miami in May and they agreed to terms on a new deal: bigger salary, bigger bonus — Namath signed. Although he declined to say how much the deal was for, Namath did tell the press that he was pleased with the new contract. "I think the Jets are happy also," he added.[2] The lack of fanfare and publicity to accompany the new deal was indicative that something was about to break. It was not like Showbiz Sonny to sign a big money contract without the attendant hoopla, but the truth is that the deal was put together in haste. There was a reason for that. The rumor was that the deal between Namath and the Jets had been made secretly by Werblin well in advance. It was also apparently made without the knowledge of Werblin's partners, which seems to have been the breaking point.

Within days of the announcement that Namath had signed a new contract, it was announced that Werblin had sold his share of the team to his partners. Werblin's price was reported to be $1,600,000, a $1.4 million profit on his original $200,000 investment. "I was disappointed," said Namath when asked about Werblin's departure. "We had much more than an owner-player relationship. He provided personal guidance. He told me what to do and what not to do. I don't do a thing without talking to him first, and I hope it'll stay that way. I'll miss him around the team."[3]

After selling his share of the team, Werblin had been trying to reach Namath to deliver the news personally. "He'll still come to me with problems," Werblin said of Namath. "I believe he's genuinely fond of me and my wife, just as I got to like him when I practically lived with him for three weeks the first time I signed him."[4]

With Werblin out, there were significant changes. Lillis retired from the Wall Street brokerage firm and assumed the presidency of the club, and Ewbank found himself with a much freer hand in running things. Whatever the situation with the coaches and owners, the players were determined that it wouldn't interfere with the job they had to do. There was a feeling among them that this would be a championship team irrespective of whatever turmoil might be brewing upstairs. The players had all been frustrated at the end of the 1967 season; they knew they had the makings of a championship team, if they could only stay focused — and healthy enough — to accomplish it. Linebacker Larry Grantham said that if the Jets didn't seize the moment and win it all in 1968, then it wasn't going to happen, and the players let Namath know that it was up to him to take them there.[5]

It was good that the players were determined not to be knocked off track by all of the outside noise, for it could have been very distracting had they allowed room for it. Werblin had been a presence — at practices, in the locker room — and his absence was noticeable, more for some players than for others. Lillis, on the other hand, made it clear from the start that he had no intention of fraternizing with the players or spending time in the locker room. Even if he had, the players would have scarcely had time to get used to him: Lillis died suddenly of a heart attack just two months after assuming the presidency of the club. The job then passed to Phil Iselin. Like Lillis, Iselin let Ewbank know that there would be no interference from upstairs — the team was Ewbank's to run.

One of Ewbank's first actions once he had the authority was to relocate the team's training camp. Werblin had always arranged for the team to hold camp at Peekskill Military Academy. His son attended the school, so perhaps Werblin had a sentimental attachment to the place, but whatever his reasons, the players did not share in his enthusiasm. The dorms, the showers, the food — nothing at Peekskill was to the liking of the players, who griped incessantly during camp. The players were very pleased when Ewbank announced that the team would be holding camp at Hofstra University in Hempstead, New York. It made a big difference: instead of spending every day and night bemoaning the conditions at camp, Maynard recalled the players began talking about important things like football, for instance. Maynard would also recall that without the pressure of having Werblin looking over his shoulder, Ewbank's relationship with the players took a different tone: there was something more respectful in the way he dealt with them.[6]

Aside from the revolving door presidency, there were personnel changes closer to home for the players to get used to. Back-up quarterback Mike Taliaferro was not satisfied with remaining second-string. He was young and capable and wanted a chance to play while he was in his prime, but with Namath ahead of him it didn't seem likely that he'd ever get much chance. Taliaferro asked Ewbank to make a deal and send him somewhere he could play. Ewbank understood, and he made a straight-up trade in July with Boston — Taliaferro for 38-year-old Babe Parilli. When Parilli got to Hofstra he let it be known that, with 14 years under his belt, he wasn't ready to fall back to second-string, and he fully intended to compete for the job of starting quarterback.

Parilli hadn't been happy about the trade. Having spent seven years in Boston, he had put down roots there beyond football, including a number of businesses, and the trade was therefore inconvenient as well as insulting. But Parilli said that the one thing that helped him decide whether or not to make the trip to Hofstra was that he saw the Jets as a serious contender for the AFL title.

The player who wound up being happiest about Parilli's joining the team was kicker Jim Turner. Parilli took over for Jim Hudson as Turner's holder on field goals and extra points, and Turner later proclaimed Parilli to be the best holder in football. Parilli moved his placement on field goals up just a couple of inches, which apparently made quite a difference as it consistently made the snap from center arrive with the laces facing toward the goalposts, eliminating delays in placing the ball or the need for Turner to kick at the laces.

But other than Turner, nobody was more pleased than Namath with the acquisition of Parilli. Both Namath and Parilli were from western Pennsylvania, and Namath remembered walking by the local Army-Navy store in Beaver Falls when he was a schoolboy and seeing the display window full of Babe Parilli football helmets. There was more than geography to link them: both of them had been coached by Bear Bryant, Parilli at Kentucky, Namath at Alabama. With all of that in mind, someone asked Namath if Parilli had been his boyhood hero. "My boyhood idol was Roberto Clemente," Namath responded with that sheepish smile. But Namath seemed genuinely pleased to welcome Parilli to the team. "Maybe Weeb can use him when I'm throwing six interceptions," he said.[7] Again, the smile.

There would be other personnel changes as camp progressed. There always is. Offensive lineman Sherman Plunkett was released and Bob Talamini was brought in. Talamini had played with the Houston Oilers from the very beginning in 1960, but retired after the 1967 season when the team would not renegotiate his contract. The Jets talked him out of retirement.

The Jets' first preseason game was scheduled for August 12 against the Oilers in the Houston Astrodome, that grotesque monstrosity that announced the unimaginative era of modern sports complexes. It was a gargantuan edifice of feces that brought to fruition the concept of arena football. It would soon enough be followed by other cavernous, carpeted arenas wherein the only hint of creativity was in the number of luxury boxes that could be squeezed in, and where.

The season had not yet begun, but with the first exhibition game the drama was already kicking into overdrive. Days before the game, Namath told Ewbank that he was experiencing pain in his left knee and that he intended to sit out the game. It was, after all, merely an exhibition and didn't seem worth the risk. Ewbank failed to inform anyone of Namath's decision not to play. With Namath coming to town, ticket sales were brisk, and announcing that the league's biggest star would not be playing wouldn't benefit anybody's purse. On game day, nobody but Ewbank seemed to know that Namath had decided not to play, and Ewbank still wasn't telling anyone. Even Namath's teammates assumed that he would play when he attended practice at the Astrodome earlier in the day. Come game time Ewbank asked Namath to suit up despite his intention not to play: Namath refused. There were more than 40,000 unhappy people in the arena that night when it was announced that Namath would not be playing. They registered their displeasure loudly, booing and taunting Namath boisterously all night as he manned the sideline phone in a double-breasted, pinstriped blue blazer.

The Oilers won the game, 28–14. After the game Namath told reporters that the plain truth was that he hadn't played because his knee was sore, but of course when it came to Namath and the media, nothing was ever that simple. On WOR-TV's broadcast of the game, Dick Young announced that he had heard (from who?) that Werblin had agreed to pay Namath $3,000 per exhibition rather than the league standard $250, but that with Werblin's departure the club was now refusing to honor the agreement, prompting Namath's refusal to suit up and play. There seemed to be nothing much to substantiate the rumor — "The way I had it," was Young's wording, without saying who it had come from[8] — and everyone from Namath to Werblin to Iselin would deny knowledge of any such arrangement. When asked about the alleged agreement, Iselin said that was the first he'd ever heard of it. In reality, there was no evidence of financial haggling between Namath and the franchise over exhibition pay.

Young was correct, however, in pointing out the power struggle at play. With Werblin around, Namath did indeed get preferential treatment. He always would, even with Werblin out of the picture, but the difference now was that Namath had an accountability to Ewbank that he hadn't before, and he was rebelling. The $3,000 was a canard: it would have been unlike Werblin to agree to such a thing without making it official and putting it in writing, particularly when he had signed a new deal with Namath at a time when he in all likelihood knew he would be stepping down as president and selling his share of the team.

What was significant was the underlying tussle beneath the silly arguing over whether or not to suit up for the game. Ewbank maintained that, even if Namath wasn't going to play, suiting up would still show some unity with his teammates, a point that Namath dismissed as frivolous. What was really at stake was who was boss, and with Werblin gone was Namath answerable to anyone anymore? It had to be considered that there was a "Namath problem" developing.

"Werblin treated Namath like an indulgent father who spared the rod and spoiled the child," wrote columnist Arthur Daley. "The owner socialized with the athlete at times and undercut the authority of the coach."[9] UPI sportswriter Vito Stellino put it succinctly: "All the Jets' strengths and weaknesses can be summed up in two words — Joe Namath." Stellino continued: "Long coddled by former owner Sonny Werblin, Namath doesn't seem to get along too well with Coach Weeb Ewbank."[10]

On the other hand, Ewbank had probably invited more controversy than needs be by not announcing until just before game time that Namath would not play. "We should at least have been warned he might not play," Houston general manager Don Klosterman said in a huff, as he found himself with some 40,000 angry patrons.[11]

The situation was not easily dismissed. "The New York Jets would do well to trade Joe Namath right now," wrote William N. Wallace in *The New York Times*. "The athlete's scant respect for the coach has so diminished that Namath calls the shots as to when he will play or not play."[12] Wallace went on to suggest that the Jets were unlikely to be a winning team with Namath and Ewbank at odds, and he suggested Ewbank talk to Al Davis and cut a deal with Oakland. Davis was known to be a great admirer of Namath's.

After he had refused to suit up for the Houston game, one of Namath's teammates asked him to address the team in a meeting to explain why he didn't play. Namath declined the request, saying that there was no need for such a meeting. He didn't play, he said, because his knee was giving him pain: it was that simple, and nothing more than that. Still begging a sore knee, Namath sat out the team's second preseason game as well. On that occasion, the Jets beat Boston 25–6 in Richmond. No one doubted for a moment that had the games been meaningful — had they *counted*— Namath would have played regardless of the pain. After all, playing with pain was nothing new to him.

There was more incentive for Namath to play in the Jets' third exhibition, however. For starters, there were only three preseason games remaining, and he needed to get some playing time to prepare for the season. But more than that, the game was being played at Legion Field in Birmingham, Namath's old home field from his days under Bear Bryant. The Jets would also be facing an NFL team, and Namath wouldn't shrink from playing against the presumed superior league. While the two leagues had already agreed to merge, that was not to become a reality until 1970, and pending that finalization the only place the two leagues would face each other outside of the Super Bowl would be in exhibition season.

The Jets' opponent for their third exhibition would be the NFL's Atlanta Falcons, which gave Namath still more incentive: two of his former Alabama teammates — tight end Ray Ogden and receiver David Ray — would be playing for Atlanta. Oh, and then there was linebacker Tommy Nobis — he was also with the Falcons then. It was Nobis who, as a linebacker for Texas, had stopped Namath just inches from scoring the winning touchdown in the 1965 Orange Bowl. Of course, no mere exhibition game could ever even that score, but on that Friday night in Birmingham, Namath put on a fine display, completing 12 of 20 passes for 140 yards and two touchdowns as the Jets easily rolled over the Falcons, 27–12. NFL? Superior league? It sure didn't look that way in Birmingham. The Jets were indeed a team envisioning a championship season. "A year ago," said Ewbank, "we coaches thought we could do it, but convincing young men — that's something else."[13]

Their championship swagger may have taken a minor ding when the Jets dropped their next exhibition to the AFL's newest team, the Cincinnati Bengals, in front of a crowd of 24,358 in Memphis on August 30. Sure it was only preseason, but losing to an expansion club was somehow degrading nonetheless, notwithstanding the fact that Paul Brown was coaching the Bengals. Leading 9–6 in the fourth quarter, the Jets lost the game when Cincinnati drove 70 yards for the winning touchdown in the game's waning minutes. Namath had completed 12 of 25 for 188 yards.

For their final game of the 1968 preseason, the Jets became the first AFL team to ever play at Cleveland's Municipal Stadium. Curiously, their opponent was not the Cleveland Browns: they would instead be facing the Detroit Lions. It was a tradition for the stadium to host a doubleheader in exhibition season. In the second game that night, the Cleveland Browns would play the Green Bay Packers.

The Lions got out to a 3–0 lead 3:20 into the first quarter when Jerry DePoyster hit a 28-yard field goal, but Namath brought the Jets back quickly, driving them 75 yards in seven plays, 57 of those yards coming on two passes that kicked the drive off. Namath first threw 20 yards to Maynard, then 37 yards to George Sauer to set the Jets up at the Detroit 18. Five plays later Matt Snell ran it in from a yard out to put the Jets up 6–3 (Babe Parilli was intercepted on the conversion attempt).

Early in the second quarter Namath hit Sauer with a 43-yard pass to the Detroit 13, but the Jets played it conservative from there and wound up settling for a field goal that increased their lead to 9–3. The Lions missed a scoring opportunity when they drove to the New York 11, only to have the Jets drop quarterback Bill Munson for an 11-yard loss and then force a turnover when running back Mel Farr fumbled on the following play. Detroit managed another field goal in the fourth quarter to cut the Jets' lead to 9–6, and then, with just four minutes left in the game, they drove to the New York nine-yard line; it was all for naught as Farr fumbled again and Carl McAdams recovered for the Jets. The Lions' final chance was snuffed out by Randy Beverly, who intercepted rookie quarterback Greg Landry with under a minute to play, preserving the 9–6 win for the Jets. Munson had been knocked out of the game with bruised ribs late in the first half when Gerry Philbin gave him a shot, but like Namath, Munson would only have played the first half anyway. In his half of play Namath had thrown for 141 yards on just five completions in nine attempts.

The Jets finished the preseason 3–2 (2–1 with Namath) and were scheduled to open their season in Kansas City on September 15. If there was any concern that Namath's sitting out the first two exhibition games was more than a matter of a sore knee — that it perhaps pointed to a lack of commitment or was otherwise suggestive of an uncooperative spirit — the coaches had a plan to help eradicate any such problem.

In the huddle, on the field, there was no question that Namath was in charge, but the truth is that his teammates had never officially voted him offensive captain before. The coaches felt that such a show of confidence from the players would go a long way toward maturing Namath's attitude, and they approached the players about voting Namath captain. Truth is, the thought had already occurred to many of the players that, as quarterback, Namath may have felt slighted at never having been voted captain, and that a quarterback who felt snubbed or otherwise under-appreciated would hardly do much for the morale or unity of the team. If he was their leader — if he was really going to take them to a championship — he needed the responsibility of being a leader.

In the week leading up to the season opener the players made Namath offensive captain. It was a vote of confidence that overwhelmed Namath. He may not have known what was behind the decision of his teammates — that they saw increased responsibility as a means of getting him to behave more responsibly — but it seems to have done the trick.

Week 1 — Sunday, September 15, 1968
Municipal Stadium, Kansas City (attendance: 48,871)

The Jets would begin the 1968 season with three consecutive road games. There were 48,871 spectators at Kansas City's Municipal Stadium when the Jets came to town: it was the largest crowd ever to attend a sporting event in Kansas City. Close to 3,000 of them had paid five dollars each for the chance to stand and watch the game from a corner terrace.

Namath started the game poorly, missing on six of his first seven throws as the Jets went nowhere on their first two offensive series; the one pass he hit was only a two-yard flare to Emerson Boozer. Fortunately for New York, the Chiefs were also spinning their wheels offensively. On the Jets' third offensive series, however, Namath lofted a beautiful long throw to Don Maynard, who had gotten behind defender Goldie Sellers. There may never have been a more perfect pass. The ball arched through the air like a guided missile, coming down over Maynard's shoulder and falling perfectly into his hands as he never broke stride and outran Sellers the remainder to the end zone. The play covered 57 yards and put the Jets up 7–0. It was the beginning of a long day for Sellers.

Kansas City did put together a drive that resulted in a 33-yard Jan Stenerud field goal to cut the Jets' lead to 7–3 at the end of the first quarter, but in the second quarter the Jets began to dominate. The New York defense would shut Kansas City out in the second period, and would only allow them two first downs.

Meanwhile, Maynard continued to vex Sellers. Halfway into the period Namath again went long to Maynard, hitting him for 45 yards in a play that took the Jets from their own 30 to the Kansas City 25. It would lead to a 22-yard Jim Turner field goal that increased the Jets' lead to 10–3. Before the half ended, Namath hit Maynard for a 30-yard score that gave the Jets a commanding 17–3 lead going into the locker room. Would it stand up? The Jets had blown better leads than that in the past.

In the second half, New York mistakes seemed to be following a familiar scenario. Six minutes into the third period Noland Smith ran a Curley Johnson punt back 80 yards for a touchdown to cut New York's lead to 17–10, and then a fumble by Boozer led to another field goal by Stenerud, trimming New York's lead to 17–13. The third period would end with Namath, under a heavy rush from Ernie Ladd and Buck Buchanan, being intercepted by linebacker Willie Lanier at the 13-yard line. That led to yet another Stenerud field goal early in the fourth quarter that drew the

Chiefs to within one point at 17–16. The Jets' saving grace had been their defense, which had managed to keep Kansas City out of the end zone following both turnovers.

New York ran four minutes off the clock in driving to a 42-yard field goal, which brought their lead back up to four points, but Kansas City volleyed back with a 28-yard field goal of their own with 5:56 remaining. Although their offense had managed nothing but field goals, one more would win it for Kansas City. All they needed now was to force a punt and give their offense a chance.

Earl Christy received the ensuing kickoff for New York; the ball appeared to be sailing out of bounds, but Christy fielded it anyway. Problem was he was so close to the sideline that he wound up stepping out of bounds — *at the five-yard line!* Short of a fumble, it was about as good a scenario as Kansas City could have hoped for. If they could hold the Jets to three-and-out, the Chiefs were almost guaranteed good field position.

A running play on first down lost a yard to the four. On second down Namath tried to hit Maynard on a slant-in pattern, but the pass was incomplete. Facing third-and-11 from the four-yard line, Namath went back to the exact same play: this time he hit Maynard for 16 yards and a first down at the 20, effectively getting the Jets out of a hole. It sent them on a 15-play drive, during which they converted three more crucial third-down plays and ran out the clock. They didn't even score — they didn't need to.

After the game, Kansas City coach Hank Stram was in disbelief. "I thought nobody in the world could do that to us," Stram said of the Jets' final time-consuming drive. That wasn't the only thing about the game that had Stram at a loss. The New York defense had really done a number on the Chiefs. Stram couldn't recall his team ever being unable to score an offensive touchdown before.[14]

Maynard proclaimed it to be his own best game (it may have felt like it at the time, but it wasn't), with eight catches for 203 yards and two touchdowns. Namath had an impressive game as well; after missing six of his first seven throws, he went on to complete 16 of the next 22 to finish 17 of 29 for 302 yards, with two TDs and one interception. But what was really impressive about Namath — perhaps even more than his slingshot bombs to Maynard — was his poise and mastery as a play-caller during the concluding drive. He may have riddled the Kansas City secondary with long throws earlier, but he had the presence of mind to opt for ball control when it needed to be done to preserve the win.

Week 2 — Sunday, September 22, 1968
Legion Field, Birmingham, Alabama (attendance: 29,192)

Although it would officially be a home game for the Boston Patriots when they met New York on September 22, they would not be hosting the Jets in Massachusetts. The Patriots' usual home venue — Fenway Park — was being used by its principal tenants, the Boston Red Sox, so the Patriots would have to look elsewhere to play on that day. They could have chosen any number of places nearer to home, but Boston's first home game of the 1968 season would be played at Legion Field in Birmingham, Alabama — Namath's old venue from his college days. Coincidence? Not likely. The choice was officially said to be a test run to see if Birmingham might spark to the professional league and possibly be awarded a franchise in the future. But everyone suspected the real reason — the Patriots, and the AFL, were anticipating that with Namath and the Jets coming to town the people would once again turn out to see their old University of Alabama hero. It had worked when Werblin had arranged for the Jets' first preseason game to be played there in 1966, so the hope was that it would work again. No such luck.

The night before the Jets-Patriots game, 63,759 people packed the stadium to see the University of Alabama play: only 29,192 showed up for the professional contest the following day.

Those that did were obviously Namath fans, for although it was officially a "home game" for Boston, the Patriots were booed throughout the contest. The low turnout was said to be a major setback for the city of Birmingham in getting a professional franchise (which it never got), but really, other than the chance to see Namath again, what was there for the people of Alabama to get excited about in watching two teams representing northeastern cities?

No doubt Babe Parilli was itching to play against his former team, which had put him out to pasture and sent him packing when they traded him for Mike Taliaferro. It is likely that Taliaferro was also keen to have a big game and show the Jets what a mistake they had made in putting him second-string to Namath.

Boston seemed to be in charge early in the game, and they controlled the ball for the better part of the first quarter, but when Taliaferro tried a pass to Jim Whalen, he was intercepted by Randy Beverly, who ran the theft back 68 yards for a touchdown. The Patriots came back with a drive that carried them from their own 25 to the New York 24 before bogging down. A 31-yard field goal by Gino Cappelletti closed the gap to 7–3, but that would soon seem insignificant.

With time winding down in the first quarter, Namath drove the Jets 74 yards to a score, hitting George Sauer with passes of 18 and 16 yards before capping the drive with a 39-yard touchdown throw to Maynard with nine seconds left in the period. The Jets led 14–3 at the end of one quarter.

In the second quarter Jim Turner kicked field goals of 30 and 27 yards to increase New York's lead to 20–3, and it certainly looked like the rout was on. But later in the period Boston closed the gap to 10 points when Taliaferro hit Aaron Marsh with a 70-yard touchdown pass. It was a beautifully executed down-and-out pattern that found Marsh wide open and going into the end zone untouched.

The score remained 20–10 going in at halftime, and less than two minutes into the third quarter the Patriots still looked to have the momentum. Facing a third-and-seven from the New York 17, Namath tried to hit Bill Mathis with a screen, but defensive end Mel Wilt stepped in front and intercepted the pass at the four-yard line. The 265-pound Wilt lumbered into the end zone to score, and suddenly it was a three-point game at 20–17.

Whatever momentum the Patriots may have had, they effectively lost it on their next offensive series. Unable to move the ball, they wound up punting from their own 24. Punter Bob Scarpitto took a problematic snap from center and had a hard time finding the handle on it: linebacker Paul Crane — another University of Alabama alumnus — broke through the line and blocked the kick. It was picked up by Mark Smolinski at the seven-yard line, and with a protective wall of five teammates to lead him, Smolinski took it in for the score and a 27–17 lead.*

Another punt would add to Boston's woes later in the period. Scarpitto had gotten off a good punt to the New York 30, but an offside penalty on the Patriots forced him to do it again: he shanked the second try and the Jets took over on Boston's 31. That five-yard offside penalty had made a 39-yard difference in field position. After a four-yard run by Matt Snell, Namath threw 27 yards to Pete Lammons for the score and a 34–17 lead. Jim Turner added another field goal — again from 27 yards — and the Jets entered the fourth quarter with a 37–17 lead.

Early in the fourth quarter Namath threw for Lammons in the end zone, and while the pass was broken up, John Charles drew a flag for pass interference. The Jets were awarded a first-and-goal on the one-yard line, and two plays later Emerson Boozer went over for the score to make it 44–17.

With such a commanding lead, Ewbank took Namath out of the game early in the fourth

---

For some reason, Smolinski is only credited with a three-yard return on the blocked punt. The play is featured in a 1968 New York Jets highlight reel included on the DVD New York Jets: The Complete History, *and Smolinski very obviously picks the ball up on the seven-yard line. All sources that say otherwise are in error.*

quarter and let Babe Parilli go at it with his former teammates. Parilli tried to hit Billy Joe with a screen pass that wound up being ruled a lateral; assuming it was merely an incomplete pass, Joe let it lay and Boston linebacker Ed Philpott grabbed the ball at the 10-yard line and carried it into the end zone. The officials were appallingly ignorant of the rules, which stated that although the defense could recover such an errant lateral, they could not advance it. Against the protests of the New York Jets, the referees allowed the touchdown to stand: it cut the Jets' lead to 20 points at 44–24. In the end it made no difference, and though it could have, it didn't affect the outcome of the contest. However, it is still hard to believe that officials in a professional sporting event would not even know the rules of the game.

Turner added another field goal for the Jets, and Boston back-up quarterback Tom Sherman came in to lead the Patriots to a late score that made the final 47–31. Boston coach Mike Holovak saw the blocked punt as the real turning point in the game, saying, "That blocked kick did it to us."[15] At the time of the blocked punt, the Patriots had cut the lead to just three points; that play did seem to open the floodgates, with the Jets going on to score 20 points before the referees gifted the Patriots a touchdown.

But Taliaferro had also hurt Boston's cause. He had thrown four interceptions, the first of which was returned for a score, while the others (two by Jim Hudson and one by Earl Christy) all led to New York field goals.

Namath finished 13 of 25 for 196 yards, two TDs and one interception, and at 2–0 the Jets were now sitting pretty atop the AFL's Eastern Division. The following week they would be concluding their three-game road swing against the Buffalo Bills. At 0–3, the Bills were an easy mark, right? Yeah, right.

Week 3 — Sunday, September 29, 1968
War Memorial Stadium, Buffalo (attendance: 38,044)

So the 2–0 New York Jets came to Buffalo to play the 0–3 Bills. Aside from their respective records, there was plenty of reason the odds makers put the Jets as high as 19-point favorites. After their 0–3 start, Buffalo had fired head coach Joe Collier and replaced him with personnel director Harvey Johnson, who would assume the job for the remainder of the season. Buffalo had also lost starting quarterback Jack Kemp for the season with a broken leg, and backup Tom Flores was out with a torn muscle in the right shoulder: that left rookie Dan Darragh to pilot the Buffalo offense. And then there was kicker Mike Mercer, who was out with a pulled hamstring. The Bills signed kicker Bruce Alford the day before the game. They certainly looked like an easy mark, but like the saying goes, there's a reason they play the games.

At first, the game looked as if it would fulfill the expectations of the prognosticators when Earl Christy received the opening kickoff at the New York six-yard line and proceeded to run it back 87 yards to the Buffalo seven. Three plays later Namath tossed a four-yard touchdown to George Sauer, and the Jets were up 7–0 just 2:11 into the game.

The Jets found themselves starting their next offensive series at the Bills' 39 after a Buffalo punt. It may have seemed at that point like things were going to be easy, but the trouble started when Namath was sacked for a nine-yard loss by tackle Tom Sestak on second down. On third down Namath was intercepted by Tom Janik, who returned the ball to the New York 36. The Jets' defense did a good job in forcing Buffalo to settle for a 35-yard field goal that let the Jets keep a 7–3 lead, but the Bills were able to capture the lead on their next series. Following a New York punt, Buffalo began at the Jets' 40, and 11 plays later Ben Gregory scored on a two-yard run to put the Bills up 10–7 just before the end of the first quarter.

It would not be until the Jets' third offensive series of the second period that they would be able to get close enough for Jim Turner to try a 37-yard field goal, but the kick was short and the Jets still trailed. For Buffalo, a blunder that looked disastrous would then turn out to be a blessing. When Darragh fumbled the ball at the Buffalo 10-yard line and Ralph Baker recovered for New York, it seemed like the kind of mistake you'd expect from a winless, luckless team, but when it came to mistakes the Jets would not be outdone.

Namath threw two incomplete passes, and then on third down he tried to throw to Curley Johnson, who was breaking toward the right of the end zone. Tom Janik stepped in front and grabbed the ball at the goal line — he took off down the sideline and there was really no one but Namath with a shot at him. Namath began to pursue, but it was obvious that with his knees he posed no threat of catching Janik. Buffalo defensive end Tom Day was in position to block Namath, but let the opportunity pass. "I didn't want to hurt him," said Day. "He's too valuable. And it wasn't necessary." There was one more reason Day refrained from taking Namath down. "I like him," Day said.[16] Besides, no one was expecting Namath to catch Janik anyway. Janik cruised 100 yards for a touchdown. The runback tied an AFL record and put Buffalo up 17–7 with four-and-a-half minutes left in the half.

After receiving the kick, the Jets started from their own 34 and Namath tried to hit Sauer with a pass on first down: the pass was intercepted by Butch Byrd at the 48-yard line. Byrd ran it back for a score, but the Jets got a reprieve — Day had been flagged for being offside, which nullified the touchdown. The Jets then moved efficiently downfield, and six plays later Emerson Boozer scored from a yard out to make the score 17–14 in Buffalo's favor with 2:12 left in the half.

Somehow Buffalo managed to avoid the letdown that a losing team usually experiences with such a change in fortune, and Max Anderson took the kickoff all the way to the New York 34, setting up another Buffalo field goal less than a minute before halftime. The Bills had increased their lead to 20–14, but even so, the Jets' defense had again done a superb job in holding them to three points.

Starting from their own 33 with 48 seconds remaining, the Jets needed all of 16 seconds to retake the lead when Namath hit Don Maynard with a 55-yard bomb that gave the Jets a 21–20 advantage going in at the half. Even so, they seemed to be in an unexpected dogfight.

Things would settle down considerably in the third period, with a 37-yard field goal by Buffalo being the only score. It did give the Bills a 23–21 lead at 8:26 of the third, but there didn't seem any reason to expect that the Jets would not overcome. There was, after all, almost a quarter-and-a-half left to play. But then came the fourth quarter, and it was a pisser.

It was just 2:34 into the final period when Byrd intercepted another Namath pass to Sauer: Byrd again proceeded to run it back for a touchdown. The difference this time was that there was no penalty to nullify Byrd's heroics, and the result was a 53-yard scoring play that increased Buffalo's lead to 30–21.

On the Jets' next series, Namath opted to throw on a third-and-one play from the 38. Right cornerback Booker Edgerson intercepted the pass at the 45-yard line and ran it back for another score. Only 62 seconds had elapsed between Buffalo's two touchdowns, and the Bills now led 37–21.

After receiving the kick, the Jets managed to put together a 65-yard drive that resulted in a three-yard touchdown pass from Namath to Matt Snell. It cut Buffalo's lead to 37–28, but time was now a major factor as the Jets needed at least two scores to catch up. The defense did its job in forcing a Buffalo punt, and the offense then drove to the Buffalo 34 when Namath threw for Sauer and was once more intercepted by Byrd; Buffalo took possession at their own five-yard line with just 2:37 left in the game.

Again the New York defense held, and there was a further blessing when Paul Crane blocked the punt and the Jets took over on the Bills' 11-yard line. Two plays later, Namath hit Sauer with a 10-yard touchdown pass that pulled the Jets to within two points. With only 1:04 left to play, everyone expected the onside kick, and Paul Costa was able to recover for Buffalo. The Bills ran out the clock after that and came away with their first victory of the season, 37–35. As it turned out, it would be Buffalo's only win of the season.

Namath had thrown for 280 yards and four touchdowns while completing 19 of 43 passes, which would ordinarily signal a good day; the problem was he had also accounted for more than half of Buffalo's points. He had thrown five interceptions, three of which were run back for touchdowns. After the game, the obvious question for Ewbank from reporters was why he had left Namath in the game, or if he had given any thought to taking him out. Yes, Ewbank said, it had crossed his mind. Ultimately, it was the explosive nature of Namath's play that had prevented Ewbank from making the decision to pull him from the game.[17]

Ewbank wound up making excuses for Namath's play, pointing out that one interception was on a tipped ball and another a busted pattern, but as usual Namath was having none of the excuse-making. "Those interceptions murdered us," Namath said. "I'm to blame for 'em. This dumb guy sitting here. I just wasn't reacting properly. I'm the guy who threw the ball, so I'm at fault."[18]

In reality there was more to it than that. Namath had been sacked three times that day, but had otherwise been under constant pressure, particularly from left-side defensive end Ron McDole. It was the job of rookie tackle Sam Walton to keep McDole out, and he just wasn't doing it. He had even taken the drastic measure of tackling McDole, about which Ewbank was in an apologetic mood afterward, saying that the coaches do not teach their offensive linemen to do such things. Ewbank took Walton out and tried both Bob Talamini and Jeff Richardson, but McDole was just a handful.

It is certainly true that the interceptions were the most glaring contributing factor to the Jets' defeat, but on the other hand, so was Turner's missed field goal. It was only from 37 yards out, and as he had made a 48-yarder the week before, it was certainly well within his range. Since the Jets only lost by two points, that field goal would have made the difference. There is also the curious fact that the Jets declined to try a two-point conversion after either of their final two touchdowns. Under the circumstances, it seems a peculiar decision from a strategic viewpoint. There was certainly enough blame to go around.

Week 4 — Saturday, October 5, 1968
Shea Stadium, New York (attendance: 63,786)

After beginning the season with three road games, the Jets finally had their home opener against the unbeaten San Diego Chargers on a Saturday night at Shea in front of an AFL record crowd of 63,786. On the heels of the debacle in Buffalo, Ewbank's game plan was simple — establish the run. It wasn't that Ewbank doubted Namath's ability, but he had been around long enough to know that after just one week even a confident player might still be reeling from such a disaster. With that in mind, the Jets ran the ball eleven straight plays during their two initial offensive series. The problem was it only got them two first downs. The New York defense came to the rescue when Randy Beverly intercepted John Hadl at the San Diego 35 to set up the game's initial score, a 26-yard field goal by Jim Turner.

Early in the second quarter, Hadl put the Chargers out in front 7–3 with a seven-yard touchdown pass to Lance Alworth, but the Jets drove back down to kick another field goal — twice. Turner hit it from 30 yards the first time, but a holding penalty on tackle Winston Hill forced Turner to try again from 45 yards out: he made that one too, and the Jets pulled to within one point, 7–6. Turner would kick a third field goal with only seconds left in the half, this time from 11 yards, and the Jets held a 9–7 lead going in at the half. Namath had been sticking to the game plan, and while he did throw 13 passes in the half (completing seven), most of them were cautious throws for short yardage.

In the third quarter the Jets increased their lead to 16–7 when they put together their first touchdown drive of the game, which climaxed with Matt Snell going over from a yard out. But the Chargers answered back almost immediately: on their first play from scrimmage after receiving the kick, Hadl threw long for Gary Garrison and connected. Garrison was able to outrun the defenders to the end zone on a scoring play that covered 84 yards. After missing the extra point, the Chargers then trailed the Jets by three points, 16–13.

In the fourth quarter the Chargers got their chance to pull back out in front when Speedy Duncan fielded a punt at the San Diego 38-yard line and returned it 37 yards to the New York 25. The Chargers would take the lead shortly afterward when Hadl again hit Garrison for the score, this time from five yards out. That put San Diego up 20–16 with 5:45 left in the game.

There was plenty of time for the Jets to work with, but even so, Namath was throwing more liberally now: he hit on three out of four throws to move his team to the San Diego 40. Then, on first down, Namath threw incomplete. On second down, he again threw incomplete. Facing a crucial third-and-10 he now had to throw: it was again incomplete. It would have brought fourth-and-10, but there was a flag on the play. The Jets were given new life when defensive end Steve DeLong was penalized for a late hit on Namath. The penalty gave the Jets a first down on the San Diego 25.

Namath then threw 18 yards to Mark Smolinski to bring the Jets to the seven-yard line. Smolinski — a fullback — was filling in at tight end for the injured Pete Lammons, and was doing a good job of it — it was his second reception of the drive.

On first down Emerson Boozer ran it four yards to the three. On second down it was Boozer again, this time picking up two yards to the one. Down by four points, a field goal was useless now — they had to get it in the end zone. On third-and-goal Namath again called Boozer's number. This time Boozer dove over for a score to put the Jets up 23–20 with 1:43 left to play.

That still left the Chargers with enough time to at least get in range for a tying field goal, but the unbeaten Chargers didn't seem content with the idea of a tie. Hadl moved his team to the New York 32 with four straight pass completions, but when he then went deep for Alworth the pass was overthrown: it came right into the waiting hands of Johnny Sample, who picked it off at the five-yard line. Alworth dove in a desperate attempt to break up the pass, but he could do nothing. Sample ran the ball back 39 yards and the Jets were then able to run out the clock.

Namath was under 50 percent on completions, hitting 16 of 34 for 220 yards, without any TDs or interceptions. The win gave the Jets a 3–1 record and a one-game lead over Boston in the AFL East. The rest of the division was looking anemic (Miami at 1–3 and Houston and Buffalo each at 1–4). The Jets would have a chance to strengthen their position the following week when they would be hosting the 1–3 Denver Broncos. Aside from Denver's poor record, there was also some comfort in knowing that in four games the Broncos had yet to intercept a pass. But they would get all caught up on that in New York.

Week 5 — Sunday, October 13, 1968
Shea Stadium, New York (attendance: 62,052)

The Jets were heavily favored over the Broncos, and while they misfired on their first offensive series, on their second they went 65 yards in just four plays. On the third play of the series, Namath threw a bomb down the right sideline to Don Maynard, who had beaten defender Charlie Greer: the play went for 60 yards to the Denver five-yard line. On the next play Emerson Boozer went around left end for the score and a 7–0 New York lead.

But the Broncos answered quickly, engineering their own scoring drive on their next offensive series. Denver went 73 yards in eight plays, the big gainer being a 35-yard pass from Steve Tensi to Eric Crabtree, and they tied the game when Fran Lynch took it through right guard from four yards out for the score.

The score remained tied until the second quarter when Pete Jaquess grabbed Denver's first interception of the season to set up the go-ahead score. Jaquess stole a Namath pass intended for Bill Mathis, and seven plays later Lynch scored again — this time from six yards out — to put Denver up 14–7.

Denver's second interception of the season came later in the second period, but did not result in any points. The Jets, on the other hand, were able to put up three more points when Jim Turner kicked a 29-yard field goal to cut Denver's lead to 14–10 at the half.

Their halftime lead may have been slim, but the Broncos wasted no time in expanding on it when the second half got under way. After the Broncos received the opening kick and started on their own 28, Tensi went back to throw on the first play from scrimmage and hit Crabtree cutting left-to-right across the middle at the New York 48. Crabtree made the catch and outran Johnny Sample to the end zone. The resulting 72-yard touchdown play gave Denver some breathing room with a 21–10 lead.

Later in the period Namath would be intercepted by John Huard, and the Jets would not mount an offensive threat until the final play of the third period when George Sauer made an outstanding one-handed catch to set the Jets up with a first down at the Denver 14. But the drive quickly fizzled out as the fourth quarter got under way, and when Namath was dropped for a five-yard loss on a third-and-eight play, the Jets were forced to kick a 24-yard field goal.

If it was frustrating for the Jets to have to settle for a field goal, the remainder of the quarter would prove more frustrating still. Namath had already been intercepted three times, but in the fourth he would be picked off twice more — both times by Charlie Greer — and while only the first of Namath's five-interception tally would lead to any Denver points, the remainder had all effectively squandered offensive opportunities.

In the final minute, three Namath-to-Sauer passes had put the Jets on the Denver three-yard line with just seconds remaining. On Namath's last pass of the game he tried to throw to Sauer in the end zone — the ball bounced off the crossbar of the goalpost, which in those days were at the front, not the back of the end zone. Denver had preserved a 21–13 win, and for the second time in three games the Jets had lost to a team they were very heavily favored to beat. The truth is that the Jets had dominated Denver in every category: 129 yards rushing to Denver's 48; 341 yards passing to Denver's 201; 460 total yards to Denver's 222. The Broncos dominated in one important statistic — they intercepted five passes to the Jets' zero. Also for the second time in three games, Namath had thrown five interceptions. He had otherwise completed 20 of 41 for 341 yards. He was in no mood to discuss it afterward. "I've been talking for four years and I've never refused to talk," Namath told reporters in the locker room, "but I ask you to respect my wishes. I want to say only one thing — I stink."[19]

The Broncos were more willing to talk about the interceptions. Could anybody blame them? They stole five — the only five they had gotten at that point in the season. But they weren't gloating. Safety Jack Lentz had intercepted Namath in the second quarter: he was asked if Denver had changed any of their pass coverage schemes. "We were just trying to confuse them," Lentz told reporters. "If Namath knows what you're in, he can pick you apart. He's that good a quarterback. But we tried not to let him know what we were doing."[20]

Over in the Jets' dressing room, Ewbank again found himself excusing Namath's play to the press. Ewbank insisted that the interceptions were not Namath's fault, and he instead blamed them on the fact that defensive end Rich Jackson was in Namath's face all day. Well … he was.

The good news for the Jets that day was that even though their record dropped to 3–2, they had still managed to stay a game up on Boston, who had also lost. Then again, the bad news was that Boston had lost to Houston, which meant that the Oilers were now creeping up on the Jets in the division. But there was more good news in that the Jets could change that the following week when they traveled to Houston to play the Oilers. More bad news — the Jets had never won a game in Houston. Well, everything in its proper time.

Week 6 — Sunday, October 20, 1968
Astrodome, Houston (attendance: 51,710)

Unlike the Jets' preseason game at the Houston Astrodome in August, there would be no controversy over whether or not Namath would suit up when they returned to Houston for their sixth game of the season. The question this time was whether or not Ewbank would keep him in if his passes were again obnoxiously wayward. Although he was not throwing interceptions, neither was Namath pitching strikes against Houston in the first quarter, as he failed to complete a pass. He would miss on his first nine throws, not completing one until hitting Billy Joe for 11 yards at the Houston 40 just six minutes before the end of the half. That play also registered New York's initial first down of the game.

Despite going the entire first quarter without a first down (Houston had three), the Jets still took a first-quarter lead when the Oilers found themselves punting from their own end zone with 25 seconds left in the opening period and had the kick blocked by Paul Crane. The resulting safety gave the Jets a 2–0 lead going into the second quarter.

When the Jets finally did get a first down, it started something — they would get four more and wound up at the Houston one-yard line. With 1:17 left in the half, it was Namath who would take it into the end zone on a bootleg around left end. The Jets then faked the extra point and Babe Parilli hit Bill Mathis in the end zone for a two-point conversion to give the Jets a 10–0 halftime lead.

It had not been a particularly impressive first half for either side. Namath had completed just three of 15 passes in the half, and the offense had only managed 33 yards; Houston had managed just 29.

The third quarter played out much the same, with neither team able to mount a threat. Finally, toward the end of the third period, the Jets put together a drive. They didn't really have far to go; they had started on their own 48 and worked their way down to the Houston five-yard line, where things stalled out as the third quarter came to an end. On the first play of the fourth quarter, Jim Turner kicked a 12-yard field goal to give the Jets a 13–0 lead.

Houston had been forced to play the whole game with their second-string quarterback, Bob Davis, because starter Pete Beathard was recovering from an emergency appendectomy. Davis had been unable to generate any offense, so it couldn't have seemed terribly dire to his team's prospects when he was carried off the carpet after being put down hard by Verlon Biggs. The Oilers' third-string quarterback, Don Trull, was a veteran who had been around; he had been Houston's quarterback the year before, but they had traded him to Boston during the season. In 1968 Boston released Trull, and he signed with Houston again three weeks prior to the game with the Jets.

Usually it is not a favorable sign when you are trailing 13–0 in the fourth quarter and are forced by necessity to send in your third-string quarterback, but as stated, Trull had seen his share of game action, and it took him just three plays to get the Oilers on the scoreboard. With passes to Mac Haik and Alvin Reed — who caught the touchdown from nine yards out — Trull cut the Jets' lead to 13–7.

When the Jets then had a fruitless offensive series and had to punt the ball away, the Oilers took possession on their own 37. Trull moved his team 63 yards in 10 plays to score on a 19-yard pass to Jim Beirne that put the Oilers up for the first time in the game, 14–13.

There were some four minutes left when the Jets got the ball back and started from their own 20. Plenty of time, to be sure—certainly plenty of time to get close enough for a winning field goal. But the Jets were not looking for a field goal. "Heck," said Namath after the game, "if you don't have the confidence in yourself to think you can score anytime, you don't have any business playing this game."[21]

On first down Namath threw a 14-yard square out to George Sauer to put the Jets on the 34. On the next play he again hit Sauer with a square out, this time for nine yards to the 43. On second-and-one, a play that might normally dictate a run, Namath again went back to pass and again hit Sauer, this time across the middle for 13 yards and a first down at the Houston 44 with 2:58 remaining.

On the next play Namath went across the middle again, this time to Emerson Boozer. The throw was low, but Boozer made an excellent catch, reaching down to the carpet and pulling it in: the play went for 17 yards to the 27. Now Namath shifted gears and called a running play to Boozer: the play only picked up two yards, but with 1:59 left Namath kept it on the ground. The call went to Boozer again, and this time the halfback gained 15 yards to the 10. There was plenty of time left to go the remaining 10 yards, so they stayed on the ground. Matt Snell gained eight yards on first down, and then on the next play it was Snell again, going the final two yards for the score with 48 seconds remaining.

If Trull still had a hot hand then the Oilers stood a chance, but on the ensuing kickoff Gerry Philbin pasted Houston return man Zeke Moore and forced him to cough up the ball. Bill Rademacher recovered for the Jets at the Houston 28, enabling New York to run out the clock. Houston coach Wally Lemm couldn't hide his disappointment. "We had stopped Namath most of the time," he said, "but then his poise and his talent showed through in that last drive."[22] Namath finished with 12 completions in 27 attempts for 145 yards, no TDs or interceptions.

The win had given the Jets a two-and-a-half game lead over Houston in the East, but Boston kept pace by beating Buffalo to stay within a game of the Jets. The Jets would have a chance to widen that gap the following week when they would host the Patriots at Shea.

Week 7 — Sunday, October 27, 1968
Shea Stadium, New York (attendance: 62,351)

Trailing New York by just a game, the Boston Patriots had an opportunity to move into a first-place tie with the Jets in the Eastern Division when they came to Shea Stadium. They had, however, lost six straight to the Jets dating back to 1965, but athletes aren't superstitious—are they?

After taking a touchback on the opening kickoff, the Jets started the game from their own 20. They were able to draw the Patriots offside with a new and theretofore unseen line shift on the first play from scrimmage, a somewhat portentous moment for Boston. Thereafter, the Jets cruised downfield with certainty, Emerson Boozer carrying for 18 yards, Namath passing across the middle to Matt Snell for 20, and Boozer taking a screen pass for 23 yards to the Boston two-yard line. Snell then took it in for the touchdown and a quick and easy 7–0 lead.

Late in the first quarter the Jets were threatening again when Namath took a hard shot from Boston tackle Tom Funches. The pass had been completed to Don Maynard for 17 yards, but after using a timeout to shake the cobwebs out of his head, Namath was intercepted on the next play by Leroy Mitchell, who ran the ball back to the Boston 38 as the first quarter came to an end.

Although the New York offense tended to get the lion's share of the attention, it was their defense that was leading the league, and it was the defense that would provide the offense with plenty of opportunities this day. In the second period Verlon Biggs knocked the ball loose from Patriots' quarterback Mike Taliaferro, and Gerry Philbin recovered for New York at the Boston 40. It led to a Jim Turner field goal and a 10–0 halftime lead for the Jets.

In the second half the New York defense would continue to present its offense with oppor-tunities. In the third period defensive back Bill Baird intercepted Taliaferro at the Boston 35 and ran it back to the 19, setting up a 23-yard Turner field goal for a 13–0 lead. Then, midway through the third, Philbin gave Taliaferro a shot that jarred the ball loose. Carl McAdams recovered for the Jets at the Boston 43, and with two passes to George Sauer, Namath had them on the one-yard line; again, it was Snell who ran it in from there for a comfortable 20–0 lead.

Namath had jammed his right thumb on his first interception in the first half (he was inter-cepted twice, both times by Mitchell), and as it was his throwing hand and it was still causing him pain in the third quarter, Ewbank decided, ahead 20–0, to send Babe Parilli into the game.

Probably more than glad to again show up his former team, Parilli guided the Jets to a touchdown early in the fourth quarter. It was Parilli who scored the touchdown, running it in from two yards out. Now leading 27–0, the Jets really began to pour it on. McAdams recovered another fumble and Jim Hudson, Al Atkinson, and Johnny Sample all intercepted Taliaferro passes (the second of the game for Sample). Midway through the fourth quarter, with the Jets by then leading 41–0 after touchdown runs of seven and 15 yards by Billy Joe, the New York defense had only allowed the Patriots to cross midfield three times, with each occasion ending in a turnover.

Then came the play that broke Gerry Philbin's heart. Rookie backup quarterback Tom Sher-man had replaced Taliaferro, and was facing a third-and-37 from his own 13 when he threw to Jim Whalen, who dodged a tackle at the New York 40 and went the distance, 87 yards, for the score. After Billy Joe scored yet again for the Jets — this time on a 32-yard run — Sherman threw another touchdown — a 33-yarder — to Bob Scarpitto with 59 seconds left. The game ended as a 48–14 Jets' victory, giving New York a surer hold on first place. "It should have been 48–0," Philbin said. "It killed me that they scored."[23]

Any defense takes pride in a shutout, but there was perhaps a bit more to it than that. Even allowing for the expected flaring of tempers in a heated first-place divisional shootout, the game grew contentious, teetering on the verge of becoming a huge brawl. Boston halfback John Charles was ejected from the game after delivering a right uppercut to the jaw of Jets' defensive back Bill Rademacher. Charles maintained that it was only payback for a cheap shot Rademacher had given him earlier that had gone unseen by officials. Otherwise, there were plenty of personal foul penal-ties being handed out, running the game's penalty yardage to 219 (111 for Boston, 108 for New York). They may not have shut Boston out, but the New York defense could at least be proud of setting a club record with five interceptions (all off Taliaferro, who had been intercepted four times by the Jets earlier in the season), while also recovering three fumbles.

Through his three quarters of play, Namath had done a serviceable, if unspectacular, job. He completed 10 of 18 for 179 yards, with two interceptions. He had thrown no touchdowns — again. It was now the fourth consecutive game Namath had gone without throwing a touchdown pass, and for all of the attention it was getting anybody would have thought they were losing. But the Jets had won three of those four games, and were ever more staking their ground atop the division.

The 5–2 Jets were now looking forward to another divisional grudge match: they would be hosting the Buffalo Bills the following week, and the Jets were looking to settle accounts for their defeat in Buffalo a month earlier.

Week 8 — Sunday, November 3, 1968
Shea Stadium, New York (attendance: 61,452)

When the Jets hosted Buffalo at Shea on November 3, the Bills' record stood at 1–6–1, Namath's comedy of errors in Buffalo back in September still being the Bills' only victory. The

Jets may have been eager to avenge that defeat, but Namath himself seemed overly-cautious, calling an extremely conservative — almost timid — game.

Namath threw little, and while the Jets did have opportunities early, they still came away empty handed when Jim Turner missed on two field goal attempts (the second being blocked). Buffalo then drew first blood when quarterback Kay Stephenson threw a 55-yard touchdown to Haven Moses.

The Jets fired back before the end of the quarter when Turner made good on a 32-yard field goal, and although the offense was not blazing a path to the end zone, the Jets would take the lead in the second quarter when Johnny Sample intercepted Stephenson at the Buffalo 36 and galloped down the sideline with the theft for a score. Jim Turner built that lead up to 16–7 by the half when he hit on field goals of nine and 32 yards.

It had not been the most inspiring of performances in the first half, and the third quarter brought more of the same: another field goal by Turner provided the only scoring in the period. Namath was not looking particularly sharp, having more misses than hits, and was still keeping mostly to the ground game, but 19–7 seemed a reasonably cushy lead going into the fourth quarter.

Halfway into the fourth, however, the Buffalo offense was able to put something together and Stephenson got them into the end zone with a 10-yard touchdown pass to Paul Costa to shave the Jets' lead to 19–14. Still, the New York offense seemed to feel no sense of urgency, and when their next series went nowhere they punted the ball away. Buffalo's Hagood Clarke let the ball drop and then fielded it on a bounce at the Bills' 18. He found a seam and took off running: Clarke went 82 yards for a touchdown with just over six minutes to play. In just a few short minutes, New York's 19–7 lead had evaporated and the Jets suddenly found themselves trailing 21–19.

But there was plenty of time to work with, and the Jets had already shown that they were capable of coming from behind late to win (San Diego, Houston); besides, Turner had already kicked four field goals, and one more was all that was needed to retake the lead. Going back to pass from his own 29, Namath found tight end Pete Lammons in the flat for 25 yards to the Buffalo 46, and the Jets were in business quickly. Then Buffalo defensive back Marty Schotten-heimer was flagged for pass interference, moving the Jets up to the 29. But the Bills shut them down at that point, and it was up to Turner to make something of the opportunity: he hit from 35 yards to put the Jets back up, 22–21.

From there it was left to the New York defense, and they came through again when linebacker Al Atkinson intercepted Stephenson at the Buffalo 18 with 52 seconds left. Turner then sealed the victory with a 21-yard field goal, and the Jets came away with a 25–21 triumph.

Turner had accounted for all of the Jets' offensive points, and his six field goals tied an AFL record set by Boston's Gino Cappelletti in a 1964 game against Denver. Turner's eight field goal attempts had also set an AFL single-game record, and his 19 points (six field goals plus one extra point) had set a club record.

As for Namath, his numbers were not terribly impressive: he had completed barely one-third of his passes, hitting 10 of 28 for 164 yards with one interception. For the fifth consecutive game he had thrown no touchdowns. But what did he care? The Jets were winning, and with Boston having lost to Denver and fallen back to third place at 3–5, second place Houston, at 4–5, was the closest threat in the division. The Oilers would be at Shea the following week, and beating them again would go a long way toward nailing down the division for the Jets.

Week 9 — Sunday, November 10, 1968

Shea Stadium, New York (attendance: 60,242)

When Houston clinched the Eastern Division in the final week of the 1967 season they had sent the Jets a bitchy telegram, crowing that they had done the Jets the favor of saving second place for them: that taunt had not been forgotten. Now, with a two-and-a-half game lead over the Oilers, the Jets had a chance to all but secure the division title with a victory when Houston came to Shea to face the Jets in a driving rain.

The Jets came out ready to make short work of their closest divisional rival. To hell with establishing the run—they wanted to put the Oilers down fast and hard. Namath threw on first down: unfortunately, George Sauer dropped the pass, but on second down Namath threw 19 yards to Don Maynard to put the Jets on the Houston 48. On the next play he threw 43 yards to Sauer who got caught from behind and taken down at the Houston five-yard line. Two plays later Bill Mathis scored on a two-yard run, and that quickly—67 yards in five plays—the Jets were up 7–0.

After the New York defense shut Houston down Namath went back to work, crossing the Oilers up with a draw play to Matt Snell. The fullback took it 38 yards from the New York 32 to the Houston 30. Larry Carwell was flagged for illegal use of the hands, and the Oilers were penalized another 15 yards. With that, the Jets found themselves on the 15. The Houston defense managed to hold the Jets off from there, but Jim Turner kicked a 14-yard field goal to increase New York's lead to 10–0. The Oilers had some success moving the ball on their next series, but Bill Baird intercepted Don Trull at the New York 32 and returned it 36 yards to the Houston 32, setting up another Turner field goal.

Houston got on the board in the final minute of the first quarter when Hoyle Granger took a draw play through the left side of the line and went 47 yards for a score. At the end of one quarter the Jets led 13–7.

The only points in the second quarter would come from another Turner field goal, this one from 28 yards out. It had been set up principally by two Namath-to-Sauer passes that accounted for 45 yards in the series: the Jets led 16–7 at the half.

As the rain continued to fall, both teams were having difficulty sustaining a drive in the third period, but the Jets finally added to their lead late in the quarter after linebacker Ralph Baker intercepted a pass. The Jets then went 35 yards in six plays, with Namath converting a third-down play with a 27-yard pass to Mathis. It was Mathis who went in for the score from a yard out three plays later, giving the Jets a 23–7 lead.

In the fourth quarter, Namath threw 40 yards to Sauer to set up yet another Turner field goal that gave the Jets a 26–7 lead. The Oilers' last chance to make it look respectable came late in the fourth quarter when punter Curley Johnson fumbled the snap from center and Houston's Roy Hopkins recovered the ball on the New York nine-yard line. But three plays later Johnny Sample intercepted Pete Beathard at the three-yard line to send the Oilers home thoroughly whipped.

The victory gave the Jets a 7–2 record and a three-and-a-half game lead over the 4–6 Oilers. The Jets had also achieved a club-record fourth-straight victory, but there was a more dubious record set that day. For the sixth straight game Namath had not thrown a touchdown pass: it was an AFL record for a starting quarterback. Namath was tired of hearing about it. "It shows you how ignorant people are," he told reporters after the game when someone brought the subject up. "What's the difference how you score? I don't care how many touchdown passes I've thrown.... If we were losing, I could understand it, but we're winning."[24] Good point, that. Still it just seemed odd for a passing team not to be scoring via the air. "It's like seeing Rocky Marciano stoop to pulling hair," wrote Larry Felser in *The Sporting News*.[25]

Namath had again completed barely one-third of his passes (seven of 20), but in just seven completions he had racked up 185 yards. The Jets were definitely in the driver's seat: in order to catch them, the Oilers would have to win three of their remaining four games, which was theoretically doable. But they would also have to count on the Jets losing all five of their remaining games, which would be a lot easier to at least fantasize about but for the fact that the Jets still had both games with Miami left on their schedule. It was conceivable that the Dolphins could shock everyone with an upset of New York at some point, but surely not twice in three weeks, which is what would have to happen. The Jets had made a habit of blowing division leads with late-season collapses, but nobody really saw that happening this time. They were too far ahead, looking too good, and had the schedule working in their favor. But the toughest part of their remaining schedule lay just ahead with a western road swing. Both the Oakland Raiders and the San Diego Chargers were 7–2, and they were the next two opponents the Jets had to face.

Week 10 — Sunday, November 17, 1968
Alameda County Coliseum, Oakland (attendance: 53,318)

Both the Jets and Raiders were 7–2 when the Jets traveled west to Oakland. To call it a grudge match would be redundant since it had reached the point where every game between the two teams was acrimonious enough to set a new precedent. Namath certainly remembered the last time the two teams had met — Ike Lassiter had fractured his cheekbone in the thirteenth game of the 1967 season. Now, as the two teams met again, the game was more important for Oakland than New York: the Jets were all but assured of an Eastern Division title, whereas Oakland was tied with San Diego for second place in the West, both trailing Kansas City. But it was important to the Jets in another way — they wanted payback for the beating they took in Oakland the year before. Besides, at 7–2, this was a team that had gotten accustomed to beating other teams. There had been some colorful and interesting contests between the two teams in recent years, but this game would top them all.

The Jets got out to an early 6–0 lead when Jim Turner hit two field goals in the first quarter, first from 44 yards and then from 18. But as the opening period was nearing an end, Oakland took the lead when Daryle Lamonica hit Warren Wells with a nine-yard touchdown throw. The Raiders led 7–6 after one quarter.

Oakland would extend that lead on their first offensive series of the second quarter when Lamonica threw a screen pass to tight end Billy Cannon and watched him take it 48 yards for a score. Nobody had laid a hand on Cannon, and the Raiders were up, 14–6.

It would take the rest of the quarter for the Jets to get into the end zone, but finally, just seconds before halftime, Namath rolled out on a bootleg from the Oakland one-yard line and ran it in himself. Now behind 14–12, the Jets tried for two-points on the conversion, but Parilli's pass fell incomplete. And so, the Jets were left trailing by two after two quarters. The first half had been marked by a rather high penalty count, the Jets already racking up 86 penalty yards after being flagged seven times, while the Raiders had been called four times for 63 yards.

Approaching the midway point of the third quarter, safety Jim Hudson intercepted Lamonica to set up New York's go-ahead touchdown, which Bill Mathis ran in from four yards out six plays later. The score gave the Jets a 19–14 lead, but Oakland came roaring back, and after Charlie Smith scored on a three-yard run, Lamonica hit Hewritt Dixon in the end zone for a two-point conversion to give the Raiders a three-point edge at 22–19.

Toward the end of the third period Oakland was driving again. The Jets appeared to have stopped them, but a face-masking penalty on Hudson gave the Raiders a first-and-goal at the New York six-yard line. Hudson was infuriated; Johnny Sample tried to restrain him, but to no avail. Hudson had some very choice words for the official, and he wound up getting tossed out of the game with 1:50 left in the third quarter. Being ejected from a game is an automatic league fine: Hudson upped his fine by flipping the jeering Oakland crowd off with both hands as he left the field.

After Hudson's dramatic departure, the quarter ended with Oakland at the New York one-yard line and poised to take a commanding lead, but on the first play of the fourth quarter,

Charlie Smith fumbled the ball and Gerry Philbin recovered for the Jets at the three. They may have avoided giving up a score, but the Jets were certainly starting from a hole — they had 97 yards of ground stretched out in front of them. No big deal. There was a rookie cornerback named George Atkinson covering Maynard: Namath decided to bully the rookie.

On first down from the three-yard line Namath went back to pass. Throwing from a good seven yards deep in his own end zone, Namath lofted the ball down the right sideline to Maynard. The ball was thrown behind Maynard, but Atkinson had fallen on his face trying to keep up with the speedy flanker, and so there was really no one to interfere with Maynard's catching the ball. Maynard turned around and caught it at the 36, then spun around and started to run. Safety Dave Grayson had the angle to cut him off, and he took Maynard out of bounds at midfield to hold the play to a 47-yard gain.

If they burned the rookie once, why night try it again? On the very next play Namath went back to pass and once more lofted it down the right sideline to Maynard. Again, the ball was underthrown: again, it didn't matter. In fact, it was for the better (was it intentional?), for after getting burned on the previous play, Atkinson was racing like a mad dog to keep pace with Maynard. Truth is, he had Maynard stride-for-stride, but when Maynard looked and saw the ball coming short, he turned and stopped; Atkinson tried to stop, but when he did he fell again. He didn't just fall — he took a good tumble. Maynard caught the ball on the 14, and when he turned and saw Atkinson on the ground he tried to cut around him, but slipped slightly himself at that point and started to go down. Question was, who could get up first? Maynard had only dropped to one knee, and when he got up at the 10-yard line Atkinson made a desperate lunge for him and missed. Grayson was again closing in to help out, but this time he would be too late — Maynard beat him to the end zone. The Jets had just gone 97 yards on only two passes to retake the lead, 26–22. It was Namath's first touchdown pass in more than six games — he picked a good time for it.

On New York's next possession they drove downfield again, but were forced to settle for a 12-yard field goal. Still, it increased their lead to a full seven points at 29–22. But the Raiders came right back at them, driving 88 yards for the tying touchdown — twice. The Raiders had appeared to score on a 65-yard screen pass to Smith, but a holding penalty nullified the touchdown and brought the play back. Undaunted, the Raiders proceeded to drive down and score again, with Lamonica passing five times to Fred Biletnikoff, the final of which was a 22-yard touchdown with 3:55 left to play.

Namath then went back to Maynard, hitting him with a 42-yard pass to set up a 26-yard field goal for a 32–29 lead with just 1:08 left to play. It is curious, to say the least, that anyone would assume a three-point lead was the final word with more than a minute remaining in a game in which the lead had changed so often, but at that point somebody at NBC decided to switch away from the game to the television production of *Heidi*. In the network's defense, they had invested a lot of money in the film, and as it was now 7:10 P.M., the game had already encroached on the movie's time slot. Still, the reaction the decision drew would let all networks know from then on how important football had become to the viewing public. The network's New York switchboard blew a fuse as thousands of phone calls came in from irate fans. Many of them may have assumed the Jets had won: many others probably knew better than to count Oakland out with more than a minute to play. It was probably better for the New York fans that they did not see the absurd conclusion of the contest.

After receiving the kick, the Raiders began on their own 22-yard line. Lamonica dumped the ball off to Smith, who gained 20 yards to the 42; another face-masking penalty on New York brought the Raiders to the New York 43. From there, Lamonica had Wells go deep and Biletnikoff cut across the middle, right-to-left. Smith then snuck out of the backfield and found the open spot in the coverage to the right side of the field, away from the flow of the coverage as dictated by the patterns run by Wells and Biletnikoff. It was Hudson's replacement, Mike D'Amato, who looked more-or-less helpless as he spotted Smith too late and tried to catch up with him: Smith caught the ball on the run and easily outraced D'Amato to the end zone. Oakland was ahead again, 36–32, and the Coliseum crowd was roaring. But there were still 42 seconds left to play; since Namath had earlier taken his team 97 yards in just two plays, everyone knew it could be done. Namath never got the chance.

As Earl Christy returned the ensuing kickoff for the Jets he was met at the 14-yard line by Howie Williams, but managed to avoid the tackle. Christy then tried to dodge a tackle by linebacker Bill Budness, but Budness dove and managed to grab an ankle. Into the picture came the Jets' Mark Smolinski; seeing Williams coming back to get in on the tackle, Smolinski tried to run past Christy to block Williams. But in trying to get around Christy, Smolinski's hand came up and punched the ball right out of Christy's hand. Christy went down with Budness at his ankles, Smolinski tripped over Budness and went down, and the only ones on hand to recover the loose ball were a swarm of black jerseys. Williams got to it first, but slipped and slid past the ball at the two-yard line. No matter, as there were none but Raiders in sight—lineman Bob Kruse, linebackers Duane Benson and Bill Fairband, receiver John Roderick. Suddenly, from out of nowhere, it was running back Preston Ridlehuber who scooped the ball up at the two and dove into the end zone. Oakland had scored two touchdowns in nine seconds. Now it was over: the Jets had lost, 43–32.

In the New York locker room the accusations were flying. Jets' defensive coach Walt Michaels had a few terse words, pointing out the need for officials who were as dedicated to their jobs as the players and coaches were to theirs. The Jets had been called for five face-masking penalties, which Michaels found too incredulous. He certainly didn't mind saying so. Michaels stormed out of the room and went next door to the officials' dressing room—it was locked, so he beat on the door while yelling vitriolic accusations.

Ewbank was in the process of telling reporters that he didn't really know why the officials had tossed Hudson from the game, but that it definitely had hurt the team, when somebody let him know that Michaels was on his way to the officials' dressing room. "Get him out of there," Ewbank said wearily, "it can only cost him money."[26]

It wasn't just Michaels—this game was going to cost the franchise money. Namath (who finished 19 of 37 for 381 yards and a touchdown) kept his head, declining to comment on the officiating, saying that anyone who had seen the game could decide for themselves what kind of job the officials did. The Jets had been penalized 13 times for 145 yards, the Raiders six for 93.

The immediate and obvious fines were the standard $50 fines to Hudson and Jets' defensive lineman John Elliott for each being ejected from the game. Hudson and Michaels received further $150 fines, Hudson for his obscene gesture to the good people of Oakland as he exited the field, Michaels for his unrestrained comments after the game, and the team was fined $2,000 for a number of offenses; in particular, Ewbank had invited the press to see some game films in the days following the contest—films that showed very obvious and egregious penalties committed by the Raiders that went uncalled by the officials. Even team physician Dr. James Nicholas was included in the rogue's gallery of offenders for barging into the officials' dressing room to give them an earful (the sneaky doc had gotten there before they had a chance to lock the door).

The truth is Michaels was justifiably disbelieving in the number of face-masking penalties. He was backed up by, of all people, Oakland offensive tackle Harry Schuh, who was right there on the play when Hudson was flagged for grabbing Hewritt Dixon's facemask. Schuh confirmed that Hudson did *not* grab the facemask, but more than that, he himself went on to criticize the officiating. "When Hudson questioned the call," Schuh said, "the official used the worst language I ever heard. The officials ruined the game for us."[27] If these officials weren't dirty they were damn sure incompetent.

To a man, the Jets wanted Oakland come January 29. The League had already determined that the winner of the Eastern Division would host the AFL Championship on that date. The Jets had no doubt that they would win their division. Now it was up to the Raiders to do their part and win the West. The Jets wanted the Raiders in a rematch — wanted them *bad*.

Week 11 — Sunday, November 24, 1968
San Diego Stadium, San Diego (attendance: 51,175)

At 8–2, San Diego was in hot pursuit of the Western Division title. The Jets' situation was not as pressing: at 7–3 they still had a good lead on Houston (5–6) in the East. But if that was supposed to give the Chargers more incentive, you would never know it from how they played.

The Jets came out and took the lead early, scoring on their first two offensive series. On the first, Jim Turner kicked a 13-yard field goal for a 3–0 lead. It being his twenty-ninth of the season, Turner set a new professional football record. On the Jets' second series, Namath and Maynard set a club record, connecting on an 87-yard touchdown pass that was not only the team's longest-ever pass play, but also the AFL's longest pass of the season. As the first quarter wound down, the Jets were leading 10–0 and were driving again, with Namath throwing to Maynard for 21 yards, then hitting him again for 23 more: they were on the San Diego three-yard line when the quarter ended.

On the first play of the second period, Matt Snell capped the 72-yard drive with a three-yard touchdown run for a 17–0 lead. Shortly afterward, Turner would kick a 20-yard field goal to increase the lead to 20–0, and it was starting to look too easy.

Speedy Duncan gave the Chargers hope when he made his own contribution to the record book by returning a punt for an AFL-record 95 yards and a score. It might have given the home crowd reason to think that San Diego could climb back into it, but the Jets snuffed that dream out when they answered with another score. Namath this time threw to Bill Mathis for a 19-yard touchdown and a 27–7 halftime lead.

It had been an impressive half for Namath, completing 13 of 25 passes for 277 yards and two touchdowns. San Diego's John Hadl, on the other hand, was having his worst game of the year by far, hitting only six of 19 passes in the half for 35 yards and three interceptions.

In the second half, with the lead decisive, Namath went to a conservative game plan with an eye toward running time off the clock and avoiding any big mistakes that might give San Diego the impetus to rise up. It seemed to work, for while the Jets only managed a 30-yard field goal in the third quarter, the Chargers could still do nothing.

In the fourth quarter, a one-yard touchdown run by Mathis gave the Jets a 37–7 lead, and when the Chargers were finally able to mount an offensive drive and scored with just under ten minutes left in the game, it was really far too late. The Jets had been dominant throughout, shutting down the league's number one offense entirely, but then, the Jets had the league's number one defense.

The Chargers knew they had lost ground they couldn't afford in their division, and they were disgusted, nobody more so than Hadl. "You can't throw four interceptions to New York, give Namath the ball that much and still beat him," he said.[28]

"The way Namath threw today," said San Diego coach Sid Gillman, "he can beat anybody. I mean *anybody*."[29] Namath was 17 of 31 for 337 yards, with two TDs and one interception.

Four days later, on Thanksgiving Day, the Kansas City Chiefs beat the Houston Oilers. It was official then — for the first time in the team's history, the New York Jets were champions of their division.

Week 12 — Sunday, December 1, 1968
Shea Stadium, New York (attendance: 61,776)

The Jets closed out the season with the weakest part of their schedule, two games against Miami with Cincinnati in-between. Having already won their division, they had the luxury of playing their starters sparingly, and giving back-up men some playing time, which would help keep everybody sharp while also cutting the risk of injury to the starters.

Although the starters took the field at Shea to begin the game against Miami, the 4–6–1 Dolphins played the Jets to a scoreless standstill after one quarter, and it was the Dolphins who got on the board first with a 15-yard field goal in the second period. But things began to go as expected when Namath got the Jets in gear with two quick scores, the first a 54-yard touchdown pass to Don Maynard, and the second a five-yard scoring toss to Pete Lammons that put the Jets up 14–3. The upstart Dolphins did not lose heart, however, and Bob Griese threw a 38-yard touchdown to Gene Milton before the end of the half.

The Jets' slim 14–10 lead after two quarters notwithstanding, Ewbank stuck to the plan and sent Parilli in at quarterback when the third quarter began. Like the first, the third quarter went scoreless, but the Dolphins surprised the Shea Stadium crowd when they put together a drive in the fourth quarter and took a 17–14 lead on a one-yard scoring run by Jim Kiick.

Alas, for the Dolphins, it would seem that the Jets were only toying with them, as Parilli answered back by taking the Jets 74 yards in seven plays to retake the lead. Parilli mixed things up, throwing 17 yards to Lammons and hitting Maynard and George Sauer for short gains to get the Jets to the Miami 47. From there he threw downfield to a very open Maynard at the 15-yard line. There may never have been a lonelier-looking touchdown: Maynard waited on the ball as if he were fielding a punt, and after catching it he could have chosen to walk the remaining 15 yards for the score — he almost did.

Now leading 21–17 with 8:44 left in the game, the Jets kicked to Miami and Milton fumbled the ball on the return: Mark Smolinski recovered for New York at the Miami 25. After a couple of incompletions, Parilli again found Maynard for the score, and the Jets were up 28–17. Before it ended, Parilli hit Bake Turner with a 40-yard touchdown throw; Turner made an excellent one-handed catch at the eight-yard line and took it in to make the final 35–17. In his half of play, Namath completed eight of 14 for 104 yards, with two touchdowns.

Week 13 — Sunday, December 8, 1968
Shea Stadium, New York (attendance: 53,318)

The Cincinnati Bengals came to Shea with a 3–10 record and hopes of becoming the first expansion club in pro football to win more than three games in their maiden season. It seemed more than a little unlikely that they would beat a 9–3 division champ, but the Bengals still had the memory of beating the Jets back in preseason to buoy them, and they seemed inspired — for a few minutes anyway. The Bengals started off well, working their way into New York territory and seemingly headed to at least a field goal when running back Estes Banks fumbled; linebacker Paul Crane recovered for the Jets at the New York 33 and the Jets proceeded to drive 67 yards to score on a 10-yard pass from Namath to Sauer.

Later in the first quarter, Matt Snell was running a sweep right when he found himself in the clutches of linebacker Al Beauchamp: as he was being pulled to the ground, Snell lofted the ball downfield to Don Maynard for a 26-yard gain to the Cincinnati 12. On the next play, Namath too found Maynard — for 12 yards and a touchdown.

With the Jets up 14–0 in the second quarter, the Bengals caught a break when Beauchamp intercepted Namath at the Cincinnati 48 and ran it back 18 yards to the New York 34. From there it was only a matter of two plays for the Bengals to get on the board. Banks ran 20 yards to the 14, and on the next play Paul Robinson found a gap off right tackle and went 14 yards for the score. Later, Jim Turner gave the Jets a 17–7 lead with a 35-yard field goal, and with that Namath's work was once more done as the first half ended. Namath would again sit out the second half, after completing 13 of 23 for 193 yards, with two TDs and one interception.

With Parilli again leading the team in the second half, Jim Turner put the Jets up 20–7 in the third quarter with a 22-yard field goal. But Cincinnati showed signs of life later in the period when Bob Kelly blocked a New York punt, and Bill Peterson gathered up the ball and ran it 38 yards to the New York two-yard line. It was a golden opportunity, but the Jets' defense was not ranked number one in the AFL for nothing. The Bengals tried to ram it into the end zone on three straight runs but could get no closer than a yard. Then, on fourth-and-goal from the one, Cincinnati went for broke — why not? What did they really have to lose? But again they failed, and as the third quarter came to a close the Jets had taken over on downs at the one-yard line.

It had to be demoralizing for the Bengals as a team. What happened next had to be just as demoralizing to the New York defense. Their opponents had taken over first-and-goal on the two-yard line, and on four consecutive plays the New York defense had stopped them and turned them away without a point. Then, just seconds into the fourth quarter, Parilli fumbled the ball in the end zone: it was recovered by Jim Griffin in the end zone for a quick and easy touchdown that shaved New York's lead to 20–14.

But beyond that, Cincinnati could muster no threat, and late in the fourth the Jets evened accounts when they too blocked a punt and Gerry Philbin recovered the ball on the Cincinnati 36. Parilli threw a 34-yard touchdown to Bake Turner to complete the scoring and give the Jets a 27–14 win. The Jets were now 10–3 and headed to Miami to close out their schedule at the Orange Bowl.

Week 14 — Sunday, December 15, 1968
Orange Bowl, Miami (attendance: 32,843)

For their second game with Miami in three weeks, the Jets got out of the gate fast: on their very first play from scrimmage Namath handed to Matt Snell, who then pitched a lateral back to Namath. Namath then threw 71 yards to Bake Turner all the way to the Miami nine-yard line. Two plays later Snell scored on a six-yard run, giving the Jets a quick 7–0 lead. Jim turner would boost that lead to 10–0 with a 49-yard field goal before the period ended.

Miami was playing without quarterback Bob Griese, who had been injured in a victory over Boston the previous week, and it was Rick Norton who was piloting the Dolphins. Norton was intercepted in the second quarter by linebacker Ralph Baker, who returned the ball 20 yards to set up a one-yard touchdown run by Emerson Boozer. That gave the Jets a commanding 17–0 lead, but a pair of New York mistakes would help Miami get on the board before the half ended.

First, George Sauer fumbled after catching a pass from Namath, and Miami's John Bramlett grabbed the ball and ran it to the New York nine-yard line. Then Randy Beverly was flagged for pass interference in the end zone on a pass from Norton to Karl Noonan. That set the Dolphins up with a first-and-goal on the one-yard line, and when Larry Csonka took it in for a score, the Jets' lead was cut to 10 points. Namath finished the half six of 10 for 120 yards.

With the Jets leading 17–7 as the second half began, Babe Parilli came in and took New York 82 yards to score on their first offensive series of the half. The big play of the drive was a 29-yard pass to Bake Turner that brought the Jets to the Miami three-yard line; Parilli then threw to Lammons for the score.

Trailing 24–7, Miami had no real reason not to let rookie quarterback Kim Hammond try his hand, but like Norton he was unable to move the team with any consistency. There would be no more scoring until the final three minutes of the game, when Bill Mathis capped a 58-yard New York drive with a two-yard touchdown run to make the final 31–7.

Griese was not the only player to miss the game: for New York, Don Maynard sat out with a pulled hamstring. Offensive lineman Bob Talamini also missed the game, and another New York lineman, Dave Herman, only came in for one play. Otherwise, Ewbank was keeping some of his big guns out: aside from Namath again playing just the first half, Snell barely stayed in the game long enough to score the initial TD. It spoke well of the team that they could win so convincingly, even while withholding their major artillery.

Now it was back to New York to wait and see who their opponent would be in the AFL Championship. Whoever it might be, the Jets were confident that they had not seen the last of the Orange Bowl for the season — the Super Bowl was scheduled to be played there.

This was the season the Jets had been working toward ever since Sonny Werblin had purchased the team in 1963. Of course, Werblin had left just a bit too soon to be a part of it all, but Ewbank had been there through it all and had seen the dream of a divisional title come to fruition. As for Namath, he had the season he wanted to have — he was a winner. His numbers were not as eye-catching as they had been in previous seasons, but Namath didn't care about personal statistics. When he had the six-game touchdown pass drought midway through the season, Namath was not simply trying to deflect criticism by dismissing his detractors as ignorant — he knew it was a non-issue as long as the Jets were winning, and they had won five of those six games.

Namath finished the season with 187 completions in 380 attempts for 3,147 yards. His completion percentage was under 50 percent (49.2), but even Lamonica and Hadl completed less than half their throws that season (49.5 for Lamonica, 47.3 for Hadl), so he was in good company. Still, Namath's passing yardage was far below his 1967 total, as were his TD passes, but that only pointed to his maturation as he began to balance the offensive attack. It is also true that in 1967 when he had his record 4,007 passing yards, he had a crippled running game most of the year, with both Matt Snell and Emerson Boozer missing half the season. And then there were the interceptions. As was becoming his custom, he had thrown a pair more interceptions than touchdowns, but with 17 interceptions on the season, that number was also considerably lower than his 1967 total. It is also significant that 10 of his 17 interceptions came in just two games, the losses to Buffalo and Denver early in the season. His interception percentage was 4.5 percent, the best since his rookie season in 1965.

From the Denver loss onward, Namath's calculated restraint had guided the team to winning eight of their nine games afterward, the only loss being the Heidi game in Oakland, which many saw as a game that was not so much lost as it was stolen by the officials. After the last game of the season, Namath's teammates voted him the team's Most Valuable Player — finally! In 1967 it had been Maynard, in 1966 Sauer — Namath's receivers were until then considered more valuable than he was; but now, his teammates recognized Namath as their true leader and the one who had guided them to their first division title.

Now the Jets waited to see who their opponent would be in the AFL championship game. Oakland and Kansas City had both finished 12–2 and would have a playoff on December 22 in Oakland to determine who would make the trip to Shea Stadium to play the Jets (San Diego, who had stayed in the race, fell back late in the season and finished 9–5). Typically, the Jets' coaches and players said publicly that they didn't really care who their opponent would be, that they would be ready for whoever it was, but that was just talk. The game in Oakland back in November still hung like a foul smell in the locker room, and the Jets all wanted another shot at the Raiders.

When Oakland and Kansas City met for their playoff game it was such a no-contest that it seemed impossible the Raiders had been chasing the Chiefs all year long. The Raiders had lost to San Diego and Kansas City in consecutive weeks during their fifth and sixth games of the season and had not lost since, riding an eight-game winning streak into the playoff with Kansas City: they proceeded to run roughshod over the Chiefs, 41–6. Daryle Lamonica threw five touchdowns — three to Fred Biletnikoff and two to Warren Wells — while passing for 347 yards. Kansas City's Len Dawson, on the other hand, threw four interceptions. The Raiders seemed strong — *very* strong.

Nobody seemed more surprised than the Raiders at the ease with which they rolled over the Chiefs, but they made it understood that they were not anticipating a similarly easy contest in New York. "We're not trying to minimize the Kansas City Chiefs," said an Oakland spokesman, "but we just feel there are many more things you have to get ready for in getting ready for the Jets."[30]

That spokesman highlighted the team's concern for the Jets' passing game, mentioning Namath's quick release and his ability to read blitzes, and noting that Don Maynard seemed to always save his best effort for Oakland.[31] The Jets had a similar high regard for Oakland's receivers. "Biletnikoff and Wells are fine ends," said New York defensive backfield coach Walt Michaels. "If you let one go, Daryle'll hit the other."[32]

Lamonica, Biletnikoff, and Wells had indeed put on a show against Kansas City, but despite Oakland's 41–6 beat-down of the Chiefs they still found themselves set as two-and-a-half to three-point underdog to the Jets. After it was final and the Raiders would indeed be coming to New York, some of the Jets were more open about their preference, admitting that they had really wanted to have the Raiders all along. In particular, Namath and Gerry Philbin were very public in expressing their pleasure, with Namath going so far as to say that he did not consider Oakland's defense to be as strong as Kansas City's. It was a very deliberate dig, and a hint of what would follow as Namath engaged in playing head games all the way to the championship.

As for the coaches, both Ewbank and Oakland's John Rauch tried to downplay talk of a grudge match, Rauch saying that his players seemed no different emotionally than they had been in preparing for any other game, and Ewbank commenting that the press — particularly in Oakland — had tried to contrive an atmosphere of hostility between the teams. But that was all just so much talk, the kind of diplomacy that coaches frequently deal in. There was a lot of respect one side for the other, but everyone knew that there was also enough ill will to go around.

The Jets had the week off as Oakland and Kansas City had their playoff, and while Rauch saw that as no real advantage for New York, saying that too much idleness could take the edge off a team's game, the truth is that the Jets needed the time. There were players who needed to rest nagging injuries, including Maynard, who had sat out the last game of the season with a pulled hamstring.

After taking Sunday and Monday off, the Jets — including Maynard — returned to practicing at Shea Stadium in 35–40 mph wind gusts on the Tuesday before the game. The Jets would hold daily workouts until game day. The Raiders would hold their workouts at home before departing for New York on Friday and being given the use of Shea for a practice session on Saturday.

The weather was going to be lousy — everybody knew it. Cold, windy: again, Rauch saw no real advantage in it for New York. Sure the Jets had more experience with it, but the wind at Shea was virtually impossible to gauge. It could blow in any number of directions in a single play. After one of the Jets' practices at Shea, George Sauer remarked that the ball was getting caught by the wind four and five times during flight on any given pass.[33] No, there was no reading it.

Oakland was coming into the game with the league's number one offense: they had gained more yards and scored more points than any other team. Conversely, the Jets had the league's number one defense: they had allowed the fewest yards and fewest points. As championships go, it was ideal. Add into the mix Namath and an Oakland front four determined to rub him out. The New York offensive line had only given up 18 sacks all year, best in the AFL. The Oakland defense had led the AFL with 49 sacks. How perfect is that?

1968 AFL Championship — December 29, 1968
Shea Stadium, New York (attendance: 62,627)

With the temperature at 37 degrees at game time, the wind promised to make it much colder. In order to combat the chilling effects of the wind, members of the Raiders organization came into Shea early in the morning and began constructing shelters on their sideline. They had gotten permission to do so from AFL president Milt Woodard, but when members of the Jets' organization arrived that morning and saw them, they complained that the shelters were going to be blocking the view of spectators who would be seated behind the Oakland bench, and Woodard reversed his decision. The shelters came down — the Oakland Raiders would have to contend with the elements just like everybody else.

Oakland won the coin toss and elected to receive and the Jets made the wise and obvious choice to play with the wind at their backs in the first quarter. The hope was that the defense could force the Raiders to punt quickly, and the Jets could get good field position early by having Oakland kick into a strong wind: that's exactly how it played out.

For starters, George Atkinson had only returned the opening kickoff to the Oakland 18-yard line, and when Charlie Smith lost a half-yard on the first play from scrimmage, the Raiders went to the pass. Daryle Lamonica was forced to run out of the pocket and lost two more yards on second down, and on third he overthrew Hewritt Dixon flaring out of the backfield. The Jets' dream scenario for their first defensive series was fulfilled when Mike Eischeid's punt died at the Oakland 43.

Starting with ideal field position and the wind at their backs, Namath decided to waste no time: on first down he threw a slant-in to Don Maynard for 14 yards to the Oakland 29, and while his pass to Maynard on the following play fell incomplete, an interference penalty gave the Jets another first down at the 20. Shifting gears, Namath then handed off to Matt Snell, who shot through the line for six yards to the 14. On second down Namath went back to the pass, again looking to Maynard, who came off the line of scrimmage and then broke left toward the sideline. When he made his break, cornerback George Atkinson lost his footing, leaving Maynard quite open as he caught the ball heading into the corner of the end zone. Three-and-a-half minutes into the game, the Jets were up 7–0.

Oakland started in much better shape on their next offensive series when Charlie Smith returned the ensuing kickoff to the 30-yard line, and after two incomplete passes, the Raiders were in business when Lamonica hit tight end Billy Cannon with a 36-yard pass that carried to the New York 34. But after Gerry Philbin caught Dixon for a three-yard loss on first down, two consecutive passes fell incomplete, and the Raiders were forced to try a 45-yard field goal into the wind. George Blanda made a valiant effort, but the wind won out and the kick failed when the ball bounced off the crossbar.

From there the game turned into something of a punting exhibition as both teams failed to gain so much as a single first down on six straight possessions, three apiece. Finally, with just over four minutes left in the first quarter, the Jets began to move the ball again.

Beginning on their own 44, the Jets crossed midfield on the first play of the drive when Emerson Boozer ran for 14 yards to the Oakland 42. Namath threw seven yards to Sauer at the 35, and a run by Snell on the next play picked up a first down at the 28. Snell then picked up another three yards to the 25, but after Namath missed on passes to Maynard and Sauer, the Jets sent Jim Turner in to try a 33-yard field goal. Turner's aim was true, and with 1:38 left in the opening period the Jets were up 10–0.

Then the Raiders began to stir. Starting at their own 20, Oakland had moved to the 49 as the first period ended, Lamonica having thrown 11 yards to Pete Banaszak and 16 yards to Fred Biletnikoff. As the second period opened, Lamonica continued with a hot hand, throwing to

Dixon for a 22-yard gain to the New York 29. Two plays later he hit Biletnikoff at the 11, and Biletnikoff ducked under an attempted arm tackle by Johnny Sample and outran Randy Beverly to the end zone. The score cut New York's lead to 10–7, and with the wind now at *their* backs, Oakland may have felt they had gained the upper hand.

Still, the two teams would resume exchanging punts until the Jets started rolling again. After receiving a punt, the Jets found themselves looking at a long field when a clipping penalty pushed them back to their own 12. Namath hit Sauer for a first down at the 24; another pass to Sauer advanced the Jets to the 31, and from there Snell ran for the first down. Namath then hit Pete Lammons for a first down at midfield. After incomplete passes to Sauer and Lammons, Namath himself ran for the first down when he scrambled out of the pocket on a third-and-10 play, gaining 14 yards to the Oakland 36. Snell then gained six yards to the 30, but after a failed pass to Sauer, Namath was dropped for a loss at the 37 on third down, forcing the Jets to send Jim Turner in to try a 44-yard field goal into the wind. Turner's kick was far short and was fielded by David Grayson, who returned it to the Oakland 18.

When the Raiders failed to gain a yard in three plays and were forced to punt, the Jets took over with reasonably good field position at their own 33. Runs by Snell and Bill Mathis gained a first down to the 43, and then Namath threw to Sauer for 25 yards to the Oakland 32. But from there, two incompletions and a short throw to Lammons had Jim Turner coming back onto the field to try another field goal. This time he put it through from 36 yards out to ring up the first score into the wind by either side, and the Jets were ahead 13–7.

Oakland responded quickly: Atkinson returned the kick to the 42, and a Lamonica pass to Dixon moved the Raiders to the New York 41. Lamonica then threw to Biletnikoff at the 23, and after an incompletion, a pass to Wells landed Oakland at the 15. But on third-and-three, a screen to Dixon failed to gain the first down when linebacker Ralph Baker dropped him for a five-yard loss. After the two-minute warning, Blanda kicked a 26-yard field goal to cut New York's lead to 13–10.

When the Jets took over at their 20 after the kick they still had time to work with, and after Boozer ran for 15 yards to the 35 and Namath followed by hitting Maynard for 12 yards to the 47, it looked like they might be onto something. A real threat failed to materialize, however, and the half ended.

As the wind was pretty well having its way with the passing game, both sides might have preferred to keep it on the ground; problem was neither team could consistently move the ball with their running game. The Jets had the league's leading defense against the run, yielding an average of just 3.2 yards per rush and 85.4 yards per game. The Raiders were only fifth in the AFL against the run (4.1 yards per rush and 128.9 per game), but were playing the Jets' ground game fairly well, and both teams had consequently found themselves in frequent passing situations. Neither side was having much success there, either: in the first half Namath had only completed a third of his passes (10 of 30); Lamonica had very similar results (nine of 28).

Aside from the wind, Namath had other problems that made him loathe the idea of going out for another half. In the first quarter he had been sandwiched by Ike Lassiter and Ben Davidson. The hit didn't fracture Namath's cheek like Lassiter had a season earlier, but it had otherwise created similar results in that it had his head feeling as though it could swell up enough to split his helmet in two. From the first quarter onward, Namath would play with a throbbing pain in his skull.

There was more — in the second quarter Lassiter had landed on Namath's left hand, badly dislocating the middle finger. As it happened on a failed third-down play, Namath merely returned to the sideline where team trainer Jeff Snedeker popped the finger back in place. Snedeker then taped the middle and ring fingers together for stability, and when the Jets got the ball back, Namath was back out on the field without missing a play.

At halftime, as Ewbank spoke to his team, Namath was in the next room being examined and medicated by Dr. Nicholas. Ewbank's pep talk was probably nothing compared to the pep that Nicholas was giving out — the painkillers were being liberally administered, but then how better to equip Namath for another half than to tell his body a lie, to convince it that it wasn't really hurting after all?

The Jets would receive the second half kick, so Oakland chose to have New York going into the wind in the third quarter. The Jets could do nothing in their first three plays of the half and had to punt the ball away, but they were handed a golden opportunity when Roger Bird fumbled the punt right into the waiting hands of Bake Turner, and the Jets took possession at the Oakland 40. Almost as quickly as the opportunity arose, the Jets pissed it away when they could only manage a single yard in three plays, and rather than attempt a 46-yard field goal into the wind they chose to punt again.

The Raiders seemed to take inspiration from having dodged one, and they wasted little time in moving downfield in their next series. Although the punt forced Oakland to begin at their own six-yard line, Lamonica got them out of the hole quickly, throwing to Biletnikoff at the 16, and then hitting him again with a pass to the 46. From there, he hit Wells with a bomb all the way down to the New York six-yard line. But the New York defense tightened after that.

On first down Lamonica handed to Charlie Smith, who carried to the three before being stopped by Jim Hudson and Ralph Baker. On second down Smith again carried, making just a yard to the two before being stopped by Hudson, Philbin, and Larry Grantham. Then, on third-and-goal, Lamonica handed to Dixon, who was stopped at the goal line — Hudson again. The Raiders were forced to settle for a nine-yard field goal and a 13–13 tie.

After a touchback on the ensuing kick, the Jets began at the 20 and launched a time-consuming drive that all but ran out the third quarter and included four key third-down conversions along the way. After Snell gained two yards to the 22 and Boozer lost three back to the 19, the Jets were facing a third-and-11: Namath hit Boozer for the first down at the 30. Three consecutive runs by Snell moved the Jets to the 47, the third providing another third-down conversion.

From the 47 Snell ran for four more yards on first down, and Namath then threw to Sauer for a first down at the Oakland 41. An incomplete pass, followed by a one-yard run by Boozer gave New York a third-and-nine at the Oakland 40, and Namath converted again with a 20-yard pass to Maynard across the middle. After two incompletions on passes intended for Maynard, the Jets faced third-and-10 from the Oakland 20. With 58 seconds remaining in the third quarter, Namath rolled out to his left and threw to Lammons at the 13. The ball was thrown perfectly, sailing just beyond the Roger Bird's reach and into Lammons' hands as he turned upfield. Taking it up the sideline, Lammons ran through an attempted tackle by David Grayson, and was able to keep his balance and stay in bounds long enough to get into the corner of the end zone for a touchdown. New York led, 20–13.

Oakland began its next series in good shape after returning the kick to the 30, and was facing a third-and-four from the 36 when the third period ended. When linebacker Al Atkinson knocked down a pass to Biletnikoff to open the final quarter, the Raiders were forced to punt; the Jets wound up being pinned back at their own four-yard line. Boozer got them out of the hole quickly with an 11-yard run to the 15, and two plays later Namath threw a 15-yard pass to Snell to move the Jets out to the 30. But when the following three plays only got them six more yards, the Jets were also forced to punt from their own 36. They did not have the same fortunes as Oakland, however, and rather than pinning the Raiders back deep, the kick only carried to the 29.

After a screen to Dixon advanced Oakland to the 33, Lamonica then went to Biletnikoff. Cornerback Johnny Sample had been benched in the first half after Biletnikoff burned him on the touchdown catch. But replacement Cornell Gordon was not handling the Oakland receiver any better, and now Sample was back in the game. Biletnikoff blew past Sample on a post pattern and Lamonica threw deep down the right sideline. Biletnikoff gathered the ball in at the New York 26, and ran it to the 11 before Sample caught up and brought him down.

From there the New York defense tightened again, yielding no ground on a first-down run, and then knocking down two passes, first a throw to Wells at the goal line that was broken up by Beverly, and then a throw to Dixon at the one: the throw to Dixon was broken up by Hudson, who almost intercepted. Oakland was forced to settle for a 20-yard field goal that brought them to within four points of the Jets at 20–16.

With 9:15 remaining in the game, one might have expected that the Jets would be looking to eat up some time in trying to increase their lead, but after Earl Christy ran the kick back to the 22-yard line, the Jets obviously had no intention of playing it safe. On first down Namath went back to pass and threw to Maynard at the left sideline. A deep out can be a dicey call in any situation, but was all the more so here, clinging to a four-point lead in the fourth quarter and from your own 22—*and with that wind*! Atkinson read it well and jumped in front, intercepting at the 37. Maynard made a diving attempt to bring him down, but Atkinson raced out of Maynard's grasp and took off down the sideline. The last man in his way as he approached the goal line was Namath, who lowered his shoulder and gave Atkinson a shot, knocking him out of bounds at the five-yard line.

The New York defense had already made some good stands, even stopping Oakland on three straight runs down close to the goal line, but it's a bit much to expect any defense to repeat such heroics after having just left the field. The Jets' defense had barely had time to put on their wind-breakers, sit down and catch their breath when the interception sent them right back on the field again. This time it took Oakland just one play, as Pete Banaszak shot through the line and managed to cross the goal line as he was being tackled. Now, for the first time in the game, the Raiders had the lead, 23–20. There was jubilation on the Oakland sideline, which became a bizarre, chaotic scene. Somehow a fire had started near the bench, and the players were jumping and celebrating in a billowing, smoky haze.

There was now 8:18 left to play and the New York offense was hungry to redeem itself and regain the lead. Maynard let Namath know that, sore hamstring or not, he could get past Atkinson on a deep pattern. Namath wanted to see what the defensive alignment would be first.

Christy did his share by returning the kickoff to the New York 32, giving the Jets decent field position to stage their rally. Namath decided to go with an audible—if the coverage by the corners was slack, he would throw a short out to Sauer: if it was tight he would send Maynard deep. Coming up to the line on first down, Namath saw that the defensive backs were laying back a little, so he called for the short out under the coverage. He hit Sauer at the left sideline for 10 yards and a first down at the 42.

Now hoping that the short pass would bring the corners in tighter, Namath again called for an audible in the huddle. When the Jets came to the line of scrimmage, Namath this time saw Atkinson move in closer to Maynard—perfect. He called his audible at the line and sent Maynard deep. When Namath took the snap and dropped back to throw, his wall of protection formed a perfect pocket. He threw long, deep and high—maybe too high. Even with the wind at his back, there was always the danger that, the higher the ball got, the more likely it was to get caught in a wind gust. The wind did seem to take the ball even higher. Maybe the wind did Namath a favor, since he at first thought he had overthrown Maynard. As Maynard turned and looked over his left shoulder, he saw that the wind was pushing the ball further toward the right. He had a step on Atkinson and could make the catch unmolested, but that counted on his being able to discern where the wind was going to bring the ball down to earth. Rather than turn the other way, Maynard looked straight up as the ball dropped like a stone directly over his head and into his hands. He gathered it in at the 15 and kept running.

"He made a hell of a catch," Atkinson said afterward. "I followed him step for step and I saw the ball all the way, but he turned the other way and caught the ball over his shoulder."[34] Atkinson was indeed right there with Maynard, and Maynard didn't get four strides before Atkinson hit him from behind. Maynard fumbled the ball out of bounds, and the official spotted it at the Oakland six-yard line. The play had covered 52 yards.

First-and-goal on the six-yard line: it had been the Jets' inclination to become rather conservative in such situations. Why not? They had a workhorse of a fullback in Snell, so situations such as this seemed suited to the run. Namath was hoping that the Raiders would assume as much. He instead called for a play-action fake to Snell, and wanted to hit Bill Mathis with a pass. Namath took the snap and faked the handoff to Snell, then began to rollout to his left. Problem was, Oakland's defense read the play perfectly. One reason may be that Mathis somewhat telegraphed the play in that when he came out of the backfield he didn't look like he was aiming to block somebody: he very obviously looked like he was running a pattern. Mathis shot out of the backfield and broke left, but cornerback Willie Brown picked him up. Snell did a good job of blocking linebacker Gus Otto, but when Namath looked to Mathis he saw that Brown had him well covered. Ordinarily Brown would have been covering Sauer, but when Namath looked to Sauer, who was running toward the left side of the end zone, he saw that he was double-covered by linebacker Dan Conners and safety David Grayson. Namath lost his footing slightly, slipping when he stopped to look to the right.

While all of this had been going on Maynard, who was a decoy on the right side well away from the flow of the play, had seen that things were not going as planned. Realizing that Namath was now in trouble, Maynard suddenly broke toward the center of the end zone and Namath spotted him. Namath threw a low bullet that just zipped past Atkinson's reach. Atkinson said that if it had been any higher, he could have tipped it. Instead, Maynard caught the ball as he fell to the ground, cradling it in his arms at the back of the end zone. The Jets were back out in front, 27–23: it had only taken them 31 seconds to regain the lead. "It was pure Namath improvisation," wrote Murray Olderman, "and a perfect example of individuality which makes both him and the Jets an exciting team."[35]

There was now 7:47 left in the game, and as quickly as the Raiders could strike with weapons like Biletnikoff, the game was certainly far from over. Atkinson returned the kick to the Oakland 34, so the Raiders were in good shape to stage a comeback of their own. After a pass to tight end Billy Cannon and a well-executed draw play to Dixon, the Raiders were already on the New York 26. On first down from there, Dixon turned what could have been a five-yard loss into a no-gain when he escaped Verlon Biggs in the backfield and got back to the line of scrimmage. On second down Lamonica threw to Wells in the right corner of the end zone, but the pass was overthrown. Then on third down Lamonica — again throwing to the right — tried to hit Biletnikoff, but the pass was almost — in fact, should have been — intercepted by Sample.

It was now fourth-and-10 at the New York 26. A field goal would only narrow the Jets' lead to 27–26, and with the clock approaching five minutes to play there was no guarantee that they would get the ball back with enough time to score a second time. Besides, kicking into the wind, even a 33-yarder was questionable. Rauch opted to go for the first down. He would be second-guessed from then until now for the decision, but the truth is it was not really that radical a choice. As it turned out, Biggs easily blew past his blocker and dropped Lamonica for a six-yard loss at the 32.

The home crowd at Shea was elated, and the Jets would have loved nothing better than to run the clock out. When Boozer gained 10 yards to the 42 on first down, it looked like they might do just that, but a pair of two-yard runs by Snell left the Jets with a third-and-six at their 46. Namath chose to pass on third down, but he overthrew Maynard at the Oakland 20-yard line. As bad as not gaining a first down, the incompletion also stopped the clock. On the punt,

Atkinson called for a fair catch at the Oakland 15, so at least the Raiders had a long field ahead of them. But once more, they moved fast.

On first down Lamonica hit Biletnikoff for a nice gain out to the 39. Lamonica then went long to Wells, who had easily gotten past Baird. Wells caught the ball at the New York 30, and wasn't brought down by Baird until he made it to the 24. To make matters worse, Hudson, who had played a superb game up to then, committed a very costly and foolish error when he gave an obvious late hit to Wells after he was already on the ground. The referee, standing two feet away, couldn't miss that. The penalty took Oakland half the distance to the goal line, setting the Raiders up nicely at the New York 12-yard line with just over two minutes left in the game.

Hudson's blunder could well have cost the Jets the championship, but fortunately for him — and the team — Lamonica and Charlie Smith were about to commit a blunder of their own. On first-and-10 from the New York 12 Lamonica went back to pass; he looked briefly downfield, but quickly turned to Smith, who was moving to the right for a safety-valve screen. Lamonica threw to Smith, but as Smith was about a yard further back than Lamonica, the pass actually wound up being a lateral. Lamonica threw it behind Smith, and the ball hit the ground at the 24-yard line. Being a lateral, it was a live ball, though Smith seemed slow to react, obviously thinking that it was merely an incomplete pass. Lamonica, on the other hand, knew the awful truth — he had just given the ball away. As the ball continued to roll backward, Lamonica tried to run to it, but was beaten by Ralph Baker, who gathered it up at the 29.

By rule, the defense could recover the ball, but could not advance it, but Baker took off running anyway. He ran all the way to the end zone with Smith chasing him, but although it was a dead ball by rule, Baker wasn't taking any chances. Earlier in the season the Jets had a similar play in which the referees had allowed Boston to run a lateral in for a touchdown irrespective of the rules, so it was wise to follow through here as well: maybe these officials were likewise ignorant of the rules. Turns out they weren't. While the Jets got to keep the ball, it was brought back to the spot where Baker grabbed possession of it.

With 1:53 left to play, surely the Jets could run out the clock this time. No such luck: three runs failed to gain a first down, and the Jets found themselves again punting the ball away with 1:01 left to play. The Raiders took possession at their 22.

Lamonica hit Cannon for 16 yards to the 38, but incomplete passes to Dixon and Wells then brought up a third-and-10. After Lamonica was forced to scramble for a yard on third down, there was nothing but to go for it on fourth-and-nine, and when Hudson tackled Dixon short of the first down on a screen pass with 10 seconds left, it was over at last. "They were trying to congratulate me with 14 seconds left," Ewbank said after the game, "but I wouldn't let them. I had a game like that before and I lost it."[36]

They had finally done it: the New York Jets were champions of the American Football League. Against the wishes of AFL president Milt Woodard, the champagne flowed freely in the New York locker room after the game. Woodard had sought to bar any alcohol from being part of the locker room celebrations of either team, but finding the idea of a championship celebration without champagne just too absurd, the Jets had 25 cases stashed away and at the ready. In Woodard's presence, and to his consternation, the Jets openly imbibed as they reveled in their triumph.

Namath was overcome by emotion after the game. "There were blood stains on his uniform, mud stains all over his shoes and what looked suspiciously like tear stains around his eyes," wrote Milton Richman.[37] Namath seemed in disbelief, saying that it was the greatest feeling he had experienced in all his years playing the game, be it high school, college, or professional.[38] His numbers read 19 of 49 for 266 yards, with three touchdowns and one interception.

As the celebration commenced, the Jets continued to receive updates on the NFL championship. Baltimore was beating Cleveland handily. It became obvious to everyone that the Jets would be playing the Colts in the Super Bowl. Ewbank deflected questions about the Colts, saying that he wanted to enjoy the triumph of the moment. They all did. Namath threw an arm around Maynard. "Are you ready for Baltimore?" he asked his flanker. Maynard smiled. "Joe," he said, "I'm always ready."[39]

In the Oakland locker room, Lamonica let it be known that he was fully rooting for the Jets in the Super Bowl, saying that he felt that Baltimore could be beaten. As the reporters left him, Lamonica had a parting message for the Jets: "Look, give my best regards to the Jets," he said, "and tell them, 'best of luck.'"[40]

Lamonica was sincere. Aside from wanting to see the AFL legitimized in people's eyes by beating the NFL, how could he not pull for the Jets? After the game Lamonica had met Namath on the field and congratulated him. Surely he too saw the tears in Namath's eyes.

Before long the Baltimore Colts were also celebrating, having waxed the Cleveland Browns 34–0. "I've heard a lot about Joe Namath and the Jets," said Baltimore quarterback Earl Morrall. "I am anxious to play against them."[41] Namath was asked about Morrall as well. "I think Daryle Lamonica is a better passer than Earl Morrall," he said.[42] Well, it was true.

6

Super Bowl III

The 1968 NFL championship game between the Baltimore Colts and the Cleveland Browns was no contest at all. Cleveland had been the only team to beat Baltimore during the regular season, besting the Colts 30–20 in week six. The Browns had beaten the Colts in Baltimore, and the Colts were eager to return the favor by humiliating the Browns in Cleveland for the league championship. In the championship, the Colts would hold Cleveland running back Leroy Kelly, the league's leading rusher, to just 28 yards. In fact, the Browns only managed to cross midfield twice in the game, and even then could get no further than the Baltimore 35-yard line.

The 34–0 bitch-slapping the Colts dealt Cleveland in the championship was the fourth shutout by the Baltimore defense in 1968; they had also beaten the St. Louis Cardinals 27–0, the New York Giants 26–0, and had annihilated the Atlanta Falcons 44–0. When they weren't shutting teams out they were frequently holding them to single digits in scoring, and winning by such lopsided scores as 41–7 (over Pittsburgh), 28–7 (over Chicago), and 42–14 (over San Francisco). They had even beaten the reigning NFL-champion Green Bay Packers 16–3. During their 13–1 season the Baltimore Colts had outscored their opponents 402–144, an incredible average of 18 points per game over the opposition. It was an awesome team.

Many were proclaiming the 1968 Baltimore Colts to be the greatest football team ever assembled. In fact, they were so good that they were considered boring. Their complete domination over opponents frequently made their games predictable and devoid of any drama. Broadcaster and former New York Giants kicker Pat Summerall noted that, while it might be great football, it could hardly be considered exciting.[1]

"The Colts are the most awesome team I have seen in football since the 1961–62 Packers," wrote New York Giants quarterback Fran Tarkenton in an article.[2] Even Baltimore coach Don Shula couldn't help but to crow a little: "I have never seen a better defensive team than this one," he said.[3]

The Green Bay Packers had been heavily favored in each of the first two Super Bowls: they had beaten the spread both times. The Packers had rolled over the Kansas City Chiefs by 25 points in the first Super Bowl, and in the second they had beaten the Oakland Raiders by 19. If it were really true that the Baltimore Colts were an even more powerful team than the Green Bay Packers, what chance did the Jets, or any other AFL team, stand against them? None at all, said the wise sages who set the odds. Las Vegas prognosticator Jimmie "the Greek" Snyder immediately put the spread at 17 points. Some felt he was being too kind to the Jets. Other oddsmakers upped the spread to 18, 18-and-a-half, and even 19 points. The presumed experts foresaw a bloodbath. "If you listen to people talk, it would be foolish for us to dress," quipped Weeb Ewbank.[4]

On paper the Jets matched up well against the Colts. The New York offense averaged 360.5 yards per game (245.6 passing and 114.9 rushing) to Baltimore's 334.3 yards per game (205.1 passing, 129.2 rushing). Both teams boasted the top defense in their respective leagues. The Jets allowed 240.2 yards per game (85.4 rushing and 154.9 passing), while Baltimore allowed ever so slightly more at 241.2 yards per game (95.9 rushing, 145.6 passing).

But the Jets' statistical edge on both offense and defense was easily dismissed by most; the perceived disparity in quality between the leagues was thought to be accountable for that. The consensus was that the Jets would be unable to run on the Colts, forcing Namath into frequent passing situations. If such were the case, it was widely believed that the Colts' front four, coupled with Baltimore's propensity to blitz, would play havoc with the Jets' passing game, and that Namath would be too harried to pose an effective threat through the air. There was also the fact that one of Namath's primary strengths — the long pass — was precisely what the Colts' zone defense would not allow, and in fact *had* not allowed all year. Without a running game or a deep passing threat, the Jets were considered dead in the water.

As for the Jets' defense, while their front four was generally considered sound, the secondary was seen as being of somewhat questionable quality. Sportswriter William Wallace was already envisioning a long day for the Jets, in particular cornerbacks Johnny Sample and Randy Beverly. "Imagine," wrote Wallace, "what Jimmy Orr and Willie Richardson, the Colts' deep receivers, will do to Sample, once a Colt himself, and Beverly. Imagine what Bubba Smith will do to Namath after he smashes through Dave Herman, the Jets' right tackle. Imagine how Mackey will knock down Larry Grantham."[5] But none of the talk seemed to bother any of the Jets, particularly Namath, who said that Bubba Smith would come away thinking he had been machine-gunned in the chest after dealing with Herman on game day.[6]

On the Sunday night that the Jets had beaten Oakland for the AFL title, Bachelors III was a madhouse. Namath had bought the small New York City restaurant on November 11, 1968 with partners Ray Abruzzese and Joe Dellapina. Abruzzese was a former teammate of Namath's, first at Alabama and then later with the Jets, and Dellapina had been the restaurant's manager under its previous owners when it was known as The Margin Call.

In an establishment cleared for a capacity of 75 people by the fire marshal, Dellapina's estimation of the crowd on the night of December 29 was in the neighborhood of 600.[7] And Namath was there through the night, laughing, drinking, greeting everyone, having a ball. The Jets would be off through New Year's before leaving for Florida on the evening of Thursday, January 2, 1969. That would give them all a good few days to bask in the glory. The day after the AFL Championship, the team held its official victory celebration at Shea Stadium's Diamond Club. Some of the players got up to speak — Gerry Philbin thanked the wives of all the players for their patience and support, Namath thanked all the women of New York for ... well, whatever they did.

The Super Bowl would be played in Miami's Orange Bowl on January 12, and before the Jets left for Florida on Thursday, January 2, they had a chance to relive their triumph. The team gathered earlier in the day to watch the game films of the AFL Championship, ostensibly to look for flaws in their play and propose corrections, but it was really as much about letting everyone enjoy the victory from a more removed vantage point.

Afterward, the team flew by chartered plane to Fort Lauderdale–Hollywood International Airport, and after arriving checked into Fort Lauderdale's Galt Ocean Mile Inn. The following day, Friday the third, they would begin workouts at Fort Lauderdale's Yankee Stadium, where the New York Yankees took their spring training.

The Colts had also taken three days off, but would continue to workout at home until flying into the same airport on Saturday. They would be staying at Fort Lauderdale's Statler Hilton, and would be taking their training slightly north at St. Andrew's School in Boca Raton. The Colts held one more practice at home on Saturday before leaving for Florida that evening.

The Jets continued to work out through Sunday before having their usual Monday off. Although they had the day free from workouts on Monday, there was one commitment to keep: the players were obligated to show up in uniform at Yankee Stadium at 10 A.M. for a scheduled press photo shoot. Getting up early on their day off? *For the press?* You must be joking. Most conspicuously absent, of course, was Namath, but Matt Snell and Emerson Boozer also failed to turn up. As usual, the reporters zeroed in on Namath; he was, after all, the one reporters clamored after for quotable copy.

Reporters were quick to inquire of Ewbank as to the star quarterback's whereabouts. Ewbank could do little but stammer and ensure the newsmen that he would look into it, while stating the obvious — that Namath was *supposed* to be there. At a briefing the following day, reporters were still asking about the lack of participation by the team's starting backfield at the press shoot and whether or not they had been reprimanded. Ewbank, eager to move past the subject, told the press that it was a non-issue and that appropriate action had been taken. When asked for an explanation of what type of action that might be, Ewbank's response was terse and dismissive: "Appropriate," he said.[8]

Over in the Baltimore camp, Don Shula was openly dismayed and wondered to reporters what kind of team Ewbank was running. Shula knew Ewbank well, and this was not the Weeb Ewbank he recalled. When Shula was a defensive back for the Cleveland Browns in the early 1950s, Ewbank was one of the team's assistant coaches. When Ewbank took the job as head coach in Baltimore in 1954, Shula was already playing in the Colts' secondary, and when Shula retired from playing he became one of Ewbank's assistant coaches in Baltimore. Obviously, there was considerable history between them.

Having been fired by Colts' owner Carroll Rosenbloom in 1963 and been succeeded by Shula, Ewbank's imprint on that team was still strong. He had coached Baltimore during its 1958 and '59 championship seasons, and many of the team's stalwart lineup had played for Ewbank on those teams, including running backs Jerry Hill and Tom Matte, defensive linemen Billy Ray Smith and Ordell Braase, defensive backs Lenny Lyles and Bobby Boyd, linebacker Don Shinnick, receiver Jimmy Orr, offensive lineman Dan Sullivan, and center Dick Szymanski. Oh, and there was another guy: Johnny Unitas.

More than that, just prior to his firing Ewbank also had much to do with drafting many young players who were still prominent in the team's lineup, among them receiver Willie Richardson, offensive tackle Bob Vogel, defensive tackle Fred Miller, defensive back Jerry Logan, and perhaps most notably John Mackey, widely acknowledged as the best tight end in football. The Jets had drafted Mackey as well, but as the story goes, Baltimore had secretly signed him before he became eligible. It was Ewbank, just arriving in New York, who prevailed over Jets' president Sonny Werblin not to reveal the illegal signing by the Colts, reasoning that the Colts might receive a mere fine or some other symbolic sanction while the only one likely to be truly effected adversely by it all would be Mackey himself. Ewbank had also drafted offensive tackle Winston Hill and safety Bill Baird for the Colts. When he departed Baltimore and subsequently signed with the Jets Ewbank learned that Hill and Baird had both been waived by the Colts, and he signed the pair in New York: they were both still with the Jets.

But even if Shula was perplexed by what he perceived to be a lack of discipline on Ewbank's team he knew better than to take the Jets lightly, and like Ewbank he gave no credence to the outrageous odds the bookies were setting. "Weeb Ewbank has been around football a long time," Shula said, "and I don't have to tell you he was in the NFL a long time. He knows what he's doing and the Jets are a good football club or else they wouldn't be where they are."[9] Shula let it be known that his team was expecting a good contest.

The Jets weren't concerned with the odds either. Middle linebacker Al Atkinson pointed out that the Jets had been favored by 18 points over the Buffalo Bills early in the season and had lost — it was Buffalo's only victory of the season.[10] "We looked at their movies," Ewbank said of Baltimore, "but my players have had no special reaction different from any other firm."[11]

As to those movies, Ewbank and Shula had agreed to an exchange, with each side being entitled to any four game films of their choosing. Ewbank chose to see both of Baltimore's games with Cleveland — the championship and the Browns' victory over the Colts in week six — as well as late-season victories over Green Bay and the Los Angeles Rams.

Shula's choices were similar; he chose to see the Jets' championship victory over Oakland and the Raiders' defeat of the Jets earlier in the season. Like Ewbank, Shula also chose to see two late-season victories, but while his choice of the Jets' win over San Diego may have been useful, the selection of the game against Cincinnati in week 13 was likely to be of little help since the Jets had played their starters sparingly in that game and the films would therefore reveal only so much. Namath, for instance, had only played the first half.

As the Jets watched the films of Baltimore, they were largely unimpressed. Sure they saw a good team, but their general impression was that they had played — and *beaten* — teams just as good during the season, and some that they considered better. It was of some concern to Ewbank, who worried that his players were becoming too cocky.

Cocky or not, the Jets had reason to be confident. The blitz was considered one of the principal strengths of the Baltimore defense, and as it turned out that was something the Jets were quite proficient at beating. With a combination of Namath's quick release and his ability to read defenses and alert his backs to pick up a blitz by calling an audible, the Jets were well equipped to handle it. In fact, they *wanted* opponents to blitz, and even though the Baltimore blitz had been playing hell with other teams all year, the Jets' only real concern about it was that the Colts might cross them up by *not* blitzing. When your main concern is that your opponent will stop doing what they do best, there really isn't much reason not to be confident.

It is now, of course, well known that the player who seemed to be least concerned with the Colts' prowess was Namath. He spoke freely — some thought too freely — and even glibly about the task at hand. Much was being made of Namath's remark to reporters after the championship game that he considered Oakland's Daryle Lamonica to be a better passer than Baltimore's Earl Morrall. It was a spontaneous, off-handed remark; it certainly didn't seem premeditated or meant to antagonize, but of course once the press got a hold of it they made it out to be the throwing down of the gauntlet.

Namath's statement continued to crop up in sports columns around the country in the days that followed, and by the time the Jets got to Florida it had been played up to be a taunt. Aside from the sportswriters slobbering over an angle, it was also kept alive by Namath's willingness to indulge the press. When asked about it, Namath was only too happy to elaborate, saying that there were at least four quarterbacks in the AFL better than Morrall. Aside from Lamonica, Namath also named John Hadl of San Diego, Bob Griese of Miami and, well, himself (naturally).

Some reporters felt obliged to caution Namath that such loose talk might invite the full fury of the Colts on Super Sunday, and they informed him that clippings were being posted on the bulletin board in the Baltimore training camp. Namath laughed the warnings off. "I said it and I meant it," he responded. "Lamonica is better. If the Colts have to use newspaper clippings to get up for a game, they're in trouble. If they're football players they know Lamonica can throw better than Morrall."[12]

Whereas the original statement was likely a simple observation, Namath seemed to now be sensing an opportunity, and he began to pile it on. He brought up his own backup quarterback, Babe Parilli, saying that the Colts would have been a better team had Parilli been their quarterback. "Babe throws better than Morrall," he said.[13] *Now* it was a taunt.

Whether or not he was succeeding in discombobulating the Colts, he was definitely getting his own coach riled up. Ewbank informed the press that he was not pleased with the statement, that he had asked Namath about it, and that he was satisfied it was an innocent remark that had been blown out of proportion by the media. Ewbank then went on to give his own thoroughly unconvincing rationalization of it all, saying that Namath was probably referring to a particular stretch of the NFL Championship game in which Morrall appeared to be struggling.[14] The only problem with that explanation is that Namath made the initial comment in the locker room after the AFL Championship, long before he had seen the game films of the NFL Championship. Ewbank's excuse was weak, and even he must have known it.

Over in the other camp the Colts seemed, for the most part, to brush it all off. "A lot of things are stuck up on the board," said Mackey. "I never even look at 'em."[15] Had Baltimore's response been limited to that, Namath might have concluded that he was fishing in a dry lakebed, but he gained the upper hand when others from the Baltimore side began chiming in. Perhaps most notable was Shula's response.

"He can say what the heck he wants," Shula said with all the élan of protest, "but I don't know how you can rap a guy like Earl who has accomplished what Morrall has accomplished for us this year. We're happy with Earl."[16] Shula went on to list Morrall's achievements in 1968, including being named Most Valuable Player in the NFL, just as Namath had been the AFL MVP, and the truth is that Shula had every reason to be pleased with Morrall. But he had played into Namath's hands nevertheless because his defense of Morrall rather came across as a case of special pleading. One should never underestimate the psychological warfare at play in sport. Whereas Baltimore may have initially been perceived as the aggressor in the impending showdown, Namath had forced them to go on the defensive.

By comparison, Morrall obviously tried to keep his own response measured. "He can express any opinion he wants," Morrall said. "That's his business … I don't have to believe it."[17] Wow. It sounded almost like Morrall was trying to convince himself. Although he wouldn't back down from his comments, after being informed of Shula's rebuttal, Namath was moved to point out that his intention was not to ridicule Morrall, but that he was merely stating the facts as he saw them.

There is no question but that Earl Morrall could be justifiably proud of the season he had in 1968. He finally had the kind of season he dreamed of having — the kind of season he always felt he could have had he ever been given the opportunity before.

Morrall was a 13-year veteran in the NFL, having begun his career with the San Francisco 49ers in 1956. He lasted one season there as a backup before being traded to Pittsburgh in 1957, where he was again a backup. He began the 1958 season as the Steelers' starting quarterback, but after just two games Pittsburgh dealt him to Detroit, where Morrall was again relegated to backup. He would stay in Detroit for seven long years, spending most of that time on the bench.

In 1965 he was shuffled off to the New York Giants, where he finally got a serious chance to play. As the Giants' starting quarterback, Morrall led them to a respectable, if unspectacular, 7–7 record and had a decent year, throwing 22 touchdowns and only 12 interceptions. While a .500 record is nothing to get too excited about, Morrall must surely have been glad to have started the entire season, and he had to have been looking forward to building on the club's record in 1966. Midway through the '66 season, however, the team had a dismal 1–5–1 record, and it was then that Morrall fractured his wrist and had to miss the rest of the season. When he returned in 1967 he was no longer the New York Giants' starting quarterback. They had acquired Fran Tarkenton in a trade with the Minnesota Vikings, and Morrall was again on the bench.

In 1968 Morrall reported to training camp, but as the preseason was set to get underway in August he was informed that he had just been traded to the Baltimore Colts. The Colts needed only to surrender a reserve tight end in acquiring Morrall. The chances of Morrall starting in Baltimore seemed somewhere less than zero, as the Colts' quarterback was the great Johnny Unitas. The Colts were merely in need of a serviceable backup as Unitas' regular backup man, Jim Ward, was lost to injury.

Morrall was fed up. At 34 years of age and with 12 years in the NFL he was tired of being a backup. He seriously considered retiring, and would recall reaching the point where he felt everyone had given up on him.[18]

But something pushed him to make the trip to Baltimore, and as fate would have it, just before the season was to begin Johnny Unitas injured his right arm — his throwing arm — and Morrall suddenly found himself thrust into the starting lineup on opening day. Baltimore beat San Francisco handily to start their season, and Morrall was awarded the game ball by his teammates. He had a pretty good game, completing 16 of 32 passes for 198 yards and two touchdowns, but giving him the game ball was really more of a symbolic gesture acknowledging his role as their de facto leader — a vote of confidence.

The team continued to win, and even when Unitas was healthy enough to retake his job, he was the first to defend the decision to keep Morrall as the starter. "He got the job done," Unitas said, "and you don't change horses in the middle of the stream. The objective is to win and Earl is the man."[19]

More than that, Unitas had nothing but praise for Morrall's performance throughout the season, which may have meant more to Morrall than any other display of respect and confidence he could have gotten. Morrall knew what an intense competitor Unitas was, and he also knew from experience how difficult it could be to watch the games from the sidelines. But Unitas not only stood aside: Morrall said that Unitas had helped him in any way he could.[20]

Unitas seemed glad to do it, and his willingness to stand aside and allow Morrall to enjoy his time in the spotlight was very indicative of character. Everybody seemed to be happy for Morrall, but then, how could they not be? The fact is he was a damn nice guy. Center Dick Szymanski recalled when Morrall first reported to Baltimore's training camp, and how he went around the cafeteria introducing himself to all the players, shaking everybody's hand: who wouldn't be glad to see a nice guy like that finally catch a break? The way things turned out, Morrall had the kind of season he had only ever dreamt of, leading his team to a championship title, completing 57.4 percent of his passes, racking up 26 touchdowns against only 17 interceptions, winning the league's MVP award. And now he was going for it all, the final, crowning achievement to his dream season. And then along comes Namath looking to pop his balloon.

Shula seemed increasingly perturbed at how the press had seized on Namath's remarks about Morrall, and he remained ever defensive. When asked if he would put Unitas in quickly if Morrall did not seem up to the challenge, Shula responded: "Morrall is not going in there with a string around his neck. If he misses with a pass or two early or has one intercepted he won't be yanked. He deserves the chance to run the team."[21]

Shula's lack of tolerance on the subject was perhaps most obvious when a reporter jokingly asked if it wasn't a luxury to have the great John Unitas as a backup quarterback. Seemingly oblivious to the inherent humor of the question, as well as the laughter of some of the reporters present, Shula testily shot back that Unitas had not been playing due to a sore arm, which he said did not make him a backup quarterback.

With Shula always on the defensive, Morrall tried to remain nonchalant about it all. He pointed out what was obvious to everyone, saying that the Colts were the best team in the NFL. He said that he expected to win, and that in watching films of the Jets he did not see anything surprising or even particularly difficult about them as a team. Saying that the Colts had played better teams during the season, Morrall added that he could think of no reason why the Colts should not be as heavily favored as they were.[22] Although he had begun casually, he wound up with a rather pale attempt at braggadocio. He was playing into Namath's hands all right.

He may have been trying to match Namath, but he just couldn't equal the insouciance of Namath's delivery. Morrall had neither the flair for it nor the swagger to pull it off, and what otherwise made his statements bland by comparison was that they did not upset the status quo. But then, how could they? He was merely voicing an opinion that most everyone concurred with anyway. Namath, on the other hand, was not only talking as though the impossible were possible, but that it was a certainty. Given his own situation, there is no way that Morrall could equal such flamboyance, even if he had the tools to do so. He could only offer the matter of fact, workmanlike attitude of the NFL, and by comparison that was just dull.

Morrall allowed that, if Namath were engaging in some form of psychological warfare, there was some rationale for it, but he quickly pointed out that Baltimore was too much of a veteran ball club to be taken in by such tactics. The truth, however, is that Namath's scheme was working. He was succeeding in planting seeds of doubt, and he was not only doing it in a vulnerable area, but a vital one — the team leader. When Morrall spoke of being relegated to second-string most of his career, he made a telling remark: "You start to question your own ability," he said.[23] No doubt: Morrall could be gotten to.

But Morrall wasn't the only card Namath was playing. The Colts had barely set foot off the plane in Fort Lauderdale when Namath started stepping on toes. The Colts arrived in Florida on Saturday night; on Sunday night defensive linemen/kicker Lou Michaels (the brother of Jets' defensive backfield coach Walt Michaels) and offensive lineman Dan Sullivan went into a Fort Lauderdale restaurant called Fazio's, and after spotting Namath and Jim Hudson there, they went over to say hello.

Michaels said hello, and by his account the first words out of Namath's mouth were "We're going to kick the hell out of your team." Michaels tried to play it off. "Haven't you ever heard of the word modesty, Joseph?" Michaels responded.

"We're going to beat you," Namath answered, "and I'm going to pick you apart."

The conversation only went downhill from there, reaching the point where Michaels, channeling the spirit of Wyatt Earp, asked Namath to step outside and settle things. Sullivan had to calm Michaels down, and interestingly enough, after all was said and done Michaels was left with a positive impression of Namath. At the end of the evening Namath paid everyone's tab and then gave Michaels a ride back to his hotel. "He strikes you as being cocky," Michaels said, "but I went away thinking he's a real gentleman. There's a lot of good under this guy."[24] Namath said it was no more than a playful verbal joust, no harm done, right? Score another round for Namath.

Shula, for once, saw the humor, saying that Namath was the 837th guy that Michaels had threatened to deck. Had Michaels followed through, Shula said, then Namath would have been only the thirty-eighth guy that Michaels actually slugged.[25]

Members of the press were starting to notice a curious trend. It may have started with Namath, but it seemed to be spreading throughout the Jets' team. The Jets — outrageous underdogs though they were — had become the aggressors. They were the ones doing all the talking. "If it was the president of the United States I'd have to tell him what I think," said Johnny Sample, "and what I think now is that we're a better ball club than Baltimore is. I think a lot of us feel that way."[26]

They sure did. Namath's confidence was infectious. "It's Joe," said Gerry Philbin, ordinarily one of Namath's harsher critics on the team. "Namath is so confident, so sure we're going to beat them, it's got me amazed."[27]

"He is not just blowing smoke," said defensive back Bill Rademacher. "We *are* good. All he is doing is reminding us. I'm telling you that if we do win, then the reason has to be his doing just that."[28]

Indeed, he was not blowing smoke. The Jets were gathering momentum; their attitude was one of assurance and their determination was very evident in their workouts. The team's mid-week practice sessions were so aggressive that it had made Ewbank nervous. He was worried that with all the hard hitting someone was bound to get hurt and wind up missing the game on Sunday, but his attempts to calm the players down could do little. For that reason Ewbank may have been glad to see the rain come on Friday, forcing the team indoors where he limited them to some light running.

One thing that Ewbank may not have welcomed as much on Friday was word that Namath had been running his mouth again. The reporters came to him looking for a reaction to Namath's latest remark. Oh, hell, what did he say this time? The reporters informed Ewbank that when Namath was at the Miami Springs Villa on Thursday evening to accept the Player of the Year award from the Miami Touchdown Club, he had made a very bold proclamation. Namath had no sooner stepped up to the microphone than a heckler sought to harangue him. So many years later, one can't help but wonder about the fellow: who he was, what his motivation or intention may have been — probably not much. He may have simply been a Baltimore fan doing what fans routinely do — harassing the opponent — or he may have been an NFL supporter. The line between AFL and NFL was very surely drawn in those days, and supporters of either side did not cross. Then again he may simply have been a guy who had enough of Namath's arrogance and was eager to see the Colts put him in short pants on Sunday. Whatever his motivation, it isn't likely that the poor slob intended to help slingshot Namath into the role of American folk hero, but that is exactly what he managed to do.

When Namath got to the microphone and began to talk, someone called out from the back of the room, informing Namath in no uncertain terms that the Colts were going to flat-out kick his ass on Sunday. Now, really, this was a bit much. It's one thing to be so ill mannered as to interrupt a guest speaker and awardee, but to do so with such obviously infantile intent, well, it would piss anyone off.

The truth is that Namath had been hearing it now for the better part of two weeks. It had begun with the ridiculous point spread, and was a common thread running through the sports columns. Nobody seemed to be taking the Jets seriously. Namath could even sense it in the demeanor of the reporters he spoke to daily. Oh, they didn't make fun of him when they were interviewing him: their job was to ask questions and get answers, that's all. But he could sense their condescension beneath the surface. Maybe it was the way some of them felt obliged to take him aside and warn him that all of his loose talk was apt to anger the Colts, as if he were inviting disaster and leading his teammates into the lion's den.

Even if the reporters weren't saying it to his face, they were saying it in the papers. They joked of the Colts being 19-point favorites but the bookies giving even money that Namath would be carried off on a stretcher; a cartoonist depicted a worker with a shovel announcing that he had come to help remove Namath from the field. It was relentless.

But *this*? Being heckled by some pathetic, drunken Shriner from the back of the room? During the preceding days, in the face of all of the derision, Namath had conducted himself with aplomb, but now he was angry. He could've said a lot of things. He could have berated the fool or gotten into a war of words with him. He could even have asked that he be removed from the room. Instead, Namath's response was certain and to the point. "The Jets will win Sunday," he said firmly. "I guarantee it."

Although he didn't say so when informed by reporters that Namath had guaranteed a victory, Ewbank wasn't pleased: he didn't feel that such talk could help the team. "He guaranteed it, huh?" Ewbank responded. He thought for a moment. "Well, I'm with him," he said. "Joe's an honest boy, and if he says that he must mean it."[29] What else could Ewbank do? He could hardly contradict his quarterback.

Shula's response was different, of course. When asked what he thought of Namath's guarantee Shula seemed amused, saying that Namath was likely the most colorful person the game had yet seen.[30] Shula allowed that all of Namath's talking had gone a long way toward generating interest in the game among the public, and he again said that he was not taking the Jets lightly. Whatever the press thought of them, Shula had respect for them as a team, and he said he was aware of Namath's ability to put points up quickly with the long pass. Then Shula may have done Namath a great favor. As much as he had been talking — and now guaranteeing a victory — one might have thought that the pressure would be on Namath to deliver on it, but Shula took the pressure off Namath and put it all on his own team. "The game is important to us," Shula said. "Very important. Everything we've accomplished this year goes on the line at 3 o'clock Sunday. If we blow it, everything we did all year is destroyed."[31]

Shula had made similar statements through the week. He had spoken of the need to avoid becoming over confident, and how the entire season hinged on the Super Bowl. He spoke of Namath's quick setup and release, his accuracy even on the long pass, his ability to read zone defenses and anticipate the blitz, his impressive timing with his receivers; Shula gave the distinct impression that even he would not be so big a fool as to give 18 points in betting on his own team. "We don't see many of the types of defense used by the Jets in our league," Shula said. "Yes, we came down here expecting a real football game and I can't see us an 18-point favorite."[32]

Maybe—*maybe*—Namath's psychological gambit was paying off. It wasn't only Shula who was viewing the Jets as worthy adversaries; other members of the Colts' team began saying so. Defensive back Lenny Lyles pointed out that the combination of Namath's passing ability and the skill of his receivers was of concern. "It's not going to be easy out there Sunday," Lyles said.[33]

Even Ewbank was losing his skepticism regarding the value of Namath's public posturing. He began to wonder if his quarterback hadn't given the Baltimore Colts a lot to think about. Surely they must have wondered why Namath was so confident. What were the Colts missing that Namath could be so bold as to guarantee victory? There must be something up his sleeve. Had he seen something in the Baltimore game films? Was there something he knew that he could exploit? Did they have a trick play or two in store for the game? *What the hell did this guy know?*

However confident the Jets were as a team, few in the press read it as any indication of a genuine shift in the tide. It was still widely believed that the Colts would make short work of the Jets, and as game day approached many sportswriters were ready with advice, mostly aimed at Namath—some sincere, some facetious, some just plain condescending—suggesting ways that he might save face, or even save his life.

Newspaper Enterprise Association sports editor Murray Olderman thought the New York offense would simply be overwhelmed by Baltimore's defense. "With their mobile zone defenses, the Colts will inhibit the long bomb proclivity of Namath," Olderman wrote. "The turnovers in the event will come so fast that the New York defense will be strained from extra duty and vulnerable to the Colts' own balanced attack."[34] Olderman foresaw a 27–13 Baltimore victory, which at least had the Jets beating the spread.

Virginia sports editor Jack Fulp of the Petersburg *Progress-Index*, seemingly unaware that the AFL and NFL had agreed in 1966 to merge come 1970, wrote that at some point in the future the AFL might reach parity and manage to defeat the NFL in a Super Bowl, but that this wasn't likely to be the year. Fulp concluded, "[I]t just doesn't seem possible that the Jets could handle the Colts, who could be just about the greatest football team ever."[35]

Dan Cook, executive sports editor of the *San Antonio Express and News*, wrote that Namath had "certainly made a mistake popping off with all that jawbone juice prior to this game." Cook saw little hope for the Jets, but did at least raise the possibility of an upset when he wrote: "If Namath can dig himself out of the deep hole he helped scratch for himself and guide the Jets to an upset over Baltimore then he must be hailed as king of the quarterbacks."[36]

Canadian sportswriter Glen May penned an open letter to Namath wherein he fantasized a private conversation with the quarterback. In May's imaginary chat, Namath confided that he knew his team had no chance of beating the Baltimore Colts and would need to play above their heads and catch every conceivable break just to make it close. May then offered a suggestion that would spare Namath the indignity and humiliation that was to come. He proposed that Namath call a quarterback sneak on the Jets' first play from scrimmage, and that after being savagely thrown to the ground he could then feign injury and allow himself to be carried from the field.

May concluded by saying that he was going out to bet his year's salary on the Colts.[37] It really is to laugh. Even while belittling the Jets, other sportswriters had the dignity to avoid the strutting pomposity exhibited by May. One can't help but wonder if he did in fact wager on the game, and if so, how much. If he did bet that much, dollars to doughnuts his wife never let him hear the end of it.

Charlie Vincent also composed an open letter to Namath, which ran in the *San Antonio Express and News* the day of the game. "If you can get the Jets on the scoreboard with a quickie TD early," wrote Vincent, "you can at least give the folks who bet on you a little breathing room." Vincent went on to point out that if the Jets could cover the point spread they would be the first AFL team to do so in a Super Bowl. He felt that the Jets could at least do that, but of more interest was the opening line of Vincent's piece. "Well, this is your big day, Joe," he wrote, "the day you can enter your name in the archives of professional football for time immemorial."[38] He could, and he would.

On Super Sunday the Jets rode the bus from Fort Lauderdale to Miami's Orange Bowl in stoic silence. Writer Lou Sahadi was in the New York locker room as they prepared for the game. In his book *The Long Pass*, Sahadi related the scene: the tension was heavy. These men may have been confident, but they were also nervous. But then, how could they not be? This was the biggest game of their lives. "The entire atmosphere had a certain stillness about it," Sahadi wrote. "You wanted to talk but were afraid to."[39]

But there was one person in that locker room who didn't seem nervous in the least. As Sahadi stood there he suddenly felt someone come up behind him and wrap their arms around him in what he described as a playful bear hug. He turned to see who it was, but he really already knew. When he turned, there was Namath, a big smile on his face as always. Namath laughed and joked with Sahadi, teasing him about his white pants and shoes, saying that they gave him the appearance of a Florida native. Maybe Namath saw the way Sahadi had been taking notice of the mood among the players. "We're going to be all right," Namath said. Sahadi hadn't asked, but Namath must have read the question in his eyes. "Yes, sir," Namath reiterated, "everything is going to be okay."[40] Namath's confidence, from the time the Jets won the AFL championship right up to the day of the Super Bowl, was remarkable. It's almost as though he didn't just *feel* that they would win — it's as though he already *knew* it, as if it were a destiny that no God would deny them, that nothing on earth could stop this train from rolling now.

Both Namath and Ewbank tried to alleviate some of the anxiety. Ewbank let the players know he felt they were going to win by telling them that he had hurt his hip when they hoisted him up and carried him off the field after the championship victory two weeks earlier, and that he would prefer that they not do it again when they won this time. Really, Ewbank was as nervous as they were. He was playing against his old league, his old team, Shula, the underling who had succeeded him in Baltimore; he was playing against the team of the man who fired him, Carroll Rosenbloom. This was his chance to show them all. This game meant a lot to Ewbank, for reasons more than just winning a championship. He reminded his players that some of them had also been cast out of the NFL before coming to the AFL and the New York Jets.

Each team had the option of introducing their starting offense or defense in the pre-game intros, and Ewbank told the players he wasn't sure which unit to choose. Namath cracked the players up by suggesting that Ewbank introduce the seniors, an allusion to the custom in high school games.

As January days in Miami go, it was a reasonably good one. Although it was overcast and the sun didn't seem likely to make much of an appearance, the temperature was 72 degrees and the winds were blowing north at 18–20 mph. The game was scheduled to begin at 3:00 P.M. EST, but as a courtesy to the many VIPs there was a slight delay in starting. Namath's carny-like ballyhoo had managed to change this from a mere game into a social event. President-elect Richard

Nixon and vice president-elect Spiro Agnew were both in attendance, as were Joseph Kennedy and his son Ted. There were also senators, governors and astronauts in attendance, and this being Miami, of course Jackie Gleason was there. So was Bob Hope. Prior to Namath, even the Green Bay Packers couldn't sell out a Super Bowl. Now there were 75,377 people in the Orange Bowl, and they had all come to see Namath, some hoping to see him do the unimaginable and defeat the NFL, others wanting to see him be taken down and put back in his place. Tickets that were priced at $12 were going for $50–75.

The Jets won the coin toss and elected to receive, and then it was on — the biggest show in sport. After Earl Christy took the opening kickoff from the end zone to the New York 23, Namath and the offense took the field. On the Jets' first play from scrimmage they went into a line shift nobody had seen before. Left guard Bob Talamini shifted over to the right guard position, while right guard Randy Rassmussen shifted to the tight end spot, and tight end Pete Lammons moved slightly to the right off the line. Left tackle Winston Hill moved over to the left guard spot and half back Emerson Boozer moved up to just behind where the left tackle position would be. With the blockers being heavily concentrated to the right, it made for a very unbalanced line, but the play was actually designed to go left. Namath took the snap and handed to Matt Snell, who ran off left tackle for three yards before being stopped by linebacker Don Shinnick and defensive end Ordell Braase. It was not a big gainer, but its purpose was more to get Baltimore thinking that there might be unexpected shifts and formations in store. In reality, the Jets had not incorporated any other new plays or formations into their repertoire.

On second-and-seven from their 26 the Jets again ran Snell off left tackle, this time from a conventional formation, and Snell picked up nine yards and a first down before being brought down by safety Rick Volk. Snell ran right over Volk, who had put his head down to make the tackle. Although he had managed to bring Snell down, Volk was shaken up on the play and had to momentarily leave the game. He would return shortly after, not yet aware that he had suffered a concussion.

On first down from the 35 Namath tried running Boozer right, but the play was well read by middle linebacker Dennis Gaubatz, who shot through the line and caught Boozer in the backfield. Boozer shook Gaubatz off but by then he was being swarmed by the entire right side of the Colts' defense — Braase, Shinnick, and defensive tackle Fred Miller. Although the play had been to the opposite side, somehow the right side of the Baltimore defense wound up taking Boozer down for a four-yard loss.

With second-and-14, Namath went to the pass for the first time and hit Snell flaring out of the backfield for a nine-yard gain. Faced with a third-and-five, Namath then ran a draw play to Snell, but the Colts had seen it coming and Miller corralled the fullback for a two-yard loss. With fourth-and-seven the Jets would have to punt, but they had at least gained a first down in the series and seen that they could move the ball. What is more, Namath took note of how they had gotten that first down — running Snell off left tackle. They were already seeing where the soft spot was.

Baltimore was offside on the ensuing punt, and although the penalty would not gain them a first down, and Tim Brown had only returned the kick to the Baltimore 23, the Jets opted to accept the penalty and kick again. It proved to be an unwise decision, as Brown this time brought the kick back a little further to the Baltimore 27.

The Colts got out of the gate quickly on their first offensive series. On first down, Morrall went back to pass and threw a screen to John Mackey. The tight end caught the pass at the 21 and took off, slipping an attempted tackle by linebacker Larry Grantham at the 30 and running right through safety Jim Hudson at the 38 before being taken down by tackle John Elliot at the Baltimore 46. The play had gone for 19 yards.

On the next play the Colts ran Tom Matte on a sweep around right end for 10 yards and another first down at the New York 44. Two plays, two first downs: it was looking as easy as so many predicted it would be. The Colts then gained another first down on three runs that got them to the New York 31, but on the next set of downs Gerry Philbin caught Jerry Hill for a three-yard loss at the 34 on first down, and Morrall then threw incomplete to Jimmy Orr on second down. The Colts were facing third-and-13, and the New York defense had a chance to halt the drive, but Baltimore converted when Morrall hit Tom Mitchell for 15 yards and a first down at the Jets' 19.

A quick lead seemed to be within easy reach now for the Colts, but when Morrall (under a heavy rush from Philbin) missed on a pass to Willie Richardson at the six-yard line on first down, and then missed on a pass to Mitchell on second down, the New York defense seemed to be regaining its composure. On third down Morrall again went back to pass, but under considerable pressure from ends Philbin and Verlon Biggs, he had to frantically flee the pocket and make a run for it. Middle linebacker Al Atkinson brought him down for no gain at the 19, and Lou Michaels came on to try a 27-yard field goal. He missed it, and despite the relative ease with which Baltimore had bolted into scoring position, they came away with nothing and the Jets took possession at their own 20-yard line with 5:33 remaining in the opening period.

Namath came out throwing in the Jets' second series. He tried to hit Snell again on a flare pass, but Snell dropped the ball. On second down Namath hit tight end Pete Lammons, but the play only gained two yards. The Jets managed to convert on third down when Namath threw to Bill Mathis (in for Boozer) for 13 yards and a first down at the 35.

With a new set of downs, Namath decided to really shake things up. He again threw on first down, dropping back to his own 27 and launching a beautiful, arching pass to Don Maynard down the right sideline. Maynard had safety Jerry Logan beat, but he reached out for the ball at the Baltimore 27-yard line and it came down just beyond his reach and fell incomplete. Defensive back Ocie Austin, who came trailing along right after, shook his head—he knew the Colts had just dodged one. Maybe it didn't connect, but the pass was very important nonetheless; had Namath taken just a little off the throw it could have gone the distance. The Colts saw the danger of the Namath-Maynard connection and were determined to stop it: Maynard would have to be double-teamed.

On second-and-10 Namath threw for six yards on a slant-in to George Sauer, but then overthrew Sauer on third down and the Jets again had to punt. In their first two possessions the Jets had failed to cross midfield, but while they may not have mounted a serious threat until then, something significant had happened. The jitters were gone and the Jets had found that the Colts were just a football team after all, much as the Jets had suspected. Sure they were good, but the mystique had flown—these guys were beatable.

After the Jets punted the Colts started from their own 42, but could do nothing with the good field position and had to punt after just three plays. The punt was a good one, catching a nice bounce and netting 51 yards. It pinned the Jets back at their own four-yard line.

With 1:58 left in the quarter, the Jets started by running Snell off right tackle for four yards, and then again on a draw to the right for five yards. On third-and-one from the 13 a run would have been expected and might have been all that was needed, but Namath chose to cross them up with a quick pass to Sauer. He threw left to Sauer at the 13, but as soon as the ball reached Sauer he took a hit from Lenny Lyles and the ball came out. It was ruled a fumble. It wasn't—it was an incomplete pass—but in the days before the errors of officials could be reversed by instant replay, there was nothing that could be done. Linebacker Ron Porter recovered the ball for Baltimore at the New York 12-yard line, and with 14 seconds left in the first quarter the Colts were poised to break the scoreless tie.

The first period ended with Jerry Hill being gang-tackled by a swarm of Jets for a yard loss, but on the first play of the second period Matte ran a sweep around left end for seven yards to the Jets' six. What happened next would be a decisive moment in the game. Now, of course, it is impossible to say what might have happened had the Colts scored, but their failure to do so seemed to light the fuse of their own destruction.

On third-and-four from the six-yard line, Morrall tried to hit Mitchell on a quick slant-in. It would have been a touchdown, but middle linebacker Al Atkinson reached out and just barely managed to get a finger on the ball. As fast as it happened, it wasn't obvious to the naked eye, but in slow motion one could see that Atkinson deflected the ball just enough to alter its path ever so slightly, and rather than hitting Mitchell in the bread basket the ball instead hit him on the right shoulder pad. It was thrown with enough velocity that it wound up ricocheting high into the air, eventually coming down into the waiting hands of cornerback Randy Beverly in the end zone for a touchback.

It often happens in sport that such a drastic reversal of fortune can be a real turning point. And so it was. When the Jets began at their own 20, they did so with a sense of purpose. While he was on the sidelines, Namath got a call from the upstairs booth: it was Jets' defensive backfield coach Walt Michaels. He was observing the Colts' secondary and saw that the long throw to Maynard had the desired result. The Colts' secondary was shading Maynard's side of the field. Michaels told Namath that he likely wouldn't have a lot of opportunity to throw to Maynard, but Sauer should be pretty easy to hit under such circumstances. Namath would keep it in mind.

When the Jets' offense came back on field, Namath returned to what had gotten them their initial first down and he sent Snell off left tackle. Although it only gained a yard on first down, Namath ran it again on second down: this time Snell gained seven. Then on third-and-two Namath again ran Snell left, this time around end—Snell gained six yards and a first down at the 34. On first down it was again Snell running left, this time for 12 yards to the 46.

The momentum was building, but on first down Namath missed on a pass to Sauer that was broken up by Shinnick. On second down Namath threw to Mathis for six yards as the Jets crossed midfield for the first time. On third-and-four from the Baltimore 48, Namath hit Sauer for 14 yards and a first down at the 34. Then on the next play he found Sauer again, this time for 11 yards and another first down. Michaels had been right: with Baltimore's attention being so focused on Maynard, it was creating a lot of other opportunities.

From the Baltimore 23 Boozer then ran for two yards to the 21, and Namath followed with a flare pass to Snell that picked up 12 yards to the nine-yard line. It was now first-and-goal. On first down Namath chose to run Snell off right tackle, and the fullback picked up five yards to the four. On second down Namath again called Snell's number, sending him around left end. In the huddle, Namath called for the ball to be snapped on the first sound he made. He could bark, cough, sneeze—whatever it was, the ball was to be snapped on the first sound he made. He was hoping to catch the Colts unprepared: it worked. When Namath shouted "Now!" the offense sprung into action and Snell took off around the left side of the line. Volk slid off a block and made a diving attempt at Snell, but failed to reach him. Snell then outran Gaubatz into the left side of the end zone for the score. After Jim Turner's extra point, the Jets led 7–0 with just under nine minutes to play in the half. It was the first time an AFL team had ever led in a Super Bowl.

After Preston Pearson gave the Colts good field position by returning the kickoff to the Baltimore 28, the Colts seemed eager to shoot back quickly. Morrall overthrew Willie Richardson on first down, but came back on second down with a flare pass to Matte, who eluded a would-be tackle by Bill Baird at the 35 and ran the ball 30 yards to the New York 42 before being knocked out of bounds by Jim Hudson. But after runs by Hill and Matte gained only four yards, Morrall's pass to Mackey on third-and-six was broken up by Johnny Sample, and Lou Michaels came in to try to salvage the drive with a 46-yard field goal. He missed again, and the score remained 7–0.

With 6:37 left in the half the Jets again began on their 20. After a one-yard run off right guard by Boozer, Namath then threw for 35 yards to Sauer to the Baltimore 44. Namath had been looking to Sauer all the way, but froze Lyles, Sauer's coverage, with a pump fake. It only halted Lyles for a split second, but it was long enough for Sauer to get past him. Namath then lofted the ball and Sauer made a great extension to pull it in and make the catch before Lyles caught him from behind.

From the 44, Snell ran for nine yards (again to the left), and then picked up the first down at the 32 with a three-yard run up the middle. But there the drive ran out of steam. Namath overthrew Maynard downfield on first down, and then underthrew Bake Turner on a slant-in on second. On third-and-10 Namath again went back to pass, but a heavy rush forced him to try and escape through the middle of the line where Gaubatz took him down for a two-yard loss. With fourth-and-12 from the 34, Jim Turner came in for a 41-yard field goal try. It was wide left, and the Jets lost a chance to build on their lead.

There was 4:13 left in the half when the Colts began at their 20. Morrall hit Richardson for six yards on first down, and on second Matte ran around right end, and after slipping an attempted tackle by Hudson, he was off to the races. It would be the longest play of the game, as Matte took it 58 yards to the New York 16 before being caught and brought down by Baird. As Matte went to the ground, Sample came down on top of him and Elliot — trailing along all the way from his defensive tackle position — tried to jump over the pile up. After the play, Matte jumped up in a fury and immediately went after Sample. As the two butted helmets, officials tried to separate them, one official losing a few teeth in the process. Matte left the field, still fuming, and would nurse a grudge against Sample all through the years, claiming that when he was already on the ground Sample had stepped on his crotch. Matte was wrong. In watching the films it is obvious that Sample did not step on Matte's crotch, but rather fell across his upper torso. However, when Elliot was jumping over the pile-up his foot came down, planting for a moment on Matte's inner thigh. All through the years Matte has been harboring a grudge against the wrong man.

With first-and-10 at the New York 16, the Colts were in excellent position to even the score before halftime, but after Hill gained a single yard on first down, disaster struck again. On second down Morrall went back to pass and tried to hit Richardson across the middle at the goal line; Sample jumped in front and intercepted the ball, falling to the ground at the two-yard line. Not having been touched, Sample could have gotten up and run, but he instead stayed on the ground cradling the ball until the official blew the play dead. The Jets took possession at their own two-yard line with two minutes left in the half.

Of course New York would have loved to run out the half, but three runs by Snell gained just five yards and the Jets found themselves punting from their own end zone with 1:04 left. They seemed to catch a break when the Colts were flagged for roughing the punter, but New York was also called for illegal procedure and the penalties cancelled each other out. On the re-kick, Tim Brown fielded the ball at the New York 46 and returned it to the 42. It set the Colts up with another good opportunity to get on the board with 43 seconds left before the half.

On first down Morrall threw to Hill for only a yard gain, and Baltimore was forced to use a timeout with 25 seconds left when Hill failed to get out of bounds. When Morrall went to the sideline, Shula gave him a play that should have worked — in fact, for the most part, *did* work. It worked in every way except its ultimate outcome.

Morrall handed off to Matte who began running right, then suddenly stopped, turned, and threw a lateral back to Morrall. The intended receiver was Jimmy Orr, and the Jets had been so fooled by the play that Orr found himself completely alone down the left side of the field in front of the end zone. There he stood, waving his arms to get Morrall's attention. "I was open from here to Tampa," Orr said afterward.[41]

Bob Oates, writing in *The Sporting News*, theorized that the play had failed because it *had* worked so well. Orr was so wide open that he had stopped running, and Oates maintained that it was Orr's lack of motion that had failed to catch Morrall's eye.[42]

What happened was unfortunate for the Colts and for Morrall, but was really quite simple. After receiving the lateral from Matte, Morrall turned to face forward and the first person in his line of vision was Hill, who appeared to be open across the middle near the 15-yard line. Even that wasn't likely to get them in the end zone, however. In fairness to Morrall, it all happened quite fast.

Hill may have been open momentarily, but Morrall's pass seemed to have been a bit soft, allowing safety Jim Hudson to move in front and intercept the ball and return it to the 21-yard line as the half expired. As the play ended, Orr threw his head back in obvious exasperation. The Colts went into the locker room at the half with nothing.

There is one more curiosity about the play worth mentioning: just before the Colts broke huddle the sun came out for the first and only time in the game. Suddenly the player's shadows fell across the ground, facing away from the end zone. When Morrall took the snap and handed to Matte the shadows were still there, and when Matte tossed the lateral to Morrall, the sun was still shining through the clouds. Then — remarkably — the very instant that Morrall threw the ball, the sun disappeared and the shadows were gone. To the superstitious, it could be seen as an omen, a foretelling that, with this last missed opportunity of the half, for Baltimore the light had gone out. Melodramatic? Maybe. It's just a curious observation.

The Jets were naturally elated to have held the Colts off yet again and to have kept their lead as the half ended. At the break the New York coaches — Ewbank, Michaels, and Clive Rush — agreed that Namath was calling an excellent game, and they told him that they saw no reason to alter the game plan in the second half.

In the Baltimore locker room there was no sense of panic, only frustration over all of the missed opportunities. Still, trailing by just seven points with an entire half to go, they had no reason to think that they couldn't change their fortunes in the second half. But there was also the momentum to consider; not only had the Jets gained momentum at the end of the half, but their confidence had been gaining steadily throughout.

Held scoreless in the first half for the first time all season, Shula had to consider putting Unitas in the game, but he still felt that Morrall deserved a shot at moving the team in the second half. With the Colts receiving the second half kickoff, Shula wanted to see if Morrall could get something started on that initial possession; if not, then he would make a change and send in Unitas. But as it turned out, the Colts' first offensive series was not a fair shot for Morrall. After receiving the kick and beginning at their 25-yard line, Morrall handed off to Matte on first down. Matte ran off right tackle and promptly fumbled the ball, which linebacker Ralph Baker recovered for the Jets at the Baltimore 33. The Jets could hardly have hoped for a better start to the half.

The Jets gained a first down at the 21 after Boozer ran left for eight yards, and Snell went right for four more. Three plays later they had gained another first down after a five-yard pass to Snell and runs by Snell and Boozer brought them to the 11-yard line. But at that point the Baltimore defense tightened, and the Jets began moving backward. First, Boozer lost five yards on a run to the left, and then Namath was caught for a nine-yard loss by Bubba Smith.

On third-and-24 from the Baltimore 25, Namath tried passing to Lammons, but the play was broken up by safety Jerry Logan. It was almost the break the Colts needed, as Logan had a real shot at intercepting the ball. It would appear that Logan dropped the ball after losing his concentration upon seeing nothing but open field in front of him. This time it was Baltimore's defense that had missed its chance. On fourth down Jim Turner came in and kicked a 32-yard field goal to boost the Jets' lead to 10–0. It was a very important score in that it necessitated Baltimore's scoring twice to catch the Jets.

When Baltimore received the kick, it was now make-or-break time for Morrall: Unitas was already warming up on the sideline. Beginning from the Baltimore 26, Morrall overthrew Mackey on first down and then threw for no gain to Hill on second. Third-and-10 would decide Morrall's fate. He again went back to pass, but a heavy rush forced him to run out of the pocket: he lost two yards. On fourth-and-12, the Colts were forced to punt and Morrall was done.

After receiving the punt, the Jets' offense took the field with 8:04 left in the third period. Starting at their own 32, the Jets ate up valuable time as they moved downfield, largely with the passing game. After gaining only a yard with a pass to Mathis, Namath came back on second down with a 14-yard completion to Sauer to the 47. After Logan broke up a long pass to Maynard on first down, Boozer then ran left for four yards, and on third down Namath hit Lammons for 11. The Jets were moving, the clock was moving: for New York, it was all good.

On first down from the Baltimore 38 Namath tried to hit Maynard with a quick throw at the line, but Maynard dropped the ball when he was thrown to the ground by Bobby Boyd. On second down Namath kept it in the air, hitting Snell with a 14-yard pass across the middle that put the Jets on the 24.

Returning to the run, Mathis gained just a yard on first down, and on second-and-nine from the 23 Namath threw for Maynard in the end zone. Maynard made the catch—out of bounds. Aside from narrowly missing a touchdown, the Jets had another problem on the play: Namath had banged his thumb on Fred Miller's shoulder pads, aggravating a nagging—and painful—injury that had been recurring since early in the season. The pain was bad enough that Namath left the field shaking his hand. With third-and-nine it was up to Babe Parilli to take them there. Parilli tried to hit Sauer with a quick slant-in but the pass fell short, and with 3:58 left in the third period Jim Turner kicked a 30-yard field goal to increase New York's lead to 13–0.

The thumb was a painful nuisance, but it would only keep Namath out for that single play. As for Morrall, he could only stand and watch the rest of the game. When the Colts started their next series from their 20 it was Unitas who trotted onto the field with the offense. Unitas began by running Matte on a sweep around right end for five yards. On second down he threw to Matte for no gain, and on third he missed on a pass to Orr. In his first series Unitas had failed to spark the Colts, and after David Lee's punt the Jets took over at their own 37 with 2:24 left in the third.

The Jets were sensing it now: victory seemed theirs for the taking. Even with the legendary Unitas in the game they had stopped the Colts from getting so much as a single first down. Soon the fourth quarter would be starting and surely the gravity of the situation would take hold of the Colts, if it hadn't already. Before long there might even be a sense of desperation among them. It would depend on how much more time the Jets could use up and whether or not they might even manage to build on their lead. A score this time could be devastating to Baltimore's chances.

After Snell ran left for three yards on first down, Namath missed on a pass to Sauer and the Jets were facing a third-and-seven from their 40. Namath managed to convert with an 11-yard pass to Sauer that gave the Jets a first down at the Baltimore 49. Then came the play that it had been suggested nobody could do against the Baltimore zone. Namath went back to pass and heaved an excellent deep throw to Sauer, who caught it over his shoulder at the 15 and took it to the 10 before Lyles brought him down from behind. It would be Namath's final pass of the game. The third period ended with Snell gaining four yards off right tackle to the six-yard line.

At the end of the period Namath went to the sideline and he and Ewbank agreed that it was best to play it safe at that point and keep it on the ground. Maybe they would score a touchdown, maybe they wouldn't, but at that point a field goal was about as good since either a touchdown or field goal would make it necessary for the Colts to score three times. The Jets did keep it on the ground, and when runs by Snell and Mathis got them no further than the two-yard line they settled for a nine-yard field goal and a 16–0 lead.

Starting their next series at their 27 with 13:10 left to play, the Colts were really up against it now. They hadn't managed a single first down in the third period, and now needed to score three times in less than a quarter. Unitas started with a short pass to Mackey to the 32, and on second down a sweep right by Matte gained the first down at the 39. Unitas then threw short again — five yards to Richardson — and Matte broke off the left side for 19 yards on the following play. The Colts were finally putting something together; Hill gained 12 yards off right tackle to the New York 25, but in the end it was as though the Jets' defense was only toying with them. After Unitas overthrew Richardson on first down, he then went downfield to Orr down the middle. The pass was underthrown, and Randy Beverly was able to move in front of Orr and intercept the ball going into the end zone. It was Beverly's second interception of the game, both in the end zone.

Starting from their own 20 with 11:06 to play, the Jets were now looking to run as much time off the clock as they could. The Colts had to have known this, and they therefore had every opportunity to key on the run and stop it. After a pair of two-yard runs by Snell and Boozer, the Jets were facing a third-and-six at the 24. This was where the Colts needed to stop them and get the ball back for their offense. They couldn't do it — Boozer ran around left end for seven yards and a first down at the 31. What is more, he stayed in bounds and kept the clock running.

The frustrations of the Baltimore defense were bubbling over now. When Snell ran left for 10 more yards on the next play the Colts were flagged for a personal foul, giving the Jets an additional 15 yards to the Baltimore 45. Snell then bolted through the middle for seven yards, and after Boozer picked up two more on second down the Baltimore defense finally rose to the occasion on third-and-one and stopped Mathis for no gain. Jim Turner then missed a 42-yard field goal attempt, and the lead remained 16.

The Colts began from their 20 with 6:34 remaining in the game and there was now a definite desperation as they tried to hurry downfield. Unitas threw incomplete to Mackey on first down, overthrew Richardson on second, and overthrew Mackey on third. With fourth-and-10 there was nothing else but for the Colts to go for broke. It paid off when Unitas hit Orr for a 17-yard gain.

Unitas again missed passes on first and second downs (overthrowing Richardson and missing short to Hill), but converted on third down with an 11-yard pass to Hill, and a personal foul on New York tacked another 15 yards onto the play. Now working from the New York 37, Matte ran for a yard on first, and Unitas hit Richardson with a 21-yard pass on second down to set the Colts up at the 15. After overthrowing Matte, Unitas then passed to Orr at the four-yard line, and a late hit by Atkinson put the ball at the two. The Colts needed to score quickly, and that being the case, it was to the credit of the New York defense that they continued to use up valuable time by forcing Baltimore to try, try, and try again. On first down Matte gained nothing behind left guard, but an offside penalty on New York moved the ball forward to the one.

On a replay of first down, Unitas tried a keeper up the middle: he was stopped by Biggs. On second down Matte ran behind right guard: he was stopped for no gain by Biggs, Hudson, and Atkinson. Finally, on third down, Hill ran through a hole off left tackle and went in for the score with 3:19 left to play. After the extra point, the score was 16–7.

Everyone knew what was coming next, but that didn't help the Jets a bit when Baltimore went for the onside kick. The ball bounced toward Sauer — the surest hands of any receiver in the AFL. Sauer dropped to his knees and prepared to receive the ball into his chest, but it went right through his arms and past him to the New York 44 where Tom Mitchell recovered for Baltimore. The Colts had not quite flatlined yet, although Rick Volk almost did. He had suffered a concussion on the game's second play, and now he was unconscious at the bottom of the pile. It took four of his teammates to drag him hurriedly off the field as they frantically tried to keep from using up a timeout.

A six-yard pass to Richardson and a 14-yard completion to Orr gave the Colts a first down at the New York 29, but after another short throw to Richardson of five yards, Unitas missed on three straight passes and Baltimore turned the ball over on downs. Again the Baltimore defense desperately needed to stop the New York ground game: again, they couldn't.

Three straight runs by Snell gained the Jets a first down on their 31. Then it really was over. The Jets took a couple of delay penalties in between runs by Snell until, faced with fourth-and-13, they punted the ball away with 15 seconds left in the game. There were only eight seconds left when Unitas took the field after the punt, and the proud old pro used every one of them. He threw incomplete to Richardson on first down, and then came back to Richardson with a pointless 15-yard completion that ended the game. It had been accomplished. The Jets had done what so many had said they couldn't. The sports columns would be rife with David and Goliath analogies, but the Jets never had seen it that way. They had always known that, at the very least, they would be in the game.

All of the things that were supposed to happen ... didn't. The Jets' defensive secondary — considered so vulnerable by the so-called experts — had turned out to be one of the team's great strengths against Baltimore, intercepting four passes, each time quashing a scoring threat. Richardson and Orr had not run them ragged; Mackey had not run over them. Nor had Bubba Smith run over Dave Herman and snapped Namath in half. The Baltimore blitz had not rattled Namath, nor had the zone defense prevented him from hitting Sauer deep when need be. It was said that the Jets would not be able to run against the Colts, but Snell had mowed through them for 121 yards. For all of the snide and condescending rhetoric in the sports columns, all of the presumptuousness and feeble attempts at wit, it was the Jets who had made fools of them all. They had beaten the Colts so soundly that one could easily conclude that, for all their presumed expertise, there was hardly a sportswriter in the country who knew his ass from his elbow. If ever there was a team that had a right to crow, it was the New York Jets after Super Bowl III. "Never were so many people so wrong," Namath said in the jubilant New York locker room. "Eighteen point favorites? I told 'em all."[43] Namath couldn't resist rubbing it in the faces of the throng of sportswriters crowding around him. "Nobody believed we would win," he told them. "Nobody but the New York fans gave us a chance. Where were you guys?"[44]

Somebody asked Namath if he didn't at least feel sorry for Earl Morrall. They seemed to be looking for some measure of contrition, but Namath was unrepentant. "Better him than me," he shot back defiantly, pointing out that had things gone the other way nobody would likely have been offering him any sympathy.[45]

Yeah, Namath was enjoying this. Part of his revenge was refusing to speak to most of the reporters. At first he said he would only talk to the reporters from New York, and he even refused to be interviewed by Kyle Rote for the NBC-TV post-game show. Jets' owner Phil Iselin eventually convinced Namath to be more sociable with the media, and Namath consented to speak with Rote on television; he used the opportunity to tell all the writers who had laughed off the Jets' chances to go eat their pencils and pads.[46]

With 17 completions in 28 attempts and 206 yards, Namath had been chosen the game's Most Valuable Player, though he would say later that he would gladly have seen Snell or Herman receive it. Even now there are many who say that Snell should have been the MVP, and the first person who would agree with them would be Namath himself. He'd be wrong, just as they would.

How, some people ask now, can a quarterback be voted MVP without even throwing a touchdown pass? But that was part of the beauty of Namath's performance that day. He could have thrown a touchdown, certainly, but he had no desire to be the show — he already was as a matter of course — but only a desire to win. If he could play it safe and still win, then what did he care about showboating?

Simpletons seldom grasp the machinations behind the game. It was Namath who was dictating the flow of the game from the start. It was Namath who was calling the plays; it was

Namath who was reading the Baltimore defense and deciding when it was good to run Snell, and which direction to run him. Namath was calling all the shots. "Namath was fabulous," said Ewbank, dripping wet after having been thrown fully clothed into the showers by his players. "He didn't make a bad call."[47] Clive Rush agreed, saying that Namath's play-calling was so superb that he found no reason to suggest any plays from his spot up in the booth. Guard Bob Talamini talked about how Namath called so many of the plays at the line of scrimmage after sizing up the defense and seeing what formation they were in.[48]

"This is so sweet," said linebacker Larry Grantham, who had been with the team since its inception in 1960 as the New York Titans. "The odds were foolish. We were confident that Joe would get the points. Baltimore undersold our defense."[49]

"He believed more than anybody else," rookie defensive back John Dockery said of Namath. Drenched in sweat in the sweltering locker room, Dockery was beaming. "He not only made me believe," Dockery said, "he made us all believe. I never saw another fella like him in my life."[50] Namath had assured everyone the Jets would win, said Herman, and they did. Herman was happy to tell reporters his quarterback was no liar.[51]

In a team sport victory is, naturally, a team effort, but ultimately a leader is the guiding hand who motivates it. If it had been another quarterback reading the defense and calling the plays that day, it is entirely possible that Matt Snell may not have fared as well. No, this victory was all about Joe Namath. Joe Namath was voted MVP — Joe Namath *was* MVP.

Over in the Baltimore locker room things were very different, of course. It was quiet — deathly quiet. The mood was so funereal that nobody wanted to talk. Many of the players almost seemed in shock, staring off in silence. When they did speak, they did it so softly that if not for the pervasive silence in the room no one would have been able to hear them at all.

The way Shula saw it, his team simply didn't do anything right: the defense didn't rise to the occasion, and the offense failed to make the big plays. The Jets simply deserved the victory, Shula said.[52] Yeah, yeah, yeah but what about Namath, the reporters asked. A faint smile crossed Shula's face. "I knew that was coming," he said. "He's everything we've heard about him." Shula praised the strength and quickness of Namath's delivery, his ability to read the blitz and to beat it. Namath could do it all, Shula said. He mixed his plays well, called a great game, and got the job done.[53]

Ten-year NFL veteran Billy Ray Smith fought back tears and spoke in a tone so hushed it was as though he were afraid that a tidal wave of emotions would come flooding out if he allowed himself to speak any louder. "They just flat walked out there and beat us," he said. The heartbreak of it seemed to overwhelm him. "When you're number one you're the best," Smith said, "but when you're number two you're nothing."[54] Like Ewbank, Rush, and Shula, Smith said that Namath did it all; the Jets won because Namath did a superb job of mixing his plays and keeping the Baltimore defense off balance. "I knew they'd be tough," Matte said. "I said earlier I'd settle for a one-point victory."[55]

Not everyone was so graceful in defeat. Unitas, for instance, who had been so magnanimous is stepping aside for the good of the team while he was less than 100 percent and Morrall was on a roll, seemed to now be distancing himself from the team, as if he had no part in the humiliating defeat. He was asked if he thought Shula should have put him in the game sooner. "That's not my decision," Unitas said, but he basically answered the question anyway when he qualified his response by adding, "I was ready to play right from the start."[56]

"I moved 'em, too," Unitas said, obviously implying that it would have been a different game had he been in sooner. In Unitas' analysis, time had simply run out on the Colts.[57] Yes, Unitas moved them, and he managed to get the Colts their only score —*with three minutes left in the game*. It's impossible to say how things would have gone had Unitas played either sooner, or even the entire game, but the truth is that Unitas came into a game that was fairly well-in-hand for

New York; the Jets' defense was not playing with the same intensity by that point, and they were getting tired as well. Shutouts are often lost in the waning minutes of a ball game precisely for those reasons. It is not difficult to imagine that, had Unitas started the game, he may well have suffered the same fate as Morrall. The reality is that Unitas did not exactly set the stadium ablaze when he did come into the game. Time ran out? Sure it did: the game is scheduled that way.

And then there was linebacker Mike Curtis. When people talk about linebackers, Dick Butkus is usually mentioned as the ultimate example of the position, but if you were looking for a linebacker you could hardly do better than Curtis. He was all the position requires and then some: big, strong, fast, aggressive, fearless. As it turned out, he was also a poor loser. In the off-season that followed the Super Bowl, Curtis gave interviews and even penned an article for a magazine in which he berated the Jets as a soft team. "The Jets don't hit like the teams in the NFL," Curtis said. "I kept waiting all day in that Super Bowl game to get hit like we're used to getting hit in our league, but it didn't happen."[58] That, more than anything, seemed to make the loss almost unbearable to Curtis.

"Maybe I'm just spilling sour grapes," he said, "but they just didn't impress me as a team, and even after all this time I'm still not impressed."[59] There's really no "maybe" about it. If the Jets weren't hitting the Colts hard enough that day, maybe it was because they didn't need to. Apparently they only hit the Colts as hard as was necessary.

Namath seemed to have no regrets about anything he had said prior to the Super Bowl, but perhaps Shula did. Shula may have regretted saying that everything the Colts had accomplished during the 1968 season would be nullified should they lose the Super Bowl. After the game, he seemed to back away from that statement, saying that it was a shame that with everything they had achieved they would now spend the off-season with this one loss hanging over their heads. Shula knew that there was nothing that could be done about it, and expressed the thought that the team would just have to man-up.[60]

People who know little or nothing about sport will not understand the burden of a competitive spirit, and there are some who may find it odd that a hulking man of 33 years like Billy Ray Smith should be so choked by emotion at having lost a game. But this was not just a game: this was their life. This was what they were, and it held the promise of what they wanted to be and how they hoped to be remembered. Almost 40 years later, interviewed for the NFL Films documentary *America's Game: The 1970 Baltimore Colts*, some of them still hadn't gotten over it. Two years after being beaten by the Jets in Super Bowl III the Colts were back to defeat the Dallas Cowboys in Super Bowl V, largely regarded as the sloppiest, dullest, and most forgettable of all Super Bowls. It was hardly the vindication that the Baltimore Colts had dreamt of. The game was won on a last-second field goal by Baltimore kicker Jim O'Brien; Bubba Smith talked in that *America's Game* interview about becoming depressed the moment that O'Brien won the game for them. This was supposed to be his second Super Bowl victory. Not even winning Super Bowl V could wipe away the crushing disappointment of losing Super Bowl III—in fact, it seemed to taunt them all the more by evoking the memory—and Smith would talk of still being haunted by dreams and having to shut off his television from time to time to avoid seeing or hearing any mention of it.

Namath really had been prophetic, not just in guaranteeing victory, but even in some of his remarks months afterward. In an interview with Lawrence Linderman for *Playboy* in 1969, Namath said that Super Bowl III would be something that the Colts would carry around for the rest of their lives; sure enough, they have. "January 12, 1969, belonged to the Jets," Namath said, "and Baltimore can't ever get even for it. They lost it; they got beat."[61]

There were eleven members of the champion New York Jets chosen to play for the Eastern team in the eighth AFL All-Star game a week after the Super Bowl. Along with Namath, the AFL East team included Don Maynard, George Sauer, Emerson Boozer, Winston Hill, Dave Herman,

Jim Turner, Gerry Philbin, Verlon Biggs, John Elliot, and Al Atkinson. They were greeted warmly by their AFL colleagues upon arriving in Jacksonville, Florida, for the game. All of the players in the AFL seemed to take their share of pride in the Jets' victory over the NFL. With the presence of so many members of the Super Bowl champions, it was expected that a record crowd would turn out for the game at the Gator Bowl, and despite rain, the 43,800 who attended did set a record for the annual event. Most attributed that record crowd not so much to the presence of eleven members of the champion Jets, but really to the presence of one — they mostly came to see Namath.

Namath himself was not eager to play, saying that the paltry $1,500 for each member of the winning team and $1,000 to each member of the losing team was really not worth the risk. "One slip and your career could be ruined," he said. "These guys are risking a lot for a little."[62] Houston Oilers coach Wally Lemm would be coaching the East team and he expressed some concern for Namath's knee, noting that he seemed unwilling to plant his right foot while throwing in practice the Friday before the game.[63]

Namath's concern about the risk/reward factor in such meaningless contests was only highlighted when Philbin suffered a dislocated shoulder in the game during a fourth-quarter goal line stand. Playing the first half in a drizzling rain, Namath led the East to a 19–3 halftime lead while completing seven of 19 passes for 98 yards. He threw one interception and no touchdowns (Houston receiver Alvin Reed dropped two sure touchdown throws from Namath), but he piloted what would turn out to be the East's only TD drive which was capped by a two-yard scoring run by Miami's Jim Kiick. Otherwise Jim Turner had kicked four first-half field goals, and added two more in the second half for a total of six. But when Miami's Bob Griese took over quarterbacking the Eastern team in the second half, and with only two field goals to show for his efforts, the West was able to overcome as Kansas City's Len Dawson took over for San Diego's John Hadl at quarterback for the Western team. Dawson led the West to 25 fourth-quarter points and a 38–25 West victory.

7

The 1969 Season

It was another busy off-season for Namath. After the Super Bowl there was the celebration back in New York, and Namath then went home to Beaver Falls where a parade was being held in his honor. The movie offers were coming in too, and he signed to co-star in a film with Glen Campbell. He was also involved in a new fast food franchise called Broadway Joe's, a burger place for which Namath received $2 million from Amos Treat Associates, who were looking to go national with it. These were the good old days all right. But the party had to end sometime, and there was trouble on the horizon.

Early in 1969, Namath had been given a list of names of people deemed "undesirable" (i.e., with ties to organized crime) who were said to be frequenting Bachelors III, the New York City establishment variously described as a restaurant, bar, nightclub, and lounge, of which Namath was one-third owner. NFL commissioner Pete Rozelle was demanding that Namath sell his share of the establishment or face suspension. There was no suggestion that Namath had done anything wrong, but Rozelle wanted to avoid even a hint of impropriety. A few years prior, Paul Hornung of the Green Bay Packers and Alex Karras of the Detroit Lions had each received a year's suspension for betting on football games, and Rozelle was very concerned about appearances.

There were talks between Rozelle and Namath and his attorneys — talks that sometimes included Jets' coach Weeb Ewbank and team president Phil Iselin. But then, quite suddenly and unexpectedly, Namath held a press conference at Bachelors III on June 6, 1969, and tearfully announced his retirement. Overcome by emotion, Namath protested that, although he had done nothing wrong, he had been given two days by Rozelle in which to sell or be suspended. Feeling unjustly persecuted, Namath chose to walk away from football. Nobody doubted his sincerity — he seemed absolutely inconsolable — only his judgment.

The announcement caught everyone off guard. Ewbank said that Namath had mentioned nothing to him about retiring, and Rozelle said that he had been told by Namath's attorney only the day before that Namath was in the process of selling his share of the club. It was obviously an impetuous decision, and with Namath being at the top of his game and in his prime, the general consensus seemed to be that he would not hold to it. Namath himself left the door open; when asked by a reporter if he and Rozelle might still be able to come to terms Namath responded, "I hope so. The last thing I want to do is quit football."[1]

Indeed, negotiations did continue after Namath's announced retirement. Rozelle wasn't eager to see the league lose the biggest superstar it ever had; for many of the public, Joe Namath *was* football. But Rozelle said in a statement that, not only was Namath's personal reputation at stake, the integrity of the sport itself was also at risk. "Constant warnings of this nature have been given to other players in professional football," Rozelle said, "and such warnings have been heeded consistently."[2] The first part of that statement may or may not have been true; the second seems to have been PR double-talk.

The truth is that Namath was not the only professional football player who owned such an establishment, and wherever athletes are, gamblers will follow, looking to get a tidbit of information that might help them further their own endeavors. But there was obviously a difference between the average grunt and the quarterback of the champions of professional football. There was Namath's celebrity to consider as well. Professional athletes didn't come any more high profile than Namath. That was something that Rozelle couldn't help but take into consideration, but whereas Namath obviously enjoyed the perks that celebrity brought, this was one occasion in which he resented the added attention.

Pete Lammons, George Sauer, and Jim Hudson, that trio of Texas Longhorns who had defeated Namath and Alabama in the 1965 Orange Bowl, were the first of Namath's New York teammates to pledge solidarity. They all said that they too would retire if Namath did not return. Poor Weeb Ewbank. Coaches frequently have to put up with a certain amount of nonsense from temperamental players, but since Namath came along the old coach had seen his share of melodrama and then some. Ewbank was exasperated. "This is what I have to put up with," the coach said in a huff when reporters told him that a healthy share of his championship team was jumping ship.[3]

Then again, Ewbank knew Namath well enough to know that this would all likely blow over. Namath loved football, and that much Ewbank was sure of. But there was something else: Namath also loved his lifestyle. Could he continue to live the life he loved without football? All of Namath's good fortunes — the movie offers, the product endorsements — had been the result of football. Would any of it continue after he was finished with the game? There was also his contract with the Jets to consider. Before selling his share of the team, Sonny Werblin had signed Namath to a new three-year contract, rumored to be worth $500,000. In retiring, Namath had thrown all of that away. He had lost some endorsements as well. Namath's friend and attorney Jimmy Walsh estimated Namath's total losses to be in the range of $5 million. "Over a long stretch of time," wrote William Wallace of the *New York Times*, "it might be interesting to see how well Namath's principles hold up in light of diminishing income."[4]

There was certainly a lot to lure Namath back, but what galled him about it was the hypocrisy of it all. "Rozelle goes to Toots Shor's and 21," Namath said, "and people make bets on football games in there."[5] Namath personally found the New York Jets' front office much to blame for the whole thing. Their inactivity in negotiating with Rozelle's office was bewildering. Had Werblin still been around, surely he would not have let it all come to this — not as much as he looked after Namath. Maybe Namath hadn't gotten used to the fact that Werblin wasn't there to defend him anymore. Iselin was certainly a different sort of president than Werblin, who had indulged Namath, paraded him, took him to parties, introduced him to Hollywood celebrities. Werblin also shielded Namath. Iselin just signed his checks. After Namath's announced retirement, Iselin had to be prodded into even telephoning his superstar.

But Iselin resented the suggestion that he had not tried to help Namath resolve the dispute with Rozelle, saying that had Namath contacted him he would have been glad to offer whatever help he could. Iselin said that in his last conversation with Namath he had told the quarterback, "You've got too much at stake. The game is bigger than anybody, you, Rozelle, or myself. It's bigger than Bachelors III."[6]

Iselin felt that, ultimately, Namath would come back. Most everyone felt that way, writers and teammates alike. "We're not figuring on those terms," said Johnny Sample when asked about the possibility of Namath not returning, "because we know he's going to play, and we know he's going to come back, and they're going to work this thing out, because a guy like that loves the game as much as any player who ever played."[7]

Toward the end of June, after returning from California where he had been marlin fishing with Gale Sayers, Rozelle got in touch with Namath to reopen a dialogue. In July, Jimmy Walsh made a proposal that offered everyone a way out without anyone having to be seen as capitulating entirely. There had been plans to open Bachelors III restaurants in other cities — Boston, for instance — and under the proposal, Namath would agree to sell his share of the New York restaurant but could remain a partner in other Bachelors III restaurants. All parties agreed to it.

Of course, Namath had many things to consider — his teammates, friends, family, *money* — but as training camp was set to get underway, he very much missed the camaraderie with his teammates. He knew he needed to be a part of it all — the game meant too much to him to just walk away.

He didn't have much time to prepare. When Namath joined camp at Hofstra, the Jets' first preseason contest was just 10 days away. As usual, exhibition season got underway with the traditional College All-Star game, an NFL tradition dating to 1934 wherein the NFL champions would square off in Chicago against the best rookies drafted that season. The Jets would be the first AFL team to ever play in the charity event. During the 35 years that the event had been held, the All-Stars had managed to win nine times, but hadn't notched a victory since shocking everyone with a 20–17 win over Vince Lombardi's Green Bay Packers in 1963.

Even Rozelle gave Namath the credit for the impressive crowd of 74,208 on that Friday night at Chicago's Soldier Field. It became obvious, however, that many in the crowd had come to jeer Namath, as he was lustily booed in the pre-game intros. Namath said afterward that, Chicago being an NFL town, he had more-or-less expected such a response. As the game progressed, the crowd continued taunting Namath, cheering enthusiastically whenever he failed to complete a pass.

But the Jets seemed to have little trouble in the first half. The All-Stars only gained a single first down in the half, and even then by virtue of a penalty. They could also do no better than 19 yards (12 rushing and seven passing), as the Jets took a 13–0 lead into halftime. It could have been worse: the one bright spot for the All-Stars was an impressive goal line stand in which they stopped three straight runs from the one-yard line.

The second half was like a separate game. Early in the third quarter, Jim Turner kicked his third field goal to boost the Jets' lead to 16–0, but on the ensuing kickoff, Utah State's Altie Taylor returned the ball 78 yards to the New York 19. Two plays later, University of Cincinnati quarterback Greg Cook hit Stanford's Gene Washington with a 17-yard TD pass to make it 16–7. Whereas Notre Dame's Terry Hanratty and Kansas' Bobby Douglass had been helpless as quarterbacks against the New York defense in the first half, Cook would ignite the All-Stars to a very productive third quarter.

On the Jets' next series Namath was intercepted by Pacific's Rudy Redmond, who fell to the ground, then got up and ran 34 yards for an apparent score. The problem for the All-Stars was that an official had blown the play dead when Redmond hit the ground. The All-Stars failed to get into the end zone on the series and settled for a 28-yard field goal by New Mexico State's Roy Gerela that cut the New York lead to 16–10.

The Jets came right back, with Matt Snell scoring on a 35-yard run that increased New York's lead to 23–10, but Cook and the All-Stars seemed undaunted. The collegians were faced with a third-and-one when Cook caught the New York secondary napping and threw to Taylor for 44 yards. It would set up a 12-yard TD pass from Cook to USC's Bob Klein, and suddenly, leading by just six points, it seemed as though the Jets were in a dogfight.

Things calmed down in the fourth quarter with Turner adding another field goal — his fourth — for a 26–17 Jets' lead, but late in the game things got ugly. There had been bad blood between All-Stars coach Otto Graham and Jets cornerback Johnny Sample for a very long time, dating to 1958 when Sample had played for Graham on the All-Star team. The two apparently did not get along, and when they met again Sample was a defensive back for the NFL-champion Baltimore Colts. The Colts won the championship in 1958 and '59, meaning Sample played against Graham's College All-Star team in both 1959 and 1960. As the Colts defeated the All-

Stars on both occasions, Sample used the opportunity to rub it in Graham's face. "I intercepted a pass," Sample said of one of the contests, "and when I ran by the All-Star bench I hollered to Otto and asked him if he still thought I wouldn't make it."[8]

Sample had maintained that after he returned to the Baltimore training camp from playing with the All-Stars in 1958, Weeb Ewbank, then coach of the Baltimore Colts, called him into the office and told him he had received a letter from Graham. Among other things, the letter accused Sample of not being a team player and concluded with Graham predicting that Sample would never make it as a professional football player. It's no wonder Sample took such glee in defeating Graham's All-Stars.

Their paths crossed again a few years later when Sample was playing for the Washington Redskins and Graham was brought in to coach the team. Sample claimed that he received a phone call from Graham in which the newly-hired coach told him he was overpaid for a defensive back. Graham promptly waived Sample.

Now here they were again at another College All-Star game. It must have vexed Graham that the man he predicted would never make it in the pros kept turning up with one championship team after another to dog him. With the Jets leading 26–17 in the last minute of the game, Graham became furious, claiming Sample clotheslined receiver Gene Washington. Graham wanted a penalty called, and he ran onto the field yelling at the nearest official. Graham got his penalty all right — he drew a flag himself for coming onto the field. Sample came over to give his rebuttal to Graham's accusation of a cheap shot, and the two had words. Sample wound up head-butting Graham in the face with his helmet: it opened a wound on the bridge of Graham's nose and the blood began to flow. Sample later made a weak attempt to alibi, saying that Graham must have charged into his helmet.[9]

After the officials restored order, Cook threw a 19-yard touchdown to Jerry Levias of Southern Methodist with 16 seconds left in the game. Levias had beaten Sample on the play. It would be the end of Sample's career. After the game, dried blood still on his face, Graham called Sample "a disgrace," and one of the Jets' coaches was anonymously quoted as saying that he was ashamed to be Sample's coach.[10] Before the end of the month, the Jets waived Sample. There would be no takers.

The Jets did manage to beat the College All-Stars 26–24, but it was hardly the dominant victory they had wanted. The Jets had placed a high priority on the contest, aiming to silence critics who were still saying that the Super Bowl victory over Baltimore was something of a fluke. Had the second half been the dominating performance the Jets had given in the first, then Ewbank would have taken Namath out of the game sooner, but as the All-Stars gained momentum in the second half Ewbank couldn't bring himself to sit Namath down and risk the embarrassment of losing to the collegians. As for Namath, he wasn't at all pleased with his own performance, but refused to excuse himself by mentioning how late he had joined the Jets in camp. He had completed 17 of 32 passes for 292 yards with two interceptions. He threw no touchdowns. "I wasn't throwing worth a flip," Namath said. "How far off am I? About five games."[11] The Jets had five exhibition games left.

Their second exhibition was a Saturday night contest with the NFL's Cardinals in St. Louis on August 9. This time Ewbank stuck with the schedule and only played Namath in the first half. It turned out to be a very uneventful 30 minutes, in which the Jets failed to score and Namath completed only six of 18 throws. The problem was not his passing, but rather the inability of his receivers to catch the ball. The Associated Press said that Namath had only thrown one uncatchable pass.[12]

The Cardinals fared little better in the half, scoring just three points on a 49-yard field goal and managing only one first down in the first quarter. Babe Parilli was in at quarterback for the Jets in the third quarter, and after they got lucky with a bad St. Louis punt that set them up at the Cardinals' 39, the Jets tied the game with a 24-yard field goal 6:20 into the second half. The Cardinals retook the lead with a 22-yard field goal with 3:44 left in the third, and increased that lead to 13–3 in the fourth quarter when quarterback Charley Johnson hit tight end Jackie Smith with a 26-yard touchdown pass. Rookie Al Woodall took over at quarterback for the Jets in the fourth quarter and managed to lead the Jets to a final score, a 45-yard field goal by Turner that made the score 13–6.

The teams seemed to have mutual respect one for the other, which no doubt stemmed from the two coaches: St. Louis coach Charley Winner was Ewbank's son-in-law. "They're a good, sound football club," said Charley Johnson after the game. "The Jets' defense has a lot of different looks, a lot of overshifts. They line up overshifted. They play to stop the run."[13]

Stop the run they did. Even if the Jets' offense seemed sloppy and lethargic, the defense did a good job, holding the Cardinals to just 74 yards rushing that night and 97 yards passing. Of course the Jets would have liked to have won, and Ewbank would have preferred to see a more inspired performance from his offense (no man wants to be bested by his son-in-law), but the Jets were really looking ahead to their next game. Although it was technically only an exhibition, the Jets' game with the New York Giants at the Yale Bowl was no mere preseason game to either team. It was a battle for the championship of Gotham, and everyone knew it. "The Jets will kill them," St. Louis center Bob De Marco said. "Namath won't be playing just for half the game. That game is going to be a blood game."[14]

The first-ever meeting of the Jets and Giants was an event that fans had been anticipating since 1966, when the two leagues had agreed to merge. The Jets, longsuffering as the redheaded stepchildren of New York, had emerged as the champions of pro football when they defeated Baltimore in the Super Bowl, but until they actually beat the Giants they knew they would never be considered the Football Kings of New York by the city's inhabitants. Even after manhandling Baltimore, the Jets were viewed with skepticism by Giants fans, who obstinately clung to the argument that the Jets had played over their heads in the Super Bowl and that they had merely caught lightning in a bottle that day. From the perspective of the Jets, both the Giants and their fans could stand to be bitch-slapped into reality. "We've been in New York ten years," said Larry Grantham, one of three remaining members of the original Titans franchise of 1960, "and there were times when they treated us like semi-pros."[15]

No, this was no mere exhibition game. It was a humid 81-degree August afternoon, yet the Yale Bowl saw its first sellout crowd — 70,784 — since the Yale-Army game of 1955. The Giants were hosting, and it was a mostly partisan NFL crowd, boisterously booing Namath when he came onto the field. True to form, Namath had been running his mouth in the days before the game, saying, "I don't think too many people are going to take the Giants seriously anymore."[16]

It was about halfway into the opening period when Namath drove the Jets 67 yards in just five plays for the first score, a 29-yard touchdown pass to George Sauer. Jim Turner added a 37-yard field goal for a 10–0 Jets' lead with 1:45 left to play in the first quarter, and even then the Jets were not finished for the period. The ball was booted by the Giants' return man on the kickoff, and rookie Cecil Leonard recovered for the Jets at the one-yard line. On the next play Bill Mathis went over for the score, and the Jets had a 17–0 lead as the first quarter ended.

The Giants were still unable to get in motion in the second quarter, and when they punted to the Jets, the game was turning into a laugher — rookie Mike Battle took the punt back 86 yards for a touchdown, and the Jets were now up 24–0. The Giants seemed shell-shocked, but finally regained their composure when quarterback Fran Tarkenton drove them 92 yards in nine plays and threw a 13-yard touchdown to Aaron Thomas.

In the third period Tarkenton threw a 40-yard touchdown pass to Bobby Duhon to cut the Jets' lead to just 10 points, but that was as close as they would get. Namath came back with a 20-yard touchdown throw to Mathis to make it 31–14. At that point Ewbank figured to sit Namath down for the day, but Namath told his coach he wanted to go one more series.[17] Ewbank relented, and Namath went back out and drove his team to one more score, throwing a two-yard touchdown pass to Pete Lammons. Now, with 7:50 left in the game, Namath was done for the day.

The Jets won by a final score of 37–14. Namath was almost flawless, completing 14 of 16 passes for 188 yards and three touchdowns. Tarkenton had a tougher time, hitting only nine of 21 throws with two interceptions to match his two touchdowns. The Jets were satisfied they had made their point; to Grantham it was all the proof necessary to demonstrate who the better team was in New York, while Don Maynard pointed out that the Jets had only given a $250 effort (that being the going rate for exhibition games).

Meanwhile, both Tarkenton and Giants' coach Allie Sherman played it off by saying that it didn't matter if they were number two in New York: they were only interested in being number one in their division. They weren't fooling anyone: the loss stung. They hadn't been merely beaten: they had been humiliated. If it hadn't been important to them, then both clubs would not have used their starters until so late in the game.

The Jets next traveled to Oakland to play the Raiders on a Monday night at the Coliseum before a crowd of 52,927 spectators. This time Namath did not play beyond the first quarter. Toward the end of the period he drove the Jets to the Oakland three-yard line only to have Emerson Boozer fumble the ball away. Oakland linebacker Dan Conners recovered the ball at the one. The Raiders had taken a 7–0 lead on a 13-yard touchdown pass from Daryle Lamonica to Warren Wells before the Jets closed the gap to 7–3 when Jim Turner kicked a 41-yard field goal with 1:51 left in the first quarter. By the end of the quarter Namath was done for the night.

In the second quarter Turner kicked another field goal, this time from 42 yards, to bring the Jets to within a point at 7–6 at the half, but after a scoreless third quarter the game changed drastically. Although he had directed them on a touchdown drive in the first quarter, Lamonica had been mostly unable to move the Raiders thereafter, and 41-year-old George Blanda took over at quarterback. After hitting Wells with a couple of throws that advanced the Raiders to the Jets' 22-yard line, Blanda threw a touchdown strike to Larry Todd to give Oakland a 14–6 lead. Then, with just 1:04 left in the game, Blanda kicked a 16-yard field goal that increased the margin to 17–6.

That would have been more than enough with a minute left, but when Mike Battle fumbled the kickoff and the Raiders took over at the New York 45, Lamonica came back in the game and wound up throwing a six-yard TD pass to Drew Bule with just 14 seconds left in the game. It rather made the final score look shameful at 24–6. The victory was Oakland's first of the preseason, as the Jets fell to 2–2.

Namath would get considerably more playing time in the Jets' next exhibition game. Held on a Saturday night in Winston-Salem, North Carolina, in front of a crowd of 31,500 at Wake Forest's Groves Stadium, the Jets would go up against the NFL's Minnesota Vikings, who were 3–0 in preseason. The Vikings had beaten Miami, Denver, and St. Louis rather easily, scoring a total of 112 points while yielding only 29. Although only preseason, it was impressive all the same.

The Jets got on the board first when Namath hit Don Maynard with a 76-yard touchdown pass in the first quarter, and in the second period Jim Turner kicked a 15-yard field goal to make it 10–0, New York. The Vikings were able to close the gap before halftime when Wally Hilgenberg ran 10 yards for a score with a blocked punt, but the Jets only returned the favor in the third quarter when linebacker Paul Crane blocked a Minnesota punt and John Elliot recovered it at the two-yard line and fell into the end zone.

Later in the period, Namath hit George Sauer with an 11-yard touchdown pass to give the Jets a comfortable 24–7 lead; Namath then exited the game. In the fourth quarter the Vikings would make it respectable with TD runs of one and 12 yards by Dave Osborn, making the final 24–21, New York.

In his three quarters of play Namath had gone 13 of 23 for 219 yards and two TDs (more than half his completions — seven — going to Maynard for more than half the yardage —156). For the Vikings, Gary Cuozzo had played the entire game at quarterback for injured Joe Kapp, and completed 15 of 22 for 186 yards. The Jets had dominated in most every statistical category, gaining 346 total yards to 226 by the Vikings.

The Jets closed out their exhibition schedule against the Dallas Cowboys in the Cotton Bowl the following Saturday night. "I've been thinking about him the whole off-season," Dallas defensive lineman Bob Lilly said of Namath. "This has to be the biggest exhibition we've ever played. I think we will be motivated a little more because of Namath."[18]

"The Cowboys' front four doesn't even compare with Minnesota," Namath said, although he allowed that Lilly was "fabulous."[19]

A week prior to the game it was already a sellout of 73,000 seats, but come Saturday night they had managed to find room for another 1,771 for a final attendance tally of 74,771. If they had come to see Namath they needn't have bothered. Three days before the game he told reporters that he had hurt his leg in the Minnesota game and might not play at all. He said he hadn't practiced during the week and would have to wait until the pre-game warm-ups on Saturday night to see whether or not he felt up to playing, but it didn't get that far. The Jets' orthopedic specialist, Dr. James Nicholas, diagnosed Namath's problem as a small blood clot in the left leg and he advised Namath to skip the game in order to be in shape for the season opener against Buffalo. Namath didn't even suit up for the game in Dallas.

He expressed disappointment at not being able to play, but pointed out that the game was meaningless and he needed to be in top shape for the season. It was a disappointment for Lilly and the Dallas defensive linemen as well: without Namath, the Jets' offense was anemic. Although they did manage to get out to a 9–0 first-quarter lead on three Jim Turner field goals, Dallas took control from the second quarter onward. Aside from Turner's kicks, the only bright spot for the Jets was a 49-yard run by Emerson Boozer that set up one of the three-pointers. The Cowboys won the game 25–9.

The preseason ended with Namath having completed 55 of 97 passes for 801 yards. Ten days later it was off to Buffalo to begin defending their title.

Week 1— Sunday, September 14, 1969
War Memorial Stadium, Buffalo (attendance: 46,165)

The Jets were very heavily favored when they opened their season against the Bills in Buffalo, but then again they had also been heavily favored to beat the Bills when they had played them in Buffalo the previous season. Despite being 19-point favorites in that game, the Jets lost it 37–35 when Namath threw five interceptions, three of which wound up being run back for touchdowns, accounting for more than half of Buffalo's points. It was the last game Buffalo had won, as they went 1–13 in 1968 and now carried an 11-game losing streak into the 1969 season.

Buffalo had reason for hope this time around as well. For starters, the Jets had not won in Buffalo in six years. And then there was Buffalo's rookie sensation, running back O.J. Simpson, who would be making his professional debut. If either Simpson would have a spectacular debut, or Namath have another of those color blind passing days, then the Bills figured they would have a shot. If both of those things occurred, hell, they might end up winning in a rout.

The previous season Buffalo's War Memorial Stadium drew some 38,044 spectators when the Jets came to town. This time it was a packed house of 46,165, a franchise record. It may have had something to do with the champions coming to town (the Jets were, after all, seen as giant slayers since the Super Bowl), but many thought it likely that the real attraction for Buffalo fans was Simpson, the most highly touted rookie since Namath.

The teams traded field goals throughout the first quarter — Jim Turner hit from nine yards, Bruce Alford hit from 35 to tie it, Turner hit from 26 and then again from 41— and the Jets held a 9–3 lead midway into the second quarter when six-foot-four, 270-pound Buffalo defensive tackle Bob Tatarek took Namath down on a pass play that was completed to Pete Lammons. After going down, Namath grabbed his right knee in obvious pain. Thinking the worst, Namath pulled his helmet off and threw it to the ground in anger. He was already envisioning surgery and a season going down the drain just as it was beginning. Dr. Nicholas came onto the field and examined him; Nicholas felt that the ligaments were not torn and that there had been no serious damage done, and after walking it off Namath resumed with the game.

On the very next play he went back to pass and threw to Maynard down the right sideline. Cornerback Booker Edgerson slipped to the ground trying to adjust his position, and after making the catch Maynard ran 28 yards, untouched, for the score. The play had gone for 60 yards, and gave the Jets a commanding 16–3 lead.

When Jim Turner added another field goal in the third period to boost the Jets' lead to 19–3, the game seemed well in hand, but a major tide shift was coming. Late in the third quarter Matt Snell fumbled, and Buffalo safety John Pitts' recovery gave the Bills possession at the New York eight-yard line. At that point, Buffalo coach John Rauch sat down his rookie quarterback, James Harris, and sent veteran Jack Kemp into the game. Two plays later, Kemp hit fullback Bill Enyart with a five-yard scoring pass. The Bills tried a two-point conversion without success, and the score stood at 19–9.

On the Jets' next series Namath was intercepted by safety George Saimes, who ran the ball back 28 yards to the New York 16. It led to O.J. Simpson's first professional touchdown when he went in from eight yards. It was early in the fourth quarter, and the score was now 19–16.

When the Jets got the ball back Namath was again intercepted, this time by linebacker Paul Guidry, who ran the ball back 39 yards to the New York four-yard line. The Jets' coaches must have been having flashbacks to Namath's five-interception performance in Buffalo a year earlier (it certainly had to have crossed Namath's mind). The New York defense did its job, keeping Buffalo out of the end zone, but Alford's 10-yard field goal tied the score at 19.

On the Jets' next series Namath decided enough was enough: he kept it on the ground, running Snell and Boozer. The Jets pounded their way downfield and eventually faced a third-and-one at the Buffalo 14: Namath ran a keeper up the middle, gaining three yards and a first down. It was Snell who then ran it in from 11 yards out for the go-ahead score with 7:31 left to play. The Jets had gone 58 yards in five plays to retake the lead.

Buffalo's final three offensive possessions all ended with Kemp being intercepted. The clincher for the Jets was when linebacker Paul Crane returned one of those interceptions 23 yards for a score to make the final 33–19. It wasn't a pretty victory, but they'd take it, of course. At 1–0 the Jets were already alone atop the Eastern Division, Buffalo, Houston, Boston, and Miami all being 0–1.

As for O.J. Simpson's professional debut, he only managed 35 yards in 10 carries, which he excused by saying he was still bothered by a cold he picked up earlier in the week. Other than his eight-yard touchdown run, the one play where he exhibited the promise of things to come was when he ran 55 yards with a screen pass.

As for Namath, he didn't look particularly sharp, hitting just seven of 19 passes for 157 yards, with one TD and three interceptions; in fact, he didn't complete a single pass in the entire second half. Jim Turner, on the other hand, had kicked four field goals. For a team with such an explosive offense, the Jets did seem to settle for three-pointers an awful lot.

Week 2 — Sunday, September 21, 1969
Mile High Stadium, Denver (attendance: 50,583)

In week two of the season the Jets traveled to Denver to play the Broncos at Mile High Stadium in front of 50,583 spectators, the largest crowd to ever attend a football game in Colorado. Favored by 10 points, it didn't take the Jets long to get started as Namath threw 54 yards to Matt Snell on just the third play of the game. It wasn't for a touchdown, but it did lead to a 15-yard Jim Turner field goal that gave the Jets an early 3–0 lead.

The Broncos put together a drive of their own, but it ended when Jim Hudson intercepted Steve Tensi at the New York 13. Hudson returned the ball 22 yards to the 35, and Namath then drove the Jets 65 yards for a touchdown and a 10–0 lead when Bill Mathis scored from a yard out. Before the end of the first quarter Jim Turner would add another field goal, this time of 49 yards, giving the Jets a 13–0 lead.

Everything was going much as expected at that point, but in the second period Floyd Little ran a punt back 52 yards to the New York one-yard line and then had the pleasure of running it in for the score two plays later. The Jets still had a 13–7 lead, but when Denver quarterback Tensi left the game with a bruised knee early in the quarter, backup Pete Liske seemed to have better luck. Liske got the Broncos moving, and put them out in front with a 23-yard TD pass to Mike Haffner that gave Denver a 14–13 lead at the half.

The third quarter saw no scoring as the teams swapped turnovers, but in the fourth quarter Liske hit Al Denson with a 41-yard scoring pass to increase Denver's lead to 21–13. It was getting late in the game when the Jets started a drive from their own 13-yard line. It looked like the drive, and the Jets chances, might come to nothing when 250-pound lineman Dave Costa put Namath down hard. The massive Costa rammed into Namath full steam, launching into him like a missile, his helmet slamming into Namath's chest and lifting him off the ground. Namath stayed on the ground for a few minutes as the team doctors came out to see if he was badly hurt. When Namath eventually was helped to his feet he opted to stay in the game, and he drove the Jets the rest of the way to complete the 87-yard drive when Emerson Boozer scored on a three-yard run.

Now trailing 21–19, the Jets had no choice: they had to go for a two-point conversion to tie the game. Curiously, Ewbank sent Babe Parilli in to quarterback the conversion attempt. Perhaps, with Namath shaken up on the drive and Parilli warming up on the sideline as Namath was being tended to, Ewbank thought that Parilli would be more fit for the situation. He was wrong. Hurried by onrushing and unblocked linebacker Carl Cunningham, Parilli's pass over the middle to Pete Lammons fell short, bouncing in front of the tight end. The score remained 21–19, and the game ended that way. For the third consecutive season, the Broncos had upset the Jets.

With the loss, the Jets fell into a first-place tie with 1–1 Houston in the East. Namath had completed 19 of 37 for 283 yards. One play that certainly deserves mention was New York punter Steve O'Neal's professional football record 98-yard punt. Kicking from the end zone, O'Neal's punt went over return man Bill Thompson's shoulder, bounced at the Denver 33 and continued to roll all the way to the other end zone. The Jets had acquired the Texas A&M rookie after waiving veteran punter Curley Johnson in August (Johnson subsequently went to the New York Giants).

Week 3 — Sunday, September 28, 1969
San Diego Stadium, San Diego (attendance: 54,042)

The Jets continued their road swing in week three, traveling to San Diego to play the 0–2 Chargers in front of yet another record crowd. The Chargers had fallen behind quickly in the Western Division, partly due to quarterback John Hadl's nursing a sore throwing arm since a preseason meeting with Deacon Jones and the Los Angeles Rams, but with his arm feeling the best it had since August, Hadl and the Chargers were hoping to change their luck.

After a first-quarter interception of a Namath pass by linebacker Pete Barnes, Hadl threw a nine-yard touchdown to Lance Alworth. San Diego added a field goal in the second period to make it 10–0, and the Jets found themselves trying to dig out of a hole. Namath hit George Sauer with a 21-yard touchdown, but the Chargers answered back with a drive that yielded a five-yard touchdown run by Russ Smith. Later in the period the Chargers would score again when Hadl threw a 13-yard touchdown to Gary Garrison. The Jets could only add a field goal before the break, enabling San Diego to take a 14-point lead into halftime.

The two teams would only swap field goals in the third period, and the Jets entered the fourth quarter down 27–13. To make matters worse for New York, safety Jim Hudson left the game with a knee injury. The Jets also lost cornerback Randy Beverly during the game, and had to use rookie Cecil Leonard in his place. Early in the fourth quarter it was Leonard who gave the Jets a lift by grabbing a Dick Post fumble at the San Diego 16 and running it back 13 yards to the three-yard line. Two plays later Emerson Boozer scored on a sweep right from two yards out to cut the San Diego lead to seven points.

But the Chargers came right back with a drive that brought their lead up to 14 when Hadl again hit Garrison with a touchdown pass, this time from 29 yards out. With time now a major factor, the Jets had to make their play, and Namath drove them 77 yards in seven plays to again trim the lead to seven points when he hit Sauer with his second touchdown of the game, this one from 14 yards out. It was now up to the defense to force a punt and get the ball back to Namath and company: this they did.

The New York offense got the ball back with several minutes remaining, and having completed 16 of his previous 18 passes, Namath had a hot hand. He again drove the Jets downfield, eventually winding up at the San Diego nine-yard line where they were facing a fourth-and-five with 2:30 left to play. Down by seven points, a field goal was useless at that point — the Jets had to go for it. As hot a hand as Namath had in the fourth quarter, suddenly, when it mattered most, he missed Bill Mathis, underthrowing him when he was within easy reach of at least the first down. It was again up to the defense to force a punt. Not this time: the Chargers ran out the clock.

The loss dropped the Jets to 1–2 and knocked them out of their first-place tie with Houston. The Oilers, who had beaten Miami, were now alone atop the East with a 2–1 record. After the game Namath was asked if he thought the '69 Jets were as good as the '68 team. "We sure as hell don't look like it right now," he said. "We've got to get it together."[20]

Namath had completed 29 of 51 passes in the game for 344 yards, with a pair each of TDs and interceptions. The 29 completions tied a team record set in 1960 by Al Dorow. The record meant nothing to Namath; the only pass that really mattered at that point was the one for Mathis that fell short.

Week 4 — Sunday, October 5, 1969
Boston College Field, Boston (attendance: 25,584)

Originally the Jets' week four meeting with the Boston Patriots was scheduled to be a home game for New York. After three weeks on the road they could have used it, but as it happened, the other residents of Shea Stadium, the New York Mets, had won the pennant and were in the National League Championship. That being the case, the Jets-Patriots game was redirected to Massachusetts and Boston College Field. As division rivals they would play each other twice anyway, so the Jets would then host the Patriots later in the season. At Boston College Field 25,584 was a sellout, and it was the first the Patriots had registered since 1966.

As the Jets were on a two-game losing streak, the Patriots seemed the ideal candidates to lift that funk. The Patriots were 0–3, really only one game behind the Jets, but that was misleading: whereas the Jets had been competitive in their losses, the Patriots were not. They had been blown out 35–7 by Denver, 31–0 by Kansas City, and 38–23 by Oakland. Aside from being outscored 104–30 in their first three games, the Patriots had allowed damn near twice the total yardage they themselves had gained (1,139 to 578). It was assumed that a mad bomber like Namath would have a field day with a team like this.

The Patriots had a new coach for the 1969 season — Clive Rush, the former offensive coach of the Jets. Rush had left the Jets after their Super Bowl triumph, accepting the offer from the Patriots, who had fired head coach Mike Holovak. If any opponent knew the Jets' offense, it would be Rush. He knew what they could do, what they could not, and everything in-between. Rush was eager for his first win as a head coach, and he knew he would have to devise something to catch the Super Bowl champions off guard.

The Patriots received the opening kickoff, and sure enough they came out with a formation not seen in their repertoire before. The offense came on field and went with no huddle, immediately lining up at the line of scrimmage with three wide receivers and only Jim Nance in the backfield. It may have been a surprise, but it didn't accomplish much. The Patriots couldn't move the ball, and quickly had to punt.

When the Jets' offense came on field, the Boston defense also had a new look for them: they went with a three-man line and four linebackers. The idea there was to inhibit the long pass, which Rush knew all too well as Namath's specialty. "He knows I don't like it," Namath said after the game of the 3–4 formation. "It takes away the sudden score with deep passes. Rush is smart."[21]

The Jets managed to drive downfield anyway, grinding it out on the ground until the drive fizzled out and Jim Turner had to try a 34-yard field goal. He missed, but on the Jets' next series they managed to get close enough for Turner to hit a 16-yard chip shot for a 3–0 lead.

In the second period the Patriots put together a 13-play, 68-yard drive that culminated with Mike Taliaferro hitting Ron Sellers with a 14-yard touchdown pass that gave Boston a 7–3 lead with 10 minutes to play in the half. Just before the half ended, however, Namath managed to drive the Jets 80 yards to retake the lead when he hit Pete Lammons with a 10-yard touchdown in the final 25 seconds of the second quarter.

Early in the third quarter Taliaferro pitched an interception that set the Jets up at midfield, and Namath promptly took the offense into the red zone. Then, facing a third-and-goal from the four-yard line, Namath shocked everyone by rolling left and bootlegging it into the end zone himself. The 10-point lead gave the Jets a little breathing room, and before the quarter ended Jim Turner added another field goal (this one from 24 yards) to make the score 20–7 going into the final quarter.

Turner would add yet another field goal in the fourth quarter before the Patriots again put something together. Midway through the fourth, Taliaferro directed an 84-yard drive that ended with a four-yard touchdown run by Jim Nance to make the final 23–14. Really, the Patriots had largely sunk themselves: all of New York's second-half points were set up by turnovers (two interceptions and a fumble). In speaking about his team's defensive formations, Rush said afterward that the idea was to force the Jets to beat them left-handed.[22] Although Rush's plan worked in taking away the long pass (Maynard, for instance, didn't catch a pass all day), it ultimately failed when Namath started throwing short to Snell and Mathis, and the running game thrived. Namath's stats read 15 of 21 for 145 yards, with one TD and one interception.

Houston beat Buffalo, which kept the Jets a game back in the East. With the Mets winning the National League Championship and advancing to the World Series, the Jets would also have to stay on the road.

Week 5 — Sunday, October 12, 1969
Nippert Stadium, Cincinnati (attendance: 27,927)

It may have only been the Cincinnati Bengals' sophomore season, but they were no pushovers. Coached by Paul Brown, the Bengals came into week five with a 3–1 record, having beaten Miami, San Diego, and — surprisingly — Kansas City (the Bengals played San Diego twice in three weeks, with the Chargers winning the rematch in week four).

Whether because the Cincinnati defense was doing that good a job, or the Jets were just being overly conservative, the first period went scoreless, but the Jets were finally driving when the quarter came to an end. The drive reached its payoff early in the second quarter, when Namath rolled out to his left and hit George Sauer with a 14-yard pass in the left corner of the end zone. The reception also put Sauer over the 4,000-yard mark in his career. The big play in the series had been a 26-yard pass from Namath to Sauer; otherwise it was Emerson Boozer who kept the chains moving, as he was on his way to his best game of the season.

Later in the second quarter, the Jets embarked on an 89-yard drive in which the running game carried the load. The big gainer was a 38-yard run by Boozer, as Namath threw only once in the series (the pass fell incomplete). It was Namath who went over from one-yard out on a quarterback sneak to put the Jets up 14–0; it was his second touchdown in as many weeks.

The game had been billed as something of a showdown between Namath and Cincinnati's rookie quarterback Greg Cook, but that didn't quite pan out. With Cook having completed only four of nine passes for just 20 yards and an interception, Brown pulled him from the game late in the first half in favor of Sam Wyche. There really wasn't much Cook could have done, as the New York defense was putting on a fine show, holding the Bengals to a lowly 39 yards in the half (30 passing, and just nine yards rushing).

Early in the third period, Jim Richards blocked a Cincinnati punt at the Bengals' 22-yard line and linebacker Paul Crane gathered up the ball at the 12 and ran it in for a score. Like Namath, it was Crane's second touchdown of the year. Cincinnati finally got rolling midway into the quarter, and managed an 80-yard drive that got them on the board when Wyche hit Eric Crabtree with a 22-yard touchdown throw to cut the New York lead to 21–7, but the Jets never seemed in any real danger.

The Bengals threatened once more in the fourth quarter, driving to the Jets' 26 before surrendering the ball on a fumble by Jess Phillips. Otherwise, it was still the New York defense calling the shots, sacking Wyche three times in the final period: they had a total of six in the game. "They aren't called the champs for nothing," Brown said after the game. "They ran right over us. We were trounced."[23]

That they were: Boozer had gained 129 yards on just 15 carries, while the team racked up 222 total rushing yards. Namath threw for 163 yards, completing 14 of 26, with one TD and one interception. The victory brought the Jets record up to 3–2, and with Houston having been blanked 24–0 by Kansas City, the Jets moved back into a first place tie with the Oilers. That made the Jets' home opener all the more meaningful in week six, as they would be hosting the Oilers at Shea.

Week 6 — Monday, October 20, 1969
Shea Stadium, New York (attendance: 63,841)

The Jets' home opener would be a Monday night first-place shootout with division rival Houston. The New York Mets had won the 1969 World Series, beating the Baltimore Orioles at Shea Stadium just four days earlier; in their enthusiasm, the jubilant Shea Stadium crowd mobbed the field after the victory, tearing out huge chunks of the turf to take as souvenirs. The groundskeepers had to quickly re-sod the field, but by game time Monday night the footing was still treacherous in spots.

Because of the Mets' postseason schedule, the Jets had been forced to play the first five weeks of the season on the road, but with the baseball season over, the Jets now had the luxury of having all of their seven home games consecutively before winding up the season with two more road games. The World Series–champion Mets were among the AFL-record crowd of 63,841 at Shea Stadium for the Jets' home opener.

Namath came out gunning: the Jets got on the board first when Jim Turner booted a 17-yard field goal after Namath had thrown for 26 yards to George Sauer and 40 yards to Don Maynard to get the Jets to the Houston 10-yard line. But early in the second quarter Namath threw the second of his three interceptions of the evening. This one would be the most costly, as cornerback Zeke Moore took it 51 yards for a score to give the Oilers a 7–3 lead.

After the Jets received the kick, Namath got the lead back quickly. Runs by Snell and Boozer advanced the Jets to their own 43, and Namath then went to the pass. With six-five Pat Holmes bearing down on him, Namath heaved a long throw to Maynard, who had a couple steps on defender Miller Farr and was racing down the center of the field. As Maynard took the ball over his shoulder at the 22-yard line, Farr made a desperate dive at him, but Maynard high-stepped away and ran the final 20 yards for the score. They play had covered 57 yards — it was Maynard's first touchdown since the 60-yarder he caught from Namath on opening day in Buffalo. Farr would say later that it seemed to be a broken play, as Maynard ran a post pattern but then cut up the middle.

Seven minutes later, with the half winding down and the Jets at their own 46, Namath again went deep to Maynard in what almost looked like an identical play. This time it was Ken Houston who was covering Maynard. Houston fell to the ground at the 25-yard line, allowing Maynard to make the catch unchallenged at the 20 and run, untouched, for a 54-yard score. Namath had only completed six of 15 passes in the first half, but those six completions were good for 227 yards. More importantly, they included two touchdowns that gave the Jets a 17–7 halftime lead.

Houston quarterback Pete Beathard hadn't fared as well, hitting only six of 18 throws, and no touchdowns; Beathard would rally his team, however. The Oilers received the second-half kickoff and were looking at a long field when they wound up starting from their own four-yard line, but after Beathard scrambled for 16 yards and a first down, Houston seemed inspired and they wound up going the 96 yards for a score. Beathard completed the drive by hitting Mac Haik with a 15-yard scoring pass that pulled Houston to within three points at 17–14.

After that brief lapse, the New York defense would tighten again as the teams only swapped field goals through the remainder of the third (Jim Turner from 48 yards, Roy Gerela from 12). The Jets put the game away in the fourth as Jim Turner added two more field goals (45 and 21 yards) to give New York a 26–17 victory. At 4–2 the Jets were now alone atop the AFL East.

Like Namath, Beathard would throw three interceptions on the evening. Namath's most costly interception had given the Oilers seven points, but Beathard had cost his team a possible seven when he was intercepted by Al Atkinson in the end zone to snuff out a Houston scoring threat in the fourth quarter. Namath completed half his throws (12 of 24) for 306 yards, and two touchdowns.

Both Farr and Houston were quick to praise Maynard after the game. "With his speed," said Farr, "he can run two or three patterns when Namath gets good protection."[24] Maynard's two touchdowns allowed him to tie an all-time AFL record with 81 career TDs. When informed of this after the game by reporters, Maynard seemed fairly unimpressed by it. He was more pleased that the Jets seemed to be getting back into their groove after a slow start. "I think we're getting better," he said. "Everything is falling into place again, and we're on our way."[25]

Week 7 — Sunday, October 26, 1969
Shea Stadium, New York (attendance: 62,298)

The poor Boston Patriots were still winless when they came to Shea Stadium in week seven. As Namath had put on such an impressive aerial show with his long throws to Maynard the previous Monday, Boston coach Clive Rush decided to stick with the defensive strategy he devised for the earlier meeting between the two teams in Boston — a 3–4 alignment that would allow double coverage of both Maynard and Sauer.

The Patriots came out fired up, receiving the opening kickoff and driving 82 yards for a touchdown. Mike Taliaferro (an ex-Jet) threw 22 yards to Bill Rademacher (also an ex–Jet) for the score.

But the Jets wasted no time in answering back, as Mike Battle fielded the ensuing kick at the New York 15 and then returned it 45 yards to the Boston 40. Having a short field to work with, the Jets went that 40 yards in eight plays and tied the game when Matt Snell scored on a 12-yard run. The Patriots had come to play, however, and before the first quarter ended they drove to the New York 32 and retook the lead with a 39-yard field goal by Gino Cappelletti.

In the second quarter, New York tied the score when Jim Turner kicked a 38-yard field goal, but the Jets soon fell behind again when Namath threw into the flat and was intercepted by John Charles, who ran it back 25 yards for a score; the Patriots kept that 17–10 lead into halftime. Rush's strategy seemed to be paying off, as Namath's first half numbers were unimpressive, completing only five of 12 passes.

In the third quarter the Jets could only trim the Boston lead to 17–13 when Jim Turner hit a 32-yard field goal, and it was not until late in the period that the champions began to rise to the occasion. After receiving a punt and starting at their own 11, the Jets began their go-ahead drive as the third period gave way to the fourth. They were faced with a third-and-10 at their own 21, and Namath went back to pass. Unable to find anyone open, he found that the coverage had dropped back far enough to give him room to run, and seeing open space to his left, Namath took off. The Patriots seemed amused. "Run, Joe, run!" they taunted as they watched his awkward, gimpy stride, but Namath managed to dodge a tackler and took it 16 yards for the first down before diving headfirst to the ground.[26]

Namath's run had advanced the Jets to the 37, and a flag on the play added more — the Patriots were penalized an additional 15 yards when linebacker John Bramlett was called for tripping Sauer. That gave the Jets the ball at the Boston 48. On first down, Namath threw to Sauer for six yards to the 42; on second down, Snell ran for 12 and a first down at the 30. Then it was Bill Mathis running for 10 yards and another first down at the 20. Snell gained seven to the 13, and from there it was all Boozer. Namath ran Boozer four straight plays, the last being a two-yard scoring run that completed the 89-yard drive and put the Jets up for the first time in the game with nine minutes left to play.

Later in the fourth quarter, the Jets' defense would seal Boston's fate when Gerry Philbin forced Taliaferro to fumble and John Elliot recovered for New York at the Patriots' 31-yard line. Namath played it safe and kept the ball on the ground, and after the Patriots managed to stop them at the six-yard line, the Jets settled for a 13-yard field goal to make the final score 23–17.

Asked about the 16-yard run that had ignited the comeback drive, Namath said, "I save those moves for emergencies, and that was an emergency."[27] Snell admitted to being apprehensive in looking for someone to block on the play, saying that his fear was that he would cause someone to fall on top of Namath's legs.

The Patriots were now 0–7, but seemed to take some pride in the fact that they had at least played the champs tougher in both their meetings than the Baltimore Colts had in the Super Bowl. Rush's defensive scheme really had taken the long pass away from the Jets (Namath threw for only 115 yards in the game, completing 10 of 21 with one interception), but had again allowed the running game to flourish. In the second half it was the Jets' defense that had taken over the game — Boston only managed two first downs in the entire second half. The New York defense did suffer a blow, however: safety Jim Hudson, who had been hurt earlier in the season, had only just been reactivated. He suffered torn ligaments in his right knee, and would now be out for the remainder of the season.

While the Jets were still atop the division with a 5–2 record, Houston managed to remain within a game of them by beating Denver, 24–21. Both teams had an easy game coming up, the Jets playing the 1–5–1 Miami Dolphins, and the Oilers going against the winless Patriots. But in week eight there was an apparent call for the division's cellar dwellers to rise up.

Week 8 — Sunday, November 2, 1969
Shea Stadium, New York (attendance: 61,761)

The Jets and Dolphins have had some spectacular showdowns through the years, and this game seems to have been the first of many classic shootouts between the two teams. November 2, 1969 was a dreary, rainy New York day. The Jets came into week eight riding a four-game winning streak: the Dolphins were coming off their first win of the season, having beaten Buffalo 24–6.

Weather conditions being what they were (there were showers off and on throughout the game), it would be expected to have an effect on the game, but its impact was obvious from the very start when Mercury Morris, receiving the opening kickoff for Miami, fumbled the ball, and the Jets recovered it at the Miami 10-yard line. But even with such ideal field position to start the game, the Jets were unable to punch it into the end zone and had to settle for a 14-yard field goal and a 3–0 lead 2:22 into the first quarter. On the Dolphins' next series, Bob Griese fumbled and the Jets recovered; Namath cashed in quickly with a 42-yard touchdown to Don Maynard, which gave Maynard an AFL-record 82 career TDs.

Before the end of the first quarter, Griese cut New York's lead to 10–7 with a five-yard touchdown pass to Jack Clancy, and in the second period the Dolphins really got their act together; Griese tossed a 29-yard touchdown to Larry Seiple that gave Miami a 14–10 lead, followed by an 11-yard touchdown pass to Larry Csonka that boosted that lead to 21–10 at the half.

It wasn't until midway into the third quarter that the Jets caught the break that seemed to wake them up. Dropping back to throw deep in his own territory, Griese was swarmed by a heavy rush and again fumbled the ball; tackle Steve Thompson recovered for the Jets at the two-yard line, leading to a one-yard touchdown run by Matt Snell. The Jets failed on a two-point conversion, and the Miami lead stood at 21–16.

Later in the third, Miami's Ed Weisacosky intercepted Namath at the New York 30, which led to a 22-yard field goal and a 24–16 Miami lead; but as the third quarter came to an end the Jets were on the move. Namath had ended the third quarter with a 15-yard throw to George Sauer, and he would find Sauer again only 12 seconds into the fourth period, this time for 27 yards and a score. The Jets were forced by necessity to go for two points again on the conversion; they ran Snell on a sweep right, and as the defense closed in, Snell flipped a quick pass to Maynard in the right side of the end zone. That evened the score at 24.

Undaunted, Griese then drove the Dolphins 65 yards to put them back up 31–24 when he again found Seiple in the end zone, this time from nine yards out. With 9:22 left to play, it was now the Jets turn to come storming back. Namath hit Maynard with a 37-yard pass that put Maynard over the 10,000-yard mark in his career. He was the only AFL player to ever reach that plateau. Namath then went back to Maynard for 25 yards and a touchdown, again evening the score with just over seven minutes remaining.

When the Dolphins' next series failed and they had to punt, John Elliot made the decisive play. He broke through the line and almost did a cartwheel while going over top of Csonka, who tried to block him low. Elliot got a hand up and was able to block Seiple's punt, which was recovered by Randy Beverly at the Miami 31. There were some three minutes left in the game, and the Jets were now in ideal position to win it. They seemed to be playing for the field goal as they remained conservative and kept the ball on the ground, but three straight runs yielded only seven yards to the 24. Turner came in for a 31-yard field goal try, but an offside penalty pushed the Jets back five yards, forcing him to kick it from the 36. Turner put it through to give the Jets a 34–31 lead with 2:41 left in the game.

The Dolphins still had plenty of time to at least get within field goal range, and although they made it as far as the New York 35-yard line in the game's final minute of play, Bill Baird quashed the threat when he intercepted Griese at the 17. The Jets were able to run out the clock from there and win their fifth straight.

The pressure was wearing on Jim Turner. After the game he pointed out that field goals had played a vital role in seven of the Jets' eight games. "I'm sure ready for one of those 50–0 games," he said. "I know I can't kick good every day. But the day I kick badly is the day I want Joe to throw 10 touchdowns."[28]

For a team with only one win, the Dolphins had put up a damn good fight. Griese had a very impressive game, hitting eight in a row at one point as he shot it out with Namath, who finished 13 of 26 for 233 yards (three TDs, one interception). It took an impressive 18-point fourth quarter by the Jets to pull it out.

Their record now 6–2, the Jets went two games up on Houston in the East, as the Patriots accomplished their first win of the season by blanking the Oilers, 24–0. The Jets continued their seven-game home stand the following week when they hosted the 2–6 Buffalo Bills.

Week 9 — Sunday, November 9, 1969
Shea Stadium, New York (attendance: 62,680)

It was another wet, drizzly day at Shea Stadium when the 2–6 Buffalo Bills came to play the Jets. The Once proud AFL-champion Bills had fallen a long way, but their superstar rookie running back O.J. Simpson held the promise of their future. With Simpson the Bills might become a contender, but it hadn't happened yet.

The Bills showed the promise of what they could be on their first offensive series, driving the length of the field to score on a three-yard run by Simpson. But they also showed the mistake-prone proclivity of a team that had yet to find its legs. The touchdown was nullified by a penalty: it was Simpson himself who negated his own score by being flagged for illegal motion, having started before the snap in his eagerness. After the penalty, the Bills failed to get the ball back into the end zone and had to settle for a 13-yard field goal try: it was blocked by linebacker Paul Crane, and for all their efforts, the Bills had driven downfield and come away with nothing.

Neither team would score in the first quarter, and by the second period a drizzling rain had started. Buffalo drove to the New York 15-yard line, but had to settle for another field goal try — it was blocked again. When the Jets took possession at their 20 they finally began a drive of their own. Namath hit Matt Snell with a 22-yard pass, but the major play of the drive was a pass interference call on cornerback Booker Edgerson. Covering Don Maynard, Edgerson had been flagged for interference in the end zone, which gave the Jets a first-and-goal at the Buffalo one-yard line. Bill Mathis scored two plays later to give the Jets a 7–0 lead.

The Bills once more managed to drive deep into New York territory, this time reaching the 18, but had to settle for another field goal attempt: it was blocked yet again. Aside from their inability to kick a field goal, the Buffalo offense was having a hard time keeping their quarterbacks protected. Starting quarterback Dan Darragh had to leave the game in the second quarter when he suffered a separated shoulder after being taken down by Verlon Biggs and Gerry Philbin. Jack Kemp came in at quarterback, but he too had to leave the game after being knocked unconscious. Receiver Marlin Briscoe wound up taking over at quarterback; having played the position in college, he was the best choice. Positioned at the New York 36, Briscoe went back to pass on first-and-10 and rolled to his right; he tried to hit Bubba Thornton but wound up being intercepted by Bill Baird. When Buffalo got the ball back again, Kemp had shaken the cobwebs out of his head and returned at quarterback.

The Bills managed to get in field goal range at the end of the half, and on the last play of the second quarter they had their fourth try at kicking a field goal — it was blocked by Larry Grantham. Fortunately for the Bills, a penalty on the Jets gave them another shot at it, and with no time left on the clock, the Bills finally got their field goal from 20 yards out, making the score 7–3 at halftime.

In the third quarter, the Bills were still making careless mistakes. They drove to the Jets' 12-yard line but Kemp, perhaps still feeling the effects of the hit he took in the first half, cost his team with a delay penalty. The Bills wound up with another field goal, which brought them to within a point of the Jets at 7–6.

Namath finally got the Jets on the move again, hitting Maynard for 23 yards and Lammons for 20 more, but when the drive fizzled out, Jim Turner came in to salvage the effort with a 37-yard field goal. In the fourth quarter, Namath hit George Sauer with a 33-yard pass to position Turner for another field goal try, which he made it from 25 yards to give the Jets a 13–6 lead. But the Bills still had plenty of chance to catch the Jets. With only a few minutes left to play, Simpson ran 18 yards to midfield and it looked like Buffalo might do it. But on the following play, Simpson fumbled the ball and linebacker John Neidert recovered for the Jets. The Jets then did an efficient job of running out the clock, as they methodically advanced to the Buffalo 40 and sent Turner in to seal the victory with a 47-yard field goal with only 23 seconds left. Turner's kick was good, making the final score 16–6.

The victory extended the Jets' winning streak to six games, which set a club record, but reporters were all asking what was wrong with the Jets. "Not a thing," said Namath. "We're 7–2 aren't we?"[29] Yes, they were 7–2, but everyone couldn't help but notice that they were struggling even against the lowliest of teams. That six-game winning streak consisted of beating last-place Boston (twice), Buffalo, Miami, Houston, and Cincinnati — only the two latter teams were playing .500 ball. Buffalo coach John Rauch noted that the Jets didn't seem to be playing as well as they had the previous season.[30]

"I don't know what it is," said Namath when pressed on the issue. "I think we've played well, but I think the big thing is we're disappointed because we haven't played as well as we think we should be playing."[31] Namath wound up 10 of 22 for 169 yards, with one interception.

In 1968 Weeb Ewbank had commented that only the great teams win when they have a bad day, and the 1969 Jets were winning on what were at best mediocre days, though only beating mediocre teams. Even with the 7–2 record, everyone had to wonder how the Jets would fare against a really good team. The following week everyone would find out when the 8–1 Kansas City Chiefs came to Shea.

Week 10 — Sunday, November 16, 1969
Shea Stadium, New York (attendance: 63,849)

Both the Chiefs and the Jets were on six-game winning streaks when Kansas City came to Shea to face New York in front of yet another new AFL-record crowd of 63,849. By the end of the game somebody's winning streak would end.

Despite their winning six straight, the Jets had been playing sloppy, uninspired football. They were able to get away with it against the likes of Boston and Buffalo, but the Chiefs were 8–1 and had the number one defense in the league. A mistake-ridden effort against them could prove costly, as the Jets would find out very early on.

Emerson Boozer fumbled on the Jets' first play from scrimmage, and Bobby Bell recovered the ball for Kansas City at the New York 18; the Chiefs would waste no time in taking advantage of the opportunity. They had devised a number of new formations to confuse the New York defense, and confuse them they did. On their first play, the Chiefs had wide receiver Otis Taylor line up in the backfield as a slot back to the right. When the ball was snapped and Taylor vacated the backfield, no one picked him up; he wound up all alone in the end zone, and Len Dawson quickly spotted him and threw. The resulting touchdown gave the Chiefs a 7–0 lead less than a minute into the game. Taylor was making his return to the lineup after having missed three games with an injury. For the Jets, he had returned a week too soon.

The two teams exchanged field goals, and with the Chiefs then leading 10–3, Namath lofted a perfect 40-yard strike down the left sideline to George Sauer that tied the score at 10 early in the second quarter. The tie was short lived, as the Chiefs drove back downfield in 12 plays and scored on another Dawson-to-Taylor pass, this one of seven yards.

The Jets had their chance to tie things up again, but after driving downfield Namath was intercepted in the Kansas City end zone by Emmitt Thomas. The Chiefs turned it back around, and drove down for a 38-yard field goal that gave them a 20–10 halftime lead. In the second half it was as though the Jets were no longer really in the game. Every time they had an opportunity to get back in it, they threw the opportunity away with turnovers. Namath was intercepted three times in the game; his two interceptions in the first half had both killed scoring threats. On another occasion, with the Jets poised to score, Namath's pitchout to Matt Snell was high and Snell fumbled it; the Chiefs recovered the ball at their three-yard line.

A two-yard TD run by Warren McVea in the third quarter increased Kansas City's lead to 27–10, and in the fourth quarter yet another Dawson-to-Taylor TD pass made it 34–10. By the time Namath found Don Maynard with a 10-yard scoring pass the game was basically over, and when the Jets failed on a fairly pointless two-point conversion, the final score read 34–16. The Jets hadn't taken such a beating since 1967 when the same Kansas City Chiefs had humiliated them, 42–18.

The loss seemed to make it official in the minds of many: there was definitely something wrong with the champions. Really, the game meant much more to Kansas City than to New York. For the second consecutive week the Houston Oilers had played their opponent to a tie, meaning that even with the loss to Kansas City the Jets still held a two-and-a-half game lead in the East. Kansas City, on the other hand, was in a real battle with Oakland for the West, holding a mere half-game lead in the division. Was Kansas City hungrier than New York? Perhaps. The truth is that the Jets looked like a team that had lost its zeal. Maybe being the champs had left them feeling they no longer had anything to prove. Then again, that's just so much talk and the Jets would have been the first to say that there is no excuse for getting beat 34–16. Still, while the Jets' winning streak ended at six, it had set a club record. Namath finished the game 24 of 40 for 327 yards, two TDs and three interceptions.

Week 11 — Sunday, November 23, 1969
Shea Stadium, New York (attendance: 62,128)

The Jets were getting tired of being viewed with suspicion. They had beaten the Colts handily in the Super Bowl, but apparently it wasn't enough. They had gone on a club-record six-game winning streak, but that didn't seem to be enough either. For all of their accomplishments, it seemed the loss to Kansas City had the Jets' critics feeling vindicated. While the naysayers were dismissing one victory after another, it only took one loss to elicit a chorus of "I told you so's."

But the yammering of the critics was nothing compared to the frustration of the beating the Jets had taken from Kansas City. They were looking to take it out on somebody, and the poor Cincinnati Bengals happened to be the next in line. At 4–5–1, Paul Brown's Bengals should have been better equipped to put up a fight than some of the Jets' other opponents, but they seem to have drawn the Jets on the exact wrong day. Weeks earlier, kicker Jim Turner, feeling the pressure of the close games the Jets had been through, said that he was ready for a 50–0 game. He wouldn't get it against Cincinnati, but damn near, and Turner would contribute more than his share with four first-half field goals.

The defense would also turn in a fine performance, giving the offense a number of choice opportunities. After Turner field goals of 29 and 41 yards gave the Jets a 6–0 lead in the first quarter, Turner would boot a 50-yarder in the second that made it 9–0. Cincinnati's rookie quarterback Greg Cook—rated second in passing in the AFL behind Namath—was having a bad day; John Dockery intercepted Cook at the Cincinnati 42 and ran it back 35 yards to the seven. It set up a five-yard TD toss from Namath to George Sauer that put the Jets up 16–0. Later in the period, a 30-yard pass from Namath to Don Maynard set up Turner's fourth field goal, a 17-yarder, and the Jets led at halftime, 19–0. The Jets had scored the first five times they had the ball, and the defense had only allowed Cook three pass completions in 10 attempts.

The Jets continued to pour it on in the third quarter. When the Bengals wound up punting out of their own end zone, the New York offense took over at the Cincinnati 30. Namath threw 15 yards to Maynard, and then 15 more to Sauer for the score and a 26–0 lead. With that, Namath's work was done, having completed 11 of 20 for 172 yards and two touchdowns. But the Jets were hardly finished: the hemorrhaging continued for Cincinnati.

After Namath's second touchdown pass to Sauer, the Bengals' Ken Riley fumbled the kickoff, and Wayne Stewart recovered for the Jets on the Cincinnati 24. Babe Parilli came in at quarterback, and with three seconds left in the third period he threw his first touchdown of the season, hitting Pete Lammons from eight yards out. The Jets led 33–0 after three quarters.

The Bengals finally put together a drive early in the fourth, averting a shutout when Cook hit Bob Trumpy with an eight-yard touchdown pass with 12:18 left in the game. New York's third-string quarterback, rookie Al Woodall, came into the game and directed the Jets to one more score; Bill Mathis capped the 80-yard drive when he ran it in from 11 yards out with 1:54 left to play. With the score 40–7, it mercifully ended there.

The Jets' defense had done a fine job, sacking Cook five times and only allowing Cincinnati to cross midfield three times in the game. Ewbank was certainly pleased, calling it the team's best defensive effort of the season.[32]

With Houston beating Miami 32–7, the Oilers stayed within two-and-a-half games of the Jets in the East, but with only three games remaining their chances of overtaking the Jets were slim. As for the critics, the Jets' win over Cincinnati, however dominating, could do little to silence them. After all, the Bengals were a last-place team. The Oakland Raiders had just beaten Kansas City to take over first place in the Western Division with a 9–1–1 record. Now, if the Jets were to beat Oakland, *that* would be impressive.

Week 12 — Sunday, November 30, 1969
Shea Stadium, New York (attendance: 63,865)

The Houston Oilers lost to the San Diego Chargers on Thanksgiving Day, which meant that the Jets could clinch the Eastern Division with a win over Oakland. It promised to be another contentious meeting between the two teams, and there was the usual back-and-forth between the players in the press. This time it did not involve Namath directly, but was instead a matter of defensive linemen complaining about the lack of holding calls by officials. The Jets' John Elliot got things started by proclaiming the Raiders to be the league leaders in holding, whether they were called for it or not. The Jets were saying that Oakland linemen held so frequently that officials were disinclined to call it for fear that the games would drag on and on with the constant stoppages. Elliot labeled Oakland center Jim Otto and guard Gene Upshaw as the worst of the bunch.

The Raiders volleyed back, saying that it was the Jets who, in their zeal to protect Namath, were holding on most every play. "They know it's their neck if they let a guy get on Joe Namath," said Ike Lassiter.[33] Oakland offensive lineman Jim Harvey said that the Jets were simply trying to influence the officials by registering their complaints ahead of time. Not an altogether bad tactic, if it were true.

The Raiders had captured first place in the West the previous week by beating Kansas City 27–24 in a game in which the Oakland defense had intercepted five passes. But with the Chiefs' Thanksgiving victory over Denver, the Raiders needed to beat the Jets in order to keep their place atop the division.

"We've never beaten the Jets here since I've been with the Raiders," said Oakland head coach John Madden. After joining the franchise in 1967 as an assistant coach, Madden had taken over as head coach of the Raiders with the departure of John Rauch following the 1968 season. "There's no doubt about it," said Madden. "This is a tough place to play in. You've got a partisan crowd working on you, the climatic conditions are usually an unknown factor, and most of all they're a good football team."[34]

The Jets would be missing two very key players on offense. Lineman Dave Herman was out with a leg injury, and would be substituted by Pete Perreault. Perhaps more significantly, Don Maynard had broken a bone in his foot the prior week against Cincinnati, and would miss the rest of the regular season. Bake Turner would take his place.

The temperature the day of the game was 40 degrees, but as always the winds of Shea added extra bite. It was late in the opening period when Oakland got the first score on a 34-yard pass from Daryle Lamonica to Warren Wells, who had beaten Cornell Gordon on the play.

The Jets shot back quickly, however, when Namath hit Bake Turner with a 54-yard touchdown pass to even the score. Turner broke in front of defender Nemiah Wilson and made the catch at the 26, then slipped Wilson's attempted tackle and ran it in.

Things got more interesting in the second quarter. With Oakland driving early in the period, Lamonica failed to convert a third-down pass, but Elliot was flagged for roughing the passer: the penalty gave Oakland a first down at the New York 24. On the next play a holding penalty took that 15 yards away again (holding penalties were a costlier 15 yards at that time), but on the following play Lamonica hit Charlie Smith with a 34-yard pass that gave Oakland a first-and-goal.

A run by Larry Todd got the Raiders to the one-yard line, and then Lamonica ran a bootleg and took the ball into the end zone himself; Lamonica was laughing as he crossed the goal line. The hit from Elliot that drew the roughing call had Lamonica spitting blood: he was still spitting blood as he guffawed his way into the end zone. The Raiders were now up 14–7, and about to add more.

Mike Battle fumbled the ensuing kickoff, and Lloyd Edwards recovered for Oakland at the New York 25. After two running plays gained five yards to the 20, Lamonica went back to pass and hit Wells in the left corner of the end zone for a score. The Raiders had scored twice in just over a minute-and-a-half, and now held a 21–7 lead.

After receiving the kick, the Jets ran just one play. Namath tried to hit Bake Turner on a square out, but threw behind him. Wilson intercepted at the 38, giving Oakland an excellent opportunity to fatten their lead some more. But when Lamonica this time failed to move the team, George Blanda came in to try a 43-yard field goal, which he missed.

Namath's interception was the only play the Jets had managed to run in a 10-minute period. But now, having dodged a bullet, they seemed inspired and embarked on an 80-yard drive for a score. Bill Mathis capped the drive by going over from a yard out to shave Oakland's lead to 21–14. The big gainer in the series had been a 30-yard pass from Namath to Bake Turner, who seemed to be filling in nicely for Maynard.

Toward the end of the half the Jets were driving again, reaching the Oakland 21 on a 12-yard pass from Namath to Bake Turner, but a holding penalty on Winston Hill took the gain away and the Jets lost their momentum. Jim Turner came in to try to salvage the effort with a 45-yard field goal, which missed wide. The half ended with the Jets still trailing 21–14.

The Jets had helped Oakland considerably with some very costly errors in the first half: in the second half the Raiders would just flat outplay them. Although the New York defense would hold Oakland to just two field goals in the second half, the New York offense would be shutout. The Jets could manage only five first downs in the second half and just 78 yards (51 rushing and 27 passing). The best they could do was to get near enough for Jim Turner to try two long field goals, which he missed from 52 and 48 yards.

The Raiders had given the Jets some different formations on defense that played hell with the passing game. Sometimes doubling on Bake Turner, other times on tight end Pete Lammons, the Oakland secondary was hard to read. Namath tried to open a lane by lining Emerson Boozer at a flanker position in an attempt to pull defensive back Dave Grayson out of the middle, but the Raiders countered by using five defensive backs.

In lining Boozer up as a flanker, Namath had also left himself more vulnerable to the blitz. With Snell the lone setback, the Raiders would blitz their outside linebackers from either side, knowing that Snell could only choose to block one angle. Namath was only sacked twice (the Raiders would also sack Al Woodall twice late in the game), but his lowly 10 of 30 passing tells the story (169 yards, one TD, one interception).

Namath praised the Oakland pass coverage after the game, noting that, whereas their usual tendency was to play man-to-man most of the time, they had presented some new looks and went to zone coverage more frequently. In the second half the Raiders used various formations (sometimes 3–3–5, sometimes 4–2–5), denying New York the long gain on passes. The strategy might have backfired had the New York running game been a more viable option, but when mistakes had put them in an early hole the Jets were forced by necessity to play catch-up.

Otherwise it was a typical New York–Oakland showdown. The two teams came very close to setting an AFL single-game record for penalties: Oakland was penalized 10 times for 165 yards, the Jets eight for 105. *New York Times* writer Dave Anderson called it "a violent, sometimes savage struggle sanctioned as entertainment by the American Football League."[35]

In the Oakland locker room after the game, defensive lineman Tom Keating was asked whose blood it was that decorated his uniform. Keating confessed that it was his own. "I'm not going to deny it, we really beat each other around," he said.[36] "It was a normal New York game," said Oakland center Jim Otto as he wiped dried blood from his face. "Every time I snapped the ball all hell broke loose."[37]

Otto explained that Oakland's enthusiasm could basically be explained by the fact that they were playing against a great team, which he said amplified their competitive spirit. When playing the champs, he pointed out, the natural inclination of a proud team was bound to be an eagerness to prove their superiority. Namath's analysis was more blunt. "Oakland is a team we don't like," he said.[38]

The sportswriters out West were purring. "They made Joe Namath a superman," *The Oakland*

Tribune's Ed Levitt said of the New York sportswriters. "But supermen don't lose the way Joe did yesterday."[39] In Oakland they were already envisioning a Super Bowl of their own.

With the loss, the Jets' unprecedented seven-game home stand came to an end. Next it was off to Houston to play the Oilers in that dimly-lit convention center called the Astrodome.

Week 13 — Sunday, December 6, 1969
Astrodome, Houston (attendance: 51,923)

The patrons at the Astrodome were a little distracted on the day the Jets came to Houston looking to wrap up their division title against the Oilers. They seemed more interested in what the Longhorns were doing a few hundred miles away in Arkansas, and as a result many seats that had been sold remained empty at game time as some fans chose to stay home and watch the Texas-Arkansas game on TV. Even among those that did show up, the arena was replete with transistor radios and portable televisions so fans could keep up on the collegiate contest.

The Jets had a reversal of fortunes right from the start against Houston. The mistakes that they had been making for most of the season were suddenly the opponent's to make. Houston quarterback Pete Beathard had injured his foot in the Thanksgiving Day game with San Diego, and Don Trull would be taking his place. After Houston received the opening kickoff, Trull was intercepted on the game's first play from scrimmage. Cornell Gordon, who had been so badly burned by Warren Wells a week earlier in the Oakland game, picked Trull off at the Houston 27 and ran it back to the seven-yard line. Three plays later Emerson Boozer went over from two-yards out to give the Jets a quick 7–0 lead.

When Houston got the ball back they only managed three plays before Verlon Biggs slapped the ball from Trull's hand and then fell on it at the Houston 21. Namath didn't waste any time, hitting George Sauer on the next play with a perfectly lofted 21-yard pass to the left corner of the end zone. The Jets led 14–0 only 3:32 into the game. In the second quarter defensive tackle Steve Thompson deflected a Trull pass at the Houston 18, and defensive end Gerry Philbin picked it off at the 21 and returned it 18 yards to the three. After a running play lost a couple yards, Namath tossed a five-yard touchdown to Bill Mathis that put the Jets up 21–0.

The Oilers made a quarterback change fairly early, sending Bob Davis in for Trull in the second quarter. Davis had been on the Oilers' taxi squad, but was activated with the injury to Beathard. Davis did throw a 20-yard touchdown pass to Jerry LeVias, and also got them in range for Roy Gerela to kick a 24-yard field goal that cut New York's lead to 21–10 at the half, but when it came to turnovers he really fared no better than Trull.

In the third quarter, with the Jets on the Houston three-yard line, play stopped momentarily when Namath was unable to call the signals for all the raucous clamor in the room. No, the crowd was not spurring the Houston defense to make a stand: the stadium scoreboard had flashed an update of the Texas-Arkansas game, letting everyone know that the Longhorns had won. It was the second time in the period that play had been disrupted by the crowd's enthusiasm for the college contest, the other time being when the scoreboard flashed the news that the Longhorns had just taken a 15–14 lead.

Two Jim Turner field goals in the third put New York out in front 27–10, and a one-yard touchdown run by Matt Snell early in the fourth made it a healthy 34–10 lead. But the Oilers seemed to wake up after returning a New York fumble 27 yards for a score. Mike Richardson ran the ball in for a two-point conversion to make the score 34–18, and when Davis led the Oilers to a late touchdown on a one-yard TD pass to Rich Johnson, another successful two-point conversion made the score 34–26 — only eight points. The problem for the Oilers was that the game was almost over.

Houston's only chance was an onside kick, which they accomplished, recovering the ball at the New York 43. But Davis then fired four incomplete passes, the last one heading for Jerry LeVias in the end zone but being tipped out of play by John Dockery with two seconds left to play. The Jets had survived a needlessly close fourth quarter to clinch the Eastern Division.

After intercepting Don Trull twice in the first half, the Jets had then intercepted Bob Davis four times to set a club single-game record of six interceptions. Aside from Gordon and Philbin's interceptions of Trull, Dockery had intercepted Davis twice, and linebackers Paul Crane and Ralph Baker had each gotten one. The New York defense had otherwise sacked the Houston quarterbacks nine times in the game for 69 yards in losses.

Namath had once more given way to Babe Parilli late in the game — perhaps too early considering how close the game wound up — but even allowing for a truncated performance, his numbers were pretty skinny, completing only six of 16 for 52 yards and two TDs. Still, the Jets had wrapped up the division title, so it was all good. And next they were off to balmy Miami to close the season against the Dolphins. It would be their first trip to the Orange Bowl since beating the Colts there in the Super Bowl.

Week 14 — Saturday, December 13, 1969
Orange Bowl, Miami (attendance: 48,168)

Although it was hardly the 75,000-plus that had packed the Orange Bowl to see the Jets beat up on the Baltimore Colts in the Super Bowl the previous January, the 48,168 fans who came to the Orange Bowl in week 14 when the champion Jets came to town was a Miami Dolphins attendance record. If they came to see Namath, they would be somewhat disappointed. Having already clinched the division title, and with a playoff game just a week off, the Jets played many of their starters sparingly.

When the Dolphins met the Jets in New York in early November, the game had been a shootout between Namath and Bob Griese; now Namath was making only a token appearance, and Griese was out with an injury, which left Babe Parilli and Al Woodall for the Jets and Rick Norton and John Stofa for the Dolphins. The Dolphins had traded Stofa to Cincinnati in 1968, but with the injury to Griese they cut a deal with the Bengals to send him back.

Just as they had done a week earlier against Houston, the New York defense presented their offense with excellent scoring opportunities early on. Bill Baird intercepted Norton at the Miami 34, and Namath took advantage quickly, hitting Bake Turner with a 34-yard touchdown 8:35 into the game. Norton was then intercepted at the Miami 31 by Mike Battle, who returned the ball to the six-yard line. After two running plays only advanced the ball to the two, Namath flipped a touchdown pass to Matt Snell on third down, and with a 14–0 lead and 1:21 to play in the first quarter Namath took a seat for the afternoon. He had completed five of eight for 99 yards and two TDs.

Although Norton would complete only three of 15 passes in the first half, he at least managed to lead the Dolphins to a second-quarter field goal of 24 yards. But that was countered, first by Jim Turner's 30-yard field goal, and then by Bake Turner's second touchdown catch of the game, a fine looking 28-yarder from Parilli that capped a 59-yard drive and gave the Jets a 24–3 lead.

After Jim Turner added another field goal in the third quarter, the Jets held a very comfortable 27–3 lead. Stofa had replaced Norton in the second half and he led the Dolphins to their only touchdown, a one-yard run by Larry Csonka with 6:34 left to play that was set up by a 42-yard pass from Stofa to Csonka. After Csonka failed to get across the goal line on a two-point conversion, the final score read 27–9 in the Jets' favor.

Meanwhile out in Oakland, the Raiders and Kansas City Chiefs were squaring off in a game that would ultimately determine who would win the Western Division. The Raiders won the game 10–6. The Jets had finished the season with a 10–4 record, and as champs of the Eastern

Division they would be hosting the West's runner-up, which meant that the Kansas City Chiefs — who had beaten them soundly 34–16 in New York just a few weeks prior — would be coming back to Shea. Oakland would play the East's runner-up, the 6–6–2 Houston Oilers, who had gotten in despite their exceedingly mediocre record only because the other teams in the East — Boston, Buffalo and Miami — were the league's bottom feeders.

Namath finished the 1969 season with a 51.2 pass completion percentage (185 of 361) for 2,734 yards, down considerably from his 3,147 yards in 1968. But he had also thrown 19 touchdowns against 17 interceptions, the first time since his rookie season in 1965 that he had thrown more TDs than interceptions. It would also be the last time. Although they had started 1–2, the Jets went on to win nine of their eleven remaining games, including the team-record six straight victories. But there were many people who weren't impressed.

Given their opponents during that six-game stretch of victories (the 4–10 Boston Patriots twice, the 4–10 Buffalo Bills, the 3–10–1 Miami Dolphins, the 4–9–1 Cincinnati Bengals and the 6–6–2 Houston Oilers) the only thing many found worth commenting on in those games was how narrowly the Jets had escaped defeat in some of them. The only teams the Jets had played with winning records were Oakland, Kansas City, and San Diego, and they had dropped all three of those games. The worst of those defeats was the 34–16 loss to Kansas City at Shea. Now the Chiefs would be returning for the playoff game with the Jets, and the Jets weren't even at full strength.

Don Maynard hadn't played since breaking a bone in his right foot in the week 11 victory over Cincinnati, and although he desperately wanted to play against Kansas City, Ewbank was holding off on making a decision almost until game time. While the Chiefs had beaten the Jets in week 10, it had still been one of Maynard's better games of the season, catching nine passes for 137 yards. Bake Turner had done a serviceable job filling in for Maynard during his absence, but there was no replacing Maynard, who wound up being the Jets' leading receiver on the season despite missing the final three games. Maynard had caught 47 passes for 938 yards (an average of 20 yards per catch) and six touchdowns. However creditable Turner's performance, a playoff game was hardly the time to be without any of your top guns.

It had been a little less than a month since Maynard's injury, but Ewbank was surprised at how well he ran in practice on the Wednesday and Thursday before the game. Still, with the game being on Saturday, it was obvious that there was not enough time for Maynard to get up to speed. He had played the AFL Championship with a bad hamstring the year before, and even wound up one of the principal heroes of the game, but a broken foot was something else. Ewbank said that any decision about activating Maynard would have to wait until Saturday morning.

Despite having dislocated his left shoulder, defensive end Gerry Philbin would still be playing in a harness. The champs were looking a bit ragged.

1969 AFL Divisional Playoff — December 20, 1969
Shea Stadium, New York (attendance: 62,977)

On game day the mid-thirties temperature was turned bitter cold by the swirling Shea Stadium winds, which promised to play hell with both the passing and kicking games. After the fans in New York had celebrated the Mets' World Series victory in October by tearing the field to pieces to take clumps of sod home as souvenirs, the field had new sod put down; it didn't really have a chance to take root, however, before the weather and the Jets' home stand beat it up all the more. With concerns about the condition of the playing surface before the game, the field was basically shorn of what grass remained and was shaved down to dirt — this would be a true sandlot game.

Kansas City had the first opportunity to score in the opening period; they drove to the New

York 40, but when the drive stalled there, kicker Jan Stenerud came out to try a 47-yard field goal. His chances might have been good under ordinary circumstances, but the wind being what it was, this was not a day for long field goals, and Stenerud missed.

Before the end of the first quarter the Jets got on the board first with a more manageable 27-yard field goal by Jim Turner, but in the opening seconds of the second period the Chiefs evened things when Stenerud hit a 23-yarder. The score would remain 3–3 at halftime. Namath was having a hard time throwing in the wind, and in the third quarter the hope was that Don Maynard might be able to help things along when he made a brief appearance in the game. Although he caught one pass for 18 yards, it was obvious that he was not up to speed, and he was only in for a few plays. Besides, Maynard could do nothing about the wind.

Stenerud had missed two more field goal attempts — from 44 and 47 yards — but in the third quarter he hit one from 25 yards out to give the Chiefs a 6–3 lead. As the fourth quarter got underway the Jets were driving, and when Namath tried to hit George Sauer in the end zone, defender Emmitt Thomas grabbed Sauer's jersey and was flagged for pass interference. That gave the Jets first-and-goal at the one-yard line, and the perfect opportunity to capture the lead. Kansas City middle linebacker Willie Lanier was the catalyst for a Herculean effort by the Kansas City defense. As they waited for the Jets to break huddle on first down, Lanier could see a despondency come over his teammates. "They can't score," Lanier told his teammates over and over.[40]

On first down Namath handed to Matt Snell, who ran off right guard for only half-a-yard as defensive back Johnny Robinson grabbed him by the ankle and Lanier closed in to bring him down. On second down Bill Mathis tried to go up the middle. It looked awfully close, but his progress was ruled just shy of the goal line. When Mathis got to the line he ran into Winston Hill's back, and linebacker Jim Lynch came around from the left side, grabbing at Mathis, but overrunning the tackle. It was Lanier, coming around from the right side, who grabbed Mathis from behind and pulled him down.

It was now third-and-goal from just inches away. Maybe a run up the middle could have powered over — *maybe*. Namath looked to catch the defense off guard with a play-action pass. "It was a fake pitch to Matt Snell but Bobby Bell stayed right with Snell, who was my only receiver," said Namath later.[41]

After taking the snap, Namath first faked the pitch to Snell flaring right then faked a handoff to Mathis going up the middle. But Bobby Bell didn't deviate, hustling to his left to pick up Snell. Namath rolled pretty deeply to his right, eventually going back as far as the 11-yard line. As he started to move forward, he saw that he couldn't hit Snell, and he kept running. By the time he reached the six-yard line defensive back Jim Kearney was on him, and Lynch was closing in fast. Kearney dove for Namath and got his arms around him, and Bell pealed away from Snell to join in the gang tackle. As Namath was going down he flipped a weak throw that fell helplessly to the ground. He was really just throwing it away, but if anything he was lucky it wasn't intercepted. The three Kansas City defenders came down on top of Namath and that was it. Now fourth down, Jim Turner had to come into the game to tie it up with a seven-yard field goal 2:16 into the fourth quarter. Namath was not pleased when he came off the field, pulling his helmet off and throwing it to the ground on the New York sideline.

Meanwhile, on the Kansas City sideline, receiver Otis Taylor had been diagramming a play in the dirt for quarterback Len Dawson. He wanted to run what the Chiefs called a camouflage slot formation, which had worked for a touchdown against the Jets when the Chiefs had played them earlier in the year. Taylor wanted Dawson to line him up in a slot formation between the left guard and tackle: Dawson agreed.

There is a reason they call the play "camouflage." Where Taylor was lined up, he was a bit inconspicuous, and was hoping to sneak through the line and hit the secondary before the Jets knew where he was. It worked perfectly. When the ball was snapped, Taylor shot through the line, and as he broke into the secondary he cut right across the middle. It took safety Bill Baird a moment to pick Taylor up, and that was all Taylor needed; he had a couple steps on Baird as he continued to run left-to-right. Dawson threw to Taylor, who made the catch at the Kansas City 49. Baird caught up at the New York 44, but Taylor made a sudden cut and eluded the tackle, running back toward the middle of the field until he was caught from behind at the New York 19 by Al Atkinson and Cornell Gordon. From the Kansas City 20-yard line, the play had covered 61 yards.

On the next play Dawson threw 19 yards to Gloster Richardson for the score. "In that corner of the stadium," said Dawson, "the wind was really whipping the ball around. You don't know where the ball is going."[42]

It went right where it needed to go, floating perfectly over Richardson's shoulder in the left corner of the end zone as Cornell Gordon fell helplessly to the ground in a vain attempt to break up the play. The Chiefs had gone 80 yards in just two plays to retake the lead. They now led 13–6, but there was still plenty of time left.

On the Jets' next series Namath drove them to the Kansas City 16-yard line, but on fourth down, and trailing by seven with under six minutes to play, a field goal would be of questionable help, so the Jets opted to go for it. Namath's fourth-down pass missed, and the Chiefs took over on downs. Even then the Jets weren't through. They got the ball back, and Namath again drove them down deep. With first-and-10 from the Kansas City 13, Namath threw to Sauer, but the pass was broken up by Thomas. On second down, he went to Sauer again; this time the ball was too far for Sauer to reach. Then on third down, Namath threw into the end zone for Bake Turner; it was intercepted by Jim Marsalis with 1:50 left in the game. Marsalis was prepared for it, saying that Turner had beaten him on the same pattern earlier in the game. "I thought Joe would try to come back with it at some time," he said. "I saw the ball was a little short and I stepped in front of him."[43]

The Jets had one last chance when the Chiefs failed to run out the clock with under a minute to play and were forced to punt. But Mike Battle fumbled the punt, and the Chiefs recovered the ball. With only 36 seconds left in the game, the Chiefs were finally able to run out the clock. The Jets' reign as champions was over. "There goes the whole season down the drain," said Ewbank.[44]

Namath was a dismal 14 of 40 passing for 164 yards with three interceptions. Yeah, the playing conditions were a problem, Namath said, adding that some of his passes were going end-over-end due to the wind, and even an eight-yard out pattern was tough because the ball would sail away in a gust. But when reporters asked if it all came down to the wind, Namath declined the alibi. It was a factor, he said, but not the only reason for the loss. "It was the wind and Kansas City's defense," Namath said.[45]

Sauer said that the Jets would have naturally fared better without the wind, but quickly added that it was no excuse since both teams had the same wind to contend with. But Sauer had reason to feel that he'd been robbed. Whereas Dawson's touchdown throw to Richardson dropped nicely in-between gusts, one of Namath's passes to Sauer didn't have the same fate. It was in one of the Jets' final two possessions late in the game when Namath threw to Sauer in the end zone. As the ball was coming down, a wind gust picked it up and floated it just beyond Sauer's grasp. Et tu, Shea?

Alas, the Jets had met their Waterloo. There was a photo that ran in many papers around the country the following day, a shot of Namath leaving the field. Hands in the pockets of his jersey, leaning forward into the wind, his head down to shield his face from the cloud of dust being kicked up off the field, he looked not unlike Marcel Marceau doing his man walking against the wind routine. Namath walked off the field that day with no way of knowing that he would never again play in a post-season game. The glory days had just ended.

The Oakland Raiders made short work of the Houston Oilers in their playoff game, running up an embarrassing 56–7 score to advance to the AFL Championship and face Kansas City. The Raiders had beaten the Chiefs twice during the regular season, so it was not unreasonable to expect that they might beat them again, particularly at home in the Coliseum. But this was Kansas City's year, and after falling behind 7–0 in the first quarter, the Chiefs went on to score 17 unanswered points and win the game. They then followed in the Jets' footsteps by going to the Super Bowl and beating a heavily favored NFL powerhouse, in this case the Minnesota Vikings.

Then came time for the AFL All-Star game. The two leagues would be merging as one the following season, so this would be the final AFL All-Star game to ever be played. There seemed little sentimentality about it among AFL quarterbacks, who mostly passed on the event, claiming injuries. Of the league's 10 starting quarterbacks, seven declined to participate. Namath, Len Dawson, Daryle Lamonica, and Houston's Pete Beathard — all the starting quarterbacks from the playoffs — were no-shows. It made for a decidedly un-star-like All-Star game. Though John Hadl did show up to quarterback the Western team, he shared duties with Kansas City second-stringer Mike Livingston, while the East was piloted by two quarterbacks whose teams went 4–10, Boston's Mike Taliaferro and Buffalo's Jack Kemp. The West won easily 26–3.

What did Namath need with another pointless All-Star game? He had better things to do: he had a date with Ann-Margret. Namath had signed to co-star with the redheaded sex kitten in a movie. What would you rather do?

8

The 1970 Season

The Jets may no longer have been the champs, but Namath still seemed more popular than ever. After the Super Bowl victory in January of 1969 Namath had gone off to play a supporting role in the film *Norwood*, starring Glen Campbell and Kim Darby, but now it was Namath who was being offered the leading roles. Following the end of the 1969 season, he went to Arizona to star in the biker film *C.C. & Company* with Ann-Margret. After completing that, he was off to Europe to star in the spaghetti western *The Last Rebel*, which was to be shot in Madrid and Rome. They were both wonderfully cheesy schlock, and today stand as fine testaments to both genres.

Working in the movies was both easy and lucrative. Frolicking with Ann-Margret sure beat getting battered by 270-pound linemen, and the pay seemed to be better, too. Namath was reportedly getting $100,000 per year under his contract with the Jets, but now that didn't seem like nearly enough. The glitz, the glamour, and the financial rewards of Hollywood were alluring, and would have given anyone plenty of reason to think seriously about a career change. Before leaving for Spain, Namath said that he felt he should be making more under his contract with the Jets. "It's true I'm stuck with the contract," he said, "and I intend to honor it — that is, if I continue to play football."[1]

Namath's contract back in 1965 had turned the whole professional sports world on its ear, but what might have gotten under his skin now was the number of professional athletes making more money than him — *and after he was the one that started it all*. Basketball stars Pete Maravich and Lou Alcindor had both signed million dollar contracts — *this for running around in shorts dribbling a ball*! Namath's knees were so bad that one shot from a defensive lineman could end his career; he was battered and bruised and abused weekly during the season, yet he was making less than guys throwing a ball through a hoop. It seemed incomprehensible. What athlete had ever done more to popularize their sport than Joe Namath? None.

Could he really be leaving the game for tinsel town? Well, he was throwing the idea out there. It wasn't the first time he had mentioned retiring from the game — a year earlier he *did* retire, albeit for only a few weeks. But back then he didn't have the blossoming show business career that he now had. When training camp rolled around, Namath was a no-show. That in and of itself was not unusual; in his six years in professional football, he was late to camp more often than not. This time he wasn't alone; there were a lot of stragglers coming late to camp. A player's strike had delayed all league camps, but once resolved, the players began turning up. As usual, the Namath situation presented a whole separate set of issues.

Namath hadn't gotten in touch with anyone from the organization, and no one had been able to get a hold of him, either. It was the last straw for one player: linebacker Al Atkinson announced that he had quite enough — he was retiring from football. Surely Ewbank was hoping that some day he might again have a training camp devoid of so much drama.

Speaking to reporters, Atkinson had gone on a rant in which he fumed over Namath's attitude, while never being able to so much as speak his name. Atkinson said there were players on the team with mortgages to pay and children to feed, and that they were working hard and looking to collect a big paycheck with a Super Bowl victory. In Atkinson's estimation, it wasn't fair of Namath to be holding everyone up by keeping them wondering about his intentions.[2] He made it sound as though the Super Bowl were Namath's for the plucking.

But Atkinson's verbal lashing went so much further — it became *very* personal. "It used to kill me," he said, "to see this guy sit back on his TV show and think everything he does and stands for is justified as long as he comes right out and says it. He thinks it makes an indiscretion correct if you admit it."[3] Throughout his tantrum, Atkinson would only refer to Namath as "that quarterback," saying, "It's more and more guys like that quarterback and the way they think. The carefree life. They don't give a damn about anybody else."[4] Atkinson said that Namath's lack of consideration was something that disgusted him.

So, Al Atkinson found it selfish of Namath to abandon his team and deprive the family men of their future Super Bowl winnings, and Atkinson's response to Namath's selfishness was … to abandon the team. Even if Atkinson were correct in viewing Namath's failure to show up as a greedy and inconsiderate maneuver, it only made Atkinson's response doubly selfish, throwing a hissy fit like he did and running out on his team in a snit.

Namath was stung by Atkinson's remarks, but he outclassed his erstwhile teammate by far with his response. "Al must feel he's right, and I'd have to consider what I do is right," Namath said, "but when someone of Al's character questions my character, I have to question myself."[5]

Namath tried explaining his position, and did say that he had tried to reach Ewbank but was unable to get a hold of him. "Football used to be No. 1 with me," he said, "but at this stage it's not my main concern. I honestly don't know what I'm going to do."[6]

The way Namath told it, he had a number of problems to work out, some business related, others personal, which were keeping him from making football his top priority. He said that concerns about a football career were considerably overshadowed by his other problems and the state of mind they had put him in.

Surely it couldn't be that bad. He had just been paid handsomely to do a couple movies, but there had also been some setbacks along the way: for instance, his fast food franchise, *Broadway Joe's*, had been a major flop. Namath said he would be meeting with Jets' president Phil Iselin to get things sorted out, but that only seemed to hint that Atkinson was correct, and the real issue was one of salary. The general consensus was that Namath was looking to hold the owners up for more money. Well, why not? If you think you're worth it and can get it, why not take your shot? But that attitude didn't sit well with many of the other players. Defensive end Gerry Philbin was also critical of Namath's tardiness, but then Philbin always had been Namath's foil on the team. Philbin denied having resentments toward Namath, but went on to say that he personally could not get away with the stunts that Namath pulled; he said very few players in sport could, and that he took it for granted that there was a double standard regarding Namath.[7]

That was no newsflash: Ewbank had already told the team as much. He had explained to the players long ago that Namath had rules that set him apart from the rest. "The facts were that Namath had to go his different way," Ewbank had said. "Everybody else had to conform with the rules. None of the men disagreed because they all realized that the only way they'd shoot the moon was on the wings of Namath."[8]

Atkinson's tirade may have been childish, but that isn't to deny the validity of some points he raised. It was all fine and good for Namath to have his own set of rules on the team, but didn't that come with some responsibility as well? One thing that Atkinson mentioned was a general lack of team unity following the Super Bowl victory, which he ascribed to the selfish nature of some players. He seemed to feel that, after their great triumph, the Jets were less a team than they were a collection of superstars and wanna-be superstars, all looking out for themselves. There is no question that the 1969 Jets, 10–4 record notwithstanding, were misfiring somewhere. Something was wrong and everybody could sense it. Even as they went on a team-record six-game winning streak, people were noticing some faulty circuitry somewhere; it's just that nobody could quite put their finger on it. Atkinson had: it was a lack of cohesion resulting from a celebrity attitude. Hey, if a monster hit record like *Hotel California* could be blamed for destroying a band like the Eagles, why not consider that a football team could also be a victim of its own success? When you get right down to it, bands, teams: they're all a collection of egos.

Meanwhile, poor Weeb Ewbank had a team to whip into shape. The Jets' first exhibition game was scheduled for Saturday, August 8, in Birmingham again: they would be playing the Buffalo Bills. Ewbank was hoping to have things squared away by then, saying that he wanted to have Namath play at least one quarter.[9]

He wasn't the only one who wanted to see Namath make an appearance; the promoters in Birmingham were playing the game up as a Namath vs. O.J. Simpson contest, although, being a preseason game, neither would probably play more than the opening half. Namath said it was very unlikely that he would be on the plane when the team flew to Birmingham, but he was going to be meeting with Iselin on the night of Thursday, August 6, to try and straighten things out.[10]

"We have met with Joe Namath in an effort to resolve some requests Joe has made," Iselin said in a statement after the meeting.[11] Iselin went on to say that, although things remained unresolved, talks were ongoing. It sure sounded like a contract dispute. Whatever it was, Iselin spoke to the team before they departed for Birmingham, telling them not to rush to judgment and that Namath should be given the benefit of the doubt where the team was concerned. But the press wasn't making that easy for anyone, reporting that Namath was demanding more money irrespective of his contract and was using his possible retirement as leverage.

Namath was hardly the only one. Football was growing in proportion to Namath's celebrity, and as a result was becoming quite the television spectacle. Advertising revenues were going up, ticket prices were going up — why not the players' salaries as well? San Diego wide receiver Lance Alworth had abruptly retired, saying that he was very underpaid given his contributions to his team (not to worry, as he would return to play another season in San Diego and two additional seasons in Dallas). There was also another quarterback named Joe who was holding out. Joe Kapp of the Minnesota Vikings was reportedly asking for a five-year contract at $250,000 per year after having led his team to the Super Bowl the previous season. They were beaten badly by Kansas City in that game, and Kapp — famous for his end-over-end passes — may have been vastly overestimating his worth to the team: the Vikings told him to take a hike. It was speculated that, with Namath holding out, the Jets might grab Kapp, but that was just talk: the Jets were not at all interested. Ewbank said that no player was worth what Kapp was asking (and wouldn't the old man choke if he were around to see the salaries today). Kapp certainly wasn't, but the truth is that he was already making the same salary as Namath, and *that* must have seemed bizarre to many, and galling to Namath.

The Jets traveled to Birmingham without Namath and went on to bully the Buffalo Bills, beating them 33–10. Buffalo's lone touchdown was the result of a fumble return, and New York quarterbacks Babe Parilli and Al Woodall both played well. Parilli hit Bake Turner with a touchdown pass in the first half, and Woodall threw a touchdown to rookie receiver Eddie Bell in the second half. Sure it was nice to win, but preseason isn't really about winning, it's about sizing your team up and getting it into shape. The Jets may have won without him, but they also wanted Namath back.

As expected, Atkinson's retirement was no more than a temper flare-up, and he was already hinting at coming back. He also seemed to have some regret about his acrimonious public tirade against Namath. "I love Joe, whether he believes it or not," Atkinson said. "If I live to be 80, he will be one of my closest friends. It's just that over the last few years I have found it harder and harder to respect him."[12]

It was already a trying start to the season for Ewbank, but in addition to missing players like Namath and Atkinson, he now had injuries to contend with. Philbin had a dislocated left shoulder and would require surgery, meaning he would not be returning immediately to the roster. After eight days, Atkinson ended his retirement, saying he felt a moral obligation to his team to help them in their time of need: aside from Philbin, Atkinson's replacement, Mike Stromberg, was also out with a bad hamstring pull. Atkinson met his teammates at LaGuardia Airport to fly with them to Winston-Salem, North Carolina, for their game with the Atlanta Falcons. Atkinson said that he had been sincere when he retired, but how could he just stand by with the team in such dire need? It was the perfect out for him—he could stick by all he had said and maintain his moral high ground, while also posturing as a selfless and saintly individual willing to set aside his own wishes for the good of the team. Had he any regrets about retiring, this was an ideal opportunity to change his mind and still save face. Meanwhile, Namath—"that quarterback"—was sunning himself on a yacht in Fort Lauderdale, Florida. The Falcons took the Jets to the woodshed, beating them 33–7.

On the Monday following the Jets' loss to Atlanta, Namath agreed to report to camp. He met with Dr. Nicholas for his physical on Monday, and after being cleared to play, it was announced that Namath would be in camp the following day. The reasons for his late arrival at camp were not made clear, but Iselin was denying it had anything at all to do with Namath's contract, which Iselin maintained had not even been discussed in his meetings with Namath. Iselin said that Namath's absence was strictly due to personal problems.

Upon arriving at camp, Namath spoke to radio and television reporters outside the training room, but specifically refused to include newspaper reporters in the gathering, claiming that the newspapers had been reporting lies about him. There were security guards present to make sure that no newspapermen got by. Namath informed the reporters that he had not been in camp sooner because he was unsure of his desire to play football any longer. As it turned out, he had taken the playoff loss to Kansas City the previous December quite badly, describing it as a humiliating experience that had stripped him of his enthusiasm for the game. It would seem that the pressure during the 1969 season had taken both a mental and a physical toll. Namath spoke of being physically ill before games, of being unable to eat, having stomach troubles, and even morning chills. He said that he began to question whether or not it was all worth it.[13] It would seem that Broadway Joe was burned out. "Physically and mentally it's getting worse," he said.[14] The pressure didn't appear likely to abate anytime soon: 2,000 spectators showed up at Hofstra to watch Namath's first practice with the team.

It was hoped that Namath would be ready to play in time for the Jets' next preseason game, a rematch with the New York Giants at the Yale Bowl. The previous August the Jets had beaten the Giants soundly, 37–14, in a game that was acknowledged to be more than just an exhibition—it was more like a title match to determine the championship of New York. Afterward, both Giants' coach Allie Sherman and quarterback Fran Tarkenton had downplayed the significance of the game, but few took them seriously in that. This time the Giants' new head coach, Alex Webster, didn't even try to hide the game's significance. "We want to win this one," Webster said. "We'll go with our starters all the way if that's what it takes to win."[15]

Ewbank was less feisty, saying that it was only an exhibition, for which he was making no special considerations. He allowed, however, that some of his players might have felt otherwise. He also cautioned the fans that if they were coming to New Haven to see Namath, they might want to save themselves the train fare: Namath was not yet ready to play, and if he did make an appearance in the game, it would likely be token. Al Woodall was listed as the starter.

Even so, 70,854 fans showed up for the game and were not pleased to see Namath in street clothes on the Jets' sideline. Many in the crowd booed him, some waving white handkerchiefs and yelling for him to go back to the movies. It isn't easy to discern the source of their ire. It was as though they felt betrayed, like he had deserted them and gone all Hollywood by making a couple films in the off-season. Or maybe they were just upset at making the trip only to witness him sit out the game. Dr. Nicholas tried to set himself up as the fall guy, saying that he was the one who had recommended that Namath not play after only four days of practice. Ewbank said that the plan for the following week would be to increase Namath's practice time in order to have him ready for the next exhibition contest.

Meanwhile, the Jets-Giants game played through the first half like a complete reversal of the previous year's meeting between the two teams. Tarkenton threw three first-quarter touchdowns, and by halftime the Giants were leading 28–3. While the Jets staged a second-half rally, they still ended up losing the game, 28–24.

There were now three preseason games remaining, and Ewbank's intention was to increase Namath's game time with each successive exhibition. Namath saw his first game action since the 1969 playoff loss when the Jets played the Minnesota Vikings on August 30. He appeared for only a brief 10 plays in the second quarter, completing two of six passes for 42 yards. The Vikings — without quarterback Joe Kapp, who was still holding out — made a laugher out of it, beating the Jets 52–21. Even the New York Titans had never allowed themselves to be that humiliated.

The Minnesota game was a brief and inauspicious return for Namath, but he made his true return the following Saturday night in New Orleans against the Saints. Playing the entire first half, Namath got started quickly, setting up a 16-yard Jim Turner field goal with a 45-yard pass to George Sauer. He then set up his own one-yard touchdown run with a 56-yard completion to rookie Rich Caster. Later in the second period he threw a three-yard touchdown to Sauer, and by the end of the half he had completed seven of nine passes for 188 yards and had orchestrated a 27–0 halftime lead.

In the second half, with his work completed, Namath watched from the sidelines in a sweatshirt and shorts, his knee wrapped in ice. He had taken quite a shot to the knee from six-foot-seven, 272-pound New Orleans tackle Mike Tilleman, but had walked it off. Without Namath in the second half, the New York offense was unproductive and the Saints managed to score a couple of touchdowns to make the final score 27–14, but it in no way took any of the shine off Namath's performance. New Orleans head coach Tom Fears was certainly impressed. "Namath was the difference," he said. "He was tough. He didn't show us anything that we didn't know he had. He threw the ball beautifully, he threw it perfect every time."[16]

Now 2–3 in their exhibition games, the Jets finished off the preseason against the Cowboys in Dallas the following Sunday night in a nationally televised game at the Cotton Bowl in front of a crowd of 55,297. Dallas had taken a 7–0 first-quarter lead on a two-yard run by Calvin Hill, but the Jets went on a tear in the second period. After a Jim Turner field goal cut the Dallas lead to 7–3, the Jets took a 9–7 lead on a 23-yard TD pass from Namath to Sauer (the extra point was blocked). A seven-yard TD run by Matt Snell and another field goal by Turner gave the Jets a 19–7 halftime lead.

Dallas quarterback Craig Morton had a very bad first half, completing just two of 12 throws for 11 yards, but Roger Staubach came in to play the second half and rallied the Cowboys with 14 points in the third quarter. Staubach hit Dennis Homan with a 15-yard TD pass that trimmed the Jets' lead to 19–14, after which Dallas took a 21–19 lead on another touchdown run by Hill, this one from a yard out.

Namath wound up playing through the entire third quarter and half of the fourth, and he recaptured the lead with a 73-yard touchdown pass to Caster that put the Jets back up 26–21. In the fourth quarter the Jets added a field goal that made the final 29–21. Namath had completed 10 of 21 for 251 yards with two TDs and two interceptions. With that, the Jets closed out their 1970 exhibition season at 3–3.

Nineteen seventy was the year of the merger. The AFL was no more. The NFL was now broken into two conferences, each with three divisions. The teams in the AFL were now in the AFC (American Football Conference), while the NFL teams were mostly in the NFC (National Football Conference). Because there were more NFL than AFL teams, some teams from the NFL were shuffled over to the AFC. Baltimore, for instance, was sent not only to the AFC, but into the Jets' division, the AFC East. The Jets' erstwhile division rivals, the Houston Oilers, were moved to the AFC Central Division. Otherwise, the Eastern Division remained in tact, with the Jets and Colts being joined by Miami, Buffalo, and Boston.

There were some significant changes to the Jets' roster before the season began. Backup quarterback Babe Parilli had reported to camp, but announced his retirement early in the exhibition season, much to the consternation of kicker Jim Turner. Parilli had taken over in 1968 as Turner's holder on field goals and extra points, and Turner had always credited his improved kicking to Parilli's excellent skills in fielding the snap and placing the ball. Getting the routine down with a new holder was no small thing. George Sauer, the surest hands on the team, was given the job.

Otherwise, the biggest changes in the starting lineup would be in the defensive secondary, long considered the team's major weak spot. Bill Baird and Cornell Gordon were gone. The Jets drafted Earlie Thomas of Colorado State to play cornerback and Steve Tannen of Florida as both corner and safety. They also picked up safety W.K. Hicks in a trade with Houston, and cornerback John Dockery would now be given a more substantial role. Safety Jim Hudson would be returning after missing most of the 1969 season with a knee injury that had required surgery.

The linebackers—Atkinson, Larry Grantham, and Ralph Baker—were the same. So was the defensive front four of John Elliot and Steve Thompson at tackle, and Philbin and Verlon Biggs at the ends. Philbin's shoulder surgery would keep him out until November, but rookie Mark Lomas of Northern Arizona was doing a good job in his place.

Aside from his favored targets through the years—Sauer and Maynard—Namath had two new receivers to throw to in Eddie Bell of Idaho State and speedy six-foot-five Rich Caster of Jackson State. On paper it looked like a hell of a team, but as has been said, they don't play the games on paper.

Week 1—Monday, September 21, 1970
Municipal Stadium, Cleveland (attendance: 85,703)

September 21, 1970, was a very significant date in American popular culture—it was the start of a national institution, the first broadcast of ABC-TV's *Monday Night Football*. MNF is no longer the culturally centric event it once was, but for many years this was what America did on Monday nights during football season. Men made bets with their co-workers earlier that day, and then went home to have dinner and watch the game. Their wives tolerated it because they understood that this was too important to be denied. Families tuned in, they griped about what a pompous ass Howard Cosell was, they laughed at Don Meredith's colorful colloquialisms and good-natured quips; Frank Gifford was too bland to take much notice of one way or the other.

How better to kick off the inaugural MNF broadcast than with Joe Namath and the New York Jets? If the NFL was going to go primetime then it only made sense that Joe Namath should be utilized to make the occasion a genuine event. After all, he was the one football player that everyone in the country had heard of, even if they knew nothing else about football. Roone Arledge, President of ABC Sports, was very specific in his request that the Jets be scheduled for the initial broadcast, and NFL commissioner Pete Rozelle concurred with the logic of it. It worked—this would indeed be a night to remember.

A record crowd of more than 85,000 people turned up at Cleveland's Municipal Stadium to watch what was also the first-ever meeting between the Browns and the Jets. After the game had begun, hundreds more showed up outside the stadium trying to get in. A riot ensued, requiring a heavy police presence to put the would-be gatecrashers down. In an on-air pre-game interview, Howard Cosell spoke to both Namath and Al Atkinson. Namath was typically honest; Atkinson, well, he might have come off less so. Despite his shrill preseason tantrums over Namath's late arrival at camp, Atkinson, perhaps out of duty, told Cosell how happy he was to have Namath back with the team. It didn't quite ring true, coming off more as an attempt to deny any problems, and after Atkinson recited what came across as a scripted statement, he trotted away.

Namath's brief interview was more interesting. After mentioning that Ewbank had declared his belief that the current New York Jets team was superior to the Super Bowl team of two years prior, Cosell asked Namath if he agreed. Without pausing, Namath responded that he did not agree, saying that the 1968 team had proven itself, whereas the 1970 team had yet to do the same. He qualified the statement by saying that he hoped Ewbank was right, but that it remained to be seen.

The Jets received the opening kickoff and immediately gave the impression of a team ill prepared. After Mike Battle's kick return set them up in good shape at their 33, the Jets ran two rushing plays, and then, facing third-and-three from the 40, Matt Snell dropped a flare pass and the Jets had to punt. On their second series they managed a couple first downs (a 13-yard run by Snell off left tackle and a 14-yard pass from Namath to Don Maynard), but then had to punt again after runs by Snell and Emerson Boozer gained a total of one yard, and Namath missed George Sauer on third-and-nine.

The Browns, on the other hand, were making it look easy. After the Jets' first punt the Browns would have started at their own 30, but in what would be an indication of how things would run for the Jets that evening, New York was flagged for interfering with the return man's attempt to field the ball — the 15-yard penalty allowed Cleveland to start from their 45. The Jets seemed up to stopping superstar running back Leroy Kelly, but they would have trouble following through on third downs. Kelly gained four yards on a third-and-three from the New York 35, and on third-and-goal from the eight, quarterback Bill Nelsen hit Gary Collins over the middle, rifling it past a diving Earlie Thomas for a score.

Cleveland's second series was helped more than a little by New York penalties. Jim Hudson and Steve Tannen were called for pass interference on consecutive plays, accounting for 33 yards. The drive climaxed when Bo Scott went two yards around left end for a score to make it 14–0 near the end of the first quarter.

The Jets finally woke up on their third series. After Battle again gave them good field position with a 38-yard runback to the 39, Namath threw 15 yards over the middle to Boozer. The Jets got into a groove as the second quarter opened, with Boozer running for six, then Snell for 11. Ultimately the Jets would cut Cleveland's lead in half 2:53 seconds into the second period when Boozer bolted into the end zone from two yards out to make it 14–7.

After the New York defense forced a Cleveland punt, the Jets were again on the march in their next series. From his own 15 Namath threw 17 yards to Sauer, and then followed up on the next play with a 40-yard throw to Sauer down the left sideline. After a holding penalty rolled the Jets back 15 yards (yes, they were still 15-yarders then) Namath hit Maynard for 16 and Boozer ran a draw for 15 yards on third-and-14. But from the Cleveland 16, yet another holding penalty knocked the Jets back to the 31, and when Namath went long for Sauer on the next play he was intercepted by Walt Sumner, who brought the ball back 34 yards from the six to the 40.

The half ended with the Jets still down by seven, but that would change mere seconds into the third quarter. Homer Jones fielded the second half kickoff for Cleveland at the six-yard line, and after running right he broke toward the middle through a wide seam. Kicker Jim Turner was the only one who got a hand on him, but as Jones cut toward the middle to evade Turner, the player with the best shot at him — rookie receiver Rich Caster — overran the play. Although Caster had a clean shot, Jones stopped him dead in his tracks when he cut back inside, and breezed past him — Caster whiffed badly. The result was a 94-yard return for a score, and a 21–7 Cleveland lead only seconds into the third quarter.

Undaunted, the Jets began their next series from the 20 and marched 80 yards to cut the lead to seven again. Namath started quick with a 20-yard gain on a slant-in to Maynard, and on the next play he hit Sauer over the middle for another 16 yards. He hit Sauer for two 13-yard gainers, and otherwise turned things over to the ground game as Boozer scored on a 10-yard run.

Again the Jets' kick coverage would let them down. It was bad enough that Cleveland ran the ensuing kick back to their 38, but a late hit by the Jets moved it up another 15 yards, allowing Cleveland to begin the series at the New York 47. It went a long way toward helping the Browns move in close enough for a 27-yard field goal and a 10-point lead.

The Jets then embarked on a time-consuming possession that only got them as close as the Cleveland 32, and ultimately saw them knocked back to the 43 after defensive end Jack Gregory took Namath down for the only time that night. The result was that Turner came in to try a 50-yard field goal, which he missed wide left with just over a minute remaining in the third quarter.

The fourth period got underway with the Jets starting a series at their 49 after receiving a punt. Snell went through left tackle for 19 yards, and three runs by Boozer gained another 10 yards to the Cleveland 22. Then an interference call on Erich Barnes set the Jets up with a first-and-goal at the Cleveland seven-yard line. The next play pretty much summed up the Jets' performance that night. There was a bad exchange between Namath and Snell on a handoff, and the ball hit the ground — Gregory recovered for Cleveland at the seven-yard line.

After beginning the game with two impressive touchdown drives in the first quarter, the Cleveland offense had been largely out of sight and out of mind through the rest of the game, but now when it really counted, they did what needed to be done. They didn't score, but they did eat up an awful lot of the remaining time. With over nine minutes remaining in the game, the Browns ran 15 plays — helped by another interference call against Tannen — and eventually made it to the New York 11-yard line with just over five minutes left. The drive should have at least resulted in a field goal, but Don Cockroft somehow missed an 18-yarder, leaving the score at 24–14.

When the Jets took over at their 20, time was short and Namath got right to it. On first down he hit Boozer up the middle for 14 yards to the 34; on the next play, Caster caught his first pass as a pro when Namath hit him for 18 yards to the Cleveland 48. Then, on the next play, Namath went to Sauer over the middle for 15 yards to the 33. With 3:22 left in the game, Namath then went for it all with a beautifully lofted throw down the left sideline to Sauer, who made the catch over his shoulder as he was crossing the goal line, easily going in to score. It had been a spectacular series — four plays and a score. It was that quick, and had looked so easy. It was now only a three-point game with over three minutes left. If the defense could force a quick punt and give the offense reasonable field position, well, no telling what they could accomplish.

The defense did its job, forcing a punt in three quick plays, and with the Browns punting from their 27, the Jets should have gotten pretty good field position out of it — *should* have. A football is a strangely shaped thing, and it can take some unexpected bounces. Battle was back to field the punt at around the New York 30-yard line, but as he saw it coming down toward the right sideline it looked like it would surely hit and go out of bounds; the Jets would have the ball at about the 30. But when the ball came down, it hit just right for the Browns — just wrong for the Jets — and took one of those weird bounces. It hit quite near the sideline, but as Battle watched it, the ball suddenly rocketed back inward, shooting well past him. Battle suddenly found himself racing after the ball as it bounced downfield. He didn't catch up with it until he reached the 11-yard line, and with his momentum going the wrong direction, he wasn't able to turn around to try and run it back until he had reached the four. By then it was too late — Cleveland defenders were all over him. With under two minutes left in the game, the Jets were looking ahead at 96 yards of ground.

The New York offense was strangely leisurely after breaking huddle. On first down they called a running play; apparently neither Boozer nor Snell could believe it either, as Namath turned around and found no one to give the ball to. Looking side-to-side and seeing a vacated backfield, Namath quickly went down at the three. Then, with the clock ticking down, the Jets casually huddled in the end zone. They came out throwing on second down, but with 53 seconds left to play Gregory batted the pass down at the goal line. On third-and-11 from the three, Namath would have to throw from the end zone again. This time he hit Sauer at the left sideline for 15 yards and a first down at the 18 with 47 seconds left. Who knows, maybe it could be done.

But on the next play the dream was definitively snuffed out when Namath tried to throw up the middle to Boozer. The pass was horribly underthrown — in fact, linebacker Billy Andrews made a hell of an effort to dive to the ground and make the interception. With a startling urgency, Andrews scrambled to his feet and took off running — he looked like his ass was on fire. He made it 25 frantic yards to the end zone, and 85,000 people went crazy as Andrews and his teammates jumped up and down in the end zone like little children. Namath was the picture of dejection, standing at the five-yard line, hanging his head in shame.

After the kickoff there was just enough time for a few plays, and with no hope of a comeback Ewbank chose to send Al Woodall in at quarterback. At first the Cleveland crowd — still overcome with giddiness over the touchdown — seemed unaware of it, but as the Jets broke huddle and the people saw Woodall coming up to the line they began to boo. They hadn't had enough — they wanted more blood. A chant of "We want Joe!" could be heard among the crowd, but there was really no point. Woodall was sacked once, threw incomplete once, and ended the game with a meaningless completion to Wayne Stewart.

After the game, the Browns were elated with the victory. Head coach Blanton Collier was beaming. "This was as tough a football game as we have ever played," Collier said. "That Joe Namath is the toughest guy we have ever met, he is just fantastic."[17] Namath was 18 of 31 for 298 yards, with one touchdown and three interceptions.

The Browns were justified in feeling as if they'd dodged a bullet. As an exasperated Howard Cosell pointed out that night, the Jets didn't lose so much as they gave the game away. The statistics favored the Jets in most every category: New York came out on top in first downs 31–20, rushing yards 168–76, passing yards 305–145, total yards 454–221. But they also set a team record with 13 penalties for 161 yards, and turned the ball over four times. This, as it turns out, would be the New York Jets of the post–Super Bowl era — so full of talent, but chronic under-achievers.

Cleveland cornerback Erich Barnes said that Namath lived up to what he was expecting. "I've played against quite a few good ones in my time and I rate him with the best," Barnes said. "It was a long evening."[18] Cleveland safety Mike Howell was also full of praise, saying that Namath's ability to read defenses was excellent. In many ways, that night would foreshadow the rest of Namath's career — so impressive, so exciting, but in a losing effort.

But as beginnings go, this did not disappoint; it was everything it was hoped to be, and everything that ABC's *Monday Night Football* would be remembered for. It was a great kickoff to a long and glorious run for ABC Sports — thanks, Joe.

Week 2 — Sunday, September 27, 1970
Harvard Stadium, New Haven (attendance: 36,040)

A crowd of 36,040 turned up at Harvard Stadium when the Jets came to town to play the Patriots in week two. That might not sound like much compared to the 85,000-plus that watched the Jets' open the season in Cleveland, but it was actually Boston's best home attendance in four years, and this despite the fact that it was going to be a rainy afternoon. The Patriots came into the game 1–0 after beating Miami 27–14 in their opening game, and in their first series against the Jets it looked like they might still be on a roll.

After the Jets had failed to move the ball on their initial series, Mike Taliaferro got the Patriots' offense out of the gate quickly when he threw 39 yards to Ron Sellers to move Boston from their own 22 to the New York 39. But that promising start dried up quickly when the Patriots were set back 15 yards by a holding penalty, and Taliaferro was then intercepted by Gus Hollomon.

After that, the Jets drove 69 yards in 12 plays, with Namath throwing only once in the drive (for a 13-yard completion). Matt Snell, who carried the ball six times in the series, ran it over from two yards out to give the Jets a 7–0 lead.

Boston answered in the second quarter after Carl Garrett fielded a New York punt at the Patriots' 10-yard line and ran it back 62 yards to the New York 28. Boston then ran Garrett on a draw play that gained 12 yards to the 16, and Jim Nance did the rest. Nance gained five yards to the 11, and then went the distance on a sweep off left tackle that knotted the score at seven.

Although the Jets failed to move on their next offensive series, their defense soon gave them the opportunity to regain the lead. Taliaferro went back to pass and was hit as he released the ball, which wound up floating right into the waiting hands of linebacker Ralph Baker. The interception led to a five-yard touchdown run by Emerson Boozer, and the Jets were up 14–7.

As the rain began to fall, Boston found themselves punting from their own 18, and the slick conditions did not agree with punter Tom Janik. His kick only went 24 yards, giving the Jets excellent field position at the Boston 42 with less than two minutes remaining in the half; it took the Jets just five plays to cash in. There were only 24 seconds left in the half when Namath—with no timeouts left to use—fired a four-yard touchdown pass to Pete Lammons, and the Jets took a 21–7 lead into the half.

Early in the third quarter, the Jets seemed to put the game out of reach when Taliaferro tried to hit another ex–Jet, Bake Turner, at the sideline and instead saw Earlie Thomas pick the pass off and race 36 yards down the sideline for a score. The play put Boston down 28–7, and it looked to be a crushing blow, but the Patriots rebounded. After receiving the kick they drove 76 yards to score on a 40-yard pass from Taliaferro to Sellers, who made a spectacular catch on the play. The pass had been tipped by Steve Tannen, but as he was falling to the ground Sellers reached up to grab the ball and pull it in. The score cut the Jets' lead in half, but obviously the Patriots still had much to do.

On their next series the Patriots drove downfield only to miss a field goal; the Jets then took over at the 20, but it was now New York's turn to be generous. As the third quarter was about to come to a close, Snell fumbled the ball and linebacker Ed Philpott gathered it up at the 25 and returned it to the six-yard line. Garrett scored around left end on the next play, and suddenly the Patriots were within seven points of catching the Jets.

The Jets responded in the fourth quarter by going on a 13-play drive that ate up much of the clock and should have resulted in a score, but instead ended when Lee White took a screen pass from Namath and then fumbled the ball away to Art McMahon at the Boston four-yard line. The Patriots' good fortune was short lived, however; they failed to move the ball, and Janik again got off a bad punt, which positioned the Jets at the Boston 28-yard line. It was by then getting quite late in the game, and Jim Turner's 25-yard field goal wound up being the final score, giving the Jets a 31–21 victory.

After the game, Patriots president Bill Sullivan came into the Jets' locker room to congratulate Namath. He complimented Namath on playing a fine game, though Namath's numbers were fairly ordinary (nine of 20 for 96 yards and a touchdown). Namath greeted Sullivan respectfully, telling him that the Patriots were always tough to beat, though Namath had lost to them just once in six years.[19]

The victory brought the Jets even at 1–1, just as the Patriots were, and for that Ewbank was pleased, but he found plenty to grumble about. "We did well until we started doing things to ourselves," he said. "We did the same thing last week when we lost to Cleveland and we have to stop it."[20]

Yes, the Jets had made some mistakes, but they were fortunate in that the Patriots had made more. Except for Buffalo, who were 0–2, the entire AFC East (New York, Baltimore, Miami, and Boston) was grouped in a cluster, all tied with 1–1 records.

Week 3 — Sunday, October 4, 1970
War Memorial Stadium, Buffalo (attendance: 46,206)

Come week three the Jets were still on the road, traveling to Buffalo to play the Bills in front of 46,206 fans at War Memorial Stadium. Things started innocently enough: the Bills received the opening kickoff but couldn't do much on offense and had to punt from their 41. The Jets' rookie defensive back Steve Tannen shot through the line, blocked Paul Maguire's kick, and then fielded it on the run. Tannen returned it for a score to give the Jets a 7–0 lead 3:01 into the game.

It didn't take Buffalo long to retaliate — 19 seconds to be exact. O.J. Simpson fielded the kickoff, and after dropping the ball at the five-yard line, he picked it up and ran it back 95 yards for the tying score. The New York offense had yet to set foot on the field and the game had already seen two scores.

After the kick, the Jets' offense came out and began from their 27. A running play gained only a yard on first down, but on second down Namath went back to pass and rifled a shot to Rich Caster — it went for 72 yards and a score that put the Jets back up 14–7.

When the Bills got the ball back, Tannen again made a big play for the Jets, this time intercepting rookie quarterback Dennis Shaw at the Buffalo 42. It set up a 22-yard field goal by Jim Turner that gave the Jets a 17–7 lead 7:12 into the first quarter.

Things slowed down considerably from there — how could it not — but Buffalo managed a 10-yard field goal at 7:44 of the second quarter to close the gap to 17–10. Then, just before the end of the half, the pace again grew frenzied. Namath hit George Sauer with a 25-yard touchdown pass to make the score 24–10 with only 31 seconds left in the second quarter. That should have been all for the half, but it wasn't. After another good kick return, the Bills managed to end the half with a 40-yard field goal that whittled the Jets' lead to 24–13 at halftime.

At 4:15 of the third period, the Bills drew to within four points of the Jets when Shaw threw a 19-yard TD to Marlin Briscoe. The Jets then came storming back, with Namath throwing 53 yards to Caster to place New York at the Buffalo 11. After a Buffalo penalty moved the Jets to the six-yard line, Emerson Boozer took it in from there, and the Jets were once more up by 11, 31–20.

But the fourth quarter was Shaw's show. The Bills closed the gap to 31–27 on a one-yard TD run by Simpson with 9:40 left in the game. The big gainers in the drive were a 45-yard pass from Shaw to Briscoe, and a 27-yarder to Haven Moses.

After that the Bills caught the Jets napping; they ran an onside kick, which Buffalo's Bill Enyart recovered at the New York 47. Two runs by Simpson picked up 22 yards to the 25, and from there Shaw threw the go-ahead TD to Briscoe.

Now trailing 34–31 with 7:20 left in the game, the Jets had plenty of time to regain the lead. Namath drove them to the Buffalo 26, but the drive stalled and Turner came in to try and tie the game with a 33-yard field goal — he missed it. Even so, there was still time. When the Jets got the ball back again, they this time drove to the Buffalo 31. With fourth down, Turner again came in to try and tie the game, this time with a 38-yarder. Again, he missed, and the Jets went down in defeat.

It is sometimes said that it is all too easy to blame the kicker for the loss of a close game, that an offense ought to put the ball in the end zone and not let it come down to a matter of winning or losing on a field goal. That's as may be, but what is the purpose of a field goal kicker but to kick field goals? Jim Turner did not miss just those two late field goals: all told, he had missed five field goals in the game. Jim Turner lost the game.

Namath was 12 of 26 for 228 yards, and two touchdowns. But the talk after the game was of Dennis Shaw, a rookie quarterback who had made the first start of his pro career and outgunned Joe Namath to bring his team from behind in the fourth quarter and win. "I think I can score on every play," Shaw told reporters.[21] Pretty big talk for a guy whose team would finish the season with a 3–10–1 record. But who knew? At that moment Shaw must have thought he *was* Joe Namath.

After three weeks, Baltimore and Miami were atop the division at 2–1, while the Jets, Bills and Patriots all fell back at 1–2. The Jets had been on the road for three weeks, but would have their home opener the following Saturday night at Shea against the Miami Dolphins. The Jets had never lost to Miami, but these were not the same old Dolphins. They had a new coach — Don Shula.

Week 4 — Saturday, October 10, 1970
Shea Stadium, New York (attendance: 62,712)

At 1–2, the Jets' situation was already looking grim. Both Baltimore and Miami were 2–1, and the Jets' prospects were not helped by the mounting injuries. In week three's loss to Buffalo, Matt Snell had torn his Achilles; he had been leading the league in rushing at the time. The loss of Snell was a real blow to the offense; Emerson Boozer was capable of good games, but he was not the workhorse that Snell had been.

As for the Dolphins, despite misfiring in their opener against Boston, they were obviously a different team than in years prior. The reason for the difference was easy to discern — Don Shula had come in as head coach. After Shula had led the Baltimore Colts to a 13–1 season in 1968, the loss to the Jets in the Super Bowl seemed to deflate them. They had finished second in the NFL's Coastal Division in 1969 with an 8–5–1 record, and like Ewbank before him, Shula felt the wrath of Baltimore owner Carroll Rosenbloom, whose impatience for non-championship seasons was acute. Shula was replaced by Don McCafferty in Baltimore, and he wound up accepting the offer to fill the vacated coaching position in Miami. The Dolphins would have settled for the 8–5–1 season that so disappointed Rosenbloom in Baltimore, but Shula would do them better than that. If the Jets were going to beat Shula's Dolphins, they would have to play sharper and forego the mistakes and blunders that had cost them so much in the first three games. But with key injuries, that was proving more difficult by the week.

There were 62,712 spectators gathered at Shea on the Saturday night of the Jets' home opener of 1970, and the Jets came out looking like they would not disappoint them. After receiving the opening kickoff, the Jets drove from their own 16-yard line to the Miami 10 in just six plays. But there they ran out of steam, and had to settle for a 17-yard field goal and a 3–0 lead. It looked as though the Jets might build on their lead when Steve Tannen intercepted Bob Griese, but the play was nullified by an offside penalty. With a new lease on the series, Griese drove the Dolphins 82 yards in 11 plays to capture the lead on a nine-yard touchdown throw to Paul Warfield, who had otherwise been key in the drive by being on the receiving end of a 40-yard pass that put the Dolphins at the New York 11.

A 35-yard field goal by Jim Turner brought the Jets to within a point of Miami at 7–6, and would be the only score in the second quarter. The Jets were having no trouble moving the ball — they just couldn't keep from shooting themselves in the foot. Two New York drives had been halted when Namath was intercepted, once at the Miami 11 and then again at the Miami 24, and the Dolphins had otherwise blocked another Turner field goal attempt. It was looking like the same old story.

Although they may have been able to move quite well offensively in the first half, in the second half the Jets seemed to fall apart. The Dolphins only managed a field goal in the third quarter, but they otherwise controlled the ball so well that they ran off 24 plays while the Jets managed only eight. The Miami field goal came with 2:05 left in the third period and gave the Dolphins a 10–6 lead. The Jets, meanwhile, had failed to gain a single first down in the period.

Griese hit Howard Twilley with a three-yard touchdown throw 4:07 into the fourth quarter to make it 17–6, and Miami later added a field goal to make the final 20–6. The Jets had been thoroughly beaten. While they had done themselves in with their usual errors in the first half, they had been completely lifeless in the second. They hadn't even managed a first down in the second half until late in the fourth quarter. Namath's numbers are a good example of how the team flatlined. In the first half he had completed 13 of 25 passes for 181 yards: in the second half he was just four of 15 for 59 yards, making his final tally 17 of 40 for 240 yards, with three interceptions. As far as Snell's absence was concerned, the game confirmed Ewbank's worst fears. Without Snell, the New York ground game was nonexistent — the team had 39 yards rushing.

As the Dolphins increased to 3–1 to continue sharing first place with Baltimore, the Jets fell into last place with a 1–3 record. But the Jets had gotten off to bad starts before: they began their Super Bowl season in 1968 with a 3–2 record and finished 11–3, and in 1969 they had started 1–2 and finished 10–4. But a 1–3 start was definitely a problem, particularly with Baltimore and Miami getting out of the gate fast in the division. A loss in week five could do irreparable damage for the Jets, especially since it would come against their new division rivals. In week five the Jets would be hosting the Baltimore Colts. It was the first meeting of the two teams since the Super Bowl, and it was a much-anticipated showdown. The Colts had certainly been counting the days.

Week 5 — Sunday, October 18, 1970
Shea Stadium, New York (attendance: 63,301)

In 1969 Namath had said that, come the AFL-NFL merger in 1970, the Colts might beat the Jets like so many were saying, but that it would never atone for the Super Bowl loss. He was right, of course, but the Colts were salivating over the opportunity nonetheless. Wanting to take two years of frustrations out on the Jets, they came to Shea Stadium in week five with visions of a massacre in their heads. Many years later, Baltimore center Bill Curry said that everyone — including the Jets — knew that Baltimore was going to kick New York's ass that day.[22] Sometimes people remember how they wanted things to be, not how they truly were.

The game certainly began like the ass-kicking Baltimore was after. The Colts received the opening kick, and on their very first play from scrimmage Johnny Unitas hit tight end John Mackey down the middle for a 48-yard catch and run. The Colts were in a two-tight end formation with only one setback, so there was no great surprise to the play, but it worked superbly regardless. Deep in New York territory after just one play, Unitas tried the run, but three straight rushing plays yielded little and the Colts settled for a 28-yard field goal and a 3–0 lead 1:59 into the game. They wouldn't have to wait long to increase their lead — 40 seconds, to be exact.

On the Jets' first play from scrimmage, Namath went back to pass and threw right. Dave

Herman had done an excellent job blocking Bubba Smith in the Super Bowl, but now he was back at his guard spot; tackle Dave Foley was blocking Smith this time. Since Herman was only six-foot-one and Foley was six-five it might have been expected that Foley was better equipped to deal with the six-foot-seven Smith. But Smith blew right past Foley on the play and got his hands up, tipping Namath's pass and sending it right into the hands of Baltimore's Jerry Logan, who had clear sailing down the sideline as he ran it 31 yards for a score. After only 2:39 of the first quarter, the Colts had a 10–0 lead.

The Jets' next series was a bust, with Namath overthrowing Don Maynard on three consecutive plays. After New York punted, Baltimore started from their own 35 and Unitas immediately threw over the middle for 32 yards to Eddie Hinton, who was brought down at the Jets' 33. Then Unitas hit tight end Tom Mitchell for 18 yards to the 15, and two plays later he hit Mitchell again, this time in the end zone from 11 yards out. Now only five minutes into the game, the Colts held a 17–0 lead. It must have felt like the vindication the Colts had been dreaming of for almost two years.

The Jets managed to get on the board and cut the lead to 17–3 when Jim Turner booted a 41-yard field goal, capping a drive that saw Namath hit Maynard with a 45-yard pass. The first quarter had started with a series of rapid-fire scores, but would trail off into a succession of bungling mistakes. Unitas had to fall on the ball after Norm Bulaich mishandled the exchange on a running play, and Unitas then gave the ball up when he threw a poor pass over the middle and W.K. Hicks made an excellent one-handed interception.

Now the real comedy of errors was beginning. Starting from the Baltimore 45, Namath took the Jets down to the Colts' nine-yard line before being intercepted by linebacker Mike Curtis. A few plays later Unitas returned the favor and threw an interception to Gus Hollomon, giving the Jets possession at the Baltimore 42.

After hitting Emerson Boozer for nine yards to the 33, Namath tried to hit Maynard in the end zone on the next play but was intercepted by Logan again. The first quarter ended there, the game having turned into a war of interceptions between Namath and Unitas: Namath was winning — or losing — 3–2.

In the second quarter everybody seemed to catch their breath, and Unitas got the Colts driving again. Baltimore drove to the New York 11, but on third down Hicks again made an excellent play, batting away a Unitas pass to Mitchell in the end zone. The Colts kicked an 18-yard field goal to go back up by 17 points, 20–3.

The Jets' best offensive play of the second quarter turned out to be a punt that forced Baltimore to start from their own four. John Elliot almost caught Unitas for a safety, sacking him at the one, and on the next play he and linebacker Ralph Baker managed to drop running back Jack Maitland in the end zone for two points. Baltimore's lead was now 20–5.

The Jets got good field position on the free kick after the safety, but they could do nothing with it and Jim Turner was very short on a 46-yard field goal attempt. Toward the end of the half, after Namath had hit Pete Lammons and Ed Bell with a couple of passes that brought the Jets into field goal range again, Turner had a 38-yard field goal attempt blocked. The half ended with Unitas passing to Roy Jefferson, who fumbled the ball away to Hicks, an appropriately sloppy end to a thoroughly sloppy half. Still, sloppy or not, the Colts had to be pleased in taking a 20–5 lead into the half.

Namath began the second half just as he had the first. The Jets received the second half kick-off, and on their first play Namath went back to pass: he threw to his right and was intercepted by linebacker Bob Grant, who ran it back 27 yards for a touchdown. Only seven seconds into the third quarter, Baltimore's lead was now 26–5 (Jim O'Brien missed the extra point).

When the Jets got the ball back, Namath tried to throw to Maynard over the middle but the pass was deflected into the air by Logan. After spinning around and doing a sort of pirouette,

Logan reached out and pulled the ball in — it was Logan's third interception of the game and the fifth thrown by Namath, who was leaving Unitas in the dust in the interception race, 5–2. Well, Unitas did his bit to catch up — he promptly threw another interception to Hicks, who returned it 35 yards to the Baltimore 17. One play later Namath equaled Unitas in touchdowns by hitting Eddie Bell in the end zone. The score was now 26–12, Baltimore.

After the New York defense forced a Baltimore punt, Namath started to move the Jets on their next series. He was not having much success long against Baltimore's zone, but he was gaining on short passes to Boozer, Lammons, and Lee White. It was a couple of slant-ins to old reliable Maynard, however, that got the Jets inside the Baltimore 10-yard line to set up a one-yard touchdown run by Boozer. The Baltimore lead was then cut to 26–19. After being down by 21 points, as well as being 17 points behind twice in the game, the Jets were now within seven.

But once more the Jets would shoot themselves in the foot. After their touchdown they kicked to Baltimore with 1:31 left in the third period, and Jim Duncan ran the ball back 43 yards from the five-yard line to the 48. From there, Unitas seemed to concede the interception sweep-stakes to Namath and tried the running game, which suddenly found its wheels. The third period ended with the Colts driving, but early in the fourth they failed to convert on third down and kicked a 28-yard field goal for a 29–19 lead.

Namath decisively won the interception derby on the Jets' next series when Duncan picked off a long throw to Maynard and ran it back 30 yards to the New York 32. The interception only hurt the Jets in as much as it allowed Baltimore to run a little more time off the clock, however, as the Colts couldn't cash in on the turnover. The Jets soon had the ball back, and Namath managed to move them downfield with short passes until being thwarted on a third down; New York had to be satisfied with cutting Baltimore's lead to seven again when Turner kicked a 42-yard field goal.

After a failed onside kick, the Jets prevented Baltimore from running out the clock, and the New York offense got one last shot with less than two minutes left. There was hope when Namath hit Maynard for 13 yards to the New York 37 and then hit Bell for 11 yards to the 48, but their march went no further and the Colts' revenge had been accomplished — sort of.

If Curry remembered an ass-kicking, it must be the only seven-point ass-kicking in NFL history. The Colts won the game, and for that they must have been gratified in some measure, but this could in no way be the dominant performance they were either needing or hoping for to exorcise the demons of Super Bowl III. It was a textbook case of winning ugly — a clumsy, slipshod performance that only managed to accomplish victory by virtue of having been matched against an even clumsier performance. It was almost a game that nobody deserved to win, the victor having won merely by making fewer costly mistakes.

Namath had set some team records: his 34 completions were a team best, as were his 62 attempts. Then again, his six interceptions tied his own personal high. It could easily have been eight, which would have tied an NFL record, but two sure interceptions were dropped by Baltimore defenders. His yardage was certainly impressive, at 397. After the game, Jerry Logan said that if Namath was off a little on his throws it wasn't his fault, but was really down to the pass coverage being tight. He was right. For the most part, the offensive line gave Namath ample time to throw, but the coverage was so good that he often held the ball a long time looking for an open man.

Unitas said that, as far as he was concerned, Namath and Sonny Jurgensen were the two best passers in football. Mackey was also full of praise for Namath's effort, saying that he thought Namath looked as good as he had in the Super Bowl. "I know we intercepted six of his passes," Mackey said, "but he keeps coming at you all the time and that's the sign of a man."[23]

Eddie Bell had set a team record with 12 receptions, but without Snell the Jets' rushing game again managed to do little. The previous week against Miami the Jets had gained only 39 yards;

against the Colts, only 37. This was a team in big trouble. Their 1–4 record made it all but impossible for the Jets to make the playoffs without running the table and winning nine straight. Maynard had been bothered with nagging injuries through the early part of the season, but he managed his best game of the year nonetheless, catching nine passes for 148 yards. It was definitely needed, as George Sauer and Rich Caster were now out. And then, the real deathblow.

In the third quarter, Namath had gone down under a heavy rush by Billy Ray Smith. He tried to break his fall and came down on his right hand. The combination of his own weight and that of Smith coming down on top of him was a bit much for the wrist to bear. Although he continued to play, there was considerable pain each time he threw the ball. Dr. Nicholas was out of town, and would have to take a look at it on Monday.

By Monday, Namath's right hand had swollen badly, and X-rays revealed that he had a broken bone just beneath the thumb. The scaphoid bone, often referred to as the navicular, helps facilitate delicate movements of the hand. Namath was outrageously optimistic. "We'll wait until the doctor sees it," he said, "maybe there's some type of cast they can put on it and I can play this week."[24]

Ewbank dismissed the idea completely, saying realistically there was zero chance of that happening. On the Tuesday after the game Namath's hand was put in a cast, which he would wear for the next four months. He became the most high-profile member of the Jets' growing casualty list. For Namath, the season was done. So was the Jets' season, really, although it could be argued that, at 1–4, their season was basically a lost cause at that point anyway.

With Namath the team had been struggling, yet there was still the hope that they would overcome all of the injuries and whatever other problems were causing them to misfire. But now, nobody seemed to take them seriously. Without Namath the team seemed in limbo, like they were just marking time pending his return the following season. The Jets would lose to Buffalo, the New York Giants, and the Pittsburgh Steelers in the three weeks after Namath's injury, dropping their record to a dismal 1–7. Namath was with the team for every game, watching from the sidelines in his street clothes (however flamboyant) and hand in a cast, standing next to Ewbank, offering his thoughts, always ready to confer. It was something that hadn't been expected by many on the team. Given his reluctance in reporting to camp, and his seeming lack of enthusiasm for the game before the season had started, many of the players weren't anticipating that Namath would stick around. They thought he might be off making another movie deal or sunning himself on a yacht in Fort Lauderdale. But Namath wanted to be with his team. That's something that he found out once he was unable to play. Having to sit out the showdown with the Giants was what seemed to hurt the most. "That's the day I remembered," Namath said. "Not being able to play just killed me."[25]

Al Woodall did a serviceable job in Namath's place, but with all respect, he was certainly no Joe Namath. After falling to 1–7, the Jets did have an impressive three-game run that brought their record to 4–7, and they even managed to beat two of the NFC's strongest contenders, first knocking off the Rams in Los Angeles, 31–20, and then beating the Minnesota Vikings at Shea two weeks later. The Vikings had the best record in the league, and the loss to the Jets would be one of only two games they would drop all season. In between those games, the Jets had beaten Boston … again.

But after the promise of those three consecutive games, the Jets went on to lose their final three games of the season to finish 4–10. Even so, they still managed to hold third place in the AFC East, ahead of the 3–10–1 Bills and the 2–12 Patriots. Baltimore won the division with an 11–2–1 record.

If anyone had cause to question Namath's contribution to the team, one need only note that in just five games he had passed for only six yards less than Woodall would throw for during the rest of the season. Namath ended his season completing 90 of 179 passes (a 50.3 completion percentage) for 1,259 yards. He had thrown five TDs, but had also thrown 12 interceptions (three in his first game of the year, six in his last).

But things would all be different the following season; at least, that's what everyone thought. After all, Namath had come to his senses. He had come to realize how much he wanted to play, and with that fire again burning in his gut, how could things not be better?

9

The 1971 Season

In 1967, Namath had left training camp and gone to New York for the evening against the wishes of his coach. During the 1968 preseason, he again disregarded the wishes of his coach when he refused to suit up for an exhibition game against the Houston Oilers. In 1969, Namath had missed most of the preseason after retiring — albeit briefly — over a dispute with NFL commissioner Pete Rozelle regarding Namath's New York City restaurant, Bachelors III. In 1970, Namath was late in reporting to training camp, citing personal problems and a general uncertainty about whether or not he even wanted to play anymore. No doubt about it: with Namath, preseason was never dull. But as has been said, you don't know what you've got 'til it's gone.

In being unable to play most of the 1970 season, Namath came to realize how much he *wanted* to play. When camp opened at Hofstra in the summer of 1971, Namath reported promptly for the first time in years, and did so with an enthusiasm he hadn't had in about as long. Having made a poor showing with what little time he had at the beginning of the 1970 season, Namath was eager to prove himself again. "I want to show people I'm the number one quarterback," he said in August.[1]

Ewbank must have felt like Christmas had come early. For once, Namath was there on time and eager to go. There was no talk of retirement or of making movies, no haggling over contracts and dickering for more money. There was just an earnest desire to play again, and to get back on top. "I know his knees feel better than they have in a long time," Ewbank said.[2]

There was considerable anticipation about the upcoming season, not merely due to Namath's return, but the Jets' chances seemed strong in light of a number of factors. Matt Snell was returning from his Achilles injury, and the running game would otherwise benefit from the arrival of rookie running back John Riggins from Kansas. Receiver George Sauer had retired prematurely, citing the game's "militaristic" and "paternalistic" qualities, which suddenly seemed to his disliking (he would be able to look beyond these onerous aspects of the sport when he made a brief return to the game, playing for the World Football League's New York franchise in 1974), but both Rich Caster and Eddie Bell were entering their second season and were fully capable of stepping in to fill his place.

On defense, the linebacking crew remained the same, and despite the departure of Verlon Biggs to the Washington Redskins, the defensive front four was strong, with Gerry Philbin and second-year man Mark Lomas at the ends, while John Elliot and Steve Thompson were back at the tackle spots. The secondary, still largely lacking experience, at least had a year behind them as Earlie Thomas and Steve Tannen were returning at the corners, while Gus Hollomon and W.K. Hicks were the safeties (the lineup would shift with injuries throughout the course of the season).

Another notable change was kicker Bobby Howfield, acquired from the Denver Broncos. Despite the season Jim Turner had in 1970, making only 19 of 35 field goals, the Broncos took him in an even-up trade.

The Jets looked to be a solid team, and for once they did not have the distractions that usually accompanied training camp. One can only hope that Ewbank enjoyed it while it lasted, for it was short lived. Namath may not have courted drama this time, but it was coming soon enough regardless.

The Jets' first preseason game was a Saturday night meeting with the Detroit Lions in Tampa, Florida, on August 7, 1971. Scheduled to play just the first half, Namath demonstrated that he was indeed getting back into his groove. After Tannen intercepted a Detroit pass at the New York 29, Namath drove his team downfield to score on an 11-yard TD pass to Snell, and in the second quarter George Nock scored on a six-yard run that put the Jets up 14–0.

Well into the second quarter, his work for the evening almost complete, Namath handed off to Lee White, who ran a sweep right. As White was running he lost the ball, and it was picked up by Detroit linebacker Mike Lucci, who took off running the other way. Namath took off too, looking to head Lucci off at the sideline; but as he tried to at least slow Lucci's progress so that someone else might catch up and make a tackle, Namath was blocked by linebacker Paul Naumoff, and the two went to the ground. Naumoff landed on top of Namath, and Lucci ran 29 yards for a score. Namath was on the ground clutching his left knee, but got to his feet and hobbled off the field; it was obvious to everyone on the sideline that he was in pain. Dr. Nicholas examined Namath on the sideline and his diagnosis was not good: Namath had torn ligaments in the left knee — the *good* knee — which Nicholas would describe to the press afterward as "severe" damage. Nicholas told Namath that he would have to go in for surgery the following morning back in New York. Namath wanted to postpone the surgery so that he might make a scheduled personal appearance in Alabama, but Nicholas denied the request.

The Detroit Lions weren't even aware that Namath had been injured until they came out for the second half and someone gave them the news. They too seemed to feel a sense of loss. "And he was throwing the ball so great," said Lucci.[3] Namath had hit eight of 14 passes.

The Lions would take over in the second half, and went on to win 28–24, but after the game the talk was mostly of Namath. Naumoff said that it was a shame, adding that he hadn't meant to hurt Namath.[4]

Upon returning to New York, it was back into Lenox Hill Hospital for Namath on Sunday morning, where Dr. Nicholas performed a 51-minute operation, removing loose cartilage and reconstructing a pair of ligaments. Namath was expected to be in a cast for six weeks. A spokesman for the hospital said that, while the injury was serious, it did not appear to be so bad as to end Namath's career. Nicholas had initially said that he expected that Namath would have to miss the entire 1971 season, but the surgery had gone so well that he revised his prognosis, saying afterward that there was a chance that Namath might be able to play by mid–November.

Naumoff certainly wanted it to be true. Often deprived of recognition among his linebacking peers in Detroit (Lucci and Wayne Walker), Naumoff suddenly found himself getting more publicity than ever, though it was hardly the type of coverage he had wanted. He was now being cast as a nefarious beast who had intentionally gone after Namath's knees with a spear block, depriving the sport and its fans of the game's biggest superstar. "I wanted to see Joe come back and have a good year," Naumoff said in protest. "I hope it's true he'll be back in November."[5] Naumoff also pointed out that Namath himself had not cried foul or accused him of a cheap shot.

With Namath again out of the lineup, the Jets certainly felt it, but there was a calmness about the team: they had weathered this storm before, and quite recently. When Namath was lost to injury the previous year, Al Woodall had stepped in to play for most of the season. Now Woodall was set to step in again, this time having the benefit of experience to draw from. The Jets felt they were a good enough team to be a contender with or without Namath, a view that Namath shared. Saying that Woodall could do the job, Namath expressed the belief that the team was too good to fall apart over the loss of a single player.[6]

The big question on a lot of minds was "Why?" Why, Joe? Why try to take on a linebacker and tackle him in a meaningless exhibition game? He was asked that question in the locker room after the game. "No way could I let him go," Namath responded.[7] "For you're information," he joked later, "that's the first tackle I've missed in seven years."[8]

Cleveland quarterback Bill Nelsen knew why Namath did it: he did it because he was a football player, and that's what football players do—try to stop the opponent from scoring. It was purely out of instinct and the basic nature of a competitor. Had the Jets been losing, Nelsen said in an interview, Namath would likely not have responded as he had, but the natural reaction of a competitor is to protect a lead.[9]

The Jets soldiered on through the preseason, losing to the Raiders 41–20 in Oakland before rebounding nicely in their annual exhibition match with the Giants in New Haven. At one point leading 20–0, it was a very inspired performance by the Jets' defense, which had held the Giants to a first-half total of minus-one-yard in offense and hadn't even allowed the Giants to get any further than their own 35-yard line until late in the third quarter. The Jets won the game 27–14.

Their next exhibition was against the Kansas City Chiefs, and losing the game was not their only problem: once more they lost their fullback when Snell suffered a knee injury. The Jets would again be playing with a patchwork backfield, but Riggins lightened that burden considerably.

After losing to the Chiefs 21–16 in Kansas City, and then falling to the Steelers 35–21 in Pittsburgh, the Jets ended their exhibition schedule by beating the Patriots 38–9 in Memphis. The Patriots, incidentally, had been re-christened the New England Patriots after moving into Schaefer Stadium in Foxboro.

As they had in previous seasons, the Jets began 1971 with an extended road swing due to the schedule of Shea's principal tenants, the Mets. They began the season badly, being blanked by the Colts 22–0, and then losing to the Cardinals 17–10 in week two. They scored their first victory of the season in week three, beating the Dolphins 14–10 in the Orange Bowl, but were then shutout again in week four, losing to the Patriots 20–0. Woodall had completed just four of 24 passes in the game; it was the first time the Jets had lost to the Patriots since 1965. Having been shutout twice in four games, the offense was obviously lacking, and after the loss to New England, Ewbank benched Woodall in favor of third-string quarterback Bob Davis. Woodall said he was not surprised by the move, adding that he deserved to be benched.[10]

Acquired from Houston, Davis had been around since 1967 but had seen limited action throughout his career—the highest number of passes he had thrown in a season was 86 in 1968. Still, Davis did have game experience and he led the Jets to a victory over the Buffalo Bills in his first start in week five.

But the Jets were up and down all season, each win seeming to be followed by a pair of losses. The most disappointing loss was a one-point defeat at the hands of the Colts at Shea in week nine. Trailing 14–7 in the fourth quarter, the Jets scored a touchdown that should have tied the game, but when the extra point was blocked they found themselves still down a point. Late in the game they were in position to kick the winning field goal, but that too was blocked. That was on November 14, and the Jets' record stood at 3–6 at that point.

Dr. Nicholas had predicted that Namath could be ready to play by November 15, but he had missed his guess slightly. In week 10, the Jets had beaten Buffalo again to bring their record to 4–6. Come week 11—November 28—Namath was ready to return. Actually, Nicholas would have been right except for one thing: while Namath had healed from the surgery and was physically able, the operation had left him with nerve pain that was also causing numbness in the left foot.

Week 11— Sunday, November 28, 1971
Shea Stadium, New York (attendance: 63,936)

When they talked about his availability to play in week 11, Namath and Ewbank both agreed that, in fairness to Bob Davis, it should be Davis who got the start. Since replacing Al Woodall at quarterback, Davis had led the Jets to three wins against three losses, making the Jets' overall record 4–6 going into week 11 (the team had begun the year 1–3 with Woodall). Still, when word got out that Woodall had been taken off the roster and that Namath had been activated, some 63,936 people turned out at Shea. Ewbank planned on having Davis play the first half before giving way to Namath in the second. That would change, of course, if the game got out of hand early and the Jets found themselves trailing badly. If such were the case, then Namath would see action sooner. The other possibility was that Namath would enter the game sooner if Davis should fall to injury.

The Jets' opponents, the San Francisco 49ers, were 6–4 and in a fight with the Los Angeles Rams for the lead of the NFC's Western Division. The 49ers very much needed a win to maintain their tenuous half-game lead over Los Angeles. For the Jets, a loss would pretty much close the door on any post-season aspirations.

In the first-ever meeting between the two teams, the Jets received the opening kickoff, but other than a good run by John Riggins on the first play from scrimmage, they were unable to make much headway and had to punt quickly. By contrast, San Francisco's first possession found them moving the ball almost at will, mostly on the ground. While the Jets were considered fairly sound defensively against the run, their secondary had for years been their soft spot. The 49ers, however, established their running game early against the Jets, with backs Vic Washington and Ken Willard carrying the ball often and far. The 49ers ran nine plays in the series — eight of them runs — and drove deep into New York territory, but came away empty-handed when Washington fumbled the ball inside the New York 15-yard line.

The Jets' next series again came to nothing, as they were unable to match San Francisco's ground attack. In their first two offensive series, the Jets would gain just two first downs. Again they punted, and when punter Steve O'Neal dropped the snap from center and then found a heavy rush bearing down on him, he got off a weak kick that allowed San Francisco to start their next series from midfield. As the first quarter gave way to the second, the 49ers were deep into New York territory again with Washington having carried the load, getting the call on seven of the drive's eight plays. Fittingly, it was Washington who carried the ball across to score from two yards out to give the 49ers a 7–0 lead.

On the Jets' next series Davis finally seemed to get something started. After a run by Riggins, Davis threw to Rich Caster for 17 yards to the San Francisco 47-yard line. But that was it for Davis — after the play he remained on the ground in obvious pain and the crowd of almost 64,000 all came to their feet. Everybody knew that with Davis down, Namath had to replace him, and as center John Schmitt and tackle Winston Hill helped Davis to the sideline the stirring of the crowd grew louder until turning to gleeful cheering as Namath trotted onto the field. There were 10:33 remaining in the first half.

"Football fans usually observe a decent quiet when a man is injured," wrote Red Smith of the *New York Times*,[11] but in this instance the fans would have to be forgiven their callous indifference to Davis' suffering. They had, after all, been waiting long for this very moment. Of course, Namath had also been waiting long, and under the circumstances he could also be forgiven his rustiness. He seemed to want to get that first pass out of the way quickly, but when he tried to hit Don Maynard with a slant-in on first down, the ball bounced off the ground well in front of its target. The crowd was understanding. After a running play did little to advance the cause, Namath threw incomplete again on third down, and the Jets turned the ball over.

When the Jets got the ball back Namath threw his first completion of the 1971 season, a 28-yarder up the middle to Emerson Boozer that advanced the Jets from their own 16 to the 44. But after that brief triumph, Namath threw to Caster on an out pattern down the left sideline and was intercepted by Bruce Taylor at the San Francisco 49; Taylor ran down the sideline, returning the ball all the way to the New York two-yard line.

The 49ers tried to run the ball in from there, but as easily as they had been running on the Jets up to then, the New York defense suddenly tightened up and prevented the 49ers from scoring on two consecutive runs. On third down, quarterback John Brodie threw to tight end Bob Windsor in the end zone; it should have been an easy six points, but Windsor dropped the ball and the 49ers had to settle for a field goal and a 10–0 lead.

With two minutes left in the half, Namath got the Jets moving. He hit Caster with a 22-yard gain to the San Francisco 32, and then threw to Maynard at the 12. A pass interference penalty on San Francisco's Johnny Fuller in the end zone then gave the Jets a first-and-goal on the one-yard line, and they were poised to get right back in the game. They came to the line with a loaded backfield, consisting of Boozer, Riggins, and rookie Steve Harkey. The call went to Harkey, and when he came to the line and got hit the ball squirted out and into the end zone. Defensive back Jimmy Johnson and tight end Pete Lammons both went for the ball; neither could get a hold of it, and they only managed to knock it out of the back of the end zone for a touchback with 40 seconds left in the half. The 49ers then ran out the half, and the Jets went in trailing 10–0 at the intermission.

San Francisco received the second half kickoff, and were still tearing off outrageous parcels of ground as Willard broke through the line and ran the ball 31 yards from the San Francisco 27 to the New York 42. In tackling Willard, W.K. Hicks had managed to grab his facemask, so the officials tacked on another 15 yards to the New York 27. A few plays later, Brodie scored on a bootleg from the one-yard line to increase the 49ers' lead to 17–0.

The Jets definitely needed to make something happen on their next series, and it happened quickly. After Boozer ran for 10 yards to the New York 43, Namath went back to pass and threw deep down the middle to Caster. Namath didn't get everything on the ball that he wanted — he would later say that the ball had slipped from his hand as he threw it — but Caster, seeing the ball, cut inside his defender, Rosey Taylor, and made the catch at the San Francisco 20. Caster outraced Taylor to the end zone, electrifying the Shea Stadium crowd with a 57-yard touchdown play. The San Francisco lead was now 17–7.

The score seemed to inspire the New York defense, and they quickly forced the 49ers to punt the ball back. Namath hit Maynard with a 23-yard pass to the San Francisco 44, but when the drive fizzled out Bobby Howfield came up very short on a 47-yard field goal try. The kick was fielded by Bruce Taylor, who fumbled it, but the 49ers recovered the ball and San Francisco took possession at their 13.

Willard was on a roll again, taking off on a 49-yard jaunt to the New York 38, but the Jets' defense pulled together after that as Larry Grantham dropped Vic Washington for a six-yard loss on first down, and John Dockery deflected two passes, first a long shot downfield to Gene Washington in the end zone, and then a throw from Brodie to tight end Ted Kwalick. The third quarter ended with the 49ers still up 17–7.

In the fourth quarter, however, San Francisco built that lead back up to 17 points when Brodie threw a 22-yard touchdown to Vic Washington, making the score 24–7. Once more, the running of Willard had been instrumental in the drive.

Only 7:30 remained in the game when the Jets got the ball back. A pass to Lammons put the Jets at midfield, and when Namath then threw incomplete across the middle to Eddie Bell, an overly eager defensive play by Bruce Taylor drew a pass interference call and the Jets were awarded a first down at the San Francisco 31. Namath threw again to Lammons, and two plays later, from the 20-yard line, he threw for Caster cutting right-to-left at the goal line. The throw was low, but Caster reached down to his knees and grabbed the ball, pulling it in as he crossed the goal line for a score. The San Francisco lead was now 24–14.

The 49ers would have loved to run some time off the clock after that, but three plays gained only two yards and they had to punt. Both Steve Tannen and Phil Wise were in on punter Jim McCann quickly, and Wise was able to get a finger on the ball, deflecting the kick and giving the Jets possession at the San Francisco 22-yard line. Namath wasted no time, hitting Bell deep in the left corner of the end zone for a score that brought the Jets to within three points with just over five minutes remaining.

The 49ers this time succeeded in getting a first down to run a good bit of time off the clock, but then on a crucial third-down play Gerry Philbin stuffed Willard behind the line to force a punt. The Jets would have one last shot.

Namath and the offense took over at their own 28 with 1:41 left in the game. Namath started by throwing to Caster for a first down at the 39. With the clock still running, he then threw down the middle to Bell, and although the ball was short, Bell made a fine catch for a 22-yard gain and a first down at the San Francisco 39. The Jets were forced at that point to use their last timeout, and Namath resumed by throwing deep to Bell down the middle of the field. The pass was underthrown and was very nearly intercepted by Bruce Taylor at the 13-yard line. With 46 seconds left, and everyone in Shea Stadium on their feet, it all seemed to end.

Namath threw across the middle, and was intercepted by linebacker Dave Wilcox. There was a collective groan from the crowd as Wilcox made a nifty little return, but it would seem they hadn't seen the end yet — defensive lineman Cedrick Hardman was flagged for being offside on the play, and the Jets had another chance. The penalty moved the ball up to the 34-yard line, and on the following play Namath crossed the San Francisco defense up by running a trap to Boozer. With only 34 seconds left and no timeouts, it was a gutsy call, but it paid off when Boozer darted and weaved through the line and then bounced outside for 15 yards to the 19-yard line. More than that, he managed to get out of bounds and stop the clock with 22 seconds left.

The people in the crowd weren't the only ones on their feet in eager anticipation. On the San Francisco sideline the players were vying with each other for position, trying to get a better view of what was happening out on the field. Namath threw to Caster in the deep left of the end zone, but the pass fell incomplete. There were now 16 seconds remaining. What happened next would somehow be adumbrative of so much of Namath's remaining career. Namath threw for Bell in the end zone. The ball seemed to have good flight, spiraling nicely toward its target, but safety Johnny Fuller was positioned well in the end zone and reached up to intercept the pass as Bell was preparing to catch it. Fuller ran the ball out of the end zone, carrying it 57 yards and running out the final seconds in the process. The Jets had lost, 24–21.

Ordinarily a home crowd might be upset by such an unfortunate turn of events to end a game, but on this occasion there seemed to be nothing that could dampen the crowd's enthusiasm. There were smiles on every face: it didn't matter if they were seven years old or 70 — there were none but little children in Shea Stadium that day. Maybe he hadn't won the game, but Namath had otherwise done what he had so many times before — he gave them a show: he had them on their feet and anxiously awaiting the outcome. The game had ended, but nobody wanted to leave. The people remained for some time, standing, applauding, smiling; fans began mobbing the field. As players from the San Francisco 49ers, as well as their coach, Dick Nolan, tried to congratulate Namath on his return, the fans began to gather, pressing in trying to pat him on the back, reaching out to touch him: anyone would have thought it was the second coming. The Jets had fallen to 4–7 and had lost their last chance of a winning season in 1971, but the fans carried on as if they had just won a championship. In a television interview many years later, center John Schmitt would pause to fight back tears at the memory of it. "It was the greatest game," he said in his charmingly lisping New York accent, "The greatest comeback I've ever seen, you know, as far as, even losing the game, but the people, and what that guy could do was unbelievable. Fifteen minutes after the game was over, the people were still clapping."[12]

Winning? Who the hell gave a damn about winning? After missing almost two full seasons, Namath had come back to thrill everyone again and add to their treasure chest of life memories, and really, wasn't that enough? His performance was more than enough for the 49ers. "That guy Namath's got charisma," said San Francisco linebacker Frank Nunley after the game.[13] Cedrick Hardman had spent the afternoon trying to take Namath's head off. When the game was over the hulking defensive end approached Namath on the field—he wanted to tell him that he still idolized him.

Fuller, who had abruptly robbed Namath of his storybook ending with the interception on the game's final play, was also impressed. "Namath really puts a lot of pressure on you," he said. "It didn't surprise me that he went for the touchdown because that's the way he plays."[14]

The only one who wasn't impressed with Namath's play was, as always, Namath himself. He had completed 11 of 27 for 258 yards, with three touchdowns and two interceptions. "I don't feel I played well," he said afterward. "I've got to improve my mental state because I didn't feel at ease."[15]

Week 12 — Saturday, December 4, 1971
Texas Stadium, Irving (attendance: 66,689)

After his semi-triumphant return to action in week 11, Namath would be making his first start in a regular season game since October of 1970 when the Jets traveled to Irving, Texas, in week 12 to play the Dallas Cowboys in Texas Stadium. The facility was one of those modern eyesores, the artificial field pristine and sterile, the arena being just less than a dome by virtue of the fact that they had left a hole in the roof for the sun to periodically squeeze through.

The 8–3 Cowboys were on their way to their first Super Bowl title while the Jets, at 4–7, had been eliminated, trailing both Baltimore and Miami quite badly in the AFC East. Being played on a Saturday, the game was televised nationally and it was hoped that after his return and three-touchdown performance the week before, Namath might lift the Jets up enough to challenge the NFC Eastern Division-leading Cowboys.

Ike Thomas took the opening kickoff for Dallas, and for the second consecutive game returned it the distance for a touchdown. A week earlier he had returned the opening kickoff 89 yards for a touchdown in the Cowboys' Thanksgiving Day game with the Los Angeles Rams—against the Jets he returned it 101 yards.

Down 7–0 only seconds into the game, the Jets were unable to do anything constructive on their first offensive series and punted. The Cowboys then started their opening offensive series from their own 14-yard line and Roger Staubach proceeded to take them on an 86-yard scoring march that ended with a screen pass to Calvin Hill that went the final 27 yards for a touchdown.

On the Jets' next series, Namath was intercepted by Herb Adderly and the Cowboys took possession at the New York 27. Staubach again threw a 27-yard touchdown to Hill, this time on a catch-and-run. Still in the first quarter, the score was already 21–0 and about to get worse.

Chris Farasopoulos fumbled the ensuing kickoff, and Claxton Welch recovered it for Dallas at the New York 15. Shortly thereafter, Duane Thomas scored from three yards out to make the score 28–0 with three minutes still remaining in the first quarter. Ewbank decided to sit Namath down. Trailing so badly so early, the Jets would necessarily be throwing, and Ewbank decided not to expose Namath to the added risk.

After Hill scored his third TD of the game on a nine-yard run to make the score 35–0 in the second period, Bob Davis got the Jets close enough for Bobby Howfield to get them on the board with a 35-yard field goal, but that did precious little to lessen the humiliation. The Cowboys added a field goal of their own to make the score 38–3 at halftime. The Jets had only managed four first downs in the half.

In the third quarter the Cowboys went up 45–3 when Staubach hit Duane Thomas with an 18-yard TD pass, but the Jets finally managed to get into the end zone as well when Davis tossed a one-yard TD to George Nock. The touchdown had been made possible largely by two runs by Davis — one of 24 yards and another of 11 — who wound up being the Jets' leading rusher in the game with 37 yards.

In the fourth quarter Staubach gave way to Craig Morton, who got in on the fun with a 20-yard touchdown pass to Lance Alworth, making the score 52–10; mercifully, it ended there. Davis had re-injured his ankle in the fourth quarter, and Namath was pressed back into duty with 6:58 remaining, but he merely presided over a handful of futile running plays, finishing the game with only one completed pass in five attempts for 20 yards, and an interception.

After the game Dallas coach Tom Landry, respectful of the Jets' feelings, was most gracious in his comments. "We were ready and it was difficult for the Jets to get as high for the game as we were," he said. "Joe gave them a little something to work on but he was off. We respect him very much."[16]

Week 13 — Sunday, December 12, 1971
Shea Stadium, New York (attendance: 63,175)

The Jets returned to Shea in week 13 to host the New England Patriots. With a 5–7 record, New England was a game up on the Jets in the division. Not that it mattered: neither team was going anywhere. Although the Patriots had beaten the Jets 20–0 earlier in the season, Namath himself hadn't lost to them since November 28, 1965, a string of nine games.

The Jets received the opening kickoff and methodically moved downfield, but after a 14-play drive that ate up 7:31 of the opening quarter they only came away with three points when the drive stalled and Bobby Howfield kicked a 16-yard field goal.

In the second period the Jets missed an opportunity to build on their lead when Namath threw 29 yards to Eddie Bell, who then fumbled the ball away at the New England four-yard line. Another significant pass in the second quarter was an eight-yarder to Don Maynard. It wasn't a big gainer, but it was made significant by the fact that it was Maynard's 600th career reception. Only Raymond Berry had more (631). Otherwise, Namath was intercepted twice in the half, and the only other scoring was a 34-yard field goal by New England that tied the game seven seconds before the end of the second quarter.

The Patriots received the second half kick and began from their own 20, but a holding penalty pushed them back half the distance to their goal. On the next play Carl Garrett ran off right tackle, and the ball was jarred loose by Al Atkinson. Defensive back Phil Wise gathered the fumble in at the five and carried it to the one before being tackled, and on the next play John Riggins scored the first rushing touchdown of his professional career. It was only 25 seconds into the third period, and the Jets were now up 10–3.

The Patriots failed to move the ball on their next series, and when they were forced to punt Tom Janik's kick was partially blocked by Steve Tannen, enabling the Jets to take possession at the New England 35. A 15-yard holding penalty set the Jets back, but a five-yard run by Riggins and a six-yard pass from Namath to Riggins got the Jets close enough for Howfield to kick his longest field goal of the season, a 42-yarder that gave the Jets a 13–3 lead.

Namath threw only one pass in the second half, as he seemed content to sit on the lead and have the ground game eat away at the clock. New England did manage a field goal in the fourth quarter to cut the Jets' lead to 13–6, but they could get no closer. It was Namath's first victory since beating the Patriots on September 27, 1970.

Afterwards, Namath and New England rookie quarterback Jim Plunkett had high praise one for the other. Namath complimented Plunkett's strong arm and said that he had a lot of potential. Namath otherwise said that he envied Plunkett for his knees.[17] Why wouldn't he? After all, Plunkett was New England's leading rusher in the game, gaining 52 yards on seven rushes.

Plunkett envied Namath's, well, Namathness, saying: "Namath has some kind of magic with that team. When he is in there he is in complete control and they respond better for him than anyone else."[18] Namath was seven of 12 for 95 yards, with two interceptions.

Week 14 — Sunday, December 19, 1971
Shea Stadium, New York (attendance: 63,151)

The Jets finished their season at home against the Cincinnati Bengals. Although they had won the AFC's Central Division in 1970, the Bengals had fallen considerably in 1971, and by week 14 they were only sporting a 4–9 record. While the Jets were in a meaningless struggle for third place with New England in the East, the Bengals were hoping that a victory would at least pull them out of the cellar in the Central.

It was a chilly 29 degrees at game time, and the Jets received the opening kickoff. But just two plays into the game, John Riggins fumbled the ball and Ken Riley recovered for the Bengals at the New York 30-yard line. Six plays later, the Bengals went up 7–0 when quarterback Virgil Carter hit Chip Myers with a five-yard touchdown pass.

The Jets' second series didn't go well either. Namath tried to hit Don Maynard but was intercepted by Lemar Parrish at the Cincinnati 40 — two possessions, two turnovers. The Bengals failed to move the ball this time, however, and were forced to punt. Under a very heavy rush, punter Dave Lewis was unable to get the kick off and wound up being swarmed and taken down at the Cincinnati 26. From there, it was only a matter of five plays for the Jets to tie the game up on a one-yard run by Emerson Boozer.

The Jets would pull away in the second period, driving 80 yards in seven plays early in the quarter and scoring on an 11-yard pass from Namath to Rich Caster. On their next series, the Jets went nearly as far on a single play. From the 26-yard line, Namath threw long to Maynard down the right sideline. Maynard cut back inside on Parrish to make the catch, and Parrish fell down in trying to adjust. Maynard made the catch at the Cincinnati 40 and ran the distance, untouched, to put the Jets up 21–7. At 74 yards, it was the Jets' longest offensive play since the 1968 season. The Jets then added to their lead late in the quarter when they drove 60 yards in nine plays, going up 28–7 on a seven-yard TD run by Boozer with 56 seconds remaining in the half.

The Bengals started the second half like they might make a game of it. After receiving the kick, Cincinnati was forced to punt but got a new lease on the series when the Jets were flagged for roughing the punter. The Bengals wound up driving 70 yards in nine plays, and scored on a six-yard run by Fred Willis that halved the Jets' lead to 28–14. But the Bengals could otherwise do no damage, and late in the third period Cliff McClain put the game out of reach for the Jets with a 63-yard TD run. It was the Jets' longest run of the season, and at that time the longest touchdown run in the team's history.

It was well into the fourth quarter when rookie quarterback Ken Anderson got the Bengals moving again, directing them 75 yards in 11 plays to score on a nine-yard pass to Bruce Coslet, making the final 35–21 in New York's favor. Despite their poor record, it was the most points the Bengals had given up all season. The Jets' 21-point burst in the second period was also the most that Cincinnati had given up in a single quarter all year.

Namath's final numbers read nine of 15 for 164 yards, two TDs and one interception. The team's performance gave Ewbank hope for the 1972 season. "When we get our guys together you see what happens," he said. "We move the ball. I hope the victory is the start of a long string for next year."[19]

During the last four games of the season Namath had completed 28 of 59 passes, only a 47.5 completion percentage, but still far and away superior to the Jets' other passers. In the first four games Woodall had only completed 43.3 percent of his passes, and Davis, who played most of the season, only had a 40.5 completion percentage. More than that, Namath's 537 yards passing was well ahead of Woodall's 395 (also in four games) and just under Davis' seven-game total of 624. As was his custom, Namath had more interceptions than touchdowns, six to five.

But there were flashes of the old Namath, primarily in the game with San Francisco, but also in the 74-yard TD pass to Maynard against Cincinnati in the season closer. If the team could only stay healthy —*if Namath could stay healthy*— then there was the chance of a return to glory. After two severely truncated seasons, it would be interesting to see what Namath could do with a full schedule of games.

10

The 1972 Season

"We called this press conference to advise you that Joe has agreed to stay on the ticket."[1] So said New York Jets president Phil Iselin at a Hofstra press conference on July 31, 1972. Namath had reported to camp a week late, bringing with him news that, as his prior contract was up, he would not be participating in any exhibition games until he had a new deal. More than that, any new deal he made should establish him as the highest paid player in the league because, as he put it, "I can play better than anyone else."[2] People can certainly debate that point, but there is far less room to dispute Namath's importance to both his team and the league in terms of commerce, for which one could easily argue his being deserving of a high reward.

There was talk that a trade was in the offing with the Los Angeles Rams, and Namath's agent, Jimmy Walsh, arrived at Hofstra to make it known that he was prepared to pull Namath from camp unless a contract could be agreed to. The next day Namath got his wish, for while he, Iselin, and Ewbank were all predictably mum on the details of the contract, the figure that was being circulated as having come from reliable sources was $500,000 for two years. At $250,000 per year, he was indeed the highest paid player in the league.

All parties seemed satisfied. At the press conference in the Hofstra dining hall, Iselin to his right, Ewbank to his left — both beaming — Namath said that he was feeling mentally sharp and his knees were feeling fine. But more than anything, he said, he was glad to have the contract out of the way so that he could concentrate on getting ready for the season. Iselin obviously felt that he had done the right thing. "Joe started with New York," he said. "He belongs to a New York team, and here's where he'll stay."[3]

Namath's teammates all seemed genuinely pleased that he was with them again. Even linebacker Al Atkinson, who two years earlier had left camp for a week in disgust over Namath's attitude, now said that the team's offense responded more positively to Namath's presence. Not that everyone was convinced Namath was worth the money. He had, after all, played little the previous two seasons, and there was some question as to his durability. Namath himself dismissed such talk, pointing out that he had played five straight seasons (1965–1969) without missing a game. "I know it's attitude that counts in this game," he said, "and when the season starts my attitude will be good, like it's always been."[4]

Namath liked the team's chances for going all the way in 1972, saying they could do it if the team managed to avoid the crippling injuries that had been so devastating in 1970 and '71. But this was not the Super Bowl team; in fact, only 15 players remained from the 1968 roster. Namath still had much the same offensive line, consisting of John Schmitt, Winston Hill, Dave Herman, and Randy Rasmussen, and he still had Don Maynard to throw to and Emerson Boozer in the backfield. Technically Matt Snell was still with them as well, but he had played even less than Namath in the previous two seasons, first missing almost all of the 1970 season with a torn Achilles, and then suffering a knee injury during the 1971 preseason. In 1972 Snell was still trying to come back. It wasn't going to happen.

On defense, Gerry Philbin and John Elliot were still on the front line, and linebackers Atkinson, Larry Grantham, Ralph Baker, and Paul Crane were still there. As usual, the defensive secondary was the big question mark. John Dockery, Steve Tannen, and Earlie Thomas were returning to the secondary, and there was also second-year man Chris Farasopoulos at free safety, and Gus Hollomon at strong safety. The Jets would also have defensive backs W.K. Hicks, Rich Sowells, and Phil Wise.

There was one very notable change on offense: tight end Pete Lammons had been sent packing and would wind up in Green Bay. Rich Caster would make the switch from receiver to tight end, and Maynard and Eddie Bell would be the starting receivers. Namath also had a new target in rookie receiver Jerome Barkum, who, like Caster, had come from Jackson State.

For their first preseason game the Jets traveled to Jacksonville, Florida, to play the San Francisco 49ers; a crowd of 42,920 packed the Gator Bowl on August 5 for the exhibition. After putting no points on the board in the first quarter, Namath gave way to Bob Davis in the second period, and with the Jets trailing 10–0, Davis hit Eddie Bell with a 30-yard TD pass to pull the Jets to within three points at the half. In the third period Bobby Howfield kicked a 40-yard field goal to tie the score at 10, where it stayed until the final minute of the game, when John Riggins ran off left tackle for a 26-yard touchdown with 33 seconds remaining. Linebacker Skip Vanderbundt was blitzing on the play and the Jets had guessed correctly, running a trap that went for the score to give the Jets a 17–10 victory. In his brief appearance, Namath was four of seven for 49 yards. Snell's appearance was even briefer, carrying the ball once for a single yard in the opening period.

The Jets were then off to Seattle to play the Pittsburgh Steelers the following Saturday. Namath played a full half this time, but the results were not terribly impressive. Under a very heavy rush throughout the first half (primarily from Joe Greene), Namath only completed three of his 15 passes for 55 yards (his completions all being to Eddie Bell). He left the game at halftime with the Jets trailing 16–3. Pittsburgh had opened the scoring in the first quarter with a 26-yard touchdown pass from Terry Bradshaw to Dave Smith, but the game was otherwise a contest of field goals, with Roy Gerela hitting four kicks and Bobby Howfield giving the Jets their only points with his 42-yarder in the second quarter. Pittsburgh won easily, 22–3. "The Steelers have a good team," said Ewbank, "but we just couldn't contain Greene. At least Namath got out of here alive."[5] Having gotten the contract he wanted in late July, people would be justified in wondering at that point if Namath was really worth it. After the first two preseason appearances Namath made, it must have seemed difficult to justify the expenditure. But then, it was only preseason.

As it tended to do, the annual August meeting of the Jets and Giants in New Haven at the Yale Bowl promised to make preseason much more interesting. It was to be the fourth showdown between New York's professional football teams in New Haven, and their fifth meeting overall. The Jets had won two of the previous three preseason games, while the Giants had won the only regular season game. Namath had only appeared in the first clash between the teams, leading the Jets to an easy 37–14 triumph in 1969. The Giants had won both games in 1970, beating the Jets 28–24 in the preseason and then besting them 22–10 at Shea during the season. Namath had missed the preseason match in 1970 due to his late arrival at training camp, and then missed the regular season game with a broken wrist. He also missed the 1971 preseason game due to his knee surgery, but that didn't stop him from contributing to that event's hype by telling reporters from his hospital bed that the Jets would kill the Giants. They did, 27–14. Now Namath was amping things up again, telling reporters that the Giants were a terrible team and that the Jets would defeat them easily. Giants coach Alex Webster brushed the remarks off, saying that it was just Namath doing his thing. Some of the players weren't as nonchalant about it: defensive end Jack Gregory, for instance, said that Namath was a marked man. As always, Ewbank played it all down. "We just want to get Joe in there long enough to get his timing down," he said.[6] The game would perhaps be the most interesting showdown between the cross-town rivals up to then.

The Giants made it interesting from the start, with Ron Johnson putting them up 7–0 on just the second play from scrimmage when he ran 63 yards for a touchdown. The Jets then took command with 17 unanswered points in the second quarter. Early in the period they went 80 yards on just three plays, the final being a 45-yard pass from Namath to Bell that tied the score. After taking the lead with a 14-yard field goal, the Jets then took a 10-point lead into halftime when Namath threw a 20-yard touchdown to Maynard.

But Giants' quarterback Randy Johnson opened the third quarter by driving his team 80 yards to score in eight plays, the payoff coming on a 12-yard throw to tight end Bob Tucker. It was the beginning of a 21-point explosion by the Giants in the third period. Down 17–14, Johnson hit Tucker with a second touchdown pass later in the quarter, this time from 21 yards, to put the Giants up 21–17, and Johnson would then score himself on a five-yard run that gave the Giants a 28–17 lead. The Giants' very productive third period was helped considerably by that old Namath bugaboo, interceptions.

The Jets fired back quickly after that, with Namath hurling an 87-yard touchdown to Maynard to cut the Giants' lead to 28–24 before the end of the third period. Then, just 1:32 into the fourth quarter, the Jets took a 31–28 lead on a two-yard touchdown run by Cliff McClain. Amid all the theatrics Namath had been making things very interesting, throwing five interceptions that helped the Giants stay in the game. The Jets' defense managed an impressive goal line stand and held the Giants to a 10-yard field goal with 7:31 left in the game, but it still tied the score at 31. It wasn't until the final minute that either team mounted another threat. The Giants had a chance to win the game with a 37-yard field goal with only 52 seconds left to play, but Pete Gogolak missed it and the game ended in a tie.

Given Namath's comments about them earlier in the week, the 31–31 tie could only be seen as a moral victory for the Giants. Namath had a laugh about it after the game. "I guess you'd have to say they're not terrible," he said. "They played a hell of a game."[7] Aside from those five interceptions, so did Namath. He completed 12 of 24 for 340 yards and three touchdowns. *But those interceptions!* That much of Namath's game hadn't changed, anyway.

The Jets' next exhibition game was a return to the site of the worst beating in franchise history. In week 12 of 1971—Namath's second game back after returning from knee surgery—the Jets had gone to Irving, Texas, and been beaten handily, 52–10, by the Dallas Cowboys. Namath was pulled from the game in the first quarter with the Jets already trailing 28–0. To make it all the more humiliating, the game was played on a Saturday and was therefore televised nationally. Now the Jets were heading back to Texas Stadium for a Saturday night meeting with the Cowboys on August 26. This game would also be televised nationally by NBC. It may have been a mere exhibition, but Dallas coach Tom Landry was not one to take preseason lightly. He maintained that it was important to win those games in order to carry that momentum into the regular season, and the Cowboys brought a 14-game winning streak into their meeting with the Jets, including winning the Super Bowl (in which they beat Miami), and going undefeated in their first four preseason games of 1972.

Ewbank, on the other hand, was more concerned with getting the bugs worked out than winning a no-count game, and Namath was coming into the game with a weak 42.2 completion percentage, so there were definitely bugs to work out. For one thing, Caster was already out with injuries, so the tight end position was uncertain. And then there was Jerome Barkum, the Jets' first round draft pick. He was only now getting started, having held out for more money through the first weeks of camp. He and Namath had yet to get accustomed to one another on pass routes. "Offensively, we're still worried about our timing," Ewbank said.[8] Ewbank had Namath scheduled to play the first half.

It was a sellout crowd of 65,000 at Texas Stadium that watched the Cowboys take the opening kickoff and get out to an early 7–0 lead when Craig Morton hit Ron Sellers with a 54-yard touchdown pass. The Jets got a field goal to cut the lead to 7–3 after one period, and in the second quarter Namath and the Jets took charge. After another field goal cut the Dallas lead to 7–6, Namath engineered two second-quarter touchdown drives, one ending with a one-yard touchdown run by Boozer, the second with a one-yard touchdown by Riggins that came with 14 seconds left in the half. Namath left the game with the Jets leading 20–7 at halftime. He looked very sharp, completing five of seven passes for 74 yards. He had also thrown a long TD pass that was nullified by a penalty.

The second half was a different story. The Cowboys got a couple third-quarter field goals to cut the Jets' lead to 20–13 before Al Woodall pitched a 13-yard touchdown to Barkum early in the fourth that increased the Jets' lead to 27–13. But the fourth quarter belonged to Dallas running back Mike Montgomery, who was playing for the injured Calvin Hill. Montgomery capped two Dallas drives with one-yard touchdown runs to tie the game at 27 with 3:24 left to play. Cliff Harris then intercepted a Woodall pass to Barkum and ran it back 37 yards, giving the Cowboys the ball at the New York 12-yard line. Two plays later Morton tossed the winning touchdown pass, a 12-yarder to — who else — Montgomery. The final was 34–27 in Dallas' favor.

But the Jets' fourth-quarter collapse only managed to accentuate Namath's importance to the team: they really did seem lost without him in the game. "With ole Broadway Joe at the throttle," wrote F.M. White in *The Odessa American*, "the Jets blew the Cowboys off the field.... You may not agree with Namath's lifestyle but watching him in action confirms that he may be the best passing quarterback who ever played the game."[9]

As impressive as Namath had been in the Dallas game, his performance the following Saturday afternoon against the Atlanta Falcons at Georgia Tech's Grant Field was a different story entirely. Again playing the first half, Namath could only lead the team to a single field goal while completing just five of 14 throws for 58 yards. Even so, the Jets took a 3–0 lead into halftime, as the Falcons were struggling themselves. Atlanta was getting its first look at their number two draft pick, Heisman Trophy winning Auburn quarterback Pat Sullivan, who played the entire game and managed only six completions in 27 attempts, with four interceptions.

The Falcons tied the game with a field goal in the third quarter, but Bobby Howfield kicked two more in the fourth quarter to give the Jets a 9–3 victory. Even in preseason, there ought to be at least *one* touchdown.

With a 2–2–1 preseason record, the Jets traveled to San Diego to close out their exhibition schedule against the Chargers on September 9. It was like old times, harkening back to the AFL days as both Namath and San Diego's John Hadl quarterbacked their teams through the first half. Hadl took the Chargers 78 yards to score on their initial series, with Lee White's one-yard touchdown run giving them a 7–0 lead. It wasn't until the second quarter that the Jets drew even when Namath drove them 75 yards to a touchdown, hitting tight end Wayne Stewart from nine yards out to tie the score. The two teams would exchange field goals later in the quarter to make the score 10–10 at halftime.

The score may have been even, but Hadl's numbers certainly bested Namath's. Hadl completed 11 of 13 passes for 177 yards: Namath was four of 10 for 57 yards. Both sat out the second half. San Diego backup quarterback Wayne Clark ran for a three-yard touchdown in the third to put the Chargers up 17–10, but in the fourth the Jets tied it again when Bob Davis threw a 23-yard touchdown to Bell. Late in the game the Chargers went back up 20–17 on a 38-yard field goal, but Davis drove the Jets from their own 35 to the San Diego 27 in six plays to give Bobby Howfield a chance to tie the game in the game's final 10 seconds. Howfield put it through from 33 yards, and the game ended a 20–20 tie. The Jets thereby finished the preseason with a portentous 2–2–2 record.

The Jets felt good about their chances as the season was set to begin. "If we don't get any key injuries we're going to be tough this year," said Riggins. "I'd be real disappointed if we didn't get into the playoffs."[10]

Namath said he was ready for the season, but he sounded ready pretty early on. After his impressive half of play against Dallas he had said: "This ball club showed what it could do in the first half and I don't think there's any doubt the Jets are capable of winning big."[11]

Expectations seemed high, and there was a lot of talk of winning a title. Given the misfortunes of the two prior seasons, most were quick to qualify such talk by saying the obvious, that it all hinged on the team staying healthy. With that, it was time to start winning — big.

Week 1 — Sunday, September 17, 1972
War Memorial Stadium, Buffalo (attendance: 46,206)

As was the custom with the Jets since playing at Shea Stadium, they would begin the season on the road so as not to conflict with the New York Mets' schedule. The Jets opened the 1972 season against the Bills in Buffalo, and they quickly looked to be living up to expectations. Establishing their running game from the start, the Jets went downfield to score 6:31 into the game on a 16-yard run by John Riggins.

The Bills failed to mount a threat, and the Jets 7–0 lead quickly grew to 14–0 at 8:20 of the first period when Chris Farasopoulos returned a Buffalo punt 65 yards for a touchdown. Toward the end of the first quarter the Jets were driving again, and as the period came to a close they were on the Buffalo 12-yard line. On the very first play of the second quarter, Namath tossed a pass to Emerson Boozer in the deep left corner of the end zone, and just five seconds into the period the Jets were up 21–0.

Buffalo finally found their feet and produced their first points of the game when they drove 67 yards in eight plays, scoring 6:44 into the quarter on a 38-yard pass from Dennis Shaw to J.D. Hill that cut the Jets' lead to 21–7. The momentum looked to have swung in Buffalo's favor, as cornerback Alvin Wyatt then intercepted Namath at the New York 38, but on the next play Shaw returned the favor and was intercepted by Al Atkinson at the Jets' 29. Atkinson returned the ball seven yards to the 36, and the Jets then seized control again. They marched 64 yards on 10 straight running plays to go ahead 28–7 on a 15-yard touchdown run by Boozer just before the end of the half.

Namath had thrown little, but then, with the running game doing so well, he didn't have to. Riggins had carried the load with 16 rushes in the first half. In the third quarter the Jets stuck with that plan, and Bobby Howfield kicked a 35-yard field goal that put New York up 31–7. The Bills did put together a drive nearing the end of the third quarter, and scored on a bit of razzle dazzle when O.J. Simpson ran an option and tossed a 21-yard touchdown to Hill that closed the gap to 31–14. But the Jets closed the door on Buffalo's comeback hopes 2:09 into the fourth quarter when Boozer scored his third touchdown of the game, going in from a yard out to increase the New York lead to 37–14.

The two teams exchanged field goals as the quarter wore on, making the score 41–17, and Buffalo managed one more touchdown with just 1:16 left in the game, but it did little to make the loss respectable for them. The final of 41–24 seemed to confirm Namath's assertion during the preseason that the New York Jets were a team that could win big.

Namath's numbers weren't very big, however, completing only five of 14 passes, but then again he did rack up 113 yards in those few completions (with one TD and a matching interception). But impressive stats or not, there was no doubt in the mind of Buffalo coach Lou Saban as to who was doing the driving. "Joe makes it go," said Saban. "He drives the Jets by his presence. He's enough to get them going."[12]

It's also true that the Jets seldom needed to pass in the game. Riggins had the first 100-yard game of his career, running for 125 yards on 26 carries, while Boozer ran for 50 more on 13. "We now have a fine running game to go along with our passing game," said Ewbank.[13]

It was lucky for Namath that the running game had been doing so well, since somehow his knee braces had been left behind and he had to play the first half without them while the team had some flown in. Having to throw so little, he didn't take a hit in the first half. After the braces arrived and he put them on for the second half, he got hit for the first time when a safety blitz took him down.

Other than the high score posted by the offense, the defense also played well, despite giving up 24 points. They had intercepted Shaw four times, linebacker Ralph Baker grabbing one and cornerback Steve Tannen stealing two. The passing game may have been less than amazing, but Namath would certainly make up for that the following week: he was about to have the greatest passing day of his career.

Week 2 — Sunday, September 24, 1972
Memorial Stadium, Baltimore (attendance: 56,626)

Since beating the Baltimore Colts in Super Bowl III in January of 1969, the Jets had lost to them four consecutive times following the AFL-NFL merger in 1970. Namath had only played in one of those four losses — the first, coming in week five of the 1970 season — and he broke his wrist in that game. As the Jets traveled to Baltimore for their week two game with the Colts, it was to be the first time Namath would play in Baltimore's fabled Memorial Stadium. He would certainly make it one to remember.

What was to be a classic shootout between Namath and the legendary Johnny Unitas actually started slowly, as both teams tried to get the ground game in motion, with very little success. Namath's first pass on the Jets' initial series floated harmlessly past its target; in fact, it was all Don Maynard could do to get a hand on the ball as it fluttered over his head and out of bounds. But on the Jets' second series, things got more interesting. After hitting Eddie Bell with a short pass, Namath went back to Bell three plays later, this time deep down the right sideline. The ball was underthrown, which actually worked in Bell's favor: when he stopped to make the catch, safety Jerry Logan tried to stop as well but slipped and went to the ground. The other safety, Rick Volk, had come over to assist, but when Bell made the catch at the Baltimore 36 and started running all Volk could do was make a diving attempt at a tackle at the 30. Otherwise, Bell had little trouble outrunning cornerback Charlie Stukes to the end zone, with Stukes also making a diving stab at a tackle at the five-yard line. The play covered 65 yards, and when Bobby Howfield missed the extra point the Jets were left with a six-point lead.

It was nearing the end of the first period when the Colts put together a drive that produced their first points. From the New York 40, Unitas handed to Tom Matte, who ran a sweep to the right. Matte suddenly stopped and tossed a lateral back to Unitas — it was the flea-flicker, the play that Baltimore had failed to cash in on in the Super Bowl, despite having completely fooled the Jets. The Jets were likewise caught unaware this time. Although Matte's lateral was high, Unitas did a good job of one-handing it and bringing it back down, and he then threw a pass down the left sideline to Sam Havrilak, who had a good few steps on the coverage. Havrilak caught the ball at the 10-yard line and easily went in to score, and with the extra point the Colts were up 7–6.

When the Jets got the ball again they ended the first quarter on a sour note, with Namath being blindsided at the 24 by defensive end Roy Hilton and coughing up the ball. Tackle Fred Miller recovered for Baltimore at the New York 27, and the Colts started the second quarter with a plum of an opportunity. But after getting inside the 10, they failed to punch it in and had to settle for a 14-yard field goal. Still, it increased their lead to 10–6.

The Jets were having trouble getting in gear again, and when the Colts got the ball back they chipped their way downfield to the New York 18. But after Mark Lomas sacked Unitas back at the 24 and Rich Sowells broke up a pass to Cotton Speyrer at the goal line, the Colts again had to settle for three on a 32-yard field goal.

Trailing 13–6 with just over four minutes left in the half, Namath tried to get something started and threw to Rich Caster for 10 yards to the New York 33. John Riggins had told Namath he could get behind linebacker Ted Hendricks on a pass route, so on the next play Namath sent Riggins out of the backfield. Riggins did indeed get by Hendricks, and ran up the left sideline. With the six-foot-six Hilton in his face, Namath fired the ball. Riggins had to slow down slightly to make the catch at the Baltimore 40, but he gathered it in and defensive back Lonnie Hepburn gave chase. The big fullback showed impressive speed, and had no trouble leaving Hepburn in the dust on his way to the end zone. The 67-yard touchdown tied the score at 13.

That lead was short lived, however, as Don McCauley took the kickoff at the Baltimore seven-yard line and proceeded to run through a crowd right up the middle of the field, and went 93 yards for a touchdown. Steve Tannen made a surprisingly feeble attempt at a tackle at the Baltimore 34, merely throwing an elbow at McCauley and whiffing badly, failing to even slow him down. The last Jet with a chance at bringing McCauley down was Matt Snell, relegated to special teams, who made a desperate dive for him at the three-yard line. The score put Baltimore back up 20–13.

Namath fired back quickly, launching a 40-yard strike to Bell that placed the Jets at the Baltimore 28, and then on the next play throwing a touchdown to Maynard, who had found the seam between safeties Logan and Volk. It was a perfect throw, a bullet rifled with pinpoint accuracy over Maynard's shoulder as he was crossing the goal line. Again, the score was tied, but once more it wouldn't be for long.

When the Colts began their next series from their 20, Unitas was sacked by Gerry Philbin and wound up fumbling the ball. Mark Lomas recovered for the Jets at the Baltimore 10-yard line, and on the next play Namath went for the throat. Dropping back to pass, Namath seemed to have tight end Rich Caster in mind all along. After shuffling to his right, Namath fired a pass to Caster in the end zone. With Logan to Caster's right, Namath threw to the left side, and Caster was thereby able to screen Logan out and make the catch. With the extra point the Jets had recaptured the lead at 27–20 with just over a minute to play in the half.

But Unitas saw that as time enough to do some damage, and after throwing short to Matte he went long down the left sideline to Havrilak, who had beaten Earlie Thomas by a good five yards. If the ball had more on it Havrilak would have scored easily, but he had to slow down considerably to wait on it, allowing Thomas to catch up. Havrilak made the catch by turning awkwardly and almost losing his balance, and Thomas was able to nudge him out of bounds at the New York four-yard line. That was unfortunate for Baltimore, as they failed to take it in from there. A penalty set them back to the 19 and they wound up sending Jim O'Brien in to try a 27-yard field goal, which he missed. The Jets kept their seven-point lead at halftime.

The scores were coming at a dizzying pace in the latter part of the second quarter — four touchdowns within three minutes — and Namath had already thrown for 281 yards and four touchdowns, so it was not surprising that things calmed as the third period got underway. The ground game for both teams was still having trouble finding wheels, so Namath continued pitching to Bell. After throwing 22 yards to Bell to the Baltimore 23 Namath came back to him two plays later, but that wound up being his lone mistake of the afternoon. Actually it may have been less his mistake than someone else's. Maynard, who was one to break patterns, seems to have led his defenders into the area, and when Namath threw down the left sideline he wound up throwing into a cluster of blue jerseys.

But other than squandering an opportunity, the interception did no damage as Baltimore failed to move the ball and quickly surrendered it back.

On the Jets' next series, Namath again tried to go long to Bell down the left sideline, but the pass was broken up by Hepburn at the Baltimore 10-yard line. All of the long passes seemed to have loosened the defense up a bit, however, and Riggins suddenly began to advance the ball on the ground. Gaining 43 yards on six runs in the series, Riggins was finally stopped on a third down play by Volk. Reminiscent of the Super Bowl, Volk took a knee to the head in making the tackle and wound up facedown on the ground and semi-conscious. In the Super Bowl he had much the same experience when he suffered a concussion on the game's second play after trying to bring down Snell and likewise taking a knee to the head. In this instance his efforts stopped the Jets from advancing further, and forced them to settle for a 14-yard field goal and a 30–20 lead.

The ensuing kickoff would be the final play of the third quarter. Taking the ball a good five yards deep in the end zone, Bruce Laird ran it back up the right sideline all the way to the Baltimore 44 before being brought down from behind by Snell. It gave the Colts a good starting point as the fourth quarter got underway.

In the fourth quarter the Baltimore running game also began to grind out yardage, and Tom Matte and Don Nottingham pounded downfield until McCauley took it over from the one-yard line to cut the Jets' lead to three points. But if the Colts were hoping for a momentum shift they missed their guess, for they hardly had time to catch their breath before the Jets went back up by 10.

After receiving the kick the Jets started at their own 21, and on the very first play Namath went back to pass and fired the ball from his own 10-yard line down the middle of the field to Caster at the New York 45. The pass was behind Caster, who had to turn around to catch it, and Hepburn came very close to getting a hand on it. But when Hepburn missed batting the ball and Caster grabbed it, the speedy tight end turned and took off running and there was no one back there to catch him. He took it the distance, 79 yards for a score that put the Jets back up by 10 at 37–27.

With 7:26 left in the game Unitas had ample time to engineer a good drive, and he worked the Colts downfield with passes to Speyrer and Mitchell before capping the drive with a 21-yard touchdown pass to Matte. Again the New York lead was down to three points, but once more the Colts scarcely had time to celebrate.

On the sideline, awaiting his chance to go back on the field after the kick, Namath was pondering whether or not to go for the jugular again on first down. There were six minutes, 12 seconds left in the game and he felt skeptical about the chances of using up that much time to protect a three-point lead. But he also knew that going for it all could backfire. There was something that helped make up his mind.

When the Jets received the kick and began at their own 20, Namath saw an unsoiled jersey joining the Baltimore huddle. With all of the firebombs Namath had been tossing — 65 yards, 67 yards, 79 yards — Baltimore coach Don McCafferty decided to send some fresh reinforcements into the secondary in Rex Kern — Namath singled Kern out immediately. Hoping to get some pressure on Namath, the Colts sent linebackers Ray May and Mike Curtis blitzing, but Caster came off the line quickly and broke left toward the sideline — right toward Kern. Again dropping back to his 10-yard line, Namath whipped a perfect pass to Caster, who again caught it at the New York 45. The ball whizzed over Kern's outstretched hand, over Caster's shoulder, and right into his hands. Caster never had to break stride in making the catch, and Kern therefore never had a prayer of catching him. As Caster raced past the Jets' bench, half of the players on the sideline were jubilantly waving him by and celebrating. The other half were the defensive unit — they were moaning. Having not had enough time to sit down and get a moment's rest, they would now have to go back out again after the kickoff. The Colts still had some five minutes left, but this time they could do nothing — they were spent. The Jets scored their first regular season victory over the Colts, 44–34.

With just 15 completions in his 28 attempts, Namath had thrown for an incredible 496 yards, which was good enough to place as the third highest total in NFL history at that time, and his six touchdowns were one shy of the NFL record — Baltimore had only given up nine touchdown passes during the entire 1971 season! Although his numbers paled in comparison to Namath's, Unitas had a fine day himself, throwing for 376 yards and two touchdowns. Unitas' 26 completions were a Baltimore record, believe it or not, and the 872 combined passing yards between the teams set an NFL single-game record that stood for years. The Jets' 573 total yards also set a team record. As for the Colts, it was the first time in team history that they had scored as much as 34 points and still lost the game.

Hilton, recalling the touchdown to Riggins, said that when he hit Namath he was sure that he was just dumping the ball off. But he turned to see the play going the distance, 67 yards for a score. "It takes something out of you," Hilton said.[14]

The conventional wisdom was that it was impossible to throw against the zone defense with such consistently incredible results. "I've never felt that way," said Ewbank. "You've just got to read the zone and Joe is the master of reading it."[15] *Time* magazine called it "a game that prospective quarterbacks should have watched with the same solemn intensity that surgical residents devote to watching a kidney transplant."[16]

Unitas seemed to think it was all a matter of luck, saying that you can beat the zone if you throw it up for grabs and catch a break, which is what he said Namath had done. If that were the case, it would have made Namath the luckiest passer in history. The hell you say. Unitas did qualify his remark, however, by adding that Namath threw well.[17]

Through the first two games of the season, the Jets were certainly validating Namath's pre-season statement that they were a team that could win big. They had scored more than 40 points in both their games, winning in outrageous, delirious, even ridiculous fashion. Could it be that after four years Namath and the Jets were Super Bowl bound again? They certainly looked to be for real. Typically, Namath was the least impressed by his incredible performance. "I know it sounds dumb, but I've had better days throwing the ball," he said. "Sometimes I threw it short, sometimes I was long and sometimes where I wanted to be."[18]

Week 3 — Sunday, October 1, 1972
The Astrodome, Houston (attendance: 51,423)

At 2–0, the Jets went to Houston in week three sharing first place in the AFC East with Miami. They were greeted at the Astrodome by the second largest home crowd in Houston history, 51,423 strong. The Oilers being 0–2, the Jets were favored, and with Houston having been blown out 30–17 by Denver and 34–13 by Miami, the Jets should have had no trouble with them. Luckily for Houston, the Jets were about to have one of those philanthropic days of theirs.

It all started well enough for New York, as they drove downfield on their first series and scored on a 26-yard pass from Namath to Jerome Barkum. Eddie Bell had caught a 32-yard pass in the drive, but had to leave the game upon being thrown down onto the wonderful concrete floor of the Astrodome — *but, hey, the footing was so good on that stuff*! Barkum came in to replace Bell and wound up with his first touchdown in the pros. He caught Namath's pass at the Houston 14, and both John Charles and Benny Johnson whiffed on tackle attempts, as Barkum spun around and out of the grasp of both defensive backs and took it in.

On the Jets' next series, they went all the way downfield only to run out of gas at the Houston one-yard line. Bobby Howfield then kicked an eight-yard field goal to give the Jets a 10–0 lead after one quarter of play. Two possessions, two scores — so far, so good. But the Oilers came to life in the second quarter, as quarterback Dan Pastorini took them 75 yards to score on a one-yard run by Willie Rodgers. Pastorini hit four of six passes on the drive to account for 55 of those 75 yards.

The Oilers then took a 14–10 lead when Pastorini hit Ken Burrough with a 52-yard touchdown. New York managed another field goal to cut the Houston lead to 14–13 at halftime, but in the third quarter the Jets' generous nature sealed their fate. The Oilers would post nine points on three field goals in the period, all set up by turnovers. Cornerback Willie Alexander grabbed a John Riggins fumble at the Houston 46 and ran it back to the New York 26 to set up one three-pointer. Houston's other cornerback, Benny Johnson, gathered a Barkum fumble at the Oilers' 48 and took it back 19 yards to the Jets' 33 to set up another. Namath's receivers seemed to have quite the butter fingers, as another pass went off a receiver's hands and was intercepted by safety Bob Atkins at the New York 24. And that was how Houston notched three field goals in the third quarter.

Trailing 23–13 in the fourth quarter, Namath managed to take the team down to score on a 10-yard pass to Rich Caster that pulled the Jets to within three points, but the Oilers booted another field goal to lead by six late in the game. Still, a touchdown for New York would tie it: add the extra point and they'd win it. In the final two minutes it looked like they would accomplish it, but after driving the Jets deep downfield, Namath was intercepted by Johnson at the Houston six-yard line with 1:21 left in the game. He finished the game 18 of 38 for 301 yards, two TDs and two interceptions.

It was really the kind of loss that the Jets had for some time come to be known for; the Jets had made a habit through the years of giving games away to lesser teams. Even in their Super Bowl season in 1968, they had gifted the Buffalo Bills their only win of the season in week three. Now here they were giving the Oilers what would turn out to be their only win of the season as well — in week three. Could it be that … nah. The shame of it was that this was a game the Jets should have won without much effort. But at least the Oilers had thereby been spared the humiliation of going 0–14 for the year, although they had no way of knowing at the time that this would be their only win of the season. With Miami winning and going to 3–0, the loss dropped the Jets into second place at 2–1.

Week 4 — Sunday, October 8, 1972
Shea Stadium, New York (attendance: 63,841)

The Jets had their home opener in week four as the Miami Dolphins came to Shea. At 3–0, the Dolphins were a game ahead of the Jets in the AFC East. Ewbank was anything but pleased with the defensive secondary, for despite their 2–1 record the Jets came into week four with the lowest-rated secondary in the AFC. The offense had been able to score enough points in the first two games to cover up for that deficiency, but the week three loss to Houston showed that, if the offense was having a sloppy day, it would not always be possible to win by running up an outrageous score. Against a first-place team like Miami, a sloppy performance by the offense coupled with a poor defensive secondary would be a fatal combination.

On the Jets' first series the offense looked fairly sharp, Namath's receivers this time managing to hold on to the ball. Passes of 11 and 15 yards to Don Maynard, and an 11-yard completion to Jerome Barkum helped the Jets drive 65 yards in 11 plays. John Riggins ran for nine yards from the Miami 10, and then Namath handed it to Cliff McClain going off left tackle. For a moment it looked like it had all been for nothing as McClain proceeded to fumble the ball into the end zone, but the Jets caught a break when guard Randy Rasmussen fell on the ball for a New York touchdown.

After that, the Jets' receivers were up to their old tricks, dropping very catchable passes laid right in their hands. Miami quarterback Bob Griese was having better luck, throwing 16 yards to Howard Twilley and 24 yards to Paul Warfield in a 55-yard march that carried over into the second period. From the New York 27 Jim Kiick ran a sweep for 11 yards to the 16, and Griese then hit Twilley in the end zone for the tying score.

Later in the second quarter, Miami drove 62 yards to take the lead. Griese was having his way with the New York secondary, hitting tight end Marv Fleming for 12 yards and Warfield for eight. Then, facing a third-and-six at the New York 24, Griese threw 18 yards to Otto Stowe at the Jets' six-yard line. On the next play, Kiick ran it in for the go-ahead score with 2:32 left in the half.

In the third period Garo Yepremian put the Dolphins up 17–7 with a 27-yard field goal, but the Jets came roaring back when Namath threw 52 yards to Barkum, who was tackled by Dick Anderson at the Miami one-yard line. From there the Jets went backward, however, and wound up settling for an 18-yard field goal that cut the Miami lead to 17–10.

In the fourth quarter the Dolphins began to pull away again, embarking on an eight-play 60-yard drive in which Griese threw 23 yards to Warfield, and was otherwise assisted by a pass interference call on Steve Tannen that put Miami at the New York four-yard line. Two plays later Kiick scored his second touchdown, going in from three yards out to increase the Miami lead to 24–10.

The Jets still had hope when Charlie Leigh fumbled a punt and Wayne Stewart recovered for New York on the Miami 20. It led to a one-yard touchdown run by Emerson Boozer five plays later that drew the Jets to within a touchdown at 24–17, but by the time Yepremian added a late field goal the Jets had run out of gas and lost 27–17.

Completing just under half of his throws (12 of 25 for 156 yards, with one interception), Namath was, as the Associated Press reported, "plagued by receivers who repeatedly dropped easy passes."[19] Griese was better served by his receivers, and graciously told reporters that he didn't consider the New York secondary to be as bad as they were being portrayed. He attributed his success to the fact that the Jets tended to favor one-on-one coverage, which was not easy to do against the likes of Warfield. Perhaps, but the truth is that, other than mental lapses by the New York receivers, the defensive secondary was the major stumbling block to the Jets' success.

The Jets were now 2–2, and a full two games behind the 4–0 Dolphins. The gap would only continue to widen from week to week.

Week 5 — Sunday, October 15, 1972
Schaefer Stadium, Foxboro (attendance: 60,999)

Although they had gotten out of the gate fast with two barnstorming victories on the road, by week five the Jets found themselves on a two-game skid and in a three-way tie with New England and Buffalo for second place in the AFC East. With a victory in week five the Jets could at least pull a game ahead of New England, as they were in Foxboro to face the Patriots at Schaefer Stadium.

With the wind gusting up to 30 mph, the Patriots chose to kick to the Jets after winning the coin toss, opting to have the wind at their backs in the first period. It's a sound tactic; the Jets themselves used it with success in the 1968 AFL Championship game with Oakland. In this instance, however, the Patriots had done themselves no particular favor.

Starting from their own 20, the Jets ate up 7:10 in driving 80 yards to score in 13 plays. Conditions being what they were, Namath was wise in keeping the ball on the ground for 12 of those 13 plays, throwing only when needing to convert a third-down play along the way with a short pass of nine yards to Rich Caster. Otherwise, John Riggins accounted for 50 of the drive's 80 yards, including the six-yard touchdown run that put the Jets up 7–0. The other 21 yards in the series were provided by Emerson Boozer.

Just 24 seconds into the second period, the Patriots got on the board with a 36-yard Charlie Gogolak field goal, and at 6:49 of the period they closed to within a point when Gogolak hit again, this time from 25 yards. But the Jets soon commenced running all over the Patriots, and Boozer scored on a 37-yard jaunt at 10:03 of the quarter to put the Jets up 14–6. Boozer made it look so easy, running through an enormous hole at the line of scrimmage, veering slightly right five yards off the line to dodge a diving attempt at a tackle by safety Rickie Harris, breezing past a splendid block by Rich Caster, who took out defensive back Clarence Scott, and then simply running straight down the middle of the field for the score.

Following a New England punt, the Jets started from their own 27 with 2:40 remaining in the half. Namath began by running Riggins on four consecutive plays, in which the fullback gained 17 yards. Namath then threw nine yards to Eddie Bell to give the Jets a first down at the New England 47. With 48 seconds remaining in the half, Namath called a timeout before resuming by throwing eight yards to Bell to the 39, and then running a draw play to Riggins that gained 12 yards to the 27. Then, with 28 seconds left in the half, Namath threw to Caster in the left corner of the end zone to give the Jets a 21–6 halftime lead.

Namath had only thrown five passes in the half, completing four and having one intercepted by Harris in the first quarter, but even had conditions been better for passing, there was really no need. Riggins and Boozer were finding gaping chasms in the front line to run through, and once in the open field they were making it all look absurdly easy. Riggins had already run for 107 yards in 20 first-half carries, while Boozer had gained 72 yards in just seven rushes.

With the wind at their backs in the third period, the Patriots came out throwing, knowing that it presented their best opportunity to catch up. But it was not until 10:43 into the period that they finally managed to get into the end zone, and even then by way of a run off right tackle by Carl Garrett that went 41 yards for the score. The third period ended with the Jets up 21–13.

Bobby Howfield kicked a 37-yard field goal 1:30 into the fourth quarter to increase the New York lead to 24–13, but theoretically the game was still within reach for New England at that point. Not for long: on the Patriots' first play of their next series, Jim Plunkett was intercepted by linebacker Paul Crane at the New England 27, and a four-yard return gave the New York offense a first down at the 23. From there, it was only a matter of one play as Boozer ran 23 yards for the score 2:09 into the fourth quarter to put the Jets up 31–13. Things got out of hand after that, with Boozer running for his third TD (this time from eight yards), with just under seven minutes left in the game, and Howfield kicking another 37-yard field goal with under two minutes to play. The final read, Jets 41, Patriots 13.

The Jets' 20-point fourth quarter had once more given them a wide margin of victory: in all three of their wins they had scored more than 40 points. Namath had only thrown three passes in the second half, making his game totals a skinny five of eight for 63 yards (one TD and one interception), but he could not have cared less. "When you get Riggins and Boozer rolling," he said, "you're in clover and don't have to put the ball in the air."[20] No doubt. Riggins had run for 168 yards and Boozer for 150. Boozer might have topped 200 but for a holding penalty on Bell that negated a 51-yard run. The 333 total rushing yards was a team record. The Patriots were left shaking their heads. "They pushed me around more than any other two backs this year," Harris said of Riggins and Boozer.[21]

New England coach John Mazur said that the Patriots knew that both Riggins and Boozer were healthy again, so the Patriots came into the game expecting the Jets to run, yet they were virtually powerless to stop them. Mazur was wrong about one thing: neither Riggins nor Boozer were healthy. In fact, they both had problems that should have hindered them considerably. Boozer had both legs taped tightly from the ankles to the hips, nursing a pulled hamstring in one and a charley horse in the other, while Riggins also had to play with one leg heavily wrapped due to a charley horse.

With Miami leading the division at 5–0, the victory kept the Jets within two games of the Dolphins while the Bills, like the Patriots, fell back at 2–3. The Colts were fading fast at 1–4. The 3–2 Jets would be returning home to host the Colts the following week.

Week 6 — Sunday, October 22, 1972
Shea Stadium, New York (attendance: 62,948)

The 1–4 Baltimore Colts came to town with a new coach. The Monday prior, Don McCafferty had been fired and replaced by John Sandusky. Anyone hoping to see another shootout between Namath and Johnny Unitas like the one in Baltimore a month earlier would be very disappointed: Sandusky was sitting Unitas down in favor of Marty Domres, a fourth-year quarterback acquired by the Colts from San Diego.

The Jets were certainly having no trouble getting early leads: for the third consecutive week they took the opening kick and proceeded to drive to a score. Starting from their own 24, they drove to the Baltimore 32, where John Riggins did the rest. Running a sweep left, Riggins eluded the grasp of defensive end Roy Hilton, but was grabbed by linebacker Ray May at the 33-yard line. As May was grappling, trying to get a hold of Riggins to bring him down, safety Rick Volk came in and gave Riggins a shot. The hit spun Riggins around, forcing May to lose his grip and fall to the ground, and freeing Riggins up. After spinning around, Riggins took off running again, eluding the reaching arms of linebacker Mike Curtis and cornerback Lonnie Hepburn and racing down the left sideline. A key block by Eddie Bell on safety Jerry Logan allowed Riggins to go the full 32 yards for the score.

The Colts closed the gap to 7–3 on a 22-yard field goal by Jim O'Brien, but after Mark Lomas recovered a Norm Bulaich fumble at the Baltimore 49, Namath took advantage by quickly hitting Emerson Boozer with a pass that went the distance, 49 yards, for a score. Heading straight up the middle of the field, Boozer caught the ball in stride at the 40-yard line and bolted, untouched, to the end zone, putting the Jets up 14–3.

In the second quarter Hepburn intercepted a Namath pass and returned it 14 yards to the New York 22-yard line, which set up an eventual one-yard touchdown run by Don Nottingham that pulled the Colts to within 14–10. But the Jets came back with a 29-yard field goal, set up by a 49-yard pass from Namath to Rich Caster, in which the six-five tight end jumped up to make the catch over Hepburn before being tackled by Volk at the Baltimore 25. The field goal put the Jets up 17–10, and they were able to keep that lead going into halftime after a holding penalty nullified a 20-yard touchdown pass from Domres to O'Brien, who was doubling as a receiver. With 18 seconds left in the half, O'Brien then missed a 40-yard field goal.

O'Brien redeemed himself with a 28-yard field goal in the third quarter after defensive tackle Fred Miller recovered a fumble at the New York 22: it would be the only score in the period. The Colts squandered another opportunity in the fourth, after Curtis intercepted Namath at the New York 33 and returned the ball to the 14. Facing a third-and-six from the New York 10, Domres went back to pass and wound up putting on a display reminiscent of Curly Howard. Domres ran a play-action fake to Don McCauley, and dropped back to the 20-yard line. With Mark Lomas closing in from his blind side, Domres caught sight of him and spun around, running back to the 27. He started forward again, looking for a receiver, but unable to find one he pulled the ball down and looked like he was planning to run. As he ran left, linemen John Elliot and Ed Galigher were closing in, and Domres stopped at the 20-yard line, turned around, and retreated to the 25, then the 30. The entire New York front four was now bearing down on him — Lomas, Elliot, Galigher, and Joey Jackson — and Domres turned around again, tried to change direction at the 36, and slipped and went to the ground. He tried to get up, but by then all four of the Jet linemen were landing on him. It was a 26-yard loss. O'Brien then missed a 43-yard field goal, and the Colts still trailed 17–13.

A little more than midway through the fourth, the Colts drove deep into New York territory, but Nottingham fumbled at the 10-yard line after being hit by Al Atkinson. McCauley tried to pick the ball up but wound up booting it, and Larry Grantham recovered for the Jets.

There were about two minutes left when the Colts got the ball near midfield for what looked to be their last shot. A pass to Sam Havrilak gained 12 yards, and runs by Nottingham and McCauley carried to the New York 30. A 15-yard pass to O'Brien put them at the 15, but after Nottingham gained only two yards on first down, Domres threw two incomplete passes. Now facing fourth-and-eight on the New York 13, the Colts were down to their last chance. Trailing by four, a field goal was useless. But on fourth down, the New York secondary showed why it was ranked last in the AFC — Domres found O'Brien all alone in the left side of the end zone, and Baltimore took a 20–17 lead. It was their first lead of the game.

The problem for the Colts was that they had left the Jets with 1:30 to work with, certainly more than enough for a quick-strike offense like New York's. To make matters worse for Baltimore, the Jets got a good kick return and began at their 32-yard line. As much time as they had, there was no need for the Jets to rush or panic, but a holding penalty on first down pushed them back to the 17, putting the situation in a different light. Still, the Jets could have methodically worked their way downfield, but Namath had other ideas. In the huddle, Namath told Eddie Bell to run his ass off.[22]

Namath took the snap and dropped back to his eight-yard line. From there he heaved the ball long down the center of the field. He threw too far for Bell to get to it, but Bell kept running, trying to catch up with the ball. It was very fortunate for the Jets that he hadn't let up. As the ball came down, Logan was poised to intercept it for Baltimore, but Charlie Stukes, coming from the other side, jumped up to make a play on the ball. The ball came down over his shoulder and hit him in the hands, but as Stukes tried to pull it in he wound up flipping it over his shoulder and right into Bell's hands at the Baltimore 40-yard line. As he took the ball on the run, Bell was able to dart right between Stukes and Logan; it happened so fast that they were unable to react in time to stop him, and Bell raced the remaining 40 yards, untouched, for what would be an 83-yard touchdown, easily outrunning his only pursuer, May, and putting the Jets back on top 24–20. Namath knew it was a lucky shot. "Down south they have an expression for things like this," he said later. "They call it 'spitting in a swinging jug.'"[23]

Now it was the Jets who had left too much time on the clock. With 1:03 left in the game, Domres was able to work the Colts to their 45 with short passes, but then with just enough time for one more play it was his turn to throw up a prayer. He heaved the ball downfield to tight end John Mosier inside the five-yard line, and Mosier out-wrestled Rich Sowells and Earlie Thomas for the ball. But as the clock struck zero, Sowells pulled Mosier to the ground at the two-yard line. The Jets escaped with a 24–20 victory.

Namath's numbers were not too impressive, hitting only five of 16 passes, with two TDs and three interceptions, but then again a quarterback is often only as good as his receivers, and on this day Namath's receivers were still dropping the ball. On one series the Jets were forced to punt after three consecutive incomplete passes — two were dropped by the receivers and the third fell incomplete when Namath's target slipped and fell. The incredible thing was that Namath had thrown for 228 yards on only five completions.

The win gave the Jets a 4–2 record and a firm hold on second place in the division, with both Buffalo and New England losing and falling to 2–4. The Colts fell further into a hole at 1–5.

Week 7 — Sunday, October 29, 1972
Shea Stadium, New York (attendance: 62,867)

In week seven the Jets hosted the New England Patriots on a soggy day at Shea Stadium. Although the Jets had beaten the Patriots badly just two weeks prior, Ewbank cautioned his team against taking them lightly. Yet Ewbank himself was willing to sit John Riggins out with nagging injuries, playing Steve Harkey in his place; that was something he hadn't done in the first game with the Patriots, when both Riggins and Emerson Boozer played with injuries. Having run all over the Patriots for 168 yards in week five, Riggins would be missed. The Jets still had Boozer, however, and he had gained 150 yards against the Patriots in the Foxboro game.

With a 30 mph wind in Foxboro that day, Namath had thrown little in the game, but this time at Shea he was easily picking the New England defense apart through the air. Even so, both teams looked sloppy in the first quarter. The Jets did have the makings of a promising drive in the opening period, but when Namath hit Harkey with a 27-yard pass to the New England 15, Harkey tried to lateral the ball to Don Maynard; the result was a fumble that was recovered by New England. The Patriots made good on the turnover by driving to the New York 12, but unable to go any further, they settled for a field goal and a 3–0 lead.

Before the end of the period the Jets tied the game with a field goal of their own (of 21 yards), and they started the second period off right when Rich Sowells intercepted a Jim Plunkett pass on the New York 47 on the first play of the quarter. From there Namath kicked the offense into gear, hitting Eddie Bell across the middle for 23 yards, and then again for 13 more on a sideline pattern. From the New England 10-yard line Namath hit Caster in the end zone, but the officials ruled that Caster hadn't maintained control of the ball. It mattered little; after a holding penalty on New England moved the Jets up to the five, Boozer ran it in from there to give the Jets a 10–3 lead three-and-a-half minutes into the second. The drive had gone 53 yards in eight plays.

In the Jets' next series they would again score in eight plays, this time driving 65 yards. Namath hit Caster on a short pass of eight yards, and otherwise relied on Boozer, who twice ran for seven yards in the series. The Patriots also did themselves some damage when Honor Jackson was flagged for interfering with tight end Wayne Stewart. The penalty advanced the Jets 21 yards to the New England 20, and after the Jets ran Caster on an end-around, Boozer took it the remaining 12 yards, running a sweep left and bouncing outside of a superb block by Dave Herman. The score gave the Jets a 17–3 lead at the half.

In the third quarter, after Namath had hit Bell for 19 yards and Caster for 17, the Jets were positioned at the New England 19 where they crossed the Patriots up with a draw play to Boozer, who went through the right side of the line and down the sideline for his third touchdown of the game. It was the second time in three weeks that Boozer had scored three touchdowns against New England, and his third three-TD game of the season. With 11 touchdowns on the season he was leading the league.

After Bobby Howfield kicked a 31-yard field goal, the Jets took a 27–3 lead into the fourth quarter. With the game so well in hand, Ewbank decided to send Bob Davis in for Namath in the final period, and Davis added to New England's woes by throwing a 14-yard touchdown to Caster to put the Jets up 34–3. The Patriots also put in their backup quarterback, Brian Dowling (Plunkett having been harassed mercilessly throughout the game), who would score New England's only touchdown on a one-yard run late in the game to make the final 34–10.

Even without Riggins, the running game had done an impressive job, with Boozer gaining 91 yards and Cliff McClain enjoying more playing time and running for 68 yards. Namath also had a good game, hitting 12 of 24 passes for 203 yards (one interception). The numbers weren't showy, but then, they didn't have to be.

Their record now 5–2, the Jets had a very comfortable second-place lead over New England and Buffalo (who had also lost), both at 2–5. The Jets were still trailing the 7–0 Dolphins by two games, however. If the Dolphins would just lose a game or two...

Week 8 — Sunday, November 5, 1972
Shea Stadium, New York (attendance: 63,962)

Now riding a three-game winning streak, the 5–2 Jets would be hosting the Washington Redskins in week eight, and a record Shea Stadium crowd of 63,962 turned out to see the first ever meeting between the two teams. The Redskins came in with a four-game winning streak; at 6–1 they would be the biggest test the Jets had faced during the season, aside from Miami. People had been hoping for a showdown between two passing greats, Namath and Sonny Jurgensen, but Jurgensen was out with a ruptured Achilles, and Bill Kilmer would be quarterbacking the Redskins. The Redskins had the NFL's leading rusher, Larry Brown, and with Jurgensen out, it was assumed that they would rely that much more heavily on the running game. He may not have been the passer that Jurgensen was, but Kilmer would turn out to have himself quite a day.

Bob Brunet took the opening kickoff for Washington and gave his team excellent field position, returning it 38 yards from the six to the 44. Knowing that the Jets would be keying on Brown, the Redskins tried to cross them up by running Charlie Harraway on three straight plays, and Harraway gained 11 yards to the New York 45. Then, on the fourth play from scrimmage, Kilmer threw his first pass. Taking the snap and rolling out left, Kilmer looked deep downfield for Roy Jefferson and threw long. Chris Farasopoulos was actually ahead of Jefferson, running inside the five-yard line, and looked like he was expecting to catch the ball, but with Earlie Thomas right behind him, Jefferson caught the ball between the two defenders and went into the end zone to score. After just four plays, the Redskins were up 7–0.

The Jets had early success running the ball on their first series, with Emerson Boozer and John Riggins banging out a couple of first downs. But on a third-down play, Namath ran an end-around to Eddie Bell rather than put the ball in the air, and Bell lost five yards. The Jets got off a good punt, forcing Washington to start from their own seven-yard line, and when the Redskins sputtered on offense they were forced to punt from their own end zone; under a heavy rush from Steve Tannen, Mike Bragg's punt only carried to the Washington 40. This time Namath came out throwing, hitting Don Maynard for 18 yards on first down. Having softened the defense a bit, Namath went back to the ground attack, and after a series of runs, Riggins tied the game when he went over from a yard out.

Through the rest of the first quarter, and much of the second, both teams were having trouble moving the ball. After the New York touchdown, the Washington defense seemed to clamp down on the Jets' running game, and they were also getting a lot of pressure on Namath. Despite the fact that Namath was no scrambler, he was forced to run from the pocket frequently. As for the Redskins, they were finding that their main weapon, Brown, was getting nowhere against the Jets. Brown had gained 841 yards rushing in just seven games, yet against the Jets he would only manage 22 in the first half.

It was well into the second period when Kilmer threw for Jefferson over the middle at the New York 45. The pass was badly overthrown and floated right to safety Gus Hollomon at the 41. Hollomon gave it a good runback to the Washington 34, and after the New York offense took over, a pass interference call helped them even further. But with first-and-goal inside the 10, the Jets failed to get into the end zone. Linebacker Harold McLinton made tackles on two running plays, and then on third-and-goal McLinton tipped Namath's pass causing it to career out of play. The Jets settled for a 13-yard field goal and a 10–7 lead.

But the lead was very short lived. After receiving the kick and starting at their 22-yard line, the Redskins ran Brown twice for eight yards to the 30. Then on third-and-two, and with the Jets obviously anticipating the run, Kilmer went back to pass. Under a blitz from Hollomon and linebacker Larry Grantham, Kilmer unloaded a pass down the middle to Charley Taylor. The ball just cleared the outstretched hand of Tannen, and Taylor pulled it in at midfield and outran Farasopoulos to the end zone. The play covered 70 yards and put the Redskins back on top, 14–10.

That lead grew very quickly. The Jets began their next series at their 26, and Namath immediately went to the air. Under a heavy rush, he threw right into a crowd; for some reason, Bell, Boozer, and Riggins had all run patterns to the exact same area, creating a huge cluster that also brought a lot of defenders. Namath's pass was intercepted by linebacker Chris Hanburger at the New York 41, and Hanburger started upfield and broke toward the left sideline. Defensive back Mike Bass did an excellent job of clearing the path with a block on Dave Herman at the 16-yard line, enabling Hanburger to take it in for a score. The Redskins now led 21–10.

With time winding down in the first half, the Jets were unable to get anything started, but interestingly enough, caught a break when McLinton blocked New York's punt at the 28-yard line. It worked in the Jets' favor because, in trying to scoop the ball up, Ted Vactor kicked it and drew a penalty flag. The penalty was designed to prevent players from trying to advance the ball on such plays by booting it further downfield, but in this case it was entirely incidental. Nonetheless, it allowed the Jets to keep possession. They did nothing with their second chance, however, as Namath was again intercepted by Hanburger, this time at the Washington 35 in the closing seconds of the half.

At halftime the Jets trailed by 11, despite having outplayed the Redskins for the most part. The Jets had controlled the ball in the half, but having given up the big plays which accounted for all of Washington's points, they were now in a position of playing catch-up in the second half.

The Jets received the second half kick, and Namath tried to get something started fast. He went right to the air, but after throwing 16 yards to Caster on the first play from scrimmage, Namath was again intercepted. On the Jets' second play from scrimmage, Namath tried to hit Boozer over the middle and McLinton, who was having himself quite a day, picked the pass off at the Washington 49 and returned it 19 yards to the New York 32. The Redskins were still having trouble moving the ball, however, and when they had to settle for a field goal try, Curt Knight missed from 30 yards and the score remained 21–10.

When the Jets took over at the 20 they looked like they meant business, gaining four first downs on four straight plays. The first was a pass interference call on Mike Bass, who was defensing Eddie Bell across the middle. The penalty gave the Jets a first down at their 31. On the next play Namath hit Caster for 10 yards to the 41, and Riggins then carried for 12 yards to the Washington 47. Namath threw another 10-yard pass to Caster at the left sideline to pick up another first down at the 37, and the drive seemed to be cruising along just fine. But despite the success Namath was now having with short passes, he went back to the ground attack and Washington stopped Riggins and Boozer on three consecutive runs, halting the drive at the 30-yard line. Bobby Howfield came in to kick a 37-yard field goal, but it was just a bit short and bounced off the crossbar.

After taking possession, Washington's running game again failed to move the chains and the Redskins punted. Namath went back to the air, throwing across the field left-to-right to Bell. After being immediately hit, Bell dropped the ball — it was incomplete, but the official didn't see it that way. It was ruled a fumble, and Washington took possession.

The only score of the third period would again be a matter of a big play — a *very* big play — by the Redskins. Although the Jets had done a good job of containing Brown on running plays, he would break the game open on a pass play. Actually it was more a run than a pass, but it went down as a pass play in the books. From his own 11-yard line Kilmer dropped back and dumped a screen pass off to Brown at the five-yard line. Brown took off down the left sideline, outrunning four diving tackle attempts along the way as he cruised 89 yards for a touchdown. The Redskins were now up 28–10.

In the fourth quarter, with the game pretty well getting away from them, the Jets got a break when Speedy Duncan fumbled a punt and John Mooring recovered for New York at the Washington 15-yard line. On the next play Namath lofted a pass to Maynard, cutting across the center of the end zone, and Maynard made a sliding catch for a touchdown. It cut the Washington lead back down to 11 points at 28–17. The play was significant in retrospect because, as it turns out, it would be the last touchdown of Maynard's career. Who knew?

Neither team was mustering much offense the remainder of the game, but the Redskins did manage one final score, which was accomplished by their defense. From the New York 27, Namath went back to pass, and as had been occurring all day, he was forced by a heavy rush into fleeing the pocket. Six-foot-five Bill Brundie was on Namath's heals as he ran to his left, and when Brundie hit Namath from behind he managed to punch the ball out of Namath's hand at the 18-yard line. It was picked up by, of all people, Verlon Biggs, who had spent most of his career with the Jets and was a member of their Super Bowl team. This was Biggs' triumphant return to Shea Stadium: he gathered the ball up at the 16-yard line and ran it into the end zone for a touchdown. The final score was a lopsided 35–17. What seems amazing is that Washington could accomplish such a score with only seven first downs in the entire game.

Namath finished 15 of 28 for 148 yards, with one TD and three picks, as the Jets' record fell to 5–3 and they dropped a full three games behind the unbeaten Miami Dolphins in their division. With only six games remaining, and the Dolphins having a fairly soft schedule, it was looking like the Jets' playoff chances would come down to landing a wild card spot.

Week 9 — Sunday, November 12, 1972
Shea Stadium, New York (attendance: 62,853)

The Jets hosted the Buffalo Bills in week nine; in the pre-game warm-ups Eddie Bell and Buffalo receiver Linzy Cole were practicing running deep patterns from opposite ends of the field, and apparently neither was looking where they were going. Each looking back for the ball, they collided into one another with enough force that both would have to sit out the game. That was about the biggest trouble the Jets would have all day with the Buffalo Bills, who came into the game with a 2–6 record.

Although the Jets failed to get on the board after receiving the opening kickoff, it was not indicative of the type of day they were to have. The Bills found themselves starting back at their 12-yard line following the New York punt, and on their very first play from scrimmage O.J. Simpson fumbled the ball and Larry Grantham recovered for the Jets at the Buffalo 10. From there it was only a matter of two plays as John Riggins ran nine yards to the one on first down, and then took it in to score on the next play.

The Bills responded by marching downfield on what would turn out to be their only sustained drive of the afternoon. Perhaps eager to redeem himself for the error that put his team in the hole early, Simpson ran for 53 of the drive's 78 yards. But things bogged down at the New York two-yard line, forcing Buffalo to settle for a field goal that made the score 7–3.

In the second quarter the Jets would begin to outdistance the Bills, taking advantage of scoring opportunities presented by Buffalo mistakes. Chris Farasopoulos set the Jets up at the Buffalo 29 with a 34-yard punt return, and six plays later Emerson Boozer scored on a one-yard run to put the Jets up 14–3. Even better than a good punt return was a subsequent shanked punt that netted only 10 yards, giving the Jets the ball at the Buffalo 16. The Buffalo defense did a good job of holding the Jets to a 23-yard field goal, but not quite good enough — a Buffalo penalty gave the New York offense another shot, and Namath pitched a four-yard touchdown pass to Boozer, who made a nifty (if needlessly dramatic) catch at the edge of the end zone.

Now trailing 21–3 with time winding down in the half, Buffalo quarterback Dennis Shaw tried to give his team a lift before the intermission and threw long on the Bills' first play after the kick. The pass wound up being intercepted by Farasopoulos at the New York 47, and a 23-yard return set Namath and company up at the Buffalo 30. That led to a 26-yard field goal by Bobby Howfield that gave the Jets a 24–3 lead with 25 seconds left in the half.

Seemingly desperate for a shot of momentum before halftime, Shaw was still firing away in the closing seconds of the quarter, hitting Bob Chandler for gains of 22 and 28 yards. Shaw eventually hit Chandler in the end zone for what appeared to be the booster the Bills needed, but the play was nullified by a penalty. Undaunted, Shaw tried again with just two seconds left in the half. He again found Chandler, hitting him with a 12-yard pass that ended the half as Chandler was knocked out of bounds at the New York three-yard line.

Obviously feeling frisky, the Jets opened the second half with a successful onside kick, which was recovered for New York by Roy Kirksey at the Buffalo 46. Four plays later the Jets upped their lead to 31–3 when Namath threw a 26-yard touchdown to Rich Caster, who did a fine job of jumping up and swiping the ball from defender Leon Garror. That would prove to be the only score of the third period, but in the fourth Howfield added a 25-yard field goal and Bob Davis, enjoying some playing time with the game well in hand, threw a nine-yard touchdown to Jerome Barkum to make the final 41–3. It was the fourth time during the season that the Jets had scored more than 40 points. Namath's numbers were not showy at six of 12 for 106 yards, two touchdowns and an interception, but they obviously didn't have to be.

The victory boosted the Jets' record to 6–3, but with Miami still unbeaten it was looking like a wild card was the only chance the Jets had of making the playoffs. In that respect, the Jets and the Cleveland Browns (also 6–3) were ahead of the rest in the AFC. The Jets would be traveling to Miami to play the Dolphins in the Orange Bowl in week 10; Miami could clinch the division with a victory.

Week 10 — Sunday, November 19, 1972
Orange Bowl, Miami (attendance: 80,010)

"Catching the Dolphins is sort've a long shot," Namath said after the Buffalo game, "but we're thinking about the playoffs ... I think our chances are pretty good for the wild card spot."[24] The wild card would go to the second-place team with the best record among the AFC's three divisions. As it stood after week nine, it was between the Jets and the Cleveland Browns, both at 6–3.

In week 10 the Jets would be up against the 9–0 Dolphins at Miami's Orange Bowl, scene of Namath's greatest triumph, the Super Bowl victory over the Baltimore Colts in January of 1969. But this was not the same Orange Bowl of Super Bowl III; the once beautiful field had been covered with carpeting, and the rain and humidity of south Florida gave the artificial turf a perpetually blotchy, discolored appearance that now made it one of the ugliest fields in sport.

One thing that would be the same as Super Bowl III was the quarterback that Namath was matched up against. Miami coach Don Shula had coached Earl Morrall in Baltimore, and in 1972 he brought Morrall to Miami. Just as an injury to Johnny Unitas had given Morrall the opportunity to play in Baltimore, so too did he get that chance in Miami when Bob Griese went down with a broken leg in the fifth game of the season. It is a testament to Shula's team that they would continue to win without their quarterback.

Super Bowl III was likely an albatross for Morrall. Baltimore had been soundly beaten that day, but more than anyone else the loss seems to have been hung on Morrall. And then there were Namath's remarks. In the two weeks leading up to the Super Bowl Namath had been widely quoted as saying that there were at least four or five quarterbacks in the AFL better than Morrall. It was the truth, but the fact that Morrall went out and played a lousy game probably made Namath's comments all the more bitter to take.

But now, in 1972, things were different. Morrall knew that this was not the New York Jet team of the 1969 Super Bowl. The few players that remained from that squad were getting older, and the younger players were green. This was a team largely in the process of remaking itself, and it was a team struggling for a playoff spot. Namath was different too. When training camp began in summer, many reporters took note of a difference in his demeanor: the brashness was largely gone. This was a man who had been away from the game for the better part of two years, and one who wanted very much to get back in it. Reporters noted a certain maturity about Namath now.

But if Namath had matured, Morrall seems to have done the opposite. Namath's remarks from 1969 seem to have been ringing in Morrall's ears ever since, festering deep within him. During the week before the game, Morrall spoke to Al Levine of the *Miami News* and went on something of an infantile rant. He told Levine that at the time of the Super Bowl he too felt that there were better quarterbacks than Namath but he simply didn't make it a point to say so publicly. Perhaps, but then why do so now?

Had he left it at that then Morrall might have kept his dignity, but he went much further. "I don't have any respect for him, that's for sure," Morrall said of Namath. "I don't want to be like him. And I hope my kids, and the younger generation, don't grow up to be like him."[25]

Coming from Morrall, the remarks were surprising in that they seemed to be decidedly lacking in class. Whereas Namath's 1969 remarks had been confined to talk of football, Morrall had the extreme poor taste of making his remarks very personal. The Dolphins might win the game, but Morrall made sure that he himself would somehow personally still look like a loser, having painted himself as bitter and catty.

Although the Jets were coming off an impressive 41–3 victory over Buffalo, the Dolphins had done even better the previous week, bitch-slapping the New England Patriots 52–0. The Dolphins could now clinch the division with a victory over the Jets.

When Miami won the pre-game coin toss, Shula put his faith in his defense and opted to kickoff. It was a move that paid off early when Namath's very first pass was intercepted by Dick Anderson at the New York 33. Seven plays later, the Dolphins got into the end zone on a nine-yard pass from Morrall to Howard Twilley. The Jets came right back, however, as Namath chipped away at the Miami defense with short passes, driving the Jets 80 yards in 13 plays and eventually tying the game on a one-yard touchdown run by John Riggins.

With the score still tied in the second quarter, the Jets caught a break when Mercury Morris fumbled a pitchout and Earlie Thomas recovered the ball at the Miami 37. It took the Jets three plays to take the lead, as Namath rifled a 29-yard touchdown pass to Rich Caster. At that point the Jets seemed to have taken over, and as Dick Lundin wrote in *The News Tribune* of Fort Pierce, Florida, they "all but blew the Dolphins out of the Orange Bowl."[26]

Unfortunately, that dominance did not translate into a tremendous point disparity as the Jets indulged in their frequent pastime of sinking their own ship. Midway into the second period Riggins bulled his way to the Miami 14 on a very impressive 40-yard run, but Namath's pass to Emerson Boozer over the middle on the next play was intercepted by linebacker Nick Buoniconti at the six-yard line and returned to the 16. The shame of it for the Jets is that, in all likelihood, the play would otherwise have been a touchdown as Boozer, cutting across the middle at the two-yard line, had a couple steps on linebacker Mike Kolen. But Buoniconti made an excellent play, reaching up to block the ball and then bring it down for the interception.

Just four plays later the Jets got the ball back when W.K. Hicks intercepted a Morrall pass intended for Otto Stowe at the New York 48. Hicks raced 43 yards down the right sideline all the way to the Miami nine-yard line, but the Jets failed to make the most of the opportunity. On first down Boozer lost a yard, and that was followed by an offensive pass interference call against Cliff McClain. The Jets found themselves backed up in the vicinity of the Miami 26 with a third-and-goal, and after Manny Fernandez batted Namath's third-down pass at the line of scrimmage, Bobby Howfield came in to kick a 33-yard field goal. It gave the Jets a 17–7 lead with 2:41 left in the half.

After receiving the kick, the Dolphins started at their 21, and Morrall hit Twilley for 22 yards on a slant-in that carried to the 43. A draw play to Larry Csonka gained 13 yards to the New York 45, and on the next play Morrall again threw for Twilley, this time deep down the right sideline. Twilley had a couple steps on Steve Tannen, and would have scored had Tannen not made a dive for him that caused Twilley to lose his balance and go out of bounds at the New York one-yard line.

From the one, Miami ran Csonka twice, but he not only failed to get into the end zone, he also fumbled the ball. Bob Kuechenberg recovered for Miami, and on third down Morris finally took it in for the score to cut New York's lead to 17–14 with 41 seconds left in the half. For the most part, the Jets had outplayed the Dolphins in the first half but had only a slim three-point lead to show for it: against a 9–0 team that would hardly suffice.

In the third quarter neither team had success on their initial offensive series, but on Miami's second possession they put together a drive and took the lead on a 31-yard run by, of all people, Morrall. After going back to pass and being unable to find a receiver, Morrall saw that the entire left side of the field was wide open and he took off running. With only linemen John Elliot and John Little chasing after him, Morrall had clear sailing. It wasn't until he approached the end zone that he met any challenge at all, and even then it was no more than a feeble attempt at a tackle by Thomas, who merely lowered his shoulder to give Morrall a weak shot at the one-yard line. Morrall's touchdown gave the Dolphins a 21–17 lead 6:05 into the third quarter.

The Jets were still unable to get into gear on their next series, but on fourth down a running into the punter penalty on Curtis Johnson gave them new life — and a new set of downs. From his own 39 Namath dropped back to pass and threw deep down the right sideline 41 yards to Don Maynard, who made a tightrope catch along the sideline and went out of bounds at the Miami 20. Maynard had easily gotten past Anderson, who bit on Namath's pump-fake.

After working their way to the Miami four, the Jets re-took the lead when Namath ran an excellent play-fake to Boozer and then rolled out left, hiding the ball at his hip. He found tight end Wayne Stewart all alone at the back of the end zone and the Jets were back up, 24–21, with 3:59 left in the third.

The lead held through the remainder of the third and into the fourth, until a New York mistake helped Miami pull out in front again. The Dolphins missed a chance to tie the game early in the fourth quarter when Garo Yepremian missed a 42-yard field goal, but just two plays later Miami got the ball back when McClain fumbled and Anderson recovered the ball at the New York 27. Four plays later, Morris put the Dolphins ahead 28–24 with a 14-yard touchdown run.

Eleven minutes, eleven seconds were left in the game, certainly enough time for a comeback, but being undefeated, the Dolphins seemed to sense that they now had the game. Conversely, the Jets, who were struggling, seemed to sense that they had let it slip away, and they now looked lethargic, like a beaten team.

The Jets squandered their last opportunity late in the game when, after stopping the Miami offense and forcing a punt, Joey Jackson was flagged for running into punter Larry Seiple, allowing the Dolphins to retain possession of the ball. Miami scored no more points, but the penalty gave them the opportunity to run out much of the game's remaining time. When the Dolphins did punt again, the field position allotted by the penalty and ensuing plays allowed them to pin the Jets very far back in their end of the field, and with so little time left, the Jets were unable to do much: Miami won the game and clinched the division. Namath finished 14 of 23 for 175 yards, two TDs and two interceptions.

It wasn't the Super Bowl, but for Earl Morrall it would have to do. It was as close as he would get to salving that still-open wound, for although the Dolphins would go on to the Super Bowl, Morrall would taste little of that glory. Bob Griese was back and able to play by the playoffs, and when the Pittsburgh Steelers seemed bound to end Miami's season in the AFC Championship game, Shula pulled Morrall in favor of Griese. It was Griese who led the Dolphins to victory in the AFC Championship, and it was Griese who won the Super Bowl. Morrall was a mere bit player again.

Week 11 — Thursday, November 23, 1972
Tiger Stadium, Detroit (attendance: 54,418)

In week 11 the Jets were scheduled for their first ever Thanksgiving Day game, traveling to Detroit to play the Lions in Tiger Stadium (Lions in Tiger Stadium? Oh, the irony). Both the Jets and the Lions came into the game 6–4 and battling for a playoff spot, but while the Jets were fighting for the AFC wild card, the Lions were only one game behind the Green Bay Packers in the NFC Central Division and still had hopes of a division title.

The Jets had come out of week 10 very banged up, and the short down time between games (Sunday to Thursday) didn't help matters. Emerson Boozer had injured his knee in the Miami game, and would not play against Detroit. Otherwise, defensive tackle John Elliot also had injured a knee, Steve Tannen had re-injured his shoulder, defensive tackle Steve Thompson had an ankle injury, and safety Gus Hollomon suffered a serious concussion that required his removal by stretcher in Miami. In all, there had been seven Jets injured in week 10, and while most were not serious injuries, there just wasn't enough time in a short week for everyone to get well.

Prior to the game many people had been anticipating an aerial shootout between Namath and Detroit's Greg Landry, but it became evident early on that this was going to be a day for running backs. The Lions got on the scoreboard first with a 15-yard field goal that was made possible largely by a 33-yard run by Altie Taylor.

On the Jets' first play, John Riggins ran for 16 yards; on their second play Cliff McClain ran for 30. But ultimately, their efforts would come to nothing when the drive bogged down at the Detroit 35 and Bobby Howfield missed a 42-yard field goal.

In the second quarter, the Jets took a 7–3 lead on a one-yard touchdown run by Riggins, but they quickly let Detroit get back on top. After Mickey Zofko gave the Lions excellent field position with a 49-yard kick return, Landry fired a pass from the New York 34 to Larry Walton at the 17; Walton shook off three tackles on his way to the end zone, giving Detroit a 10–7 lead.

Later in the second period, Landry ran for a touchdown himself from a yard out to put Detroit up 17–7, and the best the Jets could do was to answer back with a 13-yard field goal that cut the lead to seven points. But the Jets' kick coverage again let them down, this time falling for a bit of trickery when Zofko fielded the New York kick and then handed the ball to Walton on a reverse. The resulting 57-yard return led to a field goal that gave the Lions a 20–10 halftime lead.

Their playoff hopes slipping away, the Jets battled back in the third quarter; a 20-yard field goal again brought them to within a touchdown of Detroit, and then a 33-yard TD pass from Namath to Rich Caster evened the score at 20. But in the fourth period the Lions would once more gain the upper hand.

Six minutes into the final quarter, the Lions took the lead on a 37-yard field goal. The Jets were unable to answer back, and while the game had been a fairly even match throughout, the final three minutes gave the impression of a blowout. Landry scored his second TD of the game when he ran it in from six yards out to up the Lions' lead to 30–20 with 2:57 left to play.

The running game may have done quite well throughout the day, but with Howfield having missed three field goals and the Jets trailing by 10 points with under three minutes to play, they were forced to play catch-up in a hurry. Namath was intercepted by linebacker Charlie Weaver, and very shortly afterward, Taylor broke a 38-yard TD run that gave Detroit a 17-point lead with 1:49 left. There was no coming back from that.

"I thought they'd throw the hell out of us," said Detroit coach Joe Schmidt.[27] A lot of people thought the same, but the passing numbers were pretty skinny on both sides, with Namath hitting on less than half his throws (nine of 22 for 165 yards, one TD and one interception) while Landry only hit a third (six of 18 for 125, with a TD). What was surprising was the number of long gainers coming on the ground. It was only the second time in NFL history that three players ran for over 100 yards in the same game. Taylor led the pack with 123 yards in just 15 carries, while McClain (playing for the injured Boozer) gained 121 yards on only 10 runs. Riggins carried 24 times for 105 yards.

Schmidt felt that his team had an advantage from the start by virtue of the fact that the Jets had never played a Thanksgiving Day game before, whereas it was an annual event for Detroit. To Schmidt, that meant his team somehow had a psychological edge.

"We're not out of it yet," said Namath. "Anything can happen."[28] But if something was going to happen, it needed to happen soon. At 6–5 the Jets were running out of chances, as Cleveland had continued winning and after 11 games led the wild card race with an 8–3 record.

Week 12 — Sunday, December 3, 1972
Shea Stadium, New York (attendance: 62,496)

December 3, 1972, was New York Jets kicker Bobby Howfield's thirty-sixth birthday. The English, soccer-style kicker had been acquired by the Jets from Denver in an even trade in 1971 for kicker Jim Turner, but many were wondering if the Jets hadn't taken the pipe in the deal. Howfield had been getting his share of criticism, particularly after missing three field goals in the Jets' loss to Detroit on Thanksgiving Day. As it turned out, those nine points would have mattered little, but missing so many scoring opportunities in a single game never looks good on a kicker's résumé.

Now, as the Jets took on the New Orleans Saints at Shea on his birthday, it would be nice for Howfield if he could redeem himself, especially since his 75-year-old mother was visiting from England. But what chance did Howfield really have of being called on against the 2–8–1 Saints? As many high scores as the Jets had run up against lesser teams during the season, they surely wouldn't have any trouble getting into the end zone against the Saints. Would they?

It was Howfield who would score the game's first points when he put the Jets up 3–0 with a 30-yard field goal in the first period. After tying the game with a field goal of their own (from 31 yards) in the first, the Saints got out in front in the second quarter when quarterback Archie Manning led them on a 78-yard drive that used up 7:11, and culminated in a three-yard touchdown run by Bob Gresham. Trailing 10–3, the Jets could only answer with a 39-yard field goal by Howfield to cut the lead to 10–6. A 31-yard field goal by Howfield in the third period cut the New Orleans lead to a point, but as the quarter was winding down Manning was leading the Saints on another long drive.

Within a minute of the start of the fourth quarter, Manning completed the 72-yard drive with an eight-yard touchdown pass to Bill Butler that increased the New Orleans lead to 17–9.

Now the Jets were in trouble. They had almost the entire fourth quarter to stage a comeback, but having been unable to put the ball into the end zone for three quarters, they seemed under the thumb of the lowly Saints.

Namath started working the Jets downfield with short passes — 11 yards to Eddie Bell, 11 more to Don Maynard — but eventually the drive ran out of gas at the New Orleans 16, and Howfield was called on to kick his fourth field goal. He put it through from 23 yards out, thereby cutting the Saints' lead to 17–12.

The New York defense stepped up and did its share when Earlie Thomas intercepted Manning at the New Orleans 36 and ran it back 14 yards to the 22. But the New York offense could only go backwards from there, and again it was Howfield who was called on to salvage something from the opportunity. He made good from 33 yards, and brought the Jets to within two points of the Saints at 17–15. With five field goals, it was already Howfield's best game.

With only 3:02 left in the game, Howfield was sent on the field to give the Jets the lead. The Jets were stalled at the New Orleans 42-yard line, so at 49 yards it would be Howfield's longest field goal of the year. This time he missed it. Bob Davis, the Jets' backup quarterback and Howfield's holder on field goals, tried to boost the kicker's spirits, telling him that, with three minutes left, there was still time for another shot. Howfield wasn't worried. He would say later say that, with Namath at quarterback, he felt assured of getting another shot to win it.[29]

The Jets did get another shot, but after receiving a punt that set them back at their 15, it looked like a long shot. Going right to the air, Namath was helped considerably by an overzealous New Orleans defense that was called for pass interference not once, but on two consecutive plays, moving the Jets up to their 48. Namath then threw 16 yards to Rich Caster to the New Orleans 36. It was starting to look hopeful.

Namath was obviously playing for the field goal, and he ran Steve Harkey (in for Riggins, who left the game with a knee injury) for three yards to the 33. But a five-yard penalty that pushed the Jets back to the 38, followed by an incomplete pass, brought up a third-and-12. Still playing for a field goal, and just wanting to get Howfield a little closer, Namath again ran Harkey, and again he gained three yards. With fourth-and-nine at the 35 and no timeouts, the New York field goal unit rushed onto the field. Howfield looked up at the clock and saw there were 14 seconds left and counting down. It would be a 42-yard attempt, which would also be his longest of the season if he hit it. With only a few seconds remaining the ball was snapped: the final gun sounded as the ball was still in flight. Davis surmised that the ball made it inside the post by about a yard. Howfield had done it. His six field goals had accounted for the Jets' only points in the game, but it was enough for an 18–17 victory.

Although the win kept the Jets' slim playoff hopes alive, Ewbank seemed unable to enjoy it. The home crowd had booed the Jets heartily throughout the game, causing Ewbank to go on a post-game tirade, pointing an accusing finger at the press. The local press had been complaining of a perceived conservatism in the Jets' offensive scheme, feeling that they weren't passing enough. Ewbank was fuming, and said that such talk was inciting the home crowd to turn on the team and boo every running play. Namath was also not pleased by the criticism, saying that with running backs like Riggins, Boozer, and McClain, there was good reason to run the ball. "I like exciting football, too," he said, "but I don't want to be stupid about it."[30] It was an odd gripe from fans and reporters alike, since Namath had thrown 40 passes, completing 21 for 259 yards (two interceptions).

But the Jets had to play without Boozer since week 10, and now they would be without Riggins as well. Riggins left the New Orleans game with a knee injury and would be going in for what was described as minor knee surgery during the week. The Jets were facing the grim prospect of making a desperate playoff run without their starting backfield.

The win had brought the Jets' record up to 7–5, still in the race for the wild card, but also still chasing Cleveland. The Jets absolutely had to win their two remaining games (including their season-ender against Cleveland). But now they were off to Oakland for a Monday night meeting with the Raiders. Namath hadn't played them since 1969.

Week 13 — Monday, December 11, 1972
Alameda County Coliseum, Oakland (attendance: 54,843)

After the Jets-Raiders game in Alameda County Coliseum, Oakland coach John Madden was in the Raiders' dressing room talking to reporters. He offered a simple, yet unequivocal observation of what had just transpired. "If Namath's not the best," he said, "I don't know who is."[31]

The rest of the locker room was likewise abuzz with talk of the performance that Namath had just given. Rookie safety Jack Tatum said that he had waited a long time for the opportunity to play against Namath. "He's better than people say," Tatum offered. "You know what he's going to do, you defend against his passes just the way you think you should and he still hits his receiver's hands. He's the best passer I've ever seen."[32]

Oakland offensive lineman Bob Brown couldn't even sit down when Namath was on the field. He had to see what was happening. "On the sideline," Brown said, "I found myself looking at the game like a fan. He was a magician."[33]

Late in the game there had been a weird, almost surreal moment, when Namath, after being taken down hard by linebacker Phil Villapiano, had to leave the game. He got up slowly, and on swollen ankles walked gingerly from the field. As he made his was to the sideline an almost unbelievable thing happened: the Oakland fans rose to their feet roaring with applause. These same Oakland fans who had for years called for Namath's head and had cheered every miserable cheap shot that Ben Davidson, Ike Lassiter, and Dan Birdwell could tag him with, were now giving Namath a standing ovation. "I heard it," said Namath, "and I don't think I'll forget it."[34] Namath waved to the crowd to acknowledge their appreciation.

Oakland quarterback Daryle Lamonica must have felt as though he had been dropped into the *Twilight Zone*. It was like logic had been stood on its head. These fans—these very loyal fans—were heaping all their affection on the enemy, and winning seemed to be irrelevant. But the truth is that Namath hadn't played in Oakland since that very memorable Heidi game in 1968, and now, on a chilly December night in Alameda County, California, the Oakland fans realized that in the intervening four years ... they missed Namath. It was like revisiting those rough and tumble AFL days in the 1960s when the Jets-Raiders rivalry was in full swing. They missed the excitement that Namath always brought. Now, they wanted him to know that they appreciated it. Everybody appreciated it: when the final gun sounded, Oakland Raiders owner Al Davis left his luxurious owner's box atop the stadium and made his way downstairs. He wasn't going to his team's dressing room: he was headed to the New York Jets' dressing room to shake Namath's hand.

The Jets came into Oakland for their Monday night game in dire straits. They had to win both of their remaining two games to have any chance at making the playoffs, and now they had to do it all with one hand tied behind their backs. John Riggins, their main running threat, had gone in for minor knee surgery the previous Tuesday and would be unable to play. Their other starting back, Emerson Boozer, had missed two consecutive games with injuries, and while he would be available to play in the Monday night game he was far from optimal health, and how much game time he would see was uncertain. Even Boozer's backup, Cliff McClain, was out. So the Jets had a patchwork backfield. At least they still had Namath, and with so many runners hurt and out of action, everybody knew that the Jets' entire offense came down to Namath and the passing game. Problem was, Namath came down with the flu and was running a temperature the night of the game. With the temperature getting down into the mid-thirties that night, it was not exactly an ideal evening for a man with the flu to be barking signals through a hoarse, raspy, fading voice. Ewbank must've wondered what else could be thrown at him during a playoff run.

The Raiders posted the first points of the game when George Blanda kicked a 47-yard field goal* to climax a drive that was accomplished entirely on the running of Marv Hubbard, who carried six times for 32 yards from the Oakland 29 to the New York 39. It looked like that 3–0 lead would be short lived when Namath drove the Jets downfield, hitting four of four passes for 61 yards, but on a third-and-goal play from the Oakland seven-yard line Namath tried to hit Eddie Bell on a quick look-in pattern and threw ahead of his target. Oakland's Willie Brown intercepted the ball at the two-yard line to end the New York threat.

The Raiders were unable to get another drive up and running, and subsequently found themselves punting out of a hole: Jerry DePoyster's 34-yard punt was fielded by Rocky Turner at the Oakland 46, and his seven-yard return set the Jets up at the Oakland 39. But when Namath went back to pass from there, defensive ends Horace Jones and Tony Cline converged on him from either side, and tackle Art Thoms came from the middle. Jones overran the play, but Cline took Namath down at the 49 for a 10-yard loss. Namath came right back at them, going back to pass from the 49 and throwing into the seam of the left side of Oakland's zone coverage. The ball arched perfectly over the outstretched hand of Villapiano and into the arms of Rich Caster, who caught it while backpedaling. Caster spun around and avoided a diving tackle attempt by George Atkinson, then took off down the sideline, outrunning four defenders to the end zone. With the 49-yard touchdown, the Jets were up 7–3.

In the second quarter, the Jets missed a chance to build on their lead after Steve Tannen intercepted a Lamonica pass to Fred Biletnikoff at the New York 29 and returned it 31 yards to the Oakland 40. The Jets could only advance the ball eight yards to the 32, and Bobby Howfield then missed a 39-yard field goal. Lamonica may have missed Biletnikoff on that long throw, but after the Jets failed to capitalize on the mistake, Lamonica came back to Biletnikoff again. The Raiders traveled 80 yards in nine plays, with Hubbard's running once more accounting for much of the drive. Lamonica had otherwise thrown 16 yards to tight end Raymond Chester in moving the Raiders to the New York 39, and then went deep for Biletnikoff, this time hitting him in stride in the right side of the end zone for a score and a 10–7 Oakland lead.

The Jets drew even when Namath drove them from their 27 to the Oakland 18, passing 26 yards to Don Maynard and 14 to Caster, enabling Howfield to kick a 25-yard field goal that tied the game at 10–10. Namath had hit four of six passes in the drive for 52 yards. After that, Rich Sowells halted an Oakland threat by intercepting Lamonica on the New York 17 and returning it to the 31. Namath managed to get the Jets to midfield with a 19-yard pass, but able to go no further, the Jets punted. It turned out to be to their advantage, as Clarence Davis fumbled the punt and Roger Finnie recovered for the Jets at the Oakland 23 only seconds before halftime. There were nine seconds left when Howfield kicked a 30-yard field goal to give the Jets a 13–10 halftime lead.

After receiving the second half kick, the Raiders began from their 25 and proceeded to drive 75 yards in 13 plays to take the lead. Other than a pair of 14-yard passes to Biletnikoff, Lamonica kept it on the ground with 11 rushes, the last being a one-yard touchdown run by Charlie Smith that put the Raiders up 17–13. The drive had used up more than eight minutes of the third period.

The Jets didn't score in the third quarter, but on their first series of the fourth Namath again got them rolling. After hitting Bell on a short pass of seven yards, and following with two running plays for nine, Namath hit Maynard on consecutive passes of 21 and 19 yards. But again the drive

*For some reason Blanda is officially credited with a 48-yard field goal, though the ball was very obviously placed on the 47-yard line.

stalled, and Howfield came in and brought the Jets to within a point of the Raiders with a 42-yard field goal. The score now stood at 17–16 with 11:26 left in the game.

The Raiders next series was disastrous for the Jets. At halftime, the Oakland coaches had looked at Polaroid photos taken from upstairs in the coaches box, and they pointed something out to Lamonica. The pictures showed that on short-yardage plays the Jets were stacking the line of scrimmage, sometimes with all 11 of their men; even their weak side safety would often be at the line. It was a dicey maneuver: if it worked, that was all fine and good, but if the quarterback got wise and called an audible, then it could be suicidal. All the receivers would have to do is blow past one man and they'd have clear sailing. Lamonica kept it in mind.

On their first series of the fourth quarter, the Raiders began at their 23. Lamonica ran Hubbard on first down, and the fullback gained two yards. On second down Hubbard again carried, this time for seven yards to the 32. That created a third-and-one scenario, just the type of short-yardage situation that Lamonica had been alerted to watch for. Lamonica ran a play-action fake to Smith and then went back to pass. He had sent Chester through the line, and once he broke from the line of scrimmage, Chester was already all alone and in the clear. "I don't think I've ever been that wide open before in my life," he said later. "It seemed like it took forever for that pass to get to me."[35]

Chester waited on the ball, and it eventually floated to him at the New York 42. After that it was a fairly leisurely stroll to the end zone, although Phil Wise made a dash to try and make it interesting. The play went for a 68-yard score that gave the Raiders an eight-point lead with 9:26 left in the game. Now the Jets would have to score twice.

When they got the ball back Namath went right to work, hitting Maynard for 21 yards. It was a very significant play for a couple of reasons: it was the 632nd pass reception of Maynard's career, making him the all-time leader in that category, passing Baltimore's Raymond Berry. That was announced, and was known to all in attendance that night and those watching at home. What nobody could have known was that it was to be the last pass that Maynard would ever catch from Namath. That lethal combination that had terrified the AFL throughout the 1960s and had thrilled fans for almost a decade had reached its coda: after this night, Namath and Maynard would never again play together in a professional football game.

Following the throw to Maynard, Namath hit Bell for 24 yards to the Oakland 30. He then threw a swing pass to Boozer that advanced the Jets three yards to the 27. After that, Namath went for it all: he threw deep down the middle for Bell. The pass was underthrown and would likely have been intercepted by Brown but for the fact that Tatum was back there waiting as well. Tatum seemed to come from out of nowhere, jumping in front and intercepting the pass in the end zone. He proceeded to run it out and up the sideline. He broke toward the middle and was thinking of breaking left at the 45-yard line, but after seeing Namath there he cut back toward the middle again, enabling Winston Hill to trip him up and bring him down at the New York 46. When Tatum came down he lost the ball and it was recovered for New York by tackle Bob Svihus at the Jets' 44. The official on the spot ruled the ball for New York, but referee Jim Tunney came running from downfield to overrule him, and awarded the ball to Oakland. Ewbank flew into a rage.

From the New York 46, seven runs by Hubbard and Davis brought the Raiders to the six-yard line. Davis then lost three yards to the nine, and after the Raiders took a delay of game penalty, Blanda came in for a field goal try. It was only 22 yards, but somehow he missed it to the right and the score remained 24–16. The possession may have resulted in no points, but it had otherwise allowed the Raiders to run more than three minutes of valuable time off the clock.

There were 3 minutes, 12 seconds left for the Jets to get two scores. Only 2:33 remained when Villapiano took Namath down and forced him out of the game. As the crowd gave Namath an ovation, Bob Davis came in to replace him at quarterback. Davis threw an incomplete pass;

Ewbank turned to Namath and asked him if he was ready to go back in the game, but Namath said he needed a minute. Davis threw another incomplete pass; again Ewbank asked Namath if he was ready to go back in. It was fourth-and-very long, but the Jets had no other options now — they had to go for it, and Namath had to go back in.

Going back to pass from his 44-yard line, Namath threw long to Jerome Barkum: it wound up being a jump-ball at the Oakland 16. When Tatum and Atkinson went up for it and collided, the ball popped right into Barkum's hands, and after falling to the ground at the 14 he managed to get back up and get to the 10 before being taken out of bounds by Tatum and Brown. From the 10, Namath threw to Barkum again, this time all alone at the back of the end zone. The pass was a little high, but certainly catchable — it ricocheted off Barkum's hands and out of the end zone. Namath then threw a little dump-off pass over the middle to Steve Harkey, who got to the one-yard line. But then, as the clock wound down, Namath went back to pass and went down at the 10-yard line under a heavy rush from Nemiah Wilson. It was over, and the Jets were out.

Ewbank hurried across the field and shook Madden's hand, then raced up the tunnel toward the locker rooms. But he wasn't running for the locker room: he was trying to catch up with referee Jim Tunney. Still fuming over the reversal of the fumble call on Tatum's interception, Ewbank sarcastically called after Tunney. "Did they give you the game ball?" Ewbank barked.[36] But Ewbank was wrong. A look at the play shows that Tatum's knee came down at the New York 47 before the ball came out; more than that, Tatum didn't even lose the ball until his upper torso hit the turf. It was a dead ball.

Meanwhile, Namath was hobbling off the field on swollen ankles to the applause of an appreciative enemy crowd. He had completed 25 of 46 passes from an incredible 403 yards (one TD and two interceptions). Keeping in mind that this was before the five-yard rule governing pass coverage, which has since 1978 made passing a far easier task, Namath's second 400-yard game of 1972 came at a time when it was a rare accomplishment. In fact, Namath's 403 yards against Oakland that night was only the thirty-sixth time in professional football history that a quarterback had surpassed 400 yards passing in a game. Namath had three of those 36 games: only Sonny Jurgensen had more with five. Namath would have thrown for more against Oakland that night, but he was again ill served by his receivers, who had dropped eight passes in the game.

Namath had done something else that night: he had surpassed 20,000 career passing yards. Again, with the far more offense-friendly rules in today's game, that doesn't impress like it once did, but at that time Namath was one of only a small handful of quarterbacks to reach that plateau.

Nemiah Wilson said that Namath hadn't changed much. Wilson hadn't played against Namath since 1969, but he said that Namath was as sharp as ever, and as always he was ready to play hell with the Oakland secondary. "He comes to throw," Wilson said.[37]

Elsewhere in the locker room Madden was explaining the difficulty that the Raiders had in defensing Namath. When Namath was having success against the zone the Raiders went to six defensive backs, with a three-man line and two linebackers. They also tried man-to-man coverage, but they just couldn't stop him. Even with no running game and everyone knowing he would be throwing, Namath kept moving the ball. Everywhere except into the end zone, Madden pointed out. Brown said that the Raiders had given Namath every type of coverage they had, but still he kept coming at them. Everybody seemed awed.

Whoa, whoa, wait a minute. What the hell is this? The Oakland Raiders won the game. The Raiders were champions of the AFC Western Division. They were 9–3–1 and headed for the playoffs, and who knows, maybe even the Super Bowl. And for all that, all anyone wanted to talk about was the quarterback who *lost* the game? For the Jets the season was over, even with one game remaining. They weren't going anywhere but home for the holidays. There was one player in the Oakland locker room who had no interest in talking about what an incredible show

Namath had put on. Daryle Lamonica declined to give his opinion of Namath's performance, other than making one simple observation. "The quarterback's job is to get points," Lamonica said, "and I got more than he did."[38] True. It might have come off sounding a bit pissy, but true nonetheless.

But it is also true that Namath had wowed the fans and put on a hell of a show. Still, he didn't get the points. He lost the game, and he didn't get his team to the playoffs. And yet, he earned everybody's respect with his performance that night. "The young man is a professional," said Howard Cosell during the ABC *Monday Night Football* broadcast of the game.[39]

Namath's heroics had overshadowed Maynard's achievement in becoming the all-time leader in pass receptions, but Maynard didn't care. He said that the record was nice, but it could in no way take the place of winning and getting to the playoffs. There was something else bothering Maynard. As he sat in the locker room with a black eye, he editorialized a bit about the direction the sport had taken. Although the shiner was courtesy of a hit by Villapiano, Maynard refused to name names. The hit was flagged, but Maynard was more concerned by the fact that he could have lost an eye. Villapiano would claim that it was an accident, and that he hadn't hit Maynard so much as Maynard had run into the blow. For those who suspected that a part of Oakland Raider training camp included lessons in excuse giving, this seemed a case in point. "Some sportsmanship must be put back into this game or somebody's going to get permanently paralyzed or killed," Maynard said.[40]

Six years later in a 1978 preseason game, Darryl Stingley of the New England Patriots was hit while trying to catch a pass across the middle. The hit left him a quadriplegic for the rest of his life. The Patriots were playing the Oakland Raiders that day.

The Jets closed out the 1972 season at home against the Cleveland Browns. It was a miserable day for football; with 40 mph winds and a wind chill factor of 15 degrees below zero, it was a miserable day for anything. The game was meaningless for the Jets, but the Browns were still fighting to win the AFC Central Division. Aside from needing to beat the Jets, Cleveland needed Pittsburgh to lose to San Diego. But really, the Browns were going to the playoffs no matter what. If the Steelers beat San Diego, the Browns would still be the AFC wild card team, win or lose to the Jets.

Despite his ankle injury the prior Monday in Oakland, it was believed that Namath would be playing in the last game of the season. But as it turned out the ankle wasn't healing quickly, and Namath wound up sitting out the game. Backup quarterback Bob Davis claimed to have been unaware that he would be playing until Cleveland had already received the opening kickoff and run a couple of plays.

Despite the Jets' 7–6 record to Cleveland's 9–4, the Jets had been made three-point favorites, but of course that was predicated on Namath's playing. Namath's performance the previous Monday had been seen by everyone. "We know we're going to have to come up with a superb defensive effort to beat the Jets," said a spokesman for the Browns.[41]

Without Namath playing, that wasn't necessarily the case. Although the Jets kept it close in the first half, trailing 10–7 at the intermission, the Browns pulled away in the second half for an easy 26–10 victory. After the game, Davis was as bitter as the Shea Stadium wind chill. "It's just a shame that I had to go into a game like this — one that doesn't mean a damned thing — and under the conditions we had to play," he said. "Somebody decides you're second-string and that's it for the year. They look at you once and make their decision."[42]

Davis didn't mind speaking his piece, as he seemed convinced that his days with the Jets had come to an end that afternoon. A good number of other players on the team — mainly on the defensive unit — felt the same way, but then, the truth is that there were changes that needed to be made. Failing to make the playoffs had been a big disappointment to the team and fans alike, all of whom had such high expectations when the season began. During the preseason,

Namath had remarked that the Jets were obviously a team that could win big, and for the most part he and the offense had held up their end of the deal. The Jets had scored some outrageous victories, beating Buffalo 41–24, and then beating them again 41–3, beating New England 41–13, and downing the Colts 44–34. Having racked up 367 points during the season, the Jets had the second highest scoring offense in the league. The problem was that they had given up 324 points, which ranked nineteenth among the NFL's 26 teams. Consider this: in 1972, the New York Jets' offense was ranked number one in passing yardage in the NFL, while their defense was ranked dead last in passing yardage allowed. First in one, last in the other: it makes it rather clear where the strengths and weaknesses were.

As for Namath, his 2,816 passing yards led the league, and his 19 touchdown passes tied him with Washington's Bill Kilmer for tops in the NFL in 1972. Namath also led the league in average yards per attempt (8.7), yards per completion (17.4) and yards per game (216.6). As usual his interception count (at 21) exceeded his touchdown count by a pair, but overall the numbers were impressive. With a stronger defense and a backfield that could keep healthy, there is no telling how far they could have gone.

The Pro Bowl was played on January 21, 1973, at Texas Stadium in Irving, and Namath had been voted to the AFC's Pro Bowl team. He had to decline, as by then Dr. Nicholas had diagnosed his slow-mending ankle as a case of torn lateral ligaments. San Diego's John Hadl was selected to take Namath's place in the game.

11

The 1973 Season

"Both of Joe's knees look terrific this year," announced Dr. Nicholas prior to the start of training camp in 1973. "They are much stronger. He is in as good shape as I have ever seen him."[1] Namath himself seemed pleased with his physical condition as he prepared to enter his ninth season. "My arm feels fine and there's no pain in my knees," he said.[2] Namath otherwise said that he still felt that he was the number one quarterback in the league, and his numbers from the previous year seemed to support that. He had led the league in most passing statistics, and the Jets certainly had a very explosive offense in 1972: good enough to rank second in the NFL.

Even so, without a defense to complement their high-flying offense, the Jets had failed to make the playoffs. The New York Jets' defense had placed last in pass defense and was ranked nineteenth overall in 1972. Obviously it was the defense that was most in need of revamping, and so the team's number one draft choice in 1973 was Miami defensive back Burgess Owens. The Jets otherwise hoped to strengthen the defensive secondary by acquiring Delles Howell from New Orleans; the Jets gave their number three draft choice to the Saints in exchange for Howell and defensive end Richard Neal.

Neal was also considered a necessary acquisition, as the Jets needed some help on the line. Gerry Philbin was candid in telling reporters in the midst of the '72 campaign that he did not expect to be back with the Jets in '73. Philbin had seen the writing on the wall when Ewbank ceased speaking to him during the 1972 season. During the off-season, the Jets sent Philbin to Kansas City in a trade for running back Mike Adamle. As training camp opened, the Chiefs then cut a deal and sent Philbin to Philadelphia.

There were even more significant changes: the last two remaining players of the original New York Titans franchise would also be gone. Linebacker Larry Grantham had decided to retire, and Don Maynard—the very first player to ever be signed by the team—was being prodded to do the same. Ewbank did not want to cut Maynard, but he had fine young receivers in Rich Caster, Eddie Bell, and Jerome Barkum, and he now also had rookie David Knight and Margene Adkins (also acquired from the Saints). But for his long hair, Knight could have been mistaken for Maynard, having the same lean, lanky build, and even sporting the same old-school single-bar facemask. Having so many young receivers with bright and potentially long futures, Ewbank was unwilling to part with any of them for the sake of getting one more year out of Maynard. Still, Maynard was refusing to go quietly.

This was certainly going to be a different team, but Ewbank knew big changes needed to be made. Although he would remain with the Jets as general manager, Ewbank would be stepping down as head coach after the 1973 season, and he wanted to go out a winner.

But Ewbank's tightfisted ways weren't helping toward that end. Having gotten the contract he wanted the year before, Namath was at camp and ready to go, but there were other holdouts this time. The team was without a starting backfield, as both John Riggins and Emerson Boozer were demanding more money. Cliff McClain and Hank Bjorklund returned (although McClain would be playing without a contract), and the team otherwise beefed up the backfield by signing Jim Nance as a free agent. Nance was a name, and he once held the promise of a very bright future after a couple of good seasons with the Patriots in 1966 and '67, but he was definitely now on the downside of his career. If Ewbank could get things squared away with Riggins and Boozer, then the Jets were thought to be capable of taking a run at the Miami Dolphins in the AFC East. But in the meantime, they would have to begin the preseason without them.

The Jets opened their 1973 exhibition season on a Friday night in early August against the Oilers in the Houston Astrodome. In front of a crowd of 45,772, Namath played only the first quarter and threw only three passes, completing one for 16 yards. The other two were both intercepted, one by Zeke Moore at the Houston 15-yard line.

After the first quarter ended in a scoreless tie, Al Woodall (once more stepping in as Namath's backup after the departure of Bob Davis) came in to lead the Jets to a 10–3 halftime advantage. Although the Oilers had gotten out to a 3–0 lead with a 22-yard field goal in the second period, the Jets came back with a six-yard touchdown run by Adamle and a 44-yard field goal by Bobby Howfield. The Oilers tied the game in the third quarter with a 35-yard TD pass from Dan Pastorini to Clifton McNeil, and then took the lead with a 39-yard field goal. By the end of the third quarter the Jets had tied the game 13–13 with a 31-yard field goal, and after neither side was able to score through most of the fourth quarter the Jets got a break when a short punt gave them the ball at the Houston 39. With 1:35 left in the game, Howfield kicked a 23-yard field goal to give the Jets a 16–13 victory.

The Jets then traveled to Tampa, Florida, for their second exhibition game, a Saturday night meeting with the San Francisco 49ers on August 12 before a crowd of 46,477. San Francisco backup quarterback Steve Spurrier, a Heisman Trophy winner from the University of Florida, requested to start in the game, as it would be something of a homecoming for him. The request was granted.

Spurrier guided his team to an early 7–0 lead, but that was as good as his homecoming got. The Jets tied the game when tackle John Elliot intercepted Spurrier and ran it four yards for a touchdown. Before the first quarter was over Namath put the Jets up 14–7 with a 42-yard touchdown pass to Caster, and after tossing a one-yard touchdown to Nance that gave the Jets a 21–7 edge, Namath was done for the evening. The Jets went on to win 34–14. In his brief appearance (15 plays) Namath was six of eight for 85 yards.

As sharp as Namath had looked in picking apart the 49ers, he looked equally as sloppy the following Sunday in the Jets' annual clash with the Giants in New Haven. In front of a crowd of 70,874 at the Yale Bowl, Namath started well, driving the Jets downfield to a 3–0 lead, but by the end of the first quarter the Giants had gone up 7–3 on a two-yard TD run by Ron Johnson. It was early in the second period that Namath had a deflected pass intercepted by Willie Williams, who returned it 20 yards to the Jets' 38. Five plays later, the Giants upped their lead on a one-yard touchdown run by Vince Clements, which was set up by a 29-yard pass from Norm Snead to Johnson. On the second play of the Jets' next series Namath was intercepted again, this time by linebacker Pat Hughes at the Jets' 35. Snead then threw a 31-yard touchdown to Bob Grim to give the Giants a 21–3 lead.

Having suffered a bruised elbow, Namath played no more that day. Woodall came in and got the Jets back in the game, engineering a 53-yard drive that cut the deficit to 21–10 when Nance scored on a four-yard run with 3:40 left in the first half. Two minutes later Woodall took a page from Namath's book, hitting Caster with a 72-yard bomb that cut the Giants' lead to 21–17, and when the Jets added a field goal just before halftime, they trailed by only a point at the intermission, 21–20.

The teams exchanged field goals in the third period as the Jets briefly led 23–21, then trailed again, 24–23. In the fourth quarter, however, things went terribly awry for the Jets. After driving to the Giants' 17, the Jets seemed poised to take the lead again, but Woodall was hit while releasing a pass and the ball wound up being intercepted by defensive end Carter Campbell, who ran 82 yards with it for a touchdown.

Now trailing 31–23, the Jets received the kickoff, and just three plays later Woodall took another hit while passing. This time linebacker Jim Files intercepted the ball and ran it back 22 yards to score. With two touchdowns in less than a minute, the Giants then led 38–23.

With under two minutes left in the game, Spider Lockhart intercepted Woodall at the Giants' 18 and took it back 77 yards to the Jets' five. That set up a two-yard touchdown run by Rocky Thompson that gave the Giants a 45–23 lead, and even a 32-yard TD pass from Woodall to Barkum with nine seconds left in the game could do little to lessen the humiliation. With their 45–30 triumph, the Giants were once more the top dogs in New York.

Curiously, Giants coach Alex Webster attributed the Jets' first-half comeback to the Giant defense's emotional deflation after Namath left the game. Fired up to take on Namath, the Giants apparently lost their focus once he was out. "We suffered a letdown when Namath went out of the game and it took us a long time to get going again," Webster said.[3]

Now 2–1 in preseason, the Jets traveled to St. Louis the following Saturday to play the Cardinals at Busch Stadium. Namath got them out to another early lead that night with an 18-yard touchdown pass to Bell on their first series. St. Louis quarterback Jim Hart tried to retaliate quickly, but the Cardinals could only manage a 16-yard field goal to cut the margin to 7–3.

Still playing without Riggins and Boozer, the Jets relied on the running of Nance, McClain, and Steve Harkey to eventually get them close enough to post a 22-yard field goal, making it 10–3 in the fourth quarter. But the Cardinals came back to tie the game on a drive that was capped by a two-yard touchdown run by Donny Anderson.

Late in the game, St. Louis kicker Jim Bakken was just short on a 41-yard field goal try that would have given the Cardinals the lead. The Jets then drove 44 yards to the St. Louis 36, and with only seconds remaining Howfield came in to try to win the game with a 43-yard field goal. But the snap was high, resulting in a fumble that gave St. Louis the ball at their own 46 with only one second on the clock. The Cardinals obviously had no time to try to advance the ball, and so St. Louis coach Don Coryell sent Bakken in to try a 54-yard field goal. He made it, and the Cardinals managed a 13–10 victory.

During his first-half appearance, Namath had thrown for 101 yards. "Any time you can hold a passer like Namath to one touchdown you're doing well," said Coryell. "The guy's just fantastic."[4]

Riggins reported to camp just prior to the St. Louis game, but was refusing to play without a contract. Negotiations resumed following the game with the Cardinals, but short of the $120,000 he was asking, Riggins left camp on August 28. "I went for all the marbles. It was all or none," he said to reporters in departing. "The way I see it now, I don't think I'll be back."[5]

Things may have still been at an impasse with Riggins, but later in the week the Jets did come to terms with two other holdouts. Boozer and offensive tackle Winston Hill returned to camp on Thursday, August 30, just in time to make the trip to New Orleans for the Jets' next exhibition game on the night of Saturday, September 1. For the first time in the preseason, Namath played beyond the first half; in fact, he didn't leave the game until the final four minutes.

The Saints started well, scoring twice in the first quarter on a pair of long drives. On the first, Archie Manning led his team on a 72-yard march to take a 7–0 lead on a one-yard run by fullback Bill Butler. The Jets surpassed the Saints' drive in a single play: Namath promptly tied the score with a 73-yard bomb to Caster.

The Saints then pulled in front again on another one-yard touchdown run, this one by Steve Ferrughelli, that capped an 80-yard drive. But again the Jets struck back fast, tying the game on a 58-yard TD pass from Namath to Bell. It was really a bit of luck as the ball reached Bell by way of being tipped twice, first by Caster and then by New Orleans safety Tom Myers.

The Saints' scoring drives had been accomplished by keeping the New York defense off balance with a lot of rollout plays, but once the Jets made some adjustments, New Orleans' had minimal success. In fact, the Saints failed to capitalize on two New York fumbles within a few minutes.

The Jets took a 21–14 lead on a one-yard scoring run by Nance in the third quarter, and after the Saints mustered a fourth quarter field goal, Namath put the game away with an 85-yard bomb to Caster that made the final 28–17. Namath finished eight of 16 for 285 yards.

Monday, September 10, was the cutoff date for teams to trim their rosters down to the 40-man season limit. Ewbank had been trying to convince Maynard to retire, but the 36-year-old veteran was forcing the old man's hand. On the tenth, the Jets announced that Maynard had been traded to the St. Louis Cardinals for an undisclosed draft choice. Maynard said that he had no hard feelings. "The Jets have been taking care of me and watching over me for a long time," he said. "They will always have a place in my heart but now I have another bridge to cross."[6] Maynard's time in St. Louis would be brief: he played in only two games and caught one pass for 18 yards. He then retired as the all-time leading receiver with 633 catches. "I feel quite honored," said Ewbank, "to have been associated with two of the greatest receivers in Don and Raymond Berry, who is already in the Hall of Fame.... There will always be a warm spot in New York for Don Maynard."[7]

The Jets were back in Tampa the following week to close out their exhibition schedule in the rain against the Philadelphia Eagles. Despite their usual custom of increasing Namath's playing time in latter exhibitions, Ewbank chose to play Namath in only the first quarter, in which he completed two of five passes for 25 yards and led the Jets to one field goal.

The Eagles were leading 6–3 in the second quarter when Chris Farasopoulos fumbled a punt and Philadelphia recovered the ball at the New York 30. Shortly thereafter, quarterback Roman Gabriel connected with Harold Carmichael on an 18-yard TD pass to give the Eagles a 13–3 lead. The Jets added a 39-yard field goal to make it 13–6 at the half, and it stayed that way through a scoreless third quarter. It wasn't until late in the fourth that the Jets sprang to life and tied the score when Woodall threw a 17-yard touchdown to Barkum. Then, with four seconds left in the game, Howfield kicked a 24-yard field goal to give the Jets a 16–13 victory, and a 4–2 preseason record.

Just prior to the start of the season, Riggins finally settled for much less than he had wanted and signed a new deal with the Jets. Coming just before the season opener on Monday night against the Green Bay Packers, it didn't seem likely that he would be ready to play. But how ready would any of them be? Boozer had signed not long before Riggins, and had missed the majority of the preseason. As far as Namath was concerned, except for the fifth exhibition against New Orleans, his playing time was negligible, and again aside from that one game, decidedly less than spectacular.

Week 1— Monday, September 17, 1973
Milwaukee County Stadium, Milwaukee (attendance: 47,124)

When the Jets opened their season on a Monday night in Milwaukee against the Packers, John Riggins would not be starting at fullback. That was not surprising, as he had only signed his contract the prior Thursday and had just two workouts with the team. It was Jim Nance who would be starting at fullback. Nance was attempting to make a comeback with the Jets, having first been traded by the Patriots to Philadelphia in July of 1972, and then cut by the Eagles prior to the start of the '72 season. He sat out the year, but during the off-season he contacted Ewbank to inquire about trying out for the Jets. Ewbank expressed interest, but was shocked upon seeing Nance, whose weight had ballooned to 270 pounds. Ewbank informed Nance that, if he could get his weight down to 240 then the Jets would give him a shot in camp. Ewbank didn't believe he could do it, but Nance arrived at camp weighing 235. He went on to be the preseason's top ground gainer with 311 yards on 72 carries, an average of 4.3 yards per carry. With Riggins now back on the team, Nance needed to take advantage of his opportunity and have a good game against Green Bay.

The Packers received the opening kickoff and New York's defense did its job, quickly forcing a punt after three running plays. After the punt, the Jets began at their 25 and got a freebie on first down when the Packers were flagged for being offside. With second-and-five from the 30, Emerson Boozer broke through the line for 12 yards and a first down at the 42. Another offside penalty on Green Bay moved the Jets to the 47, and after a one-yard run by Boozer, Namath hit Jerome Barkum for 13 yards to the Green Bay 39. On the next play Namath hit Barkum again, this time for 19 yards to the 20, and followed with a five-yard screen to Nance. Now positioned at the Green Bay 15, everything seemed to be going well. Then somebody let the air out of the tires.

That somebody was either Green Bay linebacker Tom MacLeod or New York fullback Jim Nance, take your pick. Namath went back to pass, and MacLeod blitzed. Nance looked like he was going to go through the line and run a route, but stopped when he saw MacLeod charging through unimpeded and tried to put a block on him. Having all but run right by MacLeod, Nance whiffed badly on the block, and MacLeod blew past him and took Namath down for a 10-yard loss. Nance knew he blew it; for a moment he lay face down on the ground, but if he was worried about Namath he was probably glad that it was not a hard takedown. Still, it brought up a third-and-15 at the 25, and the Jets then tried some ill-advised trickery, running a reverse to Rich Caster that lost an additional nine yards to the 34. Bobby Howfield came in to try a 41-yard field goal, which missed wide left, and the Jets' promising start came to nothing.

When the Packers took over on their 20 they ran a couple running plays, and facing a third down at the 28 quarterback Scott Hunter threw his first pass: he hit Jon Staggers for 24 yards to the New York 48. After Green Bay wound up with a fourth-and-one at the New York 39, Chester Marcol came in to try a 41-yard field goal. Like Howfield before him, Marcol missed it, but rookie safety Burgess Owens was flagged for running into the kicker, only a five-yard penalty, but enough to give the Packers a first down and keep the series going.

After MacArthur Lane gained four yards to the 30 on first down, Hunter threw incomplete on second and then hit Lane for 20 yards and a first down at the 10. But the Packers could only advance to the two-yard line on three runs, and Marcol came back in to make good on a nine-yard field goal that gave Green Bay the lead.

Errors plagued the Jets after that. Their first series of the second quarter was sunk by consecutive holding penalties, and the series that followed ended when a third-and-three play from the 46 resulted in Namath being sacked again, this time by defensive end Aaron Brown back to the 35.

A fumble by Rich Caster on the first play of the Jets' next series gave Green Bay the ball at midfield, and from there Lane and John Brockington began gaining good yardage on traps and draws. After the Packers advanced to the 19, Hunter hit Rich McGeorge with a touchdown pass to put the Packers up 10–0 late in the half.

The Packers took over again at their own 46 after a pale three-and-out by the Jets, and following a one-yard run, Hunter passed 21 yards to rookie Barry Smith to put Green Bay at the New York 32 with 35 seconds left in the half. A couple plays later, the Packers let the clock run down to three seconds before sending Marcol in to end the half with a 37-yard field goal that put Green Bay up 13–0.

The Jets' anemic offense would collapse into utter incompetence in the second half. After his failure to pick up the blitz on the Jets' first offensive series of the game, Nance was benched by Ewbank in favor of Riggins, but Riggins was very rusty and obviously unprepared. After receiving the second half kickoff, the Jets began with a pitchout to Riggins running right: he fumbled the ball, and while he managed to scoop it up himself, he still lost five yards on the play. Boozer bailed them out with a 17-yard run off left tackle to gain a first down to the 32, but on the next play another pitchout to Riggins, this time running left, resulted in another fumble. This time, Bob Brown recovered for Green Bay at the New York 36.

Both Lane and Brockington were getting into a rhythm, and they managed to punch the ball down to the New York three before the Jets' defense tightened up. The resulting 10-yard field goal increased Green Bay's lead to 16–0.

The Jets seemed in complete disarray. A holding penalty on the kickoff forced the offense to start from their 11, and although Namath was able to hit Caster with a pair of passes for 13 and 17 yards, a 13-yard sack by Brown ultimately killed the series.

Green Bay's field goal would be the only score of the third period, but in the fourth the Packers would strike again after another New York error. From the 27, Namath threw for Barkum but the ball went through his hands and was intercepted by Ken Ellis, giving the Packers possession at the New York 38. Again, the running of Brockington and Lane pounded down deep into Jet territory until Brockington took it in from a yard out on a sweep left to make the score 23–0.

The Jets finally showed some determination on their next series. From the 25 Namath threw 15 yards to Caster to the 40, and then hit Cliff McClain at midfield. Namath then went long to Barkum for 32 yards to the Green Bay 18. The play might have scored but for the fact that the ball was underthrown, causing Barkum to go to the ground to make the catch. Namath then hit Caster for a first-and-goal at the six. After a flare pass to McClain only gained a yard to the five Namath threw for Barkum in the left corner of the end zone: the pass was tipped away by Ellis. On third-and-goal Namath again threw for Barkum in the left side of the end zone: again Ellis batted the pass away. Now facing fourth-and-goal and trailing 23–0, the Jets gave no thought to a field goal. On fourth down, Namath again went back to pass. Once more he threw to Barkum in the left side of the end zone: Ellis broke it up yet again. Green Bay took over on downs. Namath's decision to throw three consecutive passes to Barkum in the same spot was bewildering. "I thought Ellis wouldn't expect it three times in a row," Namath explained after the game.[8] Bad guess.

The Packers were able to run a couple minutes off the clock and then punted just after the two-minute warning. When the New York offense took the field it was Al Woodall who came in at quarterback, much to the chagrin of the Milwaukee crowd. "We want Joe!" some of them began to chant.

The Jets began at midfield, and after McClain gained 11 yards to the 39 and Mike Adamle gained two yards to the 37, Woodall hit Margene Adkins with a pass to the 17 with 39 seconds left to play. Then Woodall spoiled the shutout, hitting David Knight with a 17-yard touchdown with 27 seconds left. It was the first catch of Knight's professional career, and the young man who had replaced Don Maynard looked so much like him in making the play, extending himself to make a very Maynard-like catch as he went to the ground. Knight had beaten Ellis on the play.

"We know Namath can score from anywhere on the field," said Green Bay safety Jim Hill after the game, "and one of the things we wanted to eliminate was the deep pass."[9] They certainly did that. Namath completed 16 of 33 for 203 yards, and one interception. Overall, the Jets looked like a team that was completely unprepared for the start of the season.

Week 2 — Sunday, September 23, 1973
Memorial Stadium, Baltimore (attendance: 55,942)

After the very frustrating Monday night game, the Jets seemed fired up and ready in week two. Traveling to Baltimore to play the Colts, it was one year after Namath had put up the best single-game numbers of his career in the very same venue, Baltimore's Memorial Stadium. In the first quarter it looked like he might be on his way to another big game against the Colts when he marched the Jets downfield, taking them inside the Baltimore 10-yard line with passes to Jerome Barkum and Eddie Bell. Then Namath went back to pass again, and linebacker Stan White shot straight up the middle through a gaping hole in the line. Nobody made any attempt to block White: he had a clear shot at Namath all the way. "I came in clean," White said of the play afterward. "Joe ducked at the last minute. If he hadn't ducked, I don't know what would have happened to him."[10]

"I saw him coming," said Namath, "but it was too late then."[11] With White charging in unimpeded and bearing down on him quickly, Namath had no time to do anything. He hunkered down and braced for the shot. As Namath went to the ground he landed on his right shoulder and White came down on top of him. Namath stayed on the ground after the play as an official came over to check on him. He got up on his own and walked to the sidelines holding his right arm as the crowd in Baltimore gave him a standing ovation. The sack took the Jets back from the Baltimore five to the 15, and they wound up kicking a 22-yard field goal for a 3–0 lead.

With all of White's weight landing on him, it had separated Namath's right shoulder. How badly remained to be seen. After being examined in the locker room by Dr. Nicholas, Namath returned to the sideline with his arm in a sling. In the meantime, Baltimore had tied the game with a 17-yard field goal set up by a 51-yard pass from rookie quarterback Bert Jones to Glenn Doughty. Al Woodall would have to take the Jets the rest of the way. "I honestly thought he'd just bruised his shoulder," Woodall said. "I thought I'd be in for just a series or two."[12]

Just 19 seconds before halftime Jones hit Doughty again, this time for a 23-yard touchdown that gave the Colts a 10–3 lead. Trailing at the half, and without the services of Namath any longer, the Jets might have looked like a bad bet, but Woodall—and the New York defense—rose to the occasion. In the third quarter, Chris Farasopoulos intercepted Jones and gave Woodall and company the ball at the Baltimore 49. The Jets took advantage, and Woodall soon threw 12 yards to Bell, all alone in the right side of the end zone to tie the score with 9:41 left to play in the third period.

Only five plays later, linebacker Al Atkinson intercepted Jones at midfield and returned the ball to the Baltimore 39, setting up a 16-yard field goal that put the Jets up 13–10. In the fourth quarter the New York defense would turn the game into a blowout.

Early in the fourth quarter, Delles Howell intercepted Jones at the Baltimore 30 and ran it back to the 20, setting up a one-yard touchdown toss from Woodall to Emerson Boozer; the Jets then led 20–10 with just under 10 minutes left in the game. Having thrown four interceptions on the afternoon, Jones was benched. His replacement, veteran Marty Domres, fared no better.

With 5:12 left in the game, linebacker Ralph Baker intercepted Domres and ran it back 22 yards for a score to give the Jets a 27–10 lead. Just three plays later Rich Sowells made his third interception of the game, and gave a very determined 30-yard return for a touchdown, making it 34–10. Having come into the game with under 10 minutes to play, Domres wound up matching Jones with four interceptions. The New York total of eight interceptions was a team record, and was just one shy of the league record.

Ewbank said that the defense was nothing the Jets hadn't used before—just a nickel defense—but he seemed more concerned with the loss of Namath. Ewbank wouldn't name the responsible party, but he said that it was a missed assignment by a lineman who was too much a veteran to be so careless. During his brief appearance, Namath had completed three of four for 37 yards.

The victory brought the Jets' record up to 1–1, and put them in a three-way tie for first place with Miami and Buffalo in the AFC East.

After returning to New York on Sunday night, Namath was back in Lenox Hill Hospital for more X-rays. Dr. Nicholas was hoping to avoid surgery, which would put Namath out for the rest of the season. If the shoulder could mend without an operation he would miss six to eight weeks, which was still a considerable chunk of the schedule.

Nicholas wanted to keep Namath in the hospital and see how the shoulder responded overnight. The following day he was encouraged, saying that the swelling had been significantly reduced and that it looked like surgery could be avoided. "He is in considerable pain," Nicholas told reporters, "but with constant pressure it is felt at this time that the shoulder will heal by itself."[13] Ultimately the decision would be made not to operate, but with 12 games remaining to be played, and the possibility of Namath missing as many as eight of them, what position would the Jets be in when he returned? Would they still be in contention? Could the team pull itself together and stay in the race pending his return?

Eddie Bell tried to have a positive attitude, telling reporters that it made no difference to the Jets who their quarterback was.[14] Nobody was buying that: it seemed to be no more than a bit of bravado that rang hollow. Perhaps he was trying to keep up appearances, or maybe he was trying to lift the spirits of his teammates. But Bell could talk as big as he pleased: the truth was that, with Namath out, nobody liked the Jets' chances. "The Jets are no longer to be taken very seriously as a threat to Miami in the AFC East," wrote Lerry Felser in *The Sporting News* following Namath's injury.[15] That unwillingness to regard the Jets as a viable contender was always there when Namath was out with injuries. It was there in 1970 when he missed nine games with a broken wrist; it was there again when he missed 10 games in 1971 after having knee surgery. The consensus seemed to be that playing the Jets when Namath was absent was like boxing a man in a wheelchair.

Still, after Namath went down in the first quarter against Baltimore, Woodall stepped in and did an excellent job, completing 17 of 21 passes for 149 yards. If he could keep playing at that level in Namath's absence, then the Jets had a shot. But in Buffalo in week three the Jets could manage just one score, a fourth-quarter touchdown that only allowed them to avoid a shutout as they lost 9–7. The defense, however, had done its job in holding the Bills to no more than a trio of field goals.

Then in a week four meeting with the Dolphins in Miami, bad luck struck yet again. In the third period, Woodall went down with a sprained left knee; the Jets were down to their third-string quarterback, rookie Bill Demory. They lost the game and fell to 1–3. Fortunately, they were traveling to Foxboro to play the Patriots the following week: the Patsies were usually good at lifting the Jets' spirits.

Demory would have to go the distance at quarterback for the Jets, and although he only managed to complete one pass in seven attempts against the Patriots, he made that one completion count. Throwing 11 yards to David Knight, the pass set up the winning field goal in the fourth quarter as the Jets pulled out a 9–7 triumph. The New York defense had again done its job, as New England's only score came by way of their defense when linebacker Will Foster recovered a New York fumble in the end zone to put the Patriots up 7–6 in the third quarter.

But as Demory was learning, the Jets' season was slipping away, losing to the Steelers in Pittsburgh and then to Denver at home. Woodall had recovered enough to participate in the loss to Denver, and retook the starting job the following week when the Jets hosted Miami. It made little difference, as the Jets continued losing. After eight games, with a record of 2–6, the Jets were already well out of the race. They managed a victory in week nine when they hosted the Patriots, who again proved an ego boost for the Jets, despite both clubs coming in with 2–6 records that made them look like equals.

In week 10, the Jets would be off to Cincinnati to play the 5–4 Bengals. Although Woodall would get the start, Namath was sufficiently mended to be available to play if needed. At 3–6, they definitely needed him.

Week 10— Sunday, November 18, 1973

Riverfront Stadium, Cincinnati (attendance: 55,745)

In 1972, the Jets' record stood at 6–3 after nine games. By the ninth week of the 1973 season, they were 3–6. What a difference a year makes. The most notable difference, of course, was that in 1973 Namath had been out since week two. Although his separated shoulder had mended sufficiently for him to play in week 10, it wasn't expected that he would.

When the Jets came into dreary Riverfront Stadium to play the Cincinnati Bengals, they at least had history on their side: the teams had met four times since Cincinnati had entered the AFL as an expansion team in 1968, and the Jets had won each time. But with a record of 5–4, the Bengals were still in the playoff race: the game held more urgency for them than for the Jets, who by then had little more at stake than saving face.

In the first period neither team played like much was at stake. The first quarter went scoreless, but after defensive end Sherman White recovered a New York fumble at the Cincinnati 46 in the second period, the Bengals got on the board first when Boobie Clark capped a nine-play drive with a one-yard touchdown run 2:19 into the quarter.

The Bengals built on their lead quickly when linebacker Ken Avery intercepted Woodall at the New York 29 and returned it to the 14 to set up a 16-yard field goal with 7:35 left in the half. A few minutes later, Cincinnati quarterback Ken Anderson hit Isaac Curtis with a 24-yard scoring pass to give the Bengals a 17–0 lead with 4:26 left in the half.

Just before the end of the half, Woodall got the Jets back in the game when he drove them 77 yards in 12 plays, scoring on a three-yard pass to Jerome Barkum eight seconds before the intermission. Having cut the lead to 17–7, the Jets seemed to carry that momentum into the second half. On their first series of the third quarter, Woodall again led them to a score, driving the team 76-yards in 10 plays and hitting Rich Caster with a 12-yard touchdown pass. Woodall had otherwise hit Caster with a 37-yard gainer in the series. The score cut Cincinnati's lead to 17–14 midway through the third period.

The Jets were driving again late in the third period, but a 13-yard pass from Woodall to Caster that would have advanced them to the Cincinnati 20 was nullified by a holding penalty, and an additional 10-yard loss on a quarterback sack effectively ended the threat, taking the Jets out of field goal range. Then, in the opening minute of the fourth quarter, Horst Muhlmann kicked a 51-yard field goal to increase Cincinnati's lead to 20–14.

As the fourth quarter wore on the Bengals were able to hold the Jets at bay, but then it happened: after being kicked in the head, Woodall was shaken up and unable to continue playing. Ewbank hadn't planned on playing Namath that day, but after a brief appearance by Bill Demory at quarterback, he felt he had no other choice. With 4:49 left in the game, Namath trotted onto the field and into the huddle. "It gets you on your toes," said lineman Randy Rassmussen of Namath's unexpected appearance. "Just the way he says things, you believe him."[16]

But after hitting Eddie Bell for 12 yards on his initial pass, Namath was then intercepted by linebacker Al Beauchamp at the New York 41. Beauchamp promptly fumbled the ball, however, and Bell recovered for the Jets. Just two plays later the Jets gave it right back when Cliff McClain fumbled on a run, and Avery recovered for the Bengals at the Cincinnati 49. The Bengals would have naturally loved to run out the clock, but unable to move the ball, they punted back to the Jets. Namath had one more shot with 1:37 left to play.

Starting from his own 21-yard line, Namath hit Caster with consecutive passes of 21 and 16 yards to move the Jets to the Cincinnati 42. He then lofted a 31-yard pass to Bell down the right sideline that advanced the Jets to the 11-yard line. From there Namath went back to Caster, lobbing a pass to the left side of the end zone. Caster went to his knees and made an excellent catch, gathering in the ball as he slid on the turf and went out of bounds. It was a touchdown, but the official didn't see it that way and ruled that Caster had caught the ball out of bounds. He was wrong, but in the official's defense it was very close and it happened so fast. In the days before instant replay review by officials, there was no recourse: the decision stood.

Two incomplete passes brought up a fourth down, and with no other options the Jets had to go for it. Namath again threw to Caster, hitting him just inside the end zone. As Caster made the catch with both feet in the end zone, he was pushed back outside the goal line by two defenders. Still, he had received the ball in the end zone for a score. Again, the official disagreed, spotting the ball inside the one-yard line. The completion had at least given the Jets a first down.

On the next play, the Bengals were flagged for being offside and the ball was moved half the distance to the goal, putting it about a foot from the goal line. With 19 seconds left and no timeouts remaining, Namath called two running plays in the huddle. He handed off to McClain: linebackers Bill Bergey and Doug Adams stopped McClain just short of the goal. With the clock ticking down, the Bengals were naturally taking their time getting up off the carpet and referee Bernie Ulman stopped the clock with five seconds left. Namath would claim afterward that he was unaware that Ulman had even restarted the clock, but he had as the Jets were getting set. As the clock struck zero another flag flew. But this time it was on Rasmussen for illegal procedure.

There was considerable confusion as the game was abruptly declared at an end. Ewbank was completely bewildered as to what was going on, first assuming that the penalty was on Cincinnati and protesting that the game could not end on a penalty on the defense, then protesting again when finding that the call was on New York.

In the locker room, Namath seemed at a loss to make sense of the game's chaotic final moments. "So close," he said quietly as he sat in front of his locker. "Why couldn't it have been different? We lost, why?"[17] He finished the game six of 13 for 98 yards, with an interception.

If Namath was glum, Ewbank was far more animated, furiously repeating that Caster had made *two* touchdown catches in the last minute that were both disallowed. Caster concurred; about the first of the two he said: "I thought I was in. My feet were always on the ground and they were behind me."[18]

Things weren't much more upbeat in the Cincinnati locker room. Defensive lineman Steve Chomyszak said he thought the Bengals had lost the game. Anyone would have thought so to see the numbers. Other than the score the numbers were overwhelmingly in New York's favor: 21 to 11 in first downs, 310 to 96 in net passing yardage (264–76 gross), 357 to 208 in total yardage. All of which amounted to nothing as the Jets had four turnovers to the Bengals' one.

Bengals head coach Paul Brown wasn't exactly overjoyed. "I'm glad we won," Brown said, "but you're suppose to feel good after you win."[19] Beyond that, Brown told the reporters to give Ewbank a message: he felt that the Bengals' victory was down to luck, and he wanted the Jets' coach to know that.

Namath's dramatic appearance late in the game had overshadowed everything else. When he came onto the field the fans in Cincinnati grew excited, rising to their feet in joyous applause. They left the stadium that day feeling satisfied: their team had won, and more than that, they got to see an enthralling climax, courtesy of Joe Namath. Yeah, they got their money's worth.

Cincinnati defensive back Neal Craig said that the Jets had become aroused by Namath's sudden appearance in the game. In Craig's estimation, the Jets simply felt that Namath could get it done.[20] Chomyszak had his own take on the Namath effect. He noted that, after Namath came into the game the New York linemen were holding a lot more. Chomyszak figured these were men looking to protect their jobs by keeping Namath safe at any cost.[21]

"The defeat," wrote Murray Chass of the *New York Times*, "was heartbreaking and anger-provoking, but it once again pointed up the uncanny ability Namath has to lift the team single-handedly and inspire it to greater achievements than it perhaps is capable of."[22]

Week 11—Sunday, November 25, 1973
Shea Stadium, New York (attendance: 47,283)

Returning to Shea in week 11 to host the Atlanta Falcons, the Jets were 3–7 and now had no hope of achieving a winning record in Weeb Ewbank's final season in coaching. The old man would not be going out a winner. All the team could shoot for would be to do him proud with what little time remained.

The Falcons, on the other hand, were right in the thick of things. After starting the season 1–3, they came into Shea on a six-game winning streak, and at 7–3 were hot on the trail of the NFC West Division title, being just a game behind the Los Angeles Rams.

Namath would be making his first start since his shoulder separation in Baltimore in week two. Under the circumstances, he could hardly be expected to be in top form, but it was hoped that his presence might inspire the team to rise above their situation. One circumstance that both teams would have to contend with that day was the weather. Through much of the game the rain was coming in a steady downpour, which had resulted in more than 14,000 no-shows at the sold out event.

The Jets did not start well. Namath's first pass of the game was intercepted by defensive back Ray Brown—one of two he would pick off that day—which killed a New York drive, and got the Falcons started on their first scoring march. Following the interception, the Falcons drove 67 yards in six plays, taking a 7–0 lead when Bob Lee hit Tom Geredine with a 38-yard touchdown throw.

The Jets came right back and evened the score before the end of the first quarter, when Namath got his first touchdown pass of the season. From the two-yard line, Namath rolled out right and drilled a pass to Rich Caster in the right side of the end zone. The Jets then took the lead in the second quarter after Ralph Baker intercepted Lee at the Atlanta 44 and returned it nine yards to set the New York offense up at the 35. But the Jets were unable to get it into the end zone, and had to send Bobby Howfield in to kick a 14-yard field goal that gave them a 10–7 lead.

Atlanta climbed back on top, not so much by virtue of its offense, but more by way of a punt that pinned the Jets back at their own two-yard line and the foul weather that no doubt played its role when Mike Adamle fumbled the ball two plays later. Linebacker Don Hansen recovered for Atlanta at the New York one, enabling the Falcons to retake the lead on a one-yard touchdown run by Eddie Ray.

The Jets would cut the lead to a point at 14–13 when Howfield kicked a 24-yard field goal, but Atlanta built their lead back up again with just 42 seconds left in the half. Lee threw over the middle to a wide open Louis Neal at the New York 30, and the receiver took it the distance for a 47-yard touchdown play.

As the rain continued to pour down in the third quarter, the Jets again drew to within a point at 21–20 when Namath threw 38 yards to Eddie Bell for a score, but that was as close as they would get. In the fourth quarter, the Falcons put the game away with a 16-play drive that covered 62 yards and ended with Ray once more punching it over from a yard out. In the end, the Jets were done in by six turnovers (three fumbles and three interceptions). Aside from his three interceptions, Namath was 15 of 32 for 191 yards, and two TDs.

With the 28–20 victory, the Falcons extended their winning streak to seven games, and with eight victories to their credit, assured themselves of the best record in the club's eight-year history. They also remained within a game of Los Angeles in the NFC West. Ultimately, they would fail to catch the Rams, however, as the Falcons would lose two of their three remaining games and would fail to make the playoffs.

As for the Jets, at 3–8 they were only fighting to keep from finishing last in their division.

Only the 2–9 Baltimore Colts trailed them in the AFC East, and the Jets could keep it that way in week 12 when they would be hosting the Colts.

Week 12 — Sunday, December 2, 1973
Shea Stadium, New York (attendance: 51,167)

The 3–8 Jets against the 2–9 Colts — it was certainly a long way off from the 1969 Super Bowl when the Jets were 11–3 and the Colts 13–1. In sport, five years can be an eternity, teams growing old that quickly and losing their edge. It might be hard for a losing team to try and get up for a game, but there is often a renewed vigor when one losing team plays another. Perhaps it's the sensing of opportunity, the notion that a victory might lift the team a bit, and the additional win make things look slightly less bleak in the standings. Or maybe it's just the humiliation that would accompany being beaten by another bunch of losers.

Although Namath had gone down early with a separated shoulder when the Jets and Colts met earlier in the season, the Jets had pulled themselves together nicely and beat Baltimore soundly that day, 34–10. In the first half of their week 12 meeting at Shea, the Jets might have felt on their way to a similar triumph, but the Colts would ultimately make it more interesting.

In the first quarter the Jets took a 3–0 lead on a 30-yard field goal, but there would be no more scoring until the second period. The Colts were driving when quarterback Marty Domres hit tight end Raymond Chester with a pass at the New York 10-yard line, but as Chester turned he was hit by safety Burgess Owens and lost the ball. The Jets' Phil Wise tried to scoop it up on the run, but initially had a hard time getting a hold of it. It didn't slow him down much, however, as he was able to gather the ball up at the 20 and then race 80 yards up the sideline for a touchdown.

Later in the second quarter, with the Jets still up 10–0, another Baltimore drive was killed when Domres coughed the ball up, and defensive tackle John Little recovered for the Jets at the New York 43. From there it was a matter of four plays for the Jets to cash in again, with Namath passing 15 yards to Emerson Boozer for a touchdown. Namath threw left to Boozer at the six-yard line, and Boozer then darted in between linebacker Stan White and defensive back Nelson Munsey to go in for the score.

After halftime, that 17–0 lead held through a scoreless third quarter; then Baltimore made things interesting in the fourth. It was only seven seconds into the fourth quarter when Baltimore finally posted their first points of the game on a 17-yard field goal that cut New York's lead to 17–3. It took the Jets less than three minutes to answer back, as a 63-yard pass from Namath to Jerome Barkum set up an 18-yard field goal that made it 20–3. Catching the ball on the run at midfield, Barkum looked like he might go all the way, but as he tried to out-sprint Munsey to the end zone he suddenly lost the handle on the ball, bobbling it into the air at the 30-yard line. Barkum was able to gather it back in, but having broken stride, Munsey had by then caught up and took him down from behind at the Baltimore 20.

To get back in the game, the Colts dusted off a play that seemed to always fool the Jets, even if Earl Morrall had failed to successfully complete it in the Super Bowl: they went with the flea-flicker, which they had burned the Jets with for a score the prior season. This time, rather than start as a run, the Colts ran it like a screen to wide receiver Cotton Speyrer. Domres threw a lateral across the field to Speyrer, who then lobbed a very wobbly throw downfield to Glenn Doughty, all alone deep downfield — so alone that he could wait on the ball and just about walk it in. The play covered 54 yards, and cut the New York lead to 20–10.

Sensing that the Colts were getting something started and gathering momentum, Namath seemed to want to answer back quickly. He might have been wise to try and run some time off the clock, but with Riggins out with a separated shoulder since early in the Cincinnati game two weeks earlier, the running game was not at full strength. Even so, Boozer was having a good day, and wound up with his first 100-yard game of the year. But perhaps Namath was eager to kill a Baltimore rally before it could get rolling, and he chose to pass on first down. Bad move: the pass was intercepted by linebacker Ted Hendricks at the New York 25, and a six-yard return gave the Colts the ball on the 19. From there, Baltimore ran Lydell Mitchell on five straight plays, the fifth being a one-yard touchdown run that brought the Colts to within three points of the Jets at 20–17.

Unable to put a drive together on their next series, the Jets had to surrender the ball back to Baltimore, and with time winding down the Colts worked their way to the New York 25. A holding penalty on guard Elmer Collet knocked Baltimore back to the 40 (yes, holding penalties were still 15 yards at that time), and facing a third-and-22 with two minutes to play, Baltimore decided to run Mitchell on a draw play rather than pass. Mitchell only gained two yards and George Hunt came in to try and tie the game with a 46-yard field goal. It was both short and wide right, and the Jets took over with 1:51 left in the game. They then managed to run the clock out.

"We came out at the half thinking we'd try to shut them out," Ewbank said. "They really took it away from us. They scared the heck out of us."[23] Namath was 15 of 21 for 231 yards, one TD and one interception. The victory made the Jets 4–8 while the Colts dropped to 2–10.

The Jets traveled to Philadelphia to play the Eagles in week 13, but Namath's status for the game was uncertain. Namath began having trouble with his right knee during practice on the Thursday before the game, and the subsequent swelling left the Jets' quarterback position a question mark. Come game day, it was Woodall that quarterbacked the Jets in the rain in Philadelphia.

Woodall had a good game, hitting on 11 of 29 for 160 yards, but the Jets' running game was better: Boozer rushed for 160 yards in 21 carries, while Mike Adamle carried 16 times for 84 yards. After jumping out to a 14–0 lead in the first quarter, the Jets upped it to 17–0 in the second before the Eagles got on the board with a touchdown that made it 17–7 at the half. In the third quarter, the Eagles would explode for 17 points while the Jets could manage only a pair of field goals in the second half. The Jets lost by a point, 24–23, and fell to 4–9.

The Jets were returning home for their last game of the season, and Ewbank's last game as coach. The players all wanted very much to make it a memorable send off for the old man: it would be memorable for all the wrong reasons.

Week 14 — Sunday, December 16, 1973
Shea Stadium, New York (attendance: 47,790)

Everyone knew that December 16 would be Weeb Ewbank's last game as a coach. He had announced his retirement well in advance and had named his son-in-law, Charley Winner, his successor. What wasn't so certain was Namath's future with the franchise. Some were raising the question of whether or not the season-ender at Shea would also be Namath's last game with the Jets, or even his last game entirely. Namath's contract was up at the end of the 1973 season, and while he did have an option year in 1974, he seemed unsure if he would return to the Jets for another season. "Right now my immediate goal is doing a good job this week," Namath said. "I'm not looking past this week. I don't have to make that decision right now."[24]

Ewbank would not be retiring a winner, but the team hoped to at least get him one more win in his final game. If it might be Namath's last game with the Jets, then he too would very much want to go out with a victory, but all of the glory that day would not be theirs. It would, however, be a day for the record books.

The Jets were closing out the 1973 season against the 8–5 Buffalo Bills in a snowy game at Shea. Buffalo's O.J. Simpson came into the game with 1,803 yards rushing and needing just 60 yards to tie Jim Brown's single-season rushing record. He and his teammates had their sights set higher: 197 yards would give Simpson an unprecedented 2,000 yards for the season. Having rushed for more than 200 yards twice already during the season, it seemed doable. But surely the New York defense knew what Buffalo was shooting for, and certainly they would be ready for it. Right?

After receiving the opening kickoff, Buffalo went right to work without pretense. After gaining four yards on the first play from scrimmage, Simpson went off right tackle for 30 yards on the second play. That run made him only the twentieth player to surpass 5,000 career-rushing yards. Buffalo quarterback Joe Ferguson basically did what he had all year — took the snap and gave the ball to Simpson — in marching the team downfield. Aside from an 11-yard run by fullback Jim Braxton, the Bills simply gave the ball to Simpson until they had gotten to the New York three-yard line. At that point they decided to run Braxton on three consecutive plays, until he finally scored from a yard out to give Buffalo a 7–0 lead.

The Jets could do nothing in their first series, and punted after three plays. As the snow continued to fall, Simpson went back to work on achieving his team's goal of getting him the rushing record. Already within six yards of Brown's record, Simpson got it on the Bills' first play of their next series. The game was stopped while Simpson's teammates all congratulated him, and he was given the ball he carried for the record. After taking the ball to the sideline for safekeeping and making the rounds in receiving congratulations from everyone there, Simpson returned to the field and the game resumed. On the next play, Simpson promptly fumbled the ball and the Jets took over.

Namath wasted little time, hurling a 48-yard bomb to Jerome Barkum two plays later for the tying score. The game was still tied 7–7 in the second quarter, and Buffalo had been unable to get into scoring position since early in the first. It took the Bills quite some time to come to the realization that the Jets' keying on Simpson may have opened up other opportunities, but eventually they tried the passing game. With a couple passes to Braxton and Bob Chandler, the Bills loosened the New York defense up enough to return to — what else — running Simpson, and he scored on a 13-yard run that gave Buffalo a 14–7 lead with 1:12 left in the half.

The Jets were unable to mount a threat in the final minute of the second quarter, and punted with some 30 seconds left. The punt didn't travel far, and Bill Cahill fielded it on the run at his own 49, running through a seam up the middle before breaking outside and managing to outrace David Knight to the left corner of the end zone. It gave Buffalo a 21–7 lead just before halftime.

Giving up two touchdowns just before the end of the half seems to have broken the team's spirits, and it would not be until late in the game that the Jets would score again. The New York ground game, held to only 32 yards in the first half, was nonexistent in the second half, gaining only seven yards. Meanwhile Buffalo continued to run and run and run, eventually going up 28–7 on another one-yard touchdown run by Braxton.

Buffalo went up 31–7 with a 12-yard field goal in the fourth quarter, and then scored their final points — an 11-yard field goal — in a drive that accomplished the team's ultimate goal. With under six minutes to play, Simpson ran around left end for seven yards, giving him 200 for the game, and 2,003 for the season.

Namath — the entire team — had wanted to win this final game for their retiring coach, but with the score now 34–7 that obviously wasn't going to happen. Still, even as Shea Stadium was already emptying, the offense wanted to at least make one final gesture. On five straight passes Namath took the Jets down to a score, hitting Rich Caster, Barkum, Knight, and then finally Caster again for a 16-yard touchdown that made the final 34–14. It didn't count for much, but it was all they could do for the old man. In the end, Namath's numbers read 13 of 30 for 206 yards, and two TDs.

The New York Jets locker room was an emotional scene after the game. There was no shortage of tears when Dave Herman presented Ewbank with a gold watch on behalf of the team. "It's a great game," Ewbank said. "It's a great life."[25]

Like the rest of the team, Namath's regret was in not winning one last game for Ewbank. "We've had our ups and downs through the year," Namath said, "but honestly I like the guy."[26] Saying that he had to fight to hold back his own tears, Namath gave a simple yet apt summation of Ewbank's career: he said that the old man really loved the game.[27]

While the Jets lost their final two games, the Colts managed to win both of theirs, meaning that the Jets and Colts got to share last place in the division, both finishing 4–10. Technically, the Jets finished ahead of Baltimore, having beaten them twice during the season, but that was little consolation.

Nineteen seventy-three was another wasted season for the Jets. When Namath went down with a separated shoulder in the second game, many wrote the Jets off at that point, but there is no guarantee that things would have gone a whole lot better had he played the entire season (the Jets were 2–3 in the five games that Namath started in 1973). From the start of the season, the Jets seemed in disarray and lacked cohesion. The team had talent, but with the preseason holdouts of people like Riggins, Boozer, and Winston Hill, the Jets began the season looking completely unprepared. Things weren't helped with the significant losses to injury during the year; not only did Namath miss much of the season with a separated shoulder, but in week 10 Riggins also separated a shoulder and missed the rest of the schedule.

As the Jets ended the season they were a team in transition. Ewbank — the only coach the team had since becoming the Jets in 1963 — was stepping down as head coach, and passing the torch to Charley Winner. As for Namath, there was much uncertainty about his future with the team. He had completed 68 of 133 passes (51.1 percent) for 966 yards, with five TDs and six interceptions during his abbreviated season. With the team transitioning, there were some who wondered if he was worth the expense anymore. After all, he hadn't played an entire season since 1969. From 1970 through 1973 he had missed half of the team's 56 regular season games. Whereas he was once essential to the team's commerce — as well as that of the league — he now seemed unnecessary from that perspective as the Jets regularly sold out their home games irrespective of whether or not he played.

There was talk of Namath going to the upstart World Football League, which would launch in 1974 and was said to be offering him a $2 million deal. Namath declined to comment on the possibility of his going to the WFL, saying that his lawyer was in talks with them, but he himself knew little about it.

Namath seemed unsure whether he would play at all the following year. "I don't have to decide right now," he said after the last game of the year. "I'll just have to think on it and come to a decision."[28] Aside from his own uncertainty, he also raised the possibility that the Jets would not want him back in 1974. Although his two-year contract had ended with the completion of the 1973 season, he had an option year remaining. There was the possibility of a trade, but a spokesman for the team said that they had not entered into talks with any other team about trading Namath. "If I do get traded," Namath said, "it would have to be to a contender or a warm weather team. At this stage of my career, I'm not about to go somewhere where they're rebuilding."[29] Still, he said he would prefer to remain with the Jets.

For many, the idea of Namath playing anywhere else was unthinkable. He had been the franchise since 1965, but while the team had always been generous with Namath in regards to his own contracts, he hadn't always been well served when it came to the team supplying a good supporting cast (the 1973 holdouts attested to that), and while Ewbank would be stepping down as coach, he would remain with the organization as general manager. There were some who felt that did not bode well for Namath's future. In *The Sporting News*, Bob Oates summed it up thusly: "The inept Jet organization ... has doomed Namath to also-ran status for the rest of his professional life unless he can promote a trade."[30]

12

The 1974 Season

"If I find I am able to play football, I will play out my option with the Jets," Namath said in early February of 1974.[1] Later that month, Namath was in the Bahamas doing some water skiing when the towrope snapped. That wasn't all that snapped: as his body fell into the water, he got turned around and his left hamstring snapped as well.

Back in New York the next day, Dr. Nicholas took a look and decided against operating. There was not a great track record for reattaching hamstrings, Nicholas explained, and while the muscle was essential for running, with his knees nobody was expecting Namath to do much of that anyway. It was described to reporters variously as a pulled hamstring and a torn hamstring, but in reality it hadn't just torn, but was detached. It hadn't even happened on the field, yet it would be the most debilitating injury of Namath's career. For the rest of his playing days he would look the part of the creaky, hobbling old veteran.

Despite his latest injury, the Jets had decided on keeping Namath, but he declined to commit himself beyond the 1974 season. "I've already told them that I'm not going to negotiate a new contract," Namath said in late June. "This is the option year of my contract and when it's over I want to be free and clear."[2]

He was also still being wooed by the WFL, and was probably interested to see how the fledgling league would fare in its maiden season in 1974. If he found himself still able to play after the 1974 season — and if the money was right — he might consider it. But after a decade in New York, leaving would be a big decision. "I like the city of New York," Namath said, "and I'd like to keep playing there."[3]

With Charley Winner now assuming the head coaching job, 1974 would be the beginning of a new era for the New York Jets. Winner had been head coach in St. Louis for five years (1966–1970), and while he had led the Cardinals to three winning seasons, they had not made the playoffs even once during his tenure. Having decided to step down as head coach come 1974, Weeb Ewbank hired Winner as the Jets' linebacker coach in 1973 with the idea that Winner — Ewbank's son-in-law — would take over as head coach the following year.

Winner's tenure got off to a shaky start when none of the veterans turned up at camp in July due to an NFL Players Association strike. The NFLPA had given a list of demands to the NFL Management Council back in March, but the two sides were finding no middle ground as training camp was drawing near. What seemed to be the most important of the union's 63 demands was the right for players to negotiate with any team of their choosing. "The basic issue is the right of a player to move from one team to another when his contract has expired," said union president Bill Curry of the Houston Oilers.[4]

Among the other demands were the elimination of reserve and waiver clauses, the rights of players to veto any trade, and limits on the authority of coaches in imposing curfews and issuing fines for disciplinary infractions. With no agreement in sight, a strike was announced at the end of June as team camps were set to begin. Each team began camp populated by rookies and free agents, who were all ineligible to join the union until the start of the season when they would be officially listed on a team roster.

The players with most cause for concern were the second-stringers, who faced the greatest chance of being replaced. The starters and superstars could all assume their place again once the strike was over, but without a chance to prove themselves early, second-stringers stood every chance of losing a spot. The veterans tried to persuade rookies not to report to camp, but it did little good: these guys had dreamt long and worked hard for this. Few of them were willing to roll the dice and risk losing the opportunity just because a pack of fat cats who already got theirs were telling them it was all in their best interests.

As was the tradition, the NFL preseason was scheduled to begin with the College All-Star game, which was to be held on Friday, July 26, in Chicago. Throughout the month of July, as the two sides appeared nowhere near an agreement, many players were losing patience and began to trickle into camp. But as the time for the College All-Star game was approaching, the All-Stars voted by a narrow margin not to play. Two days later, the event was officially cancelled for the first time in 41 years. The charity that sponsored the event, which benefited underprivileged children in the Chicago area, was estimated to have lost some $200,000 for their cause.

More and more players — including some heavyweights — began to filter into team camps in late July, but the rosters were still largely made up of free agents and rookies as preseason was set to begin. Namath was not among the veterans to make himself available, but then he never liked training camp or exhibition games anyway. At least this time there would be no controversy as to why he reported late.

The Jets opened their preseason schedule in Denver against the Broncos on Saturday, August 3, before 27,559 fans at Mile High Stadium. Exhibition games are always a poor indicator of a team's impending season; all the more so this time with so few veterans playing, but Winner must have still been very pleased that the Jets easily rolled over the Broncos, 41–19, in his first game as head coach in New York. Rookie quarterback J.J. Jones threw a pair of touchdown passes to David Knight, and rookie running back Robert Burns scored on three runs.

A week later, the Jets would participate in a game of minor historical relevance to the league. In 1974 the NFL would for the first time be playing overtime during the regular season, and the decision was made to include sudden death overtime in the preseason as well. The Jets' game with the Chargers in San Diego would mark the first overtime game of the year, and the first not to be played in post-season. The Jets lost to the Chargers 20–14 in a game attended by only 19,036.

Finally, toward mid–August, with no union-management agreement forthcoming and players becoming frustrated, many chose to join their respective teams of their own volition. With more players crossing the picket lines and the season drawing near, a cooling off period was announced, and the union gave players the green light to report. But as New York Jets veterans began to arrive at camp on August 12, Namath was noticeably not among them. A spokesman for the team confessed that no one had been able to locate him, but word got to him somehow (the news perhaps), and at 1:15 P.M. on Wednesday, August 14, Namath arrived at camp in a chauffeured limousine.

Although the hamstring — still being described as a pulled hamstring — was making dropping back and setting up a little problematic, Namath said that he would be ready by Saturday for the Jets' annual exhibition against the New York Giants in New Haven. Winner disagreed, saying that Namath hadn't had enough practice time and that he would therefore be playing Al Woodall and J.J. Jones at quarterback. Having taken over and installed a new offensive system, Winner felt that Namath and some of the other late-arriving players had simply not had sufficient time to learn the new plays. Emerson Boozer and John Riggins would also sit out the game.

Namath didn't even make the trip to New Haven, and his absence no doubt took much of the luster off the event. The Giants won 21–13 in a game more one-sided than the score would suggest, but the real showdown between the two teams would come later, as they were scheduled to meet again in week nine of the season.

On August 23, Namath made his first appearance of the preseason in a Friday night game in St. Louis. It was something of a homecoming for Winner, having coached the Cardinals for five years, and a crowd of 43,485 turned up at Busch Stadium. Winner wasn't sure if he would play Namath beyond the first quarter, but he told reporters that he might leave him in for a half. With no score after the first period, Namath stayed in for the second quarter and put the Jets up 7–0 with a slant-in pass to Eddie Bell that went 64 yards for a score. After Burns ran for a touchdown in the third, Bell caught another touchdown, this one a 21-yarder from Woodall that gave the Jets a 20–0 lead early in the fourth quarter. The Cardinals managed to avoid a shutout when Willie Belton scored a one-yard touchdown run with 24 seconds left in the game, making the final 20–7. With the victory, the Jets evened their preseason record at 2–2. In his half of play, Namath had completed six of 14 for 122 yards.

The following Saturday, on a humid night in New Orleans, Namath threw a 31-yard touchdown to Bell in the first minute of the second quarter to give the Jets a 7–0 lead over the Saints. New Orleans added a field goal before the half, and after two quarters of play Namath's work was done, having completed five of 12 for 97 yards. The Jets' 7–3 lead held up through the third quarter, but the Saints suddenly caught fire in the fourth and ran up 21 points in rolling to a 24–7 victory. It had been a thoroughly sloppy performance by the Jets, who fumbled six times, losing three. But that could not explain away the loss, since New Orleans had lost the ball an equal number of times on eight fumbles.

The fourth quarter collapse must have been discouraging to Winner, but the Jets wouldn't wait until late in the game to fall apart in their final exhibition, a meeting with the Oakland Raiders at the University of California's Memorial Stadium in Berkeley. "We got whipped," Namath said after the game. "They got a good ball club and they just beat the hell outta us."[5]

With the season just around the corner, Winner wanted to increase Namath's playing time, but Namath left the game early in the third quarter with a hip pointer courtesy of Tony Cline and Otis Sistrunk. He didn't have a bad game to judge by the numbers (12 of 21 for 163 yards with one interception), but the Raiders were clearly the better team, gaining 32 first downs and running over the New York defense for 253 yards on the ground and 545 yards in total offense. The Jets only managed 262 yards of offense in the game, mostly through the air. The New York ground game accounted for only six yards on eight attempts in the first half, and 56 yards on 17 rushes by the game's conclusion. Of course, this was without Riggins and Boozer, who both had yet to play. Trailing 14–3 at halftime, the Jets posed no threat in the second half and went on to lose 31–6 to finish their exhibition schedule with a record of 2–4. They hardly seemed ready for the start of the season, but the season was staring them in the face nonetheless.

Week 1— Sunday, September 15, 1974
Arrowhead Stadium, Kansas City (attendance: 74,854)

The Jets opened the 1974 season with a four-game road swing, beginning against the Chiefs at Arrowhead Stadium in Kansas City. Namath got New York out to a 6–0 first-quarter lead when he hit Rich Caster with a 14-yard touchdown throw (Bobby Howfield missed the extra point). In the second quarter, the Jets built their lead to 13–0 when Namath hit Eddie Bell from seven yards for a score.

Throughout the first half the Jets had been winning the war for field position, and keeping the Chiefs pinned deep in their own end of the field. In fact, with five minutes left in the half the Chiefs had only once ventured beyond their own 30-yard line. But then Larry Brunson fielded a New York punt at the Kansas City 25 and returned it to the New York 46. It was Kansas City's first good field position of the game, and they took advantage. Five plays later, they scored on a two-yard run by Ed Podolak to cut the New York lead to 13–7.

The Jets seemed determined to quash any momentum shift, and proceeded to drive to the Kansas City eight-yard line, but when the drive stalled they had to settle for a 25-yard field goal (1974 marked the year that the NFL had the goal posts moved from the front to the back of the end zones — there would be no more eight or 10-yard field goals). Still, it increased their lead to 16–7 with only a minute left in the half.

The Jets quickly forced a Kansas City punt, and having achieved good field position, sought to further pad their lead just before halftime. The opportunity was there — the execution wasn't. Namath tried to dump a screen pass off to John Riggins, but the fullback misplayed the ball. It hit Riggins right in the hands, but he bobbled the ball while trying to pull it in and defensive end Marvin Upshaw snatched it right from his hands. Upshaw ran 52 yards for a score with only 10 seconds left in the half. "I saw Riggins set for a screen as he came around," Upshaw said. "I was lucky he didn't have complete control of it, and I came up with it."[6] The score not only cut the Jets' lead to 16–14 right before the intermission, but also caused a major tide shift in momentum.

While the Jets were unable to post any points in the third period, the Chiefs managed a 27-yard field goal late in the third that gave them the lead for the first time in the game. The Jets continued to trail by a point, 17–16, through the fourth quarter, and when they took possession at their own 25 with 2:01 remaining they still had plenty of time to at least get close enough for a field goal to win the game. But when Namath tried to hit Jerome Barkum on one of those dicey out patterns, he was intercepted by Emmitt Thomas at the New York 38. As he ran the ball down the sideline for a score, Thomas raised his hand to give Namath a wave along the way. With nobody between him and the end zone, Thomas could afford to showboat. The touchdown gave Kansas City an eight-point lead with 1:52 left to play. The Jets had that much time to score twice: it wasn't going to happen. Namath was 14 of 30 for 210 yards and two TDs, but he also had four interceptions.

An opening day loss is always disappointing, starting the season on a bad note as it does, but it was all the more disappointing in that the Jets let the game get away from them, having blown a 13-point lead. It was also disappointing for Charley Winner, of course, since it was officially his first game as head coach of the Jets.

Week 2 — Sunday, September 22, 1974
Soldier Field, Chicago (attendance: 50,213)

In week two, the Jets traveled to Chicago to play the Bears at Soldier Field. Namath and the Jets hadn't played there since beating the College All-Stars in 1969. This, however, would be their first-ever meeting with the Chicago Bears. The Jets got out to an early lead, as Namath again opened the scoring with a touchdown pass to Rich Caster, this time lofting a 30-yard throw down the middle of the field that came down perfectly over Caster's shoulder and into his hands as he crossed the goal line. Just as he had done after Caster's touchdown catch the week before, Bobby Howfield missed the extra point, leaving the Jets with a 6–0 lead after one quarter.

In the second quarter, the Jets increased their lead by way of some nifty running by John Riggins — and a very lucky bounce. Namath threw left to Riggins flaring out of the backfield, and after making the catch at the New York 39-yard line Riggins ran down the left sideline before cutting in-between two tacklers at the Chicago 45 and breaking back toward the middle. Riggins outran another tackler at the 35 and then faked out defensive back Allan Ellis at the 31, but as he was preparing to try and get around defensive back Clarence Clemons, Riggins was hit from behind by linebacker Doug Buffone and the ball popped out at the 27. Halfback Clarence "Jazz" Jackson happened to be trailing along looking for somebody to block, and the ball bounced right his way. Jackson gathered it up at the 24, and outran defensive back Bill Knox to the end zone. The score gave the Jets a 13–0 lead.

Later in the quarter the Jets drove 77 yards in eight plays, finishing the drive with a three-yard touchdown run by Emerson Boozer. This time there would be no momentum-changing late-second-quarter collapse, and the Jets took their 20–0 lead into halftime. They had fairly well outplayed the Bears in the first half, converting five of six third downs, and Namath had thrown for 179 yards in the first two quarters. But that isn't to say that the momentum wouldn't shift anyway: the Bears still had half a game to turn things around.

Early in the third quarter Howfield missed a 19-yard field goal that would have increased New York's lead to 23–0, which seemed to perk the Bears up. Chicago quarterback Gary Huff then began to put on a show of his own, throwing two third-quarter touchdowns, the first an 11-yarder to running back Carl Garrett, and the second a four-yard toss to tight end Bob Parsons that cut New York's lead to 20–14.

In the fourth quarter Howfield made good on a 39-yard field goal that increased New York's lead to 23–14 with 6:30 left in the game, but Ken Grandberry fielded the ensuing kickoff at the three-yard line and returned it 68 yards to the New York 33. Five plays later Jim Harrison scored from a yard out to cut the Jets' lead to 23–21, with 4:24 left in the game.

When the Jets got the ball back, they seemed to be doing a good job of running the clock out. They used up valuable time in crossing midfield, but with 1:25 left in the game Jackson appeared to have fumbled, and the ball was recovered for Chicago by Clemons at the Bears' 48. Quite a scene ensued when the referee declared it a dead ball, allowing the Jets to retain possession. At that point things took an ugly turn as Clemons, for whatever reason, took a swing at Boozer, for which he drew a personal foul penalty. As the officials marked off 15 yards, Clemons' demon-strative protesting—described later by referee Ben Dreith as "abusive"—drew a second 15-yard flag. Again Clemons persisted, and *again* he was flagged. With his third consecutive unsports-manlike conduct charge he was ejected from the game. The third penalty was marked half the distance to the goal, placing the Jets at the Chicago nine-yard line.

The angry crowd grew very loud at that point, causing a stoppage in play. "We couldn't hear ourselves," said Namath. "I tried to run plays a couple of times but couldn't."[7] From there the Jets seemed to have no interest in a field goal, running four straight plays and turning the ball over to Chicago on downs with five seconds left to play. The Jets won, 23–21.

After the game, Chicago coach Abe Gibron was fuming about the penalties, but having been fined $500 the prior season for criticizing game officials, he declined to comment on it. Instead he vented himself by taking aim at another target. "Namath is a great pro," Gibron said sarcas-tically. "He conned us out of 50 seconds near the end of the game by claiming his signals couldn't be heard. There wasn't that much noise."[8] Namath disagreed, saying that the officials were standing right there and could hear for themselves how loud the crowd was. Namath finished 16 of 23 for 257 yards and one touchdown.

Being his first victory as head coach, Charley Winner was awarded the game ball by the players. The victory upped the Jets' record to 1–1, putting them in a three-way tie with Miami and Buffalo for second place in the AFC East, all trailing the 2–0 New England Patriots.

Week 3 — Sunday, September 29, 1974
Rich Stadium, Buffalo (attendance: 76,978)

"It was absurd," said Namath after the Jets' week three game against the Buffalo Bills in Orchard Park. "Ridiculous."[9] In a driving rain, the two teams played in winds gusting 40 to 45 mph. It was indeed absurd. It was particularly difficult for a team like the Jets, who depended quite a bit on the pass. For Buffalo, not so big a deal: the last time the two teams played in December of 1973 Buffalo quarterback Joe Ferguson only threw the ball five times, so the wind was of little concern for Ferguson, who threw little anyway.

The Jets were a team that for years had lived and died by the pass, and on a day like this one, they would likely be committing suicide by putting the ball in the air. But unlike some quarterbacks, Namath was unafraid. In the first quarter he went to the airways and tried hitting David Knight, who had a step on defender Tony Greene. As the ball tried to cut through the maelstrom, the wind picked it up; the ball looked haunted, almost being suspended in air until Greene plucked it out of the current at the New York 25-yard line. Greene ran it back 20 yards to the New York five, and three plays later Ferguson showed that he could do more than hand the ball to O.J. Simpson — he ran it around left end himself for a one-yard touchdown that gave Buffalo a 7–0 lead 6:11 into the game.

In the second period, Buffalo kicker John Leypoldt somehow managed to float a kick through the uprights from 21 yards to increase the Bills' lead to 10–0. Trying to keep it on the ground, the Jets then managed to work their way to the Buffalo 13, where John Riggins put New York on the board with a nifty touchdown run off left tackle with just over five minutes left in the half. Due to the wind and the rain, the snap on the conversion was mishandled, and as a result the Jets wound up with only six points. The half ended with Buffalo up 10–6, and no pass completions for either side.

In the second half the Jets chose to kick into the wind, hoping to get some points in the third quarter with the wind at their backs. The plan worked — sort of. Buffalo could get no further than their own 41 in the entire period, and punting into the wind, they were giving the Jets excellent field position to work with. Bills' punter Spike Jones could do little to help his team's cause, kicking only 28 yards and giving the Jets possession at the Buffalo 37. But the Jets didn't take full advantage, and on fourth down, with the wind at his back, Bobby Howfield managed a 31-yard field goal that cut the Buffalo lead to 10–9. On Buffalo's next series they again had to punt, and Jones again lost the battle with the wind, this time kicking just 27 yards, again allowing the Jets to start from the Buffalo 37. But the Jets were stymied once more, and had to send in Howfield. It was a longer try this time — 40 yards — but Howfield put it through again, and for the first time in the game the Jets led, 12–10.

The Jets would keep the lead into the fourth quarter, but having switched sides at the end of the third period, it was now New York's turn to kick into the wind. Jet punter Greg Gantt only got off a 25-yard kick, allowing the Bills to start at midfield, and eight plays later fullback Jim Braxton put Buffalo back on top when he ran 21 yards for a score. The extra point failed when the snap was mishandled, and the Bills then led 16–12 with 6:59 left in the game.

With time running out Namath had to try to pass more than he might have liked under the circumstances, but the wind was still whipping the ball around mercilessly. As the Jets struggled to get something started, the Bills struggled to run the clock out. It wasn't until the final 1:52 that Namath accomplished the game's first completed pass, a 12-yarder to Knight. He then completed a second throw, hitting tight end Willie Brister for 21 yards, but shortly afterward he was intercepted at midfield by defensive back Robert James, who returned it eight yards to the New York 42.

Keeping the ball on the ground, Buffalo was unable to run out the clock and had to punt. Namath had one last shot, but starting from the New York 25 and having no alternative but to challenge the wind he was again intercepted, this time by linebacker Rich Lewis with 17 seconds left. Buffalo then finally managed to run out the clock.

The game's passing stats were risible: Ferguson's numbers read 0–2, but he had actually attempted four throws. The other two were intercepted, but both turnovers were nullified by

New York penalties. Less inhibited, Namath threw 18 passes, completing two for 33 yards and having three intercepted. "If it was a golf tournament, they'd have called it off," Namath said afterward.[10]

At 1–2, the Jets fell into third place behind Miami and Buffalo. The still-unbeaten New England Patriots continued to lead the division.

Week 4 — Monday, October 7, 1974
Orange Bowl, Miami (attendance: 60,727)

In week four the Jets were in Miami to play their division rivals, the reigning Super Bowl–champion Dolphins on Monday night. The Dolphins may have been the two-time defending Super Bowl champions, but they also came into the game with their "No-name Defense" ranked twenty-fourth among the NFL's 26 teams, giving the Jets some hope for changing their fortunes. It was the Dolphins who got out of the gate fast, however, receiving the opening kickoff and driving 80 yards to score on a two-yard pass from Bob Griese to tight end Jim Mandich. The Jets' opening series, on the other hand, consisted of six plays and a punt, and in the second period Miami increased their lead to 14–0 when Larry Csonka scored from a yard out.

Griese was having quite the game in the first half, completing 13 of 18 passes, to the consternation of Charley Winner. "They couldn't have completed any more passes if we didn't have anybody out there," Winner said. "It was pathetic. We should have pulled the whole 11-man defensive unit but we had nobody else to put in there."[11]

Winner's disgust with his team's pass coverage resulted in some changes at halftime. In the second half, cornerback Earlie Thomas was replaced by Roscoe Word and free safety Steve Tannen was pulled in favor of Phil Wise. It seemed to make a difference, as the Jets turned things around.

There was also a new vigor in the Jets' offense. If the first half belonged to Griese, Namath took charge in the second. The Jets received the second-half kick and Namath took them 72 yards to score, completing seven of nine passes for 63 yards along the way. The drive ended with Namath hitting John Riggins with a nine-yard touchdown pass that cut the Miami lead in half at 14–7 at 5:16 of the third quarter.

The score seemed to perk up the New York defense as well, and after they forced a Miami punt the Jets took over at their own 36. Namath again got the offense moving, but this time the drive bogged down at the Miami 26, necessitating the Jets to send in Bobby Howfield to try a 43-yard field goal with under three minutes to play in the third period. Howfield made it, and the third quarter ended with the Dolphins still ahead, 14–10.

In the fourth quarter, the Dolphins found an unlikely hero in running back Hubert Ginn. Having been drafted by the Dolphins in 1970, Ginn had played with the team until being traded to Baltimore early in the 1973 season; but the Colts had cut him prior to the start of the 1974 season. With Mercury Morris injured, the Dolphins were lacking outside speed in their running game and had therefore reacquired Ginn two weeks prior to the Monday night game. Against the Jets, it would pay off. With 8:59 left in the game, Ginn reestablished Miami's momentum and increased their lead with a 41-yard touchdown run down the right sideline.

Now trailing 21–10, and backed up at their own 11-yard line, things looked fairly grim for the Jets, but Namath was known to put up points quickly, and put them up he did. From the 11 Namath dropped back and fired the ball down the left sideline to Rich Caster, who pulled it in at the 35 and proceeded to race the remaining 65 yards, untouched, for a score. The 89-yard touchdown was a Jets team record. It was also a thing of beauty, the ball sailing perfectly between four Miami defenders and right into Caster's hands as he took it on the run.

The lead once more cut to four points, the New York defense again rose to the occasion, forcing a punt and getting the ball back into Namath's hands. But after driving the Jets to the

Miami 48, Namath missed on three consecutive passes, forcing the Jets to punt it back. Again the New York defense stopped Miami, and after the Dolphins punted the Jets began at their 42 with 1:13 left to play. After advancing to midfield, Namath just missed hitting David Knight long at the 15. The Dolphins then had an even more narrow escape on a pass to Jerome Barkum that was broken up by Tim Foley inside the Miami five. The Jets managed to get to the Miami 40 for a first down, but with time running out Namath went across the middle to Caster, and the ball went through Caster's hands and was picked off by defender Jake Scott at the Miami 20 with only 19 seconds left in the game. The Jets came up short, 21–17.

"Those were two pretty good No. 12's going after each other tonight," Miami coach Don Shula said of Namath and Griese after the game.[12] Namath's assessment was more blunt. "That old saying 'It's not whether you win or lose but how you play the game' is garbage," he grumbled in the locker room. "It's if you win."[13] He completed 17 of 39 throws for 290 yards, two TDs and two interceptions.

The loss knocked the Jets further back in a hole at 1–3, ahead of only the winless Colts in the AFC East. The following week, New York would be facing the undefeated New England Patriots.

Week 5 — Sunday, October 13, 1974
Shea Stadium, New York (attendance: 57,825)

The Jets had their home opener in week five when the unbeaten, division-leading New England Patriots came to Shea. Through the years, the Patriots had proven a boost to the Jets during lean times when a win would at least pad their record and lift their spirits, if nothing else. While the Patriots had managed to beat the Jets in 1971 when Namath was out due to knee surgery, Namath himself hadn't lost to them since his rookie season in 1965. During his career, he had amassed a record of 12–1–1 against the Patriots. But now, with the Jets 1–3 and the Patriots 4–0, the times were indeed a-changing.

Despite their record, New England came into Shea with the worst-ranked pass defense in the AFC, something that should have boded well for a passing team like the Jets. Instead, Namath would have one of his toughest days throwing the ball, being sacked four times, and getting dumped on his ass plenty more after getting the ball off.

In the first period, five-foot-five Mack Herron fielded a New York punt at his 31 and returned it 36 yards to the Jets' 33. New England quarterback Jim Plunkett threw 11 yards to Darryl Stingley, and fullback Sam Cunningham broke a draw play for 12 more yards as the Patriots went on to score in seven plays; Cunningham took it the last six yards on a sweep around left end 5:16 into the game.

The Jets managed to drive to the New England 33, but when they stalled out there a 50-yard field goal seemed beyond Bobby Howfield's range, so they punted. Greg Gantt then booted the mother of all shanks, squibbing the ball a mere four yards to the New England 29. From there, the Patriots drove to a 37-yard field goal, upping their lead to 10–0, which is how it stood at halftime.

The Jets had posed a serious scoring threat only once in the half. John Riggins had run 34 yards from midfield to the New England 16, and after a pass had advanced them to the six-yard line the Jets had a first-and-goal. On first down Riggins gained three yards to the three, but linebacker Steve King then dropped Riggins for a nine-yard loss back to the 12 on second down. On third down, Namath was intercepted at the goal line by linebacker Sam Hunt.

After a scoreless third quarter, the Patriots put the game away in the fourth with an 11-play, 61-yard drive that reached paydirt when Cunningham went over from a yard out to give New England a 17–0 lead with 6:41 left in the game. As for Namath, he was done for the day. Having completed only seven of 21 passes for 63 yards, he was benched in favor of Al Woodall. Namath had also thrown two interceptions, which Woodall would equal in the final six minutes. With three minutes left in the game, linebacker Bob Geddes intercepted Woodall and took it back 29 yards for a touchdown to make the final 24–0. It was the first time the Jets had ever been shutout at home.

Now 1–4, the Jets were well behind the 5–0 Patriots, and also trailed the 4–1 Buffalo Bills and 3–2 Miami Dolphins by a good margin. At least they were ahead of the winless Baltimore Colts, and the good news was that they would be hosting the Colts the following week. Well, it would be good news for one or the other, anyway.

Week 6 — Sunday, October 20, 1974
Shea Stadium, New York (attendance: 51,745)

Even at 1–4, the Jets had reason to be optimistic when they hosted the Baltimore Colts in week six. After all, their three-game losing streak could not match the five-game skid of the winless Colts. There is also the fact that in their first five games the Baltimore Colts had given up the most points in the league, while scoring the fewest. But when a 1–4 team meets a 0–5 team, bragging rights are minimal whichever way it breaks.

After a largely uneventful first period, the Colts drew first blood just before the quarter ended. After a 21-yard punt by Greg Gantt, the Colts drove 43 yards in eight plays with quarterback Bert Jones running the last nine yards for the score with 1:38 left in the quarter. It wouldn't take Baltimore long to increase their lead. Two plays after receiving the kick, the Jets turned the ball over when Emerson Boozer fumbled and linebacker Stan White recovered for the Colts at the New York 32. Four plays later, and 46 seconds into the second quarter, Jones threw a 15-yard touchdown to Cotton Speyrer to put the Colts up 14–0.

Later in the second quarter, the Jets cut the lead in half when Steve Tannen blocked a punt at the Baltimore 12-yard line and Burgess Owens recovered the ball in the end zone. With the score now 14–7 the Jets were back in the game, but their spirits would quickly fade. On the ensuing kickoff, Tim Berra — son of baseball Hall of Famer Yogi Berra — fielded the ball at the 12-yard line and returned it 54 yards to the New York 34. Six plays later, Joe Orduna scored from two yards out to increase Baltimore's lead to 21–7.

After a scoreless third period, The Colts widened the gap further after linebacker Dan Dickel recovered a Clarence Jackson fumble at the New York 22. A pass interference call in the end zone on Roscoe Word then positioned the Colts at the one-yard line, and two plays later Lydell Mitchell took it in. The 28–7 Baltimore lead would hold up until the final 2:23 of the game, when Namath hit David Knight with a 13-yard touchdown. Having been shutout the previous week, it was New York's first offensive score in eight quarters.

The Colts seemed to be taking their frustrations out on the Jets, and rather than run out the clock and be satisfied with a 28–14 victory, they quickly went downfield to score again when Jones ran for his second touchdown, this time dashing 32 yards for a score. Perhaps the Jets felt that the Colts were rubbing their noses in it, but they got in a parting shot of their own when Namath speedily guided them downfield and threw a seven-yard touchdown to Jerome Barkum with 27 seconds left in the game. Under the circumstances, it seemed somehow fitting that Bobby Howfield missed the extra point. The Colts had scored their first victory of the season, 35–20.

Although Namath had passed for 156 yards (hitting 12 of 20), incredibly 142 of those yards came in the game's final five-and-a-half minutes. He finished with two TDs and one interception. For Baltimore, Mitchell set a team record with 156 yards rushing. His 40 carries also set a new NFL record, breaking O.J. Simpson's record of 39 carries set the previous season against Kansas City.

Now 1–5, the Jets had allowed the Colts to either climb out of the basement, or pull New York down into the cellar with them, have your pick. Neither was posing a threat to anyone. "At this stage," Namath said, "it's not the low ebb of my career, but it's close to it."[14]

After the game, second-string Baltimore quarterback Marty Domres had a word with Namath and came away with the impression that he was just going through the motions. Namath admitted to Domres that it was difficult playing on a team in which so many other players were trying to learn the game. In Domres' estimation, Namath's heart didn't seem to be in it.[15]

Week 7 — Sunday, October 27, 1974
Shea Stadium, New York (attendance: 56,110)

All week long, Los Angeles Rams coach Chuck Knox had been telling everyone — his players most of all — that the Jets were a better team than their 1–5 record would suggest. He didn't want his team taking the Jets lightly when the Rams came to Shea in week seven. "Namath still has the best arm in football and he can beat you anytime," said Knox.[16] The Los Angeles coach knew what he was talking about. Both Knox and Namath were from western Pennsylvania, where Knox had coached one of Namath's high school rivals. As an assistant coach with the Jets years later, Knox was very instrumental in getting the Jets to draft Namath. He knew better than most what Namath was capable of. At 4–2, Knox's Rams came into the game leading the NFC Western Division. To hold their divisional lead, they could not afford to look past any opponent.

It wasn't until the closing minute of the first period that the Rams broke a scoreless standoff, when quarterback James Harris capped a 76-yard drive with a 12-yard touchdown run. The Jets' rookie defensive tackle Carl Barzilauskas blocked the extra point to hold the Rams to a 6–0 lead.

The Jets fought back midway into the second quarter when Mike Adamle — playing for injured John Riggins — scored on a two-yard run, and with punter Greg Gantt's extra point the Jets were up 7–6 (kicker Bobby Howfield had twisted his right knee during practice earlier in the week, necessitating Gantt to do all the kicking).

New York was still leading as the second half got started, and after forcing a Los Angeles punt, the Jets began their first series of the half at their 24. Namath threw five yards to Adamle, and after Boozer gained two yards on a running play, a 15-yard penalty against the Rams gave the Jets a first down at the 46. They seemed well on their way to posting some points when Namath hit Boozer with a 28-yard pass to the Los Angeles 26. After an incomplete pass and a three-yard completion to Eddie Bell, a 12-yard pass to David Knight would have accomplished a first down, but it didn't stand: Rich Caster was flagged for illegal use of hands, a 15-yard infraction that knocked the Jets back to the 38, effectively taking them out of field goal range and killing the drive. The Jets wound up punting.

Late in the third quarter, the Jets drove downfield again and managed to get into the end zone on a 14-yard run by Boozer, but when Gantt missed the extra point the New York lead stood at 13–6, meaning the Rams could tie it with a touchdown and conversion. As the third quarter came to a close the Rams were threatening, having driven to the New York 23 after Harris threw 17 yards to Harold Jackson. The drive was otherwise largely the work of running back Lawrence McCutcheon.

On the first play of the fourth quarter McCutcheon ran a sweep left from the New York 23, and after bouncing off an attempted tackle by linebacker Jamie Rivers and eluding safety Phil Wise, he found himself with nothing left but to outrace Burgess Owens to the end zone. He did, and after the extra point the game was tied 13–13 just eight seconds into the fourth quarter.

The tie wouldn't last long. Two plays after receiving the kick, Namath threw for Jerome Barkum, but cornerback Charlie Stukes picked it off at the New York 42 and ran it back to the one-yard line. Stukes said afterward that the ball was not poorly thrown, but he had simply read the play correctly. For one thing, Namath never looked him off, eyeing Barkum from the start. "Namath looked like he was determined to throw to him no matter what," Stukes said.[17]

On the play following Stukes' interception, McCutcheon scored his second touchdown in 31 seconds, and the Rams then led 20–13. It wasn't until late in the game that the Jets threatened to tie the score back up. After linebacker John Ebersole intercepted Harris, the Jets started from their 27; Namath completed four straight passes with roughly two minutes left to play, but after a pair of incompletions and a short throw of five yards to Adamle, the Jets were faced with a fourth down. There was no other choice but to go for it, and when Namath went over the middle to Caster, free safety Steve Preece intercepted the pass and quashed the Jets' last hope. Namath finished 19 of 35 for 155 yards. The 20–13 defeat dropped the Jets to 1–6.

The buzz all week had been that there was a trade in the works that would send Namath to the Rams. Just a week before, the Rams had traded veteran quarterback John Hadl to Green Bay for a wealth of draft picks, but with Harris now their starting quarterback, many thought a trade for Namath was plausible, and to the Rams' advantage. Namath declined to comment on such a possibility, but Winner dismissed it outright, pointing out that the trade deadline for the season had already passed. He also asked why anyone thought he would trade the best passer in football. Namath would, however, be free to go wherever he pleased after the season ended. "You can't trade a man who doesn't have a contract," Namath's lawyer Jimmy Walsh pointed out.[18]

Week 8 — Sunday, November 3, 1974
Shea Stadium, New York (attendance: 47,218)

After the Houston Oilers' week eight meeting with the New York Jets at Shea, Houston quarterback Dan Pastorini had much the same reaction the Los Angeles Rams had the week before. "They're not a bad team," Pastorini said of the Jets, "they've got some good talent."[19] Having suffered through consecutive 1–13 seasons with Houston in 1972 and '73, Pastorini could certainly sympathize with what the Jets were going through.

The Oilers presented the Jets with a chance to change their fortunes: for starters, at 2–5 Houston was only one game better than the Jets, and considering how well they had played the Rams the week before, there was no reason to think that the Jets could not beat a 2–5 team. Weeks earlier, when they had been shutout 24–0 by New England, Winner was disgusted with his team and had gone on a tirade, accusing his players of having no pride. But he had been very encouraged by their performance against the Rams, calling it their best game of the season.

A 1–6 team can ill-afford a bad start to a game, irrespective of the opponent, but against Houston that is just how the Jets began. On his very first pass of the game Namath was intercepted by Zeke Moore, who ran it back 22 yards for a touchdown and a quick 7–0 Houston lead. But the Jets shot right back, driving 64 yards, the last 20 of which were covered by a TD pass from Namath to Clarence Jackson. After missing the previous week's game, kicker Bobby Howfield was deemed well enough to play. Perhaps not — he missed the extra point wide left, and the Jets still trailed, 7–6.

Guard Gary Puetz was doing the Jets' kickoffs, and not booting too deeply at that. The Jets were also not getting good coverage on kicks, so the Oilers were having little difficulty with field position. Bob Gresham gave Houston a short field to work on with a 40-yard kick return, and shortly thereafter Pastorini hit Billy Johnson with a 29-yard touchdown throw that increased Houston's lead to 14–6.

Again the Jets fired back quickly, needing less than two minutes to score. After Namath hit tight end Willie Brister (filling in for injured Rich Caster) with a 21-yard pass, Emerson Boozer took a pitchout from Namath and bounced outside to run 12 yards for a score, bringing the Jets to within a point of Houston at the end of the first quarter.

The pace of the game slowed considerably during the second quarter, and it wasn't until almost 10 minutes into the period that Houston kicked a 45-yard field goal to increase their lead to 17–13. Then, with 1:17 left to play in the half, the Jets took the lead for the first time when Namath threw a 42-yard TD to David Knight, who went up over Moore to make a splendid, acrobatic catch. Howfield then missed the extra point again, this time dinging it off the left upright. Even so, the Jets held a 19–17 halftime lead.

The only scoring in the third quarter came down to a 46-yard field goal by Skip Butler, but it was enough to put the Oilers back in front, 20–19. That lead held up until the closing minutes of the game, when Howfield atoned for his two missed extra points by kicking a 35-yard field goal that gave the Jets a 22–20 lead with 3:57 left to play.

Another short kickoff by Puetz allowed the Oilers to start at their 35, and after moving to their 46, Houston delivered the backbreaker. Earlier in the game, the Jets had blown coverage on receiver Ken Burrough on a deep route. The play hadn't gone to Burrough then, but he was sure to tell Pastorini about it. The quarterback filed it for future reference, and trailing with just a few minutes remaining, it now seemed a good time. True to form, the Jets blew the coverage again, and Burrough got behind safety Phil Wise. The play went for 51 yards to the New York three before Burrough was hauled down from behind. With first-and-goal from the three, running back Willie Rodgers bulled two yards to the one, and on the following play dove across for the go-ahead score with 1:56 remaining. The Jets still had time for a score of their own, but now trailing by five points, 27–22, it would obviously have to be a touchdown. Their last hope died when Namath was intercepted by Bob Atkins with 1:40 left in the game. Namath finished 19 of 31 for 256 yards, two TDs and two interceptions.

At 1–7 there seemed no doubt about it: Joe Namath and the New York Jets ... were losers. One of the players in the New York locker room summed up the feelings on the team. "This can't be happening to us," he said.[20]

Week 9 — Sunday, November 10, 1974
Yale Bowl, New Haven (attendance: 67,740)

In week nine, the Jets would be traveling to New Haven to face the New York Giants for only the second time in regular season play. Although it usually came in preseason, a meeting between the Jets and the Giants was never taken lightly. Beginning with their first meeting in 1969, even in mere exhibition games the starters for both teams were not removed until very late. The only thing that on occasion deflated enthusiasm for the event was Namath's periodic absence due to injury (or other reasons), but it seemed that Namath's participation this time wasn't enough for some. With the Jets a pathetic 1–7 and the Giants not much better at 2–6, even the local New York television affiliates declined to carry the game, feeling that nobody would be interested in watching two of the league's worst teams. It was a bad call. As it turned out, they would miss out on broadcasting a game that had some historic significance to the league, as well as being a damn good contest.

Enthusiasm among diehard fans was still high — well over 60,000 people turned out at the Yale Bowl in New Haven — but the game meant something to the players as well. They may have been losers, but this game was important to them. Before the game, the Jets' players requested a players-only meeting, which the coaches obliged. Some of the team's veterans got up to speak — Namath among them — and try to impress upon the younger players that this was no ordinary game. Having been regarded since their inception as New York's redheaded stepchildren of football, beating the fair-haired Giants always meant something to the Jets. The game meant something to the Giants as well, as triumphing over the Jets had always symbolized their maintaining the status quo.

Both teams had significant recent additions to their squads. The Giants, having started the season 1–6, acquired quarterback Craig Morton (previously of the Dallas Cowboys) two weeks earlier; Morton then led the Giants to their second victory of the season, beating Kansas City 33–27 in week eight. The week of the game, the Jets brought in rookie kicker Pat Leahy. Bobby Howfield had been nursing an injury all season, which he was said to have initially suffered while playing soccer in the off-season, and he had been very unreliable, even on extra points. Leahy would prove so reliable that he would last the next 18 years as the Jets' kicker.

It was a beautiful, sunny November day in New Haven when the Jets and Giants met up. The Giants received the opening kickoff, and after a good return from rookie running back Doug Kotar, they began from their 31. The Jets' defense looked sharp, sacking Morton twice in the series and batting down another pass at the line of scrimmage.

After forcing the Giants to punt, the Jets began their initial series in good position at their own 44. Namath went right to the pass, throwing to David Knight for 10 yards to the Giants' 46 on the first play, then hitting Emerson Boozer for 12 yards across the middle to the 34 on the next. An offside penalty against the Giants moved the Jets to the 29-yard line, and Namath then tested the ground game. Runs by Boozer, Hank Bjorklund, and Bob Burns brought the Jets to the 19, and then Namath went back to the pass. Getting great protection from his line, he hit Knight cutting right-to-left across the middle: Knight was wide open and had no problem making the catch at the goal line and going in to score, giving the Jets the early lead.

A short kick gave the Giants good starting field position again, as Kotar brought the ball out to the 32. Largely on the running of Kotar, the Giants methodically moved the ball into Jets' territory, but after advancing to inside the five-yard line, the drive was stopped when Steve Tannen broke through the line and tripped Kotar up for a five-yard loss on a sweep left. It forced the Giants to settle for a 26-yard field goal, allowing the Jets to hold on to a 7–3 lead.

As the first quarter drew to a close the Jets were on the move again, Namath having thrown seven yards to Jerome Barkum and then 16 to David Knight, taking the Jets to the Giants' 45. On the last play of the first period, however, Namath fumbled the snap, and while the Jets managed to recover the ball at the 48, it seemed to derail the series. When the second period began, the Jets were unable to gain another first down and wound up punting the ball away.

Starting from their 17 after the punt, the Giants moved quickly as Morton first threw 13 yards to tight end Bob Tucker to the 30, and then went deep down the left sideline to Walker Gillette for 41 yards to the Jets' 29. Morton finished off the drive with a touchdown pass to Tucker from two yards out that gave the Giants a 10–7 lead.

The Jets' next series went nowhere. On first down Namath threw a screen to Barkum that lost five yards, followed by two incompletions (his first of the game), and the Jets were quickly forced to punt. Backed up at their own 12, the punt only carried to the Jets' 44-yard line, and fielding it on the run, Kotar brought it back to the 34, giving the Giants an ideal opportunity to increase their lead. But Morton could only connect on one of three passes, which gained just five yards to the 29, and Pete Gogolak came in to try a 47-yard field goal. He was wide to the right, and the score remained 10–7 in the Giants' favor.

With under four minutes left in the half, the Jets began at their 29, and pounded their way downfield on runs by Burns and Boozer. The Jets were able to grind down to Giants' 16, but when the drive ran out of wheels there, Leahy came in and kicked the first field goal of his professional career, hitting from 34 yards out to tie the game 10–10 with 2:07 left in the half. But there was still time for the Giants to work with, and Morton picked his way downfield with passes to Tucker, Gillette, Bob Grim, and running back Joe Dawkins, enabling the Giants to retake the lead, 13–10, on a 22-yard field goal 20 seconds before halftime.

When the Jets received the second-half kickoff, they proceeded to eat up a large portion of the third period with a long drive. Boozer, Burns, and Bjorklund chipped away at the defense on the ground and, usually passing only when needed, Namath kept the drive going by converting a third-and-six play with a nine-yard throw to Eddie Bell. It looked like the drive might end when a swing pass to Bjorklund only gained seven yards on a third-and-eight play from the Giants' 30, but a 1–7 team really has nothing to lose in such a situation, and so the Jets went for it on fourth-and-one from the 23; Bjorklund kept the drive alive with a six-yard run to the 17. The drive eventually ended up at the Giants' three-yard line, and Bjorklund looked to have put the Jets in the lead with the first touchdown of his career on a run around right end, but a holding penalty nullified the score and pushed the Jets back to the 13. Two runs by Burns then brought the Jets to the six-yard line, but on third-and-goal, with his intended receiver covered, Namath threw the ball away, forcing the Jets to settle for a 13–13 tie with a 22-yard field goal.

The Giants then ate up the bulk of the remaining time in the third period with a time-consuming drive of their own. This time it was running back Leon McQuay who ground out much of the yardage, but Morton had otherwise thrown 26 yards to Tucker before capping the drive with a 12-yard touchdown pass to Grim in the deep right corner of the end zone. The Giants were now up 20–13.

Beginning from their 31 after the kickoff, the Jets had time enough for just one play — an 11-yard run by Burns — before the third quarter ended. Now at their own 42 as the fourth quarter began, the Jets again methodically moved downfield, using up almost half the period. After Burns gained three yards on the ground, Namath threw to Rich Caster for 13 yards to the Giants' 42. A pair of passes to Knight and runs by Bjorklund and Burns advanced the Jets to the 21, and after Namath threw to Barkum for seven yards and Burns picked up another first down with an eight-yard burst up the middle, the Jets found themselves at the six-yard line.

With first-and-goal, Namath ran Boozer up the middle for two yards to the four. On second down Boozer carried again, this time gaining just a yard to the three. It was now third-and-goal from the three-yard line, and the Jets needed a touchdown to tie it. Namath called a run by Boozer off right tackle: well, that's what he *called*, anyway. When Namath took the snap, he turned to hand the ball to Boozer; the flow of the play was to the right, and Boozer was trusting Namath to stick the ball right in his gut. But as he passed Namath and advanced toward the line, Boozer realized he didn't have the ball. At first thinking he had missed the exchange, Boozer glanced to the ground thinking the ball had been dropped — it wasn't there. Namath hadn't even told his own teammates what he planned on doing. As he turned to hand to Boozer, Namath had faked the hand off and rolled left. Had someone anticipated it, the play would certainly have failed. Linebacker Brad Van Pelt came around the left side of the Jets' line completely unblocked, and with his sights set squarely on Boozer, ran right past Namath. But Namath had kept the ball, and by the time Van Pelt realized it, he couldn't adjust. Van Pelt tried to put on the breaks, but wound up sliding and falling to the ground as Namath — looking every bit a 75-year-old man — hobbled into the end zone. It was an almost comical sight. As he crossed the goal line, Namath held up a hand to wave off defensive back Spider Lockhart, who was bearing down on him. Lockhart let up as Namath went across the goal line to tie the score, 20–20. The Jets' bench practically emptied as the players ran to the end zone to mob Namath.

On the ensuing kickoff, Dawkins seemed to set the Giants up to regain the lead when he took the kick at the four-yard line and ran it back all the way to the Jets' 42 with 7:45 left to play. But after Morton advanced his team to the Jets' 30 with a 12-yard pass to Gillette, the Giants could go no further. McQuay gained nothing on a sweep left, and after Morton threw incomplete to the well-covered Grim in the end zone, he was sacked by Mark Lomas on third down. Now positioned at the 34, the Giants punted rather than try a 51-yard field goal.

Neither team could achieve a first down in their next series, the Jets gaining nine yards in three plays and punting with 4:25 remaining, and the Giants losing five yards in three plays and punting with 3:02 left. At that point the Jets took possession at their own 35. Namath hit Burns on a flare pass for 17 yards to the Giants' 48, and then hit Caster for 13 yards to the 35. After the two-minute warning, Boozer ran for five yards to the 30, and then Namath, moving to his right to avoid a heavy rush, threw a dump-off pass to Burns that gained 12 yards to the 18. Burns ran for three yards to the 15 on a draw and then gained a couple more yards to the 13 on the next play. The Jets called a timeout with 21 seconds left in the game. With third-and-five from the 13, Namath then threw across the middle for Barkum in the end zone — the ball was batted down by linebacker Brian Kelley. Leahy then came in to try and win it with a 30-yard field goal. Either Leahy didn't get good lift or Lockhart did — Lockhart jumped up from the back of the line and got his right hand up high enough to deflect the ball. With 12 seconds left, the game was still tied. Dawkins carried for five yards from the 20 to end regulation play, and the game was going to overtime.

Nineteen seventy-four was the first season in which the NFL would play overtime during the regular season. In the second week of the season, the Pittsburgh Steelers and Denver Broncos had gone into overtime, but after a full extra period, the game still ended in a tie. The Jets and Giants would play the first regular season game ever to be decided in overtime.

The Giants won the coin toss; at midfield, Lockhart was ecstatic: Boozer seemed crestfallen. After returning the kick to their 35, the Giants marched fairly quickly downfield. On first down McQuay ran for eight yards to the 43, and on second down Dawkins ran for six more and a first down at the 49. Dawkins then gained another five yards to the Jets' 46, and Morton threw 12 yards to Gillette; the Giants were already at the Jets' 34-yard line. From there, Morton rolled right and threw to Dawkins for five yards to the 29. It was starting to look grim for the Jets, but then the Giants got conservative, obviously eying a winning field goal. Dawkins gained only two yards to the 27 on second down, and on third-and-three McQuay only gained two more. With fourth-and-one at the 25, Gogolak came in for a 42-yard field goal try. The kick had height and distance, but the official ruled it had gone wide of the left upright. Gogolak was furious, taking off his helmet and barking at the officials in protest. He wasn't the only one: many of the players on the Giants' sideline were likewise enraged. Some spectators behind the end zone confirmed afterward that the official's call had been correct, but Gogolak was having none of it. "They took it away from me," he said. "It wasn't even close. I got a good foot on the ball and it was a good foot inside the post when it went through there."[21]

The Jets took over at their 25, and Gogolak and many of his teammates were still carping when Namath went back to pass on the very next play and fired the ball deep down the middle of the field to Caster. Had he led Caster it might have gone all the way for a score, but Namath underthrew him. Caster had to turn his upper body and then reach down to make the catch, but he made it — it was a fine catch. Having to turn around halfway did, however, take him off his stride and allowed defensive back Clyde Powers to catch him and bring him down at the Giants' 33-yard line. The play had gone for 42 yards.

On the next play Namath took a two-step drop and pump-faked right, then turned left and threw to Barkum. Making the catch at the 30, Barkum cut inside and avoided several tackle attempts before being brought down at the 20. After that, Namath called a couple running plays to Boozer, who gained five yards on the first, and then picked up six more and a first down on the second. With first-and-goal from the nine, a pitchout to Clarence Jackson gained four yards to the five. Then, on second-and-goal, Namath faked a handoff to Burns and went back to pass. Boozer looked to be the lead blocker for Burns' run, but when it was obvious that it was a play-action fake, Van Pelt tried to cover Boozer, who had broke toward the left side of the end zone. Namath's pass was tight — it was *perfect*— a quick bullet that whizzed right past Van Pelt's out-stretched hand and into Boozer's as he crossed the goal line. It was over — the Jets had just won the very first regular season game to be decided in overtime. Something else had ended: the Jets' six-game losing streak was over — that monkey was off their back. The Jets' bench emptied again, some of the players mobbing Boozer behind the end zone, but most mobbing Namath. After six straight losses, the sense of release must have been quite a feeling. Yeah, they were only 2–7, but they couldn't have looked any happier had they just won a championship.

Namath's numbers were good, hitting 20 of 31 for 236 yards and two touchdowns. Giants' coach Bill Arnsparger spoke briefly to reporters after the game, but then excused himself. He wanted to get over to the Jets' locker room and have a word. When he got there he found Namath. "Joe," he said as he shook Namath's hand, "I always thought you were the greatest. Today I know it. You're a tough man to beat."[22] That might sound odd, as it was being said to the quarterback of a 2–7 team, but the Jets had taken inspiration from Namath's bold bootleg score that had tied the game. Something magical had happened, and now Joe Namath and the New York Jets were about to embark on the last great run of his career.

Week 10 — Sunday, November 17, 1974
Shaefer Stadium, Foxboro (attendance: 57,165)

Since shutting the Jets out 24–0 in week five of the season, the New England Patriots had seen a severe reversal of fortunes. They had started the season 5–0, but had then gone on to lose three of their next four games and were on a two-game losing streak when they hosted the Jets in week 10. Just the sort of opponent that a win-starved team like the Jets were needing.

Namath got the Jets out to a 7–0 first-quarter lead with an 11-yard touchdown pass to Bob Burns, but New England cut the lead to 7–3 with a 32-yard field goal three minutes into the second period. The Jets then drove 66 yards to increase their lead to 14–3 on a four-yard TD run by Emerson Boozer with 2:23 left in the half. Namath completed three passes in the series, accounting for 42 yards in the drive.

The Patriots started the second half with a bang as Andy Johnson took the kickoff 95 yards for a touchdown, but the play was nullified by a clipping penalty that forced New England to come back and start the series from their 31. Undaunted, the Patriots wound up rolling downfield almost as quickly. On the second play of the series, Sam Cunningham broke a 40-yard run, and a personal foul penalty tacked onto the play placed the Patriots at the New York 13. Three plays later, Mack Herron scored on a five-yard sweep around right end to cut the Jets' lead to 14–10.

New England blew an opportunity midway through the third quarter when John Smith missed a 24-yard field goal, but he made up for it at 10:53 of the period when he hit from 44 yards to bring the Patriots to within a point at 14–13. Then, with 42 seconds left in the third, Namath hit David Knight with a 34-yard touchdown throw that put a serious dent in New England's comeback bid.

Trailing 21–13 in the fourth quarter, the Patriots halted a New York drive when Ron Bolton intercepted Namath at the New England 30. The Patriots then drove to the New York 18, but when they ran out of steam Smith kicked a 35-yard field goal to cut the Jets' lead to 21–16 with 4:45 left in the game. Then things got very interesting.

The Jets would naturally have loved to keep the ball on the ground and run out the clock, but facing a third down at his 20 with two-and-a-half minutes left, Namath was forced to pass. Jack Mildren made a diving interception at the New York 30-yard line — it looked like a disaster for the Jets. Jim Plunkett passed seven yards to Bob Adams, and then Cunningham ran the ball 18 yards to the New York five-yard line.

After the two-minute warning, the Patriots ran Herron. Originally planning to run an option play to the left — the weak side — Plunkett called an audible when he came to the line and saw that the Jets' defensive formation wasn't what he was anticipating. He changed the play to the right-side sweep by Herron (which had gone for a TD from the same spot earlier in the game), and Rich Sowells broke through and dropped Herron for a three-yard loss at the eight.

On second down Plunkett threw incomplete to Reggie Rucker, and then, on third-and-goal, Plunkett went back to pass again. He threw across the middle of the end zone for Randy Vataha — rookie Roscoe Word jumped in front and made the first interception of his pro career to end the threat. It was the Jets' fourth interception of the game (and Plunkett's eleventh in the last three games), almost doubling their season total of five coming into the game.

Even then it wasn't over. The Jets were still unable to run out the clock, and the Patriots got one last shot. After managing to advance to the New York 43, Plunkett had time for one more play and threw up a prayer: Eddie Hinton was unable to make the catch in the end zone.

The win improved the Jets' record to 3–7, and gave them their first consecutive victories since 1972. The Patriots, on the other hand, dropped to 6–4 and were seeing their season slip away from them. They were now a game behind second-place Buffalo in the division, and two games behind first-place Miami.

For the Jets, the season had long since slipped away, but after so many blown leads and narrow defeats, it was still a good feeling to win. "We're not in a playoff situation," Namath said, "but there's still a thing called personal pride."[23] He finished eight of 20 for 112 yards, with two TDs and two interceptions.

Week 11— Sunday, November 24, 1974
Shea Stadium, New York (attendance: 57,162)

Maybe they were only 3–7, but Charley Winner was still pleased by his team's two-game winning streak (who wouldn't be after six straight losses?), and beyond that, he was happy to note that his players were finally performing up to their potential. For most, the wins were easily dismissible: after all, who had the Jets beaten? The dismal 2–6 New York Giants and a New England team that was falling to pieces after a very promising start. The Jets were still not considered worthy of being taken seriously by most, and would not be until they could beat a more formidable opponent.

They would face such an opponent in week 11 when they hosted the Miami Dolphins, defending Super Bowl champions for two years running. The consensus was that the Dolphins would make very short work of the Jets. People seemed to easily forget that the Jets had played the Dolphins very close earlier in the year.

The Jets may have felt emboldened by the recent change in their fortunes, but no one could fault them if their confidence was shaken by word that Namath would be more than a little distracted in their meeting with Miami. Prior to the game he had received word that his father was in the hospital in critical condition. Stricken with emphysema, John Namath had been taken to the hospital back in Beaver Falls, Pennsylvania, after suffering a gall bladder attack. Namath would be flying back home immediately after the game.

Really, both teams looked distracted, each making mistakes and failing to take advantage of opportunities. Predictably, it was the Jets who most often failed to capitalize on their chances. In the first half, Roscoe Word recovered a Larry Csonka fumble at the Miami 20, but almost immediately afterward Jake Scott intercepted Namath at the two-yard line. On another occasion in the first half, the Jets had driven to the Miami 27 and seemed bound to score when a 25-yard pass advanced them to the Miami two. But the gain was wiped out by a holding penalty on center Wayne Mulligan that effectively took the Jets out of field goal range.

The lone score of the first half came when the Jets managed to cash in on a Miami blunder in the second quarter. Jake Scott fumbled a punt, and rookie receiver Lou Piccone recovered for the Jets at the Miami 25. One play later, the Jets were at the Miami 11 after Namath threw 14 yards to Rich Caster. Two runs by John Riggins (back in the lineup after an absence due to injury) advanced the Jets to the two-yard line, but the going got tougher from there. Emerson Boozer managed to run for the first down, but after two more running plays lost yardage back to the three the Jets were facing third-and-goal. Namath hit Caster at the back of the end zone for the score, and the Jets were up 7–0.

That lead held up until the third quarter, when it was Miami's turn to cash in on a New York error. Nick Buoniconti intercepted Namath at midfield, and his 16-yard return set the Miami offense up at the New York 34. Other than a short pass to Paul Warfield, it was the running of Csonka and Mercury Morris that carried the Dolphins to the six-yard line. From there Bob Griese went back to pass, but unable to find an open receiver, he took off in a dash around right end and made it into the end zone to even the score at 7–7.

Early in the fourth quarter, Namath passes to Caster and Eddie Bell put the Jets within range for Pat Leahy to kick a 34-yard field goal that gave the Jets the lead again at 10–7. It might have seemed incomprehensible to some that the 3–7 Jets could be leading the Super Bowl champions as late as the fourth quarter, but most probably assumed that the Dolphins would get it together and emerge victorious in the end. Although the New York defense had frustrated the Miami offense through most of the game, it would have surprised no one if they experienced a late-game collapse, as lesser teams so often do.

Those expectations seemed to come to pass when the Dolphins captured the lead for the first time in the game with 6:43 left to play. It all began with a 26-yard punt return by Scott, and ended with a six-yard TD pass from Griese to Jim Kiick. But the main play—the one that got the Dolphins to the six-yard line—was a bit of trickery that may have been indicative of Miami's frustration (perhaps, being so late in the game, it could even be seen as an act of desperation). From the New York 37, the Dolphins ran a flea-flicker, Griese throwing a lateral to receiver Nat Moore, who then threw 31 yards to Warfield.

Had it been earlier in the season, this would have been the point at which the Jets folded, but this was now a team with a newfound confidence. Trailing 14–10, the Jets pulled back in front quickly. After a pass interference call on Tim Foley advanced the Jets 23 yards from their 32 to the Miami 45, Namath whipped the ball down the center of the field to a wide open Caster, who caught the pass at the 20-yard line and easily ran it in for a score. "We showed them a different formation than they had seen all day and they got mixed up," said Caster.[24]

Mixed up indeed: not only did the Miami defense fail to pick Caster up when he came off the line of scrimmage, but they also left the entire center of the field vacant of coverage. The 45-yard touchdown play put the Jets back up, 17–14, with 5:05 left in the game. It was certainly more than enough time for the Dolphins to score again.

Who knows, they might have done it, too, if not for Word once more coming to New York's rescue. The previous week, Word had notched the first interception of his professional career with a late-fourth-quarter steal of a New England pass in the end zone that preserved a Jets' victory. This time Word jumped in front of a Griese pass across the middle to Warfield, and came up with an interception at the New York 38 to snuff out a Miami drive.

Unable to run out the clock, the Jets were forced to punt the ball back to the Dolphins, but desperately trying to create a break for his team, Miami's Dick Anderson tried to block the kick and wound up being flagged for roughing the punter. The Jets retained possession, ran out the clock, and won the game. They had defeated the champions of the NFL. The stadium seats emptied as the jubilant fans spilled onto the field. Winner was trying to have a word with Don Shula, and was shaking his hand when some of his players, joined by ecstatic fans, hoisted him up onto their shoulders. Now 4–7, the Jets still weren't going anywhere, but having just beaten the champs, a celebration seemed in order nonetheless.

Overall, Namath's numbers were good, hitting 13 of 22 for 182 yards and two TDs, though he also had three interceptions. It was a big win, but Namath wasn't celebrating. He showered and dressed quickly, and was then off to the airport to fly to Pittsburgh and then drive to Beaver Falls to be with his father. His greatest victory in at least two seasons, and he couldn't enjoy it. The good news is that his father would recover.

Week 12 — Sunday, December 1, 1974
Shea Stadium, New York (attendance: 44,888)

Having beaten the reigning Super Bowl champions, Winner was leery of a letdown. He knew that after such a high there was the possibility of taking a lesser opponent lightly, but at 4–7 the Jets were only one game better than the 3–8 San Diego Chargers, who they would be hosting in week 12. It turned out that Winner needn't have worried, as the Jets came out looking thoroughly prepared, and with an almost clinical efficiency proceeded to put the Chargers in short pants.

The Jets received the opening kickoff, and after a good return they went 61 yards in six plays to grab a 7–0 lead when Namath flipped a four-yard TD pass to John Riggins 3:33 into the game. Otherwise, Namath's 29-yard pass to Emerson Boozer had been the highlight of the drive.

Quickly thwarted by the New York defense, San Diego punted and Roscoe Word's 34-yard return set the Jets' up at the Chargers' 43 to start their second series. The running of Riggins and Boozer got the Jets to the San Diego three, but when they bogged down, Pat Leahy came in to kick a 20-yard field goal that gave the Jets a 10–0 advantage.

In the second quarter, Namath hit Rich Caster with a 44-yard bomb to the San Diego 17, and after throwing another nine yards to Caster, Namath again turned it over to the running game. Clarence Jackson gained five yards to the three, and Riggins took it into the end zone from there on a sweep right to give the Jets a 17–0 lead with 5:37 left in the half.

The Jets began their next series from the San Diego 42, courtesy of a 14-yard punt that was likely down to the vigorous winds of Shea. Namath threw to Riggins twice, and Caster once before Riggins ran through the right side of the line to score from two yards out. Riggins' third touchdown of the game gave the Jets a 24–0 halftime lead.

The New York defense had been especially impressive in the first half, holding the Chargers to a skinny three first downs and not allowing them to penetrate deeper than the New York 40, which they managed only in the waning moments of the second quarter. As for Namath, he looked very sharp, completing 13 of 18 passes for 189 yards. With a 24-point lead, the Jets played conservatively in the third period, adding a 45-yard field goal to make it 27–0, and after the third period was done Namath left the game to allow backup Al Woodall some playing time in the fourth quarter.

The Jets would add no more points, but in the fourth quarter San Diego managed to break up the shutout when running back Don Woods threw a 28-yard touchdown to Gary Garrison on an option play. Woods' numbers for the game were impressive, rushing for 142 yards in 25 attempts, but much of that came quite late when the game was basically long since decided. With 49 seconds left in the game Woods also ran four yards for a touchdown to make the final 27–14, giving the impression that the contest had been more competitive than it really was.

San Diego coach Tommy Prothro said that, although he was really not one to take much notice of players other than his own, he could not help but notice Namath's performance. "(Y)ou just had to notice Namath," Prothro said, adding that "he threw well and he seemed to be standing in a vacuum in that wind."[25]

In his three quarters of play, Namath had thrown for 254 yards and a TD, completing 17 of 27 passes. Now 5–7, the Jets would close out their home schedule against the 9–3 Buffalo Bills the following week.

Week 13 — Sunday, December 8, 1974

Shea Stadium, New York (attendance: 32,805)

As the Jets were preparing to play their last home game of 1974, the word going around was that it would in all probability be Namath's final game in New York. The talk throughout the year had been of Namath's possibly signing with the Los Angeles Rams for the 1975 season. Namath himself had expressed a desire to play with a contender, as well as wanting to play in a warmer climate. It was also said that Los Angeles would keep him closer to the film and television industries, of which he also had an eye on for the future.

Dave Herman, once an offensive lineman tasked with protecting Namath, but now retired and covering the Jets for a local radio station, interviewed Namath for a broadcast prior to the Jets' home closer against Buffalo. Herman asked Namath if he would be back with the Jets the following year; Namath said that he really didn't know if he'd be back, but he kind of doubted it. Jets president Phil Iselin said that until he heard it directly from Namath, he would assume that his quarterback would be back to play for the Jets in 1975.

At 9–3 the Buffalo Bills were already assured of a playoff spot, the only question being whether they would be divisional champs or the wild card. Like their meeting with the Bills in Orchard Park earlier in the season, the Jets' game with Buffalo at Shea would be played under terrible conditions, the rainfall remaining fairly constant throughout the first half, and while the wind gusts would not top the 40 mph gusts experienced earlier in Orchard Park, the winds at Shea would be clocking at 30 mph. In fact, the weather was so crummy that 28,286 paying customers stayed home.

Conditions being what they were, it was no surprise that both teams looked a bit off their game. In the first quarter the Bills did manage to pound their way through the mire to the New York 17, but when they tried a 34-yard field goal it was blocked by Burgess Owens. It was as close as either team would get to scoring in the first half. The Jets managed to drive to the Buffalo 28 in the second quarter, but when Donnie Walker broke up a pass from Namath to Rich Caster in the end zone the Jets wound up punting. On a better day they might have gone for a 45-yard field goal try, but not in this weather.

After the first half went scoreless, the rain subsided and the teams had only to deal with its aftermath in the second half. Early in the third quarter, Buffalo drove 80 yards in seven plays for the game's first points. The running of O.J. Simpson and Don Calhoun had gotten the Bills to the New York 41, and then Joe Ferguson went to the air. Looking right, he threw to J.D. Hill, who dropped to a knee and made the catch at the 27, and as both Rich Sowells and Phil Wise went to the ground in vain tackle attempts, Hill got up and spun away from them, outrunning Owens to the end zone.

The Bills were still up 7–0 when Ferguson fumbled later in the third, and linebacker Al Atkinson recovered for the Jets at the Buffalo 19. Namath wasted no time in going to the air and throwing a perfect strike to Rich Caster in the right side of the end zone. It should have evened the score, but when Pat Leahy's extra point was blocked the Jets were still down, 7–6.

The turf being in the condition it was, field position was even more important than it might ordinarily be, and the Jets seemed to score a victory in that department late in the third quarter when punter Greg Gantt pinned the Bills back at their own nine-yard line. Unfortunately, Mike Adamle was flagged for getting downfield too soon, and the Jets had to punt again. It looked like a very costly penalty, as Donnie Walker returned the re-kick 52 yards to the New York 25. Buffalo could gain only a yard in three plays, however, and John Leypoldt then missed wide left on a 41-yard field goal attempt.

In the fourth quarter, more mishaps ensued. On another New York punt, Gantt had to field a high snap and he bobbled it. Unable to get the kick off he was forced to run with the ball, and

Buffalo wound up taking possession at the Jets' 20-yard line. The flags flew heavy after that, with a brawl breaking out between Buffalo guard Reggie McKenzie and the Jets' tackle Carl Barzilauskas, both of whom wound up being ejected from the game. Leypoldt then made good on a field goal attempt from 36 yards out to increase Buffalo's lead to 10–6 with only 6:25 left in the game.

After the kickoff the Jets began at their 28 and Namath went to work, first hitting Caster for 13 yards, then Jerome Barkum for 22 to the Buffalo 36. From there, Namath went back to Barkum, heaving the ball into the end zone. Both Barkum and Walker went up for it — Barkum came down with it. There were four minutes to play, and after the extra point the Jets led for the first time in the game, 13–10.

With plenty of time to work with, Ferguson managed to direct the Bills to the New York 39, but when he tried to hit Simpson with a pass the ball went through Simpson's hands, bounced off his knee, and shot up into the air. It eventually came down into the waiting hands of linebacker Ralph Baker, who took off running down the right sideline. Baker had a convoy of blockers, led by Owens, as he sloshed down the field; slowing his pace so as not to outdistance Baker, Owens jokingly urged him to run faster.[26] There was a wild celebration in the end zone after Baker scored; the Jets' bench emptied as players rushed to mob him. Some fans behind the end zone joined in as well. Baker's 67-yard interception return put the game away, giving the Jets a 20–10 lead with 2:05 left to play. It was the Jets' fifth consecutive victory, upping their record to 6–7.

Namath finished eight of 19 for 131 yards and two TDs. "I thought Namath was great," said Buffalo safety Neal Craig after the game. "He loves to challenge defensive backs and we love to challenge him. It's a perennial battle."[27] If this really was Namath's farewell to the New York fans, Craig said, then he certainly went out in style.

Week 14 — Sunday, December 15, 1974
Memorial Stadium, Baltimore (attendance: 31,651)

After the Jets-Colts game in Baltimore's Memorial Stadium in week 14, somebody asked Namath if he had thought of the possibility that it might be his last game with the Jets. "Yes, that thought went through my mind," Namath answered, "and I was thinking, 'I'll make this a good one.'"[28] And he did, too.

Namath led the Jets to their sixth straight victory, tying a club record set in 1969 — the team's last divisional title. He got things started early, driving the team 75 yards in the first quarter to take a 7–0 lead in the first few minutes on a 25-yard TD pass across the middle to Jerome Barkum. It certainly helped that his offensive line gave him enough time to have thrown a half-dozen passes.

At 2–11, the Baltimore Colts had already accomplished the worst record in their history, having never before lost more than nine games in a season. They had also never failed to win less than three (they had finished 3–9 in 1953 and '54, when the seasons were 12 games). With their dignity at stake, the Colts battled back to tie the game in the second quarter when Lydell Mitchell caught a five-yard touchdown pass from Bert Jones. Both were on their way to record days.

The Jets regained the lead soon enough when John Riggins dove across the goal line from a yard out to end a relatively short 48-yard drive that was helped along by a number of offside penalties on the Colts. When the Jets got the ball back, a Baltimore penalty again proved useful. While breaking up a pass to Jerome Barkum at the Baltimore two-yard line, Nelson Munsey was flagged for interference, setting the stage for Riggins to score his second touchdown of the game one play later, giving the Jets a 21–7 lead.

Desperate to get back in the game, Jones was throwing in Baltimore's next series but only managed to dig a deeper hole for his team. His pass over the middle was nearly intercepted by linebacker Ralph Baker, but the ball hit his hands and shot high into the air; when it came back down it landed in the hands of safety Burgess Owens, who ran it back 29 yards for a touchdown, giving New York a 28–7 advantage. Baltimore would add a field goal before the end of the half, but the Jets held a commanding 28–10 lead after two quarters.

The Colts received the second half kick, and after a good return they drove 68 yards to score. Jones hit five straight passes in the drive, the final being a nine-yard touchdown to tight end Raymond Chester. But Namath soon enough answered back with a 39-yard TD pass to Rich Caster to put the Jets out in front by 18 points again at 35–17. The Colts would narrow the gap to 11 points before the end of the third period when Jones threw another touchdown to Mitchell, this one from 16 yards.

The Jets pretty well put the game out of reach in the fourth quarter, first hitting a 25-yard field goal, and then scoring on a three-yard TD run by Mike Adamle that made the score 45–24. The Colts managed to add two scores in closing, but having been down by 21 points it was just too late. Jones' hot hand in the second half had put him in the record books, however, when he completed an NFL-record 17 consecutive passes. He finished the game with 36 completions in 53 attempts, both Baltimore records. Mitchell had caught 13 of those throws, giving him a league-leading 72 receptions on the year, a league record for a running back.

Namath's numbers were not too shabby either, completing 19 of 28 passes for 281 yards and two touchdowns. For the third consecutive game he had not thrown an interception. But most importantly, the Jets had done it: with their six straight wins they managed, at 7–7, to avoid a losing season. Even with a record denoting mediocrity, they couldn't help but feel like winners after the way they had finished the season. It certainly gave hope for a brighter future.

Nineteen seventy-four marked the first time since 1969 that Namath had played through an entire 14-game schedule. Many attributed the Jets' turnaround in the second half of the season to Namath, but of course there was more to it than that. The defense, for instance, began to step up and make big plays at crucial moments, whereas they had been inclined to fall apart at such moments earlier in the year. Still, Namath seemed to have been the spark plug, and it could be traced back to that gutsy call in the week nine game with the Giants when Namath, without even telling his own teammates, kept the ball and took it into the end zone himself to send the game into overtime. Namath's passing would win it after that, and it changed the team's outlook entirely. They seemed to suddenly feel that he could get them there, and week after week he did. Had their winning streak begun a little sooner, the Jets would have made the playoffs. In fact, if they had beaten Buffalo in that Orchard Park typhoon bowl in week three, the Jets would have gone to the playoffs instead of the Bills. It might be said that all the Jets got out of their six-game streak was a third-place tie with New England in the AFC East, but really they got much more. They got to feel like winners through the last half of the season, and they were looking forward to 1975.

The second half of the season had lifted the team, and Namath's numbers had improved dramatically as well. His 2,616 passing yards placed second in the league, as did his 20 touchdown passes. But once more his interceptions (counting 22) had beaten his TDs by a pair. Namath's improved play during the six-game winning streak is illustrated by the turnaround in his touchdown-to-interception ratio. During the first eight games of the year, Namath threw only nine touchdowns and 17 interceptions. During the final six games he threw 11 touchdowns and only five interceptions. Namath was voted Comeback Player of the Year by the Associated Press.

Any question as to Namath's importance to the team can be settled by looking at the fact that, while they ranked eleventh in the NFL in offense, they ranked fifth in the league in passing; impressive for a 7–7 team (they only placed eighteenth in rushing). But during the 1970s it wasn't the Jets' offense that was lacking, but rather the defense, and in 1974 that would still be true. The Jets' defense ranked twenty-fourth out of 26 teams in 1974, but whereas the secondary had usually been their Achilles heel, this turned out not to be the case in 1974 when the team's defense placed twenty-fourth against the rush and tenth against the pass. A real weak spot was special teams, where the poor kick and punt coverage saw the Jets ranking dead last. The Jets had conversely ranked number one in kick and punt returns. First in one, last in the other … again. The weak spots were obvious.

The winning streak had also made Namath's situation even more of a question mark. When the season ended, he told reporters that he honestly didn't know what he was going to do. Throughout the year, there had been a good deal of talk of Namath wanting to play for A) a contender, B) a team in a warmer climate, and C) a team close to the entertainment industry, so that he might further pursue his acting career. Added together, the three things could only point to the Los Angeles Rams, but the question had always been whether or not the Rams would be willing to pay the price to acquire Namath. As the Jets struggled through the first half of the season, the talk was that the Rams would not likely consider him worth the expense, but once the Jets turned things around, some weren't so sure. In directing a six-game winning streak, Namath seemed to reaffirm his worth, to the Jets as much as any other interested team. It certainly didn't hurt his bargaining position.

But if Namath had wanted to play with a competitor, maybe the winning streak had also gone a long way toward making up his mind to stay in New York. They did, after all, look like a team that could compete the following year. It was more than a matter of money; if money were the main consideration then Namath would have gone ahead and signed with the World Football League, which was offering him millions, as well as part ownership of a franchise. There were defections taking place from the NFL already. Even before the season had begun, Larry Csonka, Jim Kiick, and Paul Warfield had all agreed to leave the Miami Dolphins after the 1974 season to go to the WFL's Memphis franchise. Had money been the main objective, then Namath would have done the same. But with his many endorsements, he was certainly not short of cash.

One thing to consider was the question of whether or not Namath would be comfortable deserting the Jets now that it looked like they could be a serious contender in 1975. Maybe he could get the Jets there again. Yes, that six-game winning streak had certainly made things interesting.

13

The 1975 Season

Football had been very good to Joe Namath. By 1975, it seemed like an awfully long time since those glory days when he shocked the sporting world by beating the Baltimore Colts in the Super Bowl. Yet that one moment in time — a moment that seemed equally as important to the sport itself as it did to Namath's own mass appeal — seemed to have bestowed him with a celebrity that transcended his continued worth to the game.

Nineteen seventy-four had been Namath's first complete season since 1969 — the Jets' last winning record — but despite his playing a full schedule, the team only managed a mediocre 7–7 record and a third-place finish in their division. Namath had only played five games in 1970, four in 1971, and six in 1973, but despite such a dramatic decrease in his playing time there was a substantial increase in his salary. With Namath having played a full season in 1974 and the Jets still failing to post a winning record, one might have expected the law of diminishing returns to come into play, but having played out his option, Namath was again requesting a bigger contract in 1975. His bargaining position was no doubt helped by the team's six-game winning streak to close out the 1974 season, but team president Phil Iselin was not very receptive to Namath's asking price of $1 million for two years. Even the length of a new contract couldn't be agreed on, with Namath wanting a two-year deal and the Jets wanting him to sign for three.

In January, less than a month after the end of the season, Namath's attorney, Jimmy Walsh, was puzzled by the fact that Iselin had not gotten in touch to negotiate. Perhaps Iselin felt there was plenty of time since Namath would not officially become a free agent until May 1, but Namath had other options to consider. There was, for instance, a very lucrative offer from the World Football League.

The WFL had managed to survive its inaugural season in 1974, even if only just barely, and had vowed there would be a 1975 season. To try and ensure their success the league was throwing around more money than one might have thought they had, offering considerable contracts to lure NFL players. Even before the 1974 season had begun, Larry Csonka, Jim Kiick, and Paul Warfield had all agreed to defect from the NFL's Miami Dolphins to the WFL's Memphis franchise. Most of the money spent on the trio went to Csonka, whose $400,000 annual salary would make him the highest paid player in any league — unless Namath got his way.

Just as Namath had been largely credited with saving the AFL in the 1960s, the WFL was banking on him saving them as well. For that reason, they were willing to offer him a $500,000 signing bonus and $500,000 a year for three years. They hoped to seal the deal with the promise of a $100,000 annual pension for 20 years upon the completion of his three-year contract in 1978. All told, that would make it a $4 million deal. Hoping to make its Chicago franchise the cornerstone of the league, the idea was to sign Namath to play two years in Chicago before having him go to New York for the third season of his contract, provided another New York franchise could be established. The WFL's original New York team, the Stars, had failed miserably and was relocated to Charlotte before the 1974 season had ended, but there were plans for the league to establish another New York franchise in the future. The WFL tried to further sweeten the deal by offering to make Namath part owner of the future New York franchise.

It was certainly an offer worthy of consideration — the WFL's Chicago franchise had even brought in Namath's old friend and former teammate Babe Parilli as head coach — but so much of it was dependent on the WFL beating the odds and surviving that long. In the end it was just too big a roll of the dice, and in May of 1975 Namath turned the offer down. In retrospect, it was a wise decision, of course, since the WFL would not even last through the 1975 season and was swept away in a tidal wave of debt. Could Namath have saved them as was hoped? We will never know.

When it came to long term, there was easier money to be made. During the off-season, Namath signed a deal with Faberge, Inc. to promote the company's cologne, among other things. It was a 20-year deal, and at $250,000 annually, it came to $5 million. No celebrity — be they athlete, film star, singer, or otherwise — had ever been offered so much to promote a product.

As training camp drew near, the sticking point in negotiations between Namath and the Jets seemed the same. Although both sides were by then agreed on the $1 million price tag, Namath wanted a two-year contract while Iselin wanted him to sign for three. Come mid–July, Namath arrived at camp on the sixteenth ahead of the team's other veterans, though he had arrived not to work out, but rather to negotiate. As 76 hopefuls were put through training drills, Namath and Walsh were meeting with Iselin. By the time the team's veterans began to turn up on the nineteenth, Namath was already back in Tuscaloosa working out on his own, having gotten nowhere with Iselin. The following week it was being reported that Namath would sooner retire than accept Iselin's offer, said to be $200,000 less than his asking price, although the Jets were apparently by then amenable to a two-year agreement. "We have made our top offer," Iselin told reporters, adding, "you can squeeze only so much juice out of an orange, and there is no orange left."[1] There must have been something left, for on Tuesday the twenty-ninth of July a press conference was called at Hempstead to announce that Namath had signed with the Jets for two more years. The $200,000 disparity between sides was bridged by the time-honored method of splitting the difference — the deal was said to be for $900,000.

Namath seemed happy; Iselin seemed happy; coach Charley Winner was beaming. "This is my eleventh season," said Namath, "and I think it's the best I've ever felt."[2] Well, sure — $900,000 will do that for you. After the joyous announcement, Namath was off to take his physical, and then joined the team in practice. He wanted to be ready in time for the Jets' first exhibition game, scheduled for August 9 against the Minnesota Vikings in Tempe, Arizona.

Two days after signing the contract that once more bracketed him as the highest paid player in the history of football, Namath participated in a controlled scrimmage against the New York Giants. It was a seven-on-seven drill, with the Jets' receivers and running backs going against the Giants' linebackers and defensive backs. Namath looked sharp, hitting 10 of 14 throws. Rich Caster caught five of those 10 completions, one of them being a 40-yard touchdown.

Come August 9, some 51,323 people in Tempe spent their Saturday night in Arizona State University Stadium, the 100-degree temperature notwithstanding: the count was just 60 shy of a record for the stadium. They came out to watch the New York Jets and the Minnesota Vikings play the first-ever professional football game in Arizona. Namath did not start the game, but rather played the second and third quarters.

The Jets got out to a 7–0 first-quarter lead when running back Bob Gresham (acquired from the Houston Oilers) scored on a five-yard run 4:30 into the game, which was set up by, of all things, a bad snap on a Jets punt. Center Joe Fields sent punter Greg Gantt chasing after a high snap, and once he'd gotten to it Gantt managed to escape being tackled and kicked the ball downfield to Jackie Wallace. Perhaps having been pulled out of position by all of the scurrying about on the bad snap, Wallace went after the ball and couldn't get a handle on it. He wound up fumbling it away, and Phil Wise recovered for New York at the Minnesota 14-yard line. Shortly afterward, Gresham took it in.

Later in the first period Fields again sent the ball sailing over Gantt's head on a punt, but on this occasion the luck was all Minnesota's as the Vikings recovered at the New York 17. It led to a Minnesota field goal that cut the Jets' lead to 7–3.

Namath made his first appearance 2:47 into the second period and led the Jets to a 24-yard Pat Leahy field goal, but Minnesota then tied the game at 10–10 when Fran Tarkenton drove the Vikings 68 yards to score on a 22-yard touchdown throw to Jim Lash. The Jets pulled back out in front late in the half when Namath drove them 62 yards to another score, with Gresham again running it in, this time from two yards out with 1:22 remaining in the second quarter. The big gainer in the series had been a 32-yard pass from Namath to tight end Willie Brister.

The Jets led 17–10 at halftime, and after a scoreless third quarter the Vikings posted a safety in the fourth when linebacker Wally Hilgenberg caught running back Clarence Jackson in the end zone. After that, the teams ended the scoring by exchanging field goals, Fred Cox hitting from 46 yards for Minnesota while Bobby Howfield—who was trying to regain his job after missing the last half of the previous season due to injury—hit from 19 yards to make the final 20–15 in the Jets' favor.

The New York passing game hadn't been exactly scintillating: Namath finished five of 11 for 45 yards, while Al Woodall was only one of seven for 14 yards, and Bill Demory was one of three for 25 yards. But extended back to the previous season, the Jets' winning streak was now seven games.

Despite a pulled muscle in his right side that occurred during the week in practice, Namath was scheduled to play the first half of the Jets' game against the Cardinals in St. Louis the following Saturday night. But that all changed just before game time, when Winner chose to keep Namath out of the game and start Woodall instead.

The Cardinals opened the game by driving to a 7–0 lead on a three-yard touchdown toss from Jim Hart to Jim Otis in their first series, and that lead expanded to 13–0 in the second quarter when Woodall was intercepted by Norm Thompson, who returned it 49 yards for a score. Woodall came back with a 31-yard touchdown pass to Gresham in the second period, but with the Jets driving late in the half he was again intercepted, this time by Greg Wojcik at the St. Louis 12-yard line to end a scoring threat. Woodall threw three interceptions in all.

New York held the Cardinals scoreless in the second half, but it wasn't until very late in the game that the Jets themselves got into the end zone again, when Gresham scored his fourth touchdown in two games. After J.J. Jones threw 30 yards to Jackson, Gresham took the ball over the goal line from less than a yard out with 1:56 left to play. Howfield's extra point gave the Jets their eighth straight victory, as they held the Cardinals off to take a 14–13 win.

Naturally, it was hoped that Namath would play the following Sunday in the Jets' annual game with the Giants at the Yale Bowl, but still nursing a case of sore ribs, the decision was again made to keep him out. While he did suit up for the game, Namath watched from the sidelines as J.J. Jones went the full four quarters. Jones surprised everyone with his performance, and he gained the Jets a 13–7 halftime lead with a long touchdown throw to Jerome Barkum. But the Giants turned things around quickly in the second half, when Clarence Jackson fumbled the opening kick and Pete Athas recovered for the Giants at the Jets' 25. From there it was a matter of six plays for Craig Morton—who also played the entire game—to throw a 13-yard touchdown to Bob Tucker that gave the Giants a 14–13 lead. Later in the period Morton hit fullback Steve Crosby with a seven-yard touchdown pass to increase the lead to 21–13, but the Jets came back to within a point when Jones threw another touchdown to Barkum.

Having driven to the Giants' 21-yard line in the game's waning seconds, the Jets might have won the game with a 38-yard field goal. From that distance, it was very doable, but with nine seconds left center Joe Fields did it again: his snap sailed over kicker Pat Leahy's head, and the Jets lost the game. Their eight-game winning streak was over, having begun and ended against the Giants at the Yale Bowl.

Namath was again held out of action the following Saturday night against the Falcons in Atlanta. This time it was Woodall who got the start, but he left the field on a stretcher after suffering a twisted knee just 3:34 into the game. Jones came in, and the Jets gained a 6–0 first-quarter lead on Leahy field goals of 33 and 39 yards. The Falcons tied the game with field goals of their own in the second and third quarters, but the Jets pulled back out in front when Jones hit his favorite target, Barkum, with an eight-yard touchdown pass; another Leahy field goal in the fourth quarter gave the Jets a 16–6 lead.

Atlanta quarterback Steve Bartkowski hit Alfred Jenkins with a 47-yard TD bomb to make it 16–13, but the Falcons missed a chance to tie the game when kicker Nick Mike-Mayer was wide left on a 35-yard field goal try with 2:42 remaining in the game. The Jets ran out the clock and won it, making their preseason record 3–1.

Namath had recovered sufficiently to play the following week against the Washington Redskins, and he got the Jets out to an early 14–0 lead, opening the scoring with a 57-yard TD pass to Rich Caster, then driving the Jets to a second score on a two-yard run by Clarence Jackson. The Redskins tied the game with a pair of TDs before Gresham scored on a nine-yard run that gave the Jets a 21–14 halftime lead.

After playing three quarters, Namath left the game with cramps in the left calf. By then the Redskins had tied the score at 21, and in the fourth quarter Washington took the lead for the first time with a 19-yard field goal. It was the Jets' defense that succeeded in recapturing the lead, when Delles Howell intercepted a pass and ran it back 37 yards for a score.

The Jets' next offensive series was short and sweet, beginning at the Washington seven-yard line after linebacker Godwin Turk blocked a punt, and lasting all of one play as Gresham scored his second touchdown of the game. His seven-yard scoring run gave the Jets an 11-point lead, which the Redskins cut to four points on a four-yard touchdown pass from backup quarterback Randy Johnson to Larry Jones with 4:46 left in the game. But the Jets ran out the bulk of the remaining time, and hung on to win the game 35–31. In his three quarters of play Namath had completed 12 of 28 passes for 219 yards with one TD and one interception.

Now 4–1, the Jets' final exhibition was a return engagement at the Yale Bowl, where they were to play the New England Patriots the following Sunday. But the day before the game, it was announced that the New England Patriots' players had voted to go on strike. The decision was sparked by the NFL Players Association's rejection of the latest contract offer made by the league's managers. The strike that had taken place during the 1974 preseason had accomplished nothing, and after more than 19 months without an agreement, the New England players apparently took it upon themselves to launch a protest. It was not a very intelligible move; even Bob Woolf, the attorney representing some of the striking New England players, was at a loss to understand it. Woolf said that he recognized the moral and emotional side of the issue, but added: "I can't quite understand the intelligence of it."[3]

Few could. The Patriots were imploring the other teams to join in their strike, but there seemed little support around the league. The night that the strike was announced, the Giants were scheduled to play the Dolphins in the Orange Bowl; the best the Giants' players could muster was a vote to delay the start of the game for a half hour as a show of solidarity with the New England players. Even that didn't hold up: Giants' owner Wellington Mara spoke to the team, as did Miami coach Don Shula and several of the Miami players. In the end the game only started eight minutes late.

But the following Tuesday, both the Jets' and Washington Redskins' players voted to join in the strike; a day later, the New York Giants and Detroit Lions joined as well. If it was hoped that enough teams would throw in to threaten a cancellation of the opening of the season, that notion quickly proved unrealistic. With the beginning of the season only several days away, no other teams were enthusiastic about the action initiated by New England, and the five teams that were out on strike faced the possibility of forfeiting their games until they returned. It all accomplished nothing in the end, and coming so close to the start of the regular season, all it really managed to do was rob the striking players of much needed practice time before the season got underway proper. As the season was set to begin the players all returned, looking none too bright.

The loss to the Giants — attributable to a bad snap on a field goal that would have won the game — was the Jets' only loss since week eight of the 1974 season. It is wise, of course, not to place too much stock in preseason, but all the same, who wouldn't be pleased with a 4–1 preseason record? While nobody was picking them to win their division, the Jets were being painted by many as the dark horse in the AFC.

Week 1— Sunday, September 21, 1975
Rich Stadium, Buffalo (attendance: 77,837)

The Jets opened the 1975 season against the Bills in Buffalo. Although the five-team strike — of which the Jets were counted among the five — had ended a few days prior to the start of the season, those teams had lost valuable practice time. With the Bills having voted not to join the strike, feelings among some of the Jets players toward Buffalo were rancorous. In particular, defensive lineman Richard Neal accused Buffalo of trying to score an easy victory by hoping that the strike would result in the Jets forfeiting the game. "They tried to get something for nothing," Neal said. "It's going to be a blood match."[4] As it turned out, the only blood being spilled was New York's.

The lack of practice on the Jets' part did seem to play a factor — though not necessarily — as a New York fumble gave the Bills opportunity to take a quick lead when safety Steve Freeman recovered the ball for Buffalo at the New York 28. It set up a two-yard touchdown run by O.J. Simpson that gave the Bills a 7–0 advantage 3:41 into the game.

About midway into the opening period, the Bills made it 14–0 when Joe Ferguson flipped a three-yard touchdown pass to fullback Jim Braxton. But the Jets would close the gap before the quarter ended, as Namath rifled a 28-yard touchdown to Rich Caster to make it 14–7.

Early in the second quarter, the Bills started to pull away again when a pass interference call helped set up a five-yard touchdown run by Simpson just 1:04 into the period. The Jets would again close to within seven points, however, when Namath hit Eddie Bell with a 12-yard touchdown. Trailing 21–14 at halftime, the Jets were not in bad shape, but the second half played out like a bad dream for New York.

It was 6:46 into the third quarter when Ferguson threw a two-yard touchdown to tight end Paul Seymour to up Buffalo's lead to 28–14, and things quickly deteriorated for New York after that. On the Jets' next series Namath was intercepted by Charlie Ford at the Buffalo 48, and a 19-yard return gave the Bills the ball at the New York 33. Even busted plays were working in Buffalo's favor: positioned at the one-yard line eight plays later, Ferguson turned to hand the ball off and found no one in his backfield. He quickly turned back around and followed his right tackle into the end zone for a 35–14 lead at 10:24 of the third period.

Early in the fourth quarter Buffalo put the game away quite nicely when defensive end Pat Toomay intercepted Namath, and the 247-pound lineman proceeded to run it back 44 yards for a score. The 42–14 final was more indicative of a blood*bath* than a blood *match*.

After the game, Simpson put the Jets' poor performance down to the strike. "It's tough to go two weeks without playing a game and it was a huge handicap in missing those days of practice," Simpson explained. "That was the biggest difference in the game."[5]

Buffalo guard Reggie McKenzie concurred, saying: "I'm sure the layoff had an effect on them."[6] New York running back Bob Gresham, who dropped two passes in the first quarter, also attributed his team's mistake-ridden performance to the down time created by the strike, but Namath (who finished 14 of 36 for 173 yards, two touchdowns, and four interceptions) was reluctant to alibi the poor performance, saying that he wasn't convinced that the strike was responsible for the Jets' sloppy execution. Not that it mattered anymore: the strike was over, the game was over, and the Jets were in an early hole. There was nothing to do now but try and climb out.

Week 2 — Sunday, September 28, 1975
Arrowhead Stadium, Kansas City (attendance: 74,169)

"(We) played a team that was heavily harassed by their writers and probably their coaches," said Kansas City coach Paul Wiggin after the Chiefs hosted the Jets in week two. "They probably came out with a vendetta to move the football. And they did."[7] No doubt.

In front of the largest Kansas City crowd in two years — 74,169 strong — the Jets took the opening kickoff and pounded 80 yards in seven straight runs, the last being a one-yard burst across the goal line by John Riggins that gave the Jets a 7–0 lead in the game's opening minutes. The Jets quickly expanded that lead on their next series. They began at the Kansas City 49, and after a running play advanced them to the 44, Namath threw his first pass of the day, good for 35 yards to Rich Caster to the nine-yard line. After Riggins gained four more yards on first down, and then another four to the one on second, Carl Garrett went through the left side of the line and into the end zone for the score at 9:31 of the first quarter.

The Jets' third series saw their first punt, and when the Chiefs began at their 42-yard line, 40-year-old Len Dawson (playing for injured Mike Livingston) got them back into the game with a 10-play drive that climaxed with Woody Green going around left end and into the end zone from four yards out.

Although the Jets were able to move the ball quite easily, they would not get into the end zone again for the remainder of the half. The Chiefs, on the other hand, would even the score with a 10-yard touchdown run by Ed Podolak in the second period. The Jets still managed to go into the intermission ahead when they got close enough for Pat Leahy to kick a 32-yard field goal on the last play of the half.

Leading 17–14 at halftime, the Jets had already rushed for 197 yards. With no pressing need, Namath had thrown sparingly, completing five of 10 passes for 92 yards. He would throw even less in the second half, as Riggins and Garrett were having their way with the Kansas City defense.

Midway into the third quarter Riggins scored his second TD, going in from two yards out to top off a 61-yard drive. After the extra point was botched, the Jets then led 23–14, but the Chiefs would retaliate with a 60-yard drive of their own, Dawson finishing the march with a 36-yard touchdown pass to Barry Pearson that closed the gap to 23–21.

Namath threw only four passes in the second half, completing two. The one that made all the difference was a nine-yard touchdown to Caster in the fourth quarter that turned out to be the margin of victory. It gave the Jets a 30–21 lead, which the Chiefs whittled down to 30–24 with a 35-yard field goal.

Kansas City's last chance saw them come awfully close in the final minute. The Chiefs were at the New York 14-yard line after Dawson hit Larry Brunson with a 36-yard pass, but two running plays and an incomplete pass brought up fourth down. With 58 seconds left in the game, and needing a touchdown, Kansas City was forced to go for broke. Dawson's pass to running back Jeff Kinney came up a yard shy of the first down at the five-yard line, and the Jets took possession and ran out the remaining 47 seconds.

If Namath's numbers — seven of 14 for 126 yards, one touchdown, and two interceptions —

were a bit slight, Riggins' and Garrett's stats were fat enough. Riggins had run for 145 yards and Garrett 135. Now 1–1, the Jets were in a three-way tie with Baltimore and Miami for second place in the AFC's Eastern division. Buffalo was in front at 2–0.

Week 3 — Sunday, October 5, 1975
Shea Stadium, New York (attendance: 57,365)

The Jets' week three home opener against the 0–2 New England Patriots was their earliest home opener since 1967. Having seen the havoc that the New York running game had caused in Kansas City the week before, the Patriots were determined to prevent a repeat performance. With that as their primary objective, they devised a defensive scheme whereby their 3–4 alignment attacked the line from every which way to thwart any blocking strategies and fill all the gaps. It worked beautifully: John Riggins and Carl Garrett, who had combined for 280 rushing yards the week before, found nowhere to run. In the first half the Jets were held to only 33 yards rushing; obviously the plan dreamed up by the Patriots achieved its goal. Problem was, it failed to supply a pass rush, which left Namath able to choose passing targets at his leisure. "Joe read the defenses as if he was in our huddle," New England cornerback Bob Howard said of Namath.[8]

Even so, the Patriots managed to play the Jets to a scoreless standoff in the first quarter. But the trouble began for New England in the second period. Pinned back at their own five-yard line, the Jets proceeded to march 95 yards to the game's first score as Namath almost effortlessly guided them, throwing 21 yards to Rich Caster, then hitting Caster again for 23 more. He also threw a 28-yarder to Eddie Bell, and the drive reached fruition when Garrett ran around left end for a six-yard score. The extra point was blocked, however, and the Jets' lead stood at 6–0.

The Patriots went nowhere on their next series, and when they punted Bell received the ball at the New York 35 and brought it back 34 yards to the New England 31. A few plays later, Namath hit Caster in the right corner of the end zone for a three-yard touchdown to put the Jets up 13–0.

The Jets again got a short field to work with when Patriots quarterback Jim Plunkett was intercepted by Phil Wise at the New England 39, and a three-yard return left the Jets with only 36 yards to travel. It took Namath all of two plays, as he threw 15 yards to Caster on the first and then whistled a 21-yard touchdown to Caster on the next play. Again the extra point failed, leaving the Jets ahead 19–0.

On New England's next series Plunkett was intercepted again, this time by Roscoe Word. But with the first half running down, the Jets failed to capitalize and kept their 19–0 lead into the intermission. By halftime Namath had already thrown for 201 yards, hitting 13 of 16 passes. New England did some drastic reworking of their defensive strategy at the break, and came out with a new mission in the second half—to stop Namath. But with a fair-sized lead, the Jets were inclined to play conservatively in the second half, anyway. That being the case, New England's reprioritizing played right into the Jets' hands. Namath threw only five passes in the second half, completing two (both touchdowns) for 17 yards, but whereas the New York running game had only managed 33 yards in the first half, it exploded for 140 in the second.

The Jets were further aided by New England mistakes. In the third quarter, New England running back Mack Herron fumbled and linebacker Godwin Turk recovered for the Jets at the Patriots' 34. It only led to a 47-yard field goal, but it still upped the Jets' lead to 22–0.

Later in the third, Herron fumbled again and rookie safety Bob Prout pounced on it at the New England 19. This time the Jets took full advantage, as Namath threw a 13-yard TD to Jerome Barkum that made it 29–0. Going into the fourth quarter, the New York defense must have been thinking about a shutout, but if they were, that notion would soon be snuffed out.

Plunkett had been pulled from the game early in the third quarter. He had suffered a separated shoulder in the preseason, and had missed the first two games of the year; week three against the Jets proved to be the wrong day for him to come back. He had completed only eight of 21 passes in his little more than half-a-game, and would be replaced by Steve Grogan. On the very first play of the fourth quarter, Grogan threw a 42-yard touchdown to tight end Russ Francis to make the score 29–7. The Jets were in no danger of losing the game — the Patriots would have to score four more times to capture the lead — but it had to be disappointing for the defense to lose the shutout.

Even if they were a tad disappointed, they likely got over it when Namath directed a 54-yard drive that resulted in his fourth touchdown pass of the game, this one a four-yard toss to Barkum that made the score 36–7 with nine minutes left to play. With that, Namath sat out the rest of the game, turning the reins over to J.J. Jones. Namath's numbers were very good, hitting 15 of 21 for 218 yards, with four TDs and one interception. It was an impressive victory in every way, and with a 2–1 record the Jets were tied with Miami for second place in the AFC East, a game behind the 3–0 Buffalo Bills.

Week 4 — Sunday, October 12, 1975
Metropolitan Stadium, Minnesota (attendance: 47,739)

The Jets traveled to Minnesota to play the Vikings in week four and found themselves down 3–0 midway into the first quarter when a 35-yard pass from Fran Tarkenton to John Gilliam set up a 40-yard field goal. But the Jets gained the lead on their next series when they went 69 yards in eight plays, including a 34-yard pass from Namath to John Riggins. It was Riggins who took it in from a yard out to put the Jets up 7–3 at the 11:34 mark of the quarter.

Early in the second quarter the Vikings drove to the New York three-yard line, but when the drive was derailed by an offensive pass interference call, Minnesota settled for a 36-yard field goal that closed the gap to 7–6. The remainder of the half was marked by missed opportunities. The Jets drove to the Minnesota 13, only to have linebacker Jeff Siemon intercept a Namath-to-Rich Caster pass in the end zone. The Vikings then drove to the New York 28, but Tarkenton was intercepted by Bob Prout at the 15-yard line. With a minute left in the half, Minnesota running back Chuck Foreman fumbled and linebacker Godwin Turk recovered for the Jets. The Jets were unable to cash in, however, and the half ended with New York up 7–6.

The Vikings got out of the gate quickly in the third quarter, when Sam McCullum took the second half kickoff and ran it back 63 yards to the New York 32. It led to Minnesota's first touchdown of the game, as Tarkenton hit Foreman four plays later with a 13-yard TD pass that gave the Vikings a 13–7 lead.

The Jets were pinned back deep on their next series, facing a third-and-long from their own 13, but when Namath converted with a 20-yard pass to Caster it sparked the team, and they went on a drive that carried to the Minnesota 29 before running out of wheels. A field goal would have cut it to 13–10, but Pat Leahy's kick was blocked by linebacker Fred McNeill, and the Vikings kept their six-point advantage.

The Vikings then built on their lead after going 71 yards in only four plays in their next series. Foreman scored his second touchdown of the game when he took a swing pass from Tarkenton, broke an attempted tackle by Ed Galigher, and went nine yards for the score. The Minnesota lead then stood at 20–7 with 5:22 left in the third period. Before the period ended, the Jets got back in the game with a seven-play, 72-yard drive. Namath hit Riggins with a pass down the left sideline that went 11 yards for a score, making it 20–14.

Early in the fourth quarter, the Jets got the break they needed when Turk blocked a Minnesota punt and cornerback Ed Taylor's recovery set New York up at the Vikings' eight-yard line. Carl Garrett ran it into the end zone from two yards out three plays later, giving the Jets a 21–20 lead.

But just as a blocked punt had made it possible for the Jets to regain the lead, it was also a blocked punt that took it away from them again. Punting from his own end zone midway through the fourth quarter, Greg Gantt had his kick blocked by Minnesota's Joe Blahak; the ball carried out of the end zone for a safety, giving the Vikings a 22–21 lead with 7:14 left in the game.

The free kick that followed the safety gave the Vikings excellent field position at their own 43, and they went 57 yards to score when Foreman notched his third TD of the game with a four-yard run that put Minnesota ahead 29–21. Unable to rally after that, the Jets lost the game. Namath finished 12 of 21 for 195 yards, one touchdown, and two interceptions.

The Jets fell to 2–2, but more than that, the loss seemed to affect the team psychologically. "We're pretty well drained after losing an emotional game like that," Namath said afterward.[9] The loss may have demoralized the Jets, but not nearly so much as would their return to Shea the following week.

Week 5 — Sunday, October 19, 1975
Shea Stadium, New York (attendance: 47,513)

"I didn't expect to do anything like this against the Jets," said Miami quarterback Bob Griese after a wet, windy no-contest at Shea.[10] "They couldn't do anything right and we couldn't do anything wrong," added Miami coach Don Shula.[11]

It was degrading. Not since 1963 — the pre–Namath era — had the Jets been beaten so badly. The 1963 loss was a 48–0 spanking by the Kansas City Chiefs: this was almost as bad. It started innocently enough, with the Jets trailing only 6–0 after the first period. The Dolphins had driven 58 yards in 10 plays to open the scoring when Griese took it in from five yards out on a quarterback draw. Jim Bailey blocked the extra point, one of the only New York accomplishments of the afternoon.

Things began to go terribly wrong in the second period. Namath was intercepted by linebacker Steve Towle at the Miami 20-yard line, and a 16-yard return gave the Dolphins the ball at their 36. A 49-yard run by Mercury Morris promptly advanced Miami to the New York 15, and four plays later Don Nottingham made it 13–0 with a one-yard TD run.

On the Jets' next series they kept it on the ground and advanced 55 yards from their own 20 to the Miami 25, but on the first pass of the series Namath was again intercepted, this time by linebacker Mike Kolen. Griese then threw a 53-yard TD to Nat Moore to make it 20–0.

Things went from bad to worse, as New York punter Greg Gantt found himself in a frantic race to escape a heavy rush and he fumbled the ball. Miami defensive back Curtis Johnson grabbed it and ran to the New York 10. One play later, Morris ran it in for a touchdown, and after the extra point again failed, the Dolphins led 26–0.

New York's nightmare continued in the second half. Griese threw another pair of TDs in the third quarter, a two-yarder to running back Norm Bulaich and a 32-yarder to tight end Jim Mandich, and with the score then 40–0, Griese left the game with 5:05 remaining in the third period. The Dolphins added an 18-yard field goal in the fourth to make the final a very humiliating 43–0.

Namath had one of the worst days of his career, completing only eight of 24 passes for 96 yards. He also threw six interceptions. Johnson, who had three of those interceptions and caused a fourth with a hit that jarred the ball loose, seemed shocked by the rout, saying that never in his years of playing football — be it high school, college or professional — had he intercepted three passes in a game. He allowed that the wind and rain may have been a factor, but said that Namath should certainly have grown accustomed to it in his years of playing at Shea.[12]

Namath could only agree. He dismissed the weather as a factor, but also pointed out that three of the interceptions were off of deflected passes. Otherwise, with the Jets so far behind and having to throw constantly, all the Miami defense had to do was lay back and wait for it. After being booed off the field by the few remaining spectators (due to the weather, there were over 14,000 no-shows), Namath was replaced by J.J. Jones, who threw no interceptions — no completions either, but no interceptions.

If Griese and Johnson were surprised by the ease of the victory, other Miami players were more analytical in sizing things up. A year earlier, Miami center Jim Langer had remarked that Jets' tackle Carl Barzilauskas was the strongest lineman he had ever faced. Now, constantly facing double-teaming every week, Barzilauskas didn't strike Langer as playing at the same level of intensity. Miami guard Bob Kuechenberg noted that Barzilauskas just wasn't hustling.[13]

Charley Winner was understandably furious with his team's performance (or lack thereof). The good news was that, at 2–3 the Jets still managed to hold third place, ahead of Baltimore and New England, both 1–4. The bad news was that things weren't going to get any better.

Week 6 — Sunday, October 26, 1975
Shea Stadium, New York (attendance: 55,137)

"Joe is the best there is," said Baltimore quarterback Bert Jones after the Colts' game with the Jets at Shea. "In fact, I think he's the best there ever was."[14]

Namath's numbers were impressive, throwing for 333 yards, his highest yardage total in a game in two seasons, and the twenty-first time in his career that he had thrown for over 300 yards (Johnny Unitas held the record at the time with twenty-six 300-yard games). He also threw three TDs, and after his six-interception performance against Miami the week before, he managed to hold his interception count to a single miscue. Unfortunately that one interception was very costly, being run back the other way for a score. Still, it was an impressive performance. He had also set a team record with a 91-yard pass to Rich Caster.

The problem was, there was another personal high for Namath that day as he was sacked seven times for a total of 74 yards in losses. Tackle Mike Barnes — who accounted for four of those sacks — and defensive end Fred Cook seemed to have no trouble blowing past Winston Hill and Gary Puetz to get to Namath. "I thought two of them were part of my backfield," Namath said of Cook and Barnes after the game.[15]

The main problem for the Jets, however, was their abysmal defense, which was proving to be the worst in the league. It didn't help matters that the Jets basically spotted the Colts 14 points in the game's opening minutes. Carl Garrett fumbled on the first play from scrimmage, and Bruce Laird recovered for the Colts at the New York 26. Jones scored on a 15-yard run three plays later to give the Colts a 7–0 lead 1:09 into the game.

When the Jets got the ball back Namath fired a 44-yard pass to Caster, but the play was nullified by a holding penalty. Garrett then fumbled again; this time it was Lloyd Mumphord who recovered the ball, giving Baltimore possession at the New York 24. Don McCauley ran it in from two yards out five plays later to give the Colts a 14–0 lead only several minutes into the game.

Things calmed down a bit after that, and in the second quarter Namath drove the Jets 62 yards, cutting the lead to 14–7 with a 42-yard TD pass to Jerome Barkum 2:47 into the period. But the Colts came right back when Jones hit rookie Marshall Johnson with a 15-yard TD pass. It was Johnson's first catch as a pro, and it upped Baltimore's lead to 21–7.

With time running out in the half, a pass interference call on Nelson Munsey placed the Jets at the Baltimore one-yard line. Namath then tossed another TD to Barkum to again pull the Jets to within seven points. The score came with just 24 seconds left in the half, but incredibly the New York defense could not stop Baltimore from scoring again in that short time. Jones quickly got the Colts within range for Toni Linhart to kick a 36-yard field goal in the last two seconds of the half to put the Colts up 24–14 at the intermission.

When the second half began the Colts again struck quickly, as Jones threw over the middle to Johnson at the New York 40; Johnson cut through the defenders, broke outside, and outran everyone to the end zone for a 68-yard scoring play that made it 31–14. It was the second pass reception of Johnson's professional career — he was certainly making them count.

Now trailing badly and backed up at his own eight-yard line, Namath went back to pass and threw from his own end zone down the middle of the field for Caster. After making the catch at the New York 40 and outrunning a diving tackle attempt by Bruce Laird, Caster was galloping downfield for what looked to be a sure touchdown when Jackie Wallace caught up and grabbed him. Munsey then joined in hauling Caster down mere inches from the goal line. The play had gone for 91 yards, and it wasn't even good for a score.

From a foot away, fullback John Riggins was usually a safe bet in such situations, but not on this occasion: Riggins fumbled the ball into the end zone. This time, however, luck was on New York's side as tight end Willie Brister fell on the ball in the end zone for a touchdown, which cut the Baltimore lead to 10 points again at 31–21.

Still trailing by 10 in the fourth quarter, Namath threw his only interception, but it was good for seven points the other way as Wallace picked it off and ran it 38 yards for a score. Even then the Jets fought back, once more making it a 10-point game when Namath threw a 22-yard TD to Eddie Bell.

But trailing 38–28 late in the game, the Jets tried in desperation to convert a fourth-and-one from their own 20: the Colts stopped them and took possession. On the next play Lydell Mitchell ran 20 yards for a score to put the game away. The 45–28 loss marked the third time in six games that the Jets had given up more than 40 points. But aside from the dismal play of the defense, the New York offensive line had been of little help to Namath. Puetz, who was tasked with blocking Barnes, ranked it the worst game of his career. But Namath refused to blame his line. "They're trying hard," he said. "I won't chew them out. They've helped me out too often."[16]

It must have been frustrating nonetheless. That frustration was apparent on a play in which Barnes was flagged for a late hit. Barnes didn't think he deserved the flag, but Namath obviously did. It was well known that Namath took his lumps and seldom groused about getting hit late, but on this occasion his frustration may have caused him to make an exception. "He got up screaming and said I was a punk if I couldn't hit him before he threw the ball," said Barnes.[17]

The game broke Baltimore's four-game losing streak, while extending the Jets' losing streak to three. Namath completed 19 of 28 for 333 yards, with three TDs and one interception.

Week 7 — Sunday, November 2, 1975
Shea Stadium, New York (attendance: 58,343)

Since they had met on opening day, the Jets and Bills had each gone in opposite directions: the Bills came into Shea Stadium with a 4–2 record, whereas the Jets were 2–4. But the good news for the Jets was that the Bills were sliding. Having begun the season 4–0, the Bills came into the game on a two-game losing streak. Of course, the Jets were on a three-game skid of their own, but having been blown out by Buffalo on opening day, there was a matter of having a score to settle.

It was the Bills who got on top quickly, however, receiving the opening kickoff and driving 74 yards to a 7–0 lead on quarterback Joe Ferguson's 11-yard TD pass to fullback Jim Braxton. But the Jets turned things around after that. A 42-yard field goal by Pat Leahy cut Buffalo's lead to 7–3 in the first quarter, and field goals of 41 and 31 yards in the second quarter put the Jets up 9–7. The momentum certainly seemed to be on the Jets' side when Namath hit Emerson Boozer with a 16-yard TD pass just 14 seconds before halftime.

The Jets came out for the second half sporting a 16–7 lead, and quickly struck again when

Namath found Eddie Bell with a 31-yard touchdown strike that made it 23–7. At that point they looked to be in pretty good shape, and even after the Bills hit a 40-yard field goal midway through the third the Jets still seemed in control.

The Jets moved downfield and were on the verge of scoring again when Namath tried to hit Bell in the end zone, and was instead intercepted by safety Tony Greene. The ball was brought out to the 20, and the Bills proceeded to drive 80 yards for a score, cutting the Jets' lead to 23–17 when Ferguson threw a 28-yard TD to J.D. Hill.

The Bills were trailing the Jets by only six points when the fourth quarter got underway, but the Jets continued to hold steady as the final period wore on. After receiving a punt and starting from their own 31, the Jets moved 49 yards to the Buffalo 20-yard line. Faced with a fourth-and-one, the obvious choice seemed to be a field goal. It would have been a 37-yarder, and Leahy had already hit from 41 and 42 yards, so the distance seemed no problem. A field goal would put the Jets up by nine points, making it necessary for Buffalo to score twice to overtake them. But Charley Winner had other ideas — the Jets went for it on fourth down. The call went to John Riggins, who went into the line and was stopped dead in his tracks by tackle Earl Edwards. Buffalo took over at the 20 with 5:19 left to play.

Trailing by six, Buffalo had plenty of time. On first down, Braxton ran for nine yards to the 29. On second down, Ferguson picked up the first down himself with a seven-yard run to the 36. Then, after an incomplete pass, Ferguson went back to pass again on second down. He found O.J. Simpson over the middle at the New York 40, and after making the catch, Simpson bounced outside to his left and outraced the defenders to the end zone. With the extra point Buffalo had retaken the lead, 24–23, with 3:46 left to play. What happened afterward was wholly predictable: inspired by the 64-yard TD that had recaptured the lead for them, Buffalo did what good teams do — they rose to the occasion — and the Jets did what not-so-good teams do — they folded.

Sure, in hindsight the decision not to kick the field goal struck some as a poor choice, but it was easy enough to explain. Winner reasoned that, as the Jets had been rushing well all day, they figured they could make one foot.[18] Riggins certainly wasn't happy about it. "I guess I have to take the responsibility," he said. "If I can't get one damned yard I must be pretty sorry."[19] It was easy to label it a bad decision after the fact, but it really wasn't. A 2–4 team has to roll the dice at some point to pull itself back up. The risk is in winding up a 2–5 team, which they did. Namath's numbers were 16 of 31 for 208 yards, two TDs and one interception.

Week 8 — Sunday, November 9, 1975
Orange Bowl, Miami (attendance: 72,896)

With their 43–0 loss to Miami three weeks earlier still fresh in mind, the Jets traveled to the Orange Bowl for a rematch with the Dolphins in week eight. Whereas the Jets were on a four-game losing streak going into the game, the Dolphins were riding a six-game winning streak and were looking to expand their lead over Buffalo for first place in the AFC East.

It was a more determined New York team that met the Dolphins this time, evidenced by their initial series in which the Jets went 67 yards in nine plays to take a 7–0 lead on a 15-yard touchdown pass from Namath to Carl Garrett. The Dolphins mounted a drive on their first series as well, but it ended abruptly when Don Nottingham fumbled at the New York 13.

The Jets missed an opportunity to increase their lead in the second quarter when Pat Leahy's 42-yard field goal attempt bounced off the left upright. Even so, the New York defense was doing a creditable job of keeping the Miami offense at bay through most of the first half. The Dolphins finally managed to get on the scoreboard toward the end of the half, however, when they drove 76 yards to tie the game on an eight-yard run by Benny Malone with under two minutes left before the break.

The 7–7 tie was broken on Miami's second series of the third quarter, when Bob Griese scrambled out of the pocket and found Norm Bulaich all alone down the sideline at the New York 20-yard line. From there, Bulaich had no trouble running it in on a play that went for a 59-yard score. Garo Yepremian missed the extra point, and Miami's lead was held to six. At that point the Jets were still in it, but just two minutes later the roof began to cave in.

After failing to pick up a first down, the Jets were quickly forced to punt. Freddie Solomon fielded the punt on the run, a dicey thing to try, but on this occasion Lou Piccone, who was bearing down on Solomon, kept going and wound up running right past him. After darting up the middle of the field, Solomon broke outside to the right and down the sideline. From there, the race was on—Solomon won, and the Dolphins took a 20–7 lead.

The Jets did have their opportunities: late in the third quarter Carl Barzilauskas recovered a Griese fumble at the Miami 13-yard line, but the Jets failed to cash in. Forced to settle for a 31-yard field goal try, Leahy's kick was blocked by Don Reese and the Dolphins maintained their 13-point lead.

Early in the fourth quarter, the Dolphins put the game away with an 80-yard drive. They needed only five plays to cover that distance, primarily due to Griese's 63-yard pass to Nat Moore that moved Miami from their own 23 to the New York 14. In the end, it was another pass from Griese to Bulaich, this one of seven yards, that got the Dolphins across the goal line.

The Jets' hard luck story continued. Namath drove them to the Miami seven-yard line, but after Reese took Namath down for a nine-yard loss back to the 16 on third down, there was nothing for the Jets but to go for it. On fourth down Namath was intercepted at the five-yard line by linebacker Earnest Rhone, sealing Miami's 27–7 victory. Namath finished the game 11 of 28 for 140 yards, with one TD and two interceptions.

The closeness of the first half was due to both an inspired performance by the New York defense and the Jets' ability to run the ball. John Riggins carried nine times for 64 yards in the first half, allowing Namath to pick opportune moments to throw. Namath didn't need to throw often, completing four of seven for 41 yards in the half. But the Dolphins eradicated the New York ground game in the second half, holding Riggins to just 26 yards and forcing Namath into more frequent (and obvious) passing situations on second and third downs. As the Jets fell behind, the situation worsened. Namath completed only a third of his second-half passes (seven of 21) for 99 yards. After stopping the run in the second half, the rest was easy for the Dolphins. "We just teed off on Namath the rest of the game," said Miami coach Don Shula.[20]

For the Jets, the season had become bitter. "I don't see anybody quitting out there," said Namath. Still, he had no explanations for what was happening. "If any of us knew what causes the breakdowns, we would fix it," he said.[21]

Week 9 — Sunday, November 16, 1975
Memorial Stadium, Baltimore (attendance: 52,097)

"We're learning to win now," said Baltimore running back Lydell Mitchell after the Colts had beaten the Jets quite soundly for the second time in the 1975 season.[22] After starting the season by losing four of their first five games, the Colts had found their rhythm. Their week nine victory over the Jets marked their fourth consecutive win, something they had not accomplished since 1970. It also put their record at 5–4, the first time they had been over .500 since 1971. Their winning streak had begun four weeks earlier—against the Jets.

As for the Jets, the loss marked their sixth in a row, and there seemed no end in sight. "It's not one individual, it's everybody," Namath explained after the game. "There's no way you can single out one guy the way we're losing."[23]

The Jets had opened the scoring with a 45-yard field goal in the first quarter. That was basically the last chance they had opportunity for optimism, as all of their subsequent points came after the game was out of reach — or out of *their* reach anyway.

The Colts captured the lead in the first quarter with a 17-yard TD run by Mitchell that finished off a 69-yard drive, and the opening quarter ended with the Colts up 14–3 after Bert Jones pitched a one-yard touchdown throw to Don McCauley on the eleventh play of a 43-yard drive.

Less than a minute into the second period came the knockout punch. The prior week Jones and receiver Roger Carr had tied a team record with an 89-yard TD pass against the Buffalo Bills. The record had been set in 1966 by Johnny Unitas and John Mackey. Now, just one week after tying the record, Jones and Carr would break it. Going back to pass from his own 10-yard line, Jones heaved the ball far down the right sideline to Carr. It was a jump-ball at the New York 35-yard line, with both Carr and Roscoe Word going up for it. Carr came down with it, sped away for the remaining 35 yards, and the Colts were up 21–3.

The play seemed to demoralize the Jets, and the best they could muster in response was a 36-yard field goal that made it 21–6. It was scarcely enough as the Colts continued to light up the scoreboard, first with a four-yard TD run by McCauley and then with a 36-yard field goal of their own that made the score 31–6 at halftime.

The third quarter was a wash, with the teams trading touchdowns, the Colts scoring on a 20-yard pass from Jones to Glenn Doughty, and the Jets finally getting into the end zone on a two-yard run by John Riggins. Late in the third Jones left the game with a rib injury, but that was no help to the Jets: Jones' replacement, Marty Domres, scored on a 20-yard keeper that made it 45–13.

With the game so far out of reach, Winner took Namath out, saying afterward that there was no reason to risk injury in a game that was virtually over. J.J. Jones came in and threw a 12-yard TD to Eddie Bell, but the Baltimore defense still had the last word. The scoring concluded when Fred Cook took a New York fumble back 49 yards for a score, making the final 52–19.

Before leaving the game after three quarters, Jones had completed 16 of 22 passes for 277 yards and three touchdowns, far and away superior to Namath's numbers (nine of 26 for 194 yards and two interceptions). Even when he was on target, Namath couldn't catch a break — one of his two interceptions had bounced off his receiver, Rich Caster, and into enemy hands.

After the game, a reporter, obviously hoping for a catty remark to spice his write-up, asked Jones if he was now a better quarterback than Namath. Jones wouldn't oblige: Namath had been his idol. "How can you ask a question like that?" Jones replied as he launched into a defense of Namath. "Joe is a helluva quarterback. He can throw with the best of them, but he's not getting the protection he needs. I still look up to him. He's far from over the hill."[24]

The Jets had suffered through five straight divisional losses, dropping games to Miami, Baltimore, Buffalo, Miami a second time, and then Baltimore again. The only team in their division that they could beat — the New England Patriots — wasn't on their schedule for another three weeks. But a game with the Patriots was just what the Jets were needing.

Week 10 — Sunday, November 23, 1975
Shea Stadium, New York (attendance: 53,169)

"When you're going to kill a gnat, it's best to do it with a sledgehammer." So said St. Louis receiver Mel Gray after the Cardinals' easy victory over the Jets in week 10.[25] So this is what it had come to: the Jets were no more than a gnat — a minor annoyance — to their opponents.

The loss was a team-record seventh straight for the Jets, and was an apropos topper to what had been a difficult week in the most difficult of seasons. On the Wednesday before the game, Coach Charley Winner was called out onto the carpet by management. Winner's father-in-law, Weeb Ewbank (who had given him the job), was no longer there to protect him, health issues having forced his retirement from the front office during the 1974 season. Winner was said to have been reduced to tears as he pled his case, but there was no stopping the inevitable: the Jets were 2–7, and somebody had to be held accountable. The coach's head is most always the first on the chopping block, and so Winner was sent packing.

Assistant coach Ken Shipp was elevated to head coach for the time being. It was Shipp's great misfortune that his first game as head coach would be played at home. Ordinarily it may have been preferable, but under the circumstances Shipp knew he would be debuting before a lynch mob. There are no fans so unruly or unforgiving as those in New York, where expectations are always high, and patience always low. That being the case, Shipp had made an appeal to the fans in New York. It was simple enough, but again, given the state of affairs it was apparently too much to ask. He merely asked the fans to help in lifting the team's morale by cheering them as they came onto the field. He might have settled for his team not being booed by their own fans, but it was useless, as he would get neither.

The Jets enthusiastically sprinted onto the field during the pre-game introductions, greeted by a wellspring of roaring boos, jeers and taunts. Even poor Shipp was not spared, being greeted most unceremoniously by a Shea Stadium crowd that was apparently unprepared to give him a chance and hope for the best. The players acted oblivious to it all, but there was no way they could fail to hear it. It would take a lot to win these folks over anymore.

The Jets tried to prove themselves by driving to the St. Louis 30-yard line on their opening series, but unable to go any further, they sent Pat Leahy in to kick a 47-yard field goal. Leahy made it, and the Jets led 3–0. The smattering of applause — barely noticeable — was indicative of a home crowd that had grown cynical. They had seen this before — an opening field goal, or even a touchdown, and then the Jets seemed to knock off for the rest of the day. The Jets would once more prove predictable in that respect. It doesn't take much to break the spirits of a 2–7 team, and the Cardinals wasted little time in doing just that.

The Cardinals were facing a second-and-eight at their own 48; the Jets guessed pass — they guessed wrong. The Jets sent their safeties blitzing as the Cardinals ran a draw play to Terry Metcalf. After breaking through, Metcalf was only five yards beyond the line of scrimmage and he was already in the clear. He took it 52 yards for a touchdown, and a 7–3 St. Louis lead.

On the Cardinals' next series Metcalf scored again, this time on a one-yard run that completed a 56-yard drive. With the extra point being botched, the St. Louis lead stood at 13–3, but they were hardly finished. On the very last play of the first quarter, St. Louis quarterback Jim Hart lofted a 74-yard touchdown pass to Gray to make it 20–3.

By the second quarter, even the booing had died down. Nobody seemed to give a damn. After the teams exchanged field goals, the Cardinals ended the first half with Hart throwing another touchdown to Gray — 20 yards this time — to give St. Louis a 30–6 halftime lead. The crowd was unable to even muster the enthusiasm to make their displeasure known any longer, having used up most of their emotional energy in jeering their own team in the pre-game intros.

For the Cardinals, the second half was like an exhibition game. After cornerback Norm Thompson picked off a Namath pass to Eddie Bell and ran it back 61 yards for a touchdown early in the third quarter, the Cardinals started putting in their reserves. Scheduled to play just four days later on Thanksgiving, St. Louis saw no reason not to rest their starters. The fans also seemed rested. Well, they were quiet, anyway. Many had already left.

The Jets were also going to their backups — Namath, who had only completed eight of 21 for 117 yards, was pulled in favor of J.J. Jones, but there was no face-saving in the end. The Jets would be hosting the Steelers in week 11, and Pittsburgh scout Tim Rooney had attended the game. But he also left early, having seen enough to know that these guys weren't hurting anybody. He could fly back to Pittsburgh early with the good news.

Shipp's debut had been a nightmare, and all he could do afterward was point to a myriad of changes that needed to be made. The only kind words, interestingly enough, came from a very sympathetic St. Louis coach, Don Coryell. "I didn't expect us to bust it open that quick," Coryell said. "It was not a laugher, though. It's just that, for once, we put the points on the board early."[26] He was too kind.

Week 11 — Sunday, November 30, 1975
Shea Stadium, New York (attendance: 52,618)

There were really no surprises when the Super Bowl–champion Pittsburgh Steelers came to Shea in week 11 to play the Jets. When it was all over, the Steelers had a team-record ninth consecutive win and the Jets had a team-record eighth consecutive loss. The only element that deviated from the expected was how passive the Steelers seemed much of the time, but apparently they were only putting as much effort into it as was necessary.

The Jets managed to play the Steelers to a scoreless tie in the first period, but Pittsburgh's sluggish performance had much to do with fullback Franco Harris leaving the field with a pinched nerve in his right arm after just a few plays. The Steelers seemed lethargic as Harris sat out the period while regaining the feeling in his arm.

In the second period the Jets managed to drive to the Pittsburgh 31, but when Namath underthrew Eddie Bell at the goal line the ball was intercepted at the two by Glenn Edwards, and his 46-yard return set the Steelers' offense up near midfield. The turnover led to the game's first points, when Roy Gerela kicked a 26-yard field goal to put the champs up 3–0.

On the Jets' next series they drove to the Pittsburgh four-yard line, but after being bumped back to the 15, Namath was again intercepted, this time by Mel Blount in the end zone. Starting from their 20 after the touchback, the Steelers drove to the New York 44 in five plays, largely on the scrambling of quarterback Terry Bradshaw, who ran for 15 and then 20 yards on consecutive plays. Harris was back in the game, and from the 44-yard line Bradshaw escaped tackle Carl Barzilauskas and threw down the right sideline for Harris. After making the catch at the 25, Harris took it in for a score, his first TD catch since the famed "immaculate reception" against Oakland in the 1972 playoffs. The score came less than two minutes before halftime, and gave Pittsburgh a 10–0 lead.

The Steelers built on that lead quickly when the second half got underway, driving 51 yards in eight plays in their first series of the third quarter. Bradshaw threw eight yards to Frank Lewis for a score that made it 17–0, and before the third period ended another interception by Blount set up a 19-yard field goal that made it 20–0. The Jets managed to avert a shutout with just 3:55 left in the game, when Namath threw a six-yard TD to Jerome Barkum.

Both Namath and Bradshaw commented afterward on the unpredictability of the swirling Shea Stadium winds. Because of the wind, Bradshaw said that he necessarily stuck to shorter passes, a less viable option for Namath, who was again playing catch-up. Namath had otherwise seen the short passing game taken away by Pittsburgh's superb linebackers. Namath completed only eight of 21 passes for 138 yards; Bradshaw completed only nine of 22 for 120. The big difference was that Bradshaw threw no interceptions: Namath threw four.

But the Jets could now rejoice, as they were on their way to Foxboro to play the Patriots. Their two-month nightmare was bound to end at last.

Week 12 — Sunday, December 7, 1975
Schaefer Stadium, Foxboro (attendance: 53,989)

The Jets hadn't won a game since beating the Patriots in week three back in early October, so they must have been happy to be traveling to Foxboro. The prospect of snapping their eight-game losing streak seemed realistic not merely in light of their 36–7 victory over New England earlier in the year, or New England's 3–8 record, but also due to a supposed psychological edge the Jets held over the Patriots. It had long been said — only half in jest — that Namath held some sort of jinx over the Patriots, having lost to them only twice in 17 games dating back to 1965.

The Jets got out to a modest 6–0 first-quarter lead on two Pat Leahy field goals. The first — a 42-yarder that came 4:24 into the game — was set up when linebacker John Ebersole intercepted New England quarterback Steve Grogan at the Patriots' 48 and brought it back to the 34. The second — a 27-yarder — was the byproduct of a shanked punt by New England's Mike Patrick that netted only three yards, and gave New York the ball at the Patriots' 30.

In the second period, the Jets went up 13–0 when they drove 80 yards — 51 through the air on four passes — to score on a four-yard run by Carl Garrett. But the Patriots managed to cut the lead to 13–7 by halftime when Grogan threw a 20-yard touchdown to Randy Vataha.

It was 4:14 into the third period when John Riggins ran off left end and broke free on a 37-yard TD run that put the Jets up 20–7, but the Patriots retaliated quickly. Don Calhoun — acquired just two weeks earlier from Buffalo — did Riggins one yard better, cutting the New York lead to six points again with a 38-yard TD run.

Five seconds into the fourth quarter Riggins scored his second TD of the game, going in from six yards out to boost the Jets' lead to 27–14. The Jets then seemed to put the game out of reach four minutes later when Leahy made it 30–14 with a 44-yard field goal after Burgess Owens had made his second interception of the game. But the Patriots wouldn't quit.

Grogan threw another TD to Vataha — this one a 10-yarder — to trim the Jets' lead to 30–21, and then, with time running out, he had the Patriots on the move again. With less than a minute remaining in the game Grogan threw to Vataha, and when he and Owens both came down with the ball it was ruled a simultaneous catch, which, of course, goes to the offense. Shipp wasn't pleased, feeling that Owens had wrested the ball from Vataha before the whistle, but the official ruling gave New England the ball at the New York two-yard line. It was Grogan who took it over the goal line from the one with 39 seconds left in the game, drawing the Patriots to within two points at 30–28. But the Jets recovered the onside kick and managed to hold on, running out the remaining time and accomplishing their third victory of the season (and second against New England).

Namath's numbers were impressive, hitting 14 of 18 passes for 160 yards. He threw no TDs, but he also threw no interceptions. This time it was the other side making the errors, as Grogan was picked off four times, twice by Ebersole and twice by Owens.

With the win, the Jets not only ended their eight-game losing streak, but also managed to drag the Patriots down into the basement with them, as both teams were then 3–9. Well, misery does love company.

Week 13 — Monday, December 15, 1975
San Diego Stadium, San Diego (attendance: 52,446)

When the Jets traveled to San Diego for a Monday night game with the Chargers in week 13, they were in an unfamiliar position — they were favored. Although the Jets were only 3–9, the Chargers had lost their first 11 games of the season before finally notching their first victory in week 12 against the Kansas City Chiefs. Against the 1–11 Chargers, there seemed no reason to think that the Jets could not achieve their fourth victory of the season, but when two losers play each other it simply comes down to who is hungriest. Both teams were coming off of victories, but it was San Diego's first taste of it, so they apparently wanted it more.

On the night before the game, the Jets had an 11 P.M. curfew; at 11:25 P.M. Coach Shipp checked Namath's room — he was not there. Shipp may have felt that, being an interim coach,

Namath was not taking his authority seriously. He made no immediate decision, however, and instead spoke to team president Phil Iselin to seek permission to impose disciplinary action. Perhaps feeling that Namath had shown him no respect, Shipp asked permission to not only fine Namath, but to withhold him from the starting lineup on Monday night as well: Iselin granted Shipp's weird request.

Shipp wanted to inform the team of his decision when they were all together, and so waited until the night of the game when he addressed them in the locker room before taking the field. "I was damn near sick when I got the news," Namath said later. "I felt I really let everyone down, especially Coach Shipp."[27]

The crowd in San Diego may not have been sick over the announcement, but when it came just before the game, they were definitely not pleased. Some 52,000 people had paid to see the game, which made it San Diego's biggest home crowd of the season, and they hadn't come to watch their 1–11 Chargers, or to glimpse Howard Cosell up in the broadcast booth — they had come to see Namath.

Coming off their first victory of the 1975 season, the Chargers seemed fired up, receiving the opening kickoff and driving 68 yards to a quick 7–0 lead. A big play on the drive was quarterback Dan Fouts' conversion of a third-and-seven play with a 20-yard scramble from the San Diego 35 to the New York 45. Later in the series Fouts threw 23 yards to Gary Garrison to the Jets' four-yard line, and on the following play Tony Baker took it in on a sweep right.

As much as the crowd may have approved of the home team's good start, they were even more vocal in voicing their disapproval when the New York offense trotted onto the field. J.J. Jones came in at quarterback to a resounding chorus of boos from the crowd, and proceeded to do … not much. Later in the period, the Jets did have an opportunity to even the score when they took possession at the San Diego 31 after linebacker Richard Wood blocked a punt. But a personal foul charged to Godwin Turk on the play pushed the Jets' starting position back to the 46, and two plays later Jones threw deep for Jerome Barkum and was intercepted in the end zone by safety Chris Fletcher.

The Jets did get on the scoreboard in the first period, however, when Pat Leahy kicked a 20-yard field goal. They had driven to the San Diego two-yard line, but when linebacker Don Goode dropped John Riggins for a one-yard loss on a third-and-one, Leahy salvaged the series.

To the roaring approval of the crowd, Namath entered the game with 9:31 left in the first half and the Chargers still up 7–3. But it was San Diego that would provide the only other scoring in the half, when they drove 64 yards for another touchdown. Fouts threw 33 yards to tight end Pat Curran for the big gainer in the series, which otherwise included a 12-yard pass to Garrison, and Rickey Young scored on a two-yard run to make it 14–3 at halftime.

Namath got the Jets back in the game early in the second half when he drove them to a touchdown, passing 29 yards to Carl Garrett and hitting Barkum with 16 and 21-yard throws to set up a one-yard touchdown run by Steve Davis that cut the San Diego lead to 14–10. The Jets might have thought they got a break when Fouts wound up leaving the game with a sprained neck in the third quarter, but backup Jesse Freitas would lead the Chargers to 10 fourth-quarter points, which proved to be the difference in the game. Of course, he had help — a bad snap on a New York field goal attempt wound up giving San Diego possession on the Jets' end of the field, and five plays later the Chargers kicked a 45-yard field goal to go up 17–10. On the Jets' next series, Fletcher picked off his second pass of the night to start the Chargers on an 80-yard march that climaxed with a one-yard touchdown run by Bo Matthews to make the score 24–10 with only 2:33 remaining.

The Jets would score again, but Riggins' one-yard touchdown run came on the game's very last play. With the score then 24–16, there seemed no reason to bother with the extra point, and so, with fans already milling about the field, both teams simply left. Namath's final numbers were 15 of 29 for 181 yards, with two interceptions.

Shipp was defensive about his decision to start Jones instead of Namath, saying that he didn't feel at all that it might have cost the Jets the game. San Diego guard Doug Wilkerson seemed to disagree. "Namath is super," Wilkerson said. "You could see the Jets change when he came out. If they had Namath in from the start, it might have made a big difference."[28] It was not the first time such an observation had been made. Regardless of their record or circumstance, when Namath was in the game the Jets seemed to feel they could accomplish something. Too bad he didn't play defense, too.

Week 14 — Sunday, December 21, 1975
Shea Stadium, New York (attendance: 37,279)

"I'm glad it's over," Namath said after the Jets' season-ender at Shea against the Dallas Cowboys.[29] He wasn't talking about the game: he was talking about the season. It would have been apt either way; statistically, he just had the worst game of his career to finish off the worst season of his career.

Dallas quarterback Roger Staubach had a case of bruised ribs, and since the Cowboys had already clinched a playoff spot by beating Washington the week before, the decision was made to start backup Clint Longley in his place. That was one small bit of good news for the Jets, and when Dallas got off to a rocky start in the first quarter, things looked hopeful for New York. Thomas Henderson fumbled the opening kickoff, and Steve Davis' recovery gave the Jets the ball at the Dallas five-yard line. It took John Riggins two runs to score and give the Jets a 7–0 lead less than a minute into the game.

On Dallas' next series, Longley attempted a screen pass but was intercepted by defensive end Jim Bailey at the Cowboys' 25. That lead to an eight-yard TD run by Carl Garrett, and the first quarter ended with the Jets leading 14–0. But of course it was too much to expect that the playoff bound Cowboys would continue to present the Jets with such easy scoring opportunities, and in the second quarter things turned around.

The Cowboys evened things in the second period; Robert Newhouse scored on a three-yard run after a blocked punt had given Dallas possession at the New York 31, and Doug Dennison later finished off a 71-yard drive with a one-yard touchdown run. The Cowboys then took the lead on their first series of the third quarter when Longley threw to Drew Pearson in the corner of the end zone. Pearson had gotten behind Rich Sowells and made a diving catch to put the Cowboys up 21–14, at 4:34 of the third period.

It was by then the Jets' turn to be generous, as Sowells inadvertently touched a Dallas punt and Mike Washington recovered for the Cowboys at the Jets' 30-yard line. The Cowboys managed to capitalize with a 22-yard field goal six plays later to up their lead to 24–14. Both sides were making their share of mistakes, however, and in the fourth quarter Dallas punter Mitch Hoopes was taken down at the Cowboys' 22 after mishandling the snap from center and being unable to get the kick off. Soon afterward, Bob Gresham scored on a seven-yard run to bring the Jets to within three points, 24–21.

In the meantime, Namath had been having a thoroughly unimpressive afternoon, despite the closeness of the score. Through the first three quarters he failed to complete a pass, and after finally connecting with Rich Caster for seven yards in the fourth quarter, he left the game with bruised ribs and a very anemic one of eight for seven yards. J.J. Jones also completed only one pass (that, too, went to Caster), but he also threw the pass that put the game away for Dallas. With the Jets desperately trying to work their way into field goal range in the final minute, safety Randy Hughes intercepted a Jones pass and returned it 33 yards for a score to make the final 31–21.

Namath had completed one of eight throws for seven yards, Jones one of five for eight, giving the team a total of 15 yards passing. With two sacks for a loss of 16 yards, the New York Jets had a net of minus-one-yard passing in the game. It was a fitting end to an awful season, and with the end of the game it was official: finishing with a record of 3–11, the Jets had just closed out the worst season in team history.

"I see Joe as part of our team next season," said New York Jets General Manager Al Ward at the conclusion of the season. "I couldn't blame Joe for what happened to our team this season. You can't blame any one individual. We just went into a tailspin and the bottom fell out."[30]

It was always said that, as Namath goes, so go the Jets. Such would seem to be the case. Namath had his worst season, so too did the Jets have their worst season. Their 3–11 record saw them sharing last place with the New England Patriots in the AFC East. Namath completed only 48.2 percent of his passes (157 of 326) for 2,286 yards and pitched 28 interceptions, almost double his touchdowns (15 TDs). He ranked tenth in the league in both yardage and TD passes, but also ranked first in interceptions. Namath was also sacked 27 times in 1975 for a total of 253 yards in losses. But still the master of the long throw, his 14.6 yards-per-completion was tops in the league.

As had been the case for quite some time, the big problem with the Jets was defense. The offense wasn't setting any records in 1975, but their 258 points placed them fourteenth in the league, whereas the 433 points the team allowed put them dead last. The Jets were ranked fifteenth in total offense and twenty-sixth (again, dead last) in team defense. Even had Namath had one of the better seasons in his career, it would have been exceedingly difficult to overcome the team's poor defense and post a winning record.

As usual, the season ended with Namath fielding questions about his plans for the future — would he be playing again the following season, and if so, would it be with the Jets? Namath said that he had a year remaining in his contract with the Jets, and that he intended to honor it. He also said that he still felt capable of playing. Beyond that, he seemed relieved that the 1975 season was over, but also expressed great disappointment in the way it had turned out. "I really thought we had a shot for the playoffs this year," he said after the final game of the season. "But everything just fell apart. Things have to get better next season. They just can't get any worse."[31] Can't they now?

14

The 1976 Season

At the close of the 1975 season, Namath was asked about his future plans. Such had been the custom for some years running, and the answer was usually noncommittal, but this time Namath seemed adamant in announcing that he would not be retiring. Saying that he still felt capable, he also pointed out that he had a year remaining in his contract with the Jets, which he intended to honor. But he soon enough let it be known that he wanted out. Namath didn't mince words when he was interviewed by Irv Cross on the CBS Super Bowl X pre-game show on January 18, 1976. Cross asked Namath if he was going to be traded to the Rams. "I hope so," Namath said. "I'd like to go somewhere else, especially with a contender."[1]

It was news to Jets president Phil Iselin, who said that Namath hadn't spoken to him at all about being traded. Iselin said that he would not rule out the possibility of a trade, provided the Jets got the deal they would want for a trade involving Namath. If they would be dealing with the Rams, there was some track record to look to: the Rams had previously acquired another aging quarterback, John Hadl, in a deal with the San Diego Chargers. That deal saw the Rams giving up five draft picks, including two first-round choices.

As for the Rams, owner Carroll Rosenbloom said that he hadn't spoken to Namath, nor could he since Namath was still under contract with the Jets. "If Joe really wants to be traded," Rosenbloom said, "why doesn't he go to Iselin and tell him so? Then Iselin could let word out that he wants to make a deal. He could call me and we could talk."[2]

Rosenbloom certainly sounded interested, but he just as quickly dismissed the possibility by pointing out that the Rams were not in the market for a quarterback, as they currently had three on their roster. There was also a matter of Namath's salary—$450,000—which Rosenbloom said the Rams would simply not pay for *any* player. Still, there was unmistakable interest on Rosenbloom's part: he seemed to simply be waiting for Iselin to pull the trigger.

On February 10, the Jets announced that they had signed 39-year-old Lou Holtz as their new head coach. Having turned winners into losers at both William and Mary and North Carolina State, Holtz at least had that going for him, and he was irrepressibly optimistic—naïve, perhaps—saying that he saw no real difference between the collegiate and professional level. It was inevitable that Holtz would be asked about Namath, and he let it be known that he definitely wanted Namath on his team.

But Namath was still heading the opposite direction. "I'm not a National Football League coach," Namath said, "but I don't understand why a new team with a new coach would want me there."[3] His point was well made. By "new team" Namath was of course referring to the fact that the Jets were in the process of rebuilding, which would necessarily bring a good many new players. For a team looking to build a future, it didn't seem practical to cling to a quarterback in the twilight of his career, and who almost certainly didn't have enough years left to share in that future. Namath pointed out that, beyond the one year remaining on his contract, the most the Jets would likely keep him around would be another year, which didn't seem very constructive for a rebuilding team. The Jets needed a quarterback to build a future on, and Namath made it clear that he was not that quarterback. But it was all moot so long as there was no other team willing to pick up his salary.

It was a point that seemed lost on Namath. He didn't see why it would not be an easy decision in regards to the Jets' interests, as well as his own, for a deal to be made even if it meant the Jets taking a loss by putting up whatever portion of his salary an interested party might be unwilling to pay. "What am I going to do for them in their rebuilding program?" Namath asked. "If they get rid of their obligation to me, that should be enough."[4]

Iselin was well enough aware that Namath's time with the Jets was winding down, as likely were his days playing the game. That being the case, the Jets did make a major investment in their future: in the first round of the 1976 draft, they chose quarterback Richard Todd. Like Namath, Todd had played at Alabama under coach Bear Bryant. Perhaps the hope was that lightning would strike twice. But even with the drafting of a new quarterback, and for all of Namath's lobbying, there seemed no way out. When training camp opened, Namath was still a New York Jet. His goal of once more quarterbacking a contender would have to wait.

The Jets opened their preseason schedule on a Saturday night in early August against the Cardinals in St. Louis. After receiving the opening kickoff, the Cardinals drove 85 yards to the game's initial score, which came on a one-yard run by Wayne Morris. The Jets tied the game in the second quarter when Namath threw an 11-yard TD to David Knight to cap an 80-yard drive. Namath had completed six of eight passes for 63 yards in the drive. But the Cardinals would regain the lead on the final play of the first half with a 47-yard field goal.

The Jets pulled to within a point at 10–9 in the third quarter on an unusual safety. A tipped pass was intercepted in the end zone by St. Louis safety Lee Nelson, but the Jets ended up with a couple points, regardless. The Cardinals' Mike Sensibaugh was flagged for clipping on Nelson's return, and as the infraction was committed in the end zone it resulted in two points for the Jets. When the fourth quarter brought no more scoring than an exchange of field goals, the Jets went down in defeat, 13–12.

The Jets' second preseason game would be their annual meeting with the New York Giants. While the event had been held at the Yale Bowl in New Haven since the teams first met in 1969, this time it would be held at the Giants' erstwhile home, Yankee Stadium. The twist was that it was the Jets who would be playing host, as the Giants were taking up residence across the Hudson River at their new home stadium in New Jersey.

Things being what they were for both teams, the annual match-up had necessarily lost much of the luster it once had, but a few of the players had been around long enough to believe that it still meant something. Giants quarterback Craig Morton was among those who still felt the game's significance. "This is without question one of the most important games of the year for us," Morton said the week of the game. "People have been downplaying the game the past few years and they shouldn't be. This game is something special. It's very important that we beat the Jets."[5]

As was the custom in the preseason rivalry, both teams played their first-stringers most of the way. The Jets opened the scoring in the first period when Namath threw a 21-yard TD pass to Jerome Barkum, but the first half ended in a 7–7 tie after the Giants scored on a one-yard run by Larry Csonka in the second quarter.

The Giants went out in front in the third quarter when George Hunt hit a 23-yard field goal, and Hunt added a 37-yard field goal in the fourth quarter to increase the Giants' lead to 13–7. But Namath hit running back Louie Giammona with a seven-yard TD pass, and with Pat Leahy's extra point the Jets led 14–13 with 2:12 left in the game. It was just enough time for Morton, who drove the Giants down close enough for Hunt to win the game on a 34-yard field goal with 16 seconds left to play. "We proved we are better than them," said Giants defensive tackle

John Mendenhall, who had run onto the field celebrating after the winning kick. "This team is going to be all right this year and beating the Jets is still a big thing."[6] Yeah, the game was still a big deal for some. Namath, who had played the entire game, completed 10 of 24 passes for 116 yards, two TDs and one interception. The Jets' preseason record had dropped to 0–2.

There was nothing slim about the margin of defeat when the Jets hosted the Oakland Raiders just two nights later. Having gone the distance against the Giants, Namath was given the night off and watched his old rivals walk all over the Jets. Todd and J.J. Jones split the quarterbacking duties: by halftime the game was already over, the Raiders by then leading 34–10. Not having gotten to play against the Giants, Todd was eager for game time and completed 18 of 35 passes for 224 yards. The embarrassing 41–17 final notwithstanding, he was glad for the significant playing time. Oakland coach John Madden was naturally pleased by his team's dominant performance, but under the circumstances couldn't make too much of it. "The Jets had played Wednesday night," Madden said. "They couldn't have been ready."[7] It certainly was an odd choice in scheduling.

The 0–3 Jets had a full seven days off before their next game, when they traveled to Houston to play the likewise 0–3 Oilers. Namath played the first half, and led the Jets to a 13–10 advantage after they had fallen behind early. Houston had posted the only points of the first quarter when Ronnie Coleman scored on a four-yard run 8:28 into the game. Almost half of the Houston drive's 46 yards were the result of New York penalties. Among the 20 penalty yards racked up by the Jets in the series was an offside call that nullified a New York interception of Houston quarterback Dan Pastorini on a third-and-four play.

The Jets tied the score early in the second period when Namath completed a six-play, 43-yard drive by throwing a 10-yard TD to Barkum. Karl Douglas came in at quarterback for Houston, and when he hit Otis Taylor with a 40-yard pass it looked like the Oilers might get into the end zone again. But the drive was halted at the New York three-yard line, and Houston had to settle for a 20-yard field goal and a 10–7 lead. Namath then led the Jets to a pair of field goals (31 and 21 yards) to give New York a 13–10 edge at the half. Namath played through the first series of the third quarter, and finished the night with 14 completions in 22 attempts.

The only points of the third quarter were awarded the Jets on a safety; pinned back at their one-yard line after a Greg Gantt punt, Houston failed to clear the end zone on a running play. The Jets were then able to further pad their lead in the fourth quarter when Houston's Ken Ellis fumbled a punt, leading to a one-yard TD run by Giammona.

Now trailing 22–10, it took the Oilers one play from scrimmage to retaliate. After Douglas and John Hadl had taken their turns at quarterback, Pastorini came back in and threw a 74-yard TD to Ken Burrough. It brought Houston to within five points of the Jets with 11:44 to play. But Pastorini went to the well once too often, and when he tried the same play on Houston's next series he was intercepted by linebacker John Ebersole. The interception led to a field goal that increased New York's lead to 25–17. The Jets then notched another safety when a bad snap sent Houston punter Leroy Clark scrambling back to the end zone. He got the kick off, but a clipping penalty in the end zone (an uncommon call that the Jets had gotten twice in three games) against the Oilers made it 27–17 with 5:01 to play.

Even then it wasn't over. With less than two minutes to play Ellis brought a New York punt back 38 yards to the Jets' seven-yard line, and when Pastorini hit Burrough with a TD pass on the next play the Oilers were within three points of the Jets. The Oilers tried an onside kick, but the Jets recovered and took possession at the Houston 33. Feeling anxious, Holtz decided to send Namath back into the game to run out the clock and put the game away. He didn't — on his first play back in, Namath fumbled the snap and the ball was recovered by Houston's C.L. Whittington. Holtz must have been wondering what it would take to win even a preseason game in the pros.

The Oilers managed to get as far as the New York 18, but with time running out they were forced to try a tying field goal. The 35-yard attempt would have sent the game into overtime, but Houston kicker Skip Butler was wide left, allowing the Jets to hang on and win, 27–24.

Yankee Stadium has seldom been so empty as it was the following Saturday night when little more than 13,000 people turned up to watch the 1–3 Jets play the 1–3 Washington Redskins. Namath did not have a good night: his first pass was intercepted by linebacker Harold McClinton, whose return helped set up a three-yard TD run by Mike Thomas that put Washington up 7–0.

After missing his first seven passes, Namath went on to hit 11 straight and led the Jets on an 80-yard drive that tied the game in the second quarter. There were a lot of new names among his receivers in the drive, as he hit rookie running back Clark Gaines for 21 yards, James Scott for 18, and Don Buckey for 15, but it was old favorite Jerome Barkum who caught the three-yard TD from Namath.

The Redskins retook the lead when Billy Kilmer threw a 17-yard TD to Roy Jefferson with just over a minute left in the first half; the Jets seemed to unravel after that. Still playing into the third period, Namath was again intercepted by McLinton, which led to another Washington TD, this one a 14-yard pass from Kilmer to Jean Fugett that made it 21–7. After that, Washington began to pile it on, eventually cruising to a 38–7 victory.

Expectations were probably not very high for the Jets when they traveled to Pittsburgh to finish off their preseason schedule against the two-time reigning Super Bowl champion Steelers the following Saturday night. Having been born and raised in western Pennsylvania, it was the first time in Namath's professional career that he would play so close to home, but it would be a disappointing homecoming—the Jets were never in the game. Namath completed 12 of 23 passes for 104 yards through three quarters, as the Jets could only muster six points on two field goals. The biggest problem for Namath was a matter of protection, as he was sacked six times. Richard Todd fared worse, playing much less of the game and still being sacked four times. In the end, the Steelers rolled to an easy 41–6 win.

The conventional wisdom is that preseason means nothing. Win, lose, what does it really matter? The games don't count. It is merely a time to try out new players and get the team in shape. Still, nobody really wants to be 1–5 even in preseason, and getting roughed up by such lopsided scores as 41–6, 41–17, and 38–7 could certainly do no good for morale.

There were plenty of new names on the New York Jets roster in 1976. It was certainly a long way from the Super Bowl team of the late '60s. In fact, only Namath, Winston Hill, and Randy Rasmussen were left from the 1968 roster. Even Emerson Boozer had retired, his string of knee injuries having finally made the continuation of his career unviable. Boozer had entered the league a year after Namath; for a quarterback, bad knees were a hindrance: for a running back, they were the kiss of death.

Even some of the familiar faces from more recent seasons were gone. Receiver Eddie Bell was sent packing for San Diego after six years of catching Namath aerials. But the most notable departure was that of running back John Riggins, who had played out his option year with the Jets in 1975. Saying that he felt under-utilized in New York, Riggins chose to sign with the Washington Redskins. "It is a pass-oriented team to begin with," Riggins said of the Jets. "That's the way the team got started in the AFL with Joe passing 40 or 50 times a game. It wasn't a running back paradise."[8]

That wasn't an entirely accurate description of Riggins' time in New York. It may have been true that Namath threw 40 or 50 passes a game in the old AFL days, but that was hardly the case by the time Riggins arrived. Both fans and writers alike in New York had been griping since 1972 about the seeming reluctance of the Jets to pass more often, which Namath always pointed out had much to do with the good running game that Riggins and Boozer provided. It had certainly been a long time since Namath had thrown 50 passes in a game, and seldom even 40 while Riggins was there. It was probably closer to the truth to say that, like Namath, Riggins merely wanted to play with a contender. As perennially dysfunctional as the Jets were, they didn't seem to hold the promise of becoming contenders any time soon.

A running back of Riggins' caliber would be very difficult to replace. The Jets acquired Ed Marinaro, who had left the Minnesota Vikings after playing out his option. Tired of playing behind Chuck Foreman, Marinaro was eager for an opportunity to start in New York. The Jets also signed promising Wake Forest rookie running back Clark Gaines as a free agent.

A new coach, a lot of new players — this was a team looking ahead at building a future. Surely a gimpy, aging quarterback nearing the end of his career had no realistic place in that future. And yet, there he was. The truth is that the Jets still needed Namath. Even if he couldn't work a miracle and make winners of them, he was still somehow good for the team's spirit. He seemed to have some ability to anchor them through the stormy times; 1976 would be the stormiest of times.

Week 1— Sunday, September 12, 1976
Municipal Stadium, Cleveland (attendance: 67,496)

The Jets opened the 1976 season in Cleveland against the Browns. While both teams had finished 3–11 in 1975, expectations seemed to be higher for the Browns than they were for the Jets in 1976. Perhaps it was the fact that Cleveland, after starting 0–9 in 1975, closed out the season by winning three of their final five games, whereas the Jets, after starting 2–1, had gone into a nosedive and lost 10 of their next 11. Then again it may have simply been that, with so many new faces — rookies at that — the Jets obviously had a longer road to travel to become contenders. The Jets were sporting four rookies on their starting defensive roster on opening day.

But whatever the crowd of 67,496 may have been anticipating, they were not too happy to find their Browns trailing 10–0 at the end of the first quarter. Cleveland cornerback Tony Peters was flagged for interfering with Lou Piccone on a long pass, and the penalty advanced the Jets 38 yards from their own 35 all the way to the Cleveland 27. It ultimately resulted in a 41-yard field goal by Pat Leahy, and a 3–0 New York lead.

On Cleveland's next series, quarterback Mike Phipps — already booed by the crowd during the pre-game introductions — fumbled the snap from center, and the Jets took possession at the Browns' 45. Four plays later, Steve Davis scored on an impressive 20-yard run to make it 10–0. The Jets were proving opportunistic, and had otherwise done well on defense, holding Cleveland to a single first down in three first-quarter possessions. If the game were only fifteen minutes long, the Jets would have been in great shape.

Early in the second period, the Browns drove 74 yards in 11 plays and scored at 4:29 of the quarter on a 13-yard pass from Phipps to Reggie Rucker. It seemed to trigger a second-quarter explosion by Cleveland, and they quickly took the lead. After forcing a punt and taking possession in good position at the New York 47, the Browns scored again four plays later when Phipps hit Paul Warfield with a 23-yard TD pass that put Cleveland up 14–10.

Toward the end of the half, the Browns were facing a third-and-nine from their own 29 when running back Greg Pruitt broke a draw play for 60 yards. Two plays later, Phipps threw another TD to Rucker — this one from four yards out — to give Cleveland a 21–10 lead with 1:35 left in the half.

Phipps seemed to have the hot hand, hitting 11 of 15 passes for three TDs in the first half, so the Jets might have felt optimistic when he left the game just 2:43 into the third quarter. After scrambling for 24 yards to the Cleveland 43, Phipps suffered a separated shoulder after being taken down hard by Shafer Suggs. But his replacement, Brian Sipe, completed the drive by getting the team in range for Don Cockroft to kick a 32-yard field goal that upped Cleveland's lead to 24–10.

Now the game was really slipping away from New York. Three plays after the Jets received the kick, Namath was intercepted by Thom Darden and the Browns took over at the New York 29. Cleveland took a 31–10 lead six plays later when Rucker caught his third touchdown of the game, this one an eight-yarder from Sipe with 5:23 left in the third. Trailing by a full three TDs, it might have seemed hopeless, but the Jets kept battling. Richard Todd came in at quarterback and drove New York to the Cleveland one-yard line, but failing to punch it in from there seemed to crush the team's spirits. Three consecutive runs—two by Ed Marinaro and one by Steve Davis—failed to score, and on fourth-and-goal Todd tried to run it in himself. Running off right guard, he was stopped inches from the goal line by linebacker Bob Babich, and Cleveland took over on downs.

Todd did manage to score midway through the final period when he capped a 58-yard drive with an eight-yard TD run, but that only cut Cleveland's lead to 31–17 with too little time remaining to make any difference. It became even more meaningless when Sipe hit Steve Holden with a 26-yard TD pass with 1:28 left in the game, making the final 38–17.

It was a most disappointing coaching debut for Holtz, but always looking for the silver lining, he was optimistic to the point of being delusional. Holtz saw the difference in the game as coming down to a few big plays by Cleveland. "If there were 140 plays," he said, "you could look at 135 of them on a reel of film and not be able to determine the winner."[9] Sure, as long as the five plays you edited out were Cleveland's five TDs. Aside from that, what the hell did they do? Namath was 15 of 31 for 137 yards, and one interception.

Week 2 — Sunday, September 19, 1976
Mile High Stadium, Denver (attendance: 62,669)

In week two the Jets were in Denver to face the 0–1 Broncos. Mile High Stadium had been expanded to accommodate the team's growing fan base, and it would be a record Denver crowd of 62,669 that would come that day to watch their team set other records. By the time they were finished with the Jets, the Broncos had amassed a club-record 543 total yards and had produced the largest margin of victory in franchise history. For the Jets, it was that kind of day.

The Broncos got out to an early 6–0 lead when Otis Armstrong scored on a 15-yard run (the extra point by Jim Turner failed—yes *that* Jim Turner, who had helped kick the Jets to championship glory with three field goals in Super Bowl III), but the Jets managed to cut the Denver lead to 6–3 with a 25-yard field goal later in the opening period. Actually, the New York field goal was more an achievement for the Broncos than for the Jets; having recovered a fumble at the Denver 18, the Jets could still do no better than three points.

Namath had taken a couple of nasty shots in the first period and wound up missing most of the second quarter with a severe headache. With Richard Todd at quarterback in the second period, the Jets failed to gain even a single first down. Meanwhile, the Broncos commenced throwing a party.

After Rick Upchurch returned a New York punt 24 yards, the Broncos went up 13–3 when tight end Riley Odoms took an end-around 15 yards for a score. Later in the second, Denver quarterback Steve Ramsey threw a 53-yard pass to Upchurch that set up a 20-yard field goal by Turner to make it 16–3. With 1:41 left in the half, Ramsey made it 23–3 when he finished an 11-play drive with a 14-yard TD pass to Haven Moses. Coming so close to halftime, the Jets might have thought the Broncos' second-quarter explosion would end there, but no such luck.

Unable to manage a first down, the Jets were quickly forced to punt and Denver was able to get close enough for Turner to try a 38-yard field goal. The Broncos were apparently feeling frisky: rather than place the ball for Turner's kick, holder Bill Van Heusen took off running, breaking to the outside and racing 20 yards to the one-yard line. From there it was fullback Jon

Keyworth, who plowed the final yard to give the Broncos a stout 29–3 halftime lead (Turner again missed the extra point).

Namath returned in the third quarter, and for just a moment the Jets appeared to show a flicker of determination. Namath threw a 31-yarder to Howard Satterwhite, but ultimately the Jets advanced no further than the Denver 31 and had to send Leahy in to try a 48-yard field goal, which failed.

Denver had added a 30-yard field goal and led 32–3 when Namath, under a very heavy rush, threw into a crowd populated mostly by Denver defenders. John Rowser intercepted the pass, and with a wall of teammates to escort him, went 41 yards for a touchdown.

In the fourth quarter, Denver backup quarterback Norris Weese came in and led the Broncos to a final TD, accomplished on Jim Kiick's one-yard run. That made the final a thoroughly humiliating 46–3.

"To hold a team like the Jets, with their explosive offense, to three points was very nice," said Denver coach John Ralston.[10] A team like the Jets? Explosive offense? This was not the 1968 New York Jets, or even the high-scoring 1972 squad. The 1976 Jets were only a very pale shadow of those teams. It was almost as if no one dared speak the truth — or even acknowledge it — that Joe Namath and the New York Jets were just … losers. Namath completed 11 of 18 for 106 yards, and one interception. Again, he threw no touchdowns.

Week 3 — Sunday, September 26, 1976
Orange Bowl, Miami (attendance: 49,754)

"I don't think Namath had much help," said Miami coach Don Shula after his team had hosted the Jets at the Orange Bowl in week three. "He really hung in there. They've got some new people. I understand Joe introduced himself to the left tackle in the huddle last Thursday."[11]

Shula had respect for Namath. He had watched him and coached against him long enough to know that what was happening to the New York Jets was not indicative of Namath's personal ability. It somehow seemed an injustice was being done, but Shula had his own problems to cope with. After opening the season with a Monday night victory over Buffalo, the Dolphins had been soundly beaten by New England, 30–14, in week two, and it was a curiously small crowd of 49,754 that came out to the Orange Bowl for the Dolphins' home opener in week three. It was the smallest home crowd the team had drawn since the 1960s. The lack of enthusiasm by the fans seemed justified when the Dolphins came out with a less-than-enthusiastic performance against the Jets. As much as the Jets had been patsies for the Browns and the Broncos in the first two games of the season, a team like Miami should have put on quite a show for their fans. Instead, the Dolphins went to the locker room at halftime to a chorus of boos from the home crowd.

After a scoreless first period, Miami had finally put together a drive in the second quarter, moving from their own 26 to the New York eight-yard line before running out of gas. Garo Yepremian kicked a 25-yard field goal to salvage the effort, and thereby gave Miami the only points of the half. A three-point lead was not terribly impressive against a New York team that had trailed Cleveland by 11 points at halftime in week one, and trailed Denver by 26 points after the first half in week two.

The Dolphins would largely rely on New York's ineptitude to expand on that lead in the second half. The Jets turned the ball over three times in their first seven plays of the third quarter. On the Jets' first play from scrimmage in the second half, Steve Davis fumbled and Jeris White recovered for Miami. It only led to a 26-yard field goal, but that 6–0 lead would have sufficed to win the game anyway.

On the third play of the Jets' next series, Davis fumbled again. Miami linebacker Steve Towle recovered at the New York 44, but this time the Dolphins couldn't even get close enough for a field goal try and had to punt back to New York. Three plays later Namath was intercepted by Charlie Babb, who returned the ball 18 yards to the New York 29. Benny Malone, Norm Bulaich, and Stan Winfrey helped advance the ball to the three-yard line, from where Bob Griese tossed a TD pass to Jim Mandich. Miami then had a more respectable 13–0 lead.

In the fourth quarter the Dolphins put together one sustained drive, covering 67 yards in 10 plays, but it only resulted in another field goal, which made the final 16–0. As for the Jets, they could get no further in the entire game than the Miami 24, but even then a clipping penalty pushed them out of field goal range. On the plus side for the Jets, their lone sack of Griese in the game was New York's first of the season.

Namath was 16 of 26 for 171 yards and an interception: still no touchdowns. Griese knew it wasn't a very impressive performance for either side, but he blamed the 84-degree temperature, saying that the heat likely effected the play of both teams. Shula wasn't as free and easy with the excuses, finding a good deal to criticize in the performance of his offense. But the Dolphins could grouse all they liked about their 16–0 victory. They were now 2–1, while the Jets fell to 0–3. The Jets hadn't even scored a touchdown in the last two games. Now there's something to grouse about.

Week 4 — Sunday, October 3, 1976
Candlestick Park, San Francisco (attendance: 42,961)

"It's kind of an honor to play on the same field with Namath," said San Francisco defensive lineman Jimmy Webb after the 49ers' week four game with the Jets at Candlestick Park.[12] Webb certainly showed Namath no honor on the field, taking him down for a loss three times in the first half. Namath would be dropped five times in all (Cedric Hardman notched the other two).

Namath spent the better part of the afternoon running for cover. So much so that when he left the locker room after the game and saw the security guards assigned to escort him to the team bus he asked them where they'd been all day.[13] Even so, the game left much to be desired by both the San Francisco fans and the team's coach, Monte Clark. "I'm glad this one is over and we are walking away on the top side of it," Clark grumbled afterward.[14]

For almost three full quarters it looked as though no one would break the scoreless tie. In the first quarter the Jets had driven to the San Francisco 30-yard line on their second series, but when the drive ran out of wheels they came away with nothing after Pat Leahy was very short on a 47-yard field goal attempt. The 49ers didn't even cross midfield until quite late in the first half, and even then it was largely attributable to a New York fumble. It would have taken an extremely incompetent performance by the 49er offense not to cross midfield after Ralph McGill recovered a fumble by New York receiver Howard Satterwhite at the San Francisco 45. The 49ers managed to make it all the way to the New York 11-yard line before quarterback Jim Plunkett was intercepted by rookie linebacker Greg Buttle with only 37 seconds left in the half.

The crowd's displeasure seemed evenly distributed as both teams walked off the field at halftime to a chorus of boos, which was the most enthusiasm the crowd had mustered through the first half. The 49ers seemed to want to make it up to their fans in the second half, and began the third quarter with a drive that carried to the New York 21. When Steve Mike-Mayer came on to kick a 38-yard field goal it looked as though somebody might put a few points up at last, but a high snap sent holder Scott Bull racing the other way after the ball. He managed to catch up with it around midfield, and his throw deep the other way served the basic function of a punt when it was intercepted by linebacker Bob Martin.

It was late in the third quarter when the 49ers caught a ridiculous break on a third-and-11 play. Usually when a defender bats a pass it is to their advantage, but on this occasion New York linebacker John Ebersole swatted it five yards into the waiting arms of San Francisco's Tom Mitchell, who turned it into a 24-yard gain. It helped the 49ers considerably in their march to the New York 14, and their eventual 31-yard field goal that put them up 3–0 with 38 seconds left in the third period.

The Jets' next series carried over badly into the fourth quarter. Just 1:28 into the fourth, Namath was blindsided by Hardman. The hit jarred the ball loose, and Cleveland Elam gathered it up and barreled — all 252 pounds worth — 31 yards for a touchdown and a 10–0 lead.

The 49ers seemed to be making up for lost time when they increased their lead a few minutes later. A pass interference call on the Jets' Shafer Suggs was a major contributing factor in the 49ers' five-play, 56-yard drive, as it accounted for 36 of those yards and moved San Francisco from their own 44 to the New York 20. Four plays later, Sammy Johnson scored from a yard out to make it 17–0.

Namath's day ended when he limped off the field following another takedown by Hardman: he had completed eight of 17 for just 70 yards. Richard Todd looked good in relief, leading the Jets 80 yards to their only score. After throwing 29 yards to Rich Caster, Todd hit David Knight with a 21-yard pass to the one-yard line, and Ed Marinaro punched it over from there with 7:24 left in the game. Leahy's extra point was blocked by Dave Washington, and the final score read 17–6.

The 49ers advanced to 3–1, and were looking to keep pace with the 4–0 Los Angeles Rams in the NFC West. That being the case, both the 49ers and their fans felt they should have had an easier time with the Jets, now 0–4.

Week 5 — Sunday, October 10, 1976
Shea Stadium, New York (attendance: 52,416)

The Jets had their 1976 home opener against the Buffalo Bills in week five. It was a fairly typical Shea Stadium day, the wind gusting 35 mph. The 2–2 Bills gifted the Jets on the game's first play, when rookie defensive back Keith Moody fumbled the opening kickoff. The Jets recovered, and it was just 2:39 into the game when Ed Marinaro scored on a one-yard run six plays later to give the Jets a quick 7–0 lead.

It was another Buffalo mistake that allowed the Jets to build on that lead. Linebacker John Ebersole intercepted Buffalo quarterback Joe Ferguson at the Bills' 25, and again it was a matter of six plays for the Jets to get into the end zone. On a third-and-goal play from the two-yard line, Namath tossed a touchdown pass to rookie tight end Richard Osborne; it was Namath's first TD pass of the season. Osborne had been waived by Philadelphia and picked up by the Jets only four days earlier. With Jerome Barkum out with a hamstring injury, the decision had been made to move Rich Caster to wide receiver, which had left the tight end position open.

Having injured his calf in the first quarter after taking a shot from Buffalo's Mike Kadish, Namath sat out the second half. He had completed only three of 11 passes for 21 yards, with a TD and an interception. Ten minutes into the third quarter Ferguson also left the game, though that had more to do with his inability to put any points on the board. Buffalo backup Gary Marangi finally got the Bills some points late in the third quarter, but that was largely courtesy of a shanked punt by New York's Duane Carrell that allowed the Bills to take possession at the Jets' 38. After the Bills converted a fourth-and-one quite nicely with a 14-yard run by Jeff Kinney, it was Marangi who scored on a six-yard run, halving the Jets' lead at 8:38 of the third quarter.

It stayed that way until the final four minutes of the game. Having contributed considerably to the Jets' first touchdown by fumbling the opening kickoff, Moody redeemed himself with a 67-yard punt return that tied the game. It somehow seemed typical of the Jets, and it would have surprised no one had they totally collapsed at that point. In his five weeks as a pro, Richard Todd had certainly not faced such a pressure situation. The expectation for many — certainly for many of the Buffalo Bills — was that the Buffalo defense would force a punt, and if the Bills didn't get close enough to kick a winning field goal, they would surely win it in overtime.

The Jets started their next series at their own 20-yard line, and Todd advanced them to the 30 with a pass to Rich Caster. Running back Louie Giammona then broke a run for 35 yards to the Buffalo 35. Two more plays got the Jets five yards to the 30, but on third-and-five Richard Todd was taken down for an 11-yard loss by defensive end Sherman White. The play would have taken the Jets out of field goal range, but Buffalo's Doug Jones was flagged for defensive holding, a penalty that gave the Jets a first down at the 25.

Very obviously playing for the field goal, the Jets ran the ball three straight plays, gaining only four yards to the 21. On fourth-and-six, Pat Leahy came in to try a 38-yard field goal: it wasn't pretty, but he managed to put it through with 48 seconds left on the clock. The Jets held on to take their first win of the season, 17–14. There was an almost comical jubilation in the New York locker room after the game. It might have seemed disproportionate for a 1–4 team, but it was understandable. This time they didn't blow it: *this day* the Jets were winners.

Week 6 — Monday, October 18, 1976
Schaefer Stadium, Foxboro (attendance: 50,883)

In week six, the Jets would be in Foxboro for a nationally televised Monday night meeting with the New England Patriots. Like the Jets, the Patriots had finished the 1975 season with a 3–11 record; unlike the Jets, the Patriots had already matched their 1975 win total. With a 3–2 record, the Patriots were trying to keep within a game of division-leading Baltimore. Former division powers Miami and Buffalo had both fallen on hard times; even at 1–4, the Jets could draw even with both clubs with a victory against the Patriots.

For years, the Jets were supposed to have some sort of jinx over the Patriots: more particularly, Namath was said to have some power over them, having amassed a record of 15–2–1 against the Patriots since he entered professional football in 1965. Even when Namath was out with injuries the Jets usually handled the Patriots easily enough, having the advantage in the series 18–3–1 during that same period of 1965–1975. But unlike the Jets, the Patriots were now on the upswing in the division's power shift. One big change was that New England had traded longtime quarterback Jim Plunkett to San Francisco, and put their future in the hands of second-year man Steve Grogan. He was proving to be up to the task.

Lou Holtz had maintained — rather naively — that there was no difference between coaching at the college and pro levels, and to accentuate his lack of comprehension he devised a New York Jets fight song, a bit of college-style rah-rah that seemed to somehow throw a spotlight on the team's desperation. The Jets were already finding it hard to be taken seriously by opponents and sportswriters: now it was official — Holtz had made a laughingstock of them. On ABC's *Monday Night Football*, broadcaster Alex Karras — trying his best to fill Don Meredith's shoes as the jovial member of the broadcast booth — mockingly sang Holtz's ditty, much to the amusement of Howard Cosell.

It was very quickly obvious that it would take more than superstitious nonsense about jinxes to help the Jets on this night. After receiving the opening kickoff, the Jets gained a total of one yard on three running plays and quickly punted. Beginning from their 41 after a less-than-stellar New York punt, the Patriots went on a 59-yard march to score in seven plays, with running backs Sam Cunningham and Andy Johnson carrying the load. The big plays were a pair of passes from Grogan to his backs; he began with a 19-yard screen to Cunningham, and otherwise hit Johnson for 12 more. Meanwhile, Cunningham and Johnson were ripping off six and nine-yard runs until Johnson plowed into the end zone from four yards out for a 7–0 lead 5:26 into the game.

Late in the first quarter, the Jets began to put together a sustained drive that carried over into the second period. The big play had been a 21-yard pass from Namath to Louie Giammona, but the drive stalled at the New England 23 and the Jets looked to close the gap to 7–3 with a field goal. No such luck—a bad snap by center Joe Fields killed the effort, and gave the Patriots the ball at their 36. That seemed to flip the switch; Cunningham and Johnson were back in business, and Grogan converted a third-and-one with a 12-yard run of his own. After an eight-yard run by Johnson gave New England a first-and-goal at the nine-yard line, he gained another three yards to set up a second-and-goal at the six. On second down Grogan handed to Don Calhoun; there was a fair-sized hole for Calhoun to shoot through, but as he came to the line of scrimmage that gap was suddenly filled by rookie linebacker Greg Buttle, who popped Calhoun at the line and forced him to cough up the ball. But on this night, the Jets would be mocked at every turn. The ball popped out and landed in the backfield: Grogan took it on a hop and darted around left end and into the end zone. It's pretty rough when even a good defensive play results in points for the opponent.

Now trailing 14–0, the Jets found themselves starting their next series from their own 15, but Namath got them out of a hole quickly with a 20-yard pass to Rich Caster. Then, after working their way to the New England 49, Namath tried to hit Caster again—Caster ran inside, Namath threw outside. The result was an interception by Tim Fox at the 25, and his 18-yard return set the Patriots up at the 43 with 4:39 left in the half. The Patriots took advantage with a 57-yard drive that ate up most of the remaining time, and climaxed with a 10-yard touchdown pass from Grogan to Johnson with 58 seconds left in the half. The extra point was blocked, but the Patriots' 20–0 halftime lead seemed virtually insurmountable to a team like the Jets.

The Patriots got started early in the third quarter; on their first series of the second half they were facing a second-and-10 at the New York 41 when Grogan took a short drop back, looked right, then turned left and took off running. With a good block by guard John Hannah, Grogan was sprung, and once in the open field he had little trouble going the distance for a touchdown. It was now 27–0, but on his final series of the game Namath salvaged some pride by taking the Jets to their only score of the night.

Starting at their own 37 after a short kick and good return, the Jets chipped their way downfield until Namath hit rookie running back Clark Gaines with a 12-yard touchdown pass. With the score 27–7 and the game pretty much out of reach, Namath was finished for the evening, having hit 16 of 27 for 135 yards, with one TD and one interception. Holtz then sent Richard Todd in for some tough learning. The Patriots would add two more touchdowns on runs by Cunningham and Calhoun, and although Todd managed to get the Jets as far as the New England eight-yard line, they would not score again, turning the ball over on downs on that occasion. The final was a very decisive 41–7.

The Jets' woes were adding up: not only had they been blown out again, but they had mounting casualties. Early in the second period Ed Marinaro—the Jets' leading ground gainer at that point in the season—caught a five-yard pass from Namath and stayed on the pale carpet in obvious pain after being taken down. He had to be carried off the field by teammates. The news reached the broadcast booth that Marinaro had a bruised foot, but it was worse than that: Marinaro had fractured his foot and was gone for the year. The other starting back, Giammona, suffered a muscle pull, and Davis would miss time with a sprained knee. At least the team's spirits could be lifted by that rousing fight song.

Week 7—Sunday, October 24, 1976
Shea Stadium, New York (attendance: 49,768)

When the 5–1 Baltimore Colts came to Shea Stadium to face the 1–5 Jets in week seven, it must've looked like the mismatch that everyone had envisioned the first meeting between the teams would be in Super Bowl III. But this time there would be no astounding upset.

After linebacker Derrel Luce intercepted a Namath pass, the Colts posted the first points

5:38 into the game when Bert Jones hit Roger Carr across the middle on a pass that went 41 yards for a score. Baltimore coach Ted Marchibroda had devised the play earlier in the week after spying a vulnerability in the Jets' game films. The play was apparently sprung at just the right time to pay off.

The Colts added a pair of field goals in the second period to go up 13–0 before the Jets finally put something together. The Jets drove from their own 28 to the Baltimore 39, and Namath then threw 24 yards to David Knight to advance to the Baltimore 15. It was Namath's fourth straight completion, and he was moving the team well in the last two minutes of the half. On the next play Bruce Laird was flagged for pass interference when he tackled Rich Caster ahead of the throw, which placed the Jets at the four-yard line. But after Bob Gresham picked up a yard to the three, Namath tried to hit Richard Osborne in the end zone on a crossing pattern on second down. Baltimore's Jackie Wallace read the play well, and stepped in front of Osborne to pick the throw off. The interception killed what would turn out to be the Jets' biggest threat of the game. Minus the two interceptions, Namath's numbers were not bad in the half, hitting 10 of 15 passes.

After a scoreless third quarter, the Jets managed to threaten again early in the fourth. Still down by 13, they started from their 20 and wound their way downfield, largely on the running of Wake Forest rookie Clark Gaines, who was slicing through the Baltimore defense with surprising ease. From the Colts' 37, Namath hit Caster over the middle for 25 yards to the 12, and the Jets looked to be in good shape at that point. But when three plays gained only four yards to the eight, they were faced with a fourth-and-six. With a 13–0 deficit and a 1–5 record, there was really no reason not to go for it, but under a very heavy rush, Namath underthrew Lou Piccone at the goal line on fourth down and Baltimore took over on downs. The play also knocked Namath out of the game, as he was put down hard by defensive end Fred Cook and suffered a mild concussion. Namath thought trainer Jeff Snedeker had magically appeared on the field like a bolt of lightning: in reality, Namath had lost consciousness and didn't come to until Snedecker was kneeling over him.

The Jets were still only trailing by 13, but three plays later the Colts iced the game when Jones went back to pass from his 21 and lofted a deep throw to Carr. He didn't have more than a step on Shafer Suggs, but the ball was so perfectly thrown that it came down right into Carr's hands; he outran Suggs and took it all the way for a 79-yard score. Jones and Carr had given a performance that was certainly reminiscent of Shea's early days when it was Namath and Maynard providing the aerial show.

Jones watched Namath intently during the game, saying later that he paid Namath more attention than any other quarterback. "The reason I do that," Jones explained, "is because he's the best."[15] Namath was 15 of 29 for 154 yards, with two interceptions.

Following the Baltimore game, Namath missed practice with a swollen knee. With the knee still swollen by midweek, it looked like Richard Todd would be getting his first start as a professional quarterback when the Jets traveled to Buffalo to play the Bills in week eight. Unsure if Namath would be able to play at all, the Jets also hurried to sign free agent Larry Lawrence as a backup quarterback. Lawrence had been waived by the Tampa Bay Buccaneers, one of the league's two expansion franchises in 1976.

It had been theorized by some that Namath's knee was being used by Holtz as an excuse to make a quarterback change with some discretion, but if such were the case that would not explain signing Lawrence (who, incidentally, didn't play a down for New York). The truth is that Namath had been playing through a number of ailments, including a pulled calf muscle, and with both the concussion he suffered against Baltimore and the subsequent swollen knee, everything did seem to point to a need for a quarterback with a bit more durability than Namath seemed to be exhibiting at that point.

Since he had been the Jets' quarterback, the routine was that if Namath said he was good to go on Sunday, then he played regardless of how much practice time he had gotten during the week (or even if he hadn't gotten any). Holtz broke with tradition in announcing that Todd would be starting if Namath hadn't practiced by Friday. While Namath claimed to be completely well by Thursday, he curiously still hadn't practiced by Friday. Perhaps it was simply a power struggle of the sort that Namath had engaged in with past coaches, but if such were the case then Holtz let it be known who was in charge.

Todd did indeed get his first pro start against Buffalo, and with the Bills' Joe Ferguson also out, Gary Marangi would be getting his first pro start at quarterback as well. It was not a spectacular game for Todd, but he did lead the Jets to a 16–0 halftime advantage and threw his first touchdown pass, a 20-yarder to David Knight. Larry Keller also blocked a punt, which Steve Poole ran in from six yards for a score, and after missing the extra point, Pat Leahy later added a 21-yard field goal.

Marangi brought the Bills back in the third quarter with a pair of TD passes to Bob Chandler (11 and nine yards), but a 35-yard field goal by Leahy in the fourth quarter helped the Jets secure their second win of the season (both coming against Buffalo), despite a 166-yard rushing performance for Buffalo by O.J. Simpson.

Todd had only completed six of 20 passes for 87 yards in the 19–14 victory over Buffalo, but the Jets had managed the victory regardless. Namath was still listed as ailing the following week, and so Todd got the start again when the Jets hosted the Miami Dolphins. Trailing 17–0 at halftime, the Jets were never really in the game; in fact, they only managed to avoid a shutout when Clark Gaines scored on a one-yard run with 3:34 left in the game. That made the score 20–7, but Miami added another touchdown with 1:52 remaining. If the Jets could only beat somebody besides Buffalo. Tampa Bay to the rescue!

Week 10 — Sunday, November 14, 1976
Shea Stadium, New York (attendance: 46,427)

The general consensus when Tampa Bay came to Shea to face the Jets in week 10 was that it was the Buccaneers' last hope of avoiding and 0–14 season. After playing the Jets, the Bucs would finish off their maiden season against the Cleveland Browns, Oakland Raiders, Pittsburgh Steelers, and New England Patriots, all contenders, so the 2–7 Jets were seen as the only realistic shot the Bucs had of escaping the humiliation of a winless season. For much of the first quarter they may have felt good about their chances. It is sometimes said that the problem with playing a victory-starved team is that you need to put them away early: the longer you allow them to entertain notions of an upset, the more momentum you allow them to collect. As the first quarter was nearing an end, the game remained scoreless; as long as they could stay in the game, the Buccaneers had to be thinking of that first victory. But then came Namath.

Namath was able to play, but as he hadn't seen action in three weeks, Holtz made the decision to again start Richard Todd. He told both of them, however, that Todd would play the first two offensive series before Namath came in for the third. Holtz assumed that the Jets' third series would come in the second quarter, and but for a Tampa error he would have been right.

With Todd at quarterback the Jets had failed to generate a threat in the first period, but they were handed a golden opportunity when Tampa's Louis Carter fumbled the ball and Phil Wise recovered for New York at the Buccaneers' 14-yard line with 2:02 left in the period. It was the Jets' third series — Namath came onto the field. The crowd was obviously glad to see him, rising to their feet in applause. If they were going to pay to sit there on a chilly November afternoon and watch a bunch of losers, at least they wanted to see a superstar loser.

Namath came into the game, and on his first play in three weeks he handed the ball to Clark

Gaines, who slipped a few tackles and went 14 yards for a score. Namath hadn't really done anything — just handed the ball off, is all — but somehow his mere presence on the field seemed to infuse the team with some spirit — it inspired the crowd and it inspired his teammates. Whereas the Jets hadn't had much success moving the ball prior, suddenly Gaines ran like a man possessed.

The Buccaneers tried to fire back, driving to the New York 23 on their next series only to bog down there and miss a 40-yard field goal 1:31 into the second quarter. The Jets then took possession at their own 23, and came out with a surprise formation. There was Joe Namath — king of the drop back passers — calling signals out of a shotgun formation. He pitched a 10-yard pass to Rich Caster, and was hammered upon releasing the ball. Still taking the snap from the shotgun on the next play, Namath again took a good shot upon releasing the ball, which this time failed to reach its mark. He wouldn't use the formation again.

Namath threw 14 yards to Lou Piccone, Gaines picked up 11 on a draw play, Steve Davis ran for 11 and 13 yards on a pair of sweeps, and before anyone knew it the Jets were on the Tampa four-yard line. Two plays later, Caster caught his first TD of the season when Namath hit him at the back of the end zone from three yards out 5:58 into the second period. The drive had gone 77 yards, and it put the Jets up 14–0.

On the Jets' next series Namath drove them 66 yards in nine plays, including passes of 26 yards to Gaines and 13 yards to Caster. The drive resulted in a 21-yard field goal by Pat Leahy that increased the Jets' lead to 17–0 with 1:54 left in the half. With so little time remaining it might have been expected that the scoring in the first half had climaxed, but on the ensuing kickoff the Buccaneers promptly fumbled the ball away, and Clint Haslerig recovered for New York at the Tampa 25. Namath threw 15 yards to Gaines to set up a five-yard sweep around left end by Davis that made the score 24–0 at halftime. His work completed, Namath returned to the bench for the afternoon. He had been in for four series, and the Jets had scored each time. For a few moments, it seemed like the good old days. He finished his cameo appearance with seven completions in 12 attempts for 94 yards, and one touchdown.

The Buccaneers received the second half kick, but very quickly punted the ball away. Piccone took the punt at his own 40-yard line and ran straight up the middle, seemingly breezing right through a swarm of outreached hands and then into the clear, 60 yards for a touchdown. That gave the Jets a 31–0 lead just 1:09 into the third quarter, and the game was basically over. With Namath sitting out the remainder, things were fairly uneventful as the Jets played conservatively, but Leahy added another field goal 4:29 into the fourth quarter to complete the scoring. The 34–0 final was the first shutout the Jets had accomplished since December 1, 1963, when they were still playing in the old Polo Grounds. They had beaten Kansas City 17–0 on that occasion.

His team now 0–10, Tampa coach John McKay may have been weary of losing, but he was still quite capable of expressing disgust with his usual acidic humor. "Our guys were pretty polite to Namath," McKay quipped. "When they knocked him down they'd pick him up — and one guy stayed back there long enough to get his autograph."[16]

"This is a nice change," Namath said. "You really look forward to going to practice after a game like this one."[17] Aside from winning, there was something else nice about the game. Namath very much appreciated the crowd's enthusiastic response when he came onto the field. "It gives you a heck of a lift," he said. "It's one of the greatest feelings you can have."[18] It was good to be cheered again. But this was New York: don't get too used to it.

Week 11 — Sunday, November 21, 1976
Shea Stadium, New York (attendance: 49,983)

"As far as Joe is concerned," said New England defensive back Prentice McCray, "the ball was not getting there. He just isn't the same man he used to be."[19] Actually, the game had started well enough for the Jets, but by the end of the first quarter it became a matter of which team was most determined to give it away: the Jets won out in that respect. The Jets would commit 10 turnovers in their contest with the Patriots at Shea in week 11, and every one of them would lead to New England points.

The Patriots gifted the Jets early when Don Calhoun caught a swing pass from Steve Grogan, and after gaining a yard fumbled the ball away to linebacker John Ebersole at the New England 25. But Richard Todd — who was once more starting at quarterback — failed to take full advantage, and when the Jets bogged down at the two-yard line Pat Leahy kicked a 19-yard field goal to give New York a 3–0 edge 3:56 into the game.

On New England's first play after receiving the kick, Andy Johnson ran for two yards before being stripped of the ball by Lawrence Pillars. Linebacker Greg Buttle gathered it up and took off running: he went 23 yards for a touchdown. The Jets had scored twice in 20 seconds and held a 10–0 lead, but New England's generosity would end there; the Jets' generosity would soon begin.

Later in the first period, Clark Gaines fumbled and New England recovered at the New York 40. Grogan threw a 15-yard touchdown pass to Johnson seven plays later that cut the Jets' lead to 10–7 with 3:26 remaining in the first period. Louie Giammona then tried to field the ensuing short kickoff on a hop: it didn't turn out well, as he fumbled it and McCray recovered the ball at the New York 20. Three plays later, Grogan hit Darryl Stingley with a 17-yard TD to give the Patriots a 14–10 lead.

Namath entered the game with 2:12 left in the opening period, but unlike the previous week when his entry fired up the team and led to a 24-point explosion, this time it seemed to only contribute to the team's unraveling. At 4:42 of the second period, Namath tried to hit Rich Caster but found McCray instead. McCray would say afterward that Namath never looked Caster off. More than that, he hesitated before throwing, allowing McCray to get a jump on the ball. When McCray jumped in front of Caster, he was able to grab the pass on the run and race 63 yards down the sideline to score.

Now trailing 21–10, the Jets were able to battle back late in the half when Namath threw an 11-yard TD to Jerome Barkum. Having torn a hamstring in preseason, Barkum was playing for the first time all season; his TD made it 21–17 at halftime. The New York defense was actually holding up fairly well, though their offense wasn't making it easy on them. Late in the third period the Patriots were still holding onto their four-point lead when it happened again — Namath went back to pass and threw down the left sideline for Caster: the ball was underthrown, and McCray again stepped in front. Again he intercepted, and *again* he took it back the distance — this time 55 yards — down the sideline for a touchdown. The score was then 28–17, and it remained that way until the fourth quarter when a Namath fumble led to a six-yard TD pass from Grogan to Pete Brock that pretty well put things out of reach at 35–17.

After Namath's fumble Holtz sent Todd back into the game, but he was quickly intercepted by Tim Fox with 3:19 left to play; it led to a 28-yard field goal four plays later. Lou Piccone gave the Jets a bit of a spark when he returned the kickoff 58 yards from the New York nine to the New England 33, allowing the Jets to make the score more respectable. Todd ran a seven-yard bootleg to the 26, and then threw a 26-yard TD to Gaines with 1:43 left.

The 38–24 victory ensured the Patriots (then 8–3) of their first winning record in 10 years. It also allowed them to keep pace with Baltimore in the AFC East. The Patriots had otherwise achieved a team-record seven interceptions against the Jets (five from Namath, and two from Todd). For the Jets, the 10 turnovers were far too much to overcome (they would have been even for far better teams), something even more apparent when one views the Jets' dominance in other statistical categories (287 total yards to New England's 237, for instance).

McCray made no secret of the fact that he felt Namath had thrown poorly that day, saying that the first interception he made was on a wobbly throw and that, despite having ample time most of the game, Namath just wasn't getting the ball there. McCray's teammate, rookie corner-back Mike Haynes, disagreed. "I've watched Joe Namath play ever since I can remember," Haynes said, "and I think he's a great quarterback. I thought he threw well today but then, I haven't seen him as long as some of the other guys."[20]

Namath defended his own play, saying that McCray's first interception "was just a damn good defensive play." He felt that his execution was there. "I don't think I passed the ball all that badly," he said, adding, "at least the passes felt good when I released them."[21] Namath completed 16 of 36 for 176 yards.

There was also the execution of others to consider. On his fourth play after entering the game Namath threw deep for Caster, who was streaking wide open downfield. It looked to be a sure touchdown. The pass was on target — Caster dropped the ball.

Week 12 — Sunday, November 28, 1976
Memorial Stadium, Baltimore (attendance: 43,823)

There were no surprises when the Jets played the Colts in Baltimore in week 12. Leading the AFC Eastern Division with a 9–2 record, the Colts seemed very much on their game. It wasn't expected that they would have any trouble with the Jets, who didn't have any game. What is interesting is how the game followed such a familiar pattern. Throughout the season, opponents had been making careless mistakes and basically spotting the Jets an early lead. The Jets would then very predictably lose the advantage with their own flurry of errors.

That pattern persisted in week 12, when Baltimore running back Roosevelt Leaks fumbled on the game's first play from scrimmage. The ball never hit the ground, but hopped right into the hands of John Ebersole, who ran it to the Baltimore six-yard line. Two plays later Steve Davis scored on a three-yard run, and after Pat Leahy's extra point failed, the Jets were up 6–0. The Colts cut the lead in half with a 34-yard field goal, but before the first quarter ended the Jets added a 26-yard field goal of their own, and held a 9–3 lead going into the second period. For the Jets, the game may as well have ended there.

Holtz was still sticking with his schizophrenic offensive strategy, starting Richard Todd, bringing in Namath after a few series, then bringing Todd back again in the second half. It once more yielded poor results. Then again, it may have been completely arbitrary at that point, since neither quarterback seemed able to get anything going.

The Colts began to run away with it in the second quarter. Early in the period, they embarked on an 80-yard march that culminated with them taking a 10–9 lead on a five-yard TD pass from Bert Jones to Don McCauley. When Baltimore then kicked to New York, Louie Giammona fumbled the kick, and Freddie Scott recovered for the Colts. That led to a 14-yard touchdown throw from Jones to Lydell Mitchell, making it 17–9. Later in the period the Colts went up 20–9 on a 34-yard field goal by Toni Linhart, and by the end of the half a 31-yard touchdown throw from Jones to Roger Carr made it 27–9. The game was basically over by halftime.

Jones exited the game early and made way for backup Bill Troup. The Colts added a pair of field goals in the second half to make the score 33–9 before the Jets finally found their way back to the end zone in the game's final two minutes, when Todd threw up a rainbow that found David Knight 44 yards downfield for a score. That made the final 33–16.

Bert Jones idolized Joe Namath. After the game he was one to defend the Jets' quarterback. "It's an inspiration playing against Joe," Jones said. "He's been the best of my lifetime and you always like to play against the best."[22] In his little more than one quarter of play, Namath completed three of eight passes for a grand total of six yards.

Lou Holtz had received some criticism for his handling of the quarterback situation. There were those who felt that he was wrong to lift Todd from the games against New England and Baltimore. The basic premise was that the Jets were leading Baltimore when Namath came in, and as Namath was unable to lead the team to any points in the second quarter and the Colts pulled in front, it would have been wiser to leave Todd in the game. It wasn't a particularly sound argument, as the Jets' small lead had little to do with Todd and everything to do with Baltimore errors. Once the Colts stopped screwing up, the Jets' points dried up: it was that simple. But Holtz seemed to take the criticism to heart, and when the Jets hosted the Washington Redskins in week 13 he decided to sit Namath out and let Todd go the distance. The results were no different.

Against the Redskins, Todd completed four of 14 passes for 61 yards and two interceptions. The Jets were trailing 17–0 by the end of the first quarter. At halftime, it was 24–3. The Jets did manage a pair of rushing touchdowns in the second half, but still wound up losing 37–16. After the game, Holtz was asked to address rumors that he was going back to coaching collegiate ball, but he dismissed such scuttlebutt outright, saying that he had a good relationship with the Jets' owners and was happy with his situation in New York. He said he intended to fulfill his contract. Four days later, he announced he was leaving.

There was no ill will between Holtz and the organization. Holtz simply came to realize that pro ball was not the place for him, and president Phil Iselin and general manager Al Ward both agreed. By all appearances it was an amicable parting, and with Holtz gone the Jets could get serious about finding a coach to build a solid foundation for the future.

In the meantime, personnel director Mike Holovak would step in as interim coach. Holovak certainly had plenty of experience: he had coached the Boston Patriots through much of the 1960s. Having coached against the Jets — and Namath — during that time, Holovak said that, as a coach, he had always wanted to have Namath as the quarterback of his team. Now he was finally getting that wish. In the end, he probably wished he hadn't.

Week 14 — Sunday, December 12, 1976
Shea Stadium, New York (attendance: 31,067)

"If it was my last game here then I'm sorry it had to end the way it did."[23] So said Joe Namath after the Jets ended their season on a cold, wet, dreary day at Shea Stadium against the Cincinnati Bengals. A team record was set that day: there were more than 23,000 no-shows, the highest in franchise history. At 31,067 it was the smallest home crowd for a Jets game at Shea that anyone could remember. Those who did come basically came to say goodbye, for everyone knew that Namath would not be back this way again. They weren't looking for anything miraculous, although that would have been nice. At this point they probably would have settled for vague reminders of the way things used to be, just one last good memory to take with them. It would be a disappointing day for everyone.

It was even disappointing for the victors. The Cincinnati Bengals had held a two-game lead over the Pittsburgh Steelers in the AFC Central with only three games left in the season — they blew it. The Bengals came into Shea having dropped two consecutive games — to Pittsburgh and Oakland — and after starting 1–4, the Steelers finished the season with a nine-game winning streak. The day before the Bengals played the Jets, the Steelers had beaten the Houston Oilers 21–0 to finish the season 10–4. The Bengals could also finish 10–4 by beating the Jets, but having lost to the Steelers twice during the season they now had no hope of winning the division. They also had no realistic hope of winning the wild card as that would go to either New England or Baltimore, both 10–3 and both playing easy marks: the Patriots drew the 0–13 Buccaneers while the Colts had 2–11 Buffalo on their schedule. Either team could trump Cincinnati in a tiebreaker. Any way they looked at it, the Bengals were screwed. It must have been very frustrating. They sure needed someone to take it out on.

With the sudden departure of Lou Holtz, Jets' personnel director Mike Holovak would take over as head coach for the last game of the season. He said he'd always wanted Namath to quarterback a team he was coaching, but this day wasn't the dream scenario Holovak had probably envisioned: it was just a lot of guys playing out the string. Surely, Shea Stadium was never so bleak. Namath threw a pair of interceptions in the first quarter, and the Bengals kicked a pair of field goals for a 6–0 lead. It was not a particularly riveting 15 minutes.

The Bengals began to open things up in the second period, when Ken Anderson threw an 85-yard TD pass to Isaac Curtis to make it 13–0. The Jets received the kick, and three plays later Namath was intercepted by safety Marvin Cobb. Cincy scored another TD, this one a seven-yard sweep by Boobie Clark: 20–0, Cincinnati.

The Jets again received the kickoff, and again on the third play of the series Namath was intercepted, this time by Ken Riley. Seven plays later, Stan Fritts scored on a two-yard run to put the Bengals up 27–0 with 3:35 left in the half. The way they were playing the Jets might have been looking at a shutout, but the Bengals let them off the hook late in the first half when Lemar Parrish fumbled a punt, and Louie Giammona recovered for New York at the Cincinnati 26. It would lead to the Jets' only points, a 26-yard field goal with nine seconds left in the half.

Holovak's fantasy game with Namath as his quarterback didn't likely include pulling Namath at halftime, but the end of the first half saw the end of Joe Namath's career as a New York Jet. He sat out the second half, having completed only four of 15 throws for an anemic 20 yards. He matched his completions with an equal number of interceptions. In the second half, Richard Todd led the Jets to a total of three first downs (which is all they'd gotten in the first half) and nine total yards of offense. Meanwhile, Cincinnati had continued to rack up points, Anderson hitting Bob Trumpy with a 39-yard TD pass and Chris Bahr adding two field goals, one of them set up after Riley grabbed his third interception of the game. Then, with just five minutes left in the season, Todd was taken down in the end zone for a safety by Coy Bacon and Gary Burley. The 42–3 final was a fittingly humiliating end to a thoroughly awful season.

It was certainly an ignominious departure for the likes of Broadway Joe. Toward the end of the first half, as Namath left the field for the last time as quarterback of the New York Jets, he was booed. Those who booed him off the field didn't realize that he wouldn't be back in the second half. There was a silence among the small crowd when Richard Todd came onto the field in Namath's place, almost as though no one understood what was happening. When it began to sink in, some of them began to call for Namath's return. But it was too late: Broadway Joe was done. Had they known he wouldn't be back, then perhaps those who booed him from the field would have kept their silence as he walked to the sideline after playing his final down with the team. Then again, maybe it would have made no difference; after all, this was New York.

After the last game that Namath would ever play at Shea Stadium, he had quite a bit of unloading to do as he sat in front of his locker. Whenever his offensive line had been criticized in the past, Namath had always been quick in jumping to their defense. This time he was the one handing out criticism. Saying that he had been taking his share of blame all year long for the team's poor showing, Namath wondered how any passing game could be expected to flourish when the quarterback was getting dumped on his ass 80 percent of the time (his estimate). He dismissed talk that the problem may have been his lack of mobility, pointing out that Richard Todd — a rookie with absolutely no mobility issues — also got knocked on his ass 80 percent of the time (again, his estimate). Throughout his career, Namath had always been one to shoulder blame and deflect criticism away from his teammates, but fair is fair and enough is enough; it turned out that 1976 was quite enough.

Amazingly, the Jets did not finish last in their division: that fell to Buffalo at 2–12. But while they did finish 3–11 for the second consecutive season, make no mistake: the Jets were worse off in 1976. They finished the season with a point differential of minus 214. While defense had been the obvious problem in 1975, with the offense middling, in 1976 both squads just looked bad.

As for Namath, he undoubtedly had the worst season of his career. His 49.6 completion percentage was comparable to some seasons past, but his paltry four TDs up against 16 interceptions was by far his worst differential ever. His average yards per attempt (4.7) and average yards per completion (9.6) were a far cry from previous seasons, and most indicative of the type of year it had been was the fact that Joe Namath — master of the long throw — had not completed a pass longer than 35 yards all season. That placed him last among starting quarterbacks in that category. Who would have thought that Joe Namath would ever place last in that respect? Just a year earlier he had finished first in that category, with his longest pass going for 91 yards.

After the end of the 1976 season, word was that defensive coordinator Walt Michaels would be taking over as head coach in 1977. Many thought Michaels should have gotten the job years earlier when Weeb Ewbank stepped down as head coach. Nepotism won out when Charley Winner — Ewbank's son-in-law — was given the job in 1974; poor judgment won out when Lou Holtz got it in 1976. How different might Namath's last three years with the Jets have been had Michaels taken over in 1974? It is interesting to wonder. It would take a few years, but Michaels would eventually lead the Jets back to the playoffs, and even the AFC Championship, where they fell a game shy of returning to the Super Bowl.

There were many big changes ahead for the New York Jets: Michaels would be the new head coach, Namath would in all likelihood be gone, and the team would soon enough need a new president as well. Phil Iselin, the co-owner who had been president since 1968, had suffered a heart attack in September while watching his team get mugged by the Broncos in Denver. He recovered and returned to work, but after the season ended he was in his Madison Avenue office sitting at his desk in late December when he suffered another heart attack and died. It was almost as though fate were wiping the Jets' slate clean and forcing them to begin anew. Soon, Namath would also get the opportunity to begin anew.

15

The 1977 Season

In early January of 1977, Los Angeles Rams executive vice-president Don Klosterman was asked if his team would be acquiring Namath. Klosterman was fairly nonchalant in his response. "We haven't talked to the New York Jets about Namath," Klosterman said, "and so far he has not figured in our plans."[1]

Klosterman went on to explain that the Rams felt confident in the quarterbacks they had (second-year man Pat Haden, seven-year veteran James Harris, and Ron Jaworski, who had three years under his belt). The Rams had won their division in 1976, and had gotten as far as the NFC Championship game, but they had also spent the season juggling their quarterbacks, unable to settle on one until late in the season when Haden took the job from Harris. A solid quarterback was thought by many to be the only missing ingredient keeping the team from a Super Bowl crown.

In January of 1977, Jets general manager Al Ward said he hadn't talked to the Rams about Namath, nor even talked yet to Namath or his attorney, Jimmy Walsh, about any future plans. The Jets still held the option on Namath's contract: they could resign him or trade him. All the Jets would say on the subject was that they would come to a decision before the April deadline, at which time Namath would become a free agent.

As for Namath himself, he wasn't being mysterious in the least. While the Jets and the Rams were claiming to have scarcely considered the matter, Namath said publicly that it was L.A. or bust. If he couldn't play for the Rams in the upcoming season, he said, then he would be retiring from the game. "I don't think I'd want to play for the Jets again under any circumstances," he said.[2]

It had been known for several years that Namath wanted to go to the Los Angeles Rams. He had made it clear for some time that he wanted to play for a contender, preferably in a warm climate: L.A. filled the bill on both counts, and being that Namath was looking to restart his acting career, L.A. was obviously the place to be in that respect as well. From the standpoint of Namath's needs, it all made perfect sense. What wasn't so obvious to many was why the Los Angeles Rams would want Namath.

As Klosterman had pointed out, the Rams already had three able-bodied quarterbacks to choose from; granted, none of them seemed to have Namath's celebrated abilities, but then again, at that point it wasn't for certain that Namath did anymore either. The ranks were thinning in Los Angeles, however: Jaworski had played out his option with the Rams and let it be known that he wanted to go elsewhere. The Rams obliged, and Jaworski was off to Philadelphia, but that still left Haden and Harris to choose from. With both of them being fairly young—although at 29 Harris had a few years on him—and having potentially bright futures, why would the Rams opt for a fragile quarterback in the twilight of his career? Perhaps the Rams bought into the idea that they could get over that last hurdle to the Super Bowl with a proven leader who had been to the top of the mountain.

There is another possibility to consider: the owner of the Los Angeles Rams was Carroll Rosenbloom, the man who had owned the Baltimore Colts when Namath and the Jets took them out to the woodshed in Super Bowl III back in January of 1969. Perhaps it appealed to Rosenbloom's sense of irony, the idea that the man who handed him his most crushing defeat might now be able to deliver to him his greatest triumph.

Whatever lay behind the decision, the Rams began giving serious consideration to signing Namath. Helping move things along was a March 15 deadline set by Al Ward. Apparently the Jets had come to a decision of their own. If the Jets chose to pick up the option on Namath's contract, they would then be required to pay him $495,000 for the 1977 season, rather than the $450,000 he had been paid in 1976. Things being what they were, that just wasn't going to happen. The Rams definitely had the upper hand, and they were rumored to be taking advantage with a meager $200,000 offer for Namath's services. That turned out to be only rumor, however, as the real numbers were considerably different. It was more in the neighborhood of $350,000, still a significant pay cut at $100,000 less than his prior contract, but for Namath it wasn't about the money. He wanted very much to go out a winner, and the Rams looked to be the answer. The rumor, interestingly enough, came from the Rams organization, which announced that any quarterback on their club would be paid, at most, between $150–200,000. It could be that the announcement was intended to head off any resentment among the team's other quarterbacks.

But before they would decide on signing Namath, the Rams had a request — they wanted to see films of Namath from the 1976 season. Good grief, anything but *that*! Namath hadn't looked good in 1976. Not much of anything about the Jets looked good in 1976. Apparently the films gave the Rams pause for thought. Ultimately, they were unwilling to give up anything in trade for Namath, preferring to wait for the deadline to expire on the Jets. If the Jets hadn't traded Namath by the first of April, then they would have to either pick up his option or put him on waivers. The prospect of the Jets picking up Namath's option was extremely remote. The Rams had the advantage — if they really wanted Namath, all they had to do was wait.

The deadline passed and Namath was waived. That was followed by a month of negotiations between Walsh and the Rams until finally on Thursday, May 12, it became official — Broadway Joe was now Hollywood Joe. Namath was joined by Rosenbloom, Klosterman, and Rams head coach Chuck Knox — yes *that* Chuck Knox — at a press conference to announce the signing. All parties were uniformly mum on the terms of the contract, which was still being given a low estimate (around $150–175,000).

As for James Harris, well, he wore number 12, and with Namath coming to town there was only room for one number 12: Harris was out. Still fuming over being benched in favor of Haden in 1976, Harris wouldn't go quietly. In his five starts in 1976 he had led the Rams to a 3–2 record. They fared better under Haden (5–1–1), but Harris chose to muddy the water with vague accusations, saying that his benching was not decided by Knox, but was rather a management decision unrelated to his performance. He made no effort to explain the claim, preferring to leave everyone to insinuate a racist taint to it all (Harris being black and Haden white). Both Knox and Rosenbloom denied Harris' insinuation. Harris maintained that he was still the one who could get the Rams to the Super Bowl, but he was turning out to be more trouble than the Rams needed to deal with in an already crowded quarterback situation. Stirring the pot even more was the fact that the Rams had chosen Nebraska quarterback Vince Ferragamo in the fourth round of the draft. Ultimately, Harris was dealt to San Diego.

Namath had his first workout with the Rams on Monday, July 8, 1977. It was announced that he and Haden would be roommates, and the two of them held a joint press conference after workouts were through. Always looking to spice things up, the reporters were no doubt hoping to seize on something catty to write about, but they would be disappointed when neither quarterback would take the bait. Namath was asked if he was the new starting quarterback for the team, and he was quick to shoot the notion down. He let it be known he intended to fight for the job, but pointed out that Haden had to be the No. 1 quarterback going in, as he was the one who had led the Rams to the NFC Championship the prior season. Otherwise, Namath joked of asking for a new roommate after learning that Haden was married and therefore didn't have any good phone numbers to share. Haden would disappoint the press as well: after joking that he was three or four years of age the first time he watched Namath play, Haden added: "I can only be a better football player for Joe being here."[3]

Namath admitted that his knees were still a problem and that they had been giving him trouble, but team physician Dr. Robert Kerland had devised a program to get him into shape for the season. Kerland's regiment leaned heavily on swimming. Namath would be in the pool at 8:15 A.M., an hour before the other players were required to be at practice. When practice ended, and the other players were running laps, it was back to the pool for Namath to swim more laps. It was a bit grueling, but he was determined to be in the best possible shape to make a run at being the starting quarterback.

Namath's presence was already getting people's attention. Whereas training camp the prior season might have attracted a dozen or so curious spectators at the practice field, the Rams were finding in the neighborhood of 200 people showing up at practice to get a look at Namath. When practice would end and it came time for Namath to be driven back to the swimming pool, it wasn't always easy to get him there. Fans often intercepted him on his way to the car, seeking autographs or just wanting to talk to him. It looked as though Namath was definitely going to be good for box office.

Namath made his public debut with the Rams on Saturday night, August 6, at the Los Angeles Coliseum against the Minnesota Vikings. Some 55,168 spectators came out to see the Rams take on the team that had prevented them from getting to the Super Bowl the previous season; if they were anxious to see Namath, they would be kept waiting: Haden played the entire first half.

The Vikings got out to an early lead when Fran Tarkenton hit tight end Stu Voight with an eight-yard TD pass. After missing the extra point, Minnesota kicker Fred Cox went on to add a 44-yard field goal to make it 9–0. Fortunately for the Rams, Tarkenton only played the first quarter, but before departing he pitched a three-yard TD to Ahmad Rashad to give the Vikings a 16–0 lead going into the second period.

Haden got the Rams on the board in the second quarter with a 36-yard touchdown pass to Willie Miller, but they still trailed 16–7 at halftime. Haden finished the half with six completions in 12 attempts for 104 yards. Namath finally entered the game in the third period and received a standing ovation as he came onto the field for the first time. He didn't see the people rise to their feet, but he couldn't fail to hear the crowd roaring its approval. "It gave me a good feeling," he said later.[4] Hearing the commotion of that many people coming to life would get anybody's attention. Even Haden felt the emotional pull of it all. "I expected that and I was excited by it," he said.[5]

The crowd continued to get excited: Namath's first pass was good for 11 yards to Terry Nelson and the crowd grew louder. His second pass was also complete, again for 11 yards, this time to running back Jim Jodat. The crowd's excitement grew. They weren't the long throws that he was famous for, but everyone likely thought Namath was just getting warmed up. Namath threw little, however, and only played the third period, ending his night three of four for 34 yards. The Rams got a field goal in the third quarter to cut the Minnesota lead to 16–10.

In the fourth quarter rookie Ferragamo came in at quarterback, and while he only completed three of nine passes for 20 yards, he also presided over the touchdown drive that put the Rams in front for the first time when Rod Phillips scored on a two-yard run with 5:05 left in the game. Now leading 17–16, the Rams forced the Vikings to surrender the ball and they could have run out the clock. They didn't. The Rams wound up punting as well, and that was their undoing.

In the 1976 NFC Championship game, the Rams had started by driving the length of the field only to have a field goal attempt blocked by cornerback Nate Allen. Bobby Bryant ran it back 90 yards for a score, and the Vikings never looked back. Now, on this August night, it must have felt like déjà vu all over again when Allen blocked Gerald Vaught's punt and then grabbed it himself and ran it back 23 yards for a touchdown with 1:27 left. Cox again missed the extra point, but it made no difference: the Vikings held the Rams at bay and won the game 22–17.

Namath's performance in his Los Angeles debut was certainly not spectacular, but it wasn't bad for a quarter's work. He would have an opportunity to make a better impression the following Saturday night when he would be starting against the Philadelphia Eagles. Again the Coliseum crowd gave Namath a standing ovation when he came onto the field, but in his three series, lasting a little more than a quarter, Namath threw only one pass (which was incomplete) and the Rams managed a net of only 13 yards. The Eagle's fared little better under Ron Jaworski's leadership, but did manage a field goal to take a 3–0 lead.

Haden came into the game in the second period and completed six of 11 throws for 75 yards, but it was the running of rookie Wendell Tyler that helped the Rams blow past the Eagles. Tyler ran for his first touchdown as a pro to give the Rams a 7–3 lead late in the first half. After getting into the end zone, Tyler made it a point to spike the ball. He recalled the last time he had spiked the ball at UCLA: it resulted in his being benched by UCLA coach Dick Vermeil. Perhaps the spike this time was a message to Vermeil, who was now coaching the Philadelphia Eagles.

Tyler then broke a 59-yard run that set up a seven-yard touchdown run by Jodat. In all, Tyler would gain 87 yards on seven carries, while Jodat gained 66 in nine rushes. Obviously the Los Angeles rushing game was having no trouble with Philadelphia, and the Rams went on to a 20–3 victory. The quarterbacks for both sides were not as impressive, but Haden made the best impression. Ferragamo was one of four for a total of three yards, while Jaworski was two of 11 for 25 yards and Philadelphia's other quarterback, Roman Gabriel (another former L.A. Ram), was three of nine for 33 yards.

His anemic numbers notwithstanding, Jaworski was one to run his mouth after the game nonetheless. Still very unhappy (apparently) with not being the Rams' starting quarterback the previous season, Jaworski had been traded to the Eagles for tight end Charles Young. He was obviously still nursing a grudge. He brought up the standing ovation given Namath: "But after the first quarter against us," he said, "they wanted him out of there."[6]

"Joe was operating under some rough circumstances," Haden said. "We didn't have very good field position for him."[7] It was a gracious comment by Haden, but Namath knew there was no real excuse. A good quarterback can always dig his team out of a hole, as Namath had done many times in New York.

The Rams were in San Francisco the following Saturday afternoon to play the 49ers in Candlestick Park. Playing the entire second half, Namath got his most significant workout of the preseason — some said it was more a work over. "Last year I would have expected to be on my back all the time," Namath said after it was over, "but not with this team."[8]

The Rams came into the second half with a 14–6 lead after Haden had thrown a 27-yard touchdown to Miller in the first quarter, and Ferragamo threw an 11-yard TD to Harold Jackson in the second quarter. San Francisco's Jim Plunkett had tossed a one-yard touchdown to tight end Jim Obradovich late in the second quarter to make it 14–6 at the half (Steve Mike-Mayer missed the extra point — he was hastening his departure for Detroit). But the 49ers largely kept their first unit in for the second half, while the Rams substituted liberally (which is, after all, what preseason is largely for), the result being a 17-point second half for San Francisco. As for the Rams, they failed to score with Namath at quarterback, their only sustained drive ending with an interception. The Rams went down in defeat, 23–14.

"He showed he could take some shots," Knox said of Namath after the game.[9] Namath wound up completing six of 15 for 80 yards. Aside from his being sacked five times, Namath otherwise had trouble with handoffs, twice turning the wrong direction and running into Jodat in the backfield. While Haden had been sacked twice in the first quarter, both he and Ferragamo had been able to avoid getting dumped a number of times with the kind of fleet-footedness that Namath couldn't accomplish. But those who assumed that the Rams' inability to score in the second half was down to Namath's performance were quick to look past the fact that both of the first-half touchdowns scored by Los Angeles were the byproduct of fumbles by San Francisco's Wilbur Jackson, one being recovered by Fred Dryer at the San Francisco 35, while the other was recovered by Ron McCartney at the San Francisco 37.

Having to learn a whole new system already put Namath at somewhat of a disadvantage in vying for the starting job, but he otherwise let it be known that he felt he needed more playing time to get the kinks worked out. Haden also wanted more playing time to get tuned up for the season, and since the starting job in all likelihood came down to one or the other, Knox chose to sit Ferragamo out the following Saturday night in Kansas City. Against the 1–2 Chiefs, Namath would get the first half, and Haden the second.

"Something about Joe Namath scares the hell out of me," said Kansas City head coach Paul Wiggin.[10] Namath might have scared his own receivers as well. His first two passes — bullets thrown right on target — were both dropped by his receivers (one of which would likely have gone for a score). But unlike the previous week in San Francisco, Namath was being given time by his offensive line, and he moved the club well. Problem was, the Rams were frequently thwarted by their own mistakes, including four holding penalties.

The Rams fell behind 6–0 when Jan Stenerud kicked a pair of field goals in the first quarter, and were down 13–0 by the time Namath got his first TD pass with the Rams, a 29-yarder to Wendell Tyler that made it 13–6 at halftime (the extra point was blocked). He finished the half three of seven for 52 yards and one interception. In the third quarter, Haden brought the Rams to within one point at 13–12 with a 28-yard touchdown throw to Harold Jackson (the extra point was blocked again), but a pair of rushing touchdowns by the Chiefs trumped Tyler's five-yard touchdown run in the fourth to put the Chiefs up 27–19. Late in the game, the Rams were driving when defensive back Gary Barbaro intercepted Haden inside the Kansas City 10-yard line to end the threat and preserve the Chiefs' victory. It was Haden's second interception of the half, while completing seven of 15 for 106 yards.

Barbaro seemed to feel that his interception would have been less likely had Namath still been at quarterback, saying that Namath had a quicker release and was better at reading zone defenses. The game did little to tilt the quarterback decision one way or the other, and otherwise dropped the Rams to 1–3 in preseason. They would be returning home to a restless and impatient home crowd.

When James Harris had been traded to San Diego in June, he stopped just shy of accusing the Los Angeles Rams of racism for having benched him in favor of Haden in 1976. Harris had been booed that season by the fans at the Coliseum, and no one gave any indication that he would be missed. That being the case, he must have been surprised upon being greeted warmly by the Los Angeles fans when the Chargers came to L.A. to play the Rams on Thursday night, September 1. In the pre-game introductions, Harris was welcomed enthusiastically by the crowd of 55,946, who probably made him feel more at home than they ever had when he was playing *for* them. Namath, on the other hand, was met by boos when he entered the game in the second half. And this just a few weeks after they welcomed him with a standing ovation. With such churlish fans, is it any wonder the city currently has no professional football team?

Harris came out looking like he was eager to show the Rams what a mistake they had made, as he got the Chargers out to an early 14–0 lead with touchdown passes to Johnny Rodgers and Chuck Bradley in the first quarter. But the scoring drives only covered 24 and 11 yards respectively, as the Chargers were gifted with Los Angeles fumbles by Haden and Lawrence McCutcheon.

Haden got the Rams back in it with a 32-yard touchdown pass to tight end Terry Nelson, and in the second quarter Dave Elmendorf's interception of Harris led to a nine-yard touchdown from Haden to Harold Jackson that tied the game at 14-all. The momentum had definitely swung in L.A.'s direction, and when San Diego punter Jeff West was mobbed in the end zone while trying to field a bad snap, the resulting safety put the Rams up 16–14. But another fumble by McCutcheon gave the Chargers the opportunity to close the half with a 36-yard field goal that gave them a 17–16 lead at the intermission.

The fans had little opportunity to rest at halftime, as the movie *Heaven Can Wait* was shooting a make-believe Super Bowl between the Rams and the Pittsburgh Steelers, and the crowd was invited to participate by cheering wildly for the fantasy game. Maybe they were spent by the start of the third quarter, but for whatever reason they still mustered a smattering of boos when Namath came onto the field. Namath quickly turned that around with a 23-yard pass to tight end Charle Young, but when Ron Jessie dropped a pass at the San Diego 25-yard line the drive ended with no points to show.

The Rams did regain the lead on their next series, however, when Namath directed them on a drive that climaxed with a seven-yard touchdown run by John Cappelletti. Extra points seemed to be an increasingly trying experience for the Rams, and a bad snap killed the point after; the lead stood at 22–17.

In the fourth quarter Harris (enjoying extended playing time) hit Rodgers with another touchdown throw to put the Chargers up 23–22 with 8:34 left in the game (San Diego also made extra points look almost impossible), but Namath got the Rams into range for a 35-yard field goal by Tom Dempsey that again put Los Angeles on top, 25–23. The second half ended as did the first, with Toni Fritsch kicking a field goal to put the Chargers up by a point. This time it was a 22-yarder in the last three seconds that gave the Chargers a 26–25 victory. The fickle L.A. "fans" must have been elated.

Namath finished the night three of seven for 53 yards, while Haden was seven of 13 for 100 yards and two touchdowns. For someone fighting for the starting job, Namath seemed to be reluctant to take full advantage of his playing time, throwing little and putting up consistently mediocre numbers as a consequence. Still, Knox claimed to be undecided going into the final preseason game as to who would get the job come opening day.

Namath would get his most significant playing time in the team's final preseason game when the defending Super Bowl champion Oakland Raiders came to the Los Angeles Coliseum. With the quarterback situation still unresolved, Knox chose to play Namath for three quarters. Namath had complained of not having enough playing time to find his groove, and perhaps Knox wanted to give him every opportunity to prove himself. The way it turned out, it looked more like he was giving Namath enough rope to hang himself.

Although the Rams would muster no offense in the first half (and would only manage one first down), they had still played the champs to a scoreless standoff through most of the half thanks to two botched Oakland field goals, the first being scuttled by a mishandled snap and the second sailing wide right. But late in the half, Namath threw for Ron Jessie and was intercepted by linebacker Monte Johnson at the Los Angeles 35. Jesse's valiant effort to bring Johnson down eventually paid off 12 yards later at the 23, but after another four plays the Raiders took a 7–0 lead on Mark van Eeghen's one-yard run off left tackle.

The last five minutes of the first half would prove very productive for Oakland. After Namath was dumped for an 11-yard loss by Pat Toomay, Ted Hendricks blocked Glen Walker's punt and the Raiders took over at the Los Angeles 30. That led to a nine-yard TD pass from backup quarterback Mike Rae to tight end Dave Casper with 29 seconds left in the half.

The score was 14–0 at the half, but it could easily have been worse. The Raiders had 167 total yards of offense while the Rams managed only 23. The Rams had gained just one first down, and had not gotten beyond their own 39 in the half. As for Namath, his numbers were anemic to the point of flatlining. He had completed one of seven passes for three yards. Subtracting the 20 yards lost on two sacks, that gave the Rams a net of minus–17 yards passing in the half. There is one other thing to consider, however: statistically, dropped passes only count against a quarterback since they go down as no more than incomplete passes. Namath should have been four of seven passing — his receivers dropped three passes.

There was a collective groan from the crowd when Namath came back onto the field in the third quarter, but he began to quiet the critics when he led the Rams on what would turn out to be their only scoring threat of the evening. Namath threw for 60 yards in the series, but came away empty-handed when he was intercepted by Hendricks at the Oakland one-yard line.

The Raiders added one more TD in the third quarter when Rae hit his other tight end, Ted Kwalick, with a 13-yard scoring pass that made the final 21–0. The crowd had cheered enthusiastically when Haden entered the game, and the general consensus seemed to be that, although he too failed to get the Rams any points, he somehow injected some life back into the team. It isn't easy to discern where this perspective came from. Namath completed less than half his passes (eight of 18 for 108 yards with two interceptions) while Haden fared worse, completing less than a third (five of 16 for 31 yards and one interception). No, there seemed no clear winner for the starting quarterback position, but many seemed to assume Haden would get it by default.

The week of the season opener against Atlanta, however, Knox surprised a good many people with the announcement that Namath would be starting. Saying that there was no great difference in the preseason performances of either, Knox cited Namath's experience as the deciding factor. Both had completed less than half their throws (Namath hitting 23 of 52 for 327 yards, and Haden 34 of 71 for 465 yards), and both had thrown four interceptions. The main difference was that Haden had thrown five TDs whereas Namath threw only one. Still, Knox saw Namath's experience as the chief asset.

For a team that had won their division four straight seasons and had gone to three straight NFC Championships, the 1–5 preseason record was puzzling. Yes, it was only preseason, but having gone 6–0, 5–1, and 5–1 in their previous three preseasons, it would certainly be understandable if the Rams were concerned. The team's poor performance had to be worrisome at some level, especially because their troubles ran deeper than an undecided quarterback situation: they were misfiring in too many areas. Knox admitted to being concerned, but the rest of the team seemed to play it off. The general feeling among the players was that things would work themselves out once the season began in earnest and the games were for real. "I'll tell you one thing," said Namath. "Atlanta is going to have its hands full with a very angry football team."[11]

Week 1 — Sunday, September 18, 1977
Atlanta Stadium, Atlanta (attendance: 55,956)

The Rams opened the 1977 season in Atlanta against the Falcons. Picked to finish last in the NFC West, the Falcons were figured as anywhere from 11- to 14-point underdogs to the Rams, who had closed out their 1976 schedule by humiliating Atlanta 59–0. The Falcons had the entire off-season to stew over that.

The Falcons had a new coach in Leeman Bennett, a former assistant to Knox who had been lured away from L.A. to try and resuscitate the Atlanta franchise. Namath presented a new wrinkle for the Rams' opponents, and Bennett geared his defensive strategy accordingly. "You can't give

Namath time," he said. "You must go and get him."[12] That they did. Namath was harassed all afternoon, and spent a good portion of the game on his back. To make matters worse, the Falcons iced the Rams' running game; even Lawrence McCutcheon, who had run for over 1,000 yards the previous season, was ineffective.

And then there were the mistakes. The Rams looked as lethargic as they had throughout the preseason, but even when they did spark to life they would soon enough shoot themselves in the foot. In the game's first minutes rookie Billy Waddy returned an Atlanta punt 48 yards only to wind up fumbling it at the Falcons' 12-yard line, where Rick Byas recovered the ball for Atlanta. But with 5:42 left in the opening period the Rams drew first blood when Namath fired a 27-yard shot to Harold Jackson in the end zone. Now came the hard part—one of those extra points that had been so elusive to the Rams through the preseason. The Rams had cut veteran kicker Tom Dempsey loose and signed rookie Rafael Septien of Mexico City, and the kid made the extra point look as easy as, well, an extra point. The problem was that the Rams were flagged for a false start and Septien had to kick over again. It was too tall an order to make the extra point twice, and Septien's re-kick was blocked by Byas. The Rams, who might have—*should* have—been up 14–0 by then (taking into account the fumble at the Atlanta 12), had to settle for a 6–0 lead.

The Falcons had problems of their own to overcome. They had lost their starting quarterback Steve Bartkowski, who went down with a knee injury a week earlier in the final preseason game. With Bartkowski having gone in for knee surgery earlier in the week, the Falcons were dependent on backup man Scott Hunter, which should have helped Los Angeles. But the Rams couldn't help themselves.

Under a heavy rush early in the second quarter, L.A. punter Glen Walker got off a 10-yard kick that gave the Falcons possession at the Rams' 37. Not long afterward, running back Haskel Stanback went over from the one-yard line to tie the game, and when Atlanta kicker Nick Mike-Mayer performed a magic act—making the extra point look as easy as, well, an extra point—the Falcons held a 7–6 lead. In the waning seconds of the half Mike-Mayer added a 33-yard field goal that gave Atlanta a 10–6 lead at the intermission.

It hadn't been good, but it wasn't a disaster. Down by four, there was still plenty of time for the Rams to awaken from their seeming somnambulism. The problem was that they had emboldened the Falcons into feeling frisky enough to be thinking upset, and Atlanta came out in the second half and drove 74 yards to another TD. This time it was Hunter himself who took it over from a yard out, giving the Falcons a 17–6 lead.

The Rams' woes continued into the fourth quarter. Waddy fumbled again, and with time running out, Los Angeles became increasingly desperate. Trailing by 11, the Rams took over at their own 33 in the game's last six minutes and were passing on most every down. Namath continued firing away, despite having been sacked three times and been constantly dumped after throwing. He threw 20 yards to Ron Jesse, 16 yards to Dwight Scales, 14 yards to McCutcheon; but then it happened again: the Rams—McCutcheon, to be precise—fumbled the ball away, this time at the Atlanta 13-yard line. And with that the Rams were finished.

The 17–6 Atlanta victory was thought to be quite an upset, but there were those who began to wonder. Maybe that 1–5 preseason record wasn't an aberration: maybe that's who the 1977 Los Angeles Rams really were. Was this really the team that had won four consecutive division titles? Was this the team that had gone to three straight NFC championship games? Was this the contender that Namath had longed to play for? "I don't like an inferior team beating us," fumed defensive end Fred Dryer.[13] There was a pall over the entire L.A. locker room after the game. Well, almost the entire locker room.

At Namath's locker it was business as usual. There were scores of reporters clamoring around him, asking how he felt (not bad), about the icepack on his knee (no big deal), about why the

Rams had lost (the Falcons played a hell of a game). Some reporters couldn't help but notice that, by comparison to the rest of the team, Namath seemed strangely jovial, particularly for a man who had lost his regular season debut with what figured to be his last hope. But then, why shouldn't he look on the bright side? He'd given a gutsy and respectable performance, completing 15 of 30 passes for 141 yards and a touchdown. He also threw no interceptions. Whatever anybody might say about the loss, no one could hang it on him. The Rams had managed only one first down rushing in the entire game. The offensive line was no more able to block for its backs than it was able to protect Namath. Yes, this was a team with problems, but on this day Namath didn't look to be one of them.

The team was grimly silent as the players filed onto the bus outside the stadium, but Namath had a smile on his face as security escorted him. There were pretty Georgia peaches reaching out trying to touch him: one of them got through security and threw her arms around Namath and planted a kiss on him. Okay, so maybe the Rams had just finished pissing down their legs, but there were still things to smile about. For Namath it was business as usual. Wouldn't you be smiling, too?

Week 2 — Sunday, September 25, 1977
Los Angeles Coliseum, Los Angeles (attendance: 46,031)

In the opening week loss to Atlanta, the Rams' plays had been sent in by the coaching staff. Two days before their home opener against the Philadelphia Eagles in week two, Knox reconsidered that strategy. "I decided it was better to have the leadership on the field with the quarterback calling the plays," Knox said. "I thought that gave the team confidence."[14]

It was a responsibility that Namath welcomed. He had been running the offense and calling the plays all through the years until that task was taken away from him in 1975 by the brilliant coaching staff that led the New York Jets to two consecutive 3–11 seasons. "I've always called my own plays since I was a little kid on the sandlot," Namath said. "It's more fun that way."[15]

But there was more to it than that. Knox was right about it boosting the offense's confidence, something Namath alluded to when he noted that it encouraged the players on the field to become more participatory in the formation of strategy. "Each guy helps me make up my mind by what he reports in the huddle," Namath said.[16] It wound up looking like a smart move.

Of course, it helped considerably that the Los Angeles defense found its game again. It also helped that the Rams were playing against the one team that they had been able to beat in preseason. But one of the biggest factors aiding the Rams was the play of the offensive line. Unable to either protect Namath or clear enough room to establish a running game the week before, the offensive line did a complete reversal in week two. Philadelphia coach Dick Vermeil sized things up afterward by saying that he hadn't seen anyone lay a hand on Namath all game long. "We tried different ways of getting to him but we didn't come close," Vermeil said.[17] It was generally acknowledged that the return of left tackle Doug France after being out of the lineup for six weeks with a knee injury was a major contributing factor to the improved play of the offensive line.

Throughout the first half the Eagles' offense looked much like the Rams' offense appeared a week earlier: the running game was flat, the passing game harried. During the half, the Eagles would venture into L.A. territory only once, and even then just barely (they got to the Rams' 48) and ever so briefly (on the next play a sack of quarterback Ron Jaworski by Larry Brooks drove the Eagles back to their own side of the field).

By contrast, the Rams seemed to move at will, with Lawrence McCutcheon and John Cappelletti finding plenty of running room and Namath having more than enough time to spot the open receiver. Namath's play-calling also seemed to set the Eagles back on their heels as he mixed his plays well and kept the defense guessing. On the Rams' first offensive series he made a call that can best be described as uncharacteristic of L.A.'s offense as it had come to be known under Knox: on a first-and-10 play he went long. The ball—intended for Ron Jessie deep down the right sideline—had good flight, but ultimately was underthrown and broken up by Johnny Outlaw in the end zone. It may have been incomplete, but it certainly gave the Eagles something to think about.

The Rams' second series saw them starting in good shape at their own 47 and crossing midfield swiftly when runs by Cappelletti and McCutcheon advanced them to the Philadelphia 42. After going 0–3 passing in his first series, Namath hit four of four on the second, throwing three yards to McCutcheon and 14 to Jessie before hitting a clutch 20-yard pass to tight end Terry Nelson on second-and-22 from the Philadelphia 36. When McCutcheon only gained a yard on third-and-two, the Rams went for broke. On fourth-and-one from the 15, Cappelletti ran around left end for two yards and a first down. The drive got its payoff when Namath ran a play-action fake to McCutcheon on second-and-goal from the one and then tossed a prefect throw to Nelson cutting left-to-right at the back of the end zone to give the Rams a 7–0 lead.

The drive had gone 53 yards in 14 plays and had taken up 6:01 of the first period. At that point the Rams had gained 97 yards on 22 plays while the Eagles had run only six plays for a total of eight yards. Philadelphia did manage to accomplish a first down on their next series, but they could advance no further than their own 37 and punted again.

In the second quarter the Rams embarked on another time-consuming drive, this one traveling 84 yards in 13 plays and accounting for almost seven minutes of the period. Starting on his own 16-yard line, Namath hit on five of five throws for 68 yards, including throws of 20 and 15 yards to Jessie. But the one that really impressed was the 13-yard TD pass to McCutcheon. With a second-and-six from Philadelphia's 13-yard line Namath ran a double fake, first faking the handoff to Cappelletti and then an end-around to Jessie. He then arched a superb pass to the right that zipped over defender John Bunting's outstretched hand and came down perfectly over McCutcheon's shoulder and into his hands as he crossed the goal line. An illegal procedure penalty forced Rafael Septien to kick the extra point twice, but he made it both times and the Rams led 14–0 with 2:09 left in the half. Los Angeles had overcome *two* holding calls against guard Dennis Harrah in the series.

The halftime numbers made Philadelphia seem awfully lucky to only be trailing 14–0. The Rams had picked up 14 first downs to the Eagles' three, and otherwise led 233–57 in total yards (109–46 passing, and 124–11 rushing), having run 41 plays to Philadelphia's 23. The time of possession was almost 2–1 (19:27 to 10:33) in the Rams' favor.

With the Rams dominating so thoroughly it might have been expected that they would come out in the second half and completely blow the Eagles out of the Coliseum. Well, defensively they did, but the offense became very conservative, more interested in running time off the clock than anything else. But the L.A. defense continued to dominate and created opportunities for the team to put further points on the board.

On Philadelphia's first series of the second half Jaworski was intercepted by strong safety Bill Simpson, whose 14-yard return gave the L.A. offense possession at the Eagles' 34. Three runs by Cappelletti and four by McCutcheon found the Rams facing a third-and-goal at the three-yard line. Namath ran a play-action, rolled to his right, but finding his receiver well-covered, wisely threw the ball away. Still, Septien's 20-yard field goal upped the Rams' lead to 17–0.

Late in the third quarter, Simpson again presented his team with a good scoring opportunity when Fred Dryer stripped the ball from Philadelphia running back Mike Hogan and Simpson fell on it at the Eagles' 28. It led to another field goal by Septien, this one of 23 yards, as the Rams continued to play it safe.

Jaworski was intercepted by rookie linebacker Bob Brudzinski, which should have led to still more L.A. points as the 23-yard return gave the Rams the ball at the Philadelphia 32, but this time Septien came up short on a 36-yard field goal attempt. Other than that, the only other play of interest in the final quarter was Jaworski's third interception, this time grabbed by Monte Jackson, which enabled the Rams to run out the clock. The interception came one play after the Eagles recovered a fumbled punt and took possession at the L.A. 38 — it was Philadelphia's only play inside L.A. territory in the second half.

The 20–0 final score did not do justice to the Rams' complete domination (21 first downs to six, 356 total yards to 112), but the Rams would happily take it as the victory evened their record at 1–1 and moved them into a first-place tie with Atlanta in the NFC West. Namath looked good, hitting 12 of 23 for 136 yards, two TDs and one interception.

Week 3 — Sunday, October 2, 1977
Los Angeles Coliseum, Los Angeles (attendance: 55,466)

Given their poor showing in preseason, the Rams' week two home opener had only drawn slightly more than 46,000 fans to the Coliseum. But with the shutout victory over Philadelphia and the Rams seemingly back on track, a more respectable 55,466 turned up at the Coliseum to watch the Rams face division rival San Francisco.

The 49ers had sacked Namath five times when the teams met in preseason, but with the protection Namath had gotten the previous week the Los Angeles offensive line now looked to be up to the challenge. It also helped that the 49ers were themselves struggling at 0–2.

The Rams got out of the gate quickly when Wendell Tyler took a short opening kickoff at the 15 and brought it back 34 yards to the L.A. 49. Then, on the game's second play, Namath threw 18 yards to Ron Jessie. The All-Pro receiver went up and made the catch, but in being taken down he also tore ligaments in his knee. Jessie would need surgery the next day and would be out for the rest of the year.

The Rams didn't waste the good field position — or Jessie's sacrifice — and managed to get a 33-yard field goal on the series after stalling out at the San Francisco 16. They got closer on their second series, but this time ran out of gas at the five-yard line. Rafael Septien kicked a 22-yard field goal that would have made it 6–0 but for a holding penalty that nullified the play. No problem: even with a 10-yard penalty assessed it was still a very doable 32-yard kick. Unfortunately, a bad snap killed the re-kick and the Rams were still left with just a three-point lead.

After that the 49ers woke up, taking over at their own 15 and embarking on an 85-yard drive that saw quarterback Jim Plunkett convert a third-and-15 with a 31-yard pass to Tom Mitchell. Plunkett also threw 35 yards to Gene Washington in the series, and ultimately put San Francisco up 7–3 with a 17-yard TD pass to running back Delvin Williams.

In the second quarter, the Rams' special teams did their share to regain the lead when Cullen Bryant fielded a San Francisco punt at the 49ers' 38 and brought it back 25 yards to the 13. Two runs up the middle by John Cappelletti got seven yards to the six, from where Lawrence McCutcheon then cut through the middle to take it in for the score. With the extra point L.A. was back on top, 10–7.

Late in the half Cappelletti scored on a one-yard run that finished off what would turn out to be the Rams' longest drive of the game. Even so, they only had to travel 53 yards, which they accomplished in 12 plays. The drive had been kept alive by the most improbable of plays, a third down conversion that came about by way of a seven-yard scramble by Namath that brought the crowd to its feet in a joyous ovation. Cappelletti's TD came with 2:07 left in the half and gave the Rams a 17–7 lead at the intermission.

The 49ers would get right back in it, however, when they took the second half kickoff and drove 63 yards to score. A three-yard TD run by Williams cut the L.A. lead to 17–14, and seemed to divert the flow of things in San Francisco's direction. On the first play of their next series, the 49ers were looking to deliver the knockout punch when Plunkett threw long for Washington. The pass was incomplete, but defender Pat Thomas was flagged for interference and the 49ers were placed at the L.A. 14-yard line. The 49ers seemed poised to take the lead, but on a third-and-two play from the six San Francisco ran Wilbur Jackson, who was thrown for a loss at the seven by defensive tackle Larry Brooks. The 49ers would have to settle for tying the game with a 24-yard field goal. But even that wasn't in the cards, as Tom Wittum's kick bounced off the upright. The third quarter ended with the Rams still clinging to a 17–14 lead.

Things quickly fell apart for San Francisco in the fourth quarter. Bill Simpson blocked a 49er punt, which Jim Jodat grabbed and ran back 10 yards to the San Francisco 30-yard line. On top of that, Mike Baldassin was penalized for unnecessary roughness in his takedown of Jodat, further advancing the Rams to the 15. It led to a 24-yard field goal for the Rams seven plays later, but down by only six, the 49ers were still in it with nine minutes left to play. Not for long.

On the very first play of San Francisco's next series Plunkett threw for Williams, who had trouble pulling it in. He juggled the ball until it was snatched away by linebacker Bob Brudzinski at the 20. His one-yard return gave L.A. the ball at the 19, and five plays later Cappelletti again went across from a yard out, giving the Rams a 27–14 lead with 6:35 left in the game.

The floodgates were open now; on the 49ers' next possession Plunket threw for Jim Lash at the 46-yard line but was intercepted by cornerback Rod Perry. Lash got a hold of Perry quickly and was in the process of bringing him down when Simpson, standing close by, got Perry's attention. Perry flipped the ball to Simpson, and the safety ran it 42 yards to the San Francisco four-yard line. McCutcheon's one-yard TD run with 4:02 left to play pretty well put the game out of reach at 34–14.

The margin of victory—20 points—was significant, but because the game had been close up until the 17-point fourth-quarter explosion by Los Angeles, many were still suspicious as to whether or not the Rams were back to form. The 49ers seemed to somehow feel cheated; linebacker Willie Harper was among the many disputing Cappelletti's fourth quarter TD, which came on a third-and-goal play. Okay, give L.A. a field goal instead of a touchdown—they still win 30–14. Imagine they miss the 18-yard field goal—they then win 27–14.

"When the ball bounces against you, it really bounces against you," said San Francisco coach Ken Meyer. "We have a field goal try hit the upright and bounce back; we get a kick blocked; and then a pass bounces off a receiver's hands."[18] News Flash: it's called "execution," and isn't poor execution the reason most teams lose? There were some sportswriters who expressed the opinion that the 49ers had played well enough to win, but when you make *that* many mistakes and it leads to *that* many points for the other side, you haven't played well enough to win—you've played badly enough to deserve the result you got.

As for Namath, his numbers were fairly light, hitting seven of 14 for 126 yards.

Week 4 — Monday, October 10, 1977
Soldier Field, Chicago (attendance: 51,412)

When the Rams came to Chicago to face the Bears at Soldier Field on Monday night, they were riding a two-game winning streak and seemed to be on the upswing. The 1–2 Bears, on the other hand, were on a two-game losing streak and were perceived as the underdogs. But there was that Monday night hoodoo to consider: the Rams were 4–7 on Monday nights and had lost their last three Monday night games. Namath had played in ABC's inaugural *Monday Night Football* game in 1970 and lost. It seemed to start a personal tradition, as he went on to lose each successive game he participated in on ABC's *Monday Night Football*—a record of 0–6. Maybe this time things would be different.

It was a lousy night, with a steady drizzling rain through the first quarter. In their initial series, the Rams drove to the Chicago 15-yard line, and Rafael Septien gave them a 3–0 lead with a 22-yard field goal. The weather seemed to be playing into L.A.'s hands, as the Bears were having a hard time coping. Chicago quarterback Bob Avellini had a pass deflected by cornerback Monte Jackson that wound up in the hands of linebacker Isiah Robertson. A 20-yard return by Robertson had L.A. assuming possession at the Chicago 15. But again the Rams were forced to settle for a field goal, this one a 29-yarder that came 7:11 into the game.

The Bears' problems persisted when Walter Payton fumbled the ball and Robertson recovered it at the L.A. 46. Namath wasted no time, firing a 37-yard strike to Harold Jackson to the Chicago 17; six plays later Lawrence McCutcheon went in from two yards out to give the Rams a 13–0 lead after 11:32 of play. But then the Bears found their feet.

With 52 seconds left in the first quarter, Avellini threw a pass to James Scott (formerly of the defunct WFL's Chicago Fire). It was intended to be a quick out pattern, but when defender Rod Perry came in close to the line of scrimmage at the snap Scott adlibbed and decided to blow past Perry and shoot upfield instead. Avellini's throw was on the money, and Scott raced down the right sideline for a 70-yard touchdown.

The rain picked up, becoming a heavy downpour as the second quarter got underway, but it no longer seemed to deter the Bears. On their next series, Avellini went back to pass from the 28 and threw down the middle for Scott again. Both Scott and Perry went for the ball, but as their arms entangled it was Scott who pulled away with it and took off running. This time it was 72 yards and a score — more than that, with the extra point the Bears had captured a 14–13 lead 2:40 into the second quarter.

Things settled down a bit until the Bears again offered up a scoring opportunity to the Rams. After recovering a fumbled punt the Rams were just 13 yards from payoff, but once more they could only manage a three-pointer as Septien kicked a 24-yarder with 2:14 left in the half. Still, it had allowed the Rams to regain the lead, and they held a 16–14 advantage at halftime.

By the second half the rain had abated and there was nothing left but the pooling water on the miserable, pale Soldier Field carpet. But even though the rain had stopped, it wasn't until late in the third period that either club would penetrate deeply into enemy territory. The Rams advanced to the Chicago five-yard line with a 30-yard gain by Billy Waddy on a double reverse, but still couldn't punch it in from there. With fourth-and-goal at the one-yard line, Chuck Knox decided against the easy field goal: hell, they already kicked three — if they couldn't put it across this time...

Really, Knox was concerned that a five-point lead wouldn't hold up, and so the decision was made to go for it. Knox sent in power runner Rod Phillips, but Phillips found no room and ran into a brick wall at the line of scrimmage — the Bears took over on downs.

The Rams quickly forced a punt, and started their next series in good field position. But just before the end of the third period, Namath was intercepted by Doug Plank at the Chicago eight-yard line: Plank brought it back 20 yards to keep the Bears out of the hole. Having missed the first three games of the season with an ankle injury, Plank was playing his first game of the season. For Namath, Plank returned a week too soon — it was his second interception of Namath that night.

Early in the fourth quarter the Bears notched a 33-yard field goal to retake the lead, 17–16. Then, approaching the midway point of the quarter, Payton broke a 51-yard run to set up Chicago's next score. From the L.A. 29-yard line, Avellini was doing his best to outrun a blitzing Jim Youngblood and he spotted tight end Greg Latta running down the middle and in the clear. Avellini threw and Latta made a superb catch to put the Bears up 24–16 with 6:08 left to play. It was very bad news for the Rams — down by eight points, they would now have to score twice to overtake Chicago.

The game's final minutes became chaotic. The Rams were looking desperate as they struggled to get downfield as quickly as possible. Then the flags were flying, and Namath was down on the carpet looking like the victim of an assassin's bullet. Guard Dennis Harrah admitted later that he hadn't even seen the hit, but when he turned and saw Namath on the carpet writhing in pain and struggling to catch his breath he just knew something dirty had happened. Harrah snapped — he balled up his fist and popped Chicago linebacker Waymond Bryant. Then came the yellow flags. It's a little confusing as to exactly what was called on who, other than Harrah getting a personal foul for punching Bryant. Harrah was also ejected. It was thought that Bryant had been flagged for a late hit on Namath, but afterward some were saying that the flag on Bryant was for engaging in the fight instigated by Harrah. In any event, the penalties were pointless as they offset one another.

Namath eventually staggered off the field, and Pat Haden came in to finish the effort. With 27 seconds left in the game, Haden hit Dwight Scales with a 26-yard touchdown pass that pulled the Rams to within a point. But it was all for nothing when the Rams failed to recover the ensuing onside kick and Chicago ran the clock out.

When the final gun sounded it seemed the real fireworks were just starting. One Chicago sportswriter almost jumped out of his shoes when Los Angeles linebacker Isiah Robertson angrily insisted on being quoted accurately as saying that the Bears played "chicken shit football."[19]

Robertson went on to accuse Payton of flagrantly clipping Bill Simpson, and said that Namath was knocked out of the game by a punch delivered by Wally Chambers. Robertson put Chambers on notice that the next time the teams met Chambers would learn what it was to take a cheap shot, and said that he wouldn't quit football until evening the score with Chambers.[20] As both were defensive players it isn't clear how Robertson intended to gain his revenge, but it was otherwise a bewildering statement because, by the reckoning of some of Robertson's own teammates, the late hit to Namath was delivered by Bryant, not Chambers. Los Angeles guard Tom Mack said that Chambers wasn't even on the field at the time.

It had been a long time since Namath had tagged any team publicly for being cheap shot artists — not since he told reporters as much about the Oakland Raiders ten years earlier — but in the locker room after the game he opened up a bit to reporters. "If you let people continue to get away with cheap shots, what happens to sportsmanship?" he said.[21] Then Namath quickly diverted the subject, saying that the only real story was that the Bears won the game and that he personally played poorly. He did seem to have a very New York Jet–like evening, throwing four interceptions.

Bryant claimed that the helmet he planted in Namath's Adam's apple was not a cheap shot, and the general response from the Chicago side was to dismiss the accusations being made by the Rams as just so much whining from a pack of crybabies. "All I saw was Joe laying there," said Harrah. "I just sort of lost my head. It was very stupid of me to get kicked out of the game. But all the Bears wanted to take cheap shots at Joe and I resented that."[22]

As for Knox, he didn't seem interested in talking about cheap shots; he was more interested in the missed opportunities, saying that the game came down to the inability of the offense to get into the end zone when they had the chance. It foreshadowed a fateful decision on the horizon. When an offense fails to score the first head to roll is usually the leader. Nobody knew it yet, but Namath would never play another down in a professional football game. So this was how it all ended — on a drizzly, chilly evening on the damp, puke-pale carpet of dreary Soldier Field. Broadway Joe Namath's career ended with a cheap shot from a player that few people even remember. He finished his final game with 16 completions in 40 attempts for 203 yards ... and four interceptions.

The brouhaha over the Monday night fracas continued through the week, as both sides hurled barbs. Reporters seemed to be sensing a major change coming in the L.A. lineup and they continued asking Knox about Namath's status. The consensus was that, although he only came into the game in the final two minutes, Haden had played better than Namath. In his customarily gracious way Haden defended Namath, saying that by the time he entered the game the rain had long since ceased, whereas many of Namath's problems that night had come when the ball was wet and conditions were miserable in the first half.

It was also true that Namath's receivers had dropped six passes. Knox himself was inclined to defend Namath. "Joe did his job," Knox told reporters. "We can't expect him to do everyone else's."[23] He added, "Receivers might as well catch the ball because they are going to get hit anyway."[24]

"I definitely believe Joe has another Super Bowl in him," said Harold Jackson. "If you give him time, he'll kill you. We've just got to get up off the floor and help the guy."[25]

But the time for helping Namath had passed. The day after the game he was examined by the team physician, who listed Namath's litany of ailments: an abrasion of one eye, a bruised sternum, swelling and inflammation in the left knee and soreness in the right knee. Knox told reporters that Namath would be starting the following week against New Orleans if he was physically able, but there were mixed signals.

By Wednesday, with the team doctor saying that Namath would be unable to even practice for a couple more days, Knox made the announcement that Pat Haden would be starting the following Sunday. Knox's statements about Namath then took on a different color; he seemed less inclined to offer excuses. Maybe he had reviewed the films by then. "The pass protection was super," Knox said of the Monday night game. "There were some dropped passes but there were also some bad throws by the quarterback. Everybody saw it. I know it. Joe knows it."[26]

The Namath acquisition hadn't turned out like it was supposed to. The Rams had won their division four straight seasons and had gotten as far as the NFC Championship the last three of those years. They had grown accustomed to being among the top teams, and the conventional wisdom was that all they needed to take them the rest of the way was a championship caliber quarterback. Namath was supposed to fill that void, but here the Rams were, struggling to keep their heads above water at 2–2. Still, how could Namath be blamed for the team's lethargy? It's true that his failure to get the team into the end zone on several occasions had cost the Rams the game in Chicago, but on the other hand Namath was not playing in the defensive secondary that allowed Bob Avellini and James Scott to connect on touchdown passes of 70 and 72 yards, nor had he played any part in allowing Walter Payton to bust loose for a 51-yard jaunt that set up Avellini's decisive touchdown pass to Greg Latta. The Rams were a team that seemed to be sleepwalking. Obviously their problems went deeper than a quarterback controversy. But a major change to a team can often shake things up — maybe in the case of the Rams it would *wake* them up.

With the announcement that Haden would be starting when the Rams hosted New Orleans in week five, the conjectures started flying free and easy. Aside from the opinion of many that Haden should have been the starter from the beginning of the season, there were those who put forth the theory that Knox had been forced to play Namath by Rams owner Carroll Rosenbloom. There were also those who were suggesting that Namath's career was officially over now that he had squandered his last chance. Namath had signed a one-year deal with the Rams; certainly they would not be inclined to negotiate a new deal with him for the following year. It was believed by some that Namath's injuries were being used as a way for Knox to discreetly turn things over to Haden.

Then there were those who saw Namath as a victim of circumstance. After all, the Rams were hardly playing like the powerhouse team they were considered to be. Clearly that couldn't all be pinned on Namath. If the team continued to play lackluster overall how much difference would a quarterback change make?

Against the 1–3 Saints in the fifth game of the season Haden played well enough, completing nine of 16 passes for 180 yards. He threw no TDs and was intercepted once, but the Rams were again doing what they traditionally did, relying on the ground game, which racked up 243 yards to the Saints' 77 rushing yards. Something was obviously still wrong, however, as the Rams found themselves in a 7–7 tie with the Saints at halftime. A one-yard TD run by McCutcheon helped the Rams escape with a 14–7 victory that put them over .500 at 3–2.

It was certainly an odd bit of scheduling that had the Rams playing their second Monday night game in three weeks when they hosted the 4–1 Minnesota Vikings in week six. With their performance in this Monday night game, many thought the Rams had finally turned the corner as they annihilated their erstwhile tormentors 35–3 in a surprisingly one-sided contest. Again the Rams' ground game carried the load, running up 283 yards and three TDs to Minnesota's 98 rushing yards. Haden also threw a pair of TDs while completing 12 of 21 for 116 yards.

But the Rams weren't finished with their Jekyll and Hyde routine, and in week seven they were once more up against the New Orleans Saints, who had by then fallen to 1–5. The Rams wound up on the short end of a 27–26 score: it was one of only three games that New Orleans would win all year. Haden even had his best game since taking over for Namath, hitting 17 of 26 for 261 yards and two TDs, but it just wasn't enough. Obviously the Rams' problems could not be solved by a quarterback. They were misfiring on too many levels.

But that loss to the lowliest of teams in their division seemed —finally— to have flipped the switch. Knowing that they were a better team than what they had been showing, the Rams were angry and in week eight they took it out on the pathetic Tampa Bay Buccaneers, who were into their second season and had yet to win a game in the NFL. The Rams' 31–0 mugging of the Buccaneers kicked off a six-game winning streak that included victories over mediocre and struggling teams like the 2–6 Green Bay Packers in week nine, the 4–5 San Francisco 49ers in week 10, the 6–4 Cleveland Browns in week 11, and the 6–6 Atlanta Falcons in week 13. Beating teams that you're supposed to beat is a good sign of stability and consistency, but the real accomplishment of the winning streak was the week 12 victory over the defending Super Bowl champion Oakland Raiders. In a 20–14 game the 8–3 Rams bested the 9–2 Raiders, making it look like they really were the team they were thought to be.

Through it all Namath dutifully continued the ritual of taping his knee braces on and then merely watched from the sidelines. Even when they were losing it had never been this way in New York. It seemed a cruel fate for the likes of Broadway Joe. On the rare occasions when Knox did take Haden out of a game, it was rookie Vince Ferragamo that came in to relieve him, not Namath. Some reporters wondered about that and asked Knox if it wasn't rubbing salt in the wounds to Namath's pride. Knox saw things differently, explaining that there was just something too distasteful about relegating somebody like Joe Namath to the role of a mere mop-up man. And so Knox chose instead to leave him standing there on the sidelines, frequently alone and looking completely disconnected from everything happening around him.

Outwardly, Namath seemed to take it well, but it's hard to imagine that it wasn't tearing his heart out. Gone were the days when reporters by the dozens gathered around his locker after a game; now he might as well have been invisible as the reporters were all off at other lockers talking to players who actually participated in the games. Namath seemed resigned to his fate. "I was there and I had my chance," he said late in the season. "I played okay sometimes and sometimes I didn't. But that's football. When Pat got his chance, he played great."[27]

Namath had only high praise for Haden, and that was something that Haden was particularly appreciative of. Haden was always quick to praise Namath and to defend him when things were not going well early in the season. Remembering that other quarterbacks had copped pissy attitudes when Knox sat them down the prior season, it was a relief to Haden to have Namath not do likewise: in fact, Haden said, he had gotten nothing from Namath but encouragement after

Knox made the switch. Whatever his inner feelings truly might have been, Namath played it classy.

The Rams closed out their schedule with a 17–14 loss to the Washington Redskins. Entering the game down 17–0, Ferragamo threw a pair of fourth-quarter TDs that made the game look closer than it perhaps was, but the Rams' 10–4 record was enough to win their division for the fifth straight year and send them to the playoffs.

The Rams had to like their chances when they drew the Minnesota Vikings in round one. Not only had they humiliated the Vikings earlier in the season, but now Minnesota would be going into the post-season without their starting quarterback, Fran Tarkenton, who was out with a broken leg.

They say that in football weather is the great equalizer. That may be true. They also say it never rains in southern California. Apparently that is not so true. A heavy downpour turned the Los Angeles Coliseum into a swamp during the NFC Divisional playoff, and the Vikings got out to a 7–0 lead in the first quarter on a five-yard TD run by Chuck Foreman. It was all the Vikings would manage in the first half, but it was still more than the Rams could accomplish. Having been unable to get anything going, the Rams trailed 7–0 at halftime and speculation arose as to whether or not Namath might see action in the second half. But Knox had long since made his decision: he had made it back in October, and now he would live or die by it. As it turned out, it would be the latter. The weather did much to assure Haden's worst game of the year, completing 14 of 32 for 130 yards. He did throw a one-yard TD to Harold Jackson in the fourth quarter, but all that did was to cut Minnesota's margin of victory as the Rams went down in defeat, 14–7. Haden had also thrown three interceptions, half as many as he had thrown all season.

If Namath had come into the game would things have turned out any differently? Who can say? It's also impossible to say how the Rams' season would have gone had Namath remained at quarterback. Would the team have finished 10–4? Would they have even made the playoffs? The team's shaky start was really more a team problem than a quarterback problem. The 2–2 record accomplished with Namath at the helm is not easily waived off by pointing the finger at Namath, but while no one seemed to fault him for the opening day loss to Atlanta, the Monday night loss to Chicago was largely hung on him. Namath came into the game with three TDs and just one interception. He threw no TDs that night but added four interceptions to his tally in a game that saw him throw 40 passes. After Haden added six more passes in the final two minutes, that made the total a very un–Ram-like 46 passes. Not generally known as a passing team, the Rams had not thrown that many times in a game since 1970 when Roman Gabriel threw 48 in a losing effort against Namath's old crew, the Jets.

Even some of Namath's own teammates were bewildered by his play-calling that night, saying that when they were ahead 13–0 the play-calling gave the general feeling that they were playing catch-up. The impression of many was that, with a national television audience watching, Namath was passing needlessly in an attempt to put on a show and convince the naysayers that he was still the Namath of old. Of course, all these years later it's all just so much speculation.

Even though there is no telling how the season would have turned out had Knox chose to stick with Namath, there is certainly no faulting his decision. Whether or not the team would have pulled itself together and righted its course regardless of who the quarterback was, the fact remains that with Namath they were 2–2 whereas with Haden the were 8–2. Haden's 56.5 completion percentage was much better than Namath's 46.7, and while Haden's numbers were in no danger of shattering any records, the Rams had never relied on gaudy numbers from their quarterbacks. Their quarterbacks had always been serviceable, and in that sense Haden seemed well suited for the job.

One person who may have been inclined to fault Knox's choice was Carroll Rosenbloom. Tired of being a bridesmaid, Rosenbloom was anxious for a coach who could at least get him to the altar, and after the season was over he handed the job to assistant coach Ray Malavasi. Two years later, with Ferragamo at quarterback, Malavasi did get the Rams to the Super Bowl, though they lost to the Pittsburgh Steelers.

As for Knox, he moved on to Buffalo, and while he never did get to the Super Bowl as a head coach, he did lead the Bills to a couple of playoff seasons before embarking on a nine-year run as head coach of the Seattle Seahawks. In his first season coaching Seattle, Knox again managed to get to within one game of the Super Bowl despite the Seahawks' entering the playoffs as a 9–7 wildcard. But they went down in defeat to the San Diego Chargers in the 1983 AFC Championship. Even though he would direct the Seahawks to the playoffs a number of times after that, they would not come so close again during Knox's tenure. Knox ended his career back in Los Angeles to coach the Rams from 1992–1994, but it was anything but the good old days. During his three-year return engagement with the Rams, Knox's combined record was 15–33.

For Namath, it ended in 1977. In his four games that season he completed 50 of 107 passes for 606 yards with three TDs and five interceptions. Professional football will not see the likes of him again.

16

Canton Was Made for
the Likes of Broadway Joe

In the DVD release *NFL Films: Inside the Vault, 1960–1970*, Steve Sabol is narrating a segment containing clips of Joe Namath and he makes a rather startling statement. "After winning Super Bowl III" Sabol informs the viewers, "Joe never again defeated a team with a winning record."[1]

Wow. That's a very interesting piece of information. It would be quite compelling if it were only true. With Namath leading the way, the New York Jets beat the reigning Super Bowl champion Miami Dolphins at Shea Stadium in 1974, more than five years after the Jets' Super Bowl III triumph. The Dolphins were 11–3 in 1974. Okay, so Sabol missed one. Whoa, not so fast. Two weeks after their victory over Miami in 1974 the Jets beat the playoff-bound Buffalo Bills. The Bills' record that year was 9–5.

Somehow, it has much less dramatic effect to say that after winning the Super Bowl Namath only *twice* beat a team with a winning record: far more jarring to say that he *never* again beat a team with a winning record. Of course, Sabol was merely parroting an erroneous bit of information that somebody else had put forth. But the fact that someone in Sabol's position would impart such misinformation is surprising. Well, you have most probably heard the axiom, repeat a story often enough...

And so it is with many revisionists who seek to size up Namath's career. Look on the Internet and you will find no shortage of Namath naysayers putting forth the opinion that Broadway Joe is overrated, this notwithstanding the fact that he really never rates a mention when the presumed experts are naming the top quarterbacks of all time. In that sense, the term "overrated" seems fairly awkward when applied to Namath. To give the naysayers the benefit of a doubt, we have to assume that what they mean in saying that Namath is overrated is that his playing career does not merit the attention his name continues to garner. Were it down to mere numbers, then the critics might earn a credit, but Namath's fame runs much deeper than that, being attributable to that most potent combination of ability and personality. Still, it seems to gall Namath's detractors that he should receive so much attention. This is hardly new: in 1977 *Sporting News* columnist Melvin Durslag wrote that "no one in the history of sports has dredged so much wealth and so much notoriety out of such modest performance."[2]

So, you see that the opinion has been around for some time that Namath was a media creation, an instant celebrity resulting from his contract in 1965 for the then-unheard of amount of $427,000. Jets president Sonny Werblin defended the amount, saying that Namath was worth it not only because of his playing ability, but also for his charisma, which Werblin reasoned would sell tickets. It did: Werblin noted that within a week of signing Namath the Jets had taken in thousands of dollars in season ticket sales. Namath may not have only saved the New York Jets franchise: he may have saved the entire AFL.

In 1965 the Houston Oilers were playing in Rice Stadium and drawing a little over 30,000 per home game; they drew 32,445 when the Boston Patriots came to town, 34,670 against the Kansas City Chiefs, 35,729 against the Oakland Raiders, 28,126 against the Denver Broncos, 34,120 against the San Diego Chargers; when Namath and the Jets came to town attendance at Rice Stadium was 62,680. Namath's ability to help the attendance of opposing teams was not always that dramatic; in Denver, for instance, at Bears Stadium (later renamed Mile High Stadium) they were drawing between 27–33,000. A visit by the Jets only increased attendance to around 35,000, but in a struggling enterprise every little bit helped.

Had Namath signed with the NFL instead, there is every reason to believe that the AFL would have continued to pose little threat to the older league and that the eventual merger of the leagues would not have occurred. If this is true, then that alone warrants his place of high standing in the game's history, as well as his place in the Pro Football Hall of Fame, which more than anything else seems to set the naysayers off.

There are those, it would seem, who feel that Hall of Fame status is merely a matter of numbers and that no other contribution is of any real consequence. They would reduce the Hall of Fame to a mere body of statistical overachievers, and are wholly ignorant of a number of very relevant facts. Herewith, then, the basic objections raised by some against Namath's induction into the Hall of Fame:

A. Namath is only in the Hall of Fame because he won the Super Bowl;
B. Namath threw more interceptions than touchdowns;
C. Namath only completed 50 percent of his passes;
D. Namath had only three winning seasons.

So, let us now look at each of these objections.

Namath is only in the Hall of Fame because he won the Super Bowl

Of all the points raised by Namath's detractors, this one bears the most legitimacy. But it would be more accurate to say that had Namath not won *that* Super Bowl he would perhaps not be the iconic figure that he is. If some other quarterback had led some other AFL team to victory in Super Bowl III, then it would not have been nearly so spectacular had Namath won a subsequent Super Bowl (say IV, V, or VI)—just ask Len Dawson. Although Dawson and the Kansas City Chiefs were still considerable underdogs to the NFL's Minnesota Vikings, Kansas City's victory in Super Bowl IV hardly generated the same media storm. But then, why would it? Whereas it was once thought impossible for an AFL team to beat any NFL team, by the time Dawson and the Chiefs got there for Super Bowl IV it had already been accomplished.

So, what if it had been the Oakland Raiders that had beaten the Colts in Super Bowl III rather than Namath and the Jets? It would have been a big deal at the time since it would still have been the AFL's first triumph over the NFL, but the simple truth is that it would not have been an event of the same magnitude. Why? Ask yourself this: Would Daryle Lamonica have commanded the attention that Namath did in Super Bowl III? Would he have boasted, cajoled, and yes, *guaranteed* a victory as Namath had? It was Namath who turned Super Bowl III into a mammoth publicity magnet, an event that riveted the public's attention. Some wanted to see Namath succeed, others looked forward to watching him fail, but they all watched because of Namath.

It may have been Namath's charisma that sucked everyone in, but that couldn't beat the Colts. Beating the Colts took a combination of Namath's football smarts and his passing skills. Namath called an excellent game in Super Bowl III, and the Baltimore blitz that was supposed to grind him into the turf was no match for his quick release. He kept the Baltimore defense on its heels all day. He wasn't supposed to be able to do it. Could anybody else have done it?

A game once regarded as no more than an afterthought to the season — Super Bowls I and II gaining little more attention than the Pro Bowl would today — became the *purpose* for the season, suddenly morphing into the biggest event in sport. It was Namath who made it so. Hell, yeah, put that man in the Hall of Fame!

In our conspiracy-oriented modern culture it is no surprise that even Super Bowl III has generated its share of nut-fudge theories. Particularly on the Internet such foolishness abounds. Some have insinuated that the game was rigged, for financial reasons, of course. The inane logic of such fantasies is that both the AFL and the NFL stood to gain a great deal from the merger, which some will say could only be brought about by an AFL victory in a Super Bowl. If one is really to believe such nonsense, then one must explain why the two leagues should need to employ covert methods in order to merge. But of course what ultimately makes the whole notion so risible is the fact that *the merger had already been agreed to two years prior*! In fact, the first Super Bowl in January of 1967 was the result of the merger agreement.

It would be tempting to conclude that there is a generation of sportswriters today populated by buffoons who are wholly ignorant of history, but it is worth reminding ourselves that we are talking here about the Internet, a place where information is frequently suspect. Let's face it, any cretin can write for a website. The truth, however, is that this kind of ignorance permeates so much of the arguments against Namath's Hall of Fame status.

Namath threw more career interceptions than touchdowns

One of the principal knocks against Namath is the number of interceptions he threw. Only twice in his 13-year professional career did his TDs exceed his interceptions in a season. The numbers were usually close, but several times in Namath's career the difference was substantial (27 interceptions to 19 TDs in 1966, 28 interceptions to 15 TDs in 1975, 16 interceptions to four TDs in 1976). That being the case, Namath wound up with more career interceptions than TDs, a concept very foreign to fans of today's game. The opinion of many nowadays is that no good quarterback — certainly no *great* quarterback — will have more interceptions than TDs, and by the standards of today's game that is a reasonable opinion. The problem for the critics is that Namath isn't playing today's game and that it is foolish to judge him, or any other quarterback from eras past, by today's standards.

The fact is that the rules of today's game are specifically designed to make passing easier. After a noticeable downward trend in offensive scoring over successive seasons in the NFL, it was decided in the late 1970s that the game needed an infusion of offense to better hold the interest of fans. The dominance of defenses like that of the Pittsburgh Steelers of the 1970s was thought to be draining excitement from the sport and it was determined that some rule changes were in order to keep the public tuned in and the gravy train rolling.

One change that favored the offense was the decision to allow blockers to extend their arms. Prior to that, blockers had been required to keep their elbows bent and their forearms across their chest. Allowing them to extend their arms would lessen the incidence of holding penalties (defensive players would often get their arms under a blocker's, increasing the chance of their arms getting hooked and a holding penalty being called) and make it easier for linemen to protect the quarterback, as well as clearing some room on running plays.

The rule that proved to be a much greater advantage to the passing game was the introduction of a five-yard zone extending from the line of scrimmage beyond which defenders would not be allowed to bump the receiver to impede his progress. It is a rule known by everyone today, but apparently not everyone knows that it hasn't always been in place, or just how dramatic an effect it has had on the game.

Nineteen seventy-seven turned out to be the lowest scoring season in the NFL since 1942, and saw the lowest number of offensive touchdowns since 1938. The new rules — which succeeded in creating opportunity for more explosive offense — went into effect in 1978, one year too late for Namath to share in reaping any benefit. There is a generation of fans — and apparently some writers — entirely ignorant of this fact today.

When Namath was playing, a defender was able to impede a receiver's route — even knock him on his ass anywhere on the field — at will, provided the ball was not in flight at that moment. Under those circumstances it was much easier for a defender to stay with a receiver, and consequently to gain position to intercept the ball. It was more difficult for receivers to run their routes and get to where a quarterback expected them to be. Considering the degree to which the rules currently favor the passing game it seems very unlikely that a quarterback of consequence will now wind up with more interceptions than touchdowns over the course of a career, or even a season. If we look at the interception percentages of Hall of Fame quarterbacks, they break down from best to worst as follows:

2.6	Joe Montana		5.1	Otto Graham
	Steve Young			Norm Van Brocklin
3.0	Troy Aikman		5.4	Terry Bradshaw
	Dan Marino		5.6	Y.A. Tittle
3.1	John Elway		5.8	Joe Namath
3.4	Warren Moon		6.6	Sonny Jurgensen
3.7	Jim Kelly			Bobby Layne
	Roger Staubach		6.8	Sammy Baugh
4.1	Fran Tarkenton		6.9	George Blanda
4.3	Dan Fouts		7.0	Ace Parker
4.4	Bart Starr		7.6	Sid Luckman
4.9	Len Dawson		7.9	Bob Waterfield
	Johnny Unitas		10.4	Dutch Clark
5.0	Bob Griese			

Even a fan of only moderate discernment should be able to tell at a glance that the top of the list is populated exclusively by players of the post–1978 era. Namath doesn't rate near the top among Hall of Fame quarterbacks in this category, but he isn't at the bottom either. His 5.8 percent places him between Y.A. Tittle and Sonny Jurgensen, both regarded by true historians of the game as among the most noteworthy of quarterbacks.

Even so, the fact that Namath threw more career interceptions than TDs is a real point of contention among critics. There are some who even suggest that *no* quarterback with more interceptions than touchdowns should be in the Hall of Fame, a sure sign of someone whose memory and knowledge of the game don't extend very far back. If you were to eliminate quarterbacks with more interceptions than TDs from the Hall of Fame then you would have to remove some of the most revered players in the game's history, including Y.A. Tittle, Norm Van Brocklin, Sammy Baugh, Bob Waterfield, Bobby Layne, George Blanda, and Ace Parker. Having said that, it also needs to be said that among Hall of Fame quarterbacks Namath's TD-to-interception ratio is tied for worst with Bobby Layne's at minus 47.

Joe Namath could certainly throw some interceptions. It just always seemed to be a part of his game. One factor may have been how often he threw. Particularly in his early career it was not uncommon for him to throw more than 40 passes in a game (in 1966 and '67 he led the AFL in both passing attempts and completions). More passes increases the odds of more interceptions — that's just simple logic, and since Namath's interception percentage was no higher or lower than a lot of other quarterbacks of his time we have to take this into account. When he led the AFL with 27 interceptions in 1967, his interception percentage was 5.7. One could then logically conclude that, had other quarterbacks thrown as many passes as Namath, they would have matched or surpassed his interception count.

Something else to consider was Namath's reputation for throwing deep. The longer the ball is in the air, the greater the chance that a defender will get under it. Unquestionably, this was also a contributing factor. Interestingly, another factor would seem to be Namath's confidence in his own ability. When it came to passing, he was something of a gunslinger — fearless, perhaps even careless — always believing he could rifle it in there. "They knock him for the interceptions," New York assistant coach Ken Meyer once said. "Well, he's intercepted because he feels he's quick and strong enough and takes chances others wouldn't."[3]

This leads us into the next category of contention:

Namath only completed 50 percent of his passes

It only stands to reason that if Namath were inclined to throw deep, then he would have a lower completion percentage. If he were one to throw more drop-off passes in the flat then his percentage would have been higher. A look now at Hall of Fame quarterbacks and their completion percentages, highest to lowest:

64.3	Steve Young	56.5	Sammy Baugh
63.2	Joe Montana	56.2	Bob Griese
61.5	Troy Aikman	55.8	Otto Graham
60.1	Jim Kelly	55.2	Y.A. Tittle
59.4	Dan Marino	54.6	Johnny Unitas
58.8	Dan Fouts	54.3	Norm Van Brocklin
58.4	Warren Moon	51.9	Terry Bradshaw
57.4	Bart Starr	51.8	Sid Luckman
57.1	Len Dawson	50.3	Bob Waterfield
	Sonny Jurgensen	50.1	Joe Namath
57.0	Roger Staubach	49.0	Bobby Layne
	Fran Tarkenton	47.7	George Blanda
56.9	John Elway	45.6	Dutch Clark

Again, the dominance of post–1978 quarterbacks at the top of the list highlights the significance of the rule changes that were enacted. Yet, if we leave more modern quarterbacks out, Namath's completion percentage is still below that of all of his contemporaries. Was he that less accurate than Len Dawson and Bart Starr? If not, then it could only mean that he was throwing longer, lower-percentage passes than they were. But was he? To determine this we need to look at the average yards-per-completion. The average yards-per-attempt is useless in making this determination since it averages in even incompletions. A tendency to throw deep will necessarily result in more incompletions, which will in turn render a lower average yards-per-attempt. On the other hand, a lower yards-per-attempt average could also result from poor throwing; or both, therefore — useless. If you really want to know if a quarterback had a real tendency to throw longer, you have to go by average yards-per-completion, and — highest-to-lowest — Hall of Fame quarterbacks break down as follows in that respect:

16.2	Sid Luckman	14.2	John Unitas
16.1	Otto Graham	14.1	George Blanda
14.8	Bobby Layne	14.0	Ace Parker
14.7	Joe Namath	13.8	Terry Bradshaw
14.6	Bob Waterfield		Norm Van Brocklin

13.7	Bart Starr	12.8	Fran Tarkenton
13.6	Y.A. Tittle	12.5	John Elway
13.5	Roger Staubach	12.4	Dan Marino
13.4	Len Dawson		Warren Moon
13.2	Dutch Clark		Steve Young
	Sonny Jurgensen	12.3	Jim Kelly
13.1	Dan Fouts	11.9	Joe Montana
13.0	Bob Griese	11.4	Troy Aikman
12.9	Sammy Baugh		

Obviously, Namath rated higher than his contemporaries (and most everyone else) in this category. Conclusion: yes, Namath was indeed a deep passer.

Namath only had three winning seasons

Of the four areas of objection raised by critics, this one is the most inherently dishonest in as much as the implication is that, of his 13 seasons as a professional quarterback Namath had a losing record in 10 of those seasons. Namath did not have 10 losing seasons: he had five. The Jets, on the other hand, had six losing seasons in that time, but it is important to remember that Namath was out with injuries much of that time.

Counting only games in which Namath played, his personal won-loss-tie record by season breaks down as follows:

Winning seasons (4)
1967 (8–5–1)
1968 (11–3)
1969 (10–4)
1972 (7–6)
Losing seasons (5)
1965 (5–7–1)
1970 (1–4)
1973 (2–4)
1975 (3–11)
1976 (2–9)

.500 seasons (4)
1966 (6–6–2)
1971 (2–2)
1974 (7–7)
1977 (2–2)

Five losing seasons, four winning seasons, and four seasons breaking even; overall, that amounts to a won-loss-tie record of 66–70–4. A losing record, but that is factoring in games in which Namath did not start. A quarterback's official record is usually calculated by games in which he started. If we go by the book, then, Namath's won-loss-tie record comes out to 62–63–4: still a losing record, even if only just barely. Ah, but wait — we're not including postseason games. Namath had a 2–1 record in postseason, which then brings his overall quarterback record to 64–64–4. Still not a winning record, but nor is it a losing record. But then, they don't count postseason in career stats. Why? They just don't, so take it or leave it and break it down however you like.

Certainly other Hall of Fame quarterbacks have better — in many cases *far* better — won-loss records, but then those quarterbacks likely didn't play for teams as dysfunctional as the New York Jets. The Jets were the football dynasty that never was: after winning the Super Bowl they should have gone on to another championship or two, but it was a team frequently fraught with an abundance of melodrama and conflict. Much of that came down to Namath, of course. There was his 1969 "retirement" over the Bachelors III commotion, as well as his occasions breaking training by leaving camp unauthorized and his tendency to arrive late to camp most times. It was often noted by players that the team had two sets of rules — one set for Namath, and another for everyone else. The players most often brushed it off by saying that they held no grudges about it, but in reality it would be much against human nature for people not to take exception.

The Jets' 1970 opener against Cleveland showed a team in which the players were frequently not on the same page. That year Namath had failed to report to camp, claiming personal reasons. His absence and perceived lack of commitment — he was very non-committal about when or if he would be ready to play — caused linebacker Al Atkinson to fly into a tantrum, and Atkinson himself quit the team (albeit briefly). Both Namath and Atkinson were back in time for the season, but by then the damage seemed to have been done, and the team was obviously short of being a shining example of congruity. In a team sport, unity is one of the most vital of components. Without it, even a talented team can sink quickly, as the Jets did that year. Of course, injuries were a major factor that year as well — Matt Snell was leading the league in rushing when he was lost for the season in week three with a ruptured Achilles, and Namath would be lost two weeks later with a broken wrist.

There were other resentments: there was talk of Namath's close relationship with team president Sonny Werblin in the 1960s. Werblin loved taking Namath to parties and nightclubs and showing him off: the type of favoritism shown Namath likely rubbed some players the wrong way, perhaps even those who liked him personally.

There is also the fact that, as Namath's star grew brighter, he became increasingly more difficult for Weeb Ewbank to manage. He struck some players as being unanswerable to anyone, and if players are not answerable to the coach then a team has lost its core of authority. It should surprise no one, then, that the ship begins to drift — there needs be a commander at the helm to ensure the team stays the course. Once that foundation of authority is lost, things can easily weaken. None of which is to suggest that Namath is responsible for the Jets not continuing as a championship team. He was, after all, one player — the most important, to be sure — and a championship team cannot rely on just one man.

The Jets, on the other hand, frequently did find themselves pinning all their hopes on him: missing that one player can still make a world of difference. Beginning in 1970, the frequent injuries that caused Namath to miss most of the 1970, '71, and '73 seasons fairly well sunk any hopes the Jets had of further championship runs. By the time Namath was back to another full season in 1974 it was hardly the same team that had won the Super Bowl years before. It was a rebuilding team then, populated mostly by players who had no knowledge of what it was to win a championship.

Now, for those enamored of numbers and such, a brief recap of some of Namath's career highlights. In 1966 Namath led the AFL is passing attempts (471), completions (232), and yardage (3,379), as well as average yards-per-game (241.4). In 1967 he again led the AFL in those categories, completing 258 of 491 passes for an average of 286.2 yards per game. He also led the AFL that season in yards-per-attempt (8.2) and yards-per-completion (15.5), but of course the big achievement that year was Namath's record-setting 4,007 yards passing, an unprecedented amount in professional football at that time. No one had ever thrown for over 4,000 yards in a season, and it would be a good while before anyone would again. It is significant that Namath's record would not be broken until 1979, after the aforementioned rule changes and the extension of the season from 14 to 16 games.

Some have suggested that leading the AFL in passing as Namath did was no big deal since the general view was that it was an inferior league, but in 1972 Namath led the NFL in passing yards (2,816), touchdown passes (19), yards-per-attempt (8.7), yards-per-completion (17.4), and yards-per-game (216.6). What drags Namath's career average down in most every category is his final two years with the Jets. The 3–11 seasons of 1975 and '76 were very detrimental to Namath's numbers across the board, the only exception being his league-leading 14.6 yards-per-completion in 1975.

But enough of all this! We can all agree that, while Namath's numbers fall short of some other Hall of Fame quarterbacks in certain categories, in a general overview he is no better than some and no worse than others (keep in mind, we are talking about that being *among other Hall of Fame quarterbacks*). We have also examined the reasons, so perhaps we can agree to set the stats aside and admit that, while Namath was certainly capable of putting up big numbers, his value to the sport went well beyond that.

It may well be the case that Namath's importance to the growth of the popularity of the sport of professional football cannot be overstated. He was a lightning rod that drew attention to the game variously through charisma, drama, and an awesome passing ability, all of which made him exciting to watch and ultimately combined to make the spectacle of the Super Bowl.

"When you think about it," wrote Joe Falls in *The Sporting News* in January of 1969, "Namath did more to change the face of professional football with his performance in the Super Bowl than any man has since … George Halas unveiled the new-fangled 'T' formation…."[4]

Many of Namath's critics today are people who would have no memory or knowledge of just how big a deal it all was, or of how big a deal *he* was. Namath's very entry into professional football amped everything up a notch. "Joe Willie Namath was a happening," wrote Dan Jenkins in *Sports Illustrated* in 1966.[5] How many athletes can be described that way? It's a description that befits a Hall of Famer, and the Hall of Fame was made for players who can be so described.

But what about the people who played alongside him? What do they say? More interestingly, what about those who played against him? And what about those coaches of opposing teams? *What about the people who were there?* In an interview with NFL Films years after the fact, former Kansas City linebacker Willie Lanier recounted a play that he said he would never forget. He recalled playing the Jets at Shea Stadium in 1969 and actually experiencing a feeling of joy come over him as he watched Namath arch a beautiful 34-yard touchdown pass to George Sauer. How often will you hear a defensive player tell of feeling joyous at the sight of their opponent scoring? It takes a kind of magic to evoke such sentiments from an opponent, a kind of magic that is crucial to sport, but hard to come by.[6]

Namath certainly had the respect of defensive backs, who got a hard tutorial on his abilities. "If he wanted to pick on you alone he'd have no sweat kicking you up to Canada," said Miami defensive back Bob Petrella. "He can make any defensive back in the league look terrible."[7]

Washington cornerback Mike Bass noted that if Namath were given even the slightest amount of time, then it was virtually impossible to defend against him[8], while Houston cornerback Miller Farr was struck by Namath's ability to look the defender off. "He can be looking at one receiver," said Farr, "and he'll suddenly whip it to another receiver."[9]

In 1968 Paul Governali, a one-time quarterback with the Boston Yanks of the 1940s and later tailback with the New York Giants, sat and watched Namath pick the San Diego Chargers to pieces. Governali seems to have been awestruck. "It's like a clinic," he said. "No one ever threw the ball like this guy."[10]

Dallas receiver "Bullet" Bob Hayes had a similar regard for Namath's passing ability, calling Namath the best passer he had ever seen. "There is a certain place a receiver wants the ball when he runs out and cuts," Hayes explained. "Namath puts it there every time. Namath is the greatest."[11]

And the coaches? They analyzed films, they stood on the sidelines watching: what did they see? Hall of Fame coach Bill Walsh said that there was no more exciting quarterback to watch than Joe Namath. Walsh spoke of Namath's dropback, of the graceful, fleet-footed motion, likening it to a ballet. It was a dropback that John Madden — another Hall of Fame coach — called the best looking drop that he'd ever seen. More than that, Madden said that Namath's release and his pass were also the best he'd ever seen. It was enough to make Madden go into an opposing team's locker room after a game for the only time in his coaching career just to shake Namath's hand.[12]

Sid Gillman, who in 18 years had coached the Los Angeles Rams, San Diego Chargers, and Houston Oilers, certainly had plenty of opportunity to see Namath firsthand. His assessment was pretty direct. "I don't believe I have seen a quarterback to equal Joe Namath," Gillman said.[13] After losing to the Jets in the 1968 AFL Championship, Oakland coach John Rauch said that in his estimation Namath was the best quarterback in the league.[14]

Maybe you have heard of Paul Brown. If not, one could easily conclude that your knowledge of the game is — let us be kind — incomplete. Brown concluded that Namath was in a class all his own.[15]

Is there any more revered name in football than Vince Lombardi? Lombardi weighed in on Namath as well. "Joe Namath is the greatest pure thrower of footballs I have ever seen," Lombardi said.[16]

But what would any of those guys know? They only lived the game. Surely they wouldn't know more than some fat-assed blogger sitting at his PC staring at rows of numbers. But who better to sum it all up than a man who spent most of his career protecting Namath. Offensive lineman Winston Hill put it simply, but there was an eloquence and a purity to his words that somehow imbued them with an unassailable truth. "Joe's special," Hill said. "And I don't like to think of him as anything other than special."[17] And there are those who will argue that someone that special has no place in the Hall of Fame? *The hell you say!*

Chapter Notes

Chapter 1

1. David Maraniss, *When Pride Still Mattered: A Life of Vince Lombardi* (New York: Simon & Schuster 1999), p. 496.

2. Maury Allen, *Joe Namath's Sportin' Life* (New York: Paperback Library, 1969), p. 118.

3. Sandy Smith, "Broadway Joe: Rebel with a Nightclub for a Cause," *Life,* June 20, 1969, Vol. 66, No. 24, p. 23.

4. Larry Bortstein, *Super Joe: The Joe Namath Story* (New York: Tempo Books, 1969), p. 58.

5. "The Rugged Path To Glory," *Super Joe Namath,* 1969, p. 36.

6. Bortstein, *Super Joe,* 20.

7. "'Bama Stuns Tulane 44–6," *Hobbs Daily News-Sun* (NM), September 30, 1962.

8. Oscar Fraley, "Namath Lauded As Top Hero In Bowls," *Daily Plainsman* (Huron, SD), January 2, 1963.

9. Bortstein, *Super Joe,* p. 42.

10. "J. Namath Suspended, Will Miss Sugar Play," *Anniston Star* (AL), December 10, 1963.

11. George Smith, "Joe Namath Guides Tide Over Georgia, 31–3," *Anniston Star* (AL), September 20, 1964.

12. George Smith, *Anniston Star* (AL), Sunday, October 11, 1964.

13. Steve Traylor, "Alabama Steps Over Volunteers," *Anniston Star* (AL), October 18, 1964.

14. "Namath, Hobbled by Injury, Shot Tech Down With Pinpoint Passes," *The Sporting News,* January 2, 1965, p. 32.

15. "Namath Signs Jets' Pact For $400,000," *Times Recorder* (Zanesville, OH), January 3, 1965.

16. Jimmy Burns, "Texas Stops Namath — When It Counts," *The Sporting News,* January 16, 1965, p. 35.

17. Dick Couch, "Texas Upsets Alabama," *Lowell Sun* (MA), January 2, 1965.

18. "Namath Greatest — Royal," *Ogden Standard-Examiner* (UT), January 2, 1965.

19. Lou Sahadi, *The Long Pass* (New York: Bantam Books, 1969), p. 97.

20. Robert H. Boyle, "Show-Biz Sonny and His Quest For Stars," *Sports Illustrated,* July 19, 1965, Vol. 23, No. 3, p. 72.

21. "The Rugged Path To Glory," *Super Joe Namath,* 1969, p. 30.

22. Lawrence Linderman, "Playboy Interview: Joe Namath," *Playboy,* December 1969, Vol. 16, No. 12, p. 94.

23. "The Rugged Path To Glory," *Super Joe Namath,* 1969, p. 31.

24. Allen, *Joe Namath's Sportin' Life,* p. 64.

25. "Ryan Sees Namath, Hikes His Own Value to Million," *The Sporting News,* January 16, 1965, p. 35.

26. Allen, *Joe Namath's Sportin' Life,* p. 65.

27. Bert Rosenthal, "'I'm the Scaredest Quarterback They've Ever Seen!'— Joe Namath," *All-Star Sports,* February 1965, Vol. 2, No. 1, p. 60.

28. Allen, *Joe Namath's Sportin' Life,* p. 61.

29. Ibid., p. 70.

30. "The Rugged Path To Glory," *Super Joe Namath,* 1969, p. 30.

31. Rosenthal, "'I'm the Scaredest Quarterback They've Ever Seen!'— Joe Namath," p. 11.

32. John Devaney, "Joe Namath: The $400,000 Challenge," *Sport,* August 1965, Vol. 40, No. 2, p. 88.

33. Rich Koster, "Injury Tab $2 Million For Pro Football in 1969," *The Sporting News,* November 14, 1970.

34. John Devaney, "Can Football Live Without Joe Namath?" *Sport,* July 1972, Vol. 54, No. 1, p. 92.

35. Sahadi, *The Long Pass,* p. 103.

36. Will Grimsley, "'I'm Gonna Try,' Says Namath in Response to Jeers of the Old Pros," *Fairbanks Daily News-Miner,* January 8, 1965.

37. Dick Young, "Namath Slated For Operation," *Post-Tribune* (Jefferson City, (MO), December 22, 1966.

38. Bert Rosenthal, "'I'm the Scaredest Quarterback They've Ever Seen!'— Joe Namath," p. 9.

39. "'Law Of Jungle' Aids Joe," *Lima News* (OH), October 8, 1967.

40. From *Broadway Joe: The Joe Namath Story* on *A&E Biography.*

41. Tex Maule, "Joe Bites the Astrodust," *Sports Illustrated,* October 9, 1972, Vol. 37, No. 15, pp. 40–41.

42. "Bonus Stars Won't Pay Price for Grid Stardom," *Appleton Post-Crescent* (WI), January 7, 1965.

43. "Jets High-Priced Namath Is Shelved," *Charleston Gazette,* August 15, 1966.

44. Bortstein, *Super Joe,* pp. 124–125.

45. "Namath of the Jets," *Newsweek,* September 15, 1969, p. 60.

46. Paul Zimmerman, "Why They Still Pick On Joe Namath," *Touchdown,* 1969, p. 8.

47. Dave Anderson, "Namath: Is He Really That Good?" *Pro Football 1969,* p. 80.

48. "Jets Coach Fumes Over Officials In Raider Game," *Big Spring Herald* (TX), December 18, 1967.

49. Devaney, "Can Football Live Without Joe Namath?" p. 92.

50. "Joe Namath and the Jet-Propelled Offense," *Time,* October 16, 1972, Vol. 100, No. 16, p. 46.

51. Devaney, "Can Football Live Without Joe Namath?" p. 94.

52. "Joe Namath and the Jet-Propelled Offense," p. 54.

Chapter 2

1. Bob Curran, *The Violence Game* (New York: Macmillan, 1966), p. 4.

2. Will Grimsley, "'I'm Gonna Try,' Says Namath in Response to Jeers of the Old Pros," *Fairbanks Daily News-Miner,* January 8, 1965.

3. Larry Fox, "Joe Namath: His Troubles and Triumphs," *Sport,* June 1966, Vol. 41, No. 6, p. 76.

4. Mike Rathet, "Jets Confident Namath Can Do the Job," *Appleton Post-Crescent* (WI), August 1, 1965.

5. Dick Couch, "Namath Telephone Operator?" *Charleston Daily Mail* (WV), September 3, 1965.

6. "Jets' Taliaferro 'Poor Man's Quarterback,'" *Gazette-Mail* (Charleston, WV), September 12, 1965.

7. "Jets Say Illegal Play Cost Game," *Corpus Christi Times,* September 13, 1965.

8. Milton Richman, "Jet Fans Boo Mike Taliaferro; Save Cheers For Joe Namath," *Simpson's Leader-Times* (Kitanning, PA), September 21, 1965.

9. "Namath: Not Good Debut," *Des Moines Register,* September 20, 1965.

10. "Namath 'Disgusted' In First Pro Start," *Oakland Tribune,* September 27, 1965.

11. George C. Langford, "Namath" $400,000 Impression," *El Paso Herald-Post,* September 27, 1965.

12. Dave O'Hara, "Joe Namath Goes Route As Jets Beat Patriots," *Bridgeport Post* (CT), November 11, 1965.

13. Frank Dyer, "'We Give 'Em Away'— Holovak," *Lowell Sun* (MA), November 15, 1965.

14. Dave O'Hara, "Joe Namath Goes Route As Jets Beat Patriots.

15. Mike Rathet, "Namath's Four Touchdown Passes Send Jets Winging," *Fresno Bee,* November 22, 1965.

16. George C. Langford, "Pats Gamble, Win, 27–23," *Lowell Sun* (MA), November 29, 1965.

17. "Parilli To Romeo Pass Upsets New York Jets," *Nashua Telegraph* (NH), November 29, 1965.

18. George Ross, "Joe Says Blame Joe," *Oakland Tribune,* December 13, 1965.

19. Jack Smith, "Raiders Eliminated Despite 24–14 Win," *Daily Review* (Hayward, CA), December 13, 1965.

20. "Namath Takes Blame, Coach Hurls Charge," *Daily Review* (Hayward, CA), December 13, 1965.

21. Ed Levitt, "Namath, Ben Feud," *Oakland Tribune,* December 13, 1965.

22. Frank Litsky, "Gogolak Blanked First Time As Pro," *New York Times,* December 20, 1965.

23. Jack Gallagher, "All-Stars Had Too Many Guns In Skinning Buffalo, 30–19," *The Sporting News,* January 29, 1966.

Chapter 3

1. "Namath Claims Jets Can Win As Teams Prepare For Games," *Jefferson City Post-Tribune* (MO), August 10, 1966.

2. Larry Bortstein, *Super Joe: The Joe Namath Story* New York: Tempo Books, 1969), p. 83.

3. "Injury to Namath Not 'Cheap Shot,' Says Coach," *San Antonio Light,* August 15, 1966.

4. Ibid.

5. Ibid.

6. Mike Recht, "Jets Coach Must Decide On Starting Quarterback," *Las Cruces Sun-News* (NM), September 8, 1966.

7. "Namath Still No. 1 QB For Jets, Ewbank Says," *European Stars and Stripes* (Darmstadt, Hesse, Germany), September 12, 1966.

8. Ibid.

9. Murray Chass, "Namath's Passing Gives Jets One-Sided Victory," *Las Cruces Sun-News* (NM), September 19, 1966.

10. Vito Stellino, "Namath sparkles in Jets' triumph," *New Castle News* (PA), September 19, 1966.

11. Chass, "Namath's Passing Gives Jets One-Sided Victory."

12. Burgin Dave, "Joe Namath Makes $400,000 Look Cheap," *Daily Times-News* (Burlington, NC), October 3, 1966.

13. George McGuane, "'Fourth Perioditis' For Patriots," *Lowell Sun* (MA), October 3, 1966.

14. "Houston Oilers Bidding For Upset Over Jets," *Big Spring Daily Herald* (TX), October 10, 1966.

15. "Jets Grounded by Oiler Gusher; Suddenly There's a Race in East," *San Antonio Light,* October 17, 1966.

16. Ibid.

17. "Jets' Namath Steams Following 24–21 loss," *Lima News* (OH), October 24, 1966.

18. "Joe the Jet Nailed by Texas Dan," *Oakland Tribune,* October 24, 1966.

19. Milton Richman, "Namath Hears His First Boos," *Bridgeport Post,* October 31, 1966.

20. Ibid.

21. Gary A. Edwards, "Division Lead Held By Bills," *Daily Messenger* (Canandalgua, NY), November 14, 1966.

22. Ed Schoenfeld, "Jets' Sideline Strategy Session Credited for Tie," *Oakland Tribune,* December 4, 1966.

23. Ibid.

24. "Mike Holovak Faults Defense for Setback," *Bridgeport Post,* December 18, 1966.

25. William N. Wallace "Victory Is Tied to Namath's Maturity," *New York Times,* December 18, 1966.

26. "Mike Holovak Faults Defense for Setback."

27. Larry Felser, "Around the AFL," *The Sporting News,* October 22, 1966.

28. Barney Kremenko, "Jets Soar on Joe's Improved Reading," *The Sporting News,* October 22, 1966.

29. Bortstein, *Super Joe;* p. 87.

30. "The Rugged Path To Glory," *Super Joe Namath,* 1969, p. 23.

31. "Knee Surgery Faces Jets' Namath Again," *The Fond du Lac Commonwealth Reporter* (WI), December 22, 1966.

Chapter 4

1. Dick Young, "'No Scrambling' for Jets' Namath," *News & Tribune* (Jefferson City, (MO), August 6, 1967.
2. Arthur Daley, "Shuffle To Buffalo," *Nashua Telegraph* (NH), September 11, 1967.
3. Ben Olan, "Dolphins Worry About Namath; Ailing Snell Will Miss Game," *Danville Register* (VA), October 1, 1967.
4. Murray Janoff, "Ouch! Those Bunions Spur Jets' Boozer," *The Sporting News,* October 21, 1967.
5. Bert Rosenthal, "'I'm the Scaredest Quarterback They've Ever Seen!'—Joe Namath," *All-Star Sports,* February 1968, Vol. 2, No. 1, p. 61.
6. Ibid.
7. George Ross, "Namath Says Ben and Dan Dirty," *Oakland Tribune,* October 5, 1967.
8. George Ross, "Look Back at Namath," *Oakland Tribune,* October 9, 1967.
9. "'Ridiculous Play,' says Namath," *Syracuse Herald Journal,* October 16, 1967.
10. Lee Andre, "Joe Namath — Superman or Myth?" *Pro Sports,* March 1968, Vol. 4, No. 2, p. 62.
11. "Green Bay Scout Respects Namath," *Times Standard* (Eureka, CA), October 30, 1967.
12. "Stram Slams Critics of Mitchell After Cornerback Intercepts Two," *Ogden Standard Examiner* (UT), November 6, 1967.
13. Vito Stellino, "Willie Makes Up, Cornerback Stars," *El Paso Herald-Post,* November 6, 1967.
14. Dave O'Hara, "Pats Hopes Eliminated; Jets Register 29–24 Win," *Nashua Telegraph* (NH), November 20, 1967.
15. George McGuane, "Patriots Bow in Thriller, 29–24," *Lowell Sun* (MA), November 20, 1967.
16. "'It was great to score'— Little," *Syracuse Herald,* December 4, 1967.
17. "Chiefs Derail Jets' Express," *Bridgeport Post,* December 11, 1967.
18. Larry Close, "'Raiders Won't Let Up'— Rauch," *Daily Review* (Hayward, CA), December 12, 1967.
19. "Raiders: 38–29 — Weeb Wails," *Fresno Bee,* December 18, 1967.
20. Ibid.

Chapter 5

1. Dick Young, "Jets have problems," *Daily Capital News* (Jefferson City, MO), January 9, 1968.
2. "Namath Signs New Contract," *Playground Daily News* (Fort Walton Beach, FL), May 20, 1968.
3. Murray Olderman, "Between you 'n' me," *Post-Register* (Idaho Falls, ID), June 2, 1968.
4. Milton Gross, "A Busy Week For Sonny Werblin," *Lima News* (OH), June 2, 1968.
5. Lou Sahadi, *The Long Pass* (New York: Bantam Books, 1969), pp. 156, 182.
6. Sahadi, *The Long Pass,* p. 147.
7. Murray Janoff, "Jets and Joe Expect to Fly Away With Kentucky Babe," *The Sporting News,* August 17, 1968.
8. "Jets, Minus Namath, Lose To Oilers In Exhibition Game," *Las Cruces Sun-News* (NM), August 13, 1968.

9. Arthur Daley, "Exit For Sonny," *Cumberland Times* (MD), June 2, 1968.
10. Vito Stellino, "Namath problems are NY Jets problems," *Las Vegas Optic,* August 20, 1968.
11. Murray Olderman, "Namath Sit-Out Rankles," *Chillicothe Constitution-Tribune* (MO), August 24, 1968.
12. William N. Wallace, "Trading of Namath Is Suggested to Solve Friction With Jets," *New York Times,* August 15, 1968.
13. Murray Chass, "New York Jets Believe This Is Their Year," *Chillicothe Constitution-Tribune* (MO), August 29, 1968.
14. "Jets Hold Ball To Beat Chiefs," *Bridgeport Post,* September 16, 1968.
15. McGuane, George. "Blocked Punt Costly," *Lowell Sun* (MA), September 23, 1968.
16. Bert Rosenthal, "Joe Namath — Why He Battles On," *All-Star Sports,* February 1969, Vol. 3, No. 1.
17. Ibid.
18. "Turnabout Bills' 5 Thefts Upset Jets," *Oakland Tribune,* September 30, 1968.
19. "'I Stink,' Says Jets' Namath," *Bridgeport Post,* October 14, 1968.
20. Ibid.
21. "Namath Leads Jets To Win," *Bridgeport Post,* October 21, 1968.
22. Ibid.
23. Larry Felser, "Gerry Philbin: Bounty Hunter," *Quarterback,* October 1969, Vol. 1, No. 1, p. 73.
24. "Critics Bugging Namath; Six-Tilt TD-Pass Drouth [sic]," *The Sporting News,* November 23, 1968.
25. Larry Felser, "AFL east," *The Sporting News,* November 23, 1968.
26. George Ross, "Sullen Jets Want Raiders in Rematch," *Oakland Tribune,* November 18, 1968.
27. Felser, "AFL east."
28. "Namath Sinks the Chargers," *Oakland Tribune,* November 25, 1968.
29. Dave Anderson, "Namath: Is He Really That Good?" *Pro Football 1969,* p. 6.
30. "Raiders Don't Expect Jets To Fall as Easily as Chiefs," *Press-Courier* (Oxnard, CA), December 25, 1968.
31. "Raiders Shocked By Ease Of Victory Over Chiefs," *Danville Register* (VA), December 25, 1968.
32. Bob Valli, "Jets Are Favored By 3," *Oakland Tribune,* December 24, 1968.
33. "Shea Meteorologist Silent," *Oakland Tribune,* December 26, 1968.
34. "Namath: Happiest day of my life," *Pocono Record* (The Stroudsburgs, PA), December 30, 1968.
35. Murray Olderman, "On the Wings Of Broadway," *Anniston Star* (AL), January 1, 1969.
36. "Joe Namath guides Jets to berth in Super Bowl," *Pocono Record* (The Stroudsburgs, PA), December 30, 1968.
37. Milton Richman, "Namath was a mess after game with Oakland team," *Delta Democrat-Times,* January 1, 1969.
38. "Namath: happiest day of my life."
39. "Namath, Maynard ... Couple Of Jets Who Are Always Ready For Foes," *High Point Enterprise* (NC), January 2, 1969.

40. Murray Janoff, "A Super Bowl Special — Can Weeb Tame Colts," *The Sporting News,* January 11, 1969.

41. "Colts Blank Browns For NFL Crown, 34–0," *Frederick News-Post* (MD), December 30, 1968.

42. "Namath: happiest day of my life."

Chapter 6

1. William Wallace, "Super 11 Vs. Super Passer," *Billings Gazette,* January 1, 1969.

2. Fran Tarkenton, "Fran Tarkenton Likes Colts Over Jets in Super Bowl," *Delaware County Daily Times* (Chester, PA), January 7, 1969.

3. "Colts' Defense Best Shula Has Ever Seen," *Post-Standard* (Syracuse, NY), January 8, 1969.

4. "Jets, Colts In Countdown," *Weirton Daily Times* (WV), January 10, 1969.

5. Wallace, "Super 11 Vs. Super Passer."

6. Larry Felser, "Gerry Philbin: Bounty Hunter," *Quarterback,* October 1969, Vol. 1, No. 1, p. 73.

7. Maury Allen, *Joe Namath's Sportin' Life* (New York: Paperback Library; 1969), p. 9.

8. "Weeb Defends Joe's Boo-Boo," *Post-Standard* (Syracuse, NY), January 8, 1969.

9. "Shula for the Defense — Colts, Jets Even," *Wisconsin State Journal* (Madison), January 4, 1969.

10. Ralph Bernstein, "Al Atkinson Believes Ball-Control Major Factor," *Abilene Reporter-News,* January 6, 1969.

11. "Jets Are Not Awe Struck by Colts," *Ogden Standard-Examiner* (UT), January 7, 1969.

12. Dave Anderson, "Namath Preps for Biggest Challenge," *San Antonio Express,* January 6, 1969.

13. Ibid.

14. "Weeb Defends Joe's Boo-Boo," *Post-Standard* (Syracuse, NY), January 8, 1969.

15. Milton Richman, "Colts Aren't Mad, Joe, But..." *Billings Gazette,* January 8, 1969.

16. Ralph Bernstein, "Namath Raps Earl Morrall," *Progress-Index* (Petersburg, VA), January 7, 1969.

17. Ralph Bernstein, "Morrall Says 'Let Joe Talk,'" *Cedar Rapids Gazette* (IA), January 10, 1969.

18. Mike Rathet, "Rag Arm to Earl the Pearl," *Walla Walla Union-Bulletin* (WA), January 4, 1969.

19. "John Unitas Isn't Miffed," *Panama City News* (FL), January 9, 1969.

20. Bernstein, "Morrall Says 'Let Joe Talk.'"

21. "Talk is of Morrall, Namath as Super Bowl kick-off nears," *Oneonta Star* (NY), January 11, 1969.

22. Maury Allen, *Joe Namath's Sportin' Life* (New York: Paperback Library; 1969), p. 157.

23. Rathet, "Rag Arm to Earl the Pearl."

24. "Namath, Colt In Hot Episode," *Dominion-News* (Morgantown, WV), January 8, 1969.

25. "Super Bowl: Joe vs. The World," *Bedford Gazette* (PA), January 11, 1969.

26. Milton Richman, "Jets Are Talking Tougher Than Colts," *San Mateo Times* (CA), January 8, 1969.

27. Felser, "Gerry Philbin: Bounty Hunter."

28. Jerry Izenberg, "And Wearing White Shoes..." *Pro!,* September 26, 1976, Vol. 7, No. 3, p. 12B.

29. "Too Hungry To Lose It, Says Shula," *Bedford Gazette* (PA), January 11, 1969.

30. "Super Bowl: Joe vs. The World."

31. Ibid.

32. "Are 18-Point Odds on Colts In Super Bowl Too Much?" *Iowa City Press-Citizen,* January 8, 1969.

33. "Jets, Colts Hone Attacks For Sunday's Super Bowl," *Ogden Standard-Examiner* (UT), January 10, 1969.

34. Murray Olderman, "NFL Mystique Shrouds Jets Effort," *Albuquerque Tribune,* January 9, 1969.

35. Jack Fulp, "Namath Real Threat..." *Progress-Index* (Petersburg, VA), January 12, 1969.

36. Dan Cook, "Greetings From Miami," *San Antonio Express and News,* January 12, 1969.

37. Glen May, "A letter to Joe Namath," *Drumheller Mail* (Canada), January 8, 1969.

38. Charlie Vincent, "Dear Joe!" *San Antonio Express and News,* January 12, 1969.

39. Lou Sahadi, *The Long Pass.* (New York: Bantam Books, 1969), p. 200.

40. Ibid. pp. 200–201.

41. Tex Maule, "Say It's So, Joe," *Sports Illustrated,* January 20, 1969, Vol. 30, No. 3, p. 15.

42. Bob Oates, "Famed Colts Defense Was Picked to Pieces By Broadway Joe, Royal Ruler of Jet Set," *The Sporting News,* January 12, 1969, p. 4.

43. Ralph Bernstein, "Jets Strafe Colts In Super Bowl Contest, 16–7," *Morning Herald* (Uniontown, PA), January 13, 1969.

44. "Broadway Joe draws spotlight in Jets' dressing room," *Post-Tribune* (Jefferson City, (MO), January 13, 1969.

45. Ibid.

46. Allen, *Joe Namath's Sportin' Life,* pp. 173–174.

47. Lowell Reidenbaugh, "Docile Colts Back Namath Guarantee,'" *The Sporting News,* January 25, 1969, p. 4.

48. Larry Bortstein, *Super Joe: The Joe Namath Story* New York: Tempo Books, 1969), p. 243.

49. Ben Funk, "Namath Called Win 'One For The AFL,'" *Morning Herald* (Uniontown, PA), January 13, 1969.

50. Milton Richman, "Broadway Joe Sparks Jets — Even On Bench," *Times Recorder* (Zanesville, OH), January 13, 1969.

51. Ibid.

52. Ben Funk, "Namath's Needles (Verbal and Aerial) True Super Upset," *Moberly Monitor-Index,* January 13, 1969.

53. Art Daley, "Colts 'Suffered Twice' After Defeat," *Appleton Post-Crescent* (WI), January 13, 1969.

54. Ibid.

55. Reidenbaugh, "Docile Colts Back Namath Guarantee," p. 8.

56. "No Big Plays For Colts," *Times Recorder* (Zanesville, OH), January 13, 1969.

57. "Colts: Time Ran Out, And We Didn't Make Big Play," *Des Moines Register,* January 13, 1969.

58. Bill Tanton, "Mike Curtis: Portrait of a Killer," *Quarterback,* October 1969, Vol. 1, No. 1, p. 65.

59. Mike Curtis, "I Don't Care What They Call Me, I Play This Game For Keeps," *All Pro 1969 Football,* p. 18.

60. "Colts: Time Ran Out, And We Didn't Make Big Play."

61. Lawrence Linderman, "Playboy Interview: Joe Namath," *Playboy,* December 1969, Vol. 16, No. 12, p. 118.

62. "Star Threats: Knee, Rain," *Pacific Stars and Stripes* (Tokyo), January 20, 1969.

63. Ibid.

Chapter 7

1. "Namath Threatens To Quit Football," *Tucson Daily Citizen,* June 6, 1969.

2. "Joe First Warned Three Months Ago," *San Antonio Express and News,* June 7, 1969.

3. "Eating the ball or words, it's still hard," *Oneonta Star* (NY), June 10, 1969.

4. William N. Wallace, "No Change Foreseen In Namath Affair," *Corpus Christi Caller-Times,* June 15, 1969.

5. "Namath Sacrifices Career for Principle," *San Antonio Express and News,* June 8, 1969.

6. "Jets Think Joe To Return," *Cedar Rapids Gazette,* June 12, 1969.

7. Ralph Bernstein, "Players Investigate Joe Namath's Case," *Corpus Christi Caller-Times,* June 15, 1969.

8. "Hassle with Sample leaves coach injured," *News & Tribune* (Jefferson City, MO), August 3, 1969.

9. Ibid.

10. Ira Berkow, "Johnny Sample's Nasty Book Getting Bigger By The Day," *Gastonia Gazette* (NC), August 16, 1969.

11. Charles Chamberlain, "Jets Squeeze Past," *Moberly Monitor-Index* (MO), August 2, 1969.

12. "Grid Cardinals Stave Off Jets," *Modesto Bee and News-Herald* (CA), August 10, 1969.

13. "Big Red displays class in 13–6 win over Jets," *Jefferson City Post-Tribune* (MO), August 11, 1969.

14. "Big Red's DeMarco says Jets 'will kill' Giants this weekend," *Jefferson City Post-Tribune* (MO), August 12, 1969.

15. "Namath-Led Jets Thrash Giants," *Raleigh Register* (Beckley, WV), August 18, 1969.

16. Robert Moore, "Jets Riddle NFL Pride," *Albuquerque Tribune,* August 18, 1969.

17. "Namath-Led Jets Thrash Giants."

18. Ted Meier, "Doomsday Gang waits for Namath," *Las Vegas Optic,* September 3, 1969.

19. "Namath belittles Cowboys' defense," *Post-Tribune* (Jefferson City, MO), September 5, 1969.

20. "Chargers Back in Race," *Oakland Tribune,* September 29, 1969.

21. "Joe Namath Leads Jets Over Boston," *Portsmouth Herald* (NH), October 10, 1969.

22. Ibid.

23. "'They Ran Right Over Us,' Says Bengal Coach Brown," *Lima News* (OH), October 13, 1969.

24. "Jets down Oilers, take AFL lead; Maynard snares seven passes," *Lowell Sun* (MA), October 21, 1969.

25. Fred McMane, "'On Our Way,' Says Maynard," *El Paso Herald-Post,* October 21, 1969.

26. "'Run, Joe, Run' Say Defenders," *Bridgeport Post,* October 27, 1969.

27. Ibid.

28. "Turner Hot Foots Miami Off a Cliff," *Oakland Tribune,* November 3, 1969.

29. Mike Bryson, "Jets Continue To Win Despite Inept Performance," *Bridgeport Post,* November 10, 1969.

30. Ibid.

31. "That Isn't Just Luck All Over The Jets," *San Antonio Light,* November 10, 1969.

32. "Defense Rests For N.Y. Jets," *Bridgeport Post,* November 24, 1969.

33. "Raiders Pounce On Jets' Gauntlet," *Oakland Tribune,* November 30, 1969.

34. Blaine Newnham, "Raiders Choice By 3-and-a-half," *Oakland Tribune,* November 30, 1969.

35. Dave Anderson, "Raiders Whip Jets As Lamonica Shines," *Charleston Gazette* (WV), December 1, 1969.

36. Ken Rappaport, "Raider Raiding Party Whips Jets," *Las Cruces Sun-News* (NM), December 1, 1969.

37. Bill Soliday, "Raiders win glorified street battle," *Daily Review* (Hayward, CA), December 1, 1969.

38. Rappaport, "Raider Raiding Party Whips Jets."

39. Ed Levitt, "Airport Love-in," *Oakland Tribune,* December 1, 1969.

40. Murray Janoff, "Air Arm of Chiefs Skyjacks Jets in Shaky Knee Duel," *The Sporting News,* January 3, 1970.

41. "2nd Place Chiefs Overthrow Jets." *Wisconsin State Journal* (Madison), December 21, 1969.

42. "Uncertain Airways Bother Namath," *Wisconsin State Journal* (Madison), December 21, 1969.

43. "Taylor Called Big Play," *Oakland Tribune,* December 21, 1969.

44. "2nd Place Chiefs Overthrow Jets."

45. "Joe Blames Wind—And KC Defense," *Oakland Tribune,* December 21, 1969.

Chapter 8

1. "Namath Sees Stars—Hollywood Style," *Des Moines Register,* May 27, 1970.

2. "Problems Pile Up—Namath Career Up in Air," *Press-Telegram* (Long Beach, CA), August 6, 1970.

3. "The Trouble With Joe Is..." *Press Telegram* (Long Beach, CA), August 6, 1970.

4. "Atkinson Quits, Rips At Namath," *The Stars and Stripes* (Garmstadt, Hesse, Germany), August 7, 1970.

5. "Problems Pile Up—Namath Career Up in Air."

6. "Problems Dog Him, So Joe May Retire," *The Stars and Stripes* (Garmstadt, Hesse, Germany), August 7, 1970.

7. "The Trouble With Joe Is...."

8. Hank Hollingworth, "Broadway Joe: A Man of His Word, They Say," *Independent Press-Telegram* (Long Beach, CA), June 15, 1969.

9. "Where did you go, Joe?" *Daily Capital News* (Jefferson City, MO), August 5, 1970.

10. "Atkinson quits Jets; blast stings Namath," *Delaware County Daily Times* (Chester, PA), August 6, 1970.

11. "Poor Ol' Joe Has Problems ... Like ... He Needs More Money," *Kokomo Tribune,* August 7, 1970.

12. Ben Thomas, "Namath plays hard-to-find," *Las Vegas Optic,* August 12, 1970.

13. Mike Rathet, "Broadway Joe finally goes to Jets Hempstead camp," *Las Vegas Daily Optic,* August 19, 1970.

14. "Namath checks into camp, complains of knee ailment," *Daily Capital News* (Jefferson City, MO), August 19, 1970.

15. "'Bragging Rights' At Stake In Jets-Giants Game," *Las Cruces Sun-News* (NM), August 23, 1970.

16. "Namath's Knee Survives Saints' Deadly Shot," *The Light* (San Antonio), September 7, 1970.

17. "Jones Sparks Browns To Win Over Jets," *Las Cruces Sun-News* (NM), September 22, 1970.

18. "Disappointed Namath draws Browns' raves," *Pocono Record* (Stroudsburg, PA), September 22, 1970.

19. George McGuane, "Namath lauds Pats," *Lowell Sun* (MA), September 28, 1970.

20. "Snell, Boozer Pace N.Y. Jet Victory over Patriots, 31–21," *Nashua Telegraph* (NH), September 28, 1970.

21. "Cocky Shaw Lifts Buffalo Past Jets," *Oakland Tribune,* October 5, 1970.

22. From *America's Game: The 1970 Baltimore Colts,* NFL Films production.

23. Milton Richman, "Unitas, Namath Have Had Better Days," *Lebanon Daily News,* October 19, 1970.

24. "Joe Namath in pain ... and Jets are hurting, too," *Jefferson City Post-Tribune* (MO), October 20, 1970.

25. Don Kowet, "What Joe Namath Learned Last Year By Not Playing," *Pro Football Almanac 1971.*

Chapter 9

1. "Hopeful After Namath Surgery," *Des Moines Register* (IA), August 9, 1971.

2. Larry Felser, "American football conference," *The Sporting News,* April 10, 1971.

3. "Namath Hurt As Lions Tame Jets," *Star-News* (Pasadena, CA), August 8, 1971.

4. Ibid.

5. Jerry Green, "NFC central," *The Sporting News,* August 28, 1971.

6. "Namath Hurt As Lions Tame Jets."

7. "Knife for Namath," *Albuquerque Tribune,* August 9, 1971.

8. "Injured Namath Speaks," *Las Cruces Sun-News* (NM), August 17, 1971.

9. Bob Oates, "QBs Lead Casualty List ... Says Oft-Injured Nelsen," *The Sporting News,* September 4, 1971.

10. "Roller-Coaster Career Of Al Woodall Heads Downhill," *Post-Herald and Register* (Beckley, WV), October 17, 1971.

11. Red Smith, "Joe Willie returns home," *Billings Gazette,* November 29, 1971.

12. From *Broadway Joe: The Joe Namath Story* on A&E Biography.

13. Murray Janoff, "Namath Dazzler of Old — But He Spots Mistakes," *The Sporting News,* December 11, 1971.

14. Gary Kale, "Namath Returns; Jets Still Lose," *Las Cruces Sun-News* (NM), November 29, 1971.

15. Bruce Lowitt, "Field generals return; Namath tosses bombs," *Lowell Sun* (MA), November 29, 1971.

16. "Cowboys in massacre," *Lowell Sun* (MA), December 5, 1971.

17. Mike Rathet, "Jets Dump Pats, 13–6; Chiefs Edge Oakland," *Nashua Telegraph* (NH), December 13, 1971.

18. "Joe Namath admires Plunkett's knees," *Billings Gazette,* December 13, 1971.

19. "Namath Will Return," *The Bee* (Danville, VA), December 20, 1971.

Chapter 10

1. Milton Richman, "Namath Matures as New York Jets' Quarterback," *News Journal* (Mansfield, OH), August 16, 1972.

2. "Namath Signs Rich Pact," *Albuquerque Journal,* August 2, 1972.

3. "'Broadway' Joe Namath inks reported $500,000 contract," *Daily Capital News* (Jefferson City, MO), August 2, 1972.

4. Herb Gluck, "Joe Namath Predicts: 'The Old Namath Will Come Back,'" *Sports Today,* October 1973, Vol. 4, No. 5, p. 47.

5. "Might be year for Pittsburgh," *Las Vegas Optic,* August 15, 1972.

6. Robert Opotzner, "New York Rivals Set for Big Tilt," *Bridgeport Post,* August 20, 1972.

7. Joe Frohlinger, "Giants Intercept 5 of Namath's Passes," *Times Standard* (Eureka, CA), August 21, 1972.

8. "Morton and Namath Slated As Starters," *Las Cruces Sun-News* (NM), August 25, 1972.

9. F.M. White, "Winners, Losers," *Odessa American,* August 28, 1972.

10. "Ewbank Pleased With Jets' Play," *Bridgeport Post,* September 11, 1972.

11. Ed Fite, "Dallas Bad, 'Had to Comeback' — Landry," *El Paso Herald-Post,* August 28, 1972.

12. Murray Janoff, "Revived Namath Scoffs at Injury Jinx," *The Sporting News,* October 7, 1972.

13. "Ewbank Praises Jets After Routing Buffalo," *Bridgeport Post,* September 18, 1972.

14. Larry Felser, "AFC eastern," *The Sporting News,* October 14, 1972.

15. "A Day Of Firsts For Joe And Jets," *Kingsport Times* (TN), September 25, 1972.

16. "Joe Namath and the Jet-Propelled Offense," *Time,* October 16, 1972, Vol. 100, No. 16, p. 47.

17. Felser, "AFC eastern."

18. Bruce Lowitt, "Wooly Joe Bombs Colts," *Silver City Daily Press* (NM), September 25, 1972.

19. "Griese Took Jets' Secondary Apart On Field, Not In Locker Room Following 27–17 Victory," *The Bee* (Danville, VA), October 9, 1972.

20. George McGuane, "Jets smother Pats; running game did it," *Lowell Sun* (MA), October 16, 1972.

21. Dave O'Hara,. "Jets Wallop Patriots, 41–13," *Nashua Telegraph* (NH), October 16, 1972.

22. "Namath, Bell Combine As Jets Nip Baltimore," *Bridgeport Post* (CT), October 23, 1972.

23. Ibid.

24. "Namath Not Quitting," *The Bee* (Danville, VA), November 13, 1972.

25. "Morrall can't respect Namath's style of life," *Montana Standard* (Butte), November 17, 1972.

26. Dick Lundin, "Morris, Morrall Pace Dolphins to Crown," *News Tribune* (Fort Pierce, FL), November 20, 1972.

27. Larry Paladino, "Roof falls on Jets in last quarter as Lions break tie for 37–20 romp," *Albuquerque Tribune,* November 24, 1972.

28. "Lions claw Jets 37–20, both eye playoff berths," *Montana Standard* (Butte), November 24, 1972.

29. "Jets' Howfield Gives Himself Big Birthday Gift," *San Antonio Light,* December 4, 1972.

30. Ibid.

31. Tom LeMarre, "Jets Out of Playoffs," *Oakland Tribune,* December 12, 1972.

32. Ed Levitt, "Joe Wins Fans," *Oakland Tribune,* December 12, 1972.

33. Dave Anderson, "Joe Namath: Why He Has To Win Again," *Pro Quarterback,* November 1973, Vol. 3, No. 10, p. 60.

34. Levitt, "Joe Wins Fans."

35. Bill Soliday, "Raiders team up on Namath, Jets," *Daily Review* (Hayward, CA), December 12, 1972.

36. *The Sporting News,* December 30, 1972, p. 10.

37. LeMarre, "Jets Out of Playoffs."

38. Joe Sargis, "Oakland Meets Pittsburgh Or Cleveland In Playoffs," *Raleigh Register* (Beckley, WV), December 12, 1972.

39. Chuck Wilfong, "Super joe is mellowing..." *Daily Chronicle* (Centralla, WA), December 15, 1972.

40. Lowell Hickey, "Maynard says NFL too dirty," *Daily Review* (Hayward, CA), December 12, 1972.

41. "Joe Namath Could End Title Race For Cleveland Browns," *Times Recorder* (Zanesville, OH), December 12, 1972.

42. "Browns Gave It Their Best Shot, But Fell Short," *Kingsport Times* (TN), December 18, 1972.

Chapter 11

1. Charles Morey, "Rating the Quarterbacks," *Sport World,* December 1973, Vol. 12, No. 6, p. 10.

2. "Namath holds key to Jets' fortunes," *Jefferson City Post-Tribune* (MO), August 8, 1973.

3. "Giants, Browns take key exhibitions," *Syracuse Herald Journal,* August 20, 1973.

4. "Cards' rally defeats Jets," *Daily Capital News* (Jefferson City, MO), August 28, 1973.

5. Frank Brown, "Nitschke Calls It Quits, Riggins Leaves Jets' Camp," *The Progress* (Clearfield, PA), August 29, 1973.

6. Joe Carnicelli, "Maynard Dealt To Cards," *Las Cruces Sun-News* (NM), September 11, 1973.

7. "Jets swap Maynard to Cards," *Pocono Record* (The Stroudsburgs, PA), September 11, 1973.

8. "Pack pounds Jets, 23–7," *Syracuse Herald Journal,* September 18, 1973.

9. Mike O'Brien, "Pack Frustrates Namath, Jets," *Fond du Lac Reporter* (WI), September 18, 1973.

10. "No surgery for Namath," *Billings Gazette* (MT), September 25, 1973.

11. "Namath hurt against Colts, at best will miss 6–8 weeks," *Bennington Banner* (VT), September 24, 1973.

12. "Namath Injures Shoulder; Jets Trounce Colts, 34–10," *Bridgeport Post,* September 24, 1973.

13. "No surgery for Jet Joe," *Syracuse Herald Journal,* September 24, 1973.

14. "Namath Injures Shoulder; Jets Trounce Colts, 34–10."

15. Larry Felser, "AFC eastern," *The Sporting News,* October 13, 1973.

16. Anderson, Dave. "'Where Did the Time Go?' Asks Namath," *New York Times,* November 19, 1973.

17. Rick Van Sant, "Jets Lose To Cincinnati; Namath's Return Too Late," *Raleigh Register* (Beckley, WV), September 19, 1973.

18. "Bengals Spoil Namath's Return," *Wisconsin State Journal,* September 19, 1973.

19. "Paul Brown: 'We were lucky,'" *The Advocate* (Newark, OH), September 19, 1973.

20. Van Sant, "Jets Lose To Cincinnati; Namath's Return Too Late."

21. "Paul Brown: 'We were lucky.'"

22. Murray Chass, "Time, Bengals Foil Late Heroics in 20–14 Setback," *New York Times,* November 19, 1973.

23. "Colts' rally falls short," *The Capital* (Annapolis, MD), December 3, 1973.

24. Joe Carnicelli, "Namath's Future Unsure, Sunday May Be End," *Daily Messenger* (Canandaigua, NY), December 13, 1973.

25. "Tears Flow At Weeb's Farewell," *The Bee* (Danville, VA), December 17, 1973.

26. "Sunday's Game May Be Namath's Last," *Raleigh Register* (Beckley, WV), December 17, 1973.

27. "Tears Flow At Weeb's Farewell."

28. "Namath Retire?" *Las Cruces Sun-News,* December 17, 1973.

29. "Namath's Future In Doubt," *Panama City News Herald* (FL), December 13, 1973.

30. Bob Oates, "NFC western," *The Sporting News,* December 15, 1973.

Chapter 12

1. "Namath Says He'll Play Out Option," *Charleston Daily Mail* (WV), February 5, 1974.

2. "Namath says no to contract," *Newport Daily News* (RI), June 26, 1974.

3. "Namath to Play Out Contract," *Charleston Gazette* (WV), June 27, 1974.

4. "NFL strike begins," *Hutchinson News* (KS), July 1, 1974.

5. Don Bloom, "Raiders Overpower Namath, Jets In 31–6 Laugher," *Fresno Bee,* September 8, 1974.

6. "Interceptions Hurt Jets In 24–16 Loss to Chiefs," *Bridgeport Post,* September 16, 1974.

7. "Bears Come to Life Too Late," *Wisconsin State Journal,* September 23, 1974.

8. Joe Mooshil, "Jets Manage 23–21 Win Over Aroused Bear Team," *Bridgeport Post,* September 23, 1974.

9. "Bills Dump Jets, 16–12, In Windy Rich Stadium," *Bridgeport Post,* September 30, 1974.

10. *The Sporting News,* October 12, 1974, p. 54.

11. John R. Skinner, "Namath's Rally Just Misses, 21–17," *Times Record* (Troy, NY), October 8, 1974.

12. "Dolphins Outlast Namath, Jets, Score 21–17 Victory," *Kingsport Times* (TN), October 8, 1974.

13. "Dolphins' Ginn Offsets Late Jets Passing Show," *Des Moines Register,* October 8, 1974.

14. Joe Carnicelli, "Jones, Mitchell Team Up to Spur Colts Past Jets," *The Sporting News,* November 2, 1974.

15. Larry Felser, "AFC eastern," *The Sporting News,* November 9, 1974.

16. "Jets Scare Rams In 20–13 Loss," *Times Record* (Troy, NY), October 28, 1974.

17. Joe Hendrickson, "McCutcheon, Stukes 'Homer,'" *Star-News* (Pasadena, CA), October 28, 1974.

18. Murray Janoff, "Namath may go to Rams," *Press-Telegram* (Long Beach, CA), October 28, 1974.

19. "Pastorini, Oilers Sabotage Jets," *The News* (Port Arthur, TX), November 4, 1974.

20. Joe Carnicelli, "Bomb by Pastorini Lands on Jets and Oilers Annex Third," *The Sporting News,* November 16, 1974.

21. "Namath passes Jets to overtime victory," *Billings Gazette,* November 11, 1974.

22. "Namath vaults Jets past foe in overtime," *North Adams Transcript* (MA), November 11, 1974.

23. "Jets' defense steals show, four passes," *Newport Daily News* (RI), November 18, 1974.

24. "Caster Hauls In Two TDs," *Post-Standard* (Syracuse, NY), November 25, 1974.

25. "Jets continue streak, waltz past Chargers," *Press-Telegram* (Long Beach, CA), December 2, 1974.

26. Bruce Lowitt, "Jets Upset Bills, 20 to 10, In Namath's 'Shea Farewell,'" *Bridgeport Post,* December 9, 1974.

27. Ibid.

28. Larry Siddons, "Namath Remains Non-Committal About Future," *Bridgeport Post,* December 16, 1974.

Chapter 13

1. "Namath, Jets Can't Agree On Right Figures," *Abilene Reporter-News,* July 26, 1975.

2. "900Gs Make Joe Highest Grid Earner," *Pacific Stars and Stripes* (Tokyo), August 1, 1975.

3. "Patriots on strike, will boycott today's game," *Independent Press-Telegram* (Long Beach, CA), September 14, 1975.

4. Joe Carnicelli, "War Drums Sound in Jets Camp For Match with Bills Sunday," *Middleboro Daily News* (KY), September 20, 1975.

5. "Bills Trounce Jets, 42–14, As O.J. Simpson Runs Wild," *Bridgeport Post,* September 22, 1975.

6. "O.J. and Bills romp past New York," *Appleton Post-Crescent* (WI), September 22, 1975.

7. "Jets Overwhelm Weak Chiefs' defense, 30–24," *Atchison Globe* (KS), September 29, 1975.

8. "Namath's arm rips Patriots," *North Adams Transcript* (MA), October 6, 1975.

9. Brent Kallestad, "Big Plays Help Vikings Beat New York, 29–21," *Albert Lea Tribune,* October 13, 1975.

10. Bruce Lowitt, "Dolphins Crush Jets, 43–0; Namath Has Six Intercepted," *Bridgeport Post,* October 20, 1975.

11. Joe Carnicelli, "Dolphins Splash 43–0 in Muddy Jet Pond," *News Tribune* (Fort Pierce, FL), October 20, 1975.

12. Bruce Lowitt, "Dolphins Crush Jets, 43–0; Namath Has Six Intercepted."

13. Larry Felser, "AFC eastern," *The Sporting News,* November 8, 1975.

14. "Jones leads Colts past Jets, 45–28," *Frederick News-Post* (MD), October 27, 1975.

15. "Young QB Passes Colts Over Namath, N.Y. Jets," *Daily Times* (Salisbury, MD), October 27, 1975.

16. Gerald Eskenazi, "Colts Sack Namath 7 Times In Defeating Jets, 45–28," *Charleston Gazette* (WV), October 27, 1975.

17. Joe Carnicelli, "Rising Colts Conquer Tumbling Jets," *The Sporting News,* November 8, 1975.

18. Bruce Lowitt, "Jets' Gamble Backfires In 24–23 Loss To Bills," *Bridgeport Post,* November 3, 1975.

19. Ibid.

20. "Miami Stops Jets, 27–7," *Albuquerque Journal,* November 10, 1975.

21. Les Kjos, "Dolphins' Long TD Plays Seal Fate of Namath, Jets," *The Sporting News,* November 22, 1975.

22. Tom Whitfield, "Prancing Colts Land Swift Kick in Teeth to Fading Jets," *The Sporting News,* November 29, 1975.

23. "Colts beat up Jets, 52–19," *The Capital* (Annapolis, MD), November 17, 1975.

24. "Namath takes back seat to Bert Jones," *Press-Telegram* (Long Beach, CA), November 17, 1975.

25. Joe Carnicelli, "Cardinal 'Laugher' Ruins Shipp's Debut With Jets," *The Sporting News,* December 6, 1975.

26. "Cardinals finally win in a walk, 37–6," *Alton Telegraph* (IL), November 24, 1975.

27. "Joe: I let everyone down," *Syracuse Herald-Journal,* December 6, 1975.

28. "Chargers Take Measure of Jets As Curfew 'Intercepts' Namath," *The Sporting News,* December 27, 1975.

29. Bruce Lowitt,. "Pokes warm up for cold future," *Paris News* (TX), December 22, 1975.

30. "Namath Will Return," *Daily Freeman* (Kingston, NY), December 22, 1975.

31. "Namath to Return After Poor Season," *Salt Lake Tribune* (UT), December 22, 1975.

Chapter 14

1. "Namath eyes Rams," *The Independent* (Long Beach, CA), January 19, 1976.

2. Will Grimsley, "Next move in trade furor up to Namath," *Des Moines Register,* January 22, 1976.

3. Bob Wolfe, "Namath works to convince Jets he must go," *Corpus Christi Times,* February 25, 1976.

4. Murray Janoff, "Broadway Joe Makes a Pitch — 'Rams Could Win Super Bowl With Me,'" *The Sporting News,* March 3, 1976.

5. "Giants take road trip — to N.Y." *Pocono Record* (The Stroudsburgs, PA), August 9, 1976.

6. "Giants Nick Jets," *Hobbs Daily News-Sun* (NM), August 12, 1976.

7. "Raiders clobber tired NY Jets," *Modesto Bee,* August 15, 1976.

8. "Riggins: face in the crowd for Redskins?" *The Bakersfield Californian*, June 11, 1976.

9. Mike Harris, "Browns take to air to down Jets," *Evening Independent* (Massillon, OH), September 13, 1976.

10. "Broncos Destroy Jets, 46–3," *Bridgeport Post*, September 20, 1976.

11. Tom Rife, "Dolphin Defense Shuts Off Jets, 16–0," *Naples Daily News* (FL), September 27, 1976.

12. Tim Hunt, "Broadway Joe slipping?" *Daily Review* (Hayward, CA), October 4, 1976.

13. Charles Tonelli, "49ers not too excited with win," *Daily Review* (Hayward, CA), October 4, 1976.

14. William Schiffmann, "49ers Win ... But The Smell," *Fresno Bee*, October 4, 1976.

15. Milton Richman, "Namath Still on Top of Game," *News Journal* (Mansfield, OH), October 10, 1976.

16. "Namath sinks Tampa," *Press-Telegram* (Long Beach, CA), November 15, 1976.

17. David Bushnell, "Jets overrun Bucs 34–0," *Times Herald Record* (Middletown, NY), November 15, 1976.

18. Bruce Lowitt, "Namath's passes foil Tampa's bid," *Times Record* (Troy, NY), November 15, 1976.

19. Bruce Lowitt, "Pats victimize Namath, upend Jets, 38–24," *Kennebec Journal* (Augusta, ME), November 22, 1976.

20. Joe Carnicelli, "Young defensive Pat players excel in win over N.Y. Jets," *Berkshire Eagle* (Pittsfield, MA), November 22, 1976.

21. David Bushnell, "Jets lose to Patriots 38–24," *Times Herald Record* (Middletown, NY), November 22, 1976.

22. Tom Whitfield, "Bert Jones Puts On Show For Old Hero Joe Namath," *The Sporting News,* December 11, 1976.

23. "Namath's Future Is In Doubt," *Daily Freeman* (Kingston, NY), December 13, 1976.

Chapter 15

1. "Namath wants Rams, but is feeling mutual?" *Wisconsin State Journal* (Madison), January 8, 1977.

2. "Namath likes Jet coach but not organization," *Post-Register* (Idaho Falls), January 28, 1977.

3. "Namath sees himself as No. 2," *Wisconsin State Journal* (Madison), July 19, 1977.

4. Rich Roberts, "Rams blocked out, 22–17," *Independent Press-Telegram* (Long Beach, CA), August 7, 1977.

5. "Can Hayden [sic] Beat Namath?" *Las Cruces Sun-News* (NM), August 14, 1977.

6. "'Quarterback clash' fails to materialize," *Daily Times* (Primos, PA), August 15, 1977.

7. Jim Cour, "Namath's Ram Debut Not Very Spectacular," *Daily Courier* (Connellsville, PA), August 15, 1977.

8. "Rams, Namath Falter," *Press-Courier* (Oxnard, CA), August 22, 1977.

9. Rich Roberts, "Rams can't protect Namath — or the lead," *The Independent* (Long Beach, CA), August 22, 1977.

10. "Chiefs force turnovers, whip Rams," *Salina Journal* (KS), August 29, 1977.

11. "Are Rams Finished Anyway?" *Nashua Telegraph* (NH), September 16, 1977.

12. Joe Hendrickson, "Falcons are smarter than Rams," *Star-News* (Pasadena, CA), September 19, 1977.

13. Rich Roberts, "Quickie Quiz: What's wrong with Rams?" *The Independent* (Long Beach, CA), September 19, 1977.

14. "Namath calls shots as Rams win, 20–0," *Wisconsin State Journal* (Madison), September 26, 1977.

15. Roberts, Rich. "Like old times for Rams: Strongarm Eagles, 20–0," *The Independent* (Long Beach, CA), September 26, 1977.

16. Joe Hendrickson, "Rams back in same fraternity," *Star-News* (Pasadena, CA), September 26, 1977.

17. "Jaworski: 'I don't think the Rams are that much better,'" *Bucks County Courier Times* (Levittown, PA), September 26, 1977.

18. Garry Niver, "Meyer — Breaks and Penalties," *San Mateo Times*, October 3, 1977.

19. Rich Roberts, "Chi Bears shock Rams," *Press-Telegram* (Long Beach, CA), October 11, 1977. The expletives were removed from the *Press-Telegram,* but were inferred and easily surmised.

20. Ibid.

21. "Namath Bashed, Bears Hold Off Rams Bid in Rain," *Press-Courier* (Oxnard, CA), October 11, 1977.

22. "Rams fuming over 'cheap shots,'" *Star-News* (Pasadena, CA), October 12, 1977.

23. "Haden to get another chance Sunday," *Valley News* (Van Nuys, CA), October 13, 1977.

24. "Rams to start Haden ahead of Namath," *Modesto Bee*, October 13, 1977.

25. "Pressure Building for Namath," *Nevada State Journal* (Reno), October 12, 1977.

26. Rich Roberts, "Knox benches Namath; Haden to start Sunday," *The Independent* (Long Beach, CA), October 13, 1977.

27. Jim Cour, "Namath Spends His Time On Sidelines," *Nashua Telegraph* (NH), December 17, 1977.

Chapter 16

1. *NFL Films: Inside the Vault, 1960–1970: Volume 3: The Merger (1970),* Warner Home Video, 2003.

2. Melvin Durslag, "Namath's Salary Is Top Secret," *The Sporting News,* June 4, 1977.

3. Murray Janoff, "Revived Namath Scoffs at Injury Jinx," *The Sporting News,* October 7, 1972.

4. Joe Falls, *The Sporting News,* January 25, 1969.

5. Dan Jenkins, "The Sweet Life of Swinging Joe," *Sports Illustrated,* October 17, 1966.

6. From the NFL Films documentary *The Legend of Broadway Joe,* NFL Productions, 2006.

7. "Namath of the Jets," *Newsweek,* September 15, 1969.

8. "Joe Namath and the Jet-Propelled Offense," *Time,* October 16, 1972.

9. Miller Farr, "I Like to Outsmart Rival Receivers, Not Dismember Them," *All Pro 1969 Football.*

10. Paul Zimmerman, "Why They Still Pick On Joe Namath," *Touchdown,* 1969.

11. Bert Rosenthal, "Joe Namath — Why He Battles On," *All-Star Sports,* February 1969.

12. Walsh's remarks are from *The Legend of Broadway Joe* (NFL Productions, 2006). Some of Madden's remarks were used in the same program, as well as being used in *A&E Biography: Broadway Joe: The Joe Namath Story*.

13. "Pro Quarterback/playback," *Pro Quarterback*, January 1971.

14. Larry Bortstein, *Super Joe: The Joe Namath Story* (New York: Tempo Books, 1969). p. 154.

15. Dave Anderson, "Namath: Is He Really That Good?" *Pro Football 1969*.

16. Jerry Izenberg, "And Wearing White Shoes..." *Pro!*, September 26, 1976.

17. From *A&E Biography: Broadway Joe: The Joe Namath Story*.

Bibliography

A&E Biography: Broadway Joe: The Joe Namath Story.

Abbott, Rudy. "The Tide Story — Coach Bryant's Love Of Players." *Anniston Star* (AL), November 27, 1964.

Addie, Bob. "Namath Works on Weak Arm." *The Sporting News,* June 12, 1971.

"Against Chiefs Namath Sparks Late TD Drive." *Jefferson City Post-Tribune* (MO), November 8, 1965.

"Alabama Defense Shines In 14–3 Win Over Houston." *San Antonio Light,* October 14, 1962.

"Alabama Drowns Vandy by 17–7." *Abilene Reporter-News* (TX), October 7, 1962.

"Alabama Slams Hurricanes 36–3," *Albuquerque Journal,* November 11, 1962.

"Alabama Tide Blanks Hapless Tulane Behind Namath, Billy Piper, 28 To)," *Anniston Star* (AL), September 29, 1963.

"Alert Defense Halts New York Title Bid." *Bridgeport Telegram* (CT), December 11, 1967.

Alexander, Ken. "Oilers Slick Test For Jets Blast-Off Plans?" *Gastonia Gazette* (NC), August 23, 1967.

Allen, Maury. *Joe Namath's Sporting Life.* New York: Paperback Library, 1969.

"Allen Need Not Have Worried." *The Bee* (Danville, VA), November 6, 1972.

"American Football League Nears Early Opening Tilt." *Hobbs Daily News-Sun* (NM), September 5, 1965.

Ammerman, Craig. "Jets join Patriots' strike, other teams considering... And NFL's 'regular season in jeopardy'..." *Bradford Era* (PA), September 17, 1975.

Anderson, Dave. "Joe Namath: The $500,000 Challenge." *Pro Quarterback,* November 1972, Vol. 2, No. 11.

_____. "Joe Namath: Football or Hollywood?" *Pro Quarterback,* January 1971, Vol. 1, No. 3.

_____. "Joe Namath: Why He Has To Win Again." *Pro Quarterback,* November 1973, Vol. 3, No. 10.

_____. "Namath: Is He Really That Good?" *Pro Football 1969,* 1969.

_____. "Namath: Jets' $500,000 Performer Lives Spartanly at Camp." *Gazette-Mail* (Charleston, WV), August 6, 1972.

_____. "New Challenge for Namath: Baltimore Defense." *Cedar Rapids Gazette,* January 6, 1969.

_____. "Raiders Whip Jets As Lamonica Shines." *Charleston Gazette,* December 1, 1969.

_____. "Streaking Chiefs Clip Jets, 34–16." *Charleston Gazette,* November 17, 1969.

_____. "Two Miscues by Simpson Help Jets Survive, 16–6." *Charleston Gazette* (WV), November 10, 1969.

_____. "'Where Did the Time Go?' Asks Namath.'" *New York Times,* November 19, 1973.

Andre, Lee. "Joe Namath — Superman or Myth?" *Pro Sports,* March 1968, Vol. 4, No. 2.

Andruskevich, Greg. "Namath Finally Proves Himself." *Nashua Telegraph* (NH), January 3, 1969.

"AP says Kansas City, Jets to be AFL's best." *Jefferson City Post-Tribune* (MO), September 11, 1969.

"Are 18-Point Odds on Colts In Super Bowl Too Much?" *Iowa City Press-Citizen,* January 8, 1969.

"Are Rams Finished Already?" *Nashua Telegraph* (NH), September 16, 1977.

"Army Won't Take Namath." *Alton Evening Telegraph* (IL), December 13, 1965.

"As Usual, Joe Namath There Late." *Hobbs Daily News-Sun* (NM), August 15, 1974.

Atkins, Stan. "Alabama Too Much For Tulane." *Anniston Star* (AL), September 27, 1964.

Atkinson, Paul. "Rivals Green With Envy Over Tulane's Goss and Steigerwald." *The Sporting News,* November 6, 1971.

"Avellini calls plays, wins." *Wisconsin State Journal,* October 12, 1977.

"Avellini Lobs Chicago Into Upset Win." *Albuquerque Journal,* October 11, 1977.

"Back by November? Knife for Namath." *Albuquerque Tribune,* August 9, 1971.

"Baltimore 17-Point Favorite in Super Bowl." *Walla Walla Union-Bulletin,* January 4, 1969.

"Baltimore steals Namath, victory: Colts top New York by 29–22." *Pocono Record* (Stroudsburg, PA), October 19, 1970.

"Baltimore's Injured Trio On The Mend For Jets." *Tri-City Herald* (WA), January 1, 1969.

"Bama Ekes Past Miami, 17 To 12." *Anniston Star* (AL), December 15, 1963.

"Bama Pushed To Beat Houston By 14 To 3." *Progress-Index* (Petersburg, VA), October 14, 1962.

"'Bama Rips Miami 36–3 In Last Half." *News Tribune* (Ft. Pierce, FL), November 11, 1962.

"'Bama Rolls Over Tulsa." *Hobbs Daily News-Sun* (NM), October 28, 1962.

"'Bama Stuns Tulane 44–6." *Hobbs Daily News-Sun* (NM), September 30, 1962.

Bauer, Steve. "Hufnagel stars for Broncos in 41–19 loss to New York." *Greeley Tribune* (CO), August 5, 1974.

Baylor, Peter. "Namath To Stay Yes Or No..." *Raleigh Register* (Beckley, WV), December 16, 1974.

"Bears Come to Life Too Late." *Wisconsin State Journal,* September 23, 1974.

"Bears Pass Over Rams, 24–23." *Post-Standard* (Syracuse, NY), October 11, 1977.

"Bears Shade Rams on Avellini's passing." *Daily Times* (Primos, CA), October 11, 1977.

"Beaver Falls Pulled For Namath, Jets." *The Morning Herald* (Uniontown, PA), January 13, 1969.

Becker, Bill. "Hadl Sets Pace." *New York Times,* December 5, 1965.

_____. "Oakland Rallies to Break 14–14 Tie." *New York Times,* December 13, 1965.

"Bengals Burn Jets, 20–14." *Albuquerque Journal,* November 19, 1973.

"Bengals, Namath end frustrating seasons." *Journal News* (Hamilton, OH), December 13, 1976.

"Bengals Romp 42–3." *Times Recorder* (Zanesville, OH), December 13, 1976.

"Bengals Spoil Namath's Return." *Wisconsin State Journal,* November 19, 1973.

"Bengals Squelch Rally." *Advocate* (Victoria, TX), November 19, 1973.

"Bengals surprise Jets for 2nd win." *News & Tribune* (Jefferson City, MO), September 1, 1968.

Berger, Phil. "The Impossible Victory." *Grit,* November 30, 1969.

Berkow, Ira. "Johnny Sample's Nasty Book Getting Bigger By The Day." *Gastonia Gazette* (NC), August 16, 1969.

_____. "Namath is true to Namath." *Great Bend Tribune* (KS), September 1, 1974.

_____. "Super Astrology: Colts See Stars." *Albuquerque Tribune,* January 9, 1969.

Bernstein, Ralph. "Al Atkinson Believes Ball-Control Major Factor." *Abilene Reporter-News,* January 6, 1969.

_____. "Jets Face Aggressive Colt Linebacker." *Evening Standard* (Uniontown, PA), January 9, 1969.

_____. "Jets Strafe Colts In Super Bowl Contest, 16–7." *Morning Herald* (Uniontown, PA), January 13, 1969.

_____. "Namath Arm, Not His Lip, Concerns Colt Counterpart." *The Times* (Hammond, IN), January 10, 1969.

_____. "Namath Raps Earl Morrall." *Progress-Index* (Petersburg, VA), January 7, 1969.

_____. "Namath starts grid war." *Las Vegas Optic,* January 7, 1969.

_____. "Players Investigate Joe Namath's Case." *Corpus Christi Caller-Times,* June 15, 1969.

"Better-Than-Ever Steelers Top Jets." *The Progress* (Clearfield, PA), December 1, 1975.

"Big Red displays class in 13–6 win over Jets." *Jefferson City Post-Tribune* (MO), August 11, 1969.

"Big Red's DeMarco says Jets 'will kill' Giants this weekend." *Jefferson City Post-Tribune* (MO), August 12, 1969.

"Big Wait Ends Sunday When Jets Meet Giants." *Gastonia Gazette* (NC), August 16, 1969.

"Bills Beat Jets but Namath 'arrives.'" *Kokomo Morning Times,* September 27, 1965.

"Bills Clinch Division As Pats Stop Jets." *Oakland Tribune,* November 29, 1965.

"Bills Drop Jets From League Lead, 33–23." *Times Record* (Troy, NY), October 31, 1966.

"Bills Dump Jets, 16–12, In Windy Rich Stadium." *Bridgeport Post* (CT), September 30, 1974.

"Bills Finally Click, Outplay Jets 31–23." *Pacific Stars and Stripes* (Tokyo), September 3, 1967.

"Bills Flip Jets, 24–23." *Bridgeport Telegram* (CT), November 3, 1975.

"Bills Humble Jets With 37–35 Victory." *Bridgeport Telegram* (CT), September 30, 1968.

"Bills' 'Juice' Was On The Loose." *Kingsport Times* (TN), September 22, 1975.

"Bills nip Jets on Simpson pass." *Argus* (Fremont, CA), November 3, 1975.

"Bills Record 1st Exhibition Victory, 31–23." *Wellsville Daily Reporter* (NY), September 1, 1967.

"Bills Swamp Jets, 34–14." *Playground Daily News* (Ft. Walton Beach, FL), December 17, 1973.

"Bills Top Jets With Late Score." *Bridgeport Telegram* (CT), September 30, 1974.

"Bills Trounce Jets, 42–14, As O.J. Simpson Runs Wild." *Bridgeport Post* (CT), September 22, 1975.

"Bills Upset Jets." *Albuquerque Journal,* September 30, 1968.

"Bills Win Over New York Jets." *Albuquerque Journal,* August 22, 1965.

"Blocked-punt safety helps Vikings tip Jets." *Wisconsin State Journal,* October 13, 1975.

Bloom, Don. "Raiders Overpower Namath, Jets In 31–6 Laugher." *Fresno Bee,* September 8, 1974.

Bock, Hal. "Joe Namath Tells All: 'Why I Had My Roughest Year.'" *Pro Football,* 1973.

"Bonus Stars Won't Pay Price." *Appleton Post-Crescent* (WI), January 7, 1965.

"Boozer, Namath Spark Jets Win." *Times Recorder* (Zanesville, OH), October 16, 1972.

"Boozer, Riggins Power Jets' Win." *Post-Herald* (West Virginia), September 18, 1972.

"Boozer's Score Lifts N.Y. Over Chargers." *Albuquerque Journal,* October 6, 1968.

"Boozer's Three TD Key Jets' 34–10 Romp." *Times Recorder* (Zanesville, OH), October 30, 1972.

Bortstein, Larry. "Long Wait For Jet Vet Bill Mathis." *The Sporting News,* January 11, 1969.

"Boston Beats Jets, 27–23, On Last-Minute Gamble." *Washington Post,* November 29, 1965.

"Boston Patriots Almost Nip Jets." *Bennington Banner* (VT), October 27, 1969.

"Bowl-Bound Crimson Tide Routs Auburn." *Albuquerque Journal,* December 2, 1962.

Boyle, Robert H. "Show-biz Sonny and His Quest for Stars." *Sports Illustrated,* July 19, 1965, Vol. 23, No. 3.

"Bradshaw, Steelers Rip Jets." *News Journal* (Mansfield, OH), September 5, 1976.

"'Bragging Rights' At Stake In Jets-Giants Game." *Las Cruces Sun-News* (NM), August 23, 1970.

"Brilliant In Defeat." *Hobbs Daily News-Sun* (NM), December 16, 1963.

"Briscoe's Only Pass Intercepted." *Dunkirk Evening Observer* (Dunkirk-Fredonia, NY), November 10, 1969.

"Broadway Joe draws spotlight in Jets' dressing room." *Post-Tribune* (Jefferson City, MO), January 13, 1969.

"'Broadway' Joe Namath inks reported $500,000 contract." *Daily Capital News* (Jefferson City, MO), August 2, 1972.

"Bronco Offense Crushes Woebegone Jets, 46–3." *Advocate* (Victoria, TX), September 20, 1976.

"Broncos Destroy Jets, 46–3." *Bridgeport Post* (CT), September 20, 1976.

"Broncos Kick Jets For 21–13 Upset." *Times Recorder* (Zanesville, OH), October 14, 1968.

"Broncos Rally In Stopping Jets, 16–13." *Oakland Tribune,* October 4, 1965.

"Broncos Stampede Jets." *Daily Freeman* (Kingston, NY), September 20, 1976.

"Broncos Stun Namath, Jets." *Albuquerque Tribune,* September 22, 1969.

"Broncos Throw N.Y. Jets." *Albuquerque Journal,* September 20, 1976.

"Broncos trample Jets." *Greeley Tribune* (CO), September 20, 1976.

"Broncos Upset Jets." *Albuquerque Journal,* October 14, 1968.

"Bronks Beat Jets." *Post Standard* (Syracuse, NY), December 4, 1967.

Brown, Doug. "Namath, as Kid Flash, Spurned Orioles' Bonus." *The Sporting News,* January 23, 1965.

Brown, Frank. "Nitschke Calls It Quits, Riggins Leaves Jets' Camp." *The Progress* (Clearfield, PA), August 29, 1973.

"Browns Gave It Their Best Shot, But Fell Short." *Kingsport Times* (TN), December 18, 1972.

"Browns rip New York 38–17; Phipps may miss Pitt clash." *Lima News* (OH), September 13, 1976.

"Browns sidelights." *Chronicle Telegram* (Elyria, OH), September 13, 1976.

"Browns' Win Turned On Goal-Line Stand." *Daily Freeman* (Kingston, NY), September 13, 1976.

Bruce, Allan. "Shaw's Passing, O.J.'s Running Leads Bills Past Jets, 34–31." *Playground Daily News* (Ft. Walton Beach, FL), October 5, 1970.

"Bryant Pleads In Vain." *San Antonio Express and News,* June 7, 1969.

Bryson, Mike. "KC Chiefs Storm Past Jets." *Las Cruces Sun-News* (NM), November 17, 1969.

_____. "'Not-So-Good' Jets Keep Right On Winning Games." *Fresno Bee,* November 10, 1969.

"Bubba Hopes To Be Set for Joe." *Albuquerque Journal,* January 10, 1969.

"Bucking Broncos deflate the Jets." *Syracuse Herald Journal,* September 22, 1969.

"Buffalo Intercepts Five Namath Passes." *Times Record* (Troy, NY), September 30, 1968.

"Buffalo Nips Jets On Goal." *Pacific Stars and Stripes* (Tokyo), September 12, 1967.

"Buffalo Scores 20 In Fourth To Hand Jets 20–17 Setback." *Times Recorder* (Zanesville, OH), September 11, 1967.

"Buffalo slips past Jets, 16–12." *Press-Telegram,* September 30, 1974.

Burgin, Dave. "Joe Namath Makes $400,000 Look Cheap." *Daily Times-News* (Burlington, NC), October 3, 1966.

Bushnell, David. "Colts come out throwing, Jets get tossed 20–0." *Times Herald Record* (Middletown, NY), October 25, 1976.

_____. "Jets crushed 42–3." *Times Herald Record* (Middletown, NY), December 13, 1976.

_____. "Jets lose to Patriots 38–24." *Times Herald Record* (Middletown, NY), November 22, 1976.

Cady, Steve. "Broadway Joe booed in Jet finale." *Independent* (Long Beach, CA), December 13, 1976.

Camen, Stu. "Kappless Vikings Defeat Jets." *Las Cruces Sun-News* (NM), August 31, 1970.

"Can Broadway Joe Namath Find Happiness With L.A. Rams?" *Grit,* June 5, 1977.

"Can Hayden Beat Namath?" *Las Cruces Sun-News* (NM), August 14, 1977.

"Cardinals, Jets take exhibition triumphs." *Daily Capital News* (Jefferson City, MO), August 19, 1969.

"Cardinals to Get Crack at Namath and Jets Tonight." *Chillicothe Constitution-Tribune* (MO), August 9, 1969.

"Cards finally win in a walk, 37–6." *Alton Telegraph* (IL), November 24, 1975.

"Cards rally defeats Jets." *Daily Capital News* (Jefferson City, MO), August 28, 1973.

"Cards to Test Jets And Joe Tonight." *Moberly Monitor-Index* (MO), August 8, 1969.

Carnicelli, Joe. "Bomb by Pastorini Lands on Jets and Oilers Annex Third." *The Sporting News,* November 16, 1974.

_____. "Cardinal 'Laugher' Ruins Shipp's Debut With Jets." *The Sporting News,* December 6, 1975.

_____. "Decision by Coach Winner Backfires as Bills Top Jets." *The Sporting News,* November 15, 1975.

_____. "Depressed Bengals Don't Show It." *Coshocton Tribune* (OH), December 13, 1976.

_____. "Dolphin Victory Blunted by Injury." *The Sporting News,* November 20, 1976.

_____. "Grieving Joe Leads Jets To triumph Over Dolphins." *The Sporting News,* December 7, 1974.

_____. "Half Million For Namath In 2 Years." *El Paso Herald-Post,* August 1, 1972.

_____. "Holtz' Amatuer Wizardry Given Opportunity With Jets." *Brownsville Herald* (TX), February 11, 1976.

_____. "Jets Go on a TD Spree ... Namath's Parting Shot?" *The Sporting News,* December 28, 1974.

_____. "Jets Jolt Critics With Fourth Victory in Row." *The Sporting News,* December 14, 1974.

_____. "Jets' Old Problem Back Again." *Times Record* (Troy, NY), September 13, 1973.

_____. "Jets, 'Skins Join Patriots On Strike." *Tyrone Daily Herald* (PA), September 17, 1975.

_____. "Joe Namath Won't Quit Yet." *Las Cruces Sun-News* (NM), December 22, 1975.

_____. "Jones, Mitchell Team Up to Spur Colts Past Jets." *The Sporting News,* November 2, 1974.

_____. "Maynard Dealt To Cards." *Las Cruces Sun-News* (NM), September 11, 1973.

_____. "Namath Shoots Down Bills In Likely Adieu to Jet Fans." *The Sporting News,* December 21, 1974.

_____. "Namath's Future Unsure, Sunday May Be End." *Daily Messenger* (Canandaigua, NY), December 13, 1973.

_____. "Namath's TD Toss Settles Jet-Giant Overtime Battle." *The Sporting News,* November 23, 1974.

_____. "New England Votes To Strike." *Denton Record-Chronicle* (TX), September 15, 1975.

_____. "Pass-Intercepting Patriots Lock Up a Winning Season." *The Sporting News,* December 4, 1976.

_____. "Quick Baptism for Ken Shipp." *Daily Freeman* (Kingston, NY), November 24, 1975.

_____. "Ram Runner McCutcheon Grounds Jets." *The Sporting News,* November 9, 1974.

_____. "Redskins' Riggins Haunts Old-Pal Jets." *The Sporting News,* December 18, 1976.

_____. "Rising Colts Conquer Tumbling Jets." *The Sporting News,* November 8, 1975.

_____. "'Should Have Made It,' Bengals Lament." *The Sporting News,* December 25, 1976.

_____. "Staubach Sub Spurs Dallas Past Jets in N.Y. Ice Box." *The Sporting News,* January 3, 1976.

_____. "Steelers Fly High and Jets Low in Shea Wind Tunnel." *The Sporting News,* December 13, 1975.

_____. "Sub QB Namath Sparks Jet Victory." *The Sporting News,* November 27, 1976.

_____. "War Drums Sound in Jets Camp For Match with Bills Sunday." *Middleboro Daily News* (KY), September 20, 1975.

_____. "Young defensive Pat players excel in win over N.Y. Jets." *Berkshire Eagle* (Pittsfield, MA), November 22, 1976.

Carroll, Bill. "16,000 See Jets Triumph Over Patriots, 55–13." *The Bridgeport Post,* August 5, 1967.

"Caster Hauls In Two TDs." *Post-Standard* (Syracuse, NY), November 25, 1974.

"CBS loses Jets' game." *Billings Gazette* (MT), November 6, 1972.

"Celeb Status for Joe No Surprise to Sonny." *The Sporting News,* November 5, 1966.

Chamberlain, Charles. "Quarterback John Huarte Overwhelming Choice As Most Valuable All-Star Player." *Danville Register* (VA), August 8, 1965.

"Chargers Back in Race." *Oakland Tribune,* September 29, 1969.

"Chargers Beat Jets, Embarrassed Namath." *Moberly Monitor-Index,* December 16, 1975.

"Chargers Jolt Jets Via Hot Hadl, 34–27." *Argus* (Fremont, CA), September 29, 1969.

"Chargers Riddle Jets, 34–9." *Gazette-Mail* (Charleston, WV), October 24, 1965.

"Chargers Romp Over Jets, 42–27." *Post-Standard* (Syracuse, NY), December 12, 1966.

"Chargers Take Measure of Jets As Curfew 'Intercepts' Namath." *The Sporting News,* December 27, 1975.

Chass, Murray. "Despite His Bad Knees, Namath Stands Alone." *Wisconsin State Journal* (Madison), January 5, 1969.

_____. "Ewbank Says Jets Will Be All Right If Joe Namath's Knee Holds Out." *Playground Daily News* (Ft. Walton Beach, FL), August 28, 1967.

_____. "Namath returns ... in style." *Independent Press-Telegram* (Long Beach, CA), August 17, 1974.

_____. "Namath's Passing Gives Jets One-Sided Victory." *Las Cruces Sun-News* (NM), September 19, 1966.

_____. "New York Jets Believe This Is Their Year." *Chillicothe Constitution-Tribune* (MO), August 29, 1968.

_____. "Now That Right Knee Is Okay, Left One Gives Namath Trouble." *Kokomo Tribune,* August 27, 1967.

_____. "Philbin Says Jets Must Get To Lamonica Early." *Appleton Post-Crescent* (WI), December 29, 1968.

_____. "Second Best QB Namath of Jets?" *Gastonia Gazette* (NC), August 23, 1967.

_____. "Time, Bengals Foil Late Heroics in 20–14 Setback," *New York Times,* November 19, 1973.

"Chicago edges Namath, Rams." *Albuquerque Tribune,* October 11, 1977.

"Chiefs beat Jets, elements 13 to 6." *Southern Illinoisan,* December 21, 1969.

"Chiefs Beat Namath, Jets in AFL." *Albuquerque Journal,* December 21, 1969.

"Chiefs Derail Jets' Express." *Bridgeport Post* (CT), December 11, 1967.

"Chiefs force turnovers, whip Rams." *Salina Journal* (KS), August 29, 1977.

"Chiefs Picked Over Jets in Playoff Game." *Ogden Standard-Examiner* (UT), December 19, 1969.

"Chiefs Regain Touch In Smearing New York." *Fresno Bee,* November 6, 1967.

"Chiefs stop Jets on interception." *Press-Telegram* (Long Beach, CA), September 16, 1974.

"Chiefs Throttle Joe, Jets." *Oakland Tribune,* December 21, 1969.

"Chiefs Trim Jets by 24–16 Despite Namath's Passing." *Bridgeport Telegram* (CT), September 16, 1974.

"Chiefs Whip Namath, Jets." *Wisconsin State Journal,* September 16, 1974.

Christopher, Rick. "Scott's jumping ability burns Rams' secondary." *Daily Herald* (Chicago), October 11, 1977.

"Cincinnati, Denver score big upsets over Chargers, Jets." *Jefferson City Post-Tribune* (MO), September 22, 1969.

"The City Belongs to Namath." *Wisconsin State Journal,* November 11, 1974.

"Clark Wasn't Fooled." *Daily Freeman* (Kingston, NY), October 4, 1976.

"Cleveland beats Jets in prime time battle." *Post-Tribune* (Jefferson City, MO), September 22, 1970.

"Cleveland Sparked By Phipps." *Times Recorder* (Zanesville, OH), December 18, 1972.

"Clock Kayoes Jets." *Times Recorder,* November 19, 1973.

Close, Larry. "'Raiders Won't Let Up'—Rauch." *Daily Review* (Hayward, CA), December 12, 1967.

"Cocky Shaw Lifts Buffalo Past Jets." *Oakland Tribune,* October 5, 1970.

"Colts admit being outplayed." *Post-Tribune* (Jefferson City, MO), January 13, 1969.

"Colts beat up Jets, 52–19." *The Capital* (Annapolis, MD), November 17, 1975.

"Colts Blank Browns For NFL Crown, 34–0." *Frederick News-Post* (MD), December 30, 1968.

"Colts Clinch Playoff Spot; Jones Talks About Namath." *Lebanon Daily News* (PA), November 29, 1976.

"Colts Club Jets to Clinch Playoff Berth." *Albuquerque Journal,* November 29, 1976.

"Colts coast by Jets 20–0." *The Capital* (Annapolis, MD), October 25, 1976.

"Colts' Defense Best Shula Has Ever Seen." *Post-Standard* (Syracuse, NY), January 8, 1969.

"Colts Down Jets, 29–22." *Frederick News-Post* (MD), October 19, 1970.

"Colts Get Berth By Whipping Jets." *Galveston Daily News* (TX), November 29, 1976.

"Colts Hurt In Title Game Will Be Ready For Jets." *Frederick News-Post* (MD), January 2, 1969.

"Colts, Jets Close Gates For Workouts." *Panama City News* (FL), January 9, 1969.

"Colts, Jets Swap Football Films." *Playground Daily News* (Fort Walton Beach, FL), January 3, 1969.

"Colts Kick Jets 35–20." *Times Recorder* (Zanesville, OH), October 21, 1974.

"Colts Practice Before Leaving." *Oshkosh Daily Northwestern* (WI), January 4, 1969.

"Colts Rack Jets." *Galveston Daily News* (TX), November 17, 1975.

"Colts' rally falls short." *The Capital* (Annapolis, MD), December 3, 1973.

"Colts Rout Jets To Clinch Crown." *Times Recorder* (Zanesville, OH), November 29, 1976.

"Colts Sack Namath 7 Times In Defeating Jets, 45–28." *Charleston Gazette* (WV), October 27, 1975.

"Colts: Time Ran Out, And We Didn't Make Big Play." *Des Moines Register,* January 13, 1969.

"Colts' victory assures a playoff berth." *The Capital* (Annapolis, MD), November 29, 1976.

"Colts Work, Jets Rest for Super Bowl." *Des Moines Register,* January 8, 1969.

Conerly, Charles. "Conerly Picks Colts and Jets in Title Games." *San Antonio Light,* December 29, 1968.

"Cool Namath ices Patriots." *Wisconsin State Journal,* October 6, 1975.

Couch, Dick. "Jets, Raiders Clash In Top Game On AFL Card." *Las Cruces Sun-News* (NM), November 30, 1969.

_____. "Namath Completes Four of 17 Passes as Buffalo Wins." *Moberly Monitor-Index* (MO), September 3, 1965.

_____. "NY Jets Are Team To Beat." *Silver City Daily Press* (NM), August 11, 1969.

_____. "NY Jets Edge Chargers, 17–16." *Abilene Reporter-News,* October 9, 1966.

_____. "Texas Upsets Alabama." *Lowell Sun* (MA), January 2, 1965.

Cour, Jim. "Namath's Ram Debut Not Very Spectacular." *Daily Courier* (Connellsville, PA), August 15, 1977.

"Cowboys Achieved Two Major Objectives." *Daily Freeman* (Kingston, NY), December 22, 1975.

"Cowboys dump Jets on Staubach's passing." *News and Tribune* (Jefferson City, MO), December 5, 1971.

"Cowboys Hijack Jets." *Albuquerque Journal,* December 5, 1971.

"Cowboys in massacre." *Lowell Sun* (MA), December 5, 1971.

"Cowboys Smother Namath," *Las Cruces Sun-News* (NM), December 5, 1971.

"Cracks Appear In Namath's Armor" *Lima News* (OH), October 31, 1966.

"Crimson Tide Over Miss St. *Albuquerque Journal,* November 4, 1962.

Curran, Bob. *The Violence Game.* New York: Macmillan 1966.

Curtis, Mike. "I Don't Care What They Call Me, I Play This Game For Keeps." *All Pro 1969 Football,* 1969.

Curylo, John. "Namath lubricates Jets with sparkling maneuvers." *The News* (Port Arthur, TX), August 22, 1976.

Daley, Arthur. "Break Up The Jets." *Nashua Telegraph* (NH), November 1, 1965.

_____. "Colts 'Suffered Twice' After Defeat." *Appleton Post-Crescent* (WI), January 13, 1969.

_____. "Exit For Sonny." *Cumberland Times* (MD), June 2, 1968.

_____. "Shuffle To Buffalo." *Nashua Telegram* (NH), September 11, 1967.

Daniel, Dan. "Joe Namath or Weeb Ewbank — Who Really Runs the Jets?" *Super Sports,* January 1970, Vol. 3, No. 1.

Dates, Bob. "Stunner: Falcons Rip Rams." *Fresno Bee,* September 19, 1977.

"Dawson, Chiefs Bomb Joe's Jets." *Wisconsin State Journal,* November 17, 1969.

"Dawson, Chiefs ruin Jets' Super Bowl dream 13–6." *News & Tribune* (Jefferson City, MO), December 21, 1969.

"Dawson Leads Chiefs Past Jets 34–16." *Ogden Standard-Examiner* (UT), November 17, 1969.

"Dawson Succeeds Where Youth Fails in AFL Game." *San Antonio Light,* January 20, 1969.

"A Day Of Firsts For Joe And Jets." *Kingsport Times* (TN), September 25, 1972.

Decker, Al. "Play-Calling Coaches in NFL Easing Task for Quarterbacks." *Grit,* November 28, 1976.

"Defense Rests For N.Y. Jets." *Bridgeport Post* (CT), November 24, 1969.

"Defiant Namath Relents For TV." *Times Recorder* (Zanesville, OH), January 13, 1969.

"Delay by Rams Puzzles Namath." *Oakland Tribune,* March 30, 1977.

"Dennis Shaw Passes for Two Scores." *Bridgeport Post* (CT), October 5, 1970.

"Denver Broncos Upset Super Bowl Champion Jets." *Albuquerque Journal,* September 22, 1969.

"Denver gives Joe, Jets big headache." *Press-Telegram* (Long Beach, CA), September 20, 1976.

Devaney, John. "Can Football Live Without Namath (& Vice-Versa)?" *Sport,* July 1972, Vol. 54, No. 1.

_____. "Joe Namath: The $400,000 Challenge." *Sport,* August 1965, Vol. 40, No. 2.

_____. "Joe Namath's Good Days and Bad." *Sport,* November 1967, Vol. 44, No. 5.

Di Pietro, Bob. "Turner's Three Kicks Beat Dallas." *Las Cruces Sun-News* (NM), September 14, 1970.

"Disappointed Namath draws Browns' raves." *Pocono Record* (Stroudsburg, PA), September 23, 1970.

"Dismal windup for dismal Jets, 31–21." *Press-Telegram* (Long Beach, CA), December 22, 1975.

"Division Lead Held By Bills." *Daily Messenger.* (Canandalgua, NY), November 14, 1966.

"Dolphins Aid Jet Tailspin." *San Antonio Light,* November 10, 1975.

"Dolphins Bombarded: Namath, Parilli Pass Jets To 31–7 Victory." *Times Recorder* (Zanesville, OH), December 8, 1968.

"Dolphins Bounce Back." *Playground Daily News* (Ft. Walton Beach, FL), September 27, 1976.

"Dolphins Clinch Title." *Post-Standard* (Syracuse, NY), November 20, 1972.

"Dolphins Club Jets; Build Up East Lead" *Playground Daily News* (Ft. Walton Beach, FL), November 10, 1975.

"Dolphins Face Vindictive Jets" *Naples Daily News* (FL), November 19, 1972.

"Dolphins' Ginn Offsets Late Jets Passing Show" *Des Moines Register,* October 8, 1974.

"Dolphins Ground Jets 27–7" *News Tribune* (Ft. Pierce, FL), November 10, 1975.

"Dolphins Flip Into Jets Net" *Gallup Independent* (NM), September 10, 1966.

"Dolphins intercept six Namath passes." *Press-Telegram* (Long Beach, CA), October 20, 1975.

"Dolphins nip Jets, 21–17." *Independent* (Long Beach, CA), October 8, 1974.

"Dolphins Outlast Namath, Jets, Score 21–17 Victory." *Kingsport Times* (TN), October 8, 1974.

"Dolphins Overwhelm Jets 43–0." *Times Recorder* (Zanesville, OH), October 20, 1975.

"Dolphins Point To Playoffs." *Naples Daily News* (FL), November 20, 1972.

"Dolphins Rally To Win." *Panama City News-Herald* (FL), November 20, 1972.

"Dolphins Splash 43–0 in Muddy Jet Pond." *News Tribune* (Ft. Pierce, FL), October 20, 1975.

"Dolphins Trounce Jets." *Post-Standard* (Syracuse, NY), October 9, 1972.

"Dolphins Wallop Jets 27–17." *Times Recorder* (Zanesville, OH), October 9, 1972.

"Don Trull Paces Late Hub Rally." *Bridgeport Telegram* (CT), November 20, 1967.

"Don, Weeb Think Alike." *Frederick News-Post* (MD), January 3, 1969.

Drolshagen, Tom. "Packers Floor Jets." *Las Cruces Sun-News* (NM), September 18, 1973.

"Dunaway Scores On Blocked FG." *Bridgeport Telegram* (CT), November 14, 1966.

Durslag, Melvin. "Are NFL Exhibitions Necessary?" *The Sporting News,* August 20, 1977.

_____. "Durslag's Column" *The Light* (San Antonio), January 9, 1969.

_____. "Future Will Decide Namath's Ranking as QB." *The Sporting News,* February 18, 1978.

_____. "Is Namath Heading for the Exit?" *The Sporting News,* November 12, 1977.

_____. "L.A. Thrilled by Namath Offer." *The Sporting News,* February 7, 1976.

_____. "Namath will cost Rams plenty." *Chronicle Telegram* (Elyria, OH), December 9, 1974.

_____. "Namath's Salary Is Top Secret." *The Sporting News,* June 4, 1977.

Dyer, Frank. "'We Give 'Em Away'—Holovak." *Lowell Sun* (MA), November 15, 1965.

"Eagles Clobber Jets as Namath Leaves With Injury." *Colorado Springs Gazette-Telegraph,* August 20, 1967.

"Eating the ball or words, it's still hard." *Oneonta Star* (NY), June 10, 1969.

Eck, Frank. "Seven Books Published About Jet's 'Super Joe.'" *Las Cruces Sun-News* (NM), September 7, 1969.

Eisenberg, Dave. "Players and Writers Drift Apart." *The Sporting News,* January 10, 1970.

_____. "Ref Gets Salute From Namath." *The Sporting News,* January 17, 1970.

_____. "Schmitt a Top-Notch Center." *The Sporting News,* January 23, 1971.

_____. "This Year Namath Talks Only Football." *The Sporting News,* March 20, 1971.

Eskenazi, Gerald. "Namath in Los Angeles—Dud or Dynamite?" *Inside Football 1977,* 1977.

"Exhibition Focus Shifts From Dallas-Jet Tilt." *Albuquerque Journal,* September 6, 1969.

"Exhibition hard on QBs." *Daily Capital News* (Jefferson City, MO), August 17, 1968.

"Ewbank Pleased With Jets' Play." *Bridgeport Post* (CT), September 11, 1972.

"Ewbank Sees Wild AFL Finish." *Oakland Tribune,* December 29, 1968.

"Ewbank Sounds Confident; Colts Talk Down 'Spread.'" *Sheboygan Journal* (WI), January 8, 1969.

"Ex-Bama Mates Ruin Patriots." *Press-Telegram* (Long Beach, CA), September 23, 1968.

"Explosive Jets Wallop Denver." *Post-Herald* (Beckley, WV), November 1, 1965.

"Falcons Edge Jets for Seven Straight." *Salt Lake Tribune* (UT), November 26, 1973.

Falls, Joe. "Brief Encounter With Namath." *The Sporting News,* January 25, 1969.

"Fans boo Namath as New York handed 28–24 defeat by Giants." *Jefferson City Post-Tribune* (MO), August 24, 1970.

"Fans Boo Namath As Rams Blanked." *Press-Courier* (Oxnard, CA), September 10, 1977.

Felser, Larry. "AFL Claims Victory in Battle With NFL Over Draft Signings." *The Sporting News,* January 16, 1965.

_____. "AFL Star of the Week: Jim Dunaway." *The Sporting News,* November 26, 1966.

_____. "AFL Star of the Week: Joe Namath." *The Sporting News,* December 31, 1966.

_____. "AFL's Gate Up 25% as Video Ratings Zoom." *The Sporting News,* November 20, 1965.

_____. "Alworth, Ewbank and Namath." *The Sporting News,* February 11, 1978.

_____. "Bad Day for QBs, But Not for Jets, Raiders." *The Sporting News,* September 27, 1969.

_____. "Coach Shoulders Blame." *The Sporting News,* October 13, 1973.

_____. "Colts Show Signs of Life While Jets Collapse." *The Sporting News,* November 9, 1974.

_____. "Cornerbacks Taking Cheap Shots." *The Sporting News,* November 2, 1968.

_____. "Ewbank a Dreamer?" *The Sporting News,* November 7, 1970.

_____. "Final Year for Wobbly Namath?" *The Sporting News,* November 20, 1976.

_____. "Gerry Philbin: Bounty Hunter." *Pro Quarterback,* October 1969, Vol. 1, No. 1.

_____. "He's No-Throw Joe." *The Sporting News,* November 23, 1968.

_____. "Holtz Wasn't Cut Out for Pros." *The Sporting News,* December 25, 1976.

_____. "Huge Task for Michaels." *The Sporting News,* January 22, 1977.

_____. "Is This Jets' Year?" *The Sporting News,* October 14, 1972.

_____. "Jet Joe Sure-Fire MVP Winner." *The Sporting News,* October 22, 1966.

_____. "Jet-Namath Divorce Not Final." *The Sporting News,* October 9, 1976.

_____. "Jets Furious Over Floyd's 'Cheap Shot.'" *The Sporting News*, September 3, 1967.

_____. "Jets Have a Problem." *The Sporting News*, December 9, 1972.

_____. "Jets Infuriated by Officials' Calls." *The Sporting News*, December 7, 1968.

_____. "Jets Owe Comeback to Namath." *The Sporting News*, December 28, 1974.

_____. "Jets Prepare for Namath Exit." *The Sporting News*, June 6, 1970.

_____. "Jets' Runners Helping Namath." *The Sporting News*, October 25, 1975.

_____. "Jets Sputter ... Colts Likely to Romp." *The Sporting News*, September 19, 1970.

_____. "Jets Take on the Look of a Winner." *The Sporting News*, October 12, 1974.

_____. "Joe the Jet Kingpin on All-AFL Squad." *The Sporting News*, January 4, 1969.

_____. "Joe's Change Is Costly." *The Sporting News*, August 28, 1971.

_____. "Lombardi Leaving Packers for Jets?" *The Sporting News*, November 4, 1967.

_____. "Namath East QB: 11 Jets to Perform In AFL Star Game." *The Sporting News*, January 18, 1969.

_____. "Namath Makes Jets Dolphins' Chief Challengers" *The Sporting News*, September 16, 1972.

_____. "Namath Quotes Bear Refreshing Honesty" *The Sporting News*, January 4, 1969.

_____. "Namath Steps Up Drills." *The Sporting News*, December 4, 1971.

_____. "Namath Tops Record 65 Free Agents in NFL." *The Sporting News*, May 17, 1975.

_____. "Offensive Line Paces Dolphins." *The Sporting News*, November 15, 1975.

_____. "O.J.'s Future Depends on Dollars and Sense." *The Sporting News*, January 3, 1976.

_____. "Passing Will Dominate Races in AFC." *The Sporting News*, September 16, 1972.

_____. "Pats' Billy Sullivan: The Joe Bflflstyk of the NFL." *The Sporting News*, November 1, 1975.

_____. "Polished Kid QBs Run Flashy AFL Show." *The Sporting News*, November 6, 1965.

_____. "Problems Beset Dolphins — Jets Tagged as Darkhorse." *The Sporting News*, September 27, 1975.

_____. "Rumors Fall Short of Paydirt." *The Sporting News*, April 9, 1977.

_____. "Snell, DeLong Due Back in Action Soon." *The Sporting News*, November 18, 1967.

_____. "Will Namath return?" *The Sporting News*, January 3, 1970.

_____. "Winner's Spirit Pervades Jets." *The Sporting News*, January 4, 1975.

"50,000 Expected at Shea Stadium: Jets, Seeking 4th in a Row, Favored to Take Second Place From Oilers." *New York Times*, November 21, 1965.

"52,000 Expected at Shea Stadium: Jets Seeking 5th in Row, get Ready for Patriots' Blitz on Quarterback." *New York Times*, November 28, 1965.

"First Title For Club In Kansas City." *Bridgeport Telegram* (CT), November 28, 1966.

Fischler, Stan. "Werblin to Try His Green Thumb on Garden." *The Sporting News*, January 7, 1978.

Fite, Ed. "Dallas Bad, 'Had to Comeback' — Landry." *El Paso Herald-Post*, August 28, 1972.

"Five Field Goals Defeat New York." *Odessa American* (TX), August 13, 1972.

"Florida Here They Come." *Pacific Stars and Stripes* (Tokyo), January 4, 1969.

"Foreman leads Vikes in win." *Daily Journal* (Fergus Falls, MN), October 13, 1975.

"Foreman Sparkles In 29–21 Triumph." *Bridgeport Telegram* (CT), October 13, 1975.

"49ers 'Joke Game.'" *San Mateo Times* (CA), August 13, 1973.

"49ers Overcome Namath, Jets." *Albuquerque Journal*, November 29, 1971.

"49ers slip past Jets, 17–6, look ahead to Rams." *Modesto Bee* (CA), October 4, 1976.

"49ers think about Rams." *Independent* (Long Beach, CA), October 4, 1976.

Fox, Larry. "Can Namath Make It All the Way Back?" *Pro Football Sports Stars of 1972*, Winter 1972, Vol. 5, No. 8.

_____. "Joe Namath: His Troubles And Triumphs." *Sport*, June 1966, Vol. 41, No. 6.

Fraley, Oscar. "Namath Lauded As Top Hero In Bowls." *Daily Plainsman* (Huron, SD), January 2, 1963.

"Fran Tarkenton quits Giants, Namath may be back by Nov. 14." *Jefferson City Post-Tribune* (MO), August 10, 1971.

Francis, Buck. "Namath's Action Limited." *Corpus Christi Times*, August 28, 1972.

"Fritsch field goal at gun beats Rams." *Argus* (Fremont, CA), September 2, 1977.

Frohlinger, Joe. "Giants Intercept 5 of Namath's Passes." *Times Standard* (Eureka, CA), August 21, 1972.

"Fu Manchu Namath A Reluctant Dragon." *The Sporting News*, December 21, 1968.

Fulp, Jack. "Many Played For Ewbank..." *Progress-Index* (Petersburg, VA), January 7, 1969.

Funk, Ben. "Jets Enjoy Scoff at Oddsmakers." *Appleton Post-Crescent* (WI), January 13, 1969.

_____. "Namath Called Win 'One For The AFL.'" *The Morning Herald* (Uniontown, PA), January 13, 1969.

_____. "Namath's Needles (Verbal and Aerial) True Super Upset." *Moberly Monitor-Index*, January 13, 1969.

Gallagher, Jack. "All-Stars Had Too Many Guns In Skinning Buffalo, 30–19." *The Sporting News*, January 29, 1966.

_____. "'Beware of Namath and the Jets' — Gino." *The Sporting News*, August 14, 1965.

_____. "Jets Placing High Price Tag on Huarte." *The Sporting News*, November 27, 1965.

_____. "Namath in Spotlight, But You Might See More of Jets' Biggs." *The Sporting News*, September 4, 1965.

_____. "Old-Guard QBs Face Hot Fight To Keep Jobs From Strong Kids." *The Sporting News*, September 11, 1965.

_____. "Werblin Joins Jets' Book-of-Year Club." *The Sporting News*, December 11, 1965.

Gallas, Bob. "Bears beat adversity, Rams, 24–23." *Daily Herald* (Chicago), October 11, 1977.

"Garrett, Chiefs Pound Jets 42–18." *Times Recorder* (Zanesville, OH), November 6, 1967.

"Garrett's Record 192 Yards Spur Chiefs, 42–18." *Des Moines Register,* November 6, 1967.

"Georgia Tech Upsets Alabama." *Albuquerque Journal,* November 18, 1962.

"Gerela Sets Mark, Pitt Stops Jets." *Lawton Constitution-Morning Press* (OK), August 13, 1972.

Gergen, Joe. "John Huarte is $200,000 Jet telephone operator." *Chronicle-Telegram* (OH), November 1, 1965.

Gerheim, Earl. "Namath Not Talking." *Silver City Daily Press* (NM), August 2, 1972.

"Giants, Browns take key exhibitions." *Syracuse Herald Journal,* August 20, 1973.

"Giants Crush Jets." *Times Recorder* (Zanesville, OH), August 20, 1973.

"Giants Nick Jets." *Hobbs Daily News-Sun* (NM), August 12, 1976.

"Giants Oppose Jets Tonight With Nothing to Brag About." *Bridgeport Post* (CT), August 9, 1976.

"Giants Pull Out Win Over Jets," *San Antonio Light,* August 12, 1976.

"Giants take road trip—to N.Y." *Pocono Record* (Stroudsburg, PA), August 9, 1976.

"Giants Top Jets In Exhibition." *Daily Times* (Salisbury, MD), August 18, 1974.

Gluck, Herb. "Joe Namath Predicts: 'The Old Namath Will Come Back.'" *Sports Today,* October 1973, Vol. 4, No. 5.

Goldstein, Richard. "James Nicholas, 85, Leader in Treating Sports Injuries, Dies." *New York Times,* July 17, 2006 (http://www.nytimes.com/2006/07/17/sports/17nicholas.html).

Graham, Otto. "Memo to Joe Namath: What a Rookie Quarterback Must Learn." *Inside Football,* 1965.

"Graham and Jets Hit With Heavy Fines by Rozelle." *The Sporting News,* December 14, 1968.

Green, Bob. "Five Swipes Key To 37–35 Shocker." *Daily Times* (Salisbury, MD), September 30, 1968.

Green, Jerry. "Naumoff Becomes a Villain." *The Sporting News,* August 28, 1971.

_____. "So Long, Sonny—and Thanks for the Memories." *The Sporting News,* May 24, 1975.

Green, Ted. "Pat Haden—He's Forever on the Rams' Spot." *The Sporting News,* October 7, 1978.

"Green Bay Scout Respects Namath." *Times Standard,* October 30, 1967.

"Grid Cardinals Stave Off Jets." *Modesto Bee & News-Herald* (CA), August 10, 1969.

"Grid Fans' Interest At Jet Game Divided." *Progress-Index* (Petersburg, VA), December 7, 1969.

"Griese Took Jets' Secondary Apart On Field, Not In Locker Room Following 27–17 Victory." *The Bee* (Danville, VA), October 9, 1972.

Griffin, John G. "New York's Defense, Snell's 121 Yards Help Top Baltimore." *Times Recorder* (Zanesville, OH), January 13, 1969.

Grimsley, Will. "'I'm Gonna Try,' Says Namath in Response to Jeers of the Old Pros." *Fairbanks Daily News-Miner,* January 8, 1965.

_____. "Namath Still Wants To Win." *Naples Daily News* (FL), January 16, 1977.

_____. "Namath's departure not flashy." *Jefferson City Post-Tribune* (MO), January 27, 1978.

_____. "Next move in trade furor up to Namath." *Des Moines Register,* January 22, 1976.

_____. "Will the real Joe Namath please stand?" *Columbus Telegram* (NE), November 18, 1974.

"Grogan 'scrambles' Jets." *Times Record* (Troy, NY), October 19, 1976.

"Grogan Too Much for the Jets." *Oakland Tribune,* October 19, 1976.

Gross, Milton. "Gross On Sports" *Lima News* (OH), June 2, 1968.

Guest, Larry. "$733,358 for Simpson in '77, Namath Earned $350,000," *The Sporting News,* February 18, 1978.

"Haden to get another chance Sunday." *Valley News* (Van Nuys, CA), October 13, 1977.

"Haden To Go For Injured Namath Sunday." *Press-Courier* (Oxnard, CA), October 13, 1977.

"Hadl's 'Best Game' Beats Jets, 42–27." *Oakland Tribune,* December 12, 1966.

"Hadl's passes spark Chargers over Jets." *Syracuse Herald-American,* December 5, 1965.

Hagen, Ross. "Jets Nip Oilers; Namath Injured." *Denton Record-Chronicle* (TX), August 14, 1966.

Hairston, Jack. "Joe No Cuddly Cat in Jacksonville." *The Sporting News,* February 1, 1969.

Hall, Cody. "Namath Leads Tide Past Vols, 35–0; Tennessee Is A Balm For Bama." *Anniston Star* (AL), October 20, 1963.

Hall, John. "Nothing Preempts Namath." *Las Cruces Sun-News* (NM), December 13, 1972.

Hand, Jack. "Chiefs Capture 13–6 Victory To Smash Joe, Jets' Dream." *Las Cruces Sun-News* (NM), December 21, 1969.

"Hanner Remarks On Fat Bonuses." *Independent Record* (Helena, MT), January 7, 1965.

Harrigan, Tom. "Jets Rout Patriots, 55–13." *Appleton Post-Crescent* (WI), August 5, 1967.

Harris, Mike. "Browns take to air to down Jets." *Evening Independent* (Massillon, OH), September 13, 1976.

"Harris claims unfair treatment by L.A. Rams." *Post-Register* (Idaho Falls), May 27, 1977.

"Hassle with Sample leaves coach injured." *News & Tribune* (Jefferson City, MO), August 3, 1969.

Hendrickson, Joe. "Ex-Rams turn on old teammates." *Star-News* (Pasadena, CA), September 2, 1977.

_____. "Falcons are smarter than Rams." *Star-News* (Pasadena, CA), September 19, 1977.

_____. "Joe: from Broadway to Skid Row." *Star-News* (Pasadena, CA), August 22, 1977.

_____. "Rams back in same fraternity." *Star-News* (Pasadena, CA), September 26, 1977.

_____. "Rams lose Ron Jesse for season." *Star-News* (Pasadena, CA), October 3, 1977.

Henkey, Ben. "Namath Horsewhips the Broncs." *The Sporting News,* October 7, 1967.

_____. "Youthful Flair to AFL's All-Time All-Star Team." *The Sporting News,* January 31, 1970.

Hickey, Lowell. "Maynard says NFL too dirty." *Daily Review* (Hayward, CA), December 12, 1972.

"High-powered Jets play Cards Saturday; Butz still won't budge." *Jefferson City Post-Herald* (MO), August 24, 1973.

Hollingworth, Hank. "Broadway Joe: A Man of His

Word, They Say." *Independent Press-Telegram* (Long Beach, CA), June 15, 1969.

"Hollywood Joe will face Chiefs for half." *Daily Capital News* (Jefferson City, MO), August 27, 1977.

"Holtz Shows A Flair For the Dramatic." *Daily Freeman* (Kingston, NY), November 15, 1976.

Hoobing, Bob. "'Bama' Rides Big Crest." *Albuquerque Tribune*, January 2, 1963.

"Houston Oilers Bidding For Upset Over Jets." *Big Spring Daily Herald* (TX), October 16, 1966.

"Houston Rallies To Tie New York." *Post-Standard* (Syracuse, NY), October 16, 1967.

"Houston Upsets Jets by 6." *Albuquerque Journal*, October 2, 1972.

"How Namath and the Jets Beat the Colts." *Sports Extra*, Fall 1969, Vol. 2, No. 2.

"Howfield Toes Jets by Oilers." *Pacific Stars & Stripes* (Tokyo), August 6, 1973.

"Howfield's late field goal enables Jets to tie S.D." *Daily Review* (Hayward, CA), September 10, 1972.

Hunt, Tim. "Broadway Joe slipping?" *Daily Review* (Hayward, CA), October 4, 1976.

"Hunter paces Falcon win." *The Argus* (Fremont, CA), September 19, 1977.

"'I Stink,' Says Jets' Namath." *Bridgeport Post* (CT), October 14, 1968.

"Injured Jet Namath Lost At Least Three Months." *The Sporting News*, August 21, 1971.

"Injured Namath Speaks." *Las Cruces Sun-News* (NM), August 17, 1971.

"Injury Halts Namath, Haden Back." *Fresno Bee*, October 13, 1977.

"Injury to Namath not 'Cheap Shot.' Says Coach," *San Antonio Light*, August 15, 1966.

"Inspired Jones Leads Colts to Wild Card." *Daily Freeman* (Kingston, NY), November 29, 1976.

"'Instant Rivalry' To Be Born Monday Night." *Lima News* (OH), September 20, 1970.

"Interception Halts Namath Rally." *Las Cruces Sun-News* (NM), October 8, 1974.

"Interceptions Help Jets Withstand New England." *Wisconsin State Journal*, November 18, 1974.

"Interceptions Hurt Jets In 24–16 Loss to Chiefs." *Bridgeport Post* (CT), September 16, 1974.

"Iselin Suffers Heart Attack At Jets' Game." *Press-Telegram* (Long Beach, CA), September 20, 1976.

"'It was great to score' — Little." *Syracuse Herald*, December 4, 1967.

"It Was the Wind — Joe Namath." *Albuquerque Journal*, December 21, 1969.

Iwasaki, Carl. "A Game That gets a Good Man Down." *Sports Illustrated*, August 17, 1970, Vol. 33, No. 7.

Izenberg, Jerry. "And Wearing White Shoes..." *Pro!*, September 26, 1976, Vol. 7, No. 3.

"J. Namath Suspended, Will Miss Sugar Play." *Anniston Star* (AL), December 10, 1963.

Janoff, Murray. "AFL Grabs Brawny Linemen in 18-Hour Drafting Marathon." *The Sporting News*, December 11, 1965.

_____. "Air Arm of Chiefs Skyjacks Jets in Shaky Knee Duel." *The Sporting News*, January 3, 1970.

_____. "Broadway Joe Makes a Pitch — 'Rams Could Win Super Bowl With Me.'" *The Sporting News*, March 13, 1976.

_____. "Docs to Repair Injured Tendon In Namath Knee." *The Sporting News*, March 23, 1968.

_____. "It's a New Namath With Half-Million Pact." *The Sporting News*, August 19, 1972.

_____. "Jet Stickout Sauer Proves Father Knows Best." *The Sporting News*, October 19, 1968.

_____. "Jets and Joe Expect to Fly Away With Kentucky Babe." *The Sporting News*, August 17, 1968.

_____. "Jets' Boozer Already Romping After November Knee Surgery." *The Sporting News*, March 23, 1968.

_____. "Jets' Philbin Never Quits, He Always Rushes." *The Sporting News*, December 23, 1967.

_____. "Most Dangerous? Jet Vet Maynard." *The Sporting News*, November 18, 1967.

_____. "Namath Dazzler of Old — But He Spots Mistakes." *The Sporting News*, December 11, 1971.

_____. "Ouch! Those Bunions Spur Jets' Boozer." *The Sporting News*, October 21, 1967.

_____. "Parlor Magician Lou Holtz Will Try Rope Trick on Cellar-Dwelling Jets." *The Sporting News*, February 28, 1976.

_____. "Revived Namath Scoffs at Injury Jinx." *The Sporting News*, October 7, 1972.

_____. "Sample Thirsting for Shot at NFL." *The Sporting News*, November 16, 1968.

_____. "A Super Bowl Special — Can Weeb Tame Colts?" *The Sporting News*, January 11, 1969.

_____. "Unhappy Tarkenton Rejoins Giants." *The Sporting News*, August 28, 1971.

_____. "'We Can Do It Again!' — Namath." *Pro Football Sports Stars of 1969*, Winter 1969, Vol. 2, No. 3.

_____. "Willie Joe — A Barrel of Boos With Bouquets." *The Sporting News*, December 28, 1968.

"Jaworski: 'I don't think the Rams are that much better.'" *Bucks County Courier Times* (Levittown, PA), September 26, 1977.

Jenkins, Dan. "The Sweet Life of Swinging Joe." *Sports Illustrated*, October 17, 1966, Vol. 25, No. 16.

"Jet Coach Ewbank Criticizes Officials." *The New Mexican* (Santa Fe), December 18, 1967.

"Jet Defender Calls Team 'The Best I've Played For.'" *Daily Review* (Hayward, CA), January 5, 1969.

"Jet Ground Attack Whips Bengals, 21–7." *Las Cruces Sun-News* (NM), October 13, 1969.

"Jet Linemen Must Protect Joe Willie's Knees Again." *Las Cruces Sun-News* (NM), August 23, 1974.

"Jet Namath Will Be Free Agent After '71 Season." *Press-Courier* (Oxnard, CA), May 20, 1970.

"Jets Advance to Super Bowl." *Albuquerque Journal*, December 30, 1968.

"Jets Ahead." *Beckley Post-Herald* (WV), November 8, 1965.

"Jets and Giants Play 31–31 Tie." *Post-Standard* (Syracuse, NY), August 21, 1972.

"Jets Annex 6th Straight." *Post-Standard* (Syracuse, NY), December 16, 1974.

"Jets Are Not Awe Struck by Colts." *Ogden Standard-Examiner* (UT), January 7, 1969.

"Jets Are Pleased To Have Joe Back." *Gallup Independent* (NM), August 18, 1970.

"Jets Ask Waivers On Johnny Sample." *Anniston Star* (AL), August 27, 1969.

"Jets Beat Bills On Turner's Toe." *Panama City Herald* (FL), November 4, 1968.

"Jets beat Colts in aerial show." *Morning Herald* (Hagerstown, MD), December 16, 1974.

"Jets Beaten, But Namath Is Big Hit." *Des Moines Register,* September 3, 1965.

"Jets Beaten 14–10 By KC; Namath Plays." *Times-Record* (Troy, N.Y.), September 20, 1965.

"Jets bid to bolster defense." *Lima News* (OH), August 17, 1975.

"Jets Blast Boston's Bid to Clinch, 38–28." *Albuquerque Journal,* December 18, 1966.

"Jets Blitz Cincy, 40–7." *Oakland Tribune,* November 24, 1969.

"Jets Bomb Boston Out Of 1967 AFL Title Race." *Lowell Sun* (MA), October 30, 1967.

"Jets bop Chargers to clinch tie for title." *New Castle News* (PA), November 25, 1968.

"Jets capture first AFL crown." *Jefferson City Post-Tribune* (MO), December 30, 1968.

"Jets Capture First Victory of Season." *Albuquerque Journal,* October 11, 1976.

"Jets Cash in on Bills, 20–10." *Post-Standard* (Syracuse, NY), December 9, 1974.

"Jets Clinch Eastern Title." *Albuquerque Journal,* December 7, 1969.

"Jets Clip Redskins 35–31." *Pacific Stars & Stripes* (Tokyo), September 10, 1975.

"Jets Clobber Dolphins, 29–7, To Take First." *Bridgeport Telegram* (CT), October 2, 1967.

"Jets Close Exhibition Slate; Colts in Action." *Jefferson City Post-Tribune* (MO), September 1, 1966.

"Jets Clout Broncos, 45–10, for First Win." *Bridgeport Telegram,* November 1, 1965.

"Jets Club Patriots, 47–31, Behind Namath, Turner." *Bridgeport Telegram* (CT), September 23, 1968.

"Jets Coach Fumes Over Officials In Raider Game." *Big Spring Herald* (TX), December 18, 1967.

"Jets Coast To 31–7 Victory." *Panama City News* (FL), December 16, 1968.

"Jets, Colts In Countdown." *Weirton Daily Times* (WV), January 10, 1969.

"Jets continue streak, waltz past Chargers." *Press-Telegram* (Long Beach, CA), December 2, 1974.

"Jets Continue To Win Despite Inept Performance." *Bridgeport Post* (CT), November 10, 1969.

"Jets continue to win in AFL, but fail to display 'super team.'" *Jefferson City Post-Tribune* (MO), November 10, 1969.

"Jets Cop Title With 34–26 Win." *Lima News* (OH), December 7, 1969.

"Jets crush Atlanta Falcons 27–12." *News & Tribune* (Jefferson City, MO), August 25, 1968.

"The Jets Decide." *Times Record* (Troy, NY), September 8, 1965.

"Jets Defeat Dolphins; Boozer Runs 96 Yards." *Bridgeport Telegram,* November 21, 1966.

"Jets Defeat Vikings, 20–15." *Evening Tribune* (Albert Lea, MN), August 11, 1975.

"Jets' Defense Stars In Win Over Raiders." *Times Recorder* (Zanesville, OH), October 9, 1967.

"Jets' defense steals show, four passes." *Newport Daily News* (RI), November 18, 1974.

"Jets Discipline Namath: 'I Let The Team Down.'" *Las Cruces Sun-News* (NM), December 16, 1975.

"Jets, Dolphins Clash In AFL Feature Friday." *Jefferson City Post-Tribune* (MO), September 8, 1966.

"Jets Down Dolphins." *Albuquerque Journal,* December 15, 1969.

"Jets down Oilers, take AFL lead; Maynard snares seven passes." *Lowell Sun* (MA), October 21, 1969.

"Jets Drop 49ers." *Albuquerque Journal,* August 6, 1972.

"Jets Dump Bengals In AFL Title Tuneup." *Times Recorder* (Zanesville, OH), December 9, 1968.

"Jets Dump Houston Move Nearer Title." *Times Recorder* (Zanesville, OH), November 11, 1968.

"Jets Easily Top Bengals." *Albuquerque Journal,* October 13, 1969.

"Jets Edge Bills, 14–12." *Times Recorder* (Zanesville, OH), December 20, 1965.

"Jets Edge Buffalo." *Times Recorder* (Zanesville, OH), November 4, 1968.

"Jets Edge Buffalo By 25–21 Score." *Albuquerque Journal,* November 4, 1968.

"Jets Edge Dolphins With 2nd Half Rally." *Times Recorder* (Zanesville, OH), November 3, 1969.

"Jets edge Falcons on Howfield FGs." *European Stars & Stripes* (Germany), September 4, 1972.

"Jets Edge Oilers On Late Field Goal." *Del Rio News-Herald* (TX), August 5, 1973.

"Jets Edge Oilers, 13–7." *San Antonio Light,* August 27, 1967.

"Jets Eke Out Victory Over Saints." *Post-Standard* (Syracuse), December 4, 1972.

"Jets Embarrass Cincy In Final Game, 35–21." *Journal News,* December 20, 1971.

"Jets End Road Slump, 13 to 10, Over Chiefs." *Bridgeport Telegram* (CT), November 8, 1965.

"Jets end tailspin, thanks to Patriots." *Newport Daily News* (RI), December 8, 1975.

"Jets expected to be better this year without Namath." *Las Vegas Daily Optic,* August 18, 1971.

"Jets face same old dilemma, no Namath." *Daily Capital News* (Jefferson City, MO), August 20, 1971.

"Jets finish with a flourish, 45–38." *Press-Telegram* (Long Beach, CA), December 16, 1974.

"Jets Get Back On Right Track." *Panama City News* (FL), October 6, 1969.

"Jets get first victory." *Daily Review* (Hayward, CA), October 11, 1976.

"Jets, Giants Battle To Wild 31–31 Tie." *Albuquerque Journal,* August 21, 1972.

"Jets, Giants fire blanks." *Press-Telegram* (Long Beach, CA), October 25, 1976.

"Jets, Giants Play Tie." *Panama City News-Herald* (FL), August 21, 1972.

"Jets, Giants Still Have That Losing Touch." *Independent* (Long Beach, CA), December 1, 1975.

"Jets given underdog role." *Arizona Republic* (Phoenix), December 20, 1969.

"Jets Grind Out Oilers in AL Exhibition Grid Test." *Colorado Springs Gazette-Telegraph,* August 27, 1967.

"Jets Ground Attack Beats Bengals, 21–7." *Bridgeport Telegram* (CT), October 13, 1969.

"Jets Ground Giants in OT." *Post-Standard* (Syracuse, NY), November 11, 1974.

"Jets Grounded by Oiler Gusher; Suddenly There's a Race in East." *San Antonio Light,* October 17, 1966.

"Jets grounded by Steelers." *Valley Independent* (Monessen, PA), December 1, 1975.

"Jets' High-Priced Namath Is Shelved." *Charleston Gazette,* August 15, 1966.

"Jets Hold Ball To Beat Chiefs." *Bridgeport Post* (CT), September 16, 1968.

"Jets hold Namath out, shade Cards." *Independent Press-Telegram* (Long Beach, CA), August 17, 1975.

"Jets hold off All-Star rally to take 26–24 triumph." *News & Tribune* (Jefferson City, MO), August 3, 1969.

"Jets' Howfield Gives Himself Big Birthday Gift." *San Antonio Light,* December 4, 1972.

"Jets in Running if Namath Stays Healthy." *San Antonio Light,* September 10, 1972.

"Jets' Joe Namath Suffers Broken Bone in Right Wrist." *Albuquerque Journal,* October 20, 1970.

"Jets Jolt Bills 20–10 In Namath's Farewell." *Times Recorder* (Zanesville, OH), December 9, 1974.

"Jets Jolt Colts, 34–10." *Albuquerque Journal,* September 24, 1973.

"Jets Jump Bengals By 27–14." *Albuquerque Journal,* December 9, 1968.

"Jets Keep Hex." *Panama City News-Herald* (FL), December 13, 1971.

"Jets Look For First Win In Oakland Game." *Post-Register* (Idaho Falls, ID), October 17, 1965.

"Jets Lose, But Namath Looks Good," *Ogden Standard-Examiner* (UT), September 27, 1965.

"Jets lose 4th in row." *Times Herald Record* (Middletown, NY), October 4, 1976.

"Jets Lose; Namath Hurt." *Daily Gazette* (Xenia, OH), August 21, 1967.

"Jets may finally believe they can win 'division.'" *Jefferson City Post-Tribune* (MO), August 29, 1968.

"Jets, Minus Namath, Lose To Oilers In Exhibition Game." *Las Cruces Sun-News* (NM), August 13, 1968.

"Jets: Namath Back." *News & Tribune* (Jefferson City, MO), August 31, 1975.

"Jets, Namath Nip Chargers For 4th Win." *Times Recorder* (Zanesville, OH), October 9, 1966.

"Jets' Namath Proves Worthy Of Big Bonus." *Grit,* September 25, 1966.

"Jets, Namath Romp Over Tampa Bay." *Times Recorder* (Zanesville, OH), November 15, 1976.

"Jets' Namath Steams Following 24–21 loss." *Lima News,* October 24, 1966.

"Jets' Namath To Undergo More Knee Surgery For Torn Cartilage." *Burlington Daily Times-News* (NC), December 22, 1966.

"Jets Near Title." *Albuquerque Journal,* November 11, 1968.

"Jets nip Big Red." *News & Tribune* (Jefferson City, MO), August 17, 1975.

"Jets Nip Chargers, 23–20, On 4th Quarter Boozer TD." *Bridgeport Post* (CT), October 6, 1968.

"Jets Nip Chiefs By One Point." *Times Record* (Troy, NY), September 16, 1968.

"Jets Nip Eagles On Goal." *Pacific Stars & Stripes* (Tokyo), September 12, 1973.

"Jets Nip Raiders, 27–23." *Frederick News-Post* (MD), December 30, 1968.

"Jets Nip Saints 18–17." *Times Recorder* (Zanesville, OH), December 4, 1972.

"Jets Not A Complete Team." *Raleigh Register* (WV), January 1, 1969.

"Jets not acting like world champs—on field or off." *Daily Capital News* (Jefferson City, MO), August 6, 1969.

"Jets not certain who'll be playing." *Jefferson City Post-Tribune* (MO), August 13, 1970.

"Jets nudge past San Diego 23–20." *News and Tribune* (Jefferson City, MO), October 6, 1968.

"Jets, Oakland Deadlock." *Kingsport Times-News* (TN), December 4, 1966.

"Jets Offer $400,000 For Namath." *Standard-Examiner* (Ogden, UT), December 30, 1964.

"Jets Outlast Baltimore." *Wisconsin State Journal,* December 3, 1973.

"Jets Outlast Bears." *Post-Standard* (Syracuse, NY), September 23, 1974.

"Jets Overcome Dolphins." *Bridgeport Telegram* (CT), November 3, 1969.

"Jets overrun Bucs 34–0." *Times Herald Record* (Middletown, NY), November 15, 1976.

"Jets Overwhelm Weak Chiefs' Defense 30–24." *Atchison Globe* (KS), September 29, 1975.

"Jets pin hopes on Namath." *Pocono Record* (Stroudsburg, PA), September 12, 1967.

"Jets pull out last-second 17–14 victory over Bills." *Times Herald Record* (Middletown, NY), October 11, 1976.

"Jets, Raiders In 28–28 Tie." *Times Recorder* (Zanesville, OH), December 4, 1966.

"Jets Rally, Beat Dolphins, 35–17." *Panama City News* (FL), December 2, 1968.

"Jets Rally For Tie." *Abilene Reporter-News,* October 3, 1966.

"Jets Rally to Beat Bills, 17–14." *Bridgeport Telegram* (CT), October 11, 1976.

"Jets Ran Bills Ragged." *Daily Messenger* (Canandaigua, NY), September 18, 1972.

"Jets Rebound To Tie Raiders." *Fresno Bee,* October 17, 1965.

"Jets Rip Miami In Playoff Tuneup." *Oakland Tribune,* December 16, 1968.

"Jets Roll Behind Namath." *Albuquerque Journal,* November 25, 1968.

"Jets rout 49ers." *European Stars & Stripes* (Darmstadt, Hesse, Germany), August 13, 1973.

"Jets Run Over Bengals Easily, 21–7." *Troy Record* (NY), October 13, 1969.

"Jets Say Illegal Play Cost Game." *Corpus Christi Times,* September 13, 1965.

"Jets Scare Rams In 20–13 Loss." *Times Record* (Troy, NY), October 28, 1974.

"Jets, 6–37." *Press-Telegram* (Long Beach, CA), November 24, 1975.

"Jets Slim Favorites In AFL Tilt." *Lima News* (OH), December 29, 1968.

"Jets Spoil Pat Sullivan's Pro Debut." *Florence Morning News* (SC), September 4, 1972.

"Jets Squeak To Victory At Chicago." *Salt Lake Tribune* (UT), September 23, 1974.

"Jets Squeeze Past." *Moberly Monitor-Index* (MO), August 2, 1969.

"Jets sting Patriots 47–31." *Jefferson City Post-Tribune,* September 23, 1968.

"Jets Struggle Again, 16–6." *The Bee* (Danville, VA), November 10, 1969.

"Jets Stun Dolphs, 17–14." *Playground Daily News* (Ft. Walton Beach, FL), November 25, 1974.

"Jets Subvert Patriots for Third in Row." *Washington Post,* November 15, 1965.

"Jets swap Maynard to Cards." *Pocono Record* (Stroudsburgs, PA), September 11, 1973.

"Jets' Taliaferro 'Poor Man's Quarterback.'" *Gazette-Mail* (Charleston, WV), September 12, 1965.

"Jets Think Joe To Return." *Cedar Rapids Gazette,* June 12, 1969.

"Jets Thrash Patriots, 34–10." *Bridgeport Telegram* (CT), October 30, 1972.

"Jets tie Chargers on Howfield's FG." *European Stars & Stripes* (Darmstadt, Hesse, Germany), September 11, 1972.

"Jets Tip Colts, 45–38, Behind Namath, Defense." *Bridgeport Telegram* (CT), December 16, 1974.

"Jets top Cards." *Daily Capital News* (Jefferson City, MO), August 24, 1974.

"Jets Top Pats To Halt Losing Skein." *Galveston Daily News* (TX), December 8, 1975.

"Jets Topple Buffalo, 41–24." *Panama City News-Herald* (FL), September 18, 1972.

"Jets Trim Bills, 16–6 For Sixth Straight Win." *Aiken Standard and Review* (SC), November 10, 1969.

"Jets Trim Seven Veterans." *Brownsville Herald* (TX), August 27, 1969.

"Jets Trip Vikes." *Star-News* (Pasadena, CA), August 10, 1975.

"Jets Trounced by Broncos 46–3." *Times Herald Record* (Middletown, NY), September 20, 1976.

"Jets Tumble Raiders." *Lowell Sun* (MA), October 8, 1967.

"Jets Upend Pats." *Las Cruces Sun-News* (NM), December 18, 1966.

"Jets Upset by Bills." *Post-Standard* (Syracuse, NY), October 5, 1970.

"Jets View Own Films." *Frederick News-Post* (MD), January 3, 1969.

"Jets Wallop Bills, 41–3." *Panama City News-Herald* (FL), November 13, 1972.

"Jets Wallop Patriots, 41–13." *Nashua Telegraph* (NH), October 16, 1972.

"Jets Whip Bills By 41–3 Margin." *Post-Standard* (Syracuse), November 13, 1972.

"Jets Whip Broncos for 3d Straight." *Post Standard* (Syracuse), September 26, 1966.

"Jets Whip Colts, But Lose Namath." *Times Recorder* (Zanesville, OH), September 24, 1973.

"Jets Whip Miami." *Times Recorder* (Zanesville, OH), December 2, 1968.

"Jets Whitewash Tampa." *Albuquerque Journal,* November 15, 1976.

"Jets Whiz Past Cincy." *Albuquerque Journal,* November 24, 1969.

"Jets Win, 415 Yards for Namath." *Press-Telegram* (Long Beach, CA), October 2, 1967.

"Jets Win Fourth Straight, 27–14." *Post-Standard* (Syracuse, NY), December 2, 1974.

"Jets Win On Toe, Defense." *Oakland Tribune,* November 10, 1969.

"Jets win opener, Namath on job." *Syracuse Herald Journal,* September 10, 1966.

"Jets win thriller from All-Stars." *Daily Capital News* (Jefferson City, MO), August 2, 1969.

"Jets Win 27–14 Behind Riggins." *Times Recorder* (Zanesville, OH), December 2, 1974.

"Joe Blames Win — And KC Defense." *Oakland Tribune,* December 21, 1969.

"Joe Calls 'Automatic.'" *The Bee* (Danville, VA), July 14, 1969.

"Joe Cool On Dolphins: No. 1." *Fresno Bee Republican,* October 8, 1974.

"Joe First Warned Three Months Ago." *San Antonio Express and News,* June 7, 1969.

"Joe Had the Right Answer: His New Car Is Jet Green." *The Sporting News,* January 16, 1965.

"Joe Has Presence Of Star." *San Antonio Express and News,* June 7, 1969.

"Joe: I Let everyone down." *Syracuse Herald-Journal,* December 16, 1975.

"Joe, Jets Try To Get Back On Win Side." *The Bee* (Danville, VA), August 30, 1969.

"Joe Laughs Off Michaels' Dare." *Delaware County Daily Times* (PA), January 8, 1969.

"Joe Namath admires Plunkett's knees." *Billings Gazette* (MT), December 13, 1971.

"Joe Namath and the Jet-Propelled Offense." *Time,* October 16, 1972, Vol. 100, No. 16.

"Joe Namath Appears Ready to Start Today." *Albuquerque Journal,* December 17, 1972.

"Joe Namath Could End Title Race For Cleveland Browns." *Times Recorder* (Zanesville, OH), December 17, 1972.

"Joe Namath Directs Jets To Victory Over Cardinals." *Ogden Standard-Examiner* (UT), August 24, 1974.

"Joe Namath Guarantees Win, Ewbank Hedges." *Albuquerque Journal,* January 11, 1969.

"Joe Namath guides Jets to berth in Super Bowl." *Pocono Record* (Stroudsburg, PA), December 30, 1968.

"Joe Namath: Hey, folks, it's not end of the world." *Independent* (Long Beach, CA), September 19, 1977.

"Joe Namath, However, Won't Lambast Raiders." *The New Mexican* (Santa Fe), December 18, 1967.

"Joe Namath hurt, but will face Cards." *Post-Register* (Idaho Falls), August 17, 1975.

"Joe Namath in pain ... and Jets are hurting, too." *Jefferson City Post-Tribune* (MO), October 20, 1970.

"Joe Namath Is The Heart Of Crimson Tide Offense." *The Star* (Anniston, AL), November 11, 1963.

"Joe Namath Leads Club To Deadlock." *Bridgeport Telegram,* October 3, 1966.

"Joe Namath Leads Jets Over Boston." *Portsmouth Herald* (NH), October 6, 1969.

"Joe Namath leads Jets over Dallas." *Post-Tribune* (Jefferson City, MO), September 14, 1970.

"Joe Namath Leads Jets to 30–23 Win Over Patriots." *Bridgeport Post* (CT), October 30, 1967.

"Joe Namath Not Likely To Forget Texas' Goalline Stand

In Orange Tilt." *The Star* (Anniston, AL), January 2, 1965.

"Joe Namath On His Way To The Rams?" *Clovis News-Journal* (NM), March 22, 1977.

"Joe Namath Paces Jets To Victory." *Albuquerque Journal,* December 25, 1967.

"Joe Namath Rallies Jets Over Broncos." *Albuquerque Journal,* September 25, 1967.

"Joe Namath Saves Tie For Jets." *Albuquerque Journal,* October 16, 1967.

"Joe Namath Sparks Jets To Victory." *Bridgeport Telegram* (CT), September 26, 1966.

"Joe Namath Starts Super Bowl Feud." *Capital Times* (Madison, WI), January 7, 1969.

"Joe Namath tells all about his woes after workout at Jets' training camp." *Jefferson City Post-Tribune* (MO), August 19, 1970.

"Joe Namath To Start in Senior Bowl." *Fairbanks Daily News-Miner,* January 8, 1965.

"Joe Namath Triggers Jets Past Chargers." *Albuquerque Journal,* October 9, 1966.

"Joe not budging as Jets open camp." *Brandon Sun* (Manitoba), July 14, 1969.

"Joe the Jet Injured." *The Sporting News,* December 30, 1967.

"Joe the Jet Nailed by Texas Dan." *Oakland Tribune,* October 24, 1966.

"Joe Willie on target, Weeb was, too." *Journal News* (Hamilton, OH), December 16, 1972.

"Joe Willie true to self." *Daily Chronicle* (Centralia, WA), August 31, 1974.

"Joe's Back, Jets Happy." *The Sporting News,* August 29, 1970.

"Joe's experience wins out." *Pacific Stars & Stripes* (Tokyo), September 17, 1977.

"Joe's future uncertain." *Daily Capital News* (Jefferson City, MO), August 8, 1970.

"Joe's handshake hurt." *News & Tribune* (Jefferson City, MO), September 7, 1969.

"Joe's Impressive 'Farewell.'" *Nevada State Journal,* December 9, 1974.

"John David Crow Carries 49ers Hopes In NFL; Namath, Huarte Fight For New York AB Spot." *Post-Tribune* (Jefferson City, MO), August 27, 1965.

"John Unitas Isn't Miffed." *Panama City News* (FL), January 9, 1969.

Johnson, William. "Mod Man Out." *Sports Illustrated,* June 16, 1969, Vol. 30, No. 24.

"Jones Helps Colts Romp by Jets, 52–19." *Press-Courier* (Oxnard, CA), November 17, 1975.

"Jones leads Colts past Jets, 45–28." *Frederick News-Post* (MD), October 27, 1975.

"Jones Sparks Browns To Win Over Jets." *Las Cruces Sun-News* (NM), September 22, 1970.

"'Juice' Powers Bills Past Jets by 24–23." *Salt Lake Tribune* (UT), November 3, 1975.

Kaegel, Dick. "Grantham, Namath Gun Down Raiders." *The Sporting News,* October 21, 1967.

_____. "Namath Has Big First Half." *The Sporting News,* November 4, 1967.

_____. "Will Boozer Injury Clog Jet Fuel Line?" *The Sporting News,* November 18, 1967.

Kale, Gary. "Crane joins Namath in pacing Jets." *Columbus Daily Telegram* (NE), September 23, 1968.

_____. "Jets and Raiders In Title Contest." *Times Recorder* (Zanesville, OH), December 29, 1968.

_____. Namath Returns; Jets Still Lose." *Las Cruces Sun-News* (NM), November 29, 1971.

Kallestad, Brent. "Big Plays Help Vikings Beat New York, 29–21." *Albert Lea Tribune* (MN), October 13, 1975.

"Kansas City Bops NY Jets, 34–16." *Albuquerque Journal,* November 17, 1969.

"Kansas City Clinches Title." *Albuquerque Journal,* November 28, 1966.

"Kansas City Edges Jets." *Tri-City Herald* (Pasco, WA), September 19, 1965.

"Kansas City Sputters to 30–17 Win." *Colorado Springs Gazette-Telegraph,* August 13, 1967.

"Kemp, Namath, Dawson Sparkle in AFL Action." *Albuquerque Tribune,* November 15, 1965.

"Kilmer Leads 'Skins Over Jets." *Albuquerque Journal,* November 6, 1972.

"Kilmer leads Washington to fifth straight victory." *Pocono Record* (PA), November 6, 1972.

"Kilmer paces 'Skins over Jets 38–7." *Times Herald Record* (Middleton, NY), August 29, 1976.

King, Joe. "Grid Pros' Battle For Talent Flares With Dual Signings." *The Sporting News,* January 16, 1965.

_____. "Jet Threat to Giant Popularity Bursts in Late-Season Collapse." *The Sporting News,* December 30, 1967.

Kjos, Les. "Dolphins' Long TD Plays Seal Fate of Namath, Jets," *The Sporting News,* November 22, 1975.

"Knee Surgery Faces Jets' Namath Again." *Fond du Lac Commonwealth Reporter* (WI), December 22, 1966.

"Knee Will Be Key To Namath Draft." *Fresno Bee Republican,* August 12, 1965.

"Knox' move gave Namath edge over Eagles." *Bucks County Courier Times* (Levittown, PA), September 26, 1977.

Kois, Dennis C. "Explosive Jets No So This Time." *Fond du Lac Reporter,* September 18, 1973.

Koppett, Leonard. "Break Up the Jets." *New York Times,* November 1, 1965.

_____. "Jets Reward Fans With First Victory Of Year." *Morgantown Post* (WV), November 1, 1965.

_____. "Namath Case Raises Sticky Issues." *The Sporting News,* January 3, 1976.

Koster, Rich. "Injury Tab $2 Million For Pro Football in 1969." *The Sporting News,* November 14, 1970.

Kowet, Don. "What Joe Namath Learned Last Year By Not Playing." *Pro Football Almanac 1971,* 1971.

Kremenko, Barney. "Jet Star Namath Listed in Met Files as '61 Baseball Prospect." *The Sporting News,* January 7, 1967.

_____. "Jets Eye 3rd Straight Champion in Lammons." *The Sporting News,* December 10, 1966.

_____. "Jets Skim Cash Clouds in Landing Alabama Star: $400,000 Namath Viewed As Short Cut to AFL Title." *The Sporting News,* January 16, 1965.

_____. "Jets Soar on Joe's Improved Reading." *The Sporting News,* October 22, 1966.

_____. "Llama Rug and Oval bed All Part of Namath's Pad." *The Sporting News,* November 5, 1966.

_____. "Success Won't Spoil Namath, AFL's Regal Rookie." *The Sporting News,* January 1, 1966.

Krikorian, Doug. "Pat Haden Is Everything a QB Shouldn't Be." *The Sporting News,* December 17, 1977.

"LA Rams Upset By Atlanta." *Albuquerque Journal,* September 19, 1977.

LaMarre, Tom. "Jets Out of Playoffs." *Oakland Tribune,* December 12, 1972.

"Lammons' Touchdown Snaps Tie." *Bridgeport Telegram* (CT), October 30, 1967.

"Lamonica Stars In Coveted Win." *Bridgeport Telegram* (CT), December 18, 1967.

Langford, George C. "Namath: $400,000 Impression." *El Paso Herald-Post,* September 27, 1965.

Larson, Al. "Eagles impressed, depressed after being pounded by Rams." *Independent* (Long Beach, CA), September 26, 1977.

_____. "Harris surprised by reception." *Independent Press-Telegram* (Long Beach, CA), September 2, 1977.

"Last Second TD Tallied By Dixon." *Bridgeport Telegram,* October 24, 1966.

"Last-minute Namath pass nets Jets victory." *Independent* (Long Beach, CA), October 23, 1972.

"Late Rally Lifts Saints." *Lincoln Star* (NE), September 1, 1974.

"Late Touchdown Allows Raiders to Edge Jets." *Abilene Reporter-News,* October 24, 1966.

"'Law Of Jungle' Aids Joe." *Lima News* (OH), October 8, 1967.

"Lee, Ray Guide Falcons by Jets." *Albuquerque Journal,* November 26, 1973.

The Legend of Broadway Joe NFL Productions, 2006.

"Len Dawson Passes Beat New Yorkers." *Mansfield News Journal* (OH), September 19, 1965.

"Len Dawson Rallies West To 38–25 Win Over East." *San Antonio Express,* January 20, 1969.

Levitt, Ed. "Airport Love-in." *Oakland Tribune,* December 1, 1969.

_____. "Joe in Longies." *Oakland Tribune,* November 30, 1969.

_____. "Joe Wins The Fans." *Oakland Tribune,* December 12, 1972.

_____. "Love-in Taboo." *Oakland Tribune,* December 21, 1969.

_____. "Namath, Ben Feud." *Oakland Tribune,* December 13, 1965.

"Lions claw Jets 37–20, both eye playoff berths." *Montana Standard,* November 24, 1972.

"Lions edge Jets." *News & Tribune* (Jefferson City, MO), August 8, 1971.

Lipsyte, Robert. "Giants Hurt; Jets Capture All of Gotham." *Albuquerque Tribune,* August 18, 1969.

_____. "Namath's Thumb Set Him Up For KC's 'Walking Wall,'" *Fresno Bee,* December 11, 1967.

Liska, Jerry. "Jets Survive Upstart All-Stars Attack; Cook, Taylor Take Glory From Namath." *Las Cruces Sun-News* (NM), August 3, 1969.

Litsky, Frank. "Fans, Bills Turn on Namath, 33–23." *Independent* (Long Beach, CA), October 31, 1966.

_____. "55,000 Expected at Shea Stadium: Jets Seeking First Victory of Season — Taliaferro Starting Quarterback." *New York Times,* October 31, 1965.

_____. "59,001 See Game: Jets' Pass Receivers Have a Hard Time Holding Onto Ball." *New York Times,* October 24, 1965.

_____. "53,717 at Shea Stadium See Jets Rout Broncos, 45–10, for First Victory." *New York Times,* November 1, 1965.

_____. "Giants and Jets to Face Tasks In 2nd-Place Battles Tomorrow." *New York Times,* December 11, 1965.

_____. "Giants' Sights on Playoff Bowl; Jets Also Hope to Finish Second." *New York Times,* December 18, 1965.

_____. "Giants Underdogs, Jets Picked In Cleveland, Boston Tomorrow." *New York Times,* November 13, 1965.

_____. "Gogolak Blanked First time as Pro." *New York Times,* December 20, 1965.

_____. "Jets Are Favored Over Oilers; Cardinals Choice to Top Giants." *New York Times,* November 20, 1965.

_____. "Jets to Meet Best in the West; Giants Facing Least in the East." *New York Times,* December 4, 1965.

_____. "Jets Top Chiefs, 13–10, as West Stars on Defense." *New York Times,* November 8, 1965.

_____. "Late Pass Clicks." *New York Times,* October 17, 1965.

_____. "Namath Passes for 2 Scores as Jets Top Patriots, 30–20, for Third in Row." *New York Times,* November 15, 1965.

_____. "Namath Throws 4 Scoring Passes." *New York Times,* November 22, 1965.

_____. "Patriots Upset Jets, 27–23, With Last-Minute Pass from 2-Yard Line." *New York Times,* November 29, 1965.

_____. "Taliaferro Gets Jet Starting Job." *New York Times,* October 23, 1965.

"Long Namath Pass Saves Jets." *Panama City News-Herald* (FL), October 23, 1972.

"Long Runs By Nelson Wins For Bama's Tide." *Anniston Star* (AL), October 6, 1963.

"Longley-Led Cowboys Slip Past Jets, 31–21." *Playground Daily News* (Ft. Walton Beach, FL), December 22, 1975.

"Lowe's Runs, Hadl's Passes Dazzle Jets As Chargers Roll." *Fresno Bee,* October 24, 1965.

Lowitt, Bruce. "Cardinals Rout Jets." *Danville Register* (VA), November 24, 1975.

_____. "Dolphins Crush Jets, 43–0; Namath Has Six Intercepted." *Bridgeport Post* (CT), October 20, 1975.

_____. "Field generals return; Namath tosses bombs." *Lowell Sun* (MA), November 29, 1971.

_____. "Hapless Jets 'Bombed,' 27–22." *Times Record* (Troy, NY), November 4, 1974.

_____. "Jets' Gamble Backfires In 24–23 Loss To Bills." *Bridgeport Post* (CT), November 3, 1975.

_____. "Jets have more than Joe Namath." *Las Vegas Optic,* August 8, 1973.

_____. "Jets Upset Bills, 20 to 10, In Namath's 'Shea Farewell.'" *Bridgeport Post* (CT), December 9, 1974.

_____. "Namath's passes foil Tampa's bid," *Times Record* (Troy, NY), November 15, 1976.

_____. "Pats Remain Undefeated." *Nashua Telegraph* (NH), October 14, 1974.

_____. "Pats victimize Namath, upend Jets, 38–24." *Kennebec Journal* (Augusta, ME), November 22, 1976.

_____. "Pokes warm up for cold future." *Paris News* (TX), December 22, 1975.

_____. "Wooly Joe Bombs Colts." *Silver City Daily Press* (NM), September 25, 1972.

Lundgren, Hal. "Hadl Hero of AFL's Anti-Climactic All-Star Game." *The Sporting News,* January 31, 1970.

Lundin, Dick. "Morris, Morrall Pace Dolphins to Crown." *News Tribune* (Ft. Pierce, FL), November 20, 1972.

MacFeely, F.T. "Len Dawson Brings Comeback Triumph." *Morning Herald* (Hagerstown, MD), January 20, 1969.

Madden, Bill. "Jets, Without Namath, Lose." *Las Cruces Sun-News* (NM), August 24, 1970.

Maraniss, David. *When Pride Still Mattered: A Life of Vince Lombardi.* New York: Simon & Shuster, 1999.

Maule, Tex. "Joe Bites the Astrodust." *Sports Illustrated,* October 9, 1972, Vol. 37, No. 15.

_____. "Say It's So, Joe." *Sports Illustrated,* January 20, 1969, Vol. 30, No. 3.

May, Glen. "A letter to Joe Namath." *The Drumheller Mail* (Canada), January 8, 1969.

May, Julian. *Joe Namath: High-Flying Quarterback.* Mankato, MN: Crestwood House, 1975.

"Maynard Gets Endorsement From New York Quarterback." *Times Recorder* (Zanesville, OH) December 19, 1965.

"Maynard, Namath Reach Landmarks Despite Loss." *Raleigh Register* (Beckley, WV), December 12, 1972.

"Maynard Sets Mark With 2 TD Catches." *Bridgeport Telegram* (CT), October 21, 1969.

"Maynard Snaps Berry's Record." *Billings Gazette* (MT), December 2, 1968.

"Maynard Was Secondary Receiver On 52-Yard Pass Which Won Tilt." *Albuquerque Journal,* December 30, 1968.

"Maynard's Grab Provides New York With Deadlock." *Bridgeport Telegram* (CT), October 16, 1967.

"Maynard's Pass Record: 87 Yards Longest In Jets' Play." *El Paso Herald-Post,* November 25, 1968.

Mazzeo, Frank. "Namath fails test as Raiders coast." *Valley News* (Van Nuys, CA), September 10, 1977.

"McCutcheon, Stukes 'Homer.'" *Star-News* (Pasadena, CA), October 28, 1974.

McGowen, Deane. "Jets' Precision Sends Mathis on a Long Journey." *New York Times,* November 22, 1965.

_____. "Patriots Cross Up Jets on Key Play." *New York Times,* November 29, 1965.

McGuane, George. "Blocked Punt Costly." *Lowell Sun* (MA), September 23, 1968.

_____. "Jets smother Pats; running game did it." *Lowell Sun* (MA), October 16, 1972.

_____. "Jets victory elates Namath; 'won't be around next year.'" *Lowell Sun* (MA), October 6, 1969.

_____. "Namath lauds Pats." *Lowell Sun* (MA), September 28, 1970.

_____. "Namath subdues Pats." *Lowell Sun* (MA), December 13, 1971.

_____. "Parilli humiliates Patriots." *Lowell Sun* (MA), October 28, 1968.

_____. "Patriots Bow in Thriller, 29–24." *Lowell Sun* (MA), November 20, 1967.

_____. "Pats continue to fade." *Lowell Sun* (MA), November 18, 1974.

_____. "Pats nearly upset." *Lowell Sun* (MA), October 27, 1969.

_____. "Pats right Rx for Jets; Namath Keeps hex intact." *Lowell Sun* (MA), December 8, 1975.

_____. "Pats Sit and Wait." *Lowell Sun* (MA), December 18, 1966.

_____. "Pats smash Jet jinx." *Lowell Sun* (MA), October 19, 1976.

_____. "Win had Arizona St. flavor." *Lowell Sun* (MA), November 22, 1976.

McMane, Fred. "Broadway Joe Jolted as Jets Drop 27–14 Clash to Raiders." *Bennington Banner* (VT), December 1, 1969.

_____. "Namath turns runner to clinch victory for Jets." *Chronicle Telegram* (Elyria, OH), October 6, 1969.

_____. "'On Our Way,' Says Maynard." *El Paso Herald-Post,* October 21, 1969.

_____. "Pro Football Sizeup." *Sheboygan Journal* (WI), September 14, 1970.

Means, Ray. "Hadl Wins Personal Duel With Namath." *Anderson Herald* (IN), December 5, 1965.

Meier, Ted. "Doomsday Gang waits for Namath." *Las Vegas Optic,* September 3, 1969.

_____. "Namath's Pro Debut Doesn't Stack Up to That of Huarte." *Charleston Gazette* (WV), August 9, 1965.

"Miami, Bengals Nab Wins." *Salt Lake Tribune* (UT), November 10, 1975.

"Miami Devastates Jets." *Victoria Advocate* (TX), October 20, 1975.

"Miami Dolphins Surprised By Namath Scoring Pass." *Nevada State Journal,* November 25, 1974.

"Miami Dolphins Trip Weakened Jets, 20 to 6." *Bridgeport Post* (CT), October 11, 1970.

"Miami Dumps Jets." *Albuquerque Journal,* September 27, 1976.

"Miami has little trouble with Jets." *Billings Gazette* (MT), September 27, 1976.

"Miami Now 4–0, Jumps Jets 27–17." *Playground Daily News* (Ft. Walton Beach, FL), October 9, 1972.

"Miami, Shula Not Happy Despite Win Over Jets." *News Tribune* (Ft. Pierce, FL), September 27, 1976.

"Miami Stops Jets, 27–7." *Albuquerque Journal,* November 10, 1975.

"Miami Tops Jets, 20–6." *Playground Daily News* (Ft. Walton Beach, FL), October 11, 1970.

"Might be year for Pittsburgh." *Las Vegas Optic,* August 15, 1972.

"Mike Holovak Faults Defense for Setback." *Bridgeport Post* (CT), December 18, 1966.

"Mike Mercer Boots Bills Past Jets; Oakland Romps." *Lima News* (OH), September 11, 1967.

Miller, Norm. "Huarte Unclaimed In AFL; Placed On Taxi Squad." *Jefferson City Post-Tribune* (MO), September 9, 1965.

"Mitchell Carries Colts." *Post-Standard* (Syracuse, NY), October 21, 1974.

"Mitchell stars as Baltimore beats Jets for first victory." *Frederick News-Post* (MD), October 21, 1974.

Mizell, Hubert. "Miami Dolphins Ground Namath-Jets 27–17." *Gallup Independent* (NM), October 9, 1972.

Moeller, Bill. "Lucky Bengals finally snatch one from Jets." *Journal News* (Hamilton, OH), November 19, 1973.

Moore, Robert. "Jets Riddle NFL Pride." *Albuquerque Tribune,* August 18, 1969.

Moran, Sheila. "Jets have woeful night." *Las Vegas Optic,* August 26, 1969.

_____. "Namath Doubtful Starter In Jets-Cowboys Clash." *Moberly Monitor-Index* (MO), September 5, 1969.

Morey, Charles. "Is Joe Namath Looking For Big Trouble?" *Pro Sports,* January 1967, Vol. 3, No. 1.

_____. "Rating the Quarterbacks." *Sport World,* December 1973, Vol. 12, No. 6.

Mooshil, Joe. "Bears' rally falls short; Jets, Namath win 23–21." *Daily Leader* (Pontiac, IL), September 23, 1974.

"Morrall can't respect Namath's style of life." *Montana Standard* (Butte), November 17, 1972.

"Morrall Considered Retiring." *Winona Daily News* (MN), January 6, 1969.

"Morrall Mauls Critics." *The Sporting News,* December 21, 1968.

"Morrall Says 'Let Joe Talk.'" *Cedar Rapids Gazette,* January 10, 1969.

"Morrall Says Namath May Be Good Quarterback, But Does Not Respect Him," *The Register* (Danville, VA), November 17, 1972.

"Morton and Namath Slated As Starters." *Las Cruces Sun-News* (NM), August 25, 1972.

Murray, Jim. "Super Sunday: The Mouse Roars." *Des Moines Register,* January 13, 1969.

"'Mystery Men' to Aid Raiders." *San Mateo Times* (CA), December 25, 1968.

"19-Point Spread Doesn't Bother Jet Al Atkinson." *Frederick News-Post* (MD), January 7, 1969.

Namath, Joe. *Namath.* New York: Rugged Land, 2006.

_____. "Namath." *Las Cruces Sun-News* (NM), August 21, 1977.

Namath, Joe; and Bob Oates. *A Matter of Style.* Boston: Little, Brown, 1973.

Namath, Joe; and Dick Schaap. *I Can't Wait Until Tomorrow... 'Cause I Get Better Looking Every Day.* New York: Random House: 1969.

"Namath Ace In Gotham's Quick Start." *Bridgeport Telegram* (CT), October 23, 1967.

"Namath Acquires New Face Mask." *Grit,* August 10, 1969.

"Namath Aerial Show Sends Colts Spinning." *Moberly Monitor-Index* (MO), September 25, 1972.

"Namath AFL Star." *Albuquerque Tribune,* November 22, 1965.

"Namath agrees to play for Rams." *Daily Inter Lake* (Kalispell, MT), March 24, 1977.

"Namath and Jets Rally To Tie Patriots, 24–24." *Bridgeport Post,* October 3, 1966.

"Namath Apparently Wants More Money." *Independent-Record* (Helena, MT), August 7, 1970.

"Namath Arm Sharp, But Jets Beaten." *Des Moines Register,* September 27, 1965.

"Namath Baffles Colts." *Independent* (Long Beach, CA), December 3, 1973.

"Namath Bashed, Bears Hold Off Rams Bid in Rain." *Press-Courier* (Oxnard, CA), October 11, 1977.

"Namath belittles Cowboys' defense." *Post-Tribune* (Jefferson City, MO), September 5, 1969.

"Namath, Bell Combine As Jets Nip Baltimore." *Bridgeport Post* (CT), October 23, 1972.

"Namath Bitter as Reporters Jam Dressing Room of Jets." *Appleton Post-Crescent* (WI), January 13, 1969.

"Namath Bombards Dolphins by 29–7." *News Tribune* (Ft. Pierce, FL), October 2, 1967.

"Namath Bombs Saints." *Pacific Stars & Stripes* (Tokyo), September 4, 1973.

"Namath-Boozer TD Pass Leads Jets Over Giants." *Playground Daily News* (Ft. Walton Beach, FL), November 11, 1974.

"Namath, Bowing Out at 35, Left Mark on Pro Football." *The Sporting News,* February 11, 1978.

"Namath calls shots as Rams win, 20–0." *Wisconsin State Journal,* September 26, 1977.

"Namath Certain Now, Wants To Play in 1971." *Iowa City Press-Citizen* (November 17, 1970).

"Namath checks into camp, complains of knee ailment." *Daily Capital News* (Jefferson City, MO), August 19, 1970.

"Namath Claims Jets Can Win As Teams Prepare For Games." *Jefferson City Post-Tribune* (MO), August 10, 1966.

"Namath, Colt In Hot Episode." *Dominion-News* (Morgantown, WV), January 8, 1969.

"Namath Considers Retirement." *Las Cruces Sun-News* (NM), December 13, 1976.

"Namath decides to report to Jets." *Jefferson City Post-Tribune* (MO), August 18, 1970.

"Namath, defense key Rams." *Argus* (Fremont, CA), September 26, 1977.

"Namath 'Definitely' Out For This Week." *Valley Morning Star,* October 20, 1970.

"Namath Demanding More Money." *Gallup Independent* (NM), August 7, 1970.

"Namath Directs Jets' Win, 20–14." *Press-Telegram* (Long Beach, CA), October 21, 1968.

"Namath directs Jets to victory." *Pocono Record* (Stroudsburg, PA), September 28, 1970.

"Namath disappointed with job against Stars." *News & Tribune* (Jefferson City, MO), August 3, 1969.

"Namath 'Disgusted' In First Pro Start." *Oakland Tribune,* September 27, 1965.

"Namath Drives AFL All-Stars To 30–19 Victory Over Buffalo." *The Times Recorder* (Zanesville, OH), January 16, 1966.

"Namath Engineers All-Star Win." *Albuquerque Journal,* January 16, 1966.

"Namath Expected To Ink Jet's Pact." *Daily Times* (Salisbury, MD), January 2, 1965.

"Namath Expected to Sign Today for $400,000 Plus." *Lowell Sun* (MA), January 2, 1965.

"Namath eyes Rams." *The Independent* (Long Beach, CA), January 19, 1976.

"Namath Faces First NFL Team Tonight." *Warren Times-Mirror and Observer* (PA), August 19, 1967.

"Namath Finds TD Touch as Rams Pass Philadelphia." *Albuquerque Journal,* September 26, 1977.

"Namath, Flores Opposing Passers." *New York Times,* December 12, 1965.

"Namath Foils Giants." *Press-Telegram* (Long Beach, CA), November 11, 1974.

"Namath Fumble Paves Way to Chiefs' Win." *Lowell Sun* (MA), September 19, 1965.

"Namath Gets Big Test." *Albuquerque Tribune,* August 7, 1965.

"Namath given crowd credit." *Las Vegas Optic,* August 1, 1969.

"Namath Grabs Headlines: Colts' Morrall Just Plodding Along." *The Light* (San Antonio), January 9, 1969.

"Namath Greatest — Royal." *Standard-Examiner* (Ogden, UT), January 2, 1965.

"Namath: happiest day of my life." *The Pocono Record* (The Stroudsburgs, PA), December 30, 1968.

"Namath, Hart in." *Daily Capital News* (Jefferson City, MO), August 23, 1974.

"Namath Has Last Chance." *Pro Football,* Fall 1967, Vol. 1, No. 5.

"Namath has praise for Jones as Colts romp over Jets, 52–19." *News* (Frederick, MD), November 17, 1975.

"Namath Has Puffed Knee." *El Paso Herald-Post,* December 8, 1973.

"Namath Headed for Rams." *The Sporting News,* April 16, 1977.

"Namath Hears His First Boos." *Bridgeport Post,* October 31, 1966.

"Namath Helps Jets Down Colts, 20–17." *Syracuse Post-Standard,* December 3, 1973.

"Namath Helps Jets Snap Losing Streak." *Press-Courier* (Oxnard, CA), December 8, 1975.

"Namath Hits Early For Jets." *Panama City News* (FL), December 15, 1969.

"Namath, Hobbled by Injury, Shot Tech Down With Pinpoint Passes." *The Sporting News,* January 2, 1965.

"Namath holds key to Jets' fortunes." *Jefferson City Post-Tribune* (MO), August 8, 1973.

"Namath Hot, But ... Mercer Field Goal Sinks Jets, 20–17." *Press-Telegram* (Long Beach, CA), September 11, 1967.

"Namath hot, Jets roll to 27–9 win." *Argus* (Fremont, CA), December 15, 1969.

"Namath Hurls Jets To Victory." *Post-Standard* (Syracuse, NY), October 23, 1967.

"Namath hurt against Colts, at best will miss 6–8 weeks." *Bennington Banner* (VT), September 24, 1973.

"Namath: 'I Don't Talk About Knees.'" *Daily Review* (Hayward, CA), January 5, 1969.

"Namath In Top Form For Season Opener." *The Bee* (Danville, VA), September 14, 1970.

"Namath Injured As Jets Triumph." *Jefferson City Post-Tribune* (MO), August 15, 1966.

"Namath Injures Shoulder; Jets Trounce Colts, 34–10." *Bridgeport Post* (CT), September 24, 1973.

"Namath involved in suit." *Daily Capital News* (Jefferson City, MO), August 30, 1967.

"Namath Is Back." *The Bee* (Danville, VA), September 7, 1970.

"Namath Is Disappointed In His NFL Grid Debut." *Florence Morning News* (SC), September 20, 1965.

"Namath, Jets Bomb Oilers." *Times Recorder* (Zanesville, OH), November 22, 1965.

"Namath, Jets Clinch Tie For Title In Eastern Division Of AFL Race." *Tri-City Herald* (Pasco, WA), November 25, 1968.

"Namath, Jets Drop Dolphins Into Tie With Buffalo, 17–14." *News Tribune* (Ft. Pierce, FL), November 25, 1974.

"Namath, Jets Jolted — Hard." *Albuquerque Tribune,* October 17, 1966.

"Namath, Jets Ready For First NFL Clash." *The Advocate* (Victoria, TX), August 19, 1967.

"Namath joins Rams, makes no promises." *Color Country Spectrum* (St. George, UT), May 13, 1977.

"Namath Just 'Running Out' On Exhibition Games, View." *Capital Times* (Madison, WI), August 8, 1970.

"Namath keys Jets' rout, 36–7." *Des Moines Register,* October 6, 1975.

"Namath Landslide MVP Pick." *Oakland Tribune,* December 24, 1968.

"Namath Leads Alabama To 35–0 Rout of Georgia." *European Stars & Stripes* (Darmstadt, Hesse, Germany), September 24, 1962.

"Namath Leads Jets By Inept Patriots." *Albuquerque Journal,* October 30, 1972.

"Namath leads Jets past Oilers 27–24." *Big Spring Herald* (TX), August 22, 1976.

"Namath Leads Jets To Win." *Bridgeport Post* (CT), October 21, 1968.

"Namath Leads NY Jets To Win Over Bengals." *Albuquerque Journal,* December 20, 1971.

"Namath likes Jet coach but not organization." *Post-Register* (Idaho Falls), January 28, 1977.

"Namath Makes Camp." *Gallup Independent* (NM), August 15, 1974.

"Namath may jump." *Bennington Banner* (VT), December 12, 1973.

"Namath May Not Need Operation." *Albuquerque Journal,* September 25, 1973.

"Namath may start Sunday." *Daily Capital News* (MO), August 22, 1970.

"Namath, Maynard ... Couple Of Jets Who Are Always Ready For Foes." *High Point Enterprise* (NC), January 2, 1969.

"Namath-Maynard Duo Leads Jets' Victory." *Albuquerque Journal,* October 21, 1969.

"Namath not discouraged." *Albuquerque Tribune,* September 25, 1973.

"Namath: Not Good Debut." *Des Moines Register,* September 20, 1965.

"Namath Not Quitting." *The Bee* (Danville, VA), November 13, 1972.

"Namath of Jets Is named Top American League Rookie." *New York Times,* December 17, 1965.

"Namath of the Jets." *Newsweek,* September 15, 1969, Volume LXXIV, No. 11.

"Namath Out to Silence Critics." *Sunday Tribune* (Albert Lea, MN), January 10, 1965.

"Namath out until November." *Jefferson City Post-Tribune* (MO), August 9, 1971.

"Namath Paces 'Bama Over Vols By 35–0." *Progress-Index* (Petersburg, VA), October 20, 1963.

"Namath Paces Jets." *Albuquerque Journal,* September 6, 1970.

"Namath Paces Jets." *Lincoln Star* (NE), August 22, 1976.

"Namath Paces Jets, 41–14." *Troy Record* (NY), November 22, 1965.

"Namath Paces Jets In Comeback Victory." *Times Recorder* (Zanesville, OH), September 25, 1967.

"Namath Passes Beat Bills." *Independent* (Long Beach, CA), December 20, 1965.

"Namath Passes for 496 Yards, 6 TDs." *Albuquerque Journal,* September 25, 1972.

"Namath passes Jets to overtime victory." *Billings Gazette* (MT), November 11, 1974.

"Namath Passes Jets To 20–19 Victory." *Albuquerque Journal,* September 16, 1968.

"Namath Passes Jets To Victory." *Times Recorder* (Zanesville, OH),November 15, 1965.

"Namath Passes Jets to Win." *Albuquerque Journal,* September 23, 1968.

"Namath performs as usual at practice." *Daily Capital News* (MO), September 1, 1970.

"Namath picks apart Pats." *Press-Telegram* (Long Beach, CA), December 8, 1975.

"Namath Pitches Jets To Win." *Panama City News-Herald* (FL), December 20, 1971.

"Namath plans for the big date." *Pocono Record* (The Stroudsburgs, PA), December 27, 1968.

"Namath Player-Owner? Joe Declines Comment." *The Sporting News,* November 23, 1974.

"Namath pondering future." *Advocate* (Newark, OH), November 18, 1974.

"Namath praises O.J.; arrives as new idol." *Lowell Sun* (MA), September 15, 1969.

"Namath Preps for Biggest Challenge." *San Antonio Express,* January 6, 1969.

"Namath Propels Jets by Boston." *Albuquerque Journal,* November 20, 1967.

"Namath, Rams Waiting for Jets to 'Do It.'" *Abilene Reporter-News,* January 21, 1976.

"Namath Raps Foul-Mouthed Coliseum Fans." *Oakland Tribune,* December 4, 1966.

"Namath Rates 4 AFL QBs Ahead of Morrall." *Delaware County Daily Times* (Chester, PA), January 7, 1969.

"Namath remaining quiet, Jets don't want Joe Kapp." *Jefferson City Post-Tribune* (MO), August 12, 1970.

"Namath Retire?" *Las Cruces Sun-News* (NM), December 17, 1973.

"Namath retired at right time." *Jefferson City Post-Tribune* (MO), January 26, 1978.

"Namath Sacrifices Career for Principle." *San Antonio Express and News,* June 8, 1969.

"Namath Says He'll Play Out Option." *Charleston Daily Mail* (WV), February 5, 1974.

"Namath Says He's Hanging 'Em Up," *San Antonio Express and News,* June 7, 1969.

"Namath Says Newsmen Lie." *Gallup Independent* (NM), August 19, 1970.

"Namath says no to contract." *Newport Daily News* (RI), June 26, 1974.

"Namath sees himself as No. 2." *Wisconsin State Journal* (Madison), July 19, 1977.

"Namath Sees Stars — Hollywood Style." *Des Moines Register,* May 27, 1970.

"Namath Sets Aerial Mark As Jets Win." *Post Standard* (Syracuse, NY), December 25, 1967.

"Namath Shatters Pro Passing record: Piles Up 4,007 Yds. For Season," *The Independent* (Pasadena, CA), December 25, 1967.

"Namath shuns quitting gridiron." *Daily Capital News* (Jefferson City, MO), August 17, 1971.

"Namath Signs Jets' Pact For $400,000." *Times-Recorder* (Zanesville, OH), January 3, 1965.

"Namath sinks Tampa." *Press-Telegram* (Long Beach, CA), November 15, 1976.

"Namath Sinks the Chargers." *Oakland Tribune,* November 25, 1968.

"Namath Sparkles Against Giants." *Bridgeport Telegram* (CT), August 1, 1975.

"Namath Sparks Late TD Drive: Jets Rally To Top Oilers 20–14." *Times Recorder* (Zanesville, OH), October 21, 1968.

"Namath stands behind guarantee in 16–7 Jet victory." *Post-Tribune* (Jefferson City, MO), January 13, 1969.

"Namath, Starr play but Jets, Packers fall." *Jefferson City Post-Tribune* (MO), November 29, 1971.

"Namath Starts First 'Super' Feud." *News-Palladium* (Benton Harbor, MI), January 7, 1969.

"Namath still pondering." *Star-News* (Pasadena, CA), March 31, 1977.

"Namath Suffers Shoulder Injury." *Moberly Monitor-Index* (MO), September 24, 1973.

"Namath takes back seat to Bert Jones." *Press-Telegram* (Long Beach, CA), November 17, 1975.

"Namath Takes Blame, Coach Hurls Charge." *Daily Review* (Hayward, CA), December 13, 1965.

"Namath TD gives Jets 30–24 win." *Daily Review* (Hayward, CA), September 29, 1975.

"Namath TDs Win for Jets." *Post-Standard* (Syracuse, NY), November 18, 1974.

"Namath Threatens To Quit Football." *Tucson Daily Citizen,* June 6, 1969.

"Namath to Be Free Agent After 1971?" *Charleston Gazette* (WV), May 20, 1970.

"Namath to Maynard Too Much for Bills." *Advocate* (Victoria, TX), December 20, 1965.

"Namath to Play Out Contract." *Charleston Gazette* (WV), June 27, 1974.

"Namath to Return After Poor Season." *Salt Lake Tribune* (UT), December 22, 1975.

"Namath to talk with Jet owners after blasts from mates." *Jefferson City Post-Tribune* (MO), August 6, 1970.

"Namath Tosses Jets to Victory Over Faltering Chargers, 37–15." *Salt Lake Tribune* (UT), November 25, 1967.

"Namath Turned Tackler, Saved Jets From Defeat." *The Sporting News,* October 28, 1967.

"Namath, Turner Pace Victors In Steady Rain." *Times Record* (Troy, NY), November 11, 1968.

"Namath Undergoes Surgery." *Moberly Monitor-Index* (MO), August 9, 1971.

"Namath vaults Jets past foe in overtime." *North Adams Transcript* (MA), November 11, 1974.

"Namath very close to becoming a Ram." *Frederick Post-News* (MD), March 25, 1977.

"Namath wants Rams, but is feeling mutual?" *Wisconsin State Journal* (Madison), January 8, 1977.

"Namath Well, Jets Win 13–7." *Waterloo Daily Courier* (IA), August 27, 1967.

"Namath Will Return." *The Bee* (Danville, VA), December 20, 1971.

"Namath Will Return." *Daily Freeman* (Kingston, NY), December 22, 1975.

"Namath won't quit." *Albuquerque Tribune,* November 24, 1975.

"Namath's arm rips Patriots." *North Adams Transcript* (MA), October 6, 1975.

"Namath's Back." *Billings Gazette* (MT), November 29, 1971.

"Namath's Bid Denied, 20–14." *Independent* (Long Beach, CA), November 19, 1973.

"Namath's 5 Touchdown Aerials Pace Jets, 52–13." *Fresno Bee,* September 19, 1966.

"Namath's Future In Doubt." *Panama City News Herald* (FL), December 13, 1973.

"Namath's Future Is In Doubt." *Daily Freeman* (Kingston, NY), December 13, 1976.

"Namath's Knee Hurt In 28–24 Jet Loss." *Albuquerque Journal,* August 8, 1971.

"Namath's Knee Survives Saints' Deadly Shot." *The Light* (San Antonio), September 7, 1970.

"Namath's Late Bomb Saves Jets." *Albuquerque Journal,* October 23, 1972.

"Namath's late entry didn't affect game." *Albuquerque Tribune,* December 16, 1975.

"Namath's Mark: 4,007 Yards." *Fresno Bee,* December 25, 1967.

"Namath's Passes Beat Baltimore." *Wisconsin State Journal,* September 25, 1972.

"Namath's passes massacre Boston: Jets turn un-Patriotic, 38–28." *Post Standard* (Syracuse, NY), December 18, 1966.

"Namath's Passes Ruin Vikings 24–14." *Cedar Rapids Gazette* (IA), August 31, 1969.

"Namath's Passing Sinks Miami, 29–7." *Albuquerque Journal,* October 2, 1967.

"Namath's Pinpoint Passing Carries Jets Past Boston." *Albuquerque Journal,* October 30, 1967.

"Namath's Play 'Erratic.'" *San Antonio Express,* August 9, 1965.

"Namath's Playing Status Indefinite Rest of Year." *The Sporting News,* October 31, 1970.

"Namath's Tosses Tip Pokes 29–21," *Pacific Stars & Stripes* (Tokyo), September 16, 1970.

"Nance Caps Amazing Comeback With Jets." *Bedford Gazette* (PA), September 15, 1973.

Nelson, John. "Five balking teams return as strike ends." *Greeley Tribune* (CO), September 19, 1975.

_____. "Jones' Pin-Point Passes Like A Dream, Says Carr." *Daily Times* (Salisbury, MD), October 25, 1976.

"New England Pummels Jets." *Albuquerque Journal,* November 22, 1976.

"New England Shows Little Mercy to Hapless New York." *Albuquerque Journal,* October 19, 1976.

"New Orleans beats Jets." *Argus* (Fremont, CA), September 1, 1974.

"New York Can Still Have Hand In Determining Central Title." *Piqua Daily Call* (OH), December 12, 1972.

"New York Choice To Win at Boston." *New York Times,* November 14, 1965.

"New York In 13–10 Triumph." *Times Recorder* (Zanesville, OH), November 8, 1965.

"New York Infantry Rolls Over Cincy." *News Journal* (Mansfield, OH), October 13, 1969.

"New York Jets." *Moberly Monitor-Index* (MO), August 21, 1972.

"New York Jets Advance to Super Bowl: Jets Sneak By Oakland, 27–23." *Albuquerque Journal,* December 30, 1968.

"New York Jets lose role of favorite to win tonight." *Las Vegas Optic,* August 1, 1969.

"New York Jets Outlast Houston's Oilers, 26–17." *Post-Herald* (Beckley, WV), October 21, 1969.

"New York Jets stars return to scene of dramatic game." *Chronicle Telegram* (Elyria, OH), December 29, 1968.

"New York Surges in Last Period." *Bridgeport Telegram* (CT), October 27, 1969.

"Newest Cowboy Faces Keep Win String Alive." *Galveston Daily News* (TX), August 28, 1972.

Newhouse, Dave. "A 1-Handed Defense." *Oakland Tribune,* November 29, 1971.

_____. "49ers Only Win, Don't Excite the Faithful." *Oakland Tribune,* October 4, 1976.

_____. "The Real Namath? Shy Guy Says Maynard." *The Sporting News,* September 2, 1972.

Newnham, Blaine. "Oakland vs. Jets, Cold, Crowd." *Oakland Tribune,* November 30, 1969.

_____. "Raiders Baffle Joe." *Oakland Tribune,* December 1, 1969.

"NFL owners claim need for pre-season games." *Daily Capital News* (Jefferson City, MO), August 9, 1972.

"NFL preparing to 'cool off.'" *The News* (Port Arthur, TX), August 13, 1974.

"NFL Strike Roundup." *Gallup Independent* (NM), August 15, 1974.

"NFL Veterans Get Last Licks." *Lincoln Evening Journal* (NE), August 31, 1974.

Nichols, Ed. "Colts Big Favorite, But Jets Add Zest To Super Bowl Game..." *Daily Times* (Salisbury, MD), January 3, 1969.

"$900Gs Make Joe Highest Grid Earner." *Pacific Stars & Stripes* (Tokyo), August 1, 1975.

Nissenson, Herschel. "Chiefs Look for Jet Scalp." *Moberly Monitor-Index* (MO), September 14, 1968.

_____. "Record Crowd Watches As Jets Beat Bills, 33–19." *Las Cruces Sun-News* (NM), September 15, 1969.

_____. "Those Bengal Babes Corral Namath, Jets." *Moberly Monitor-Index* (MO), August 31, 1968.

Niver, Garry. "Meyer — Breaks And Penalties." *The Times* (San Mateo, CA), October 3, 1977.

"No Big Plays For Colts." *Times Recorder* (Zanesville, OH), January 13, 1969.

"No surgery for Jet Joe." *Syracuse Herald Journal,* September 24, 1973.

"No surgery for Namath." *Billings Gazette* (MT), September 25, 1973.

"'Nothing Wrong with Jets,' says Namath." *Daily Review* (Hayward, CA), November 10, 1969.

"NY Defense Intercepts Five Times." *Bridgeport Telegram* (CT), October 28, 1968.

"N.Y. Jets expect Maynard to be ready for Oakland." *Pocono Record* (The Stroudsburgs, PA), December 27, 1968.

"N.Y. rivalry picks up with heat." *Lowell Sun* (MA), August 20, 1972.

"NY Survives Buffalo Scare." *Albuquerque Journal,* September 15, 1969.

"Oakland Crushes Los Angeles," *Gallup Independent* (NM), September 10, 1977.

"Oakland Downs NY Jets." *Albuquerque Journal,* December 1, 1969.

"Oakland, Houston set to dominate AFL race." *Jefferson City Post-Tribune* (MO), September 4, 1968.

Oates, Bob. "Broadway Joe Takes Road Back Via Water Route." *The Sporting News,* August 13, 1977.

_____. "Falcons Do Things Right." *The Sporting News,* December 15, 1973.

_____. "Famed Colt Defense Was Picked to Pieces By Broadway Joe, Royal Ruler of the Jet Set." *The Sporting News,* January 25, 1969.

_____. "Knox Tightens Reins on Rams." *The Sporting News,* October 1, 1977.

_____. "QBs Lead Casualty List ... Says Oft-Injured Nelsen." *The Sporting News,* September 4, 1971.

O'Brien, Jim. "Joe Namath: 'I Want To Be A Winner Again.'" *Football Digest,* December 1975, Vol. 5, No. 4.

O'Brien, Mike. "Pack Frustrates Namath, Jets." *Fond du Lac Reporter* (WI), September 18, 1973.

"'Odds Don't Bother Me': Weeb Says." *Delaware County Daily Times* (Chester, PA), January 7, 1969.

"Oddsmakers Pick Colts By 18," *Red Bluff Daily News* (CA), January 8, 1969.

"Oh Joy! Namath Back With Team." *Playground Daily News* (Fort Walton Beach, FL), August 18, 1970.

O'Hara, Dave. "Namath Quarterbacks Jets To 30–20 Victory; Fumbles, Interceptions Hurt." *Nashua Telegraph* (NH), November 15, 1965.

_____. "Pats Hopes Eliminated; Jets Register 29–24 Win." *Nashua Telegraph* (NH), November 20, 1967.

"Oiler Defensive Backs Account for 245 Yards." *The Sporting News,* October 28, 1967.

"Oilers Deny 'Cheap Shot' Injured Namath Knee." *Press-Telegram* (Long Beach, CA), August 15, 1966.

"Oilers Halt Jets, Namath." *Playground Daily News* (Ft. Walton Beach, FL), October 17, 1966.

"Oilers rally to handle Jets 28–14." *Daily Capital News* (Jefferson City, MO), August 14, 1968.

"Oilers Stun Jets, 26–20." *Times Record* (Troy, NY), October 2, 1972.

"Oilers Surprise Jets by 26–20." *Post-Standard* (Syracuse), October 2, 1972.

"Oilers Topple Jets On Late Score, 27–22." *Bridgeport Telegram* (CT), November 4, 1974.

"O.J. and Bills romp past New York." *Appleton Post-Crescent* (WI), September 22, 1975.

"O.J. Off, & Running." *Independent* (Long Beach, CA), September 22, 1975.

"O.J. Rips Jets As Bills Romp." *Post-Standard* (Syracuse, NY), September 22, 1975.

"O.J. scores twice as Bills swamp Jets." *Wisconsin State Journal,* September 22, 1975.

Olan, Ben. "Dolphins Worry About Namath; Ailing Snell Will Miss Game." *Danville Regsiter* (VA), October 1, 1967.

_____. "Namath's Arm, Gino's Toe in Grid Limelight." *Moberly Monitor-Index* (MO), August 24, 1968.

Olderman, Murray. "AFL Seen Ready For NFL By '67." *Progress-Index* (Petersburg, VA), September 20, 1965.

_____. "Between you 'n' me." *The Post-Register* (Idaho Falls), June 2, 1968.

_____. "Between you 'n' me." *Nashua Telegraph,* January 2, 1969.

_____. "Namath Sit-Out Rankles." *Chillicothe Constitution-Tribune* (MO), August 24, 1968.

_____. "NFL Mystique Shrouds Jets Effort." *Albuquerque Tribune,* January 9, 1969.

_____. "On The Wings Of Broadway." *Anniston Star* (AL), January 1, 1969.

"Once again Super Bowl less than Super." *Pocono Record* (The Stroudsburgs, PA), January 11, 1969.

Opotzner, Robert. "Giants, Jets Faceoff in Subway Bowl IV Today at Yale." *Bridgeport Post* (CT), August 20, 1972.

Oppedahl, John F. "Sports Gambling Case Now in Grand Jury Hands." *The Sporting News,* February 7, 1970.

O'Quinn, Karl. "Ewbank Influential." *San Antonio Express,* January 8, 1969.

Ostrum, Bob. "Cowboys Drub Jets, 25–9 As Namath Sits Out Game." *San Antonio Light,* September 7, 1969.

"Otto, Sample Stage Own 'Warfare' on Sideline." *Times-Reporter* (Dover, OH), August 2, 1969.

"Pack pounds Jets, 23–7." *Syracuse Herald Journal,* September 18, 1973.

"'Pack' thrashes Namath, Jets." *Albuquerque Tribune,* September 18, 1973.

"Packers Stop Jets." *Albuquerque Journal,* September 18, 1973.

Padwe, Sandy. "Joe Namath's $400,000 Tag Shows Signs of Paying Off." *Daily Times-News* (Burlington, NC), December 13, 1965.

"Pain pays the bills for Joe's good life." *Life,* November 3, 1972, Volume 73, No. 18.

Paladino, Larry. "Roof falls on Jets in last quarter as Lions break tie for 37–20 romp." *Albuquerque Tribune,* November 24, 1972.

"Parilli To Romeo Pass Upsets New York Jets." *Nashua Telegraph* (NH), November 29, 1965.

Pascale, Don. "Morton Passes Giants To Victory Over Jets." *Naugatuck News* (CT), August 25, 1975.

"Pass Protection Super Bowl Key." *Winona Daily News* (MN), January 6, 1969.

"Pass record For Namath." *Oakland Tribune,* October 2, 1967.

"Pass Thefts Add Up, Namath Finds." *The Sporting News,* October 12, 1968.

"Pastorini, Oilers sabotage Jets." *The News* (Port Arthur, TX), November 4, 1974.

"Patriots Edge Jets With 54 Seconds Left." *Post Standard* (Syracuse, NY), November 29, 1965.

"Patriots Fall To Jets, 23–14." *Albuquerque Journal,* October 6, 1969.

"Patriots on strike, will boycott today's game." *Independent Press-Telegram* (Long Beach, CA), September 14, 1975.

"Patriots Remain Unbeaten." *Times Recorder* (Zanesville, OH), October 14, 1974.

"Patriots whip bobbling Jets." *North Adams Transcript* (MA), November 22, 1976.

"Pats Crush Jets, 24–0." *Bridgeport Telegram* (CT), October 14, 1974.

"Pats Dump Jets 38–24." *Coshocton Tribune* (OH), November 22, 1976.

"Pats Gamble, Win, 27–23." *Lowell Sun* (MA), November 29, 1965.

"Pats Rip Jets, 38–24." *Valley Morning Star* (Harlingen, TX), November 22, 1976.

"Paul Brown: 'We were lucky.'" *Advocate* (Newark, OH), November 19, 1973.

"Peace Is Symbol Of Namath Plight—He Wishes He Had It." *Daily Times-News* (Burlington, NC), August 19, 1970.

Peters, Gil. "Jets Cast Their Old Spell Over Pats." *The Sporting News,* December 20, 1975.

_____. "Namath Fires for 2 TDs As Jets Slap Pat Hands." *The Sporting News,* November 30, 1974.

_____. "Pats pummel Jets 41–7 with Steve Grogan the star." *Berkshire Eagle* (Pittsfield, MA), October 19, 1976.

"Playboy Interview: Joe Namath." *Playboy,* December 1969, Vol. 16, No. 12.

Pollack, Joe. "Far Off the Mark on Namath's Effect." *The Sporting News,* November 27, 1976.

"Poor Ol' Joe Has Problems ... Like ... He Needs More Money." *Kokomo Tribune* (IN), August 7, 1970.

Porter, John. "Rams Make 49ers Kick Themselves." *Oakland Tribune,* October 3, 1977.

Porter, Steve. "Cardinals' famine results in 20–7 defeat." *Alton Telegraph* (IL), August 24, 1974.

Powers, Roger. "Double Standard for Superstars." *Grit,* August 23, 1970.

_____. "Jets Count on Q-Back Al Woodall." *Grit,* October 7, 1973.

"Praises go out to Broadway Joe Namath." *Chillicothe Constitution-Tribune* (MO), January 26, 1978.

"Predicted Powers, LA Rams & Bengals, Lose." *Las Cruces Sun-News* (NM), September 19, 1977.

"Pressure Building for Namath." *Nevada State Journal* (Reno), October 12, 1977.

Prewitt, Eric. "Even in Defeat, Joe Steals Show." *Fond du Lac Reporter* (WI), December 12, 1972.

Price, Bob. "Bum Knee Prevails Over Old Toe in AFL Thriller." *The Sporting News,* February 3, 1968.

_____. "Snubbed by Voters, Dawson Shows 'Em How in Star Game." *The Sporting News,* February 1, 1969.

"Pro Football Exhibitions." *Walla Walla Union-Bulletin* (WA), August 20, 1967.

Putnam, Pat. "The Rookies Give It a Shot." *Sports Illustrated,* August 11, 1969, Vol. 31, No. 6.

"'Quarterback clash' fails to materialize." *Daily Times* (Primos, PA), August 15, 1977.

"Rag Arm to Earl the Pearl." *Walla Walla Union-Bulletin,* January 4, 1969.

"Raiders are glad to be playing Oilers, not Jets." *Jefferson City Post-Tribune* (MO), December 15, 1969.

"Raiders Bop NY, 24–14." *Nevada State Journal,* December 13, 1965.

"Raiders clobber tired NY Jets." *Modesto Bee* (CA), August 15, 1976.

"Raiders Dim Jet Chances For Crown," *Albuquerque Journal,* December 18, 1967.

"Raiders Don't Expect Jets To Fall as Easily as Chiefs." *Press-Courier* (Oxnard, CA), December 25, 1968.

"Raiders Front Four Rips Namath." *Charleston Gazette* (WV), December 19, 1967.

"Raiders Glide By Jets, 41–17." *Hobbs Daily News-Sun* (NM), August 15, 1976.

"Raiders In Simple Bid." *The Argus* (Fremont, CA), December 15, 1967.

"Raiders KO Jets 43–32 On 2 Last-Minute TDs." *Times Recorder* (Zanesville, OH), November 18, 1968.

"Raiders Prepare For Rough Battle With Jets." *San Antonio Light,* December 25, 1968.

"Raiders Prevent Jets From Clinching Division, 27–14." *Bridgeport Telegram* (CT), December 1, 1969.

"Raiders Rebound To Trim Jets, 24–14." *Times Record* (Troy, NY), December 13, 1965.

"Raiders See Rough Game." *Billings Gazette* (MT), December 26, 1968.

"Raiders Seek 2nd AFL Title Against Jets Today." *Albuquerque Journal,* December 29, 1968.

"Raiders Shocked By Ease Of Victory Over Chiefs." *The Register* (Danville, VA), December 25, 1968.

"Raiders Slip By Namath, Jets 24–14." *Fresno Bee,* December 13, 1965.

"Raiders Stop Dolphins' Win Streak; Namath Injured." *Ogden Standard-Examiner* (UT), September 24, 1973.

"Raiders Stop Jets In Wild One." *Troy Record* (NY), November 18, 1968.

"Raiders: 38–29—Weeb Wails." *Fresno Bee,* December 18, 1967.

"Rams Edge Jets, 20–13." *Bridgeport Telegram* (CT), October 28, 1974.

"Rams fuming over 'cheap shots.'" *Star-News* (Pasadena, CA), October 12, 1977.

"Rams get Namath for free." *Star-News* (Pasadena, CA), March 30, 1977.

"Rams, Namath Falter." *Press-Courier* (Oxnard, CA), August 22, 1977.

"Rams' Namath Tarnished By Bennett's Falcons, 17–6." *Press-Courier* (Oxnard, CA), September 19, 1977.

"Rams Run Over 49ers." *Press-Courier* (Oxnard, CA), October 3, 1977.

"Rams sink floundering 49ers." *Modesto Bee* (CA), October 3, 1977.

"Rams to start Haden ahead of Namath." *Modesto Bee* (CA), October 13, 1977.

Rapoport, Ron. "Joe Namath To Undergo Knee Surgery." *Gettysburg Times,* December 22, 1966.

Rappoport, Ken. "Pro Exhibition Football Season Opens; Namath, Kapp Just Fans." *Silver City Daily News* (NM), August 8, 1970.

_____. "Raider Raiding Party Whips Jets." *Las Cruces Sun-News* (NM), December 1, 1969.

Rathet, Mike. "Broadway Joe finally goes to Jets Hempstead camp." *Las Vegas Daily Optic,* Aug 19, 1970.

_____. "Broadway Joe: He Wonders if It's Worth It." *Idaho State Journal* (Pocatello), August 19, 1970.

_____. "Broadway Joe Target Of Fans' Wrath." *Silver City Daily Press* (NM), August 24, 1970.

_____. "Chicago Does Not Like Him, Says NY Jets Quarterback." *Las Cruces Sun-News* (NM), August 3, 1969.

_____. "Cleveland Tops Jets, Broadway Joe In Opener." *Silver City Daily Press* (NM), September 22, 1970.

_____. "'Extracurricular' Activity Adds Zest to Tilt." *Times-Reporter* (Dover, OH), August 2, 1969.

_____. "Jets Blister Chargers, 37–15." *Las Cruces Sun-News* (NM), November 25, 1968.

_____. "Jets Coach Must Decide On Starting Quarterback." *Las Cruces Sun-News* (NM), September 8, 1966.

_____. "Jets Confident Namath Can Do the Job." *Appleton Post-Crescent* (WI), August 1, 1965.

_____. "Jets Dump Pats, 13–6." *Nashua Telegraph* (NH), December 13, 1971.

_____. "Joe Namath Is Offered $389,000." *Anniston Star* (AL), December 30, 1964.

_____. "Joe's Undesirable Clients Identified," *Corpus Christi Caller-Times,* June 15, 1969.

_____. "Namath Has $$ — And Smart Mouth." *High Point Enterprise* (NC), August 1, 1965.

_____. "Namath May Quit Football, New York Jets." *Silver City Daily Press* (NM), August 6, 1970.

_____. "Namath Passes Click, Jets Clip Pats." *Fresno Bee Republican,* August 14, 1965.

_____. "Namath Rich, but He May Be Cut." *Moberly Monitor-Index* (MO), August 27, 1965.

_____. "Namath Shines, AFL Stars Romp." *The Lawton Constitution-Morning Press,* January 16, 1966.

_____. "Namath's Four Touchdown Passes Send Jets Winging." *Fresno Bee,* November 22, 1965.

_____. "Pete Gogolak Leads Bills' Win." *Moberly Monitor-Index* (MO), August 9, 1965.

_____. "Tired of Second Fiddle, Earl Almost Quit Band." *Wisconsin State Journal* (Madison), January 5, 1969.

Recht, Mike. "Jets Retain Lead in AFL By Downing Bills, 20–10." *Bridgeport Post* (CT), November 13, 1967.

_____. "New York Jets Put Unbeaten Record On Line In Top Test." *News Journal* (Mansfield, OH), October 16, 1966.

_____. "NFL Ends Pre-Seasons." *Las Cruces Sun-News* (NM), September 9, 1968.

_____. "NY Jets Worried Over Star Players." *Gallup Independent* (NM), August 13, 1970.

"Red-Hot Raiders Cool Jets 24–6." *Pacific Stars and Stripes* (Tokyo), August 28, 1969.

"Redskins roll over Jets." *Troy Record* (NY), August 29, 1976.

Reidenbaugh, Lowell. "Docile Colts Back Namath Guarantee." *The Sporting News,* January 25, 1969.

"Reject, Playboy Tip Scales." *Albuquerque Tribune,* January 9, 1969.

"Rest, Travel, Diet for Namath." *San Antonio Light,* January 20, 1969.

"Revenge-Minded Raiders Tackle N.Y. Jets Today." *Standard-Examiner* (Ogden, UT), December 17, 1967.

Richards, Charles. "Jets Win Without TD Passes." *Albuquerque Tribune,* November 11, 1968.

_____. "Taliaferro returns to New York arena." *Chronicle Telegram* (Elyria, OH), October 27, 1968.

Richardson, Bill. "Seven Jet Quarterbacks." *The Sporting News,* September 16, 1972.

Richman, Milton. "Broadway Joe Sparks Jets — Even On Bench." *Times Recorder* (Zanesville, OH), January 13, 1969.

_____. "Colts Aren't Mad, Joe, But..." *Billings Gazette* (MT), January 8, 1969.

_____. "Colts get back at Joe six times." *Chronicle-Telegram* (Elyria, OH), October 19, 1970.

_____. "Don't Worry, Joe: Baltimore Not Mad at You." *Times Standard* (Eureka, CA), January 9, 1969.

_____. "Ewbank doesn't need reminder about Colts."

Valley Independent (Monessen, PA). January 3, 1969.

_____. "Jets Are Talking Tougher Than Colts." *San Mateo Times* (CA), January 8, 1969.

_____. "Jets, moral support flop as Shipp bombed in debut." *Times Standard* (Eureka, CA), November 24, 1975.

_____. "Joe Namath Defends Self." *Weirton Daily Times* (WV), January 10, 1969.

_____. "Joe Possibly In Last Home Game With Jets." *Altoona Mirror* (PA), December 9, 1974.

_____. "Last Time It Will Be Broadway Joe?" *Chronicle Telegram* (Elyria, OH), December 9, 1974.

_____. "Namath Matures as New York Jets' Quarterback." *News Journal* (Mansfield, OH), August 16, 1972.

_____. "Namath Still on Top of Game." *News Journal* (Mansfield, OH), October 26, 1976.

_____. "Namath Thinks Jones Is Tops." *Weirton Daily Times* (WV), October 25, 1976.

_____. "Namath was a mess after game with Oakland team." *Delta Democrat-Times,* January 1, 1969.

_____. "Namath's Knees Didn't Hurt After First Title Win." *Albuquerque Tribune,* January 2, 1969.

_____. "Terry takes charge." *New Castle News* (PA), December 1, 1975.

_____. "Unitas, Namath Have Had Better Days." *Lebanon Daily News* (PA), October 19, 1970.

_____. "'We're Better Than Baltimore': Jets' Johnny Sample: He's No Diplomat." *Press-Telegram* (Long Beach, CA), January 9, 1969.

"'Ridiculous Play,' says Namath." *Syracuse Herald Journal,* October 16, 1967.

Rife, Tom. "Dolphin Defense Shuts Off Jets, 16–0." *Naples Daily News* (FL), September 27, 1976.

"Riggins: face in the crowd for Redskins?" *Bakersfield Californian,* June 11, 1976.

"Riggins, Garrett Run Wild." *Bridgeport Telegram* (CT), September 29, 1975.

"Riggins, Jets Triumph." *Argus* (Fremont, CA), December 8, 1975.

"Riggins Leaves Jets' Camp." *Panama City News-Herald* (FL), August 29, 1973.

"Riggins reported only Jet holdout." *Hutchinson News* (KS), August 31, 1973.

"Riggins talking to Jets." *Hutchinson News* (KS), September 12, 1973.

"Riggins' three touchdowns helps Jets to 27–14 victory." *Montana Standard,* December 2, 1974.

"Riggins Touchdown Gives Jets Victory." *Albuquerque Journal,* December 13, 1971.

"Right Knee Good; Left Now Problem." *Walla Walla Union-Bulletin,* August 27, 1967.

Roberts, Rich. "Another surprise — Knox gets new contract." *Independent* (Long Beach, CA), September 16, 1977.

_____. "Cheers for Harris ... boos for Namath." *Press-Telegram* (Long Beach, CA), September 2, 1977.

_____. "Chi Bears shock Rams." *Press-Telegram* (Long Beach, CA), October 11, 1977.

_____. "For 49ers, it's the Pitts." *Independent* (Long Beach, CA), October 3, 1977.

_____. "It's Series time, and here come the clichés." *Independent* (Long Beach, CA), October 12, 1977.

_____. "Knox benches Namath; Haden to start Sunday." *Independent* (Long Beach, CA), October 13, 1977.

_____. "Like old times for Rams: Strongarm Eagles, 20–0." *Independent* (Long Beach, CA), September 26, 1977.

_____. "Quickie Quiz: What's wrong with Rams?" *Independent* (Long Beach, CA), September 19, 1977.

_____. "Rams blocked out, 22–17." *Independent Press-Telegram* (Long Beach, CA), August 7, 1977.

_____. "Rams can't protect Namath — or the lead." *Independent* (Long Beach, CA), August 22, 1977.

_____. "Rams 'get together' just in time." *Press-Telegram* (Long Beach, CA), October 28, 1974.

_____. "'What, me worry?' Rams minimize record." *Independent* (Long Beach, CA), August 29, 1977.

Rombach, Jerry. "Browns entertain 67,496 fans." *Chronicle Telegram* (Elyria, OH), September 13, 1976.

_____. "Browns turn out lights on 'Broadway.'" *Chronicle-Telegram* (Elyria, OH), September 22, 1970.

_____. "Sport Scope." *Chronicle-Telegram* (Elyria, OH), January 9, 1969.

"Rookie Aids Jet Win Over Miami." *San Antonio Express,* November 21, 1966.

"Rookie Wayne Morris big hit as Cards win, 13–12." *Alton Telegraph* (IL), August 2, 1976.

Rosenberg, Ken. "Joe Namath Heads 20–7 Jet Triumph." *News Journal* (Mansfield, OH), August 24, 1974.

Rosenthal, Bert. "'I'm the Scaredest Quarterback They've Ever Seen!'— Joe Namath." *All-Star Sports,* February 1968, Vol. 2, No. 1.

_____. "Joe Namath — Why He Battles On." *All-Star Sports,* February 1969, Vol. 3, No. 1.

Rosenthal, Harold. "WFL Eyes Namath as Rescue Artist." *The Sporting News,* May 3, 1975.

Ross, George. "AFL Stars Rip Bills On Namath Passes," *Oakland Tribune,* January 16, 1966.

_____. "Charlie's Return to Shea." *Oakland Tribune,* November 30, 1969.

_____. "Daryle Lowers Boom." *Oakland Tribune,* December 1, 1969.

_____. "$400,000 Bargain." *Oakland Tribune,* December 13, 1965.

_____. "Joe Says Blame Joe." *Oakland Tribune,* December 13, 1965.

_____. "Look Back At Namath." *Oakland Tribune,* October 9, 1967.

_____. "Namath Says Ben and Dan Dirty." *Oakland Tribune,* October 5, 1967.

_____. "Sullen Jets Want Raiders in Rematch." *Oakland Tribune,* November 18, 1968.

_____. "Weeb Picks the Raiders." *Oakland Tribune,* December 1, 1969.

"Royal Praises Namath." *Lowell Sun* (MA), January 2, 1965.

"'Run, Joe, Run,' Say Defenders." *Bridgeport Post* (CT), October 27, 1969.

"Running, Defense Give Chiefs Edge." *New York Times,* November 7, 1965.

"Ryan Sees Namath, Hikes His Own Value to Million." *The Sporting News,* January 16, 1965.

Sachare, Alex. "Namath Injured: Jets Lose." *Silver City Daily Press* (NM), August 20, 1973.

Sahadi, Lou. "The Day the Pro Football World Stood Still." *Pro Quarterback,* October 1969, Vol. 1, No. 1.

Sainsbury, Ed. "Jets Win, but Cook's Passing Steals Show from Broadway Joe." *Times-Reporter* (Dover, OH), August 2, 1969.

"Saints rally for 24–7 win." *Waterloo Courier* (IA), September 1, 1974.

"Saints Thankful They're Finished With Namath & Co." *Playground Daily News* (Fort Walton Beach, FL), September 3, 1973.

Sample, Johnny; Fred J. Hamilton, and Sonny Schwartz. *Confessions of a Dirty Ballplayer.* New York: Dell 1970.

"Sample Sparks Jets Victory." *Times Recorder* (Zanesville, OH), November 13, 1967.

"San Diego Gets #2 With 24–16 Victory." *Albuquerque Journal,* December 16, 1975.

"San Diego Mauls Jets." *News-Journal* (Mansfield, OH), October 24, 1965.

"San Diego Nets First Win Of Year." *Bridgeport Telegram* (CT), September 29, 1969.

"San Diego Pummels N.Y. Jets And Namath By 38–7." *Great Bend Daily Tribune* (KS), December 5, 1965.

Sargis, Joe. "Oakland Meets Pittsburgh Or Cleveland In Playoffs." *Raleigh Register* (Beckley, WV), December 12, 1972.

"Saturday exhibitions open pro grid season." *Jefferson City Post-Tribune* (MO), August 1, 1969.

"Scare for Bills' Back." *The Sporting News,* November 25, 1967.

Schaap, Dick. "'I still do what I want to do — only I don't want to do as much.'" *Life,* November 3, 1972, Vol. 73, No. 18.

_____. "Old Quarterbacks Never Die ... They Get Hurt." *Sport,* December 1973, Vol. 56, No. 6.

_____. *Quarterbacks Have All the Fun.* Chicago: Playboy Press, 1974.

_____. "Sporting Life with Joe Namath." *Sport,* November 1975, Vol. 61, No. 5.

Schiffman, William. "49ers Win ... But The Smell." *Fresno Bee,* October 4, 1976.

Schoenfeld, Ed. "Image as a Swinger Helpful, Namath Admits." *The Sporting News,* November 23, 1974.

_____. "Jets' Sideline Strategy Session Credited for Tie." *Oakland Tribune,* December 4, 1966.

Schuyler, Ed, Jr. "Namath, Jets Win Over Dallas To Close Out Exhibition Season." *Moberly Monitor-Index* (MO), September 14, 1970.

Scott, Jim. "Hawkins Recalls When Raiders Were Ragged Outcasts of AFL." *The Sporting News,* September 18, 1965.

_____. "Namath Talks of Retiring, Opens New Pub in Boston." *The Sporting News,* October 18, 1969.

_____. "Stabler's Air Strikes Impress Raiders' Coaches." *The Sporting News,* August 29, 1970.

_____. "Top Pro QBs Have Ball in Celebrity Golf Meets." *The Sporting News,* April 7, 1973.

"SD Chargers Top New York, 34–27." *Albuquerque Journal,* September 29, 1969.

"2nd-Half Rally Powers Alabama To 17–9 Victory." *Logansport Pharos-Tribune* (IN), November 8, 1964.

"2nd Place Chiefs Overthrow Jets." *Wisconsin State Journal,* December 21, 1969.

"Shatter Namath's Cheek, Jets' Hopes." *Independent* (Long Beach, CA), December 18, 1967.

"Shea Meteorologist Silent." *Oakland Tribune*, December 26, 1968.

Sherwin, Bob. "Jets Comment on Setback." *News Journal* (Mansfield, OH), September 13, 1976.

Shrake, Edwin. "A Champagne Party for Joe and Weeb." *Sports Illustrated*, December 9, 1968, Vol. 29, No. 24.

"Shula Compares Jets To Green Bay Packers." *Delaware County Daily Times* (PA), January 8, 1969.

"Shula for the Defense — Colts, Jets Even." *Wisconsin State Journal* (Madison), January 4, 1969.

"Shula, Namath Find Bright Spots." *Daily Freeman* (Kingston, NY), September 27, 1976.

Siddons, Larry. "Namath Remains Non-Committal About Future: Quarterback Guides Jets' 45–38 Victory." *Bridgeport Post* (CT), December 16, 1974.

"Simpson Reaches 2003." *Albuquerque Journal*, December 17, 1973.

"Six Turner Field Goals Give Jets 25–21 Victory." *Panama City News* (FL), November 4, 1968.

Skinner, John R. "Namath's Rally Just Misses, 21–17." *Times Record* (Troy, NY), October 8, 1974.

_____. "Soul-Searching Dolphins Blank Winless Jets, 16–0." *Bridgeport Post* (CT), September 27, 1976.

"Sluggish Rams Collapse Around Namath." *Oakland Tribune*, September 19, 1977.

"Slumping Jets Beaten 21–7 by Kansas City." *Albuquerque Journal*, December 11, 1967.

Small, Ken. "With Griese it's a constant mental battle." *Pro!*, September 26, 1976, Vol. 7, No. 3.

Smith, George. "Alabama To Use Namath In Spots." *Anniston Star* (AL), December 30, 1964.

_____. "Auburn Defeats Tide By Slim 10–8 Score, Accepts Orange Bowl." *Anniston Star* (AL), December 1, 1963.

_____. "Bulldogs Take Drubbing." *Anniston Star* (AL), September 22, 1963.

_____. "Crimson Tide Buries Georgia, 32–7; M. Fracchia, Namath Star." *Anniston Star* (AL), September 22, 1963.

_____. "Crimson Tide Clobbers Tech, 27–11; Benny Nelson Leads Attack." *Anniston Star* (AL), November 17, 1963.

_____. "Gator Rally Dies At Horn." *Anniston Star* (AL), October 25, 1964.

_____. "Gators Grow Up." *Anniston Star* (AL), October 13, 1963.

_____. "Gators Shock Alabama Tide, 10 To 6; T. Shannon, Dupree Star For Florida," *Anniston Star* (AL), October 13, 1963.

_____. "Glad To Win." *The Star* (Anniston, AL), October 27, 1963.

_____. "Joe Namath Guides Tide Over Georgia, 31–3." *The Star* (Anniston, AL), September 20, 1964.

_____. "Joe Namath, Nelson Star In 20–19 Win." *The Star* (Anniston, AL), November 3, 1963.

_____. "Namath Bombs Tech; 80 Seconds Used By Joe For 2 TD's." *The Star* (Anniston, AL), November 15, 1964.

_____. "Namath Leads Tide To 24–0 Victory." *The Star* (Anniston, AL), October 4, 1964.

_____. "Namath, Nelson Too Much For Cougars; Bama Tide Is Victor By 21 To 13." *The Star* (Anniston, AL), October 27, 1963.

_____. "Ole Indian Joe Outshines Mira." *The Star* (Anniston, AL), November 11, 1962.

_____. "A Real Cliff-Hanger." *The Star* (Anniston, AL), November 3, 1963.

_____. "Steve Sloan Guides Alabama To Seventh." *The Star* (Anniston, AL), November 1, 1964.

_____. "Talladega's Pride Sets New Tide Mark." *The Star* (Anniston, AL), October 11, 1964.

_____. "Though Joe Left Gridiron Memory, Texas Rolls Tide For Bowl Victory." *The Star* (Anniston, AL), January 2, 1965.

_____. "Underdog Tigers Put Bama To The Wall, Lose, 21–14." *The Star* (Anniston, AL), November 27, 1964.

Smith, Jack. "Raiders Eliminated Despite 24–14 Win." *Daily Review* (Hayward, CA), December 13, 1965.

Smith, Red. "Joe Namath on stage." *Lowell Sun* (MA), November 29, 1971.

_____. "Joe Willie returns home." *Billings Gazette* (MT), November 29, 1971.

Smith, Sandy. "Broadway Joe: Rebel with a Nightclub for a Cause." *Life*, June 20, 1969, Vol. 66, No. 24.

"Snead Leads Eagles, 34–19." *Independent Press-Telegram* (Long Beach, CA), August 20, 1967.

"Snell, Boozer Pace N.Y. Jet Victory over Patriots, 31–21." *Nashua Telegraph* (NH), September 28, 1970.

"Snell, Joe Pace Jets Win." *Times Recorder* (Zanesville, OH), October 28, 1968.

Snider, Steve. "Jets Stay Undefeated," *News Journal* (Mansfield, OH), October 9, 1966.

Soliday, Bill. "Namath, Jets Test Raiders Tonight." *Daily Review* (Hayward, CA), August 25, 1969.

_____. "Namath's aerial show interrupted at goal line." *Daily Review* (Hayward, CA), December 12, 1972.

_____. "Raiders better looking every day." *Daily Review* (Hayward, CA), September 8, 1974.

_____. "Raiders dominate Rams, win, 21–0." *Argus* (Fremont, CA), September 10, 1977.

_____. "Raiders team up on Namath, Jets." *Daily Review* (Hayward, CA), December 12, 1972.

_____. "Raiders win glorified street battle." *Daily Review* (Hayward, CA), December 1, 1969.

Spander, Art. "Joe Namath, the Man and the Myth." *The Sporting News*, September 21, 1974.

"Sports Editor Files Suit Against Namath." *Chillicothe Constitution-Tribune*, August 29, 1967.

Spriggs, Dave. "Super Bowl Mismatch." *Tucson Daily Citizen*, January 9, 1969.

"Star Threats: Knee, Rain." *Pacific Stars and Stripes* (Tokyo), January 20, 1969.

Steadman, John. "Colts' Matte a Thoroughbred by Any Standard." *The Sporting News*, January 18, 1969.

_____. "Like Truman, Jets Laughed at the Odds." *The Sporting News*, January 25, 1969.

_____. "Some Queries on Namath, Grogan and Ringo." *The Sporting News*, September 24, 1977.

"Steelers bombard hapless Jets." *Syracuse Herald-American*, September 5, 1976.

"Steelers Breeze Past Jets, 20–7 To Pad AFC Lead." *Valley Morning Star* (Harlingen, TX), December 1, 1975.

"Steelers Rip Jets." *Panama City News-Herald* (FL), August 13, 1972.

"Steelers will play; strike weakening." *New Castle News* (PA), September 18, 1975.

Stellino, Vito. "Blanda Bursts Namath Bubble." *Lowell Sun* (MA), October 17, 1966.

_____. "Jets Hurtle Oilers, Joe Throws For 5." *Lima News* (OH), September 19, 1966.

_____. "Jets' Namath Injured As Oilers Bow, 16–10." *Daily Messenger* (Canandaigua, NY), August 15, 1966.

_____. "Namath Missing From Camp; Alworth Threatens To Retire." *Las Cruces Sun-News* (NM), August 5, 1970.

_____. "Namath problems are NY Jets problems." *Las Vegas Optic*, August 20, 1968.

_____. "Willie Makes Up, Cornerback Stars." *El Paso Herald-Post*, November 6, 1967.

Stevenson, Jack. "Namath, Jets Fight Back To Tie Raiders." *Fresno Bee*, December 4, 1966.

_____. "Namath Nervous, Anxious." *Daily News-Record* (Harrisonburg, VA), July 19, 1977.

_____. "Namath to be at controls for L.A. in weak NFC West." *Pacific Stars & Stripes* (Tokyo), September 16, 1977.

"Still AWOL from Jets: Joe's problem — cash," *Jefferson City Post-Tribune* (MO), August 7, 1970.

Stone, Ed. "Bear QB called his own plays — they were the right ones." *Press-Telegram* (Long Beach, CA), October 11, 1977.

"Story of a 400 Grand Rookie." *Sunday Tribune* (Albert Lea, MN), January 10, 1965.

"Stram says Chiefs in '72 best ever." *Albuquerque Tribune*, August 7, 1972.

"Stram Slams Critics of Mitchell After Cornerback Intercepts Two." *Ogden Standard Examiner* (UT), November 6, 1967.

Sturgeon, Kelso. "'Bama Defense Beats LSU, 17–9." *Gastonia Gazette* (NC), November 8, 1964.

"Sullivan not yet ready," *Delta Democrat-Times* (Greenville, MS), September 4, 1972.

"Sunday's Game May Be Namath's Last." *Raleigh Register* (Beckley, WV), December 17, 1973.

"Super Bowl Crusade For Johnny Sample." *Panama City News* (FL), January 6, 1969.

"Super Bowl: Joe vs. The World." *Bedford Gazette* (PA), January 11, 1969.

"Super Bowl, Namath against whole world." *Pocono Record* (The Stroudsburgs, PA), January 11, 1969.

"Sweet victory for Harris." *Daily Review* (Hayward, CA), September 2, 1977.

Tanton, Bill. "Mike Curtis: Portrait of a Killer." *Pro Quarterback*, October 1969, Vol. 1, No. 1.

Tarkenton, Fran. "Fran Tarkenton Likes Colts Over Jets in Super Bowl," *Delaware County Daily Times* (PA), January 7, 1969.

Taylor, Charles E. "Jet Coach Guarantees Super Upset," *Billings Gazette*, January 11, 1969.

_____. "Jets fight odds." *New Castle News* (PA), January 7, 1969.

_____. "Mackey and Namath Causing Most Talk." *Middlesboro Daily News* (KY), January 9, 1969.

"Taylor Called Big Play." *Oakland Tribune*, December 21, 1969.

"Taylor pains Jets." *Daily Review* (Hayward, CA), November 17, 1969.

"Tears Flow At Weeb's Farewell." *The Bee* (Danville, VA), December 17, 1973.

"10,000 Kibitzers Bug Jet Coach." *Pacific Stars and Stripes* (Tokyo), January 4, 1969.

"Tensi, Namath Are AFL Stars; Denver Winner." *Albuquerque Tribune*, October 3, 1966.

"That Isn't Just Luck All Over The Jets." *San Antonio Light*, November 10, 1969.

"There's a Lot on the Line for Colts, New York." *Wisconsin State Journal* (Madison), January 5, 1969.

"'They Ran Right Over Us,' Says Bengal Coach Brown." *Lima News* (OH), October 13, 1969.

"Third Ranked Alabama Racks LSU, 17–9." *Albuquerque Journal*, November 8, 1964.

Thomas, Ben. "Namath plays hard-to-find." *Las Vegas Optic*, August 12, 1970.

_____. "Unitas Was Sure He'd Move Colts." *Morning Herald* (Uniontown, PA), January 13, 1969.

_____. "Vikings Humiliate Namath, Jets 52–21." *Moberly Monitor-Index* (MO), August 31, 1970.

Thomas, Tommy. "Since When Does Crowd Bother Joe Namath?" *Chillicothe Constitution-Tribune* (MO), August 16, 1968.

"Three TDs for Freitas." *The Times* (San Mateo, CA), August 12, 1974.

Tonelli, Charles. "49ers not too excited with win." *Daily Review* (Hayward, CA), October 4, 1976.

_____. "San Francisco good, but not good enough." *Argus* (Fremont, CA), October 3, 1977.

"Too Hungry To Lose It, Says Shula." *Bedford Gazette* (PA), January 11, 1969.

Traylor, Steve. "Alabama Steps Over Volunteers," *Anniston Star* (AL), October 18, 1964.

"Trench wars are won by Bears against Rams." *Alton Telegraph* (IL), October 11, 1977.

Tucker, Bud. "Rams find Monday night football is for the birds." *Press-Telegram* (Long Beach, CA), October 11, 1977.

"Turnabout Bills' 5 Thefts Upset Jets." *Oakland Tribune*, September 30, 1968.

"Turner Boots New York To 25–21 Win Over Bills." *San Antonio Express*, November 4, 1968.

"Turner Hot Foots Miami Off a Cliff." *Oakland Tribune*, November 3, 1969.

"Turner, Namath Spearhead New York Jet Victory, 40–7." *Nevada State Journal*, November 24, 1969.

"Turner Ties Kick Record." *Lima News* (OH), November 4, 1968.

"Turner's 'kicking' helps." *New Castle News* (PA), November 25, 1968.

"Turnovers, Poor Punt Set Up TDs." *Bridgeport Telegram* (CT), September 28, 1970.

"Two Fourth Period TDs Give Bills 14–3 Win." *Albuquerque Journal*, November 14, 1966.

"Two Plays By Sample Halt Bills." *Bridgeport Telegram* (CT), November 13, 1967.

"289-Pound Tackle Scores on 72-Yard Run As Bills Jolt Jets." *Post Standard* (Syracuse, NY), November 14, 1966.

Twombly, Wells. "The Great Namath — All Dignity, Charm." *The Sporting News*, September 16, 1967.

"Uncertain Airways Bother Namath." *Wisconsin State Journal*, December 21, 1969.

"Uncle Sam Writing to Joe Namath." *Moberly Monitor-Index* (MO), August 12, 1965.

Usher, George. "Joe Namath: From Ann-Margret to Ben Davidson ... Smack!" *Complete Sports*, Fall 1970, Vol. 6, No.3.

Usiak, Dick. "Todd Makes Jets Forget Joe Namath." *The Sporting News*, November 13, 1976.

Valli, Bob. "Brrr ... Winter Awaits Raiders." *Oakland Tribune*, December 26, 1968.

_____. "Division Champs Repeat." *Oakland Tribune*, December 13, 1965.

_____. "Frustrated Raiders Post 24–24 Tie." *Oakland Tribune*, October 17, 1965.

_____. "Jets Are Favored by 3." *Oakland Tribune*, December 24, 1968.

_____. "Jets Roll Over Raiders, 27–14: Streak Ends at 3 Games." *Oakland Tribune*, October 8, 1967.

_____. "Jets Score At 0:53." *Oakland Tribune*, December 4, 1966.

_____. "Jets Topple —0:02 Left." *Oakland Tribune*, October 24, 1966.

_____. "A Momento Don Maynard Really Doesn't Cherish." *Oakland Tribune*, December 12, 1972.

_____. "Raiders Display an 'Air of Confidence.'" *Oakland Tribune*, December 29, 1968.

_____. "Raiders Favored To Beat Jets." *Oakland Tribune*, December 12, 1965.

_____. "Raiders Go For Broke." *Oakland Tribune*, December 29, 1968.

_____. "That Clutch Raider Win: Frantic 14-Point Minute." *Oakland Tribune*, November 18, 1968.

Van Sant, Rick. "Jets Lose To Cincinnati; Namath's Return Too Late." *Raleigh Register* (Beckley, WV), November 19, 1973.

"Vikes Nail Rams on Blocked Punt." *Press-Courier* (Oxnard, CA), August 7, 1977.

"Vikings Comeback Nips Jets 29–21." *Times Recorder* (Zanesville, OH), October 13, 1975.

"Vikings Edge Jets, 29–21," *Albuquerque Journal*, October 13, 1975.

"Vikings humble Jets 52–21; Namath flops." *Jefferson City Post-Tribune* (MO), August 31, 1970.

"Vols Battered By 'Bama, 27–7." *News & Tribune* (Jefferson City, MO), October 21, 1962.

Wallace, Paul. "Blocking for Neighbor Namath Isn't All That Bad, Rams' Harrah Says." *Charleston Gazette* (WV), October 12, 1977.

Wallace, William N. "Bowl Build-Up Begins." *Press-Courier* (Oxnard, CA), January 1, 1969.

_____. "No Change Foreseen In Namath Affair." *Corpus Christi Caller-Times*, June 15, 1969.

_____. "Snell Is Expected to Rejoin Jets For Game With Bills on Sunday." *New York Times*, December 16, 1965.

_____. "Super 11 Vs. Super Passer." *Billings Gazette* (MT), January 1, 1969.

Ward, Joe. "Jets Thundering Herd Runs Over Patriots." *Portsmouth Herald* (NH), October 16, 1972.

"Warfield's presence helps Rucker." *Chronicle Telegram* (Elyria, OH), September 13, 1976.

Watson, Michael. "Last minute Jet run beats 49ers, 17–10." *Daily Review* (Hayward, CA), August 6, 1972.

"Weeb Defends Joe's Boo-Boo." *Post-Standard* (Syracuse, NY), January 8, 1969.

"What's Namath Future?" *Las Cruces Sun-News* (NM), December 2, 1974.

"Where did you go, Joe?" *Daily Capital News* (Jefferson City, MO), August 5, 1970.

Whitfield, Tom. "Bert Jones Puts On Show For Old Hero Joe Namath." *The Sporting News*, December 11, 1976.

_____. "Prancing Colts Land Swift Kick in Teeth to Fading Jets." *The Sporting News*, November 29, 1975.

Wielenga, Dave. "Winless 49ers are down, but not about to give up." *Independent* (Long Beach, CA), October 3, 1977.

"Wiggins Likes Chiefs Role As Giant Killer." *Atchison Daily Globe* (KS), August 29, 1977.

Wilfong, Chuck. "super joe is mellowing..." *Daily Chronicle* (Centralla, WA), December 15, 1972.

Wilkinson, Bud. "Joe Namath on Spot." *Advocate* (Victoria, TX), January 2, 1969.

Wilkinson, Jack. "Boozer's TD gives Jets win." *Chronicle Telegram* (Elyria, OH), October 6, 1968.

"Win Over Boston Could Change Joe's Tune." *Pacific Stars and Stripes* (Tokyo), October 6, 1969.

"Winners Surge In 2nd Period." *Bridgeport Telegram* (CT), December 4, 1967.

Wolfe, Bob. "Namath works to convince Jets he must go." *Corpus Christi Times*, February 25, 1976.

"Woodall Injured; Jets Cage Falcons." *Pacific Stars & Stripes* (Tokyo), September 2, 1975.

"Workouts Differ For Colts, Jets." *San Antonio Express*, January 8, 1969.

Young, Dick. "Jets Are Very Good At Wisecracks, Too." *The Sporting News*, January 25, 1969.

_____. "Namath Slated for Operation." *Post-Tribune* (Jefferson City, MO), December 22, 1966.

_____. "'No scrambling' for Jets' Namath." *News & Tribune* (Jefferson City, MO), August 6, 1967.

"Young QB Passes Colts Over Namath, N.Y. Jets." *Daily Times* (Salisbury, MD), October 27, 1975.

Zimmerman, Paul. "Why They Still Pick on Joe Namath." *Touchdown*, 1969.

Index